Sud
Sud   SO-BJI-863

Sudlersville Memorial Library
Sudlersville, Md. 21668

Ocean
and
Marine
Dictionary

Ocean
and
Marine
Dictionary

David F. Tver

Cornell Maritime Press, Inc.

Centreville   1979   *Maryland*

Copyright © 1979 by Cornell Maritime Press, Inc.

All Rights Reserved

No part of this book may be used or reproduced in any manner whatsoever without written permission except in the case of brief quotations embodied in critical articles and reviews. For information address Cornell Maritime Press, Inc., Centreville, Maryland 21617

Library of Congress Cataloging in Publication Data

Tver, David F
  Ocean and marine dictionary.

  1. Oceanography--Dictionaries.   2. Marine engi-
neering--Dictionaries   3. Marine biology--Dictionaries.
I. Title.
GC9.T86   551.4'6'003   79—1529
ISBN 0—87033—246-5

Printed and Bound in the United States of America

CONTENTS

Other Books by Author

Dictionary of Business & Science
Dictionary of Astronomy
Petroleum Industry Dictionary
Nutrition Handbook

INTRODUCTION

The oceans are the last frontier on this planet. The interest in marine activities has never been higher. From fishing to farming; from drilling for oil, to exploring for new sources of minerals; from commercial diving to scuba diving for pleasure; from sailboating, motorboating, water-skiing, to swimming, the ocean is a never ending source of pleasure and interest. Man, if he is to survive on this Earth, may well depend in the future on the sea as a major source of food and minerals.

Man is constantly probing the ocean depths, exploring farther and deeper, forever looking for new challenges, better understanding of the environment and trying to satisfy an insatiable curiosity.

Jacques Yves Cousteau states in his book, *The Ocean World of Jacques Cousteau;* "Man exists only because his home planet, Earth, is the one celestial body we know of where life is at all possible on earth because earth is a water planet. Water is not only rare, not only infinitely precious, it is peculiar, with many oddities in its physical and chemical makeups. . . . The ocean is life. . . . That is why we must change our attitude toward the ocean. We must no longer regard it as a mystery. . . . We want to explore the theme of the ocean's existence, how it moves and breathes, how it experiences dramas and seasons, how it nourishes its hosts of living things, how it harmonizes the physical and biological rhythms of the whole earth— not least of all what are its stories."

For untold millions of people the ocean is a source of recreation and pleasure. For others it is a livelihood. For still others, it is an infinite source of scientific study about its past and its future potential.

The marine environment is a complex one with many facets, each needing its own understanding and each being used to accomplish a particular objective. Those who go to sea, who love to sail, need to know sailing nomenclature, the various types of ships, the weather, the currents, and any other information relating to sailing. The fisherman needs to know about marine life. The scuba diver explores the ocean from plant life to every living thing in its depth. He is watching an endless drama unfold before his eyes. Anyone who has anything to do with the ocean, from collecting shells to studying crustacea, plankton, seaweeds, plants, fish, mammals, algae, and marine life in general, needs a reference manual to refer to.

For the first time, all aspects of marine and ocean environment, and activities relating to the oceans and seas, are defined under one cover—from sailing ships and nautical terms to seashells and seaweeds. This is believed to be one of the most comprehensive marine dictionaries ever published. For anyone who is in any way interested in the ocean or marine environment, this dictionary covers almost everything related to oceans and ocean life—which is a world unto itself.

D.F.T.

PREFACE

The purpose of this dictionary is to provide a ready reference to most aspects of ocean life above and below, from the history of ships that sail its waters to the animals and vegetation that exist in its environment.

The subject is almost endless and would take volumes to list and define every detail of ocean life. The definitions selected include most of the more important aspects, and have been made short, concise but sufficiently comprehensive. Included are in-depth coverage of marine vegetation, sporting and food fishes, the various classifications of Phylum such as Protozoa (the simple animals), Porifera (sponges); Coelentera (polyps); Ctenophora (comb jellies); Platyhelmia (flatworms); Nemertea (ribbon worms); Nemathelmia (roundworms, threadworms); Trochelmia (wheel animalcules); Annulata (segmented or ringed worms); Arthropoda (crustacians, arachnoids, myriapods, insects); Mollusca (snails, bivalves, chitons, octopuses, squid); Chaetognatha (arrow worms); Echinoderma (sea stars, brittle stars, sea urchins, sea lilies, sea cucumbers), Bryozoa (moss animals); Brachiopoda (lamp shells); Chordata (protochordates and vertebrates).

Included also are descriptions of ancient marine life including the nautiloids, cephalopods, worms, trilobites, arthropods, sharks, and bony fishes.

There are descriptions of a variety of ships and sailing vessels that have been built since the earliest of times. In addition there are a detailed listing of ship nomenclature and short explanations of how certain words relating to ocean and ocean life came about.

David F. Tver
San Diego, Ca.

A

A: International Code *burgee* or swallow-tail flag, white and blue vertically divided, which, hoisted singly, denotes *"I am undergoing a speed trial"*; and, as a towing signal, shown by towing vessel, *"Is the towing hawser fast?"* or, by vessel towed, *"Towing hawser is fast."* Its uppermost place in a four-flag hoist, or *geographical signal*, distinguishes such signal as that denoting the name of a place. Also, in a two-flag hoist, or urgent or important signal, as upper flag it indicates signal concerns *abandoning* vessel, an *accident,* or *afloat* and *aground.*

A1 [*A-one*]: 1) a rating mark given a vessel in a classification society's records, generally indicating first class condition. Lloyd's uses this mark for classifying equipment, as distinct from hull ratings. Steel hulls are classed 100-A1, 90-A1, etc., according to condition at latest survey. 2) the very best.

A.A. [*Always afloat*]: abbreviated form of phrase used in charter parties when referring to stipulated port of discharge, as in "or as near thereto as it can safely get, being *at all times afloat.*"

A.B. [*Able-bodied*]: abbreviation used in crew lists and shipping articles for rating of *able seaman.*

aback [ships]: condition of receiving wind from ahead, as when a vessel's sails are caught by wind in such a way as to press them aft against the mast; a sudden or unexpected check in the forward progress of a ship brought about by pressure of wind on the sails ahead, causing ship to drive astern.

abaft [ships]: behind, in or at the back or hind part of a ship; the part which lies toward the stern; opposed to forward; relatively further aft or toward the stern. As abaft the mainmast. Abaft the beam is behind a line drawn through middle of ship at right angles to keel.

abalone: large marine mollusks of the class *Gastropoda,* with single, oval, shallow shell containing beautifully colored interior (source of mother-of-pearl). Sought for their edible flesh, abalone are the object of a well managed fishery.

abandonment: act or state of being abandoned; relinquishment of damaged property to its insurers, party insured claiming total loss. Abandonment is possible in cases of shipwreck, capture, seizure, vessel posted missing, constructive loss, and circumstances of catastrophic nature.

abandon ship: order given for all on board to leave a stricken vessel by boats or other means available, there being no hope of her survival.

abapical [*Gastropoda*]: direction opposite that of apex along axis.

abdomen: in *Arthropoda,* main division of body behind thorax; in crayfish and lobsters, often miscalled the tail. Mammalian abdomen lies behind diaphragm and contains liver, stomach and intestines.

abeam [ships]: at right angles to the keel of the ship; directly opposite middle part of ship's side and on line with main beam; as *"We had the wind abeam."*

aberration: a small periodical displacement in position of a heavenly body, due to relative motions of Earth and body, combined with progressive motion of light from such body.

abioseston: nonliving particles suspended in water.

ablation: combined processes (such as sublimation, melting, evaporation) which remove snow or ice from surface of a glacier, snowfield, etc.; in this sense, opposite of alimentation. Particularly in glaciology, term may be applied to reduction of entire snow-ice mass, and may also include losses by wind action and calving.

ablation zone: wastage area of a glacier where along the surface at lower altitudes more snow is lost to evaporation and melting (ablation) than is gained.

aboard [ships]: on the deck or in the hold of a ship. In or upon a ship.

aboral: away from middle; at opposite pole of the body from the mouth.

about [ships]: to take different direction as in tacking, when a ship is beating to windward and changes course by allowing wind to exert its pressure upon opposite side of sails. To change from starboard to port tack or vice versa.

abrasion: wearing away or rounding of surfaces by friction; e.g., the action of glaciers, wind and waterborne sand on rocks or rock fragments.

1

abrasion platform: surface of marine denudation formed by wave erosion which is still in original position at or near the wave base, with marine forces still operating on it.

abreast [ships]: lying or moving side by side, or opposite to. On a line with the beam.

abrid [ships]: bushing plate around a hole in which a pintle works.

A.B.S. [*American Bureau of Shipping*].

absorption: when a sound wave travels outward from a source into the sea, some of the sound energy is converted into heat by friction caused by viscosity of the water.

aburton: stowed athwartships or crossways in a vessel's hold; as casks, cases, pipes, rod iron, etc., laid end to end.

abyss: region of the deep sea where depth is from 8,000 to 19,000 ft. and temperature does not exceed 39° F.

abyssal: referring to the deep sea from about 2,500 to 6,000 meters (roughly 8,000 to 19,000 ft.) where temperature does not exceed 4° Celsius (39° F.). Usually describes marine organisms especially adapted to great pressures, low temperatures and lack of light at these depths. Abyssal animals may be blind or luminescent.

abyssal hill: relatively small topographic features of deep ocean floor, ranging from 2,000 to 3,000 ft. high and a few miles wide. Usually found in large numbers seaward of the abyssal plain and bordering the mid-ocean ridge area.

abyssal plain: large area of ocean bottom which receives major portions of marine sediments, characterized by extreme flatness and gentle slope less than 5 ft. per mile. A large, extremely flat and smooth area in the deep ocean floor.

abyssobenthal: in or near the bottom in the abyssal zone.

abyssopelagec: pertaining to that portion of the ocean which lies below depths of 2,000 fathoms (3,700 meters).

abyssopelagic: in the water well above the bottom in the abyssal zone.

Acanthodians: often miscalled "tiny sharks," the least progressive placoderms. Early forms were not much larger than minnows but were most unminnowlike in appearance and anatomy. *Climatius*, e.g., was 3 in. long with a blunt head, a sharklike tail, and hard diamond-shaped scales covering entire body. Paired fins numbered 14 but 10 were little more than spines and strong spines supported unpaired dorsal and ventral fins.

acceleration: rate of change with time and speed and/or velocity; strictly the rate of change with time of velocity of a particle. In the cgs system of physical measurements, it is expressed in terms of centimeters per second per second.

accelerometer: device which measures forces of acceleration acting on a body within the instrument. Among its many uses is measuring wave effect on ship at sea.

accepted depth: best possible determination of the true depth of each Nansen bottle at time of reversal.

accessory muscle scars [*Mollusca*]: small circular impressions supplementary to the adductor scars.

accommodation ladder [ships]: stairs slung at gangway down a vessel's side to a point near water for ship access from small boats.

account: latitude (or longitude) by account; latitude and/or longitude deduced from courses and distances sailed since last position obtained by observation.

accretion: natural accretion is gradual buildup of land over a long period of time solely by action of the forces of nature on a beach by deposition of water or airborne material.

accretionary limestone: limestone which has formed in situ by slow accumulation of organic remains such as coral or shells.

accumulation: in glaciology, the quantity of snow or other solid form of water added to a glacier or snowfield by alimentation.

aces [ships]: hooks for the chains.

Achnernar: first magnitude star in the group *Eridanus*, about 30° from the south pole in about 1 hr. 35 min. of right ascension.

acicular ice: freshwater ice consisting of numerous long crystals and hollow tubes, having variable form, layered arrangement and a content of air bubbles. It forms at the bottom of an ice layer near its contact with water.

aciculum: in *Polychaete Annelida*, large setae, larger and more distinct from the ordinary setae, and almost completely buried in the fleshy parapodium.

acid rock: igneous rock containing a high proportion of silica, contrasted with basic rock in a two division classification of rocks.

aclinic: having no inclination or dip; situated where the compass needle does not dip.

aclinic line: line through those points on earth's surface at which magnetic inclination is zero. In South America the aclinic line lies at about 15° S; while from central Africa to about Vietnam it coincides approximately with parallel of 10° N. An irregular, variable line encircling the earth near the equator, where a magnetic needle has no dip; the *magnetic equator*.

acorn [ships]: solid piece of metal shaped like an acorn and used to finish off the top of an upright in a railing constructed of pipe.

acorn barnacle: cone-shaped marine crustacean found attached to coastal rocks. Feeds by extending curved, jointed legs or cirri, from its calcareous shell into seawater to catch food; is an important fouling organism on pilings.

acoustic: science of sound, including its production, transmission and effects.

acoustic dispersion: scattering or spreading of sound. Separation of complex sound wave into its various frequency components, usually caused by variation with frequency of wave velocity of the medium. Rate of change of velocity with frequency is used as measure of dispersion.

acoustic impedance: for given surface area of acoustic medium perpendicular, at every point, to direction of propagation of sinusoidal acoustic waves of given frequency and having equal acoustic pressures at equal volume velocities per unit area at every point of surface at any instant.

acoustic intensity: limit approached by quotient obtained by dividing power of the acoustic energy being transmitted at a given time through a given area by the magnitude of this area as magnitude of this area approaches zero.

acoustic pressure: difference at a point between instantaneous sound pressure and hydrostatic pressure.

acoustic scattering: irregular reflection, refraction or diffraction of sound in many directions.

acoustic screen: blanket of air bubbles that effectively entrap backscattered sound energy.

acoustic waves: waves which contain sound energy and by which sound energy is transmitted in air, water, or in the earth. The waves may be described in terms of change of pressure, of particle displacement or of density.

acre foot: volume of water required to cover one acre to a depth of one foot, hence 43,560 cu. ft.; convenient unit for measurement of irrigation water, runoff volume and reservoir capacity.

Acropora: colonial scleractinian of the madreporarian group of coral, extremely common in tropical and subtropical seas; found in green, mauve or blue, and its formation takes the form of branches or "umbrella." The latter of considerable size, sometimes attaining a height of 7 to 8 ft.

across: to moor; to secure a vessel by anchors dropped on each side of a stream.

Acrotretacca [*Brachiopoda*]: ventral valve generally conical with very high interarea with a median furrow or trough. Pedicle foramen apical or just behind apex. Dorsal valve weakly convex and may have a median septum.

Acteon [snails]: egg-shaped or slender snail whose varied species range from Pierre and Bearpaw formations to modern temperate seas; also typify the *Opisthobranchia*, class that has progressed largely by degeneration. Some such as acteon retain well-developed shell, mantle and one gill,

though it is twisted around to the rear. Appears in Mississippian and continues through later formations.

actinometry: science of measurement of radiant energy, particularly that of the sun, in its thermal chemical (octinic) and luminous aspects.

actinopterygian: means "ray fin." Virtually all these fish have fins stretched over bones which extend directly from body, not as fringes on both sides of a bony and muscular lobe. As in coelacanths, one lung has been lost while the other has become an air bladder lying above midline of the fish, reducing its weight helping it remain upright. Heavy organs below bladder serve as ballast.

actinotrocha: planktonic larva of bottom dwelling worm.

actinotroch larva: larval form in *Phoronidea*, somewhat related to trochophore larvae but bearing ciliated arms.

active glacier: glacier which has been accumulating in an area, in contrast to a stagnant glacier—need not have an advancing front.

active sonar: method or equipment by which information concerning a distant object is obtained through evolution of the sound signal reflected from object to generating equipment.

adductor muscles [*Brachiopoda*]: muscles that close shells or valves in certain bivalve mollusks such as oysters and scallops; form edible part of a scallop.

adductor muscle scars: striated depressions in interior of bivalve shell marking attachment site of muscles that control movement of the 2 valves.

ad freezing: process by which one object becomes adhered to another by binding action of ice.

adiabatic changes: adiabatic changes in temperatures of seawater take place without heat transfer. Changes generally due to variation in pressure brought about by changes in depth. These processes are less important in the ocean than the atmosphere due to relatively low compressibility of water.

adiabatic phenomena: those phenomena which occur without a gain or loss of heat.

adiabatic process: thermodynamic change of state of system in which there is no transfer of heat or mass across boundaries of the system. In an adiabatic process, compression always results in warming; expansion in cooling.

adiabatic temperature changes: compression of a fluid without gain or loss of heat to surrounding areas is work performed on the system and provides rise or fall of temperatures. Such a rise or fall of temperature occurs with changing depth.

adipose [fish]: thick fin without rays.

adjacent seas: semi-enclosed seas adjacent to and

connected with the oceans. The North Polar, Mediterranean, and Caribbean Seas are examples.

adjusted: term applied to a coastline, drainage pattern or individual stream with placement controlled by rock hardness or structure, or both.

adjusted stream: stream which tends to flow parallel to the strike of a rock formation.

adjuster muscles [*Brachiopoda*]: two pairs of muscles in articulate brachiopods that insert in brachial and pedicle valves and originate in the pedicle bases. They adjust position of shell on pedicle.

admeasurement: process of ascertaining various dimensions, capacities, and tonnage of total spaces in a vessel as required for official registration.

Admiralty, Board of: department of the British government entrusted with management of all matters concerning the navy.

adnate [fish]: fused; grown together.

adradial: in tetramerous radial symmetry of most medusae, the sector midway between main radial (perradial) canals; adradial canals are additional canals occupying this position in some medusae.

adrift [ships]: floating at random; not fastened to moorings; at mercy of winds and currents.

adsorption: adhesion of thin film of liquid or gas to solid substance. Solid does not chemically combine with the adsorbed substance.

ad valorem: Latin phrase meaning *according to value;* used in levying customs duties when such are fixed at rates proportioned to estimated value of goods concerned; opposed to duties designated as *specific*, or fixed at a specified amount.

advance: 1) distance a vessel moves in the line of its original course after putting down the helm, as for a tack, and until it has turned through 90°. **2)** payment of money before it is due: as, that paid to a seaman at an intermediate port in a voyage and charged to his account; or that paid upon signing articles for a voyage, usually amounting to a month's pay.

advance (of a shoreline): continuing seaward movement of a shoreline. A net seaward movement of the shoreline over specified period of time.

advection: process of transport of an atmospheric property solely by mass motion of the atmosphere; rate of change of volume of the advected property at a given point. In oceanography advection refers to horizontal or vertical flow of seawater as a current.

advection fog: type of fog caused by the advection of moist air over a cold surface, and consequent cooling of that air to below its dew point.

Aequorea vitrina [zooplankton]: species of *Aequorea* are immediately recognizable even when partially grown by their immense size. When full size they outrival many proper jellyfish *(Scyphozoa)*, although their hydroids are insignificant. *A. vitrina* can reach diameter of 170 mm.; has flattened bell bearing up to 600 marginal tentacles and at all stages of growth these are more than 3 times the number of radial canals; gonads are in thin strips on each side of radial canals; mesogloea is thick and velum narrow; large stomach has diameter half that of the umbrella, usually somewhat less; margins of mouth are drawn out into tentaclelike projection with crenelated margins.

aerobe: organism which can live and grow only in presence of oxygen; organism which employs aerobic respiration.

aesthetask: sense organs in the antennae of certain copepods.

affirmative: signal flag by which assent or an affirmative reply is expressed; International Code flag *"C."*

afloat: borne in water in a floating condition; to be afloat.

"A" frame [ships]: **1)** gallows used for leading wires over side of ship for lowering instruments and other devices. **2)** steel frame used for outboard suspension of oceanographic gear in shipboard survey work, so named because of its A-shape.

aft (after) [ships]: aft is part of boat toward the stern. After also refers to parts of boat which are toward stern as the "after cabin," the "afterdeck."

afterbody [ships]: part of ship's hull which is abaft the midships.

afterdeck [ships]: term applied to deck aft to midships portion of vessel.

after frames [ships]: radiating cant frames fastened to transom plates.

afternoon effect: solar heating of surface water which causes shallow negative temperature gradient. Net result is downward refraction of sound rays and reduction in near surface rays.

afterpeak [ships]: compartment just forward of the sternpost. It is almost entirely below the load waterline.

after perpendicular [ships]: vertical line through intersection of load waterline, and after edge of the sternpost. On submarines or ships having a similar stern, is a vertical line passing through points where design waterline intersects stern of ship.

after rake [ships]: that part of stern which overhangs the keel.

aftershock: earthquake which follows a large earthquake and originates at or near focus of larger earthquake. Generally, major earthquakes are followed by a large number of aftershocks, decreasing in frequency with increasing time. Such a series of aftershocks may last at sea many days or even months.

against the sun: counterclockwise rotary motion; contrary to diurnal motion of the sun, as viewed from a latitude higher than that body's northerly declination.

agar-agar: gelatinous solidifying agent obtained from certain red algae such as *Gelidium*, widely used for solidifying bacteriological media and for other purposes.

age: stage of development of sea ice; usually refers to length of time since its formation and to its thickness.

age of diurnal inequality: time interval between maximum semimonthly north or south declination of the moon and maximum effect of declination upon range of tide or speed of tidal current.

age of parallax inequality: time interval between perigee of the moon and maximum effect of parallax (distance of moon) upon range of tide or speed of tidal current.

age of phase inequality: time interval between new or full moon and maximum effect of these phases upon range of tide or speed of tidal current.

age of the tide: time elapsing since the moon's transit that originated a tide and occurrence of that tide. Such interval varies from 0 to 7 days; generally from 1 to 2, average for the world being nearly 1½ days.

age of water: time elapsed since a water mass was last at surface and in contact with atmosphere. Water's age gives indication of rate of overturn of ocean water, an important factor in use of oceans for dumping radioactive wastes and determining rate of replenishment of nutrients.

agglomerate: objects or structures closely crowded into a cluster.

agglutinated [*Foraminifera*]: test composed of grains of foreign material, sand, sponges, spicules, etc., cemented together.

aggradation: 1) upward building of surface by deposition of sediment. 2) natural filling up of head of a water course, at any point of weakening of current, by deposition of detritus.

aggrade: to deposit sediments on a stream bed or valley floor.

Agnatha [fishes]: 1) jawless fishes, lack hinged lower jaws and have rather simple mouth openings in the end of the snout or underside of head. Living agnathans do not have gill slits like those of other fishes; gills are in two rows of spherical pouches on sides of throat, connected with gut and with surface by small tubes. Agnathans are divided into 2 groups; those with single central

nostril and those with usual double nostril; single nostriled group includes living cyclostomes such as lamprey which have cartilaginous skeletons; agnathans with 2 nostrils include armored *Heterostraci* which are known from Lower Ordovician to Upper Devonian. 2) (class: phylum *Chordata*). Ordovician to Recent. Notochord large; gill chambers; elongate, fishlike, but without paired appendages or jaws. In most, head is covered by bony armor. Most lineages extinct after Devonian. Freshwater and marine. Sluggish to active, benthonic and nektonic; filter feeders and mud grubbers.

Agnostida [Trilobites]: minute creatures range from early Cambrian to late Ordovician; lack eyes, have marginal facial sutures, and possess only 2 thoracic segments. In shape they resemble eodiscids. Excellent specimens are common in Burgess shale.

agonic line: line through all parts or points on earth's surface at which magnetic declination is zero; that is, the locus of all points at which magnetic north and true north coincide. Position of this line exhibits variation in time.

aguaje: annual condition noted in coastal waters of Peru resulting in discolored water (usually red or yellow) and various degrees of destruction of marine life. Aguaje usually occurs from April through June and is local term used along certain portions of Peruvian coast.

Agulhas Current: warm current, continuation of south-flowing Mozambique Current from eastern side of Africa, around southern end of continent to Cape Agulhas.

Ahnfelt's seaweed: abundant genus that lies half buried in sands or grows on rocks between 1.0 and 1.5 ft. tide levels. Outstanding feature of this genus of seaweed is presence of naked, wiry, rigid, erect branches. Fruiting bodies form conspicuous wartlike growths nearly the thickness of branches bearing them; very deep purplish red to black. Erect thalli grow from a prostrate branched, cylindrical rhizome.

aids to navigation: buoys, beacons, fog signals, lights, radio beacons, range marks, and, generally, any charted or published information serving the interests of safe navigation.

air bladder: 1) gas-filled sac in fish; pressure in the bladder usually equalizes with depth so fish does not have to swim against positive or negative buoyancy. 2) in many teleost fishes, a gas-filled sac originating as an outgrowth from the pharynx and serving as a hydrostatic organ.

airborne expendable bathythermograph: buoyant canister which is ejected into water from aircraft to provide measurements of water temperature with depth. Temperature information is transmitted to aircraft. Instrument is designed to measure temperature from the surface to 1,000 ft. with an accuracy ± 5 percent in depth and temperature accuracy of ± 0.5° F. within range of 28° to 90° F.

airborne radiation thermometer: infrared sensing device which measures sea surface temperature from aircraft.

airborne sea and swell recorder: frequency modulated continuous wave radar system used to measure wave height from aircraft.

air casing [ships]: ring-shaped plate coaming surrounding the stack and fitted at upper deck just below umbrella; protects deck structure from heat and helps ventilate fireroom.

air embolism: blockage of an artery by an air bubble; serious potential injury among divers or personnel escaping from submarines; caused by an expansion of air inside lungs, which increases when the breath is held during ascent. Lung tissues rupture, air is forced into capillaries of lung, and resulting air bubbles are carried to heart and into arterial system.

air lift: simple but important device used in underwater archaeology, first utilized by Jacques Yves Cousteau in 1952 on excavation of Roman wreck in Mediterranean. Compressed air is pumped into bottom of vertical tube underwater. As air rises to surface, it creates powerful suction which draws up water, mud or sand, and any nearby small objects including artifacts.

air port [ships]: opening in side of ship or deckhouse, usually round in shape, and fitted with hinged frame in which thick glass is secured; purpose of air port is to provide light and ventilation to and vision from interior.

air stone: aquarium device made of amalgamated pieces of stone that releases compressed air in form of tiny bubbles. Air stones are connected with air pump by small plastic hose.

akaryotic: without definite nucleus with nuclear membrane.

akineton: plankton without any power of self-movement, such as many spores or planktonic eggs.

aktological: refers to nearshore shallow water areas, environment, sediment, or life.

alar septum [Coelenterata]: one of a pair of the initial septa (protoseptal) of Rugosa located about midway between cardinal and counter septa. Secondary septa may insert pinnately in side away from cardinal.

Alaska Current: current that flows northwestward and westward along coasts of Canada and Alaska to Aleutian Islands; contains water from North Pacific Current, and has character of warm current; it therefore exercises an influence on climatic conditions of region similar, but on smaller scale, to that which North Atlantic and Norway Currents exercise on climates of northwestern Europe.

alate [Brachiopoda]: shell form in which valves are drawn out of lateral ends of hinge line to form winglike extensions.

albacore: a long-finned tuna, like other tunas has long spiny dorsal fin almost continuous with posterior soft-rayed portion; differs in extremely long and tapering pectoral fins that may be half length of body; small, smooth scales contribute a sleek surface to this fast swimmer, and added speed comes from deeply forked and crescent-shaped tail fin. All fins fit into grooves, another adaptation for swift locomotion through water. Has dark blue head and back and silvery yellow sides. Usually less than 36 in. in length and under 30 lbs. in weight; primarily a warm-water fish.

albatross, black-browed [Diomedea melanophris]: head, neck, rump, upper tail coverts and underparts, including underwing coverts, except those at edge of wing, white; through the eye a slaty streak; back and tail slaty black; wings above dark brownish-black; bill yellow, rosy pink at tip; with narrow black line around base; feet yellowish or pinkish-white, webs and joints washed with pale blue; length 32 to 34 in.

albatross, black-footed [Diomedea nigripes]: sooty brown, paler on the forehead, cheeks, neck and abdomen, area around bill and behind and below the eyes white; bill dark reddish-brown; feet black; length 28 in.

albatross, Buller's [Diomedea bulleri]: head and neck pale grey; dark patch in front of eye; back wings and anterior edge of lower surface sooty brown; rump, upper tail coverts and underparts, including undercoverts white; bill grey; with yellow stripe along middle of upper mandible broadening at base; feet bluish-white; length 34 in.

albatross, grey-headed [Diomedea chrysostoma]: head and neck slaty grey (becoming white on old birds); backs and tail dark grey; wings above blackish-brown; dark patch above and in front of eye; rump, upper tail coverts, except at edge of wing, white; bill blackish, with yellow stripe down middle of upper mandible which is red at tip, and yellow band at base of lower mandible; feet pinkish-grey; length 28 to 32 in.

albatross, Laysan [Diomedea immutabilis]: head, neck, rump, upper tail coverts and underparts white; spot before eye sooty black; back wings and end of tail dark sooty brown; underwing coverts blackish-brown and white, irregularly mingled; bill grey, darker at base and tip, base of mandible pale yellow; feet fleshy pink; length 32 in.

albatross, light-mantled sooty [Phoebetria palpebrata]: head dark greyish-brown, nearly black on lores; back and undersurface ashy-grey; wings dark brownish-grey; primaries and long, wedge-shaped tail greyish-black; shafts of quills whitish; white ring around eye broken in front; bill black, with groove along side of lower mandible pale blue or pearl grey; feet pale flesh color; length 28 in.

albatross, royal [*Diomedea epomophora*]: entirely white, except primaries which are black and some of scapulars and wing coverts, which are mottled with grey; bill whitish; feet bluish-white; length 48 in.

albatross, short-tailed [*Diomedea albatrus*]: mostly white, washed with buff on head and neck; primaries and tip of tail dark brown; bill pinkish flesh color; feet bluish-white; length 37 in.

albatross, shy [*Diomedea cauta*]: whole undersurface including underwing coverts and axillaries white; head, neck and upper back white, more or less suffused with grey, especially on cheeks and nape; line over eye greyish-black; back wings and tail greyish-brown; bill yellow or grey with yellowish streak down center of upper mandible usually with narrow band of black at base of upper mandible and belt of orange at base of lower mandible, feet bluish flesh color; length 35 to 39 in.

albatross, sooty [*Phoebetria fusca*]: sooty brown, paler below and in middle of back, darker on wings and face; quill feathers with white shafts; a ring of short, white feathers, broken in front, around the eye; tail long and wedge-shaped; bill black, lower mandible with yellow or orange groove along side; feet pale flesh color or hazel; length 33 in.

albatross, wandering [*Diomedea exulans*]: mainly white, primaries black; tail and upper wing coverts mottled with black and white, whitish on portion nearest body, amount of white increasing with age; some feathers on back and sides usually freckled with narrow zigzag dark crossbars; peak or orange patch frequently present on sides of head; bill yellow or pinkish-white; feet pale flesh color; length 44 to 53 in.

albatross, waved [*Diomedea irrorata*]: head and neck white, nape tinged with buff; back wings and tail greyish, sooty brown; dusky, minutely freckled with white; bill yellow; feet bluish-white; length 35 in.

albatross, yellow-nosed [*Diomedea chlorohynchos*]: head and neck white; sides and back of head sometimes suffused with grey, usually with dark grey patch above and behind eye; rump, upper tail coverts and underparts white; underwing coverts white, except edge of wing; back slaty brown; wings above brownish-black; tail ashy brown; bill black with yellow line down center of upper mandible which is orange at tip, usually little yellow at base and tip of lower mandible; feet pinkish or bluish flesh color; length 29 to 34 in.

albedo: ratio of the amount of electromagnetic radiation reflected by a body to amount incident upon it, commonly expressed as percentage. Should be distinguished from reflectivity, which refers to one specific wavelength (monochromatic radiation). In the oceans albedo of water's surface (direct solar radiation) ranges from about 6 to 11 percent between 40° N and 40° S.

Alberta low: low-pressure area centered on eastern slope of Canadian Rockies in province of Alberta, Canada.

Alcyonarians [phylum *Coelentera*]: members of subclass *Alcyonaria*. Usually colonial, these marine creatures are distinguished from other corals by their 8-sided symmetry, 8 branched tentacles, and 8 septal or wall partitions. Alcyonarians are surrounded by their hard mineral deposits; are often brightly colored and luminescent. They include soft corals, horny corals, red or precious coral, organ-pipe coral, sea whip, sea pen, sea feathers and sea fan.

Aldebaran: first magnitude reddish star, often called the *Bull's Eye* (also *Cor Tauri*) in the group *Taurus* (the Bull). *Aldebaran* or *a Tauri* lies about 20° northwest of *Orion's Belt* and about midway between that constellation and the *Pleiades*. It was probably named for its following the last-named group in *ascension*, or rising. Ancient Greeks gave the name *Hyades* to the v-shaped group of five stars in *Taurus* of which *Aldebaran* is chief.

alee [ships]: toward the side away from the wind.

Aleutian Current: low-pressure center located near Aleutian Islands on mean charts of sea level pressure; represents main centers of action in atmospheric circulation of Northern Hemisphere.

Aleutian low: low-pressure center located near Aleutian Islands on mean charts of sea level pressure; represents one of main centers of action in atmospheric circulation of Northern Hemisphere. Aleutian low is most intense in winter; in summer is displaced toward North Pole and almost nonexistent.

alewife: small deep-bellied fish of the herring family, abundant in North American Atlantic waters north of Florida. Of poor food value, is used extensively for bait.

alewife [*Alosa pseudoharengus*]: moderate-sized, laterally compressed silvery fish; body rather deep and compressed, heaviest anterior to dorsal fin; head short, about as deep as long; lower jaw protruding; eyes large, gill rakers long, peritoneum white; dorsal fin slightly higher than long with 16 rays; caudal fin forked, lower lobe slightly longer than upper; color bluish above, silvery on sides and vertically; dark spot behind opercle.

Alexander's Acre: unusual, but easily recognizable type of deep scattering layer record (possibly caused by tent fish) in which train of echoes forms series of crescentic or mound-shaped traces. This type of layer record usually occurs at depth of about 180 fathoms and has been recorded most consistently in slope water off northeastern United States.

algae: 1) marine, brackish, and freshwater plants (including marine seaweeds), ranging in size from microscopic unicellular plants to giant kelps. Marine algae often have leaflike and stemlike parts similar to those of terrestrial plants, but differ in cellular structure. 2) group of lower photosynthetic plants varying greatly in color and habitat. They live in land or water and range in size from very tiny one-celled planktonic species to large attached forms such as kelp.

algae, blue-green [*Myxophyta*]: modern blue-green algae are filamentous growths of very simple cells joined together and adapted for life in aquatic environments. Some are effective as agents of deposition of calcium carbonate secreted outside cells or between them in a manner not suited to show distinctive structural features. Many fossils are characterized by obscure to well defined laminated concentric structures. They include numerous fossils called stromatolites, common in some Cryptozoic and many Phanerozoic formations; blue-green algae are important as rock builders and sometimes exhibit distinctive growth as guide fossils.

algae, brown: many of brown algae (seaweeds) secrete lime. Some seaweed fossils from Silurian deposits are more than 100 ft. long and 2 ft. wide; have contributed greatly to high carbon content of some of pre-Cambrian rocks. Whole series of parallel or concentric layers of fossil algae apparently formed reefs as early as Proterozoic era.

algae, golden: in California there are deposits of soft light diatomaceous earth many feet thick and many square miles in area. This material, seen under microscope is composed of remains of group of golden algae called diatoms. Shell of each diatom consists of 2 valves made of silica, fitting over each other at top and bottom like a pillbox.

algae, grass green [*Chlorophyta*]: in this group belong a host of marine freshwater algae distinguished by grass-green color of their pigment; consist of cells grouped together in bundles that give to calcium carbonate secreted around them a characteristic pattern of small tubes. A considerable number of these are common as fossils. One type distinguished by relatively complex repro-

ductive structures is the so-called stonewort *(Chara)* assemblage in which calcareous spheroidal spore capsules are prominently marked by spiral grooves and ridges; such capsules are common in various freshwater deposits from Devonian to Neogene. (Recent in age.)

algae, red [*Rhodophyta*]: characteristically grow as colonial structures that in living forms are distinguished by their red pigment. Some of them secrete calcium carbonate and are preserved as fossils, identified by rows of closely packed cells with polygonal cross sections.

algal biscuits: spherical and disk-shaped bodies up to 20 cm. in diameter, composed of algal limestone and often dolomitic.

algal bloom: unusual growth of small planktonic algae. Blooms often color the water and give it an unpleasant taste. Blooms of certain species can be fatal to other organisms.

algal film: growth of small to microscopic algae, mixed with other small organisms, which forms on all surfaces exposed to marine waters in euphotic zone; source of food for many animals, especially Chitons and many Gastropods that graze upon it, using filelike lingual ribbon, radulae, to scrape it off rock surfaces into mouth.

algal limestone: limestone composed largely of remains of calcium-secreting algae.

algal reef: reef composed largely of algal remains.

algal ridge: elevated margin of windward reef built by actively growing calcareous algae.

algal rim: low rim built by actively growing calcareous algae on lagoonal side of leeward reef, or on windward side of reef patch in a lagoon.

alignment: in nearshore wave study, a line drawn on chart parallel to general direction of section of coast; waves calculated to strike midpoint of alignment are assumed to be characteristic of those reaching shallow water of entire section.

alima larva: second larval stage of certain Stomatopoda, following pseudozoea stage.

alimentation: generally, the process of providing nourishment or sustenance; thus in glaciology, the combined processes which serve to increase mass of glacier or snowfield; opposite of ablation. Deposition of snow is major form of glacial alimentation, but other forms of precipitation along with sublimation, refreezing of meltwater, etc., also contribute.

alist: listed or canted to one side; inclined; heeling; not on an even keel.

all hands on deck [ships]: manner of calling the watch which is off duty, or "below," to assist in some work with sails or gear which watch on duty cannot accomplish quickly enough alone.

allocherm: marine sediment formed by chemical precipitations; includes fossils and pellets.

allochthonous: acquired from elsewhere, non-native.

allogenetic plankton: carried into region by currents, winds, etc., but normally living and breeding elsewhere.

allogenic: term applied to rock or sediment constituents which originated at different place and at previous time to rocks of which they now constitute a part.

allogenous detritus: detritus carried into a region from some other area.

allopatric: with separate, mutually exclusive areas of geographical distribution.

alluvial: referring to alluvium (sand, silt or similar material) deposited by running water that can no longer transport it.

alluvial fan: land counterpart of delta; assemblage of sediments marking place where stream moves from steep gradient to flatter gradient and suddenly loses its transporting power; typical of arid and semiarid climates, but not confined to them. Alluvial fans are built by rivers rising from mountains up lowlands; low, cone-shaped heaps, steepest near mouth of valley and sloping gently outward with ever decreasing gradient.

alluvium: general term for all detrital deposits resulting from operations of modern rivers, thus including sediments laid down in riverbeds, floodplains, lakes, fans at foot of mountain slopes and estuaries; unconsolidated detrital deposits ranging from clay to gravel sizes, generally poorly sorted, typically fluviatile in origin.

Almanac, Nautical: publication containing computed places of celestial bodies at successive regular intervals throughout the current year, their changes in apparent motion, parallaxes, semi-diameters, Greenwich hour angles, and other numerical data required for navigational purposes.

almucantar: small circle of the celestial sphere parallel to the horizon; a circle of equal altitude. An instrument for determining apparent places of heavenly bodies by observing the time they cross a given almucantar. The word is also written *almucanter, almicantara,* and *almacantar.*

aloft [ships]: in or into the top; at masthead on higher yards or rigging; above decks of ship.

alongshore current: movement of sand and other loose particles in given direction along coast becauseof prevailing angle of wave trains to coastline.

alongside [ships]: along, or by side of vessel.

alphacca: *a Coronae Borealis,* principal star in the *Northern Crown (Corona Borealis)* having a decli-nation of 26° 53' N. and right ascension 15 hrs. 32½ min. With the *Big Dipper's* tail star and *Arcturus, Alphacca* occupies the right-angled corner of a triangle. Also written *Alphecca.*

alphard: *a Hydrae,* chief star in *Hydra* located in 8° 26' S. declination and 9 hrs. 25 min. right ascension. It lies at the southern extremity of an almost equilateral triangle formed with *Procyon* and *Regulus.*

alpha rise: rise in floor of Arctic Ocean in Canadian Basin, roughly paralleling Lomonosov ridge.

Altair: *a Aquilae,* a first magnitude star in the group *Aquila* (Eagle) near the equator. It completes as southern apex, a right-angled triangle outlined through *Deneb* and *Vega.* A line from the *Great Bear* through *Vega* will pass close to *Altair.* Declination 8° 44' N.; R.A. 19 hrs. 48 min.

altar [ships]: step in a graving dock.

altitude: vertical distance between a point and a datum surface such as mean sea level; vertical angle between plane of horizon and line to observed point, as a star.

altocumulus: fleecy cloud formation averaging about two miles in altitude.

altostratus: cloud formation appearing as a thick sheet of gray or bluish color, averaging about 3 miles high.

Alvania crassa [*Rissoidae*]: larvae are common in summer and autumn plankton; newly hatched larva are 0.1 mm. with spiral sculptured shell. Later whorls not sculptured; larva colorless or yellowish; shell reaches 0.4 mm. before metamorphosis; foot brown at this stage.

alveolae surface [reptile]: crushing surface of jaw of turtle.

alveolus: pit or cavity in surface, as in lorica of various tintinnids. Differs from pore in not passing all the way through.

ambatche: canoe of White Nile River, made of bundles of ambatche reeds found along banks; bow tapers to point, while stern is cut off square.

ambergris: foul-smelling pathological waxy material formed largely from squid beaks in digestive tract of certain toothed whales such as sperm whale; was valued as stabilizer added in minute quantities to fine perfumes.

amberjack, greater [yellowtail]: common fish in Florida waters. It is delicately tinted with silvery lavender sides and dusky back; body covered with very small scales. Spiny dorsal much smaller than tapering soft-rayed fin, which extends back to tail. So named because it turns an amber color after capture. Average weight about 15 lbs.

amberjack, Pacific: somewhat larger blue and silvery fish with conspicuous yellow stripe extending from eye to tail. Found south of 32° N during summer.

ambient: environment surrounding a body but undisturbed or unaffected by it.

ambient dry and wet bulb temperatures: wet and dry bulb temperatures are obtained from 2 thermometers, one wrapped in damp material. Material cools due to evaporation, the rate of which depends upon relative humidity computed by comparing reading of the 2 thermometers.

ambient noise: background noise produced in sea by marine animals, ships and industrial activity, terrestrial movements, precipitation and other underwater or surface activity.

ambient temperature: temperature of medium surrounding an object.

ambulacrum: radial band of porous plates in test or shell of echinoderms. During life, ambulacra contain tube feet. In crinoids and other relatively primitive echinoderms, ambalacra are grooves along which cilia take food to mouth.

amidships [ships]: in or toward middle of ship; over and in line with keel. Term is used to convey idea of general locality but not definite extent.

amino acid: one of group of organic acids which are "building stones" of proteins. Produced by animals and plant tissues, amino acids are important in metabolism and formation of body tissues.

ammocoetes larva: larval stage of lampreys, remarkable for resemblance to *Cephalochordata*.

ammonia nitrogen: intermediate product of nitrogen cycle of sea present where organic matter decomposes in quantity.

ammonite [Ammon's horn]: octopus-type animal possessing either coiled or uncoiled chambered shell, usually snaillike, but with segments separated by sutures. Extinct species sometimes reached diameter of 6 ft.; nearest living relative is chambered nautilus. True ammonites lived from Triassic through Cretaceous, but earlier Paleozoic ammonoids were related to earlier nautiloids and later squidlike belemnoids.

ammonites [Ammon stones]: name given to fossil shells whose wrinkled whorls suggest ram's horns which often appeared on Egyptian god, Ammon. Ammonites are a genus, as a subclass of cephalopods that developed increasingly complex septa. Shells ranged from thick to thin, broad to narrow and smooth to almost incredibly ornate; could close shell with a horny plate (anaptychus) or double calcareous structure (aptychus) when body was completely drawn into the living chamber. Body, eyes and arms probably resembled those of nautiloids.

ammonoid: externally shell-covered cephalopod, characterized by strongly curved angulated or complex suture patterns and generally by position of syshuncle inside shell differing from that of nautiloids; includes ammonites, ceratites and goniatites.

Amphibia [class]: phylum *Chordata*. Internal nostrils and typically well developed lungs. Paired limbs; most have ossified vertebrate; except in primitive forms, no fishlike tail. Eggs laid and develop in freshwater only. Freshwater and terrestrial; predominantly predaceous, some herbivorous. Included are any tetrapod with naked skin. Amphibians descend from crossopterygian fish of Devonian time. Frogs, salamanders, newts and toads belong to this class.

amphiblastula larva: larval stage developing from fertilized egg cell in certain sponges, comprised of small flagellated cells in one hemisphere, which eventually give rise to choanocytes and bulkier, nonflagellated cells in the other hemisphere, which gives rise to other cells in sponge body.

Amphicelids [turtles]: typified by *Proganochelys*, found in late Triassic strata of Europe; jaws were already toothless, but tiny teeth remained in palate. Neither head nor tail could be tucked into shell but both were protected by spines. The legs, remaining outside the shell, were protected by long, sharp-edged scutes. Amphicelids ranged the world during Mesozoic and early Tertiary times and found refuge in Australia when competition became too keen elsewhere.

amphidromic: term refers to type of tide in which high water rotates counterclockwise in Northern Hemisphere around a point of zero range, i.e., the amphidromic point. The phenomenon is caused by the modifying effect of rotation of the planet on a standing oscillation.

amphidromic point: point in which the cotidal lines radiate from the no-tide point and progress through all hours of the tidal cycle.

amphineura [chitons]: chitons compose one of 5 great groups of molluscs. They are bilaterally symmetrical in form, dorsoventrally flattened and bear a series of 8 transverse plates in longitudinal row down their backs. These plates which overlap much like shingles of a house, are bordered by encircling band of muscles called a girdle; lower side of body usually bears large foot upon which the animal creeps. Gills lie between this foot and mantle. Chitons are divided into 2 large groups. One group, *Polyplacophora* (with plates), includes those chitons which possess series of 8 overlapping plates upon upper surface and have head marked off from body. In this group, sexes are separate and gills are numerous and placed upon each side of body between foot and mantle. Second group known as *Aplacophora* (without plates) have bodies more wormlike in shape and appearance. Conspicuous plates, so characteristic of other chitons are missing and the broad foot is much reduced in size; chitons are all slow-moving marine molluscs widely distributed through all oceans. They subsist upon vegetation.

amphioxus: genus of marine chordate animals placed in the family tree just beneath the simplest vertebrates; members of the subphylum *Cephalochordata*.

amphipod: member of mainly aquatic crustacean order *Amphipoda* that includes the beach flea. Usually marine, amphipods lack shells and possess 4 pairs of front legs and 3 pairs in back; prominent members of plankton.

Amphipoda [mysids]: Peracaridans without carapace and with a body flattened from side to side; sessile, compound eyes. One thoracic segment is welded to head and appendages form maxillipeds, remaining 7 segments forming a mesosome (thorax). The 6 abdominal segments are in 2 groups of 3 forming a metasome and a urosome (which bears the telson) so that the typical malacostracan segmentation of 6; 8; 6; become 6 + 1; 7; 3 + 3. Most amphipods are benthonic, but one family *Hyperiidae*, are sometimes rated as a suborder; *Hyperiidae* are fully planktonic, although in shallow sea area many bottom dwelling amphipods may appear in plankton collections, particularly in samples taken at night.

amphitrite: large inflatable ship; 65 ft. long, weighing 6 tons, drawing only 14 in. when fully loaded; has been used as tender in sea-diving operations.

amplitude: 1) magnitude of displacement of a wave from mean value. For simple harmonic wave, it is maximum displacement from the mean. For more complex wave motion, amplitude is usually taken as one-half the mean distance (or difference) between maximums and minimums. An ocean surface wave has amplitude equal to vertical distance from still-water level to wave crest, i.e., one-half wave height. 2) in engineering usage, loosely, the wave height from crest to trough. 3) semi-range of constituent tide.

anabolism: constructive processes in metabolism, building up of compounds and structural elements that comprise the tissue or substance of an organism.

anadromous: form of life cycle among fishes in which maturity is attained in ocean, and adults ascend streams and rivers to spawn in fresh water, e.g., salmon and shad.

anaerobe: organisms for whose life processes a complete or (in some forms) nearly complete absence of oxygen is essential. Facultative anaerobes can utilize free oxygen; obligate anaerobes are poisoned by it.

anaerobic sediment: highly organic sediment rich in H_2S formed in absence of free oxygen. Characteristics of some fiords and marine basins where little or no circulation or mixing of bottom water occurs.

anal fin: in fish, a mid-ventral fin behind the anus.

anal plate: single or divided scale lying just in front of anus in reptiles.

anal warts [amphibian]: small, white warts on each side of anus in some frogs.

Anapagurus [Paguridans]: antennal scale is relatively short. Zoea of *Anapagurus* species resemble those of *P. cuanensis* in that longest spine on telson is less than half the greatest width of the telson, but differ in that the 5th abdominal segment bears only short lateral spines. The final zoea has only 2 or 3 pairs of pleopods as opposed to 4 pairs in *Pagurus sp.*

Anapagurus hyndmanni [Paguridans]: zoea of this species differ from those of *A. laevis* in absence of chromatophores in center of carapace. Instead, chromatophores are present on base of maxillipeds and one on rostrum. Rostrum is appreciably longer than antennal scale. First stage zoea is approximately 2.7 mm. and reaches 4 mm. before metamorphosis into megalopa which has only 2 pairs of pleopods and is 2.7 mm. long.

Anapagurus laevis [Paguridans]: zoea is characterized by presence of a chromatophore in mid-dorsal surface of carapace and one on each eyestalk; posterior margin of the telson is straight or even slightly convex, in early stages. First stage zoea is approximately 3 mm. and final stage 5.5 mm. long. The megalopa has 3 pairs of functional pleopods and eyestalks only slightly longer than broad; is about 3.5 mm. long.

anaspids: though related to osteostracans, these creatures were torpedo-shaped and had ventral fins; eyes lay near side of head; hind end of body bent downward producing a reversed heterocercal tail which drove the animal upward as it swam.

anastomosis: union of 2 or more hollow organs, such as blood vessels.

ancestrula: in *Bryozoa*, first zooecium of a colony; zooecium formed by larva upon settling.

anchialina agilis [mysids]: body short and stout and cuticle covered with minute bustles. Carapace is large and covers not only all the thoracic segments but also first abdominal one; has a straight posterior margin and large triangular rostrum. This species, as name implies, is a rapid swimmer and caught at varying depths; mainly a coastal species with summer maximum.

anchor [ships]: device for securing vessel to the ground underwater by means of attached cable.

anchorage [ships]: area where a ship anchors or may anchor, either because of suitability or designation.

anchorate: 1) held by an anchor. 2) something anchor-shaped.

anchored: fastened to an anchor; held by, or, as if by, an anchor; fixed.

anchor ice: 1) ice formed on bottom of stream (also called "ground ice" or "bottom ice"). 2) ice found attached or anchored to bottom irrespective of its nature or formation.

anchor light or riding light [ships]: a 32-point white light by a ship or anchor.

anchor phraseology; at anchor: in a legal sense, means that a vessel is attached to the ground by anchor and cable, by being fixed to a buoy made fast to the ground, or by being moored to a dock.

anchor's aweigh [ships]: when anchor has broken free of bottom.

anchovy, bay [*Anchoa mitchilli*]: small, slender, green fish with silvery lateral stripe and deep, undershot mouth. Mouth subterminal and deeply cleft; dorsal fin entirely of soft rays; anal fin with 24—26 rays, silver stripe along side. Color pale greenish or whitish, very translucent; diffused silvery stripe about as wide as the eye along each side of body; about 2½ in. long.

anchovy, striped [*Anchoa hepsetus*]: small, slender, green fish with silvery lateral stripe and deep undershot mouth. Mouth subterminal and deeply cleft; dorsal fin entirely of soft rays; anal fin with 19 to 20 rays; silver stripe along sides. Color pale greenish or whitish, very translucent; silvery lateral band (about as wide as the eye) on each side, from head to base of tail; up to 6 in. long.

andesite: volcanic rock having little or no quartz; along with basaltic lava it forms beach sands of volcanic islands.

andesite line: postulated geographic and petrographic boundary between the andesite-daciterhyolite rock association of the margin of Pacific Ocean and olivine basalt-trachyte rock association of Pacific Ocean basin and its included islands.

Andromeda: constellation directly south of *Cassiopeia*, containing navigational stars *Alpheratz*, *Mirach*, and *Almach*, and located in 28 to 42 degrees north declination and 0 to 2 hours right ascension.

anemometer: device that measures wind speed, usually by 4 revolving vanes with cuplike structures on the ends.

anemone: soft-bodied complex polyps of the coelenterate class *Anthozoa;* most common in warm shallow waters but also found in a wide variety of environments all over the world. Slow-moving carnivores, they catch prey with stinging tentacles on their flower-shaped oral discs.

anemone crab, hairy [*Polydectus cupulifer*]: entire body and legs of this crab are covered with thick coat of long, yellowish hair. Body reaches width of at least 1 in.; usually found carrying a sea anemone in each of its pinchers. These anemones are held firmly by the crab, and may be used to ward off real or imaginary enemies. The anemone crab lives under stones in shallow water from shoreline to depths of at least 50 ft.

anemone crab, tessellated [*Lybia tesselata*]: has a carapace which is somewhat hexagonal in shape, smooth in texture, and marked with yellow, pink and brown; back covered with maze of irregular lines, and legs are marked with narrow bands of purple; body about 1½ in. in width. This crab carries small anemones in its pinchers and uses these anemones to ward off crabs and other animals which it fears.

aneroid: literally, "not wet," containing no liquid; applied to a barometer which contains no liquid; an aneroid barometer.

aneroid barometer: an instrument to measure air pressure. A band moves across a graduated dial, activated by the rise and fall of one surface of a partially evacuated, sealed metal chamber.

angaria: in maritime law, forcible seizure of a ship for public use; in international law, use or destruction by a belligerent, subject to a claim for compensation, of neutral property within its territory in time of war, a privilege claimed by belligerents under title of *jus angaria,* or *right of angary.*

angelfish, French: also black angelfish; has small mouth that limits its diet to sedentary aquatic forms of life. Is a dusky fish speckled with gold; dorsal fin sweeps gracefully backward terminating in a prolonged tip. Dorsal and anal fins are dusky gray becoming darker at margins; pectoral fins are yellow; ventral fins, black.

angelfish, queen: attains a length of 24 in.; fittingly named "the queen" for it is one of the most beautiful marine fishes. Its detailed coloring is difficult to describe. Predominantly blue and gold; has blue lips, blue margins to the long tapering dorsal and anal fins; sides are pearl grey or fawn-colored, speckled with brown. The tapering flame-yellow tips of dorsal and anal fins suggest the jet exhaust of an airplane engine.

angel wing [*Pterosiphonia dendroida*]: extremely delicate; grow in crevices and on protected faces of rocks between mean low and the 1.5-ft. tide levels. They are dainty, lacelike and rose-red to bright red. Varies from 1 to 3 in. in height, with branches not more than 1/16 in. wide. A number of erect branches arise from a short stipe on plane and divide into several orders. In the angel wing seaweed the older branches trail along the ground; younger ones are erect. The trailing branches eventually form rhizoids which act as holdfasts.

angle: inclination of two lines or planes to each other, or difference in direction of two lines. A common term for an *angle-bar* or an *angle-iron*.

angle bars [ships]: bar of angle-shaped section used as a stiffener and on riveted ships ties floors to the shell.

angle collar [ships]: angle bent to fit a pipe, column, tank or stack, intersecting or projecting through a bulkhead or deck for the purpose of making a watertight or oiltight joint.

angle of roll [ships]: the angle between the lateral and horizontal axis of a craft; considered positive if port side is higher than starboard side, but may be designated starboard or port depending upon which side is lower.

angle of yaw [ships]: horizontal angular displacement of the longitudinal axis of a ship from its neutral position, during a yaw; designated right or left according to direction of displacement of the bow.

anglerfish: anglerfish is far from being a beautiful fish; head is broad and flattened; enormous mouth lines have 4 rows of sharp inward pointing teeth; dwarfed body tapers rapidly to a small tail. A fringe of barbels hangs from chin like a scraggly beard; other barbels extend in a line on either side of body, some of them resembling bits of vegetation and so serving as camouflage; entire fish is mottled, chocolate brown color that harmonizes with dingy tones of ocean bottom.

angula: Singhalese double-dugout, platform canoe used at Kunsdale, Ceylon, for ferrying passengers. Hulls are similar to the "Varagum orri" except that bottoms are flat instead of round, making the craft better adapted to landing on shallow shore. The canoes lay parallel, with a platform built across amidships and range from 25 to 30 ft. long and 14 to 16 in. wide with strongly raking overhangs.

angular spreading: lateral extension of ocean waves as they move out of the generating area as well.

angular spreading factor: in ocean wave forecasting ratio of actual wave energy present at a point to that which would have been present in absence of angular spreading.

angular velocity: representation of rate of rotation of a particle about the axis of rotation, with magnitude equal to time rate of angular displacement of any point of the body.

animal exclusion theory: theory that the patchiness and inverse relationship in surface distribution of zooplankton is caused in part by failure of zooplankton to make it to surface waters when impeded in their diurnal vertical migration by dense clouds of phytoplankton.

anisogamous: characterized by a fusion of different gametes.

annelid: member of *Annelida*, phylum of worms with soft, cylindrical, segmented bodies that often bear stiff bristles. Phylum includes rock-worms, lugworms (used for fish bait), sea "mice," nereids, earthworms and leeches. A phylum of invertebrate animals in which the body is typically made up of a series of rings or segments covered by a soft cuticle and lacking jointed appendages; e.g., earthworms, leeches, and many marine worms.

anniversary winds: general term for local winds or larger scale wind systems (such as monsoons, etesians, etc.) that occur annually.

annual inequality: seasonal or yearly variation in water level or in tidal current speed.

annulus: transverse groove bearing the horizontal flagellum in dinoflagellates.

anomalistic tide cycle: average period of about 27½ days measured from perigee to perigee, when the moon completes one revolution around the earth.

anomaly: in oceanography, difference between conditions actually observed at a serial station and those that would have existed had the water all been of a given arbitrary temperature and salinity.

Anomura [tribe]: larvae of 2 main families frequently occur in plankton of the Galatheidae and of Porcellanidae. The first stage larva hatched from the egg is a zoea, unique in that carapace bears a long rostral and 2 long posterolateral spines. First zoeal stage has 2 fully formed maxillipeds but only rudimentary 3rd one. Only in later stages does 3rd maxilliped become a porcellanid, later ones being comparable to what in brachyuran crabs would be called megalopae.

anoxia: absence of oxygen; abnormal condition produced by breathing air which is deficient in oxygen.

anstau: process resulting in the piling up of water, such as occurs in convergence.

answer the helm: respond to action of a rudder.

antagonism: relationship between species in which at least one species is harmed; also known as antibiosis.

antapex: the end opposite the apex; base.

Antarctic: of, pertaining to, or designating South Pole regions; opposed to *Arctic*.

Antarctica: name given to the great continent lying near the South Pole, for which *Magellanica* was at one time proposed. Others have suggested

Victorialand, as now given to a part of it, be extended to the whole.

Antarctic air: type of air whose characteristics are developed in an antarctic region. Antarctic air appears to be colder at surface in all seasons, and at all levels in autumn and winter, than arctic air.

Antarctic anticyclone: glacial anticyclone which has been said to overlie continent of Antarctica; analogous to Greenland anticyclone.

Antarctic Circle: the parallel of latitude 66½° S of the equator.

Antarctic Convergence: 1) important zoogeographical feature in the Southern Hemisphere where northeast-drifting surface waters from the Antarctic meet and sink beneath southeast-drifting warmer waters; lies for most part, in or near the 50° to 60° latitude band south. 2) the Southern Hemisphere polar convergence; best defined convergence line in the oceans, being recognized by relatively rapid northward increase in surface temperature. It can be traced around the world in the broad belt of open water between Antarctica to the south and Africa, Australia and South America to the north.

Antarctic Divergence: regions near shores of Antarctica where water of intermediate depths rises to surface in extensive upwelling replacing surface waters that are drifting in a northern and eastern direction in the West Wind Drift.

Antarctic Ocean: name commonly applied to those portions of the Atlantic, Pacific and Indian Oceans which reach the Antarctic continent on the south, and are bounded on the north by the Subtropical Convergence. This feature is not recognized as an ocean body.

Antares: *a Scorpii*, principal star in the group *Scorpio*, its name in Greek meaning *similar to Mars*, because of its reddish color; called also *Cor Scorpii (Scorpion's Heart)*. Located in 26° 19′ S. with a right ascension of 16 hrs. 26 min., it forms with *Arcturus* and *Spica* a conspicuous triangle, nearly right-angled at *Spica*.

Antecedent Platform: postulated submarine platform, 50 meters or more below sea level, from which barrier reefs and atolls grow upward to water surface.

antecedent platform theory: theory of coral atoll and barrier reef formation which postulates a submarine platform 50 meters or more below sea level from which barrier reefs and atolls grow upward to water surface without changes in sea level.

antecedent stream: a stream that maintains during and after uplift, the course it had established prior to uplift.

antenna: in arthropods, a preoral sensory appendage of the head. Antennae are paired. In crustacea there are 2 pairs; first pair commonly called antennules, whereas the term antennae is reserved for second pair; feelers.

antennal scale: short, flattened exopodite or outer branch of 2nd antennae in mysids and various decapod crustaceans.

antennules: in crustacea, 1st pair of feelers.

anteriad: toward anterior end.

anterior [*Brachiopoda*]: direction of shell margin where valves separate when open; opposite position of hinge line.

antherozoid: swimming male gamete in certain algae and other primitive plants.

Anthomedusae [*Gymnoblastea*]: medusae of gymnoblast hydroids, distinguished by having polyps not retractile into cups or hydrothecae; bell-shaped and bear gonads on the stomach or manubrium. As a rule, tentacles around margin of the bell are few. The sense organs are eyespots (ocelli). Statocysts are observed.

anthozoan: 1) one of a class *(Anthozoa)* of the coelenterates in which the medusoid stage is absent and the polyp (hydroid) stage is better developed than in other coelenterates; sea anemones, sea pens and corals are members of this group. 2) member of the coelenterate class *Anthozoa*. Anthozoans are all marine and may be colonial or solitary. There are none of the jellyfish-like medusae forms but only sedentary polyps in this class; these polyps reach highest development in the entire coelenterate phylum; e.g., sea anemones, corals, alcyonarians, sea fans, sea pens, sea pansies and sea feathers.

antibiosis: relationship between species in which certain substances produced or excreted by organisms are generally harmful to others. Mass kills of fishes and other organisms due to outbreaks of red tide are examples of antibiosis.

Antiboreal Convergence: second greatest zone of convergence in Southern Hemisphere, located approximately 10° north of the Antarctic Convergence; often called Subtropical Convergence.

anticline: term applied to strata which dip in opposite directions from a common ridge or axis, as does the roof of a house.

anticyclone: atmospheric anticyclonic circulation; a close circulation. With respect to relative direction of its rotation, is the opposite of cyclone.

anticyclonic: having a sense of rotation about the local vertical opposite to that of the earth's rotation; i.e., clockwise in the Northern Hemisphere, counterclockwise in the Southern Hemisphere, undefined at the equator; opposite of cyclonic.

antifouling paint: substance applied to a surface to prevent the attachment of fouling organisms when submerged. The principle applied is the gradual release of compounds toxic to fouling organisms.

Antilles Current: current formed by parts of the North Equatorial Current that flows along northern side of the Greater Antilles; joins the Florida Current north of Grand Bahama Island to form Gulf Stream.

Antipatharia: compound corals with slender and branching colonies and a horny skeleton, 6, 10 or 12 complete mesenteries in each corallite.

antitrades: deep layer of westerly winds in the troposphere above surface trade winds of the tropics. They comprise the equatorial side of the mid-latitude westerlies, but are found at upper levels rather than at the surface.

antizoeal stage: first larval stage of various stomatopods.

antoeci: two places on same meridian and on opposite parallels of latitude equidistant north and south of equator.

anus: 1) posterior opening of the digestive tract through which food wastes are generally excreted. 2) in *Gastropoda*, in recent snails it lies either to right or left of the head. 3) in *Mollusca*, opens into posterior portion of mantle cavity in midline body.

aperiodic motion: any nonperiodic motion; for example a pulse from a shot in a shot hole.

apertural face [*Foraminifera*]: flattened surface of chamber adjacent to aperture.

aperture: 1) opening. In shelled organisms such as foraminifers the main or largest opening in the test. 2) in *Bryozoa*, opening in wall of skeleton (zooecium) through which living animal extends lophophores and partitions of body. 3) in *Foraminifera*, relatively large opening to exterior in chamber formed last.

aperture [ships]: space provided between propeller and sternpost for the propeller.

apex: initial part of gastropod shell.

aphanite: closely grained rock; individual crystals cannot be seen with naked eye.

aphelion: point on earth's orbit farthest from the sun.

aphotic zone: that portion of ocean waters where light is insufficient for plants to carry on photosynthesis.

apical [*Gastropoda*]: direction of apex or its vicinity.

apogean range: average of all monthly tidal ranges occurring at the time of apogee.

apogean tidal current: tidal current of decreased speed occurring at time of apogean tide.

apogean tide: tides of decreased range occurring monthly near the time of the moon's apogee.

apogee: that point on the orbit of the moon (or any other earth satellite) farthest from the earth; opposite of perigee.

apophysis: 1) in *Radiolaria*, a horizontal growth at right angles to longitudinal axis of the radial spines. 2) projection peglike or fingerlike in structure.

Aporrhais pes-pelicani [*Aporrhaidae*]: only the later larvae are recognizable with certainty. In these the shell is composed of 3 whorls of which last half of the body whorl is striated and the rest smooth. The shell is yellowish and the foot bilobed anteriorly but pointed posteriorly. The most characteristic feature is enormous 6-lobed velum (2.8 mm. across). Each lobe bears a brown spot near its tip and the whole velum is bordered with brown.

aport [ships]: toward the left or port side.

apparent velocity: velocity with which fixed phase of a seismic wave, usually its front or beginning, passes an observer.

appendage: movable, projecting part of an animal's body, e.g., leg, antenna, etc.

appendages [ships]: relatively small portions of a vessel projecting beyond its main outline, as shown by cross sections and water sections. Word applies to following parts of stern and sternpost: keel below its shell line, rolling keel or fin, the rudder, rudder post, screw, bilge keel, struts, bossing and skeg.

appendicularian: one of a class *(Larvacea)* of small transparent planktonic tunicates in which body is covered by a large tunic and is composed of a trunk and long tail. Some species are luminescent.

appendix interna: in *Euphausiacea*, a median process uniting the 2 pleopods of a given somite; also termed stylambis.

approach, right of: privilege claimed by a naval vessel to approach a private craft for ostensible purpose of verifying flag and character of such craft.

approximate absolute temperature scale: a temperature scale with the ice point at 273° and boiling point of water at 373°.

apron: sloping underwater extension of an iceberg, or an outspread deposit of ice or rock material in front of a glacier.

apron plate [ships]: plate fitted in continuation of the shell plating above the forecastle sheer strake at the stem; sometimes fitted one in each side of stem, and serve as foundation for the bow mooring pipes.

aquaculture: fish and shellfish farming; development of new seafoods, and methods of rearing larvae of clams and oysters.

aquafact: an isolated boulder which has been worn smooth on its seaward face by wave abrasion.

aqualung: self-contained underwater breathing apparatus (SCUBA), of the demand or open-circuit type.

Aquarius: constellation close to the equinoctial through which the sun passes in February. Located in 21½ to 23 hours right ascension, it contains no navigational stars, *a*, *β*, and *δ Aquarii* being of only magnitude 3.2; 3.1; and 3.5; respectively.

aquarter: on the quarter; in or from a direction approximately 45° abaft the beam; said of wind or sea.

aqueous: pertaining to or containing water, as an aqueous solution.

aqueous desert: marine bottom environment in which there is little or no macroscopic invertebrate shelled life, usually a bottom of shifting sands.

aquifer: water-saturated bed or stratum of rock that can supply a well or spring.

Aquila: northern constellation in the *Milky Way*, close to the equinoctial in about 19 to 20 hours of right ascension, containing the bright star *Altair (a Aquilae)* of magnitude 0.9.

Ara: southern constellation adjacent to, and south of, the tail in *Scorpio*, containing navigational stars *a Arae* and *β Arae*. Also called the *Altar*.

Arachnida: class of phylum *Arthropoda* which includes spiders, scorpions, ticks and mites, etc. Most are land-dwelling forms, although a few mites are aquatic. Some distinguishing characteristics are 4 pairs of thoracic legs, book lungs for breathing, simple eyes, chitinous exoskeleton and body divided into 2 parts: unsegmented cephalothorax and an abdomen.

aragonite: a form of calcium carbonate which is same mineralogically as calcite but has a rhombic form; often deposited from strongly saline waters and is not stable, the mineral altering eventually to calcite.

arbor [ships]: principal axis member or spindle of a machine by which a motion of revolution is transmitted.

arcacea: ligament is nearer the narrow end and provinculum bears numerous small teeth equal in size and not clearly separated.

Archaeogastropoda [gastropod larvae]: eggs of most archaeogastropods are shed singly into water, e.g., in *Acmaea virginea* and *Gibbula cineraria*, and larva hatches as a trochophore. In many genera eggs are laid in gelatinous masses attached to substratum and larva hatches as a veliger, i.e., trochophore stage is omitted. Typically, the veliger is provided with a round ciliated velum.

archaepocyathan: reef-building calcareous invertebrate with porous double-walled skeleton of cylindrical or conical form, known only from Lower and Middle Cambrian rocks, worldwide in distribution.

arched iceberg: iceberg with large opening at waterline, extending through the iceberg forming an arch.

Archelon [turtles]: giant turtle more than 12 ft. long with narrow head, hooked beak, huge flippers and a weight of about 6,000 lbs. Lived in late Cretaceous seas of South Dakota, Kansas and adjacent regions. Archelon was one of the turtles that lost most of their armor. Tough skin covered the bones that remained.

archerfish: small deep-bellied fish of the East Indies *(Toxotes jaculator)* about five inches in length, which is said to capture insects flying near the water's surface by ejecting small spurts of water at them from its mouth.

archibenthal: on continental slope; between the relatively shallow continental shelf and the main ocean bottom, or abyssal plain.

archibenthic: pertaining to a zone extending from a depth of about 650 ft. (200 meters), continental shelf edge, to between 2,625 and 3,000 ft. (800 to 1,100 meters).

Archimedes' principle: statement that a new upward or buoyant force, equal in magnitude to the weight of displacement fluid, acts upon a body either partly or wholly submerged in a fluid at rest under the influence of gravity. This force is known as the Archimedean buoyant force (or buoyancy) and is independent of the shape of the submerged body and does not depend upon any special properties of the fluid.

archipelagic apron: gently sloping sea floor with a generally smooth surface, particularly found around groups of islands or seamounts.

Archipelago: group of islands more or less adjacent to each other and arranged in groups covering portions of the sea.

arch piece [ships]: principal axis member of spindle of a machine by which motion of revolution is transmitted.

arch shooting: term applies to method of refraction; seismic prospecting in which variation of travel time with the azimuth from a given shot point is used to infer geologic structure.

arctalia: as defined in zoögeography, northern marine realm which extends southward as far as floating ice is found.

Arctic: of, pertaining to, or designating North Polar regions within the Arctic Circle; opposed to *Antarctic*. Also, pertaining to constellations *Great Bear* and *Little Bear*.

arctic air: type of air whose characteristics are developed mostly in winter over arctic surfaces of ice and snow; cold aloft and extends to great heights; surface temperatures often higher than those of polar air.

Arctic Convergence: Northern Hemisphere polar convergence. Because of configuration of oceans in the northern latitudes, this convergence zone is poorly defined.

Arctic high: weak high that appears on mean charts of sea level pressure over the Arctic Basin during late spring, summer and early autumn.

Arctic pack: sea ice more than 2 yrs. old. This nearly salt-free ice has a smoothly undulating surface due to smoothing of pressure ice by weathering. It has a thickness of more than 2.5 meters (8.2 ft.) and often is colored in different tints of blue.

Arctic sea smoke: same as steam fog; often specifically applied to steam fog rising from small areas of open water within sea ice.

Arctos: *Ursa Major* and *Ursa Minor*, or Big Bear and Little Bear, a collective name sometimes given these constellations.

Arcturus: brightest star in the northern sky and principal one in the group *Bootes*; easily located by following a curve started by the *Dipper* handle, or tail of *Ursa Major*, the name is sometimes applied, incorrectly, to that constellation itself. In declination about 19° 27′ N. and right ascension 14 hrs. 13 min.

arcuate: arched or curved.

arcuate delta: curved or lowered delta with convex side toward the sea.

arenaceous: applied to rock or sediments derived from or containing sand.

Arendal yawl: sharp-ended, open, clinker-built skiff used in the fishing industry around Arendal, Norway. Stem and stern are alike with curved raking posts. An outboard rudder is hung from the sternpost. Length is roughly 4 times the beam. Rig consists of a single lugsail, wide at the foot, and boat is equipped with 2 sets of oars and oarlocks.

areolation: crowding of a surface with small alveoli or pits, forming a sort of network or meshwork.

arete: 1) narrow, rugged ridge formed by glacial plucking on opposite sides of the ridge. 2) narrow, sharp divide between 2 glacial cirques.

argillaceous: containing clay particles or of the nature of clay.

Argonautidae [family]: argonauts have no shell and are free-swimming creatures which live in open sea. The "paper nautilus" of shell collectors is not the shell of a nautilus, but the egg case of the female argonaut formed by secretion from the expanded weblike ends of upper pair of arms of female. Prior to mating sperm of male is stored within 3rd arm on left side. Arm becomes detached (hectocotylized) during mating and is thereafter found in the mantle cavity of the female. Male argonaut is smaller than female, reported to be less than 1 in. long. There are about 3 present-day species.

Argus Island: oceanographic research tower erected in Plantogenel Bank, 22 miles southwest of Bermuda.

Aries: *The Ram*, a sign of the Zodiac. A star group lying west of, and next to, *Leo*, containing *Hamal (a Arietis)* and *Sheratan (β Arietis)*, about 4° apart and, respectively, of magnitudes 2.2 and 2.7. *Hamal* lies in R.A. 2 hrs. 4 min. and Dec. 23° N.

arm: any deep and comparatively narrow branch of the sea extending inland, as opposed to gulfs and firths.

arrival: chronologic appearance (such as first, second, third) of different wave energies in seismic or acoustic record.

arrow worm: one of a phylum *(Chaetognatha)* of small, elongated transparent, wormlike animals, pelagic in all seas from the surface to great depths; abundant and may multiply rapidly into vast swarms.

artemon [ships]: sail used on Roman ships; rectangular in shape, similar to a spritsail, and set from a mast that was raked to a sharp angle over the bow.

artesian: pertaining to subsurface water under pressure sufficient to make it rise above the level of the aquifer.

arthrodires ["jointed necks"]: these fish lost most of their body armor but developed a massive head shield that was hinged to plates on the shoulder region. During late Devonian some also became the largest and most savage vertebrates of the time.

arthropleura: true arthropod, now extinct. It had a rather simple head, 29 segments and diminutive tail. Exoskeleton covered head, tail and body segments, each of which carried one pair of jointed legs that divided into two. Arthropleura apparently inhabited moist lowlands or swamps for its remains are found in coal-bearing Pennsylvanian formations from England to Czechoslovakia. Largest species was 5 ft. long and must have looked like a huge broad-bodied centipede.

Arthropoda [phylum]: class *Trilobita*. Greek "arthron" joint; *"podos"* foot. Name trilobite refers to division of body into 3 longitudinal lobes. Cambrian to Permian. Extinct group of arthropods averaging 1 in. in length but ranging up to 27 in. Highly developed in Cambrian but they reached their peak in Ordovician and had entered evolutionary graveyard by end of Permian.

arthropods ["jointed feet"]: from head to whatever serves as a tail, the typical arthropod is a series of segments or somites connected by movable joints. More may be traced in grooves and constrictions where segments once movable have been fused into shields or plates. Joints show plainly because they bend, being soft parts of an exoskeleton that often becomes hard enough to be called a shell.

article: in arthropods, one of the segments of a jointed appendage.

Articulata [order *Orthida*]: 1) Cambrian to Permian. Typically unequal biconvex shells with relatively wide, straight hinge lines and with interareas on both valves. Shell impunctate, rarely punctate or pseudopunctate. 2) in this varied group of stalked and stalkless crinoids the cups are small and contain few plates. Plates of the cup are united by slightly flexible joints; tegmen is a leathery affair that bears the mouth and open food grooves and may be studded with small plates. Early Triassic to Recent.

Articulata [*Pentameracea*]: Cambrian to Ordovician; biconvex; spondylium in pedicle valve; delthyrium open or partly closed by deltidium; impunctate shell; interareas commonly small; hinge line short or moderately long.

Articulata [*Rhynchonellacea*]: Ordovician to Recent; typically biconvex shell with strong beaks on one or both valves, short hinge lines, functional pedicle; impunctate, rare punctate.

Articulata [*Sqiriterida*]: Ordovician to Recent; typically biconvex; interareas, pedicle and hinge length highly variable; punctate or impunctate; spiral brachidium.

Articulata [*Strophomenacea*]: Ordovician to Jurassic; plane to concave—convex, less commonly biconvex, interareas high variable; hinge line typically long, pseudodeltidium rarely absent, pedicle opening much reduced or absent; typically pseudopunctate.

Articulata [*Terebratulina*]: Devonian to Recent; typically biconvex, short hinge line, interarea on pedicle valve only; punctate, functional pedicle; looped brachidium.

artificial upwelling: concept of having a nuclear reactor or other unnatural source, sitting on bottom of the ocean in cold, low productivity parts of the sea to create warmth needed to generate turbulence and subsequent fertility to area.

ascendant: vector representing rate of increase of property.

ascension: rising or elevation of a point or star above the celestial horizon.

ascidian: either colonial or solitary member of class *Ascidiacea* in subphylum *Tunicata*. Common in marine littoral waters; attached to seaweed, piers, rocks, etc. Ascidians have free-swimming larvae before they become sedentary, baglike adults. Best known are sea squirts.

Ascoceras [nautiloids]: Ascoceras began by building slender shells with gentle curvature and no ballast except a siphon that moved closer to the venter. Living chamber also became longer and during late Ordovician times it began to swell, allowing septa to cut off gas-filled chambers that curved broadly over dorsal region, allowing the body to become its own ballast. As the body moved into enlarged living chamber, the siphuncle closed and the rest of the shell dropped off. Thus a long pointed shell became short and better suited to active life than it had been during youth.

asdic: British echo-ranging equipment.

aseismic: not subject to earthquake; as an aseismic region.

ash breeze: absence of wind; calm.

ash fall: rain of airborne volcanic ash falling from an eruption cloud characteristic of volcanic eruptions.

ashore: land adjacent to water; opposed to aboard or afloat.

aspect: angle made by a target with the line joining it to the observation point.

aspinose: without spines, as in some *Radiolaria*. In aspinose pores, the opening of the pores is not armed with a spine.

astacin carotenoid: animal pigment found especially in the covering of adult planktonic crustacea. Measurement of this carotenoid in seawater samples gives some measure of microscopic animal matter.

Astacura [lobsters and crayfish]: these animals range from large to small size with well-developed symmetrical body and extended abdomen. As in the case with Palinura, they are well armed, but without spines characteristic of that tribe. The tailfan is broad; there is a well-developed rostrum. The outer plate of the terminal uropods is jointed by means of a transverse, suturelike joint. The 2nd antennae have flagella.

asterionella [subclass *Pennatae*]: elongated cells are thicker at one end and stick together by thicker ends to form colonies of variable shape. *A. japonica* forms star-shaped clusters which unite into spirals.

astern [ships]: signifying position, in rear or abaft the stern; as regards to motion, opposite of going ahead; backwater.

asteroid: starfish of class *Asteroidea* in phylum, *Echinodermata*. Radially symmetrical, starfish are either star-shaped or pentagonal; generally possess 5 flexible, tapering arms but some species may have up to 50 arms.

Astraeospongia: bowl-shaped organism that seems to lay on bottom without attachment. Its coarse spicules have 6 rays arranged like a star and 2 more forming buttonlike bumps at right angles to others. A single species, *A. meniscus*, is common in middle Silurian (Nigarian) rocks of Kentucky and Tennessee.

Astrocoenina [*Scleractinia*]: compound; corallites small; septa formed by relatively few (up to 8) simple trabeculae; Triassic to Recent.

astronomical: pertaining to, or in accordance with, methods or principles of astronomy.

astronomical position: a point on earth whose position has been determined by celestial observations.

astronomical tide: tide due to attractions of sun and moon in contrast to meteorological tide.

ASWEPS: Antisubmarine Warfare Environmental Prediction System. Analyzes data and prepares predictions of oceanographic conditions useful to ASW-connected personnel.

asymptotic radiance distribution: radiance distribution which is the limit of distribution in the hydrosphere as earth increases infinitely; symmetrical around the vertical and independent of sun zenith distance.

athwart: across; from side to side; transverse; at right angles to the fore-and-aft line; across a vessel's course.

athwartships [ships]: crosswise, from side to side; transversely across the line of ship's course. Athwart the ship; crosswise of the ship.

atka fish or atka mackerel: valuable food fish of the North Pacific coasts, called also *greenling* and *rock trout*.

Atlantic Ocean: extends from Antarctic northward to southern limits of the Greenland and Norwegian Seas; separated from Pacific Ocean by the meridian of Cape Horn to the Antarctic Continent. Boundary between the Atlantic and Indian Oceans is placed at the meridian of Cape Agulhas to the Antarctic Continent.

atmospheric pressure: that of the air at sea level, under standard condition in which a mercury barometer reads 29.94 in. or 760 millimeters.

atoke: nonsexual and nonpelagic anterior part of body in certain polychaete worms.

atoll: roughly circular, elliptical or horseshoe-shaped island or ring of islands of reef origin; composed of coral and algal rock and sand rimming a lagoon in which there are no islands of noncoral origin.

atollom: large reef ring in Maldive Islands consisting of smaller reef rings. The word atoll was derived from this name.

atoll reef: ring-shaped coral and limestone reef often carrying low sand islands enclosing a body of water.

atomic number: number of positive charges on nucleus of atom of given element, and also number of electrons normally around nucleus, or number of protons within nucleus.

Atremata: inarticulate *Brachiopoda* with horny and calcium phosphate shells except in *Trimerillacea* where shell is composed of calcium carbonate; pedicle emerging between the divergent valves shows little or no tendency to enclose it in a delthyrium; has ill-defined pedicle opening formed by shallow notches in both valves, allowing stalk to emerge between them. The original shape probably is that of *Lingulella*, i.e., an elongated, pointed pedicle valve and a shorter, blunter brachial both with gently curved margins.

atrium: enclosed space in an animal body, lined with ectodermal epithelium and morphologically outside the animal surrounding the pharyngeal region, into which water from pharynx flows and into which excretory and reproductive organs usually empty; open to exterior by the atrial opening or atropore. Found in tunicates, cephalochords, etc.

Atterberg grade scale: decimal grade scale for particle size, with 2 mm. as reference point and involving the fixed ratio 10. Subdivisions are the geometric means of grade limits: 0.2, 0.6, 2.0, 6.3, 20.0.

Atterberg limits: indices (LL, PL) of water content of sediment at the boundary between semiliquid and plastic state (liquid limit) and plastic and semisolid state (plastic limit).

attitude: position of a body as determined by inclination of the axis to some frame of reference. If not otherwise specified this reference is fixed to earth.

Atyidae [family]: bubble shells are among the most frail and fragile of shells and very difficult to collect without breaking. They are too small for the molluscs which inhabit them and consequently, nearly concealed by the animal which they are supposed to cover. These shells are oval or cylindrical in shape; very light, frail, thin texture; low or concealed spire; usually light brownish or greenish in color.

augite: black, silicate mineral of granular structure, occurring in igneous rocks.

augmentation of moon's semi-diameter: increase of moon's angular semi-diameter with increase in altitude of that body, being at a maximum when in the zenith and zero when in the horizon. This is due to an observer being nearer the moon by approximately the length of the earth's radius (about 4,000 miles) when overhead, as compared with an altitude of zero. Used in correcting moon's observed altitude, augmentation is applied to *horizontal semi-diameter* as given in the *Nautical Almanac* for each day. Its value attains a maximum of 18 seconds, which is considered, generally, as negligible in practical navigation.

augmenting factor: factor used in harmonic analysis of tides or tidal currents; correction factor for tabulating hourly heights or speeds used in summation for constituents other than S not occurring in the exact constituent hour to which they are assigned, but at times may differ as much as a half hour.

auks [*Charadriiformes*]: members of this order are very small sea birds with comparatively short necks, small, narrow wings and very short tails of 12 to 18 feathers. Legs are short and placed very far back near the tail. They have only 3 toes connected by webs. In coloring, auks are usually dark above and white below. Immature birds and adults in winter plumage are frequently much whiter than in breeding plumage. Auks are peculiar to seas of colder parts of the northern hemisphere.

auks, razor-billed: head, neck and upperpart black with narrow white line from bill to eye; in winter, cheeks, throat and foreneck white, secondaries tipped with white; underparts, including axillaries and underwing coverts, white; tail wedge-shaped, of 12 feathers; bill deep and very narrow, black, crossed by a white band; inside of mouth, yellow; feet black; length 16.5 in.

aulodonts [sea urchins]: these urchins range from Triassic to Recent and have just 20 rows of plates in the test. Early members evidently were flexible, with simple ambulacral plates; later genera became rigid and developed compound plates. Spires generally are thin and may be hollow, 2 characteristics that help distinguish these urchins from stirodonts and cidaroids.

Aulopura [coral]: consists of small tubes with thick, wrinkled walls, faint septal ridges and few or no tabulae; polyps are reproduced by budding, forming chains, networks or crusts that spread out over firm though muddy bottoms or by attaching to shells, stromatoporoids and other corals.

Aulostoma: genus of sea fishes found in tropical waters; about 20 in. in length, of elongated form, and having a long tubular snout; generally called *flutemouths*.

aural null: null detected by listening for minimum signal or complete absence of audible signal.

auricle: chamber in vertebrate heart which receives blood from veins which is then pumped into the ventricle.

auricular crura: in shells like *Amussium, Pernopecten* and *Entolium* there is a pair of internal ridges diverging from the beak of each valve along juncture of the auricles with the shell body. These internal ridges or crura are in direct opposition and cannot function as teeth.

auricularia larva: free-swimming, ciliated larva of certain halothurians; possesses earlike, blunt extensions of body rather than long, slender larval arms.

Auriga: northern constellation lying about halfway between *Orion* and the *Pole Star*, containing the bright star *Capella* (a *Aurigae*).

aurora: sporadic radiant emission from upper atmosphere over middle and high latitudes. In northern latitudes these displays are called aurora borealis, aurora polaris, or northern lights; in southern latitudes, aurora australis.

aurora australis: phenomenon in Southern Hemisphere corresponding to aurora borealis in Northern Hemisphere.

aurora borealis: luminous phenomenon in Northern Hemisphere, usually forming streamers of light from clouds of ionized bases in upper atmosphere; the northern lights.

auroral zones: areas in higher latitudes where polar lights (aurora australis and aurora borealis) occur. These displays usually are associated with sunspot activity and magnetic storms and visible only at night.

austral: of, pertaining to, or in the south; southern; hence, *torrid*.

authigenic: term applied to products of chemical and biochemical action which originated in sediments at time of or after deposition and before burial and consolidation, e.g., calcium carbonate or managanese oxide deposition.

autochthonous: of local origin; indigenous.

autogenic plankton: plankton organisms that live and breed in the region in which they are found.

autopelagic plankton: surface-living plankton.

autotheca [*Graptolithina*]: large tubes produced at each budding in development of dendroid colony.

autotrophic: literally "self-feeding." Said of organisms, such as plants, that synthesize needed organic foodstuffs from inorganic substrates.

autumn ice: sea ice in early stages of formation; brackish and crystalline in appearance. Like young ice, it is not yet affected by lateral pressure.

autumn maximum: secondary flowering of phytoplankton. Flowering results from regeneration of nutrients after decomposition of organisms that have died during the summer and from vertical mixing after summer stratification.

auxiliaries [ships]: various winches, pumps, motors, engines, etc., required on ship, as distinguished from main propulsion machinery (boilers and engines on a steam installation).

auxiliary cell: in certain red algae, cell to which zygote extends a tubular extension, ooblast through which it migrates to auxiliary cell. This cell participates in formation of fruit of sexual plant.

auxiliary foundation [ships]: foundation for condensers, distillers, evaporators, pumps, or any of auxiliary machinery in engine or boiler rooms.

auxiliary thermometer: mercury-in-glass thermometer attached to stem of a reversing thermometer. It is read at same time as reversing thermometer so that the correction to reading of the latter, resulting from change in temperature after reversal, can be computed.

auxospore: in diatoms, enlarged cell (in some cases, resulting from union of gametes) which restores size to that line of cells in which size was diminished at each cell division during last few preceding divisions.

avast [ships]: order to stop or halt, as in "avast there, ye lubbers."

average: 1) to calculate arithmetical mean of; divide proportionately; as, to *average insurance losses among underwriters*. 2) financial loss arising by damage to a ship or cargo; also, proportion of such loss being equitably borne by each party interested, viz., ship, cargo, and freight, considered as entities concerned.

average depth: average water depths based on soundings reduced to low-water datum.

average limit of ice: average seaward extent of ice during a normal water.

Aves [class]: phylum *Chordata*. Jurassic to Recent. Forelimbs modified into wings. Feathers; endothermal; terrestrial and aerial; secondarily aquatic. Predators and herbivores.

avicularia: beaklike zooids in some *Bryozoa* colonies, such as *Bugula*, thought to function in keeping the colony free from debris or from larvae of other organisms that might settle on it.

avulsion: rapid erosion of shoreland by waves during a storm.

awash: 1) tossed about or battered by waves or tide. 2) rock exposed or one just bare at any stage of tide between datum of mean high water and the sounding.

awash [ships]: even with surface of water.

aweigh: atrip; said of an anchor when its flukes are just clear of bottom; as, *the anchor's aweigh*.

axenic: said of a culture of some organism that contains no other organisms.

axial [*Mollusca*]: parallel to axis of coiling in a gastropod.

axial vortex [*Coelenterata*]: longitudinal structure in axis of corallite formed by twisting together of inner ends of setae.

axis of channel: center line of channel.

Axius stirhynchus [*Thalassinidea*]: larva has long rostrum with toothed margin and dorsal spines on abdominal segments 2 to 6; pair of anterolateral spines on carapace; long median spine on telson. Exopodites of maxillipeds bear 4 terminal bristles and thoracic exopodites behind these are setose. Uropods and the first pair of pleopods are not formed until post-larvae stage is reached.

axonic: referring to the axon; long thin appendage of the nerve cell that normally conducts impulses away from the cell. A nerve cell generally has one axon.

axopodium: in *Protozoa*, a pseudopodium containing an axial filament.

azimuth: coordinate used in astronomy, surveying and navigation. The azimuth of a celestial body or other object is horizontal angle, or arc, measured between a fixed reference point and the vertical (plane perpendicular to horizon) passing through the celestial body or object.

azimuthal projection: map projection on which directions of all lines radiating from a central point or pole are the same as directions of corresponding lines on the spheres. When centered on one of the poles, it is sometimes called polar projection.

azoic: without life; however, most ocean areas described as azoic contain at least a bacterial flora.

B

B: in the International Code of Signals, denoted by a *red burgee*, which, flown by itself, indicates *"I am taking in or discharging explosives."* In ships' logbooks, *"b"* is often used for *"blue sky"* and *"B"* for *"broken sea."* b corresponds to Greek letter *beta* (β), used from ancient times in designating the second brightest star in a particular constellation, as β *Orionis*, or *Rigel* of *Orion*.

Bacillaria [subclass *Pennatae*]: *Bacillaria paradoxa* has very long narrow cells sticking together to form colonies of various sizes which look like a pile of matches. The cells slide over one another quite rapidly, being at one time almost end to end and at another neatly arranged side by side.

bacillus: any rod-shaped bacterium.

back bar [ships]: used on opposite side of bosom bar.

back bay: small bay into which streams drain; connected with sea through passes between barrier islands.

backbone: of a ship, main longitudinal strength assemblage of keel, keelson, stem, and sternpost.

backdeep: oceanic depression in concave side of an island arc.

backing: according to general international accepted usage, change in wind direction in counterclockwise sense in either hemisphere of the earth; opposite of veering.

back reef: shallow sea or lagoon shelf area behind a reef or between it and land; commonly characterized by nonfossiliferous deposits of limestones, dolostones, and evaporites as in western Texas area of Permian reefs.

back rush: seaward return of water following uprush of waves.

backshore: that part of beach which is usually dry, being reached only by higher tides, and by extension, a narrow strip relatively flat coast bordering the sea.

back slope: gentler sloping sides of a ridge; in contrast with escarpment, the steeper slope.

back splice: method of keeping end of a line from unlaying by tucking ends back in and under.

backstays [ships]: 1) long ropes or guys extending backward from heads of all masts above the lower mast and fastened in each side of ship to chain plates, serving to support the masts. 2) supporting lines on a sailboat usually running from a point about 2/3 up a mast to deck on windward side. Each time vessel comes about on a new tack and the boom swings over, backstays are set up on side opposite the boom and cast off on leeward side.

backwash: water forced astern by action of propeller; receding of waves.

backwater: 1) water turned back by obstruction, opposing current, etc. 2) water held back from main flow, as that which overflows land and collects in low places or that forming an inlet approximately parallel to main body and connected by narrow outlet. 3) arm of the sea, usually lying parallel with coast behind narrow strip of land.

Baffin Bay pack: drifting ice floes of Greenland between Davis Strait and southern limit of North Open Water, which is roughly a line from Cape York to entrance of Lancaster Sound.

baffle: 1) to struggle ineffectually, or strive in vain as, *a vessel baffles with a current*. 2) to fluctuate, as light varying winds.

baffle area [ships]: area of approximately 30° to either side of stern in which the chance of holding sonar contact is nearly impossible.

baggala: large dhow used by Arabs on Red Sea. This is a true dhow that averages about 85 ft. in length, beam one-quarter and displacement of 200 tons.

baguio: native name for a hurricane or typhoon in the China Sea and Philippine Islands.

bail [ships]: to scoop water from bottom of ship to give stability.

balanced frames [ships]: midships frames of equal shape and square flanged; 30 or more on a cargo vessel, equally divided between starboard and port sides.

balanced rudder [ships]: rudder with axis halfway between forward and after edge.

balancing: maneuver that enables stationary submarine to float in density layer.

Balandra: crude craft used on west coast of South America, sloop- or schooner-rigged.

Balanus balanoides [crustacean larvae]: nauplii are widely distributed. From above, outline of body is triangular and in later naupliar stages has pair of posterior spines. Labrum is truncated. First stage is about 0.3 mm., reaching 0.9 mm. in 5th stage.

Balcis alba [*Eulimidae*]: shell is 0.16 mm. across and 1½ whorls in early veliger which is characterized by broad apex, which soon becomes pointed. Velum is 0.2 mm. across and bilobed. Very conspicuous feature, even in retracted larva, is presence of black pigment around mouth and beside the oesophagus.

Balcis devians [*Eulimidae*]: larvae of this species are common between July and September. The veliger is approximately same size as *B. alba* but apex to the spire is blunter and there is no black pigment; digestive gland is yellow-brown. Shell of late larva reaches 0.64 mm. before velum is lost and animal settles.

baldie: double-ended fishing boat of 25 ft. on the keel and upwards used on Scottish East Coast. Built on lines of a fifie with little or no rake to stern; decked over; sleeping and cooking accommodations for full crew. They are lug-rigged, larger ones carrying mizzen and jib extending to a long bowsprit. Mizzen trims to a boomkin; mainmast is stepped well forward.

bale cubic: space in a ship's hold available for cargo, as measured inside the frame cargo-battens and to underside of beams. In a general cargo of mixed commodities bale cubic applies, since stowage of such cargo usually is confined to the limits indicated. From data taken from an actual case, bale cubic amounts to 470,000 ft., while *grain cubic*, which includes spaces between frames and deck beams, measures 641,000 ft.

baleen: horny material comprising plates in mouth of whalebone whale, through which water is strained in feeding; used to capture macroplankton. Also termed whalebone.

baleen plates: whalebone plates found instead of teeth in *Mysticeti*, a suborder of whales. Triangular plates each with a fringe or filter of hairlike material, may number in the hundreds and are attached at bases to upper jaw. They filter out and retain many small animals or plants (plankton) before the whales swallow them.

baleen whale: member of cetacean suborder *Mysticeti*, including right whales, gray whales and vorquals. Baleen whales are distinguished from *Odontoceti*, or toothed whales (including porpoises and dolphins) that prey on many organisms.

balk [ships]: in carpentry, piece of timber from 4 in. to 10 in. square.

ball: low sand ridge extending generally parallel with shoreline and is submerged by high tides; generally separated from beach by an intervening trough.

ballam: Singhalese dugout canoe of Ceylon, with round bottom (transversely); no sheer; sides that tumble home. It is open, double-ended, ends vertical above waterline; curved below with short solid section at each end; 20 to 30 ft. long, width 2 to 3 ft.

ballast: weight carried by ship to insure proper stability to avoid risk of capsizing and to secure greatest effectiveness of propelling power. When ship is "in ballast" it is without cargo and laden only with ballast.

ballastage: fee levied for the privilege of taking ballast at a port.

ballast tanks [ships]: tanks carried in various parts of ship for water ballast to add weight or to produce a change in trim in stability of ship.

ball breaker: device used in oceanographic operations, such as coring; to determine when bottom is reached. It is a metal frame containing a glass ball with a weight suspended above it. When bottom contact is made, weight drops on glass ball and causes it to implode. The sound wave generated by implosion is received aboard ship by a listening device.

ball ice: sea ice consisting of large number of soft, spongy spheres 1 to 2 in. in diameter; rare.

balloon jib [ships]: large triangular headsail of light material with wide foot used on yachts and "fishermen" in light weather when wind is abaft the beam.

balloon spinnaker [ships]: type of spinnaker (large, loose triangular sail).

ball valve: valve in which rise or fall of a fitted ball controls an opening; used in small air and water pumps.

ballycadder: an ice foot.

balsa: canoe-shaped boat constructed of bundles of grass or reeds, used in various parts of world where other materials for boatbuilding are not available.

Baltic Dandy: ketch or dandy-rigged shallow-draft vessel of Baltic Sea. Mizzenmast is lofty, which sometimes gives the rig the appearance of a schooner; leeboards are carried on craft of Southern Coast; 3 of 4 head sails run to long jibboom and when running free square sails are often set on mainmast. Hull is beamy and well built with sort of a clipper bow and old-fashioned round stern with davits and dinghy above.

Baltimore Clipper: fast, sharp-hulled vessels originated on Chesapeake Bay; used when speed was of prime consideration, as in slave trade, privateering, etc. Chief characteristics were masts with extreme rake aft, raking stem and sternpost, high bow with good sheer to low stern, low freeboard, great dead rise at midship section and 2- to 5-ft. drag to keel. The schooner rig was most popular, although some were rigged as brigs, brigantines and hermaphrodites.

banca: double outrigger canoe of Mindanao Island to Southern Philippines. Four bamboo outrigger booms to a side are conward end. Rectangular sail with a yard laced to each of longer sides is set obliquely to a tripod mast. Sail is painted with wide varicolored stripes and ornamented with tassels.

bang choon: "net boat" used in fisheries of Singapore. The hull is open, sharp-ended, with rounded "V" section. Stem and sternpost are straight, raking and extend above gunwale. There is considerable sheer; keel is parallel to gunwale; when light, forefront and keel are above water. Helmsman sits on a small seat set athwart gunwales at stern.

bangkong: long canoe-shaped, open boat used by Dyaks of Borneo for fighting. Larger ones could accommodate 80 men and were often built with flat roof from which warriors fought while others paddled below.

bank: elevation of sea floor located on a continental or island shelf where depth of water is relatively shallow but sufficient for safe surface navigation. It may support shoals or bars on its surface which are dangerous to navigation.

bankfisker-skoite: large decked vessel, rigged variously, used in cod fishing off West Coast of Norway. The hull has a curved, strongly raking stem, full bow and stern, raking sternpost, moderate sheer and rudder hung outside. Average size is 60 ft. overall by a 20-ft. 6-in. beam.

bank-inset reefs: coral reefs situated well within the environment or unrimmed outer edges of continental and insular shelves.

bank reefs: reef which lies within outer margin of rimless shoals, in contrast to barrier and atoll reefs which rise directly from deep water.

bank suta: Swedish fishing vessel of the Island of Tjorn on Bohuslan Coast. It is a carvel-built keel with flush decks, beamy and deep, flaring bow with great rakes to stem, stern shaped like bow, narrow rudder, hollow waterlines, ketch-rigged with bowsprit, fore-and-aft mainsail, spritsail mizzen, 2 jibs and square-headed gaff topsails.

banting [Atcheen]: fast, open, sailing dugout of Johore on southern tip of Malay Peninsula. One of the most remarkable forms of dugout in the world, it has fine sailing qualities: 30 to 35 ft. long, 1/6 the beam, long, hollow, clipper bow and sharp hollow floor, shaped to form a keel. Rig consists of 2 balanced lug or setee sails and jib carried to short bowsprit.

bar: submerged or emerged embankment of sand, gravel or mud built on sea floor in shallow water by waves and currents. A bar may also be composed of mollusk shells. When it is a ridge generally parallel to shore and submerged by high tides, it is a longshore bar. Offshore bars and barrier bars or beaches are built principally by wave action on sand or gravel at a distance from shore and separated from it by a lagoon.

bar: unit of pressure; 1 bar equals 10^6 dynes per square centimeter.

barbed tributary: tributary entering main stream in upstream direction.

barbels: thin, sensory appendages found near mouths of some fishes, e.g., catfishes. Barbels are sensitive to touch giving the fish tactile awareness.

barber: severe storm at sea during which spray and precipitation freeze on decks and rigging of boats.

barbette [ships]: cylindrical structure built of armor plate extending from protected deck of a war vessel to lower side of turret shelf plate. They form protective enclosures where turret stools, shell stowage flats and ammunition hoisting gear for turrets are located.

bare poles [ships]: sailing without any canvas raised, usually in strong wind.

bar finger sand: elongated lenticular sand body underlying a distributary in a bird-foot delta.

bark [barque]: 1) sailing vessel of 3 or more masts, square-rigged on all masts, except after ones, which are fore-and-aft rigged. 2) in American colonial period term "bark" was not applied to a rig, but to a type of hull, square-sterned and flush-decked. The name was often used instead of "ship" or "vessel." 3) small Mediterranean craft with combination of square, lateen, and fore-and-aft sails; long beak forward providing a stout support for lower end of forward lateen sail.

barkentine: sailing ship with at least 3 masts of which the foremost is square-rigged (having rectangular sails hanging across length of ship and supported by yards carried athwart the masts); the other masts are fore-and-aft rigged (sails more or less parallel to length of ship). The barkentine was very popular in Pacific Ocean.

barnacle: sedentary marine crustacean of the order *Cirripedia* with free-swimming larvae. Barnacles live in calcareous shells, feed by extending featherlike cirri or feet out of the shell into seawater to catch prey, are parasitic and burrow into shells of other sea animals or attach themselves to fixed or floating objects. They frequently grow on ships' bottoms and must be regularly removed. After molting 1 to 3 times they develop shells much like those of astracodes; then settle down on their heads, lose the bivalved shells and secrete others made of plates that overlap or are held together by tough skin. Food is brought to the mouth by branched fringe that resembles curved feathers; legs sweep to and fro with rhythmic movements, catching food which is then raked off by comblike organs near mouth. They are of 2 general types, acorn barnacles and stalked barnacles.

barnacle, giant [*Balanus nubilus*]: grows to be 3 or 4 in. in diameter at base and nearly the same height. Often 12 or more are found growing upon one another in irregular clusters. This species has large opening at top which can be closed by strong operculum with pointed beak. The barnacle sheds covering of its legs, body covering and lining of shell with each moult; but protective shell itself is permanent and is enlarged as animal grows. When it settles down permanently, after attaching itself by its head, it loses shell, eye and swimming legs, then acquires curled, feathery appendages and new shell covering.

barnacle, goose [*Mitella polymerus*]: attaches to objects by means of flexible, leathery peduncle, 3 in. long. The crown, 1 in. across, is covered with 18 or more plates; plates resemble scales. General color is red-brown except for plates which are white. Line crevices in rocky shores, frequently forming huge masses. When larva settles down to sedementary life, head region becomes attached and greatly elongated to form peduncle.

barnacle, rock [*Balanus cariosus*]: varies in size from ½ in. in diameter at base and 1 in. in height to 1½ by 2 in. Body is fastened securely within shell by strong muscles and surrounded by fold of skin. Thick, calcareous shell, made up of 6 or more plates, has porous wall and many irregular ribs with projecting points. Projecting points are produced by successive periods of growth.

barnacle, sharp acorn [*Balanus balanus*]: normally ¾ in. in diameter at base and ½ in. in height. Six plates of shell are smooth and distinct, overlapping somewhat at base. At top, aperture is diamond-shaped with plates ending in acute points; posterior plate folds back slightly and is curved like a beak. Calcareous shell is clear white. Barnacles are hermaphroditic, male and female sex organs being in same animal. Barnacles have a brain and chain of 5 nerve ganglia, but have no special respiratory or circulating system.

baroclinity: state of stratification in fluid in which surfaces are of constant pressure (isobaric). Number per unit area of isobaric-isosteric solenoids intersecting a given surface is measure of baroclinity.

barograph: aneroid barometer that operates a pen held against moving chart making permanent record of day-to-day atmospheric pressure.

barometer: instrument for measuring weight of pressure of atmosphere. Marine barometer is adapted to ship's motion by being suspended by gimbals and having structure in the tube to lessen oscillation of mercury.

barometric pressure: air or atmospheric pressure.

barometric wave: any wave in atmospheric pressure field. Term is usually reserved for short period variations not associated with cyclonic-scale motions or with atmospheric tides.

barong: native fishing craft used by Milanaus of West Borneo. Hull is square-ended at gunwales, with v-shaped raking end boards at bow and stern, being similar to stern of a dory; good rounding sheer with low freeboard amidships.

barotropy: state of a fluid in which surfaces of constant density or temperature are coincident with surfaces of constant pressure; zero baroclinity.

bar port: harbor entered only when tide rises sufficiently to permit passage of ships over a bar.

barque: lateen-rigged, commercial sailing vessel used in Lake Geneva, Switzerland. It is two-masted; hull is decked with walkway projecting beyond gunwales on which scullers stand; freeboard in low, no sheer except at bow which rises sharply meeting the high, concave stem in a point; slab sides meet flat bottom in a chine. There is a cabin forward with porthole on each side of stem.

barquentine: sailing ship with at least 3 masts of which foremast was square-rigged and other masts were fore-and-aft rigged.

barque provencale: the "bark" was also a Mediterranean craft of the 18th century. It had 3 masts and no bowsprit, but sometimes had long, slender extension protruding from the bow. Mainmast was a pole mast and carried 3 square sails, like the "salacre." Foremast had a severe rake forward and carried a lateen sail. Mizzenmast was small and carried a topmast with lateen course and one or two topsails.

barquette: a small, half-decked craft, common to Spanish and French Riviera. They are 18 to 20 ft. long, with high stempost, sharp rounded stern and carvel built. The single lugsail has a long yard and a short luff.

barracuda: family of voracious fishes notorious because of attacks of one species, the great barracuda or swimmers. There are over 20 species of the family, common to all warm seas. A barracuda is a streamlined fish with body proportion of a pike. Dorsal fins are small and widely separated from each other; soft rayed dorsal and anal fin are located far back on body near tail.

barracuda, great: ranges north along Atlantic Coast to Carolinas. This killer among fishes has lines of an underwater missile with pointed head, long cylindrical body and tapering tail. It is light blue with silvery sides that are at times indistinctly barred or spotted. The large mouth is full of sharp, knifelike teeth. The bite of a barracuda is straight and clean, made by single strike so swift and powerful it can cut a fish in two or easily sever an arm or leg (the bite of a shark leaves a more curved edge). Most are under 5 ft. long and weigh about 10 lbs.

barracuda, northern: smaller and more northern species found along Atlantic Coast as far north as Cape Cod. It is olive-green usually under 12 in. long. The miniature predator hovers over sandy bottoms in bays where it preys on smaller fishes, but is harmless to man. Also known as a sennet.

barracuda, Pacific: similar in appearance and habit to great barracuda, but smaller, less vicious and usually under 12 in. long. This species is found from Monterey southward along California coast.

barrarra: Arab dhow similar to baggala having true dhow characteristics: long overhang forward, raking transform stern, raised poop deck, main and mizzenmast. While Arabic in origin, it is found as far east as Rangoon, India.

barrator: one who, being master of a ship or crew member thereof, commits any fraud or fraudulent act in management of ship or cargo by which owners, freighters, or insurers are injured, as by running away with the ship, sinking or deserting her, willful deviation from a fixed course, or embezzlement of cargo.

barratry: fraud or offense committed by a *barrator*.

barrier: in polar terminology an early term for ice shelf; first used by Sir James Clark Ross for face of Antarctic ice shelf named for him, i.e., "Ross Barrier."

barrier basin: basin produced from natural damming by glacial moraine, landslides, etc.

barrier beach: offshore bar. Sand ridge parallel to shore, slightly above high-tide level; commonly separated from shore by a lagoon.

barrier chain: series of barrier islands, barrier spits and barrier beaches extending along considerable length of coast.

barrier ice: edge of a great glacier which enters the sea but remains attached to land.

barrier iceberg: bay roughly parallel to coast and separated from ocean by barrier islands; body of water encircled by coral islands and reefs, also known as an atoll lagoon.

barrier island: wave-built deposit of sand, raised above sea level by waves and separated from shore by a lagoon. Height may be increased by dune formation.

barrier reef: coral reef parallel to and separated from coast by a lagoon too deep for coral growth.

baruio: tropical cyclone in Philippines.

basal disk [*Coelenterata*]: fleshy wall closing off lower (aboral) end of a polyp.

basalt: 1) dark-colored igneous rock that may have crystals or glass in its composition. There is a 4½ km. thick (3 miles) layer of basalt underlying the earth's crust, e.g., the Giant's Causeway in northern Ireland in which the rock resembles vertical columns. 2) basic igneous (extrusive) rock composed primarily of plagioclase, pyroxene and with or without olivine. Also an inner layer of worldwide extent underlying ocean and granitic continents.

base [molluscs]: part of the gastropod shell below periphery of body whorl and to left of aperture.

base line: line between master and slave stations in Loran or other hyperbolic navigation systems.

base line [ships]: horizontal fore-and-aft reference line for vertical measurements; perpendicular to vertical center line and fore-and-aft base line.

base stations: geographic position whose absolute gravity value is known; point from which a survey begins. In exploration particularly magnetic or gravity surveys, a reference station where quantities under investigation have known values or are under repeated or continuous measurement in order to establish additional stations in relation to it.

basin: depression of sea floor more or less equidimensional in form and of variable extent.

basipodite: in biramous crustacean appendages the basal portion of appendage before branching.

bass [black seabass]: also known as blackfish. More sluggish bottom-feeding species found along Atlantic Coast from Cape Cod to Virginia. It is a dark brown fish with bluish gray back; rounded tail fin has a prolonged ray at its upper lip; pectoral fins are wide and rounded. Average black bass is under 18 in. long and less than 3 lbs. in weight. Male differs from female in having longer fin rays and fatty hump in front of dorsal fin.

bass [California Kelp bass]: olive-gray fish with pinkish belly and green fins; average individual measures about 20 in. and weighs under 5 lbs. Kelp bass are caught for most part in winter as they feed on small organisms living in kelp beds. The species are most common south of San Francisco.

bass, channel [*Sciaenops ocellatus*]: reddish fish with round, black spot toward upper margin of base of tail. Scales along lateral line 40—45; rays in soft dorsal fin 23—25; no barbels present on chin. Body elongate, only slightly compressed laterally; back slightly arched; mouth moderate; teeth in both jaws in villiform bands, outside series in upper jaw enlarged. Color reddish to reddish brown above, somewhat pale below, distinct round black spot on upper portion of base of caudal fin.

bass, chipola [shoal bass]: moderate to large bass with small scales; notch between spiny and soft portions of dorsal fin shallow; pyloric mostly simple, unbranched; maxillary not extending beyond level of posterior margin of eye; 14 rows of cheek scales. Body stout, not strongly compressed; mouth large, sturdy, but slightly oblique. Color pattern of adult rather uniform.

bass, Florida largemouth [*Micropterus salmoides floridanos*]: heavy-bodied bass with large mouth. Notch between spiny and soft portions of dorsal fin deep; pyloric caecae forked; maxillary extending beyond level of eye when mouth is closed. Body somewhat elongated, not strongly compressed; mouth large, sturdy; fins moderately high.

bass, giant sea [California black bass]: largest member of family on Pacific Coast, few are caught under 50 lbs. This is a dusky brown or black bass whose stout dorsal spines can be lowered into a groove along back. They live on rock bottoms where they feed on crustaceans and small fishes.

bass, largemouth: olive-green fish often marked by dark longitudinal stripe along the side; jaw extends backwards beyond eye hence the common name. It prefers warmer water than does the small mouth and is found more frequently in sluggish streams and weedy ponds. It is largest member of sunfish family; average individual is 12 to 24 in. long and some have been caught up to 32 in. and weighing 22 lbs. The largemouth feeds mainly on other fishes.

bass, northern largemouth [*Micropterus salmoides salmoides*]: heavy-bodied bass with large mouth. Notch between spiny and soft portions of dorsal fin deep; pyloric caecal forked; maxillary extending beyond level of eye when mouth is closed. Body somewhat elongate, not strongly compressed; mouth, large and sturdy; young with broad, dark lateral stripe which becomes broken into series of blotches anteriorly.

bass, northern spotted [*Micropterus punctulatus*]: clean cut, slender bass with spots on back. Notch between spiny and soft portions of dorsal fin shallow; pyloric caecae mostly unforked; maxillary extending almost to posterior margin of eye; 13—16 rows of cheek scales; body somewhat elongate, not strongly compressed. Mouth large, sturdy and little oblique. Row of confluent spots form a stripe along side with generally a row of discrete spots above the line.

bass, smallmouth [tiger bass and brown bass]: its reputation as a game fish is surpassed by no other freshwater fish its size. Body is longer and not so thin as that of sunfishes; upper jaws extend back only to point below the eye. Color is dark greenish-brown above and lighter shade on sides with irregular dark markings. It is usually 10 to 20 in. long and weighs less than 8 lbs. Smallmouth bass prefer flowing streams and cool, clear lakes with gravelly shorelines feeding on insects, crayfishes and other small fishes.

bass, southern rock [*Ambloplites rupestris ariommus*]: fairly thick-bodied, big mouthed pan fish with high spiny dorsal fin. Tail emarginate; anal not so long as dorsal; anal fin with VI-VII spines; body an elongate oval, not strongly compressed; mouth sturdy; fins moderately high; color brownish or greenish with indistinct mottling or marbling of dark shade on sides of head, body and vertical fins. Size of adults up to 8 in.

bass, striped [rockfish and greenhead]: brassy pink or brownish fish with dark green head and back and silvery belly; lengthwise stripes occur along sides. Ventral fins are set far forward beneath pectoral fins; average individual weighs up to 10 lbs. Native to Atlantic Coast from New England to Florida, this bass is found near shore feeding on smaller fishes, crustaceans and worms.

bass, Swannee [*Micropterus notius*]: small, relatively slender bass with dark blotches along sides. Notch between spiny and soft portions of dorsal fin shallow; pyloric caecae mostly unforked; maxillary extending to about level of posterior margin of eye; 12—13 rows of cheek scales. Mouth large, sturdy but slightly oblique; fins moderately high. Pattern of about 12 vertical dark brown blotches along sides in a background of light brown or tan.

bass, white: Pacific Coast member of the family, abundant from Santa Barbara southward along California coast. This relative of the croaker is an elongated, metallic blue fish with silvery sides; chin lacks barbels and pectoral fins are unusually long and narrow; large species, attaining weight of 80 lbs.

bateaux: this class of boat was flat-bottomed, sharp at both ends, carried 1 or 2 guns and had weather cloths all around to protect crew from bullets. They were sometimes equipped with single lateen sail, 60-ft. lengths were not uncommon. Bateaux were used on Lake Champlain and small lakes and rivers during American Revolution.

batfish: small but unusual family of fishes. They are flat, of angular shape with triangular head that tapers into pointed bony snout; winglike pectoral fins, attached to expanded sides of body, have some peculiar wrist joint as those of frogfishes.

batfish, common: about 9 in. long, a West Indies species. It lives in shallow water, crawling over sandy bottoms by means of fleshy pectoral fins.

Its toadlike appearance is accentuated by warty skin.

batho-, bathy-: prefixes used in construction of compounded terms, especially with relation to sea depths.

batholith: large igneous intrusive mass featuring an exposed area greater than 40 sq. miles and no clearly inferable or visible floor.

bathometer: instrument for measuring ocean depths; also, one which determines depth of water on basis of gravitational force.

bathy: indicator group in coded bathythermograph message.

bathyal: pertaining to ocean depths between 100 and 2,000 fathoms (180 and 3,700 meters); also to ocean bottom between those depths sometimes identical with continental slope environment.

bathyconductograph: device to measure electrical conductivity of seawater at various depths from moving ship.

bathycurrent: ocean current flowing at a considerable depth below, and unaffecting, the surface water.

bathymeter: apparatus primarily designed for measuring depth of water. Echo sounders and precision depth finders, used in bathymetric surveys, have replaced lead line of yesterday.

bathymetric: referring to bathymetry, the science of deep-sea sounding. Measurement of water depths to determine bottom contours; also refers to various depths inhabited by aquatic organisms.

bathymetric chart: 1) topographic map of bed of ocean showing ocean depth contours. 2) map delineating the form of bottom of body of water usually by means of depth contours (isobaths).

bathypelagic: living in deep water below euphotic zone but above abyssal zone from about 100 meters to above 4,000 meters; free in water, not living on bottom.

bathypelagic fish: any of variety of oceanic fishes which, at least part of the time, inhabit depth range between about 500 to 2,000 fathoms (900 to 3,700 meters). Many of these fishes characteristically undergo extensive diurnal vertical migrations and are thought to contribute to sound-scattering layers in the sea.

bathyscaphe: deep-diving submersible comprised of 2 parts; fluid-filled bag (float) and spherical cabin. Seawater enters the hull for negative buoyancy and fluid in the float (usually gasoline) provides positive buoyancy. Iron pellets that can be jettisoned are used as ballast. Should electricity fail, they are released automatically and bathyscaphe rises to surface.

bathyscope: submarine-type research vessel. Usually composed of gasoline filled ballast tank with

a manned sphere capable of operating at depths to 35,000 ft.

bathysphere: round, steel diving chamber that can be lowered into deep ocean by cable.

bathythermocouple: coupling device used in oceanographic instrumentation to make or break electrical contact by changes in temperature of water.

bathythermograph [BT]: 1) rigged instrument used by vessel at anchor or underway. It automatically draws a graph showing temperature as function of depth when lowered in sea. 2) device for determining water temperature; it is dropped overboard from ship. A stylus inside the instrument scratches a trace, indicating temperature as function of depth, on to coated glass slide.

bathythermograph grid: transparent glass slide marked with calibration lines of temperature and depth. When superimposed against bathythermograph slide it is possible to read off observed values of temperature and depth. Each instrument has its own grid.

bathythermograph print: enlarged photographic print of bathythermograph slide superimposed against appropriate bathythermograph grid annotated with particulates of location and data.

bathythermograph slide: 1 in. by 1¾ in. glass slide with a coated surface on one side. A stylus on bathythermograph scratches depth versus temperature trace on coated surface.

bathythermograph viewer: small magnifying device used in reading temperature and depth values from bathythermograph slide overlaid by bathythermographic grid.

batten [ships]: strip of wood or iron used to fasten edges of tarpaulin over a hatch. To batten down the hatches of a ship is to secure covering with strips of wood or iron; to secure firmly.

battens [ships]: narrow flat strip or strips of wood, usually ash, fitted into pockets to preserve shape of a sail and keep the after end from curling.

battens, cargo [ships]: term applied to planks that are fitted to the inside of frames in a hold to keep cargo away from shell plating; strips of wood or steel used to prevent shifting of cargo.

batter: referred to a vessel's form, indicating topsides of hull having less breadth than that measured at waterline. Inward slope of a ship's side above her waterline; more commonly known as tumble home.

baurua: outrigger sailing canoe of Gilbert Islands in western Pacific. The sharp, double-ended hull had flattened lee side characteristic of islands of Micronesia. Due to lack of timber other than coconut palm, it was carvel-built of varying lengths of planking sewed together and to ribs;

keel was sharp "V" in section, preferably to single length.

bawley: small English vessel common to Thames Estuary, rigged similar to a cutter, but without a main boom. It is wide-beamed, shallow-draft, with high freeboard forward, designed for fishing and trawling in all kinds of weather.

bay: 1) recess in a shore or inlet of sea between two capes or headlands; not as large as gulf but larger than cove. 2) an inward bend in ice edge formed either by wind or current. 3) when Isidore of Seville wrote on nautical matters in about the middle of 7th century, he used *baia*, (probably formed from some long lost colloquial form of Latin term for "opening") to describe a wide mouth indentation of sea. A bay offers a comparatively sheltered mooring place that can be reached without passing dangerously through narrow channels. Not every bay has placid waters. In the 233 km. (145 mile) long Bay of Fundy in Canada, the tide sometimes rises 12 to 15 meters (40 to 50 ft.). No coastline known to early Spanish voyagers had a feature remotely comparable to this bay where surging water can cause small vessel to lift anchor and drift in the fast current.

bayamo: violent blast of wind, accompanied by vivid lightning and heavy rain, from the Bight of Bayamo, in Cuba, and its neighborhood.

bay deltas: deltas formed at mouths of streams which discharge into bays or estuaries. Their advance toward bay mouths often extinguishes lagoons behind bay bars or completely fills open bays, simplifying the shoreline. Where delta forms at head of bay, it is a bay-head delta.

bay-head bar: bar built a short distance out from shore at head of a bay.

bay ice: level ice of more than one winter's growth which has remained free of hummocks and is nourished by surface layers of snow.

bay-mouth bar: bar extending across mouth of bay.

bayou: small sluggish stream or estuarial creek with slow imperceptible current, in coastal swamps or river deltas.

beach: zone of unconsolidated material that extends landward from low water line to the place where there is marked change in material or physiographic form or to line of permanent vegetation. A beach includes foreshore and backshore.

beach berm: nearly horizontal portion of beach or backshore formed from deposit of material by wave action.

beach cusps: beach deposits of sand and gravel in form of ridges with sharp points facing water.

beach erosion: carrying away of beach materials by wave action, tidal currents, littoral currents or wind.

beach face: section of beach normally exposed to action of wave uprush; foreshore zone of beach.

beach ridge: essentially continuous mound of beach material behind the beach that has been heaped up by wave or other action. Ridges may occur alone or as a series of approximately parallel deposits.

beach rock: friable to well cemented rock consisting of calcareous skeletal debris and in many places mineral grains and rock fragments cemented by calcium carbonate; formed only in intertidal zone and occurs in thin beds dipping seaward at angles of less than 15°.

beach scarp: almost vertical slope along beach caused from erosion by wave action; may vary in height from few inches to several feet depending on wave action and nature and composition of beach.

beach width: horizontal dimension of beach as measured normal to shoreline.

bead coral [*Calliarthron manza*]: found on beaches adhering to rocks or mollusc shells between 0.5 and 1.5-ft. tide levels. Bead coral, like other coraline algae, has calcified, crustlike base of indefinite extent from which arise many erect, branched, jointed flexible shoots. Most noticeable feature of this seaweed is resemblance to beads strung on a wire. The segments or beads are so brittle they break at slightest touch; erect shoots are 2 to 5 in. high with widely spaced forks or branches; color when alive is reddish-purple, but when dead or dry, chalky white.

beak: 1) in *Brachipoda*, pointed extremity of valve adjacent to or posterior to hinge line and in midline of valve. 2) in *Mollusca* small tip of bivalve shell near hinge, also any spoutlike elongation of shell.

beam [ships]: 1) width of ship at its widest point. 2) timber running athwartships and supporting deck.

beam ends [ships]: vessel is said to be on beam ends when it lies over on side.

beaminess: term expressing degree of breadth proportional to a vessel's length.

beam knees [ships]: angular fittings which connect beams and frames.

beam line [ships]: line showing top of frame lines.

beam plate angles [ships]: beam made from flat plate with flange bent at right angles by an angle-bending machine.

beam sea: waves moving in a direction approximately 90° from heading.

beam tide: in navigational usage, tidal current setting in direction approximately 90° from heading of ship.

beam trawl: type of trawl which has a rigid front or beam fastened between 2 metal shoes the soles of which slide over bottom. As the trawl passes over bottom, fish and other natural marine life are captured in attached net.

beam wind: nautical term for crosswind, especially wind blowing 90° from ship's heading.

beamy: having much beam or breadth, considering length-breadth ratio of an average vessel, which is approximately 8 to 1.

bean cod: small fishing or pilot boat used by Portuguese a century or two ago; rigging was similar to tartane.

bearding [ships]: line of intersection of plating and the stem or sternpost.

bearer [ships]: term applied to foundations, particularly those having vertical web plates as principal members. The vertical web plates themselves are called bearers.

bearing: horizontal direction of one terrestrial point from another; usually measured from 000° at reference direction clockwise through 360°.

bearings: to take a bearing is to ascertain on what point of the compass an object lies; to determine the situation or direction of object in relation to some part of ship, as "on the beam" or "abaft the beam."

bearings [signaling]: made by a ship pointing out an object or referring to position; reckoned from the ship making the signal or from point of departure, that is invariably toward objective.

beat: to tack back and forth to windward in sailboat.

beating: wave phenomenon which occurs when 2 or more waves of different frequencies become superimposed. The resultant wave has maximum amplitude (beats) and frequency equal to difference of frequencies of initial waves.

Beaufort force: number denoting speed of wind according to Beaufort wind scale.

Beaufort scale: scale for measuring wind force consisting of 13 levels numbered 0 to 12 accompanied by descriptions of the wind's effect at various levels; used today in modified form, it was invented by British Admiral Francis Beaufort in 1805.

Beaufort wind scale: system of estimating and reporting wind speeds, devised in 1805 by Admiral Beaufort of British Navy. In its present form for international meteorological use it equals (a) Beaufort force or Beaufort number (b) wind speed (c) descriptive terms and (d) visible effects upon land objects or sea surface.

beauty bush [*Callithamnion pikeanum*]: grows on faces of rocks and on other seaweed between 3.5- and 1.5-ft. tide levels; abundant everywhere. It has many erect, alternate fronds borne on strong cylindrical axis; branches are arranged in densely crowded spirals on all sides of axis and are curved inward with the ultimate branches sharply pointed. Generally, it is 3 to 7 in. tall with primary branches 1 to 3 in. long. The entire seaweed is a uniform dark purplish-brown. The holdfast is a rhizoid formed by filaments which emerge from basal cells.

becalmed [ships]: to be deprived of wind or delayed by a calm.

becket [ships]: short piece of line usually spliced into a circle or with an eye in either end.

becueing: method of securing a hawser to a small anchor by a light seizing to the ring, its end being made fast to the crown. Upon the anchor's flukes being caught among rocks, its release is effected by a sharp upward jerk, which carries away the seizing.

bed: 1) smallest division of layered rock series separated from material above or below by well defined change in character. 2) ground upon which body of water rests, usually based on a modifier to indicate type of water body, as sea bed.

bed plates [ships]: structure fitted for support of feet of engine columns and to provide support for crankshaft bearings and to help distribute engine weight and stresses to the ship's structure. They consist of series of transverse girders connecting fore-and-aft members or girders.

before the mast: as a common sailor, the crew of a ship being berthed in forecastle forward of the foremast.

before the wind: in direction of wind. To sail before the wind is to sail in direction in which wind blows.

belay [ships]: to make fast. To cease performing an action.

belaying pin [ships]: stout pin of wood or metal set in pin or fife rail near foot of mast and used to secure halyards and other lines on mast.

belemnoids: fossil group that may represent a link between nautiloids and existing cephalopods.

Belgian lugger: similar to Havre trawler. Rig consists of tall mainmast with dipping lugsail and topsail for fair weather, shorter foremast stepped in bow, tiny mizzenmast with triangular sail set out at stern and jib to bowsprit. Hull had transom stern with outboard rudder, straight stem and curved forefoot.

bell: unit used on shipboard to announce each half-hour of a watch. The day is divided into 6 watches of 4 hours each, first half-hours of which are, respectively, indicated on ship's bell by one *stroke*, or *one bell*; next half-hour by *two bells*; and so on, eight bells corresponding to 4, 8, and 12 o'clock a.m. and p.m., thus:

1 bell at 12:30; 4:30; and   8:30 o'clock.
2 bells at   1:00; 5:00; and   9:00 o'clock.
3 bells at   1:30; 5:30; and   9:30 o'clock.

4 bells at   2:00; 6:00; and 10:00 o'clock.
5 bells at   2:30; 6:30; and 10:30 o'clock.
6 bells at   3:00; 7:00; and 11:00 o'clock.
7 bells at   3:30; 7:30; and 11:30 o'clock.
8 bells at   4:00; 8:00; and 12:00 o'clock.
British practice modifies the preceding in *2nd dog watch* (6 to 8 p.m.) to 1, 2, 3, and 8 bells at 6:30, 7:00, 7:30, and 8:00 o'clock, respectively.

Bellarmine jug: pear-shaped stoneware jug usually decorated with figure of bearded man.

Bellerochia [phytoplankton]: broad, flat cells united in chains by their corners. Chloroplasts are numerous. This is a tropical diatom.

bell rope [ships]: short length of line made fast to clapper of ship's bell. Often referred to in the navy as the only "rope" on board ship.

belly: broadest part of a ship's hull at and below her waterline, especially in vessels having much *tumble home.*

below [ships]: used in referring to any part of ship below upper decks and also when speaking of the forecastle, as when the watch "goes below."

belt: long area of sea ice bounded by open water or land. Depending on their length, belts can vary from a few kilometers to more than 100 km. in width.

Beluga: cetacean of the dolphin family, white in color when adult and growing to about 10 ft. in length; the *white whale;* found in northern seas and well-known in the Gulf of St. Lawrence. Also, the *huso,* or great sturgeon, of southeastern Europe.

bench: level or gently sloping erosion plane inclined seaward.

bench mark: 1) permanently fixed point of elevation used as reference for elevations. Primary bench mark is one close to tide station to which tide staff and tidal datum originally are referred. **2)** level or gently sloping erosion plane inclined seaward. **3)** nearly horizontal area at about level of maximum high water on sea side of a dike.

bend [ships]: to fasten by means of a bend or knot, as one rope to another or to an anchor; to shackle, as a chain-cable to an anchor; to bend a sail, to make it fast to its proper yard, boom, gaff or stay.

bending: upward or downward motion on sheet of ice caused by lateral pressure. This is the first stage in formation of pressure ice and is characteristic of thin and very plastic ice.

bending sails [ships]: securing sails to a yard or other spar.

bending slab [ships]: heavy cast iron blocks with square or round holes for "dogging down" arranged to form large solid floor on which frames and structural members are bent and formed.

bend on [ships]: to attach; to make a sail fast to a spar or a chain to an anchor.

bends: painful and dangerous condition created in divers or in any air-breathing animals in deep water by too rapid a release of hydrostatic pressure upon rising, causing formation of bubbles of nitrogen gas in the blood.

Benguela Current: strong current flowing northward along southwest coast of Africa; formed by West Wind Drift and Angulhas Current. Benguela Current flows toward the Equator, gradually leaves the coast, and becomes the South Equatorial Current.

benthic: that portion of marine environment inhabited by marine organisms which live permanently in or on bottom. Pertaining to all submarine bottom terrain regardless of water depth.

benthic division: primary division of sea which includes ocean floor.

benthonic: of or pertaining to sea-floor types of life or marine bottom-dwelling forms of life; pertaining to the Benthos.

benthos: bottom-dwelling forms of marine life. Many authorities include certain fishes such as stingrays and flounders which spend much of their lives in close association with the bottom in this category. Also applied to the floor or deepest part of sea or ocean.

benthoscope: deep-sea exploration sphere lowered by cable.

bentinck [ships]: triangular course sail used on square-rigged ships.

bergschrund: deep arcuate crevasse or series of crevasses between glacial ice and cirque wall of valley glacier.

bergy bit: medium-sized piece of ice generally less than 5 meters (16.4 ft.) high and about the size of a small cottage; originates from glacier ice but occasionally from massive piece of sea ice or hummocked ice.

bergy seltzer: sizzling sound comparable to that of seltzer water which icebergs emit when melting. It is caused by release of air bubbles retained in the berg at high pressure.

berm: generally flat part of beach leveled by previous erosion and sometimes bounded at lower side by ridge; occur above high-water mark; formed by deposition of material by wave action.

berm crest: seaward limit of a berm for shore profile.

Bermuda high: semipermanent, subtropical high of North Atlantic Ocean, so named especially when located in western part of ocean. This same high, when displaced toward eastern part of Atlantic is known as Azores high. On mean charts of sea level pressure, this high is a principal center of action.

Bermuda sail [ships]: fore-and-aft sail, so-called because of its great hoist, narrow lead and broad foot; has much rake aft.

Bermuda sloop: type of sloop built and developed in Bermuda which was popular about 1690. Protective type of the sharp model schooners and similar to Jamaica sloop preceding it. The mast had sharp rake aft and later models used lofty leg-of-mutton mainsail.

berth [ships]: 1) to assign an anchoring ground; space to lie in at a dock or alongside a wharf. 2) shelflike space allotted to passengers in a vessel as sleeping space.

berthon boat: collapsible lifeboat frequently used on destroyers and small craft.

beset: surrounded so closely by sea ice that steering control is lost; does not imply pressure.

best depth range: detection range of submarine target which is at the best depth to escape detection by ship with hull-mounted sonar.

Beta Centauri: first magnitude star in the group *Centaurus*, in about R.A. 14 hours and declination 60° south; one of the *pointers* to *Crux (Southern Cross)*.

Betelgeuse or Betelgeux: star *a Orionis*, or first in *Orion;* reddish in color and of magnitude varying from .1 to 1.2; about 5 hrs. 52 min. in R.A. and Dec. 7° 24′ N.

between decks [ships]: space between 2 decks of ship or space between upper and lower decks.

between wind and water: outside hull surface in vicinity of the waterline; *awash.*

Bezaan sail: fore-and-aft sail of 18th century with a boom and very short gaff.

biconic [*Mollusca*]: with diamond-shaped outline especially in gastropods, spire being about same shape and size as body whorl.

bidarka: Russian term for long, narrow canoe made of skin used by Aleuts in Alaska. It is skin-decked with 1 to 3 holes cut for occupants; kayak is similar to single-holed bidarka.

Biddulphia [phytoplankton]: cells often occur singly or in 2's and 3's although longer chains can be formed; ends of the cells bear 1 sometimes 2 pairs of projections; valves often triangular in end view; chloroplasts numerous.

biennial ice: sea ice between 1 and 2 years old.

bifid [*Mollusca*]: divided by a groove into two parts; especially applied to hinge teeth in bivalves.

bifilar current indicator: apparatus used for obtaining only the direction of current at different depths.

bifoliate [*Bryozoa*]: colony consisting of 2 layers of zooecia growing back to back.

bifurcate: forked; divided into 2 branches.

bifurcation: forking or division into 2 branches; point of forking; branch.

bight: 1) bend or loop of a rope in distinction from ends. Any bent part or turn of a rope between ends. 2) bay formed by natural bend of coastline.

bilander: term used as far back as 1550. The 18th century vessel's distinguishing feature was a trapezoidal mainsail similar to cutoff lateen, the forward end going to middle of ship.

bilateral symmetry: organization of a body so that the longitudinal axis of the body divides into 2 equivalent sides, right and left, and 2 nonequivalent sides, dorsal and ventral.

bilateria [*Coelenterata*]: characterized by primary bilateral symmetry and generally having 3 tissue layers.

bilge [ships]: bottom of ship below flooring; curve of hull below waterline. Vessel with sharp curve is said to have hard bilges; vessel with gradual curve is said to have easy bilges.

bilge keel [ships]: longitudinal angles welded and riveted back to back on bilge of vessel to check ship's tendency to roll.

bilge plates [ships]: curved shell plates that fit bilge.

bilge pump [ships]: pump that removes water from ship's bilge.

bilge well [ships]: located in lowest part of the compartment; used for drainage and is shaped like a box and fitted to underside of inner bottom with strainer on top.

bill: point of an anchor's fluke, also called the *pea.* End of a curved timber or knee. Any written statement of particulars.

billet head [ships]: wooden scroll used in place of figurehead.

billfish: members of this and swordfish family differ from other species in having upper jaw prolonged into long spear or sword. The billfish family bears a cylindrical spear at tip of head; body is covered with scales and possesses ventral fins; includes some trophy game fishes, e.g., marlin and sailfish.

billow: great wave or surge of water; any wave.

billy-boy: flat-bottomed, round-ended coasting vessel of Dutch origin used on east coast of England. The rig is that of a sloop, ketch or yawl with sometimes a square sail in foremast. Clinker-built, with high sheer fore and aft. Leeboards are carried.

Biloxi mean gulf level: tidal datum at Biloxi, Mississippi, of 0.78 ft. above *mean level* of the Mississippi River at its mouths.

binabina: canoe of the "mon" type of Solomon Islands.

binary fission: form of asexual reproduction in

which an organism divides into 2 equivalent parts, each of which continues to live as a whole organism.

binnacle [ships]: stand or case for housing a compass so that it may be conveniently consulted. Binnacles differ in shape and size according to where used and size of compass to be accommodated. A binnacle for ship's navigation compass consists essentially of a pedestal whose upper end is a bowl-shaped cover. This receptacle accommodates gimbals supporting the compass. Compensating binnacles are provided with brackets or arms on either side, starboard and port, for supporting and securing iron cylinders or spheres used to counteract quadrantal error due to earth's magnetization of vessel. This type of binnacle is usually placed immediately in front of steering wheel, having its vertical axis in vertical plane of fore-and-aft center line of vessel.

biocenosis: community of organisms found in a given area, region or habitat.

bioclastic rock: rocks produced from material broken or arranged by animals or plants and consisting of fragmental organic remains.

biogenetic: describing a product of activities of living organisms.

biogenetic deposit: deposit resulting from physiological activities of organisms.

bioherm: reef or mound built principally by sedimentary organisms such as corals, mollusks, etc.

biological clock: inherent physiological rhythm in organisms that usually manifest itself in changes in behavior or physiology timed to certain recurrent changes in normal environment of the organism and that may continue for a time even when the environmental stimulus has been removed.

biological oceanography: study of ocean's plant and animal life in relation to marine environment, including effects of habitat, sedimentation, physical and chemical changes in environment and other factors in the spatial and temporal distribution of marine organisms as well as action of organisms on environment.

bioluminescence: production of light without sensible heat by living organisms as result of chemical reaction, either with certain cells or organs or extracellularly in some form of secretion. Luminescence usually is induced by external stimuli, especially mechanical, such as wave action or shock waves. It is produced by variety of marine organisms in displays of 3 general types: sheet type, spark type and glowing ball type.

bioluminescent display: production of biological light of sufficient intensity to make water or disturbance of water conspicuously illuminated.

biomass: amount of actual living organism in given

area expressed as weight or volume of organisms per unit area of volume of environment.

biometer: instrument for measuring amount of life by assessing respiration.

biometry: statistical methods applied to biological problems.

biophore: hypothetical particle of minute size assumed to be capable of growth and reproduction.

biorealm: geographical location of living animals and plants whose limits are generally suggested in context.

biosection: living particulate matter in water and organic particles derived directly from living organisms.

bioseries: in evolution, historical sequence formed by changes in any single heritable character.

biosphere: that portion of surface of world, its waters and atmosphere permeated with living organisms or their products.

biostrome: bedded structure such as shell beds consisting of and built mainly by sedimentary organisms.

biota: animal and plant life of a region; flora and fauna collectively.

biotic community: group of species of organisms living in and characteristic of a given habitat.

biotic factors: factors of biological nature, such as availability of food, competition between species, predator-prey relationships, etc., which besides purely physical and chemical factors also affect distribution and abundance of given species of plant or animal.

biotic succession: natural replacement of one or more groups of marine organisms growing in specific habitat by other groups, preceding groups in some way preparing or favorably modifying habitat for succeeding groups.

biotope: area with uniform environment and uniform population of plant and animal life.

bipinnaria [*Asterias rubens*]: all arms in this species are extremely elongated from early stage so that the bipinnaria is easily distinguished from *L. sarsi* and *Astropecten*; larvae are about 2 mm. long and occur in the plankton from May to September.

bipinnaria [*Asteroidea*]: this species has no skeleton and may be regarded as having arisen from dipleurula by further growth of 2 anterolateral, pre-oral lobes which have fused in median plane at distal ends. The band of cilia, which in auricularia is a continuous ring, later becomes split into 2 independent rings enabling the 2 larval forms to be distinguished. The sides of the larva become drawn out into symmetrical lobes called arms and bear lateral extensions of ciliated field.

bipinnaria [*Astropecten*]: bipinnaria are perhaps

the least modified from dipleura condition, lateral arms being short. But a characteristic feature, circum-oral ciliary bands are drawn out into arms.

bipinnaria [*Luida sarsi*]: pre-oral lobe is elongated and medo-dorsal arm is also long. These differences from Astropecten result in larva having distinctive shape. Larvae are in plankton from August to October and reach 2.5 to 3.0 cm. in length.

bipolarity: term describing geographical distribution of species or closely related forms in both Northern and Southern hemispheres but not in intervening equatorial belt.

biramous: two-branched as various crustacean appendages.

bird-foot delta: delta formed by the outgrowth of pairs of natural levees making the digitale or bird-foot form.

bird's nest: 1) same as *crow's nest*. 2) distended strands in a wire rope caused by a kink.

bireme: long narrow ship or galley of ancient times having two superimposed banks of oars. Phoenicians are credited with origination of the bireme and perhaps the three-banked vessel, or trirene. Double and triple banks gave increased oar power without lengthening hull.

birthmarks [ships]: builder's irregularity in construction.

biserial [*Foraminifera*]: test with 2 rows of chambers. Chambers alternate on either side of the plane between rows.

Bismarck Archipelago: group of islands northeast of New Guinea.

bisquine: two-masted, lug-rigged fishing boat used in vicinity of St. Malo, France. Hull has good sheer, high freeboard forward, straight vertical stem, raking sternpost, long overhanging counter, transom stern, short, straight keel, and much dead rise. Average size is 40 to 45 ft. long, 1/3 to 1/4 the beam, about 6-ft. draft and 15 to 20 tons displacement.

bit: actual cutting portion of drilling tool.

bitheca [*Graplotithina*]: small tube formed at each budding in the development of a dendroid colony.

bitter end [ships]: end of a line; inboard end of anchor chain made fast in chain locker.

bitter lakes: lakes with high content of dissolved sulfates and alkaline carbonates, as distinct from salt lakes.

bittern: liquid remaining after seawater has been concentrated by evaporation until salt has crystallized.

bitts [ships]: strong posts of wood or iron to which cables are made fast; generally in pairs and named according to uses, such as riding bitts, towing bitts, windlass bitts, etc. Heavy fittings on vessel's deck, usually 2 short, heavy posts used to secure lines on hawsers.

bitumastic [ships]: black, tarlike composition largely of bitumen or asphalt containing such other ingredients as rosin, Portland cement, slaked lime, petroleum, etc.; used as protective coating in ballast and trimming tanks, chain lockers, shaft alleys, etc.

bivalve [*Pelecypoda*]: one of a class of mollusks generally sessile or burrowing into soft sediment, rock or other materials. Individuals possess hinged shell and hatchet-shaped foot used in digging. Clams, oysters and mussels belong to this class; many are notable fouling organisms; several are marine borers.

B/L: bill of lading.

black and white iceberg: iceberg having dark opaque portion containing sand and stones separated from white portion by definite line of demarcation.

blackfish: *Globicephala melas*, or *caaing-* or *pilot whale* of the North Atlantic, a toothed cetacean of about 20 ft. in length; usually found in large schools and often confused with the *grampus*, a smaller member of same family. Any of several *fishes* so called from their color.

black ice: thin, new ice on fresh or salt water appearing dark in color because of transparency.

black mud: dark fine-grained sediment in poorly aerated bays, lagoons and fiords; contains large quantities of decaying organic matter and iron sulfide and generally exudes hydrogen sulfide gas.

black pine [*Rhodomela larix*]: seaweed which grows on rocks between 2- and 0.5-ft. tide levels; an Arctic species that has traveled into warmer waters. It is named for tufts of short, dark, closely set, spirally arranged branchlets or needles on branches and stems resembling pine needles in texture and stiffness. When dry, this seaweed is jet black; when alive, brownish-black. The holdfast is a small, thin disc attached to stone or shell.

black tassel [*Pterosiphonia bipinnata*]: this alga grows from rhizoidlike base at mean tide level. Tassel effect is brought about by curling back of branches which causes them to mat together. Average black tassel is 4 to 8 in. long and ½ in. wide when matted. Individually, branches are threadlike. The black tassel has tierlike structure with 11 to 13 cells around central filament.

Blackwell frigate: passenger and cargo ship of England. The "Blackwallers" represented the supreme development of the packet ship of the period. These "frigate-built" ships resembled those of the Royal Navy and were exceptionally well built of teak.

black zone: band of growth of microscopic blue-green algal cells and other minute microplants at extreme upper limit of intertidal zone, in splash zone. Black zone represents transition from essentially terrestrial to essentially marine habitat.

bladder: urinary bladder, thin-walled sac which can expand to temporarily store urine before it is excreted.

bladder leaf [*Cystophyllum geminatum*]: abundant bladder leaf often form a conspicuous belt just below low-tide mark in sheltered places. The seaweed is 3 to 4 ft. long with soft, flexible branches 18 to 24 in. long and ¼ in. wide extending at fairly regular intervals from prominent main axis; tiny 1/16 to 1/8 in. air bladders like miniature balls are suspended from very short stems on secondary branches helping to suspend seaweed at surface of water. The bladder leaf is dark olive-brown, often showing lovely, iridescence when underwater. Holdfast is a solid, fibrous, conical disc.

blade: expanded or elongated leaflike part of larger algae, especially kelp.

blanket deposit: sedimentary deposit of uniform thickness which covers wide region.

blast: strong squall or sudden wind. Discharge of an explosive. Sound made by a wind instrument or a steam whistle.

bleeders [ships]: term applied to plugs screwed into bottom of a ship to provide for drainage of compartments when vessel is in dry dock.

blind rollers: long, high swells which have increased in height, almost to breaking point, as they pass over shoals or run in shoaling water.

blink: light reflected from ice at sea; *ice-blink. Land-blink* appears over distant snow or ice-covered land.

blinker: searchlight for signalling by code usually fitted with spring-controlled shutter. Some are operated by push-button contact.

blip: echo trace or recurrence on radar or sonar indicator screens.

blister: flaw in iron found in plates and flat bars. An outer skin built on a vessel's hull to increase beam or provide tank space. An air or water chamber built to the lower outside part of a warship's hull for protection from torpedo attack; may be constructed over entire underbody, or may extend only a few feet below her waterline.

blister wrack [*Laminaria bullata*]: distinguishing feature is distinct row of blisters (bullae) an inch or 2 within margins. Blisters are about an inch wide and an inch long; blade is dark olive-brown and as thick as tough rubber. Holdfast is a mass of branched fibers.

blizzard: 1) gale or hurricane accompanied by intense cold and driving snow. 2) general discharge of guns; a rattling volley; a general *blazing away.*

block [ships]: 1) frame of wood, steel or other metal within which are fitted sheaves or pulleys over which rope may be led; increases pull in ratios of sheaves used. Blocks are designated as single sheave, double sheave or simply as single, double or treble. 2) sea ice fragment more than 6 ft. but less than 30 ft. in diameter.

block and tackle [ships]: complete unit of 2 or more blocks rove up with adequate amount of rope.

block, cheek [ships]: block with shell on only one side, other side being bolted to spar or deck.

block, fiddle [ships]: double block with 2 sheaves in same plane, one being smaller than the other, giving the block a somewhat violin-shaped appearance.

Block Island boat: sharp-ended, open keel boat used at Block Island, Rhode Island. It had good sheer, with raking stem and sternpost; rig was that of cat schooner with gaff and boom mainsail and loose-footed gaff foresail; sails had light hoist and narrow heads.

block, snatch [ships]: single-sheave block with one end of frame hinged and able to be opened so as to admit a line other than by forcing end through the opening.

blower [ships]: fan device in an air duct to ventilate interior of vessel; exhaust air and fumes from below decks, particularly from engine compartment.

blowing spray: spray lifted from sea surface by wind and blown about in such quantities that horizontal visibility is restricted.

blubber: 1) layer of oil-yielding fat beneath the skin of whales and other cetaceans, which amounts to from 40 to 50 cwt. in a large whale. 2) large jellyfish.

bluefish, Atlantic: only species in the family. It is a streamlined greenish-blue fish with silvery sides; spiny dorsal fin is much smaller than long soft-rayed portion and division between the 2 is very slight; ventral fins are set far forward beneath pectorals as in perch and bass; tail is deeply forked. Large powerful jaws, armed with sharp teeth reveal carnivorous habits of the bluefish often called the wolf of the sea because of killing much more prey than it can eat. Average bluefish is under 24 in. long and less than 2 lbs. in weight.

bluegill [bream, copperbelly]: pan fish with dark opercular spot and dark round spot at posterior end of dorsal fin. Tail emarginate; pectoral fin long and pointed; opercular spot without red margin; body ovate, compressed; mouth small, oblique; about 5 rows of scales on cheeks; fins moderately high; caudal fin emarginate; color variable depending on age and sex. Young with distinct broad dark bars on sides; adults with bars obsolete. Adults often have copper-colored head and breast.

blue-green alga: one of a division or phylum (*Cyanophyta*) of single-celled or simply filamentous plants in which blue color is imparted by water-soluble accessory pigment, c-phycocynin. In planktonic form for whose color the Red Sea was named, red pigment dominates. Attached forms have characteristic scummy or velvety growth on boat bottoms, rocks and other underwater surfaces. Large masses of planktonic forms cause "sliming" of water.

blue ice: oldest and hardest form of glacier ice distinguished by slightly bluish or greenish color.

blue mud: combination of terrigenous and deep sea sediments having bluish-gray color due to presence of organic matter and finely divided iron sulfides. Calcium carbonate is present in variable amounts up to 35 percent.

blue runner [hardtail jack]: similar in appearance to a crevalle jack but a smaller fish, averaging 2 lbs. in weight. It lacks the dark blotch in pectoral fins typical of crevalle jack. This species occurs along Atlantic Coast north to Cape Cod.

blue tang [surgeon family]: grows to length of 12 in. This surgeonfish is deep blue; sides bear irregular horizontal stripes of yellow and fins are striped with dark blue or black.

bluff: headland or cliff with bold almost perpendicular front; precipitous lofty headland on a seacoast.

boarding: act of going on board a vessel or boat.

boatage: 1) charge for carriage by boat. 2) transportation by boat.

boat channel: shallow, narrow channel on reef flat which separates fringing reef from shore; parallel to shore and generally only few feet deep.

boatman: one who works on, manages, sails, or rows a boat. Also, *boatsman*.

boatswain [ships]: subordinate officer of a ship who has charge of rigging, anchors, cable and cordage. Boatswain's chair is narrow wooden seat, like that of a swing, suspended by rope tackle and used by seamen when working aloft or overside. Petty officer or seaman in position of authority who is in charge of deck hands aboard ship is a boatswain or "bos'n."

boatwoman: woman who sails or otherwise handles a boat.

boatwright: one who builds or repairs boats.

bobao: crude, outrigger, dugout, paddling canoe of Tongan Archipelago. Outrigger has 2 straight booms with U-type connections to the float; round bottom with tumble home sides; not over 15 ft. long and 16 in. beam.

bobstay [ships]: one of 2 ropes or chains extending from outer end of bowsprit to cutwater. Their function is to hold bowsprit to cutwater, to hold bowsprit in place and to counteract upward strain exerted by headstays.

bodkin: sailmaker's tool for piercing holes in canvas; a pricker.

body plan [ships]: pair of half transverse end elevations with common vertical center line. Right side gives the ship as seen from ahead, the left side from astern. Waterlines, buttock and low lines, diagonal lines, etc., are shown.

body waves: either transverse or longitudinal seismic waves transmitted in interior of an elastic solid or fluid and not related to boundary surface.

body whorl [*Gastropoda*]: last and largest complete loop in spiral. The last formed, it terminates in aperture.

boeier: slope-rigged yacht of Netherlands. It is a roly-poly craft with round bottom; husky and well built, as are all Dutch boats.

boiler [ships]: any vessel, container or receptacle that is capable of generating steam by external or internal application of heat. Two general classes of boilers are fire tube and water tube.

boiler casing [ships]: wall protecting different deck spaces from heat of boiler room.

boiler foundation [ships]: structure upon which boiler is secured and consisting of girders built up from plates and shapes. In a cylindrical boiler athwartship girders are often called saddles.

boiler room [ships]: compartment in middle or after section of a vessel where boilers are placed.

bold: deep, as water close to a shore; said of waters navigable very near to land, as, "soundings showed *bold water* to the Cape."

bold coast: prominent landmass that rises steeply from sea.

bollards [ships]: cast steel heads or short columns secured to a wharf or dock used for securing lines from a ship. Bitts on a ship may also be called bollards.

bolometer: instrument for measuring thermal radiation.

bolster plate [ships]: piece of plate adjoining hawsehole to prevent chafing of hawser against cheeks of a ship's bow; plate for support like a pillow cushion.

bolt: 1) rod of metal employed as a fastening. With few exceptions, such as *drift bolts*, a head or shoulder is made on one end and a screw thread is cut at the other. Bolts are named according to their use, as a *fender-b.*; from their construction, as *double ended b's*; and from method of adjustment, as a *flush b.* 2) to fasten together or make secure as with a bolt. 3) *bolt-rope.*

Bombarda: Italian pole-masted, polace-rigged brigantine.

bomb ketch: naval ketch carrying mortars used for bombarding fortifications; used mostly in French navy in 18th century.

Bombschuite: odd, decked, tube-shaped fishing craft of Netherlands; 39 to 45 ft. long; beam about 2/3 the length; almost square-ended, with large outboard rudder and leeboards.

bonaventure [ships]: mizzensail carried in after mast of a four-masted vessel in Middle Ages.

bonefish: sleek silvery fish found in warm waters northward on Atlantic Coast to Cape Cod and to San Diego on Pacific Coast. Long and slender body midway along the back lacks elongated tapering ray found in tarpon. Bonefish are bottom feeders, subsisting on crabs, mollusks and other small invertebrates. Mouth is located on underside of snout, adapted for bottom feeding. Usually under 36 in. long and less than 5 lbs. in weight.

bone in her teeth, carry a: 1) to throw up a foam or spray under the bows; said of a ship turning up a curl of water and foam at her stem when sailing fast. 2) to "carry a bone in the mouth."

bonification: estimation of fertility and standing crop.

bonito, Atlantic: marvel of compact strength and beauty; its torpedo-shaped body and smoothly polished surface reduce water resistance to a minimum and place bonito among champion ocean swimmers. It has the coloring of a mackerel but upper sides are marked by numerous oblique dark blue bars extending upward and backward from lateral line. Sharply pointed finlets give tail a saw-toothed appearance and long spiny dorsal fin is continuous with soft rayed portion of the fin. Although average size is under 24 in. and 5 lbs., larger individuals up to 30 in. and 15 lbs. are sometimes hooked. It gathers in schools near surface as far north as Cape Cod and preys on mackerel and menhaden.

bonnet [ships]: long, narrow, rectangular piece of sailcloth laced to bottom of sail to increase area and removed to shorten sail. This method was used before reef points were employed to shorten sail.

bonnet shark: shovelhead, or *Sphryna tiburo,* of the hammerhead family of sharks found in warmer parts of Atlantic and Pacific Oceans; length about 6 ft. with a head narrower and less hammer-shaped than the so-named hammerhead.

boobies [*Pelecaniformes*]: members of this family are large, long-winged seabirds with stout, conical, pointed beaks, fairly short necks, stout bodies and long wedge-shaped tails. Legs are short and all their toes are connected by webs. On the throat they have small pouch of naked skin and there are unfeathered areas of naked skin in the face.

booby hatch [ships]: cover of scuttle-way or small hatch, such as that which leads to forecastle or forepeak of vessel.

book lung: breathing apparatus in arachnids. It is made of leaflike lamellar folds of one side of ventral abdominal wall through which air circulates and oxygenates blood in lamellae.

boom [ships]: 1) long rounded, wooden or metal support for the bottom of a sail. 2) pole used to extend bottom of a sail. 3) spar to which foot of a sail is affixed.

boom cargo [ships]: on cargo carrying ships, a cranelike arrangement for moving merchandise between dock and ship's hold.

boomkin [ships]: short spar extending horizontally beyond stern to take the sheet block of overhanging sail.

boom sail [ships]: when a boom was added to the 18th century "mizzen course" it was known as a "boom sail" or "driver boom sail."

boom table [ships]: outrigger attached to mast or structure built up around mast from the deck to support keel bearings for booms. Boom tables are necessary to promote working clearance when number of booms are installed on one mast.

Boötes: northern constellation whose brightest star is *Arcturus,* a Latin word meaning *bear guard,* which star and its group being considered, in ancient times, as guard or ward of the constellation *Ursa Major* or *Great Bear.* Boötes is located about 30° southward of *Alkaid* (or *Benetnasch*), tail star in *Ursa Major.*

boot-top [ships]: area on ship's hull along waterline usually painted a contrasting color.

boot-topping [ships]: operation of painting that part of ship's sides just above water with narrow strip of paint usually of different color from that of bottom or sides. Special antifouling, grease-resistant paint applied for extra protection at waterline or "between wind and wave."

bora: fall wind whose source is so cold that when air reaches lowlands or coast dynamic warming is insufficient to raise air temperature to normal level for the region; hence it appears as a cold wind.

bore: high breaking wave of water advancing rapidly up an estuary. Bores occur at mouths of shallow rivers if tide range at the mouth is large. They can also be generated in a river when tsunamis enter shallow coastal water and propagate up the river.

boreal: term descriptive of cool or cold temperate regions of Northern Hemisphere. Corresponding region of Southern Hemisphere is sometimes termed antiboreal.

borehole: hole drilled into earth to obtain samples of and measure physical properties of rock and sediments penetrated.

boring [ships]: forcing a ship under power through ice, by breaking a lead.

Bornholm herring boat: typical to Danish island of Bornholm in Baltic Sea. It is dandy-rigged, sprit-sail main and mizzen, with straight leech. A yard topsail is sometimes used. This has a sliding ganter topmast, the heel of which comes within reach of deck. Hull is about 22 ft. long with 8 ft. beam and has straight stem and sternpost.

borrow: to approach closely to a coast; to bring a vessel closer to the wind, or to *luff*.

bosom [ships]: inside of an angle bar.

bosom bar [ships]: one angle fitted inside another.

bosom plate [ships]: plate bar or angle fitted to angle bar to connect ends of two angles.

boss [ships]: part of propeller to which blades are attached. Also the aperture in stern frame where propeller shaft enters.

boss frame [ships]: frame bent around to fit the boss in way of stern tube or shaft.

boss plate [ships]: plate fitted around the boss of propeller post or around curved frames in way of stern tubes.

botter: shallow-draft, sloop-rigged yacht of Netherlands. It is perhaps, the best sea boat of all Dutch craft. Being contrary Hollanders designed the botter with rounded bow and pointed stern; bottom is flat and sides are slightly curved and flare out a bit. Average size is about 40 ft. length over-all with beam about 1/3 and draft of 2 ft. with leeboards raised.

bottle papers: blanks furnished by U.S. Hydrographic Office or other interested authority to shipmasters which are filled in with requested data prior to throwing overboard in sealed bottles. This is done at sea for determining set and drift of surface currents, subject to subsequent reports of recovery of bottles at places and dates indicated.

bottom: any ground covered by water. Bed refers more specifically to whole submerged basin and floor is essentially horizontal surface of ground beneath water.

bottom bounce: technique by which acoustic energy is reflected off ocean bottom one or more times before reaching target.

bottom flow: current denser than any part of surrounding fluid flowing along the sea bottom.

bottom friction: force resulting from interaction between ocean bottom and water particle motion over it. In the case of currents, it is a retarding force acting in direction opposite to current flow. It is proportional to roughness of bottom water density, velocity of current and water depth.

bottom outer [ships]: term applied to bottom shell plating in double bottom ship.

bottom plating [ships]: that part of shell plating which is below waterline.

bottom pressure: pressure at a point on bottom of a bottom water due to weight of column of water above it.

bottom pressure fluctuation: change in pressure at a point on bottom of body of water as surface wave passes over it.

bottom reflection: return of transmitted sound from bottom of ocean. Characteristics of reflected sound depend on nature of the bottom and on wavelength of the sound.

bottom resistivity: resistance in ohms between opposite face of a unit cube sediment; governed more by electrolyte concentration of liquid filing interstices than by intrusive conductivity of sediment grains.

bottomry: marine contract whereby an owner or master of a vessel borrows money at an agreed rate of interest solely for meeting expenses necessary to complete a voyage. Vessel and any freight she earns are pledged as security in such a contract and, if ship is lost, a lender loses his money. If more than one *b.* is involved, last lender must be repaid first. A similar contract pledging laden cargo as security is called a *respondentia* and must be repaid only upon safe arrival of some part of such cargo. When both ship and cargo are pledged, bond is termed *bottomry and respondentia.*

bottom sample: portion of material forming the bottom, brought up for inspection.

bottom sediments: in general, all sedimentary material regardless of origin found on or in submarine bottom, including ballast or other material dumped into the sea by man. More specifically it is limited to unconsolidated mineral and organic material forming sea bottoms, not including coral reefs or bedrock.

bottom set beds: layers of fine alluvial sediments carried out and deposited on bottom of sea in front of a delta.

bottom temperature: temperature observed at bottom of sea.

bottom water: water mass at deepest part of water column. It is dense water that is permitted to occupy that position by original topography.

Bougainvillia ramosa [phylum *Coelenterata*]:

medusa of hydroid bearing same name. Despite wide occurrence of the hydroid, the medusa has seldom been recorded in British waters. It seems to be a summer and southern species. Most distinguishing feature is presence of 4 branched tentacles around the mouth.

Bouguer anomaly: method of stating isostatic anomaly derived from gravity observations. It allows for height above sea level and visible excess or deficit of mass. It is called after Bouguer who first noticed that the Andes did not disturb gravity as much as their mass would suggest.

Bouguer correction: correction made in observed gravity values for altitudes (elevation) above sea level of station and rock between station and sea level.

boulder barricade: coast bordered with lines of innumerable large boulders visible between low water and half tides.

boulder clay: unstratified or little stratified and unsorted deposit of silty and clayey materials in which are embedded particles of sand to boulder size.

Boulogne drift-boat: ketch-rigged vessel engaged in drift net fishery, which works out of the port of Boulogne, France. These drifters are large and husky, ranging in length to over 90 ft.

boundary current: fast flowing current concentrated near edge of an ocean, relatively close to western shore.

boundary layer: term referring broadly to layer of fluid in immediate vicinity of bounding surface; layer in which frictional forces are not negligible.

bounding bar [ships]: bar connecting edges of a bulkhead to tank top, shell, decks or another bulkhead.

Bourbon tube: part of temperature sensing element in bathythermograph consisting of hollow brass coil connecting to a xylene-filled tube with one end fixed and other free to move with temperature expansion and contraction.

bovo: two-masted, lateen-rigged fishing vessel of Gulf of Genoa, Italy. The rig is comprised of mainmast, stepped just forward of amidships, with lateen mainsail, short mizzenmast on stern, lateen mizzen sheeted to boomkin and 2 or 3 headsails to a long bowsprit.

bow [ships]: forward part or head of a ship beginning where sides trend inward and terminating where they unite in stem or prow; opposite end to stern.

bow, bullnosed [ships]: bow with large, rounded bow point underneath waterline.

bow, clipper [ships]: bow with extreme forward rake, once familiar on sailing vessels.

bowfin [family *Amiidae*]: primitive fishes with stout bodies covered with heavy, smooth scales.

Head is covered with smooth plates; mouth is horizontal and rather large; jaws have 2 kinds of teeth: larger and outer are conical, vomer, palatine and pterygoid bear small teeth. This North American family consists of single species and like gars the bowfin is often called a bony fossil. This fish can survive in oxygen-deficient stagnant ponds where other fishes die because the air bladder functions as respiratory organ when the bowfin rises to surface and gulps air.

bowfin, American [mudfish]: unprepossessing fish inhabiting sluggish streams and swampy ponds of New York to North Dakota southward to Gulf of Mexico. It is a chunky, olive-green fish with yellowish underparts and covering of large cycloid scales; blunt head terminates in large mouth well provided with sharp teeth. The feature that names the fish is long, low dorsal fin that undulates as fish swims. Paired fins and tail fin are greenish hue and during breeding season an orange-bordered black spot appears at base of tail fin of male. Bowfins grow 2 or 3 ft. long and attain a maximum weight of 12 lbs.

bow, flared [ships]: bow with extreme flare at upper and forecastle deck.

bowline [ships]: rope leading forward and fastened to leech of square sail; used to steady weatherleech of the sail and to keep it forward making the ship sail nearer the wind. Also knotted loop in a rope as a "bowline on a bight."

bow lines [ships]: curves representing vertical section of bow end of a ship. Similar curves in aft part of hull are buttock lines.

bowling along [ships]: with most sails set and in brisk sailing breeze, ship is said to be "bowling along."

bow, ram [ships]: bow protruding underneath waterline considerably forward of forecastle deck.

bowsprit [ships]: large spar that extends forward from ship's bow carrying sails and ropes to help support masts. Beyond it extends the jib boom. Round or flat timber extending forward from bow of boat and carrying headstay and forestay to a point forward of the deck, providing extra sail area.

box gage: tide gage that is operated by a float in long, vertical stationary box to which the tide is admitted through an opening on bottom.

box the compass: to name points of compass in order, beginning with north.

brace [ships]: to swing or turn around yards of ship by braces; to brace up; to lay yards fore-and-aft so that the ship will sail closer to wind. Braces are part of running rigging used to regulate position of yards. On a square-rigged ship, line attached to yard to turn it in trimming the sail.

braced up [ships]: referring to a ship whose yards (long timbers or spars supporting sails) have been brought closer to fore-and-aft axis of ship by pulling on ropes or braces controlling horizontal motion of yards.

braces [ships]: on a sailing ship, pair of ropes attached through blocks to ends of a yard so that the yard may be adjusted horizontally.

brachial: pertaining to armlike structures, such as to rays of starfishes.

brachial valve [*Brachiopoda*]: valve to which brachidium is attached; in most brachiopods a smaller valve with small or indistinguishable beak and bearing only a small part of pedicle opening.

brachidium [*Brachiopoda*]: calcareous support for lophophore.

brachiolarian larva: last stage in starfish larvae just prior to metamorphosis into starfish form. Brachiolarian larvae develop additional larval arms, not involving the ciliated band, in connection with fixation to substrata.

brachiophore [*Brachiopoda*]: short, typically stout process that projects from hinge line of brachial valve into interior of valve; serves for attachment of lophophore.

brachiopod: literally means "arm foot." One of a phylum *(Brachiopoda)* of sessile, marine, molusklike animals in which the body, whose construction differs considerably from that of mollusks, is enclosed in calcareous or horny bivalve shells. Most species live in shallow water. The brachiopod is a living body whose 4 main parts are mantle, brachia, internal organs and stalk or pedicle. Mantle is a sheet whose twin halves are folded over rest of body and secrete the shell; edges of mantle bear fringes of hairlike setae, which are long and stiff.

Brachiopoda [phylum]: Greek "bracheo" arm; "podos" foot. Referring to internal paired appendages which were thought at first to function for locomotion but are really food-gathering organs. Cambrian to Recent. Brachiopods have same structural plan as *Bryozoa* and similar way of life but evolved in different direction. Some adult forms attach themselves to ocean floor, other shells or rocks by means of a fleshy stemlike anchoring attachment (pedicle) which protrudes through opening in one of shells. Others cement themselves to bottom. Phylum is represented by sessile benthonic individuals. They are typical of shallow marine water, although a few forms exist on Continental slope.

Brachyura [phylum *Arthropoda*]: the true crab, hatch as protozoeae changing into first zoea stage which is flattened from side to side with a carapace that has rostral and dorsal spine and, in many species, short lateral spines also. Compound eyes, not as yet on stalks, mouth parts and natatory first and second maxillipeds, walking legs hidden beneath carapace, long abdomen consisting of 6 segments ending in a forked spiny telson are other important features. Number of zoeal stages varies with species and seems to be 2, 4 or 5 but never 3. It culminates in a megalopa which swims by means of abdominal appendages (pleopods), maxillipeds by now functioning as accessory mouth parts. A suborder which is divided into 5 tribes: (1) Dromiacea; (2) Oxystomata; (3) Cyclometopa; (4) Catometopa; (5) Oxyrhyncha (Maioidia).

bracket [ships]: steel plate, commonly with a reinforcing flange, used to stiffen beam angles to bulkheads, frames to longitudinals, etc.

brackish: salty in a moderate degree, as fresh water adulterated by seawater.

brackish water: water in which salinity values range from approximately 0.50 to 17.00 parts per thousand.

bract [*Siphonophora*]: thick gelatinous structures of various shapes that aid in swimming and in protection of the colony; regarded as modified medusoids, or more recently, as modified tentacles.

bragagna: three-masted, lateen-rigged sailing vessel similar to felucca of the Mediterranean. The bragagna was a native of Dalmatia, seen on the Adriatic and Mediterranean until middle of the last century.

bragozzi: two-masted, double-ended fishing craft of Venice. Very small lug foresail is carried on mast stepped in the bow and large balance lugsail is on mainmast. A feature of Venetian boats is the painting of sails in gay colors and designs.

braided stream: stream choked with sandbars that divide it into an intricate network of interlacing channels.

brail [ships]: line secured to after end of a sail and used to gather it up against spar or stay.

brakeka: open boat used in herring fishery from Blekinge, Sweden. It is clinker-built with 8 strakes to a side and has a curved and strong raking stem, flaring sides and thin narrow stern.

branch fiord: bifurcation of a narrow deep arm of the sea.

branchia: in aquatic animals a respiration organ consisting of series of lamellar or filamentous outgrowths; gill.

branchial septum: septum of wall of connective tissue in center of fish's gill arch between 2 "halves" of a gill.

branchiopods: class, *Crustacea*, members of which are distinguished by possession of numerous pairs of flattened, leaflike, lobed swimming feet which also serve as respiratory organs; mandible is without a pair in adult; mainly freshwater forms, e.g., fairy shrimp, brine shrimp, tadpole shrimp, clam shrimp and water fleas.

branchiostagals: bony rays that support membranes on lower side of the head of a fish.

branchiostegite: expanded lateral part of carapace serving as a gill covering or gill chamber in certain crustaceans.

Branchiura: body flattened dorsoventrally; carapace shieldlike, covering head and thorax; compound eyes; abdomen bilobed; small, limbless and not segmented; antennae small; 4 pairs of swimming legs on underside of body; sucking mouth; some appendages with claws for clinging; suction cups; ectoparasites on skin or gill cavities of freshwater and marine fish.

brash ice: fragment of sea ice or river ice less than 2 meters (6.6 ft.) in diameter.

brave west wind: 1) nautical term for strong and rather persistent westerly winds over oceans in temperate latitudes. They occur between 40° and 65° N in Northern Hemisphere and 35° to 55° S in Southern Hemisphere where they are more regular and strongest between 40° and 50° (roaring forties). 2) first European who sailed to the New World discovered that in oceans of Southern Hemisphere westerly to northwesterly winds are quite strong between latitudes of 40° and 50°. A shipmaster who kept to this region could depend upon making many more knots a day than vessels north or south of the wind belt. Sixteenth century usage made "brave" equivalent to "splended, excellent or fine." Hence, brave west winds was a logical name for "splended currents" found in just one region. "Brave" has dropped out of speech as a general term of praise or admiration, but the praise formed from it remains in use among captains of modern vessels whose power make them virtually independent of "the splended winds."

Brazil Current: warm current that flows southward along Brazilian coast below Natal.

breach: 1) breaking of water, as waves or a surf; a surge. 2) leap of a whale out of water. 3) infraction of a law or violation of any obligation or agreement, as a *breach* of contract. 4) break in continuance of friendly relations; a quarrel. 5) to cause a rupture in a ship's side or dock wall.

bread and butter mode [ships]: type of ship model's hull built up with layers of wood, one placed upon the other.

breadth [ships]: side-to-side measurement of a vessel at any given place.

breadth extreme [ships]: maximum breadth measured over plating or planking, including fenders.

breadth molded [ships]: greatest breadth of a vessel, measured from heel of frame on one side to heel of frame on other side.

breadth, registered [ships]: measured amidships at its greatest breadth to outside of plating.

break [ships]: of poop or forecastle; point at which partial poop or forecastle decks are discontinued.

breakage: 1) empty space left after stowing cargo in a hold. 2) broken stowage, goods broken in transportation. 3) allowance for packaged cargo damaged by being crushed or broken during carriage.

breaker: wave breaking on shore, over a reef, etc. Breakers may be roughly classified into 3 kinds, although the categories may overlap: (1) spilling breakers break gradually over considerable distance (2) plunging breakers tend to curl over and break with a crash (3) surging breakers peak up, but then instead of spilling or plunging they surge up the beach face.

breaker depth: still-water depth at point where wave breaks.

breakhead: the strengthened bows of an icebreaking vessel.

breaking off: shoving and holding a vessel broadside off a quay or wharf by means of long heavy spars in order to permit lighters, bunkering equipment, floating cranes, etc., to work between ship and quayside; also termed *booming off*.

break of the poop: forward end of poop deck; break of the forecastle; after end of forecastle deck, just at the place where bulkheads are placed.

breakwater: structure protecting shore area, harbor, anchorage or basin from waves.

breakwater [ships]: term applied to plates fitted on forward weather deck to form a V-shaped shield against water that is shipped over the bow.

bream: to clear a ship's bottom of barnacles, seaweed, ooze, etc., by burning, scraping, and brooming off.

breaming [ships]: cleaning barnacles, paint, etc., from ship's bottom with blowtorch.

breast beam [ships]: transverse beam nearest to midships on poop and forecastle deck.

breast hook [ships]: horizontal plate secure across the forepeak of vessel to tie the forepeak of vessel and untie bow.

breast rail [ships]: upper rail of a balcony on quarter deck.

breech block: plug in breech of a large gun that blocks rearward escape of explosive force of charge.

breeze: influenced by early terms for "northeast" the Spanish and Portuguese of 16th century used *briza* to name a gentle northeast wind that was always cool because of its direction. In parts of

West Indies where the term for movement of air was transplanted very early, *briza* meant welcome relief from stifling heat. English seamen are explorers who adopted the term, modified it to breeze and extended it to include "any gentle fresh wind," regardless of direction. Today the once technical term is loosely used to name an air movement not strong enough to be called wind.

bridge [ships]: navigating deck of a ship, usually with enclosed pilothouse in center and open wings on either side for observations.

bridge, flying [ships]: open deck above bridge usually with duplicate set of engine controls and navigating facilities.

bridge house [ships]: erection or superstructure fitted about amidships on upper deck of ship. The officer's quarters, staterooms and accommodations are usually in the bridge house.

bridge, navigating or flying: uppermost platform erected at the level of the top of pilothouse. It consists of a narrow walkway supported by stanchions running from one side of the ship to the other and space over top of the pilothouse.

bridle: two or more parts of rope or chain rigged to distribute stress on a single part of another rope or chain to which they are connected at a common point; often used in slinging cargo-trays, vehicles, and heavy cases where such articles must be steadied in trim during hoisting. In hoisting such bulky and easily damaged objects as automobiles, engines, large crates, and the like, a stout piece of wood called a *spreader* is placed to separate the parts of a bridle in order to avoid crushing, or chafing against, objects thus slung.

brig: two-masted, square-rigged vessel with spanker and crossjack. A brig's main braces lead forward to foremast; hardy and fast.

brigantine: two-masted vessel, square-rigged, but without main course, mainsail being a fore-and-aft sail. Crosstrees are used on mainmast instead of usual "top."

brightwork: 1) those metal objects or fittings on a vessel which are kept bright by polishing. **2)** scraped and cleaned woodwork which may, or may not, be varnished, but never painted.

brine: seawater containing a higher concentration of dissolved salt than that of the ordinary ocean. Brine is produced by evaporation or freezing of seawater, in latter case, sea ice formed is much less saline than initial liquid, leaving adjacent unfrozen water with increasing salinity.

brine slush: mixture of ice crystals and salt water which retards or prevents complete freezing, often found between young sea ice and cover of newly fallen snow.

brink: margin of land bordering on water.

Brisinga: deep-sea starfish of the family *Brisingidae.*

bristol fashion: in seamanlike style; ship-shape; in good order.

brit: 1) young of the common herring; any of certain small herring. **2)** plankton upon which right whales feed. **3)** any of the silversides.

brittle star: 1) starfishlike echinoderm belonging to class *Ophiuroidea.* Unlike true starfish, they have long, slender, jointed arms distinctly separated from small disc shaped bodies. These flexible limbs have a remarkable power of regeneration. **2)** one of a class *(Ophiuroidea)* of echinoderms having 5, sometimes 6, rarely 7 or 8, elongate, slender, cylindrical arms radiating from a flat central disc; range from shallow water to great depths.

Brixham trawler: large ketch or dandy-rigged fishing vessel working out of and originating in Brixham, Devonshire, England. Latter-day Brixham boats run up to 70 ft. in length and over 60 tons.

broach, broach to [ships]: **1)** to turn sideways to seas when running before them, usually as result of losing control; to come suddenly up into wind by accident or by fault of helmsman. **2)** dangerous position in a gale caused by sudden shift of winds.

broadhorn: rough scow used in early days on Mississippi River. They were guided with long sweeps and floated downstream with the current, carrying passengers and freight from Ohio River ports to New Orleans and then sold for lumber at the latter port.

broadside [ships]: whole side of a ship above waterline, from bow to quarter.

broken-backed: said of a ship when so weakened as to be *hogged*, or drooping at each end; having keel or lower longitudinal members fractured or badly strained.

broken belt: transition zone between open water and consolidated ice.

broken ice: ice that covers from five-tenths to eight-tenths of sea surface.

broken stowage: stowage of unusually bulky units of cargo which leaves broken up and unoccupied space in a hold.

broken water: water having surface covered with ripples or eddies and usually surrounded by calm water.

bromeliad: member of family of plants, *Bromeliaceae*, common in tropical Western Hemisphere; characterized by spiky leaves and flowers occurring in thick clusters attached to trees, e.g., pineapple. Bromeliads are frequently mistaken for orchids.

brood pouch: chamber where eggs develop in certain crustaceans.

broom: long prevailing custom in American ports is display of a broom in the rigging, as far aloft as possible, when the vessel is offered for sale.

brow [ships]: 1) gangplank extending a dock, usually with rollers on the dock to allow for movement of vessel. 2) small curved angle or flanged plate fitted on outside of shell of a ship over an air port to prevent water running down ship's side from entering open port. Also called a watershed.

brown alga: one of a division or phylum *(Phaeophyta)* of greenish-yellow to deep brown, filamentous to massively complex plants, in which color is imparted by predominance of carotenes and xanthophylls over chlorophylls; includes rockweeds, gulfweeds and large kelp; most abundant in cooler waters of the world.

brown sieve [*Punctaria latifolia*]: brown sieve floats on quiet waters or attaches to other seaweed. Striking feature of this alga is presence of holes that dot the single mature blade. Thin, flat blade varies in shape, sometimes long and narrow, other times almost as broad as long. It is fragile, paper-thin seaweed, olive-brown when in water, green when removed from water. Blades are smooth, without markings of any kind, and taper abruptly into short stipes. When seaweed is mature, reproductive spores project above blade, forming on surface.

Bryophyta [phylum]: this small phylum, including mosses and liverworts, represents simplest stage of adaptation to land life. Like algae, these plants lack vascular tissue, therefore remain very small and thrive only in moist places. Almost nothing is known of them as fossils.

bryophyte: member of group of nonflowering plants that includes mosses and liverworts. Usually land plants, they prefer to live where there is plenty of moisture.

Bryozoa [phylum]: *Bryozoa* or moss animals form important phylum. Anatomically the bryozoan is very simple and in many respects more like a brachiopod than other animals, but unlike the brachiopod, it is invariably minute and always grows in colonies. Individual rarely attains diameter greater than that of a period, but thousands of them living together may form a colony some inches across. Locally they combine to make reef limestones. Unlike the brachiopod, the bryozoan forms a simple skeleton in form of slender tube or boxlike cell, with opening at or near one end through which front end of body can be thrust out while feeding. Greek *"bryon"* moss; *"zoon"* animal, referring to tufted, mosslike growths of some modern bryozoan colonies. Ordovician to Recent.

bryozoan: one of phylum *Bryozoa* or *Polyzoa* of minute, mostly colonial, aquatic animals with body walls often hardened by calcium carbonate and growing attached to aquatic plants, rocks and other firm surfaces. Colonies may be encrusting, creeping, or erect and branching. Encrusting colonies may be white, yellowish or brick red and consist of many tiny, beautifully formed shells. Members of this phylum are widespread and notable fouling organisms.

bryozoan, encrusting [*Membranipora membranacea*]: irregular moldlike spot which does not look like an animal. Form thin, flat colonies, one or two in. in diameter, upon floats or fronds of kelp and on rocks. Encrustations are calcareous patches filled with small rectangular spaces marked off by narrow, white ridges. Within these spaces are individual members of colony which radiate out from older, central part of the mass.

bryozoan, lace coral [*Phidolopora pacifica*]: not true coral but resembles one because of clear white color and open meshes of hard parts. Forms encrusting base and from it a thin, perforated, semicircular lacy frill. Lacelike colonies grow to 1 or 1½ in. high and nearly same width. Attached to rocks in intertidal zone or in deep water. Within each limy capsule of the lace, lives an individual of bryozoan colony. Colony increases in size by system of budding.

bryozoan, sea mat [*Dendrobeania lichenoides*]: often covers rocks in shallow sea bottom. Colonies grow erect with number of broad, flexible branches attached by narrow base. Each leaflike branch may be 1 in. long and 1½ in. wide. Observed through microscope, one sees hard, outer walls (zooecia) in which individual animal lives which are arranged in 2 rows and in 2 layers and are more or less quadrangular in shape.

bryozoan, staghorn [*Bugula murrayana*]: gets name from blunt, forked branches. Can be found on rocky beaches. Branches are approximately 1/8 in. wide and entire colony may stand from 1½ to 3 in. high. One long root fiber or holdfast may have dozens of stems that form a bushy tuft arising from it. Species of individuals of colony may be clearly seen, each one appearing as small perforation on the frond.

bryozoan, stiff stalk [*Bugula pacifica*]: small plantlike animal, 1 or 2 in. high, commonly found attached to rocks. Branches grow around central stem in spiral manner, forming dense clusters or erect tufts. Color usually white, but they may be pale yellow, green or purple. Individual members of colony are called zooids and are so small that they cannot be seen without a microscope.

B.S.: official abbreviation for *Boiler Survey*, as in records of, and certificates issued by, a classification society.

bubble pulse: pulsation attributed to bubble produced by seismic charge fired in water.

bubble sextant: device used for measuring altitude of celestial bodies. A bubble similar to one found in a surveyor's level is used as horizontal reference instead of the true horizon which a standard sextant uses. The device is used almost exclusively in air navigation.

bubble shell [Adam's]: bubble shell is oval in shape and has large and long aperture. The aperture is bordered by a lip which is nearly straight along its middle. Both the columellar and outer sides of the aperture have a white callus upon them. Shell is marbled and flecked with light and dark markings upon a somewhat tan background reaching a length of about 1½ in.

bubble shell [open]: shell of this mollusc is oval in outline and somewhat swollen in the middle; smooth and thin in texture and finely, longitudinally striate. It is of whitish transparent color and with reach about ½ in. long.

bubble shell [Pease's]: quite oblong in shape, and light and thin in texture. It is peculiar in having edge of outer lip straight for considerable portion of its length. Surface of the shell is marked with fine longitudinal strias and with extremely fine spiral striae. It is mottled and flected with various shades of brown and white and reaching a length of about 1 in.

bubble shell [Saffron yellow]: this bubble shell is oval in shape and presents a shining surface which shows growth wrinkles and extremely fine spiral striations. It is of transparent yellow or orange tint with opaque white at extremities, reaching a length of about ½ in.

bucca: sailing and rowing ship of Crusade period of Venetian origin.

buccal mass: in molluscs and various other organisms, the mouth and pharynx when heavily muscularized and used as organ of prehension and mastication.

Buccinidae: whelks are large, thick, oblong or spindle-shaped shells with few body whorls and large apertures which are usually terminated in a notch in front. Outer lip is simple, though often thickened, and columella is without folds. Operculum which closes the aperture is horny in composition. Whole outside of shell is covered by thick periostracum. Members of this family are a carnivorous, aggressive lot, distributed from warm waters of tropics nearly to the poles.

Bucentaur: state barge of Venice in time of the Doges; propelled by sweeps on main deck.

bucket thermometer: simplest measurement of sea temperature. Consists of dropping of a bucket or other container into sea, retrieving a sample of water and measuring temperature with relatively standard glass thermometer.

buckle plate [ships]: plate that has warped from

original shape; also a plate that is wider at center than at ends.

buckler: block or shutter used to close a hawse-pipe or other opening against ingress of water; a hawseplug.

buckling: 1) dangerous bending or bowing of a spar under stress. 2) warping or distortion under stress of any member of a structure.

budding: asexual reproduction in which small portion of an organism grows out from and eventually develops into another individual or another equivalent part of a colony.

buffalo fish: chunky species with large head; mouth is located farther forward than suckers and lips are not as thick and fleshy. The small-mouth buffalo fish is pale silver in color and grows to a length of 36 in.; it lives in lakes and rivers of Mississippi River valley. A largemouth buffalo fish is the same size but more olive in color; found from Minnesota to Louisiana.

buffer: salts and other substances that are to some degree amorphoteric, able to remove either hydrogen or hydroxyl ions from solution, thus retarding changes in pH of solution when either acids or bases are added and making for greater constancy in pH.

bugala: lateen-rigged Arab trading vessel of Red Sea of true dhow type; fast and seaworthy.

bugalet: small square-rigged craft used along coast of Brittany in 17th century. Rig consists of tall aftermast with large square sail and topsail; foremast was much shorter, with a square sail and 1 or 2 jibs carried to a bowsprit.

bugeye: type of vessel typical to and found only in Chesapeake Bay region, where it is employed largely in oyster fishery and as a pleasure craft.

bugfish [*Brevoortia smithi*]: silvery fish with forked tail, dark shoulder spot and series of smaller spots behind shoulder spot; no lateral line; 60—80 scale rows; dorsal fin with 19 soft rays; head large and deep; mouth large, weak maxillary reaching behind posterior margin of eye; color silvery; round dark shoulder spot followed by 15 much smaller spots arranged in about 3 rows.

built platform: bank of sediment which flanks marine-cut terrace or wave-cut platform on its seaward margin. The sediment is derived from marine erosion and rivers.

bulb angler bar [ships]: angle with one edge having a bulb or swell.

bulb plate [ships]: narrow plate generally of mild steel, rolled with a bulb or swell along one of its edges; used for hatch coamings, built up beams, etc.

bulk: hull or hold space in a ship; hence the cargo.

bulker: person who determines bulk measurement

of goods in freight assessment, or that for dock or warehouse charges.

bulkhead [ships]: partition in ship which divides interior space into various compartments.

bulkhead, afterpeak [ships]: term applied to first transverse bulkhead forward of sternpost. This bulkhead forms forward boundary of afterpeak tank.

bulkhead, collision [ships]: watertight bulkhead approximately 25 ft. aft of the bow, extending from keel to shelter deck. This bulkhead prevents entire ship from being flooded in case of collision.

bulkhead, corrugated [ships]: bulkhead made from plates of corrugated metal or from flat plates; alternately attached to opposite flanges of bulkhead stiffeners. Corrugated metal bulkheads are used around staterooms and quarters.

bulkhead, forepeak [ships]: bulkhead nearest stern forming after boundary of forepeak tank.

bulkhead, screen [ships]: light bulkhead fitted between engine and locker rooms, designed to keep dust and heat out of engine room.

bulkhead, transverse [ships]: partition wall of planking or plating running in an athwartship direction across a portion or whole breadth of a ship.

bulk kelp: one of a genus (*Nereocystis*) of large brown algae, consisting of massive holdfast, a long tough stipe terminated by elongate bulbous pneumatocyst from which 4 lamina-bearing branches radiate. This genus occurs only on Pacific coast of North America from southern California northward into Alaska and may reach lengths of 100 ft. or more.

Bull: 1) northern constellation *Taurus*, the *Bull*, in which are located the group *Pleiades* bright reddish star *Aldebaran* (*dec.* 16½° n.; *r.a.* 4½ hrs.). 2) not usu. cap.; male whale, sea lion, sea bear, or fur seal.

bull boat: North American Indian bowl-shaped "coracle" made of buffalo hide, stretched over frame of saplings. This crude craft was used on Missouri River and its tributaries by women of the Sioux, Arikara, and Hidatsa tribes for carrying their goods.

bullhead, flat [snail cat]: medium-sized (10 in. or less), slender catfish with pattern of rounded gray or golden spots; caudal fin more or less square-cut or slightly immarginate; 16—20 rays in oral fin; body elongate; head flat, upper jaw somewhat projecting; 8 barbels on head; no teeth on roof of mouth; color dark bluish brown, sides with numerous small rounded, light spots.

bullhead shark: fish of Pacific tropical waters about 5 ft. in length, having 2 dorsal fins and teeth adapted to crushing shellfish. Called *Port Jackson shark* in Australia (genus *Heterodontus*),

the species now appears to be growing extinct.

bullhead, southern brown [speckled cat]: moderate-size, mottled catfish with square tail; adipose fin free at posterior end; anal rays 20—24; mottled pattern. Head and body moderately elongate; upper jaw longer than lower, mouth subterminal; eye small; profile nearly straight. Color brownish with splotches or mottlings of black along sides; belly generally mottled.

Bullidae: shells of these molluscs are egg-shaped, thin and smooth in texture and have smooth lip bordering a large flaring aperture which is longer than body whorl. These molluscs have large, fleshy, muscular bodies which enable them to burrow through sand in search of other molluscs on which they feed. Most members of this family live in warm waters.

bull trout: 1) in England, any of several kinds of sea trout. 2) the *Dolly Varden* trout of the Pacific coast of North America from Oregon to Alaska.

bulwark [ships]: upper section of frames and side plating, which extends above and around upper deck.

bulwark stay [ships]: brace extending from deck to a point near top of bulwark, to keep it rigid.

bumastus [trilobites]: opisthoparians were much larger, with smooth pygidia and cephalons, and compound eyes that were carried well above rubbish and mud. The animals were probably crawlers that plowed into bottom only when they were feeding. If pygidium was thrust into mud it provided leverage for thrusting movements of thorax and cephalon.

bummock: from point of view of the submariner, a downward projection from underside of ice canopy; submerged counterpart of a hummock.

bumper: 1) a buffer; a fender; 2) the *pompano* or *amberfish* of the West Indies and southern United States.

bumpkin [ships]: 1) short horizontal spar projecting on either side of stern, to which leads the main brace, and at the bow to take the fore-tack. 2) on sailing vessels, simple spar or V-shaped frame at stern to carry permanent backstay outboard of the deck, allowing free crossover of boom.

bunk [ships]: wooden compartment in a vessel used as sleeping berth.

bunker [ships]: coal or fuel oil space between decks.

bunkering: rate per ton or sum of money charged for placing fuel on board; the operation itself.

bunker oil [ships]: type of oil used for fuel, particularly aboard ship.

bunker stays [ships]: stiffening angles connecting frames to bunker bulkheads.

buntline cloths [ships]: lining sewed up a sail in direction of buntline to prevent chafing.

buntlines [ships]: one of the ropes attached to footropes of square sail and led up to masthead, from there to the deck to assist in hauling up sail.

buoy: floating object fettered at a fixed point used to mark a channel, mooring or objects hidden underwater, e.g., shoals, reefs, rocks, etc.

buoyage: buoys collectively; a system or series of buoys for marking channels or navigable fairways frequented by shipping.

buoyancy: property of an object that enables it to float on surface of a liquid or compressible fluid such as the atmosphere. Quantitatively, it may be expressed as the ratio of specific weight of the fluid to specific weight of the object; or in another manner, by weight of fluid displaced minus weight of object.

burbot: freshwater member of codfish family; dusky, mottled fish with 2 dorsal fins: forward one small, posterior long and low. Chin bears a single but prominent barbel. Average individual is 15 in. long and weighs less than 1 lb.

burdened vessel [ships]: of 2 ships meeting, the one which does not have right of way and is obliged to keep clear.

burger [ships]: swallow-tailed signal pennant.

Burgess shale: fossil deposit in British Columbia. Among other things, it is noted for well preserved jellyfish fossils.

burr edge [ships]: rough uneven edge of punched or burnt hole or plate.

burrfish [striped]: also spring boxfish; cream-colored or yellowish-green fish with irregular horizontal brown stripes and larger dark brown spots. It is a smaller fish, usually less than 10 in. long, with prominent spines along the back.

Bursidae: family of shells resembling family of triton shells in many ways, often included in that group. They differ from tritons in having large longitudinal ridges on opposite sides of shell. These ridges are really the thickened lip of the shell which has been left behind as the animal grew larger, moved farther along and formed new lips as it continued to grow.

buss: small rotund, bulgy fishing boat with 3 masts and narrow poop. The buss was employed mainly in herring fishery.

butt [ships]: end of a plank where it meets end of another plank.

butterfish: any of several fishes so called from their slippery coating, including the *dollarfish* of U.S. Atlantic coast, the *gunnel* of the North Atlantic, *niggerfish* of West Indies waters, and *kelpfish* of New Zealand.

butterfly fish: name for the group is appropriate, for these fishes seem to flit about coral hummocks much like butterflies above a field of flowers. Body is covered with smooth scales; small mouth with frail brushlike teeth suitable only for nibbling at algae and eating small invertebrate animals. Most butterfly fishes are under 12 in. long.

butterfly fish, foureye: similar in appearance to spotfin but marked by faint diagonal stripes extending upward and backward above lateral line. This species also has a black stripe through eye. A large eye-spot on each side near base of tail gives the fish a double-ended appearance and might well confuse a pursuing predator.

butterfly fish, spotfin: common butterfly fish, about 8 in. long with gray body and yellow fins; forward position of dorsal fin is spiny. Distinctive feature is dark spot on posterior part of dorsal fin, also the dark vertical stripe extending from mouth through eye to top of head.

butterman schooner: topsail schooner used for carrying dairy products from island of Guernsey to London in 19th century until the advent of steam.

butt joint [ships]: joint made by fitting 2 pieces squarely together on their edges, welded or butt strapped.

buttock [ships]: counter. The rounded overhanging part on each side of the stern in front of rudder, merging underneath into the run.

buttock lines [ships]: curves shown by taking a vertical longitudinal section of after part of ship's hull, parallel to keel.

butt strap [ships]: bar or plate used to fasten 2 or more objects together with their edges butted.

Buys Ballot's law: law describing relationship of horizontal wind direction in the atmosphere to the pressure distribution; if one stands with his back to the wind, the pressure to the left is lower than to the right in Northern Hemisphere. In the Southern Hemisphere, relationship is reversed.

byssal threads: long, strong, adhesive threads secreted by byssus glands found on foot of some bivalve mollusks, e.g., mussels; these mollusks attach themselves to rocks or other objects with the threads.

byssus [*Mollusca*]: bundle of tough conchiolin strands issuing anteriorly from between valves of certain pelecypods, for temporary attachment.

by the head [ships]: describing a foundering ship which is sinking bow first.

by the mark [ships]: calls used by leadsman when taking sounding to indicate depth of water. "By the mark five" indicates 5 fathoms of water. "By the deep six" indicates the spot between markings on lead line, equal to 6 fathoms.

C

C: 1) square flag denoting the letter *C* in International Code of Signals, when flown singly, indicates *Yes* or *Affirmative;* in semaphore signalling, letter *C,* indicated by the right arm stretched upward at a 45° angle from vertical, is given by receiver at end of each word in message as acknowledgment of its receipt. *C* stands for *centigrade thermometer* reading. 2) common abbreviation in ships' logbooks for *cloudy,* or for *choppy* or *cross sea.*

caaing whale: *pilot whale* or *blackfish* of the North Atlantic, resembling the *grampus* but greater in size, reportedly numerous in vicinity of Iceland, the Orkney, Shetland, and Faroe Islands. Also called *rorqual,* it is closely related to the *Orca,* or killer whale, but has a timid disposition.

cabaling: mixing of 2 water masses with identical in situ densities but different in situ temperatures and salinities, so that resulting mixture is denser than its components.

caballito: Peruvian reed fishing boat; balsa composed of cigar-shaped bundles of coarse grass lashed together to form open boat or canoe; propelled by a paddle.

cabin [ships]: interior of deckhouse, usually space set aside for the use of officers and passengers.

cable: 1) chain of metal links or strong hemp or wire rope used to anchor ships or buoys; underwater or overhead ropelike wire carrying an electric current. 2) unit of distance equal to 720 ft. in U.S. Navy.

cable-laid rope: 3 or 4 plain-laid, 3-stranded ropes twisted together in opposite direction to twists in each rope; used for ropes much exposed to water.

caboose: 1) small deckhouse used as a galley on a merchant vessel; also, *camboose.* 2) cooking stove used on canal boats and small coasting vessels, usually on the open deck.

cabotage: coasting trade; navigation along a coast; coast pilotage.

cabrilla: in West Indies and Spanish America, the *red hind* or any of the *groupers;* any of various edible fishes of genus *Serranus,* found in Mediterranean and in warmer parts of the Pacific.

cadophore: in *Thaliacea* of family *Doliolidae,* a posterior dorsal extension of body that carries the trids in aggregate phase of life cycle.

caique: small, open Turkish boat with hull on order of a skiff; various sizes and rigs; rowed or sailed. Smaller boats are actually rowboats.

caisson: watertight structure used in underwater construction.

cake ice: ice pack composed of fragments of flat sea ice.

calamary: one of ten-armed cephalopods having a pen-shaped internal skeleton or cuttlebone. Its body is about a foot long, tapering to a point flanked by 2 caudal triangular fins, soft, and fleshy and contains 2 sacs from which a black fluid is discharged, if it is disturbed. It is found in most seas and is more commonly called a *squid;* also termed *sea-sleeve, preke, inkfish, pen-fish,* and, improperly, *cuttlefish.* As the *squid,* it is numerous on Atlantic coast of North America, where it is extensively used for fishing bait.

Calanoida [phylum *Arthropoda*]: by far the most numerous in bulk and species of all truly planktonic copepods. Head and thorax form a compact, usually ovoid forebody clearly distinct from abdomen; line of demarcation between the 2 regions lies behind the 6th thoracic segment. Only 1 thoracic segment has fused with head and the abdomen consists of 4 segments plus telson and furcal rami. Abdomen is devoid of appendages. Antennules (first antennae) are long and composed of numerous segments or joints. Antennae (2nd antennae) are short.

calcarenite: limestone or dolomite rock composed of 50% or more coral sand whose particle size ranges from 1/16 to 2 mm.; sometimes designates calcareous sand.

calcareous [tests]: limy, but not agglutinated; consisting of calcite secreted by living protists, as snail shells are made of calcite secreted by living snails. Calcite may be either grainy or crystalline and shells may be impunctate or filled with foramina.

calcareous algae: marine plants which form a hard, external covering of calcium compounds. They are found in all oceans and frequently form reefs.

calcareous sponges [*Calcispongiae*]: this group includes simple sponges. Calcareous or limy sponges have skeletons made of calcite or the related mineral aragonite. Though some spicules are needle-shaped, others have three or four branches: may also be separated or fastened together in firm but porous masses. Members of this group live near shores of shallow seas. They appear as small branched colonies of Cambrian age, become chains of overlapping spheres in late Paleozoic formations and achieve moderate variety in Jurassic and Cretaceous formations in Europe. Most American species are found in Pennsylvanian and Permian rocks of the Southwest.

calcilutite: very fine grained limestone or calcareous sediment, often containing some clay matter; mean grain diameter is less than 0.0625 mm.; lime-mud rock of aphanitic texture.

calcirudite: limestone conglomerate or sediment composed of fragments of coral, shell or limestone; cemented or mixed with calcite and calcareous sand or mud.

calcisiltite: limestone or limy sediment composed of silt-sized calcareous fragments.

calcisponge: sponge having calcareous spicules loosely embedded in soft tissue or knit together to make a firm skeleton.

Calcispongiae: with calcareous skeleton. There are several orders with 3-rayed spicules not forming a continuous skeleton. Little is known of them in the fossil state. Each spicule is mineralogically a crystal of calcite.

calcite: limy material found in coral, shells, etc. It is softer than a knife and bubbles when weak acid is dropped on it. Calcite also forms beds of limestone.

calclithite: limestone containing 50% or more of fragments of older limestone eroded from land.

caldera: large basin-shaped volcanic depression the diameter of which is many times greater than that of included volcanic vent or vents. Calderas are classified into 3 major types: explosion, collapse and erosion. Numerous islands are drowned remnants of calderas.

caledonian [*Fundulus seminolis*]: slender, olive-green little fish that makes good bass bait. No lateral line; scales along side 50—55; anal fin with 13 rays. Body slender, not compressed; head long and pointed; mouth small, terminal; teeth pointed and arranged in 2 rows. Ground color olive green, but with many of the scales having narrow dark edges giving the fish a speckled appearance.

calf: piece of floating ice which has broken away from larger piece of sea ice or land ice. Specifically, a piece of ice which rises to surface after breaking away from submerged portion of its parent formation.

calibrate: to correct errors of scale readings of any graduated instrument, as to calibrate a radio direction finder.

calice [*Coelenterata*]: upper (or at) end of corallite on which basal disk of polyp rests; typically bowl-shaped.

California clipper: clipper ship engaged in carrying passengers and cargo from east coast of U.S. around Cape Horn to San Francisco during the decade following discovery of gold in California in 1848.

California current: ocean current that flows southward along West Coast of U.S. to northern part of Baja California; formed by parts of North Pacific Current and Subarctic Current; a wide current that moves sluggishly toward southeast. Off Central America, California Current turns toward the west and becomes the North Equatorial Current.

Caligoida: body with distinct carapace and mostly fused segments; sucking mouth; 2nd antennae and 2nd maxillipeds prehensile; swimmerets modified; articulation between 3rd and 4th thoracic segments; adults parasitic on fish; freshwater and marine. *Caligus.*

calk [ships]: to tighten a lap or other seam with chisel tool, either by hand or mechanically.

calking: process of making tight seams of planking, plating, etc.

call: 1) peculiar silver whistle or *pipe* used by the boatswain and his mates in navy ships to attract attention to orders about to be given and to direct performance of duties by various strains and signals. In former times a gold *call* and chain was the badge of an admiral. 2) *call* may also be sounded on a bugle, a drum, or a bell, for boat-calls, fire-alarm, etc. 3) to make a brief stop at a port.

Callao Painter: mariner's reference to catastrophic destruction of marine life which causes blackening of paint on ships within harbor of Callao, Peru. Hydrogen sulfide released during decomposition of organisms is responsible for the phenomenon.

Callianassa subterrana [*Callian assidae*]: larvae of this species are fairly abundant in spring to early autumn plankton. After 1st stage there are 5 which correspond to zoeae; each of these has long, serrated rostrum and dorsal serrated on abdominal segments 3—5. Telson has 1 median and 7 lateral spines on each side; anterior scale is unsegmented in 1st larva, in which swimming exopodites are present on 3 maxillipeds.

callograptus [graptolites]: fanlike, consisting of branches that keep dividing and are connected by dissepiments or crossbars. There is either a short stalk or none with a base attached to sea bottom. They lived much like busy dendroids and their species did not spread widely.

callum: shell material filling gap between valves of certain boring bivalves.

callus: deposit of enamel, mostly around aperture in gastropods.

calm belt: belt of latitude in which winds are generally light and variable. Principal calm belts are horse latitudes (calms of Cancer and Capricorn) and doldrums.

Calms, Belt of: zone on either side of Trade Winds where calms of long duration prevail.

cal-sapropel: sediments containing principally sapropel but also remains of calcareous algae.

calve: to break off or discharge pieces of ice from larger ice mass, as from tidal glacier.

calved ice: piece of ice floating in body of water after calving from mass of land ice or iceberg.

calving: wastage of ice from terminus of a floating glacier; breaking off of huge masses that usually float away as icebergs.

Calycophora [phylum *Coelenterata*]: these are siphonophores with one to many swimming belts at upper end of colony; no float.

calyx: depression or cup at top of coral skeleton. Also the structure of plates enclosing body of a crinoid or similar echinoderm.

camarae: ancient rowing boat, broad of beam and tubby; sometimes wholly or partially roofed over; used in Asia Minor.

camber [ships]: 1) athwartships curvature. Camber of deck is usually the arching which drains water off into the scupper; may be reversed. 2) slope upwards toward center of surface, as on deck amidships for shedding water. This deck camber is usually 1 in. or 50 in. 3) small basin, usually with narrow entrance, generally situated inside harbor.

cambium layer: thin interior layer in higher plants that produces new cells for secondary growth (primarily an increase in plant's diameter).

Cambrian: last period of Paleozoic era characterized by much sea movement. All major groups of invertebrates were established by end of this period and first clear fossil record dates from this period.

camel [ships]: in engineering a decked vessel having great stability designed for use in lifting of sunken vessels or structures. Submersible float used for same purpose by submerging, attaching and pumping out.

Camerata [crinoids]: all plates of the calyx are rigidly united and thick. Tegmen covers both mouth and lower food grooves; lower brachial plates form part of cup and so, in most genera, do interradials; arms are uniserial or biserial and pinnulate. Middle Ordovician to late Permian; especially abundant during Mississippian.

Canadian Current: south-flowing, cold current from Atlantic Ocean along Northern Coast of Canada.

canal: artificial watercourse cut through land. Long, narrow arm of sea extending inland, between islands or between islands and mainland.

canal [*Mollusca*]: channel, especially in gastropods for enclosing siphons.

Canary Current: prevailing southward flow along Northwest Coast of Africa; helps to form North Equatorial Current.

can buoy: red or red-striped buoy of round shape.

cancellate [*Mollusca*]: sculpture lines intersecting at right angles.

Cancer: a northern constellation between *Leo* and *Gemini*; fourth sign of the zodiac. Cancer has no stars of sufficient brightness for navigational purposes.

Cancer pagurus [*Cancridae*]: most common member of the family. Zoeal stages closely resemble those of Portunus, but when alive can be distinguished by being redder with less black pigments, having shorter rostral spines and having an antennal expodite about 1/3 of length of antennal spine, whereas in *P. puber* it may be as much as half. Megalopa is easily distinguished from that of *Portunus* or *Carcinus* by very pointed rostrum and prominent dorsal spine projecting to the rear but bending upwards near lip.

candlefish: a fish of northern Pacific coasts of America allied to the smelt, excellent for food, and 8 to 10 in. in length. It is said that the fish contains so much oil that, when dried, it may be used as a candle by drawing a wick through it.

candle ice: form of rotten ice; disintegrating sea ice; disintegrating sea ice or lake ice consisting of ice prisms or cylinders oriented perpendicular to original ice surface.

candy stowage: stevedore's term for stowage of goods that are perishable or adversely affected by heat.

Canis Major: constellation lying southeast of *Orion* and containing the brightest fixed star in the heavens, *Sirius* (declination 16½° South; R.A. 6 hrs. 43 min.), the *Dog Star*.

Canis Minor: constellation located to the east of *Orion* and north of *Canis Major*, containing the bright star *Procyon* (magnitude .5; declination 5½° North; R.A. 7 hrs. 37 min.).

canoa: sloop-rigged fishing boat used by natives of parts of Amazon delta, in northeastern Brazil.

canoe: light craft, usually sharp-ended, made of wooden frame over which is stretched a watertight covering of thin wood, bark, woven fabrics, hides, etc., or in case of the dugout, hollowed out of log.

canoe yawl: small English yawl-rigged cruising boat with a keeled deck hull having rounded stem and canoe-shaped stern.

cant [ships]: inclination of object from perpendicular. As a verb, to turn anything so that it does not stand square to given object.

cant beam [ships]: any of beams supporting deck

plating or planking in overhanging part of stern of a vessel. They radiate in fan shape, from the transom beam to cant frames.

cant body [ships]: that portion of vessel's body either forward or aft in which planes of the frames are not at right angles to center line of the ship.

cant frames [ships]: frames (generally bulb angles) at the end of ship which are canted; i.e., which rise obliquely from keel.

canthals [reptile]: scales forming edge of a ridge extending from eye to nostrils.

canvas [ships]: closely woven, dense, heavy cloth of hemp, flax or cotton especially for sailcloth. Also applied to sails in general, as "to spread as much canvas as the ship will carry."

canyon: relatively narrow depression with steep slopes, bottom of which grades continuously downward.

canyon delta: variation and more specific definition of a type which is described as a sloping, cone-shaped accumulation of sediments at mouth of a canyon having a single deep channel and high natural levees on upper portion and multiple shallow distributary sea channels on lower portion.

cape: body of land jutting from a continent or large island which prominently marks a change in or interrupts coastal trend.

Cape Horn Current: that part of West Wind Drift flowing eastward in immediate vicinity of Cape Horn and then curving eastward to continue as Falkland Current.

Cape Horner: name applied to vessels engaged in West Coast of South America trade from North America and England.

capelin: small fish of the smelt family, about 8 in. in length, abundant on the coasts of Greenland, Iceland, Newfoundland, and Alaska; used for food and as bait for codfishing.

capella: the brightest star in the constellation *Auriga (alpha Aurigae)*, magnitude 0.2; declination 46° north; R.A. 5 hrs. 13 min. It lies nearly halfway between the belt in Orion and Pole Star *(Polaris)*.

capillary wave: wave whose velocity of propagation is controlled primarily by surface tension of the liquid in which the wave is traveling. Water waves of less than 1 in. in length are considered to be capillary waves.

capitulum: part of a barnacle enclosed in the mantle; swollen end of hair or antenna.

capping [cap-rail]: fore-and-aft finishing piece above sheer strake in a boat, often improperly termed *gunwale;* called a *covering board, margin plank,* or *plank sheer* in a decked boat or vessel.

caprellid amphipods: members of genus *Caprella;*

small crustaceans of order *Amphipoda* which usually live in seaweed and resemble praying mantis.

Capricorn, Tropic of: parallel that marks farthest south position of sun's vertical rays, 23½° S.

capstan [ships]: apparatus working on the principle of wheel and axle used for raising weights or applying power. At the bottom of the barrel is a pawl to catch the ratchet ring. Capstan differs from windlass in having a vertical axis instead of a horizontal one. It is worked by levers called capstan bars inserted into holes in the head and is revolved by men working about it and pushing against bars.

capsule: cluster of ganglia in annelids, sometimes called the follicle; investing sheath of connective tissue.

captacula: tentacles with suckerlike tips on head of certain scaphopods for sensory functions and food-getting.

car: 1) in U.S., a perforated floating box or crate for keeping fish, lobsters, etc., alive. 2) an old name for the constellation *Ursa Major;* also called *Charlie's Wain* or *Wagon,* the *Dipper,* and the *Plough.*

caracore: light vessel of 18th century used on Island of Borneo, Dutch East Indies, and also by the Dutch as coast guards in those latitudes. It was high at each end and propelled chiefly with paddles.

carapace: hard, external, skeletal shell that covers upper surfaces of many animals like a shield, e.g., familiar shells of crabs, lobsters, turtles, tortoises and even armor of armadillos.

caravel: 1) one of most romantic types of ships through the ages. It had high bulwarks, square stern, bowsprit with spritsail and fore-and-aft castles, latter being high; 3 or 4 masts were carried and rig varied according to locality and period. 2) kind of light ship at the poop, wide at bow, with double tower at stern, one at bow; it had 4 masts and a bowsprit and principal sails were lateen. Two of Columbus' vessels were caravels.

carbon 14 dating: means of dating, of measuring amount of carbon 14 (a radioactive isotope of carbon) present in organic matter. Carbon 14 disintegrates by radioactive radiation at a constant rate; its half-life is about 5,700 yrs., meaning that after this period of time has elapsed one-half of what was previously present is gone.

Carboniferous: period of Paleozoic era characterized by abundance of amphibians, appearance of reptiles and mountain building in U.S.

carbon tested: use of heavy carbon isotope, carbon 14, for dating organic matter, especially archaeological artifacts. The carbon disintegrates, giving off radioactivity at constant rate. Actual dating is accomplished by measuring how much radioactive carbon is left.

carcharodon: man-eating shark found in all tropical and sub-tropical seas. It has triangular serrate-edged teeth, is a voracious fish, and grows to over 30 ft. in length.

carcinology: study of crustaceans.

Carcinus maenas [*Brachyura*]: each of 4 zoeal stages can be distinguished from those of *Portunus* by absence of lateral spines on carapace and on abdominal segments, the megalopa lateral spines on carapace and on abdominal segments. Megalopa can be separated from that of *P. depurator* by absence of dorsolateral knobs on carapace and from that of *P. puber* by rostral spine in the same straight line as main axis of body. Moreover, there are only 5 bristles on uropods of megalopa of *Carcinus* as compared with 10 on those of *Portunus*. Zoeal of *Carcinus* have a distinctive dark chromatophore extending along each side of carapace.

Cardiidae [*Heterodonta*]: provinculum of left valve is thicker than that of the right and has a number of gaps along edge into which project spiky teeth of right provinculum. Some species of *Cardium* have high umbo while others have low umbo, but all are of similar general appearance and all possess an obvious pallial groove some distance from edge of shell.

cardinal area: flat or curved surface between beak and high line of pelecypod or brachiopod. Cardinal area of brachiopods is also termed interarea. Flattened area of each pelecypod valve which diverges upward the hinge line of the 2 valves.

cardinal axis: axis of rotation for pelecypod valves.

cardinal margin [*Brachiopoda*]: curved posterior margin along which valves are hinged; equivalent to hinge line in shells with straight margin.

cardinal process [*Brachiopoda*]: ridge or boss in inner surface of brachial valve between or part of "scars" marking inserting of deductor muscles.

cardinal septum [*Coelenterata*]: one of initial septa. Lies in plane of bilateral symmetry of corallite; presumably formed between "ventral" pair of mesenteries. Distinguished by pinnate insertion of secondary septa on either side.

cardinal teeth [*Mollusca*]: in heterodont pelecypods, those teeth which radiate on hinge plate immediately below beaks; lateral teeth, if present, are anterior or posterior to them.

Cardium echinatum [*Heterodonta*]: larva of this species is much larger at metamorphoses than *C. ovale*, *C. edule* or *C. scabrum* and reaches 480μ in length. Valves are very convex, giving globular appearance to larva.

Cardium edule [*Heterodonta*]: shell is about 160μ in 3-week larva and reaches 300μ in 5-week larva.

Shell is round and smooth, ribs appearing only after metamorphosis.

Cardium ovale [*Heterodonta*]: length of shell is variable, normally about 240μ but may reach 340μ. Umbones of the shell are high but valves are not so convex as in other species.

Cardium scabrum [*Heterodonta*]: shell of larva of this species bears characteristic concentric striations and reaches 160μ in length before metamorphosis; more oblong than *C. edule*.

cargo hatch [ships]: large opening in deck to permit loading of cargo.

cargo port [ships]: opening, provided with watertight cover or door in side of vessel of 2 or more decks, through which cargo is received and discharged.

Caribbean Current: current flowing westward through Caribbean Sea. Formed principally by major part of North Equatorial Current setting through Lesser Antilles.

Caribe: a remarkably voracious freshwater fish native to the Amazon and other South American waters. It will attack men and animals, inflicting dangerous wounds with its unusually sharp teeth. Though rarely more than one foot in length, it will tear another fish to pieces when latter is hooked and before the fisherman can haul it from the water.

carina [*Mollusca*]: keel or prominent, knife-edge ridge.

carinate: having keel or ridge.

carlines or **carlings** [ships]: short beam running fore and aft between or under transverse deck beams. Also called headers when supporting ends of interrupted deck beams.

carotenoid: yellow or orange pigments chemically related to carotene. Carotenoid pigments are lipid-soluble and are an important coloring matter in many marine organisms.

carotid: describing the carotid arteries which supply blood to the head.

carp [*Cyprinus carpio*]: robust fish with tiny mouth and long dorsal fin; lips thin, not thick and fleshy; dorsal fin with 20 or more rays preceded by stout bony spine. Head rather pointed with rounded snout; mouth rather small, anterior in position with 4 barbels; color variable from brownish-tan to yellowish and olive green; size generally less than 5 lbs.

carp [minnow group]: another giant-sized member of minnow group, native to Asia. Introduced into U.S. in 1877. Carp varies in color, being brassy or silvery in clear ponds, brownish-green in muddy waters. Distinctive carp features are long dorsal fin that tapers to rear and presence of 4 barbels beneath mouth. The carp is a hardy fish able to live in warm and polluted waters where most species cannot survive; omnivorous and greedy, consuming great quantities of beetles, worms and other invertebrates found in mud, as well as algae and parts of water weeds.

carpogonium: unicellular female sex organ in many red algae.

carposporangium: in red algae, a spore-bearing organ on gonimoblast filament; derived from zygote.

carpospore: spore resulting from division of zygote in red algae.

carrack: term generally applied to larger ship of 14th, 15th and 16th centuries; designed to carry large cargoes. The type was distinctive in that it had high topsides and greater draft than other ships of that period.

carrageenin: extract of Irish moss, with gel properties, used in puddings and as stabilizer in various food products.

carronade: cannon made by Carron gun factory; their most famous pieces were small.

cartel: vessel used to negotiate with enemy under a flag of truce and to carry prisoners of war.

cartilage: translucent, elastic tissue that supplements ligament in binding bivalve shell together; it is attached to resilifer and may be reinforced by calcareous cowling, the lithodesma.

cartography: art and science of making charts or maps.

carvel: mode of boatbuilding whereby planks are laid side by side smoothly, as distinguished from lapstrake construction.

carvel-built: built with external planks edge to edge, meeting flush at seams; flush-sided.

cascade: mass of spray thrown outward from around base of waterspout.

cascajo: reef-derived material consisting of coral debris and other sediment in old deposits.

casco: canoe about the size of a dory used by Brazilians of Amazon delta. It is made of dugout bottom with flaring sides of planks and raking, V-shaped endpieces.

case: cavity in upper front of the head of a *cachalot*, or *sperm whale*, which contains spermaceti and a fine quality of oil.

casing: extra case or bulkhead built around ship's funnel to protect decks from heat.

cassiduloids [sea urchins]: this order appeared in early Jurassic times and exists today. They are not primitive, for ambulacra have lost their compound plates, are limited to dorsal surface and are bluntly shaped. A double ring of flowerlike plates surrounds mouth, structure that exists in no other group of urchins. Fossil cassiduloids are widespread in Mesozoic and Cenozoic formations of North America.

cassinoceras [nautiloids]: short and thick with closely spaced chambers curving partway around siphuncle and its massive endocones. Aperture is tipped downward just a little, as if the heavily weighted cone raised it well above mud on which the animal lived.

Cassiopeia: constellation consisting of 5 stars, 3 of which are of 2nd magnitude, in approximately 60° north declination and 0 to 2 hrs. in right ascension. It may be recognized as a distorted *W*, lying on nearly the opposite side of the *Pole star*, and at about same distance from that star, as the *Great Bear.* Also called *Cassiopeia's Chair* and *The Lady's Chair.*

cast: 1) to throw; to cause to fall; to let down; to toss. 2) to turn from the wind or cause a vessel to fall off, especially in getting underway from an anchorage; to tack; to put about. 3) act of throwing, as a *cast of the lead.*

castings: castings are indigestible remnants of meals swallowed by burrowing invertebrates. Lugworms, e.g., swallow sand in order to eat small organisms. Once this food has been extracted sediment is regurgitated in form of contorted castings.

Castor and Pollux: two brightest stars of the group known as *Gemini,* Latin name for *twins,* located in the zodiacal belt between *Taurus* and *Leo* and having a declination of about 30° north and 7½ hrs. right ascension. In ancient sailor's lore, a twin flame appearance of *St. Elmo's fire* in the rigging, believed to portend the near end of a storm.

catadromous: form of life cycle among fishes in which maturity is attained in fresh waters and adults migrate into ocean to spawn. Common eel is an example.

catamaran: 1) Tamil (Ceylon) term is "kattumaram"; Singhalese term is "theppama." Ceylonese kattumaram is sailing craft of 20 to 30 ft. long, used for boarding ships when surf is too heavy to effect a landing. It is generally made of 5 logs lashed together. False bow or breakwater is built on forward end. Rig consists of single triangular sail, dyed red with a yard on the foot, stepped amidships. Steered with an oar. 2) any craft having 2 hulls side by side whether propelled by machinery, sails, or oars. 3) life-saving raft carried on ships, made of two parallel cylindrical tanks with a rectangular slatted floor between them. 4) raft fitted with a windlass and grapples for recovering sunken logs.

catanadromous; catandromous: ascending and descending streams from the sea, as the salmon, shad, and other fishes.

catascopiscus: fast Roman sailing ship of about 200 A.D. employed for reconnoitering and scouting.

catazone: deepest zone of rock metamorphism where very high pressures and temperatures both prevail.

catboat: small present-day sailboat very beamy in proportion to length, having single mast with fore-and-aft sail almost to bow.

catenary: curve assumed by flexible cord in equilibrium when suspended from both ends. Wire on which instruments are lowered into sea forms half a catenary in presence of currents.

Catenipora [coral]: consists of small oval tubes that grow side by side in rows called ranks which resemble chains in cross section. Each tube contains 12 ridgelike septa whose edge is set with spines, but tabulae may not appear. Ranks are covered with wrinkled epitheca.

catfish: in U.S., members of freshwater catfish family number about 24 species and are found for most part in rivers and lakes of Mississippi River valley; no species are native to Pacific Coast. The family includes, in addition to catfishes, the smaller bullhead, madtoms and stonecats. They lack scales and have long barbels on head giving the fish a catlike resemblance. Head is broad and rounded, mouth large and jaws contain small conical teeth. Single dorsal fin is located well forward in the back and adipose fin is situated in front of tail fin as in salmon family. Catfish are greedy and omnivorous feeders on anything they can grub from bottom; diet consists of insects and their larvae and other smaller aquatic invertebrates.

catfish, black bullhead: found in brooks and ponds from New York westward. Coloring is dark olive-green to dusky black; distinctive white bar marks base of slightly forked tail fin.

catfish, blue: largest member of family. Formerly large individuals weighing up to 100 lbs. were caught, but today one 5 ft. long and weighing 30 lbs. is considered a large specimen. Blue cat is a fish of streams, ponds and bayous of lower Mississippi River valley and Gulf states. It is a slaty-blue fish; sides are silvery and unspotted.

catfish, brown bullhead: has wide range in sluggish streams and weedy ponds from New England to central U.S. and south to Texas. It is a mottled greenish-brown fish usually under 12 in. long and seldom weighs more than a pound or two. Brown bullheads feed on bottom-dwelling snails, crayfish and insects.

catfish, channel [*Ictalurus punctatus*]: slim catfish with forked tail and distinct spots on side; 8 barbels on head; unbroken bony ridge from head to origin of dorsal fin; dark spots along side. Body long and slender; head not broad; mouth comparatively small, upper jaw slightly longer than lower; no teeth in roof of mouth. Color above light

gray, merging to nearly white below with scattered, small, rounded dark spots along sides.

catfish, flathead: large species, growing to a length of 4 or 5 ft. and 50 lbs. or more in weight. Head is flattened and adipose fin is very large; tail fin is only slightly forked in contrast with deeply forked tail fin of blue catfish. This species is known also as yellow cat because of yellowish-brown color and as mud catfish because of preference for bottom of muddy streams; common in lower Mississippi River valley.

catfish, gaftopsail [*Bagre marinus*]: broad-headed, silvery blue catfish with forked tail; long filaments extend from dorsal and pectoral spines; only 4 barbels on head. Head broad and depressed; mouth large, upper jaw slightly longer than lower; color above bluish, with definite silvery sheen and ventrally, color is silvery. Attains weight of several pounds.

catfish, sea [*Galeichthys felis*]: slender, steel-blue to silvery catfish with forked tail. No long filaments on spines; sea barbels on head. Head and body somewhat elongate; mouth not greatly enlarged, upper jaw slightly longer than lower. Color steel-blue to silvery with silvery side and belly. Attains a length of 2 ft., but averages smaller.

catfish, stonecat: small members of catfish family less than 12 in. long. Found in creeks and rivers of central and western U.S. Unusual feature is a poison gland at base of pectoral spines.

catfish, white [*Ictalurus catus*]: dark, robust catfish with forked tail; 8 barbels on head; incomplete bony ridge from head to origin of dorsal fin. Pattern uniform generally bluish-black, without distinct small spots. Head very broad, body robust; no teeth on roof of mouth; dorsal fin inserted about halfway between tip of snout and adipose fin; dorsal and pectoral fins without long filaments.

catfish, yellow [butter cat]: catfish usually slightly less than a foot long with adipose fin free posteriorly and square or slightly rounded tail; yellowish in color. Tail square or slightly rounded; anal fin with 25—27 rays. Head and body stout, at times obese; eye small; 8 barbels on head. Ground color brownish yellow, darker above, fading to yellow on belly.

catfish, yellow bullhead: yellowish-brown species of sluggish waters from New York and Great Lakes south to Texas. It has the same size and living habits as brown bullhead.

cathead [ships]: large timber projecting from each bow of a ship and having sheaves in outer end; used to afford support by which to lift anchor after it has been raised to water's surface by chain.

cat-schooner: two-masted vessel which was cat-rigged, carrying no jib, foremast being set right in bow.

cat's-paw: puff of wind; light breeze affecting small area, as one that causes patches of ripples on surface of water area.

catter: short form of bellicatter, meaning ice foot.

caudal: posterior; toward tail; caudal fin.

caudal peduncle: region between caudal fin and dorsal and anal fins; fleshy portion in front of caudal fin.

caustic: envelope of a sequence of underwater sound rays which defines boundary of sound field.

cavalla: a food fish found on the coasts of tropical America on U.S. east coast as far north as Nantucket; 10 to 12 in. in length, a fast swimmer and beautifully colored, has a slender well-defined forked tail, and a deep body with back from mouth to tail forming in profile an almost perfect 90° arc of a circle. The *cero*, of like habitat but of the mackerel family, is often improperly called a *cavalla*.

cavitation: creation of bubbles by friction of vessel or propeller moving through water.

cay: low float island or mound of sand built up on reef flat slightly above high tide which may contain large admixture of coral or shell fragments.

cay sandstone: friable to firm sandstone cemented by calcium carbonate and formed from coral sand near base of coral reefs and extending to above high-tide level.

cayuca: dugout canoe used by Indians of Panama.

C.C. or C.E.: common abbreviation for *chronometer correction* or *chronometer error*, which is applied to time shown on chronometer to obtain Greenwich mean time *(G.M.T.).* It is additive if chronometer is slow and subtractive if fast.

ceiling [ships]: inside skin of vessel between decks; in small vessel from deck beams to bilge.

celestial: of, or pertaining to, the heavens.

cell membrane [*Foraminifera*]: indistinct layer forming periphery of animal cell.

cellular double bottom [ships]: term applied where double bottom is divided into numerous rectangular compartments by floors, longitudinally.

celoces: swift, single-banked Greek galley.

Centaurus: southern constellation lying east, north, and west of *Crux* (the Southern Cross). A line joining its 2 brightest stars, a^2 *Centauri (Rigil Kentaurus)* and β *Centauri*—called the "pointers," and extended westward about 12 degrees, enters its neighboring group close to β *Crucis. Rigil Kentaurus* (named from the Arabic *al rijil al Kentauros,* the Centaur's foot), of magnitude 0.3, is said to be nearest to the earth of all so-called fixed stars.

center: in a fleet, division or column between van and rear, or between weather and lee divisions, in order of sailing.

centerboard [ships]: flat wood or metal plate used in shallow draft sailboat to provide auxiliary keel area to reduce leeway; raised or lowered on a point from box inside hull.

center line [ships]: horizontal fore-and-aft reference line for athwartships measurements, dividing ship into 2 symmetrical halves. Vertical reference line in center of body plan, midship section or another section.

center line bulkhead [ships]: fore-and-aft or longitudinal bulkhead erected in center line or in same plane as keel. Also a reference line scrived on transverse bulkhead to indicate center of ship.

center of action: any one of semipermanent highs and lows that appear on mean charts of sea-level pressure.

centerplate rudder: common type of rudder fitted to vessels of moderate speed, consisting of a single heavy plate shaped as required at its after edge and riveted to several stout arms extending at right angles to, and shrunk on to alternate sides of, the rudderstock. Also called *single-plate rudder* and *flat-plate rudder.*

centipedes: members of class *Chilopoda,* phylum *Arthropoda;* usually found in high moisture environments; exclusively carnivorous.

central capsule: in *Radiolaria,* inner portion of protoplast bounded by membrane and containing nucleus or nuclei.

centrals [reptile]: median row of laminae of turtle's carapace.

centric: in diatoms, having valves arranged radially symmetrical around central point; member of order *Centrales.*

centrifuge: machine that uses centrifugal acceleration to separate solids from liquids by whirling them at high speeds.

centrioles: self-replicating organelles that lie near nucleus in a cell and function during reproduction. Also, may be present at base of cilia and flagella.

cephalic: pertaining to head or cephalon; toward head.

cephalic fins: pair of rolled-up finlike lobes extending forward on either side of manta ray's mouth; when feeding, it unrolls fins to help direct prey toward mouth.

Cephalocarida [phylum *Arthropoda*]: body is shrimplike with primitive organization; head is horseshoe-shaped with short, paired antennae; trunk of 19 or 20 segments, of which first 9 bear similar biramous appendages; eyes absent; hermaphroditic with larval stages; marine.

Cephalochordata [subphylum]: phylum: *Chor-*

data. Recent. Notochord large, extends to tip of head; gill basket large; body segmented and fish-like. Vagrant benthos; marine and brackish; filter feeders.

cephalon: head region.

cephalopod: one of class *Cephalopoda* of benthic or free-swimming mollusks possessing large head, large eyes and a circle of arms or tentacles around mouth; shell is external, internal or absent; ink sac usually is present.

Cephalopoda: cephalopods are divided into 2 groups or orders, *Dibranchiata* and *Tetrabranchiata*. *Dibranchiata* have 2 gills, horny jaws, 8 or 10 arms and usually no shell or, if any, an internal one. This group is further divided into *Octopoda* (8 arms) and *Decapoda* (10 arms). *Octopoda* includes *Octopus* and *Argonauta*; *Decapoda* includes squid and small *Spirula*. *Tetrabranchiata* have 4 gills, shelly jaws, many more arms without suckers and external shell. This group includes nautiloids. Well-developed head is surrounded by circle of prehensile tentacles, at least partially derived from foot tentacles mostly provided with suckers; body lengthened along dorsoventral axis to become functional anteroposterior axis; shell external, internal or absent; mouth with horny jaws and radula; muscular funnel or siphon for "jet propulsion" beneath head; mantle bulky and fleshy with extensive mantle chamber, sometimes modified into fins; coelom continuous with pericardium; 1 or 2 pairs of gills; nervous system centralized in head and contained in cartilaginous capsule; eyes well developed; dioecious.

cephalosome: in copepods, the apparent head when viewed dorsally, consisting of head plus one or more fused thoracic somites.

cephalothorax: in *Crustacea*, head and thorax when united under single carapace.

Cepheus: constellation located between the group *Cygnus* and the star *Polaris*. A gentle curve from *Deneb (a Cygni)* to *Polaris* passes at nearly halfway mark through *a Cephei (Alderamin)* and β *Cephei (Alphirk)*.

ceratid [*Coelenterata*]: corallite with angle of about 20° between sides expanding from apex.

Ceratite: ammonoid cephalopod characterized by distinctive suture pattern of smoothly rounded saddles curved toward shell aperture and jaggedly crenulate lobes pointed away from aperture; typical of Triassic deposits but not confined to them.

Ceratium [phytoplankton]: genus outrivals *Peridinium* in number of important species it contains. All species are flattened cells with ornamental theca drawn out into 1 spica and 2 lower ones.

cercaria: larval stage of diagenetic trematodes. The *Cercaria* leaves mollusc host and either directly or indirectly by way of metacercarial stave invades the vertebrate host, where it matures into secual adult worm.

cercopod: one of pair of long filamentous projections of posterior end of certain crustaceans.

cerebral ganglion [*Mollusca*]: one of pair of large nerve bundles passing from posterior dorsal head.

Ceriantharia: small crabs without skeleton; having 2 rings of tentacles.

ceriantipatharia [*Coelenterata*]: black corals and some without hard parts.

Cerithidea [Mesogastropods]: larvae of this family are characterized by small size, rounded bilobed velum and presence of a process from outer lip of velum.

Cerithiopsis barleei [*Cerithidae*]: larvae common in spring and summer plankton. Very similar in structure to *Triphora perversa* except that shell is dextral. The veliger spends about 5 wks. in the plankton and settles when shell has reached 4½ whorled stage. Distinguished from *C. tubercularis* by smooth shell.

Cerithiopsis tubercularis [*Cerithidae*]: larvae common in both inshore and offshore plankton. Youngest larvae are about 0.24 mm. and shell has 2½ whorls. Outer lip of shell bears characteristic large platelike process which protrudes anteriorly and bears a number of concentric striations. Largest larva is 0—64 mm. long and suture lines of shell are dark. Shell is characteristically smooth and final whorl shows traces of adult tubercles. Velar lobes are round, one being larger than the other. Animal is yellowish but foot acquires dark pigment in late veliger.

cero: food and game fish of the mackerel family, in length from 2 to 3 ft.; found in West Indies and on Atlantic coast of U.S.

ceroid [*Coelenterata*]: type of colonial coral skeleton (corallum) in which walls of individual corallites are closely united.

cervical groove: transverse groove indicating general boundary between head and thoracic areas of carapace of certain crustaceans.

cesser clause: clause usually inserted in a charter party indicating that charterer's liability ends upon completion of loading of his cargo, shipowner then taking a lien on cargo for freight, dead freight, and demurrage.

Cestoda [phylum *Platyhelminthes*]: class of flatworms. Body with outer covering of living cells connected to deeper cells and permeated by pore canals; no digestive system; body usually of few to many segments; complicated life cycles, usually involving 2 or more hosts.

cetacean: member of *Cetacea*, an order of aquatic, mainly marine mammals in phylum *Chordata* (vertebrates); it includes whales, grampuses, dolphins and porpoises, all distinguished by no visible hind legs, layer of blubber, large head, paddlelike front flippers and horizontal tail unlike vertical tail of fishes. These are divided into toothless baleen whales *(Mystacoceti)* and toothed whales *(Odontoceti)*.

cetus: constellation lying near the equator, its greater part in the southern sky, extending through right ascension 0 to 3 hrs. and declination 5° N. to 20° S. Its only 2 navigational stars, *Menkar (a Ceti)* and *Deneb Kaitos* or *Diphda (β Ceti)*, with *Algenib (γ Pegasi)*, present a nearly equilateral triangle with sides of about 30°, *β Ceti* occupying the south corner. *β Ceti* is almost on the line joining *Alpheratz (a Andromedae)* and *Algenib (γ Pegasi)*—the east side of "Square of Pegasus"—extended to twice the distance these are apart in a direction a little east of south from *Algenib*.

cgs system: system of physical measurements in which fundamental units of length, mass and time are centimeter, gram and second, respectively.

Chaetoceros [phytoplankton]: cells are usually oval in cross section and have nearly flat ends. Pair of long, thin spines is found at each end of the frustule which, by fusion with those of neighboring cells, unite them into chains. This large and variable genus is truly planktonic but some species are more typical of inshore water than others.

Chaetognatha [phylum]: chaetognaths or arrowworms are active planktonic predators which have practically a worldwide distribution. Characteristics by which they can readily be recognized in plankton samples are fairly large size; elongated, torpedolike shape; transparency; paired lateral and expanded caudal fins; head bearing pair of eyes and series of curved spines around mouth. In mature specimens shape and proportions of body as well as position and shape of gonads and seminal vesicles are important specific characters.

chafing-gear [ships]: mats or other soft substances such as rope yarn and spun yarn fastened on rigging, spars, etc., to prevent chafing.

chain: string of connected metal rings or links, as, a *mooring chain*. A series of things following or related to each other, as, a *chain of soundings*. Metal chain on board ship is usually described as *close link* or *stud link*, latter being almost exclusively used as anchor cable. Next to the anchor chain *(chain cable)* in size, largest close link chain is usually that found in steering arrangement of *quadrant chains, quarter chains,* and *barrel chains* in the case of steering engines placed amidships or near engine room. Size of a chain is described as diameter of metal forming the link, as, a ¾-*in. short link* or *close link c.,* or 1½-*in. stud link c.*

chain locker [ships]: compartment for storing anchor chains, located near hawse pipes in bow of ship.

chain locker pipe [ships]: iron-bound opening or section of pipe leading from chain locker to deck through which chain cable passes.

chain mesh dredge: bottom sampler constructed of rectangular steel collar attached to chain mail purse lined with screens of netting; used on continental shelf to collect coarse-grained sediments and bottom dwelling organisms.

chain of the Hebrides: appears as edge of platform, sinking towards east under its covering of Cambrian and abruptly cut off at west by subsidence that gave birth to Atlantic.

chain plates: plate attached to a flat along outside of ship; shrouds (ropes extending from masthead to laterally support masts) are fastened to chain plates.

chalk: very soft white to light gray limestone composed of tests of floating microorganisms and some shells of bottom-dwelling animals in matrix of finely crystalline calcite. Chalk is classed as rock on bottom sediment charts.

chamber [*Foraminifera*]: space within test as well as enclosing walls. Tests may be divided into several chambers separated by partitions.

chamfer [ships]: bevel surface formed by cutting away angle of 2 faces of piece of wood or metal.

champan: flat-bottomed vessel used by Chinese and Japanese. It had one mast, rigged the same as mainmast of junk with single sail made of cane; seldom exceeded 80 tons burden and was constructed without iron or nails. It was used in 18th century and was about the same as sampan of present day.

champlong: double-ended, decked, keel sailing craft of Java and Pulau Klapa. Curved stem and sternpost rising above the gunwale curving inboard and terminating in oval-shaped elaborately carved end.

change of the moon: beginning of a new synodic month (29 days, 12 hrs., and 44 min.), as measured from the time of new moon; the new moon.

change of tide: reversal of direction of motion (rising or falling) or a tide. Sometimes applied to reversal in set of tidal current.

channel: 1) natural or artificial waterway which either periodically or continually contains moving water, or which forms a connecting link between 2 bodies of water. 2) part of body of water deep enough to be used for navigation through an area otherwise too shallow for navigation. 3) ledge or narrow platform bolted to and projecting from outside of vessel's hull to spread rigging.

channel islander: local type of fishing and pilot boat typical to Channel Islands in English Channel; 3-masted and about 36 ft. long. Jib is carried on long bowsprit.

channel wave: any elastic wave propagated in sound channel because of low velocity layer in solid earth, ocean or atmosphere.

chantey: song used by sailors in chorus during the work of heaving anchor, hoisting a yard, or any operation requiring united effort of a number of men.

chapeiro: Brazilian term for isolated coral structures which often rise like towers to height of 40 to 50 ft., sometimes spreading out in mushroom-like top.

character of the bottom: type of material of which the bottom is composed and its physical characteristics such as hard, sticky and rough.

charges clause: clause in a charter party stipulating which of contracting parties agrees to pay wharfage, harbor dues, pilotage, towage, customs duties and fees, etc., incident to the chartered employment of vessel.

Charlies' Wain or Charlie's Wagon: the seven bright stars of the group *Ursa Major*, commonly called the *Dipper*.

chart: draft or map of navigable water with its connected land surfaces. To lay down on a map or chart the ship's course. To regulate course of ship on its voyage.

chart datum: 1) plane or level to which soundings on hydrographic chart are referred, usually taken to correspond to low-water stage of tide. 2) permanently established surface from which soundings or tide heights are referenced (usually low water). Surface is called tidal datum when referred to certain phase of tide.

charted depths: vertical distance from tidal datum to bottom.

charter: to hire or lease a vessel according to conditions agreed upon in a document known as the *charter party*. The leasing or hire of a vessel, usually indicated as a *time, voyage,* or *bare-boat charter*, depending upon agreement between charterer and owner.

chart house: room on ship's bridge where charts, chronometers and other equipment needed for navigation are kept.

chase joint [ships]: kind of plate joint by which an overlap can gradually be made flush. This is done with aid of liners and used on bow and stern to give vessel a finer trim.

chasse maree: French vessel of lugger type, carrying 3 masts (each with lugsail), bowsprit and jibs. Fore and mizzenmasts are stepped in extreme bow and stern, respectively, mizzensail being sheeted to long boomkin extended beyond tern.

chatte: lighter used in loading and unloading larger vessels in French ports.

chebacco: small sailing vessel originated and built in parish of Chebacco of Ipswich, Massachusetts, and used extensively in fisheries of New England during half century following Revolutionary war. It was characterized by narrow overhanging "pink" stern and "cat-schooner" rig, no bowsprit or headsails.

cheeks: the bilgeways; curve or "turn" of the bilges.

cheiropteraster [starfish]: had very large opening for mouth but no arms; ambulacra being directly attached to buglike body of skin without place or spicules.

chela: in *Crustacea* and some other arthropods, a pincer formed when terminal articles of limb are opposable to a process from penaltomate article, as in crabs. An appendage ending in this manner is termed a chelate appendage.

chelate ring: ring containing at least one coordinate covalent bond.

Chelicerata: subphylum of *Arthropoda* including horseshoe crabs, sea spiders and arachnids.

cheliped: large, grasping claw in many crustaceans.

chemical oceanography: study of chemical composition of dissolved solids and gases, materials in suspension and acidity of ocean waters and their variability both geographically and temporally in relationship to adjoining domains, namely atmosphere and ocean bottom.

chemoautotrophic: deriving metabolic energy from oxidation of inorganic chemicals occurring outside organisms; combination or condition found in a few minor groups of bacteria, non-photosynthetic autotrophic forms. Chemotrophic; chemolithotropic.

chemosphere: ozone layer.

chemotrophic nutrition: that process by which an organism manufactures its food by using energy derived from oxidizing organic matter.

Chenier plain: sandy offshore barriers having become linked to coast by deposition of clay in lagoons between them and shore. These features are well developed on coast of South America between Amazon and Orinoco Rivers.

chert: usually dark, hard, flintlike rock composed of chalcedony or quartz.

Chesapeake Bay schooner: type of schooner extensively used in oyster fishery of Chesapeake Bay and tributaries. Moderately sharp bow and sharp stern; flat floor and low bilge; lofty schooner rig; masts rake aft sharply; maintop carried. Average size 45 to 55 ft., with ¼ the beam.

chess tree [ships]: timber in which sheave is set; bolted to topsides of old-time square-rigged vessel at a point convenient for hauling down main tack, tack leading to inside of bulwark.

chilarium: one of pair of appendages at posterior end of cephalothorax in certain arachnids.

chilidial plate [*Brachiopoda*]: plate at side of opening (notothyrium) in brachial valve for pedicle.

chimaera: odd-looking fish of the ray family, or group *Holocephali*, about 2 ft. in length, having a large head and body tapering to a pointed tail; found on the coasts of Europe, the north Pacific, and South Africa.

chine: in flat-bottom or V-bottom boats, chine is the line fore and aft formed by intersection of side and bottom.

chip log: line marked at intervals (commonly 50 ft.) and payed out over stern of moving ship. By timing intervals at which markers appear as the line is pulled out by a drag (the chip) the ship's speed can be determined.

chipping: act of removing thick scale from iron or steel surfaces, or dressing edges of metal plates, etc.

chiro: fish of the tarpon family (*Elops saurus*), growing to about 5 ft. in length and found in all tropical seas under many different names; like the tarpon, it is a fine game fish, but of poor edible quality.

chitin: 1) polymer of glucosamine that forms an impervious stable substance synthesized by many animals, such as arthropods, as an external covering. Impregnated with calcium salts, it may form a firm, rigid exoskeleton. 2) horny subpart of outer integument in arthropods, mollusks and other invertebrates. 3) nitrogenous substance similar to fingernails.

chitinous: composed of chitin, light-colored often hard substance found in external skeletons of insects and crustaceans and in other invertebrates.

chiton: marine mollusks of order *Polyplacophora*. Chiton live on rocks and either attach themselves or slowly creep by means of muscular foot. Long oval bodies are covered by calcareous plates which in turn are partially or totally covered by thick, bristly girdle.

chiton, black or leather [*Katharina tunicata*]: easily distinguished by 8 calcareous plates of dorsal shell. Plates arranged longitudinally, overlapping like shingles on a roof. Along outer edge, plates are covered by girdle which is exposed part of mantle. Exposed parts of plates are brown, sometimes with tiny barnacles adhering to them. Almost all ventral side is a foot. Large mouth is at one end just anterior to foot, anal opening just behind foot. Mantle completely covers head without tentacles or eyes; foot and other soft parts salmon colored; 3 in. long and 1½ in. across. Found under rocks at low-water mark and in shallow water.

chiton, giant [*Cryptochiton stelleri*]: abundant near low-tide mark. Brick-red body covered with minute, bright-red tubercles is oblong and measures from 6 to 8 in. long, 4 in. across. External plumed gills extend around animals between girdle and foot.

chiton, greenish thorny: possesses broad foot; 8 plates encircle girdle; tufts of bristles around body. Plates are semilunar in shape, smooth in middle, granulated upon sides of light blue color. Animal has greenish color and is often marked with white or light-colored line down middle of body. Bristles are darker green color than body of animal.

chiton, lined [*Tonicella lineata*]: has smooth, shiny surface, moderately arched. Ground color of calcareous plates light buff or yellow marked with wavy, dark brown lines. Approximately 1½ in. long, nearly 1 in. wide. On posterior plate are 8 or 10 teeth. Between mantle and foot is a groove in which there are many pairs of gills.

chiton, mossy [*Mopalia muscosa*]: has flattened, broadly ovate body with 8 wide dorsal plates. Plates are much exposed and surface lusterless. Central areas of plates have close, longitudinal ribs or markings. On narrow girdle many hairs give animal mossy appearance. Species usually dull brown or gray color. Normally measures 2½ in. long, 1½ in. wide.

chloragogue: special spongy tissue that envelops the intestine of certain annelids; probably aids in excretion.

chlorine equivalent: represents total amount of chlorine, bromine and iodine in grams per kilogram of seawater, with assumption that bromine and iodine have been replaced by chlorine. Chlorine equivalent is dependent on changes in atomic weights whereas chlorinity is independent of such changes.

chlorinity: measure of chloride content by mass of seawater (grams per kilogram of seawater, or per mile). Originally, chlorinity was defined as weight of chlorine in grams per kilogram of seawater after bromides and iodides have been replaced by chlorides.

chlorosity: chlorine content of one liter of seawater; equal to chlorinity of sample times its density.

chlorosity factor: ratio between various substances in seawater and chlorosity; obtained by dividing concentration of substance in milligrams-atoms per liter by chlorosity.

choanocytes: flagellated, collared cells lining internal cavities of sponges.

chock [ships]: wedge-shaped piece of wood inserted under sides of ship's small boat on deck or elsewhere to prevent movement. Oval-shaped castings, fore and aft, through which anchor line and dock lines may pass. Also wedges which are used to secure anchor or other bulk objects in place.

chock-a-block [ships]: halyard is said to be chock-a-block when 2 blocks used for purchase are so tight that no further hauling is possible.

chocolatero: brisk northwest wind in the Gulf of Mexico, so called from resemblance of the sea during the breeze to a variety of chocolate confection; also, *chocolate gale.*

choke: to foul: said of a rope in a block.

Chondrichthyes [class]: phylum *Chordata.* Devonian to Recent. Skeleton entirely of cartilage; notochord reduced; cartilaginous, vertebral elements. Jaws propped against by hyoid gill arch; 2 pairs of paired appendages. Predominantly marine, nektonic and predaceous. Sharks and their kin, descendants of placoderms that lost the power to produce bone and so reverted to skeletons of cartilage. Even when hardened by limy deposits, it was not ossified.

Chondrostei: during early stages of Mesozoic, most fishes belonged to *Chondrostei.* Characterized by heavy diamond-shaped scales, asymmetrical tails, somewhat scaly fins and considerable cartilage in skeletons. Toward middle of era, these fish were gradually replaced by *Holostei.*

chop: short crested waves that may spring up quickly in fairly moderate breeze and break easily at crest.

choppy: descriptive term for a short rough sea caused by meeting currents, or a breeze blowing against a current; also said of the wind when changeable and baffling.

choppy sea: short, rough waves tumbling with short and quick motion.

chops: shores or headlands forming entrance to a harbor or channel; mouth or entrance of a channel or strait; as, *chops of the English Channel.*

chordate [phylum *Chordata*]: Ordovician to Recent. Coelomate; level of organization approximately that of arthropods. Notochord and series of paired gill slits, both of which are present only in embryo of air-breathing members and dorsal central nervous system. Representative chordates are tunicates, fishes and mammals.

chord method: in navigation, determination of a line of position according to the principles first used by *Sumner.* The altitude of a heavenly body is observed and two values of latitude are assumed in calculation of the longitude, or 2 values of longitude in calculating the latitude. Line joining the 2 resulting positions, being a *chord* of an arc of the circle of equal altitude, is required Sumner line, or line of position, on which vessel was located at some point at time of observation, displacement of such chord from the intercepted arc being considered negligible.

choroid: pigmented membrane in rear of eye behind retina. It contains numerous blood vessels to nourish the retina and in many vertebrates, generally either nocturnal land animals or deep-water fish, it is capable of reflecting light rays where light is poor. Usually the "mirror" is produced by crystals of material called guanine in choroid.

chromatin: protoplasmic substance in nucleus of living cells that forms chromosomes and contains genes.

chromatography: means of separating gaseous, liquid or solid mixture into identifiable components by passing mixture through solvent and then an absorbent.

chromatophore: one of pigment cells in animal's skin that are responsible for coloration; some animals, such as octopus and squid, can expand or contract their chromatophores and thus change color. In plant cells, plastids containing yellow or brown pigments, in addition to chlorophyll, give them a color other than clear green.

chromoplast: small, colored body found in cells of plants and some one-celled animals; composed of specialized cellular material or protoplasm and lies outside of cell's nucleus.

chromosome: any of minute rod-shaped bodies into which chromatin separate during nuclear cell division; carries genes; constant in number for each species.

chronometer: very precise clock used for maintaining time standard necessary for navigation.

Chthamalus stellatus [crustacean larvae]: barnacle of exposed rocks at high shore levels on western coasts. It has nauplius with rounded outline. Caudal end is very short and limb setae are finely plumose. Fifth nauplior stage is approximately 0.5 mm. long.

chubasco: violent thundersquall on west coast of Central America.

chub mackerel: small mackerel occasionally found in large schools off Atlantic coast of America, but generally widely distributed. The species is termed *Scomber japonicus.*

chub, southeastern creek [*Semotilus atromaculatus*]: big, forked-tail minnow with dark stripe on side. Scales along lateral line 45—55; small barbel at base of each maxillary; dorsal fin with 8 rays. Head moderate; eye relatively small; body stout, arched in front of dorsal fin. Bluish-dusky above, creamy below with broad lateral dark stripe which is black on young, but which fades in larger individuals. Dark spot at base of origin of dorsal fin.

chub, southern bigeye [*Hybopsis amblops*]: graceful, pale-colored minnow with narrow, pale stripe down side, small barbel at base of each maxillary; 34—36 scales along lateral line; dorsal fin short

(7—8 soft rays), body moderately robust, spindled-shaped and somewhat compressed; inconspicuous, narrow lateral stripe along side from opercle to base of the tail. Flesh colored above and below lateral stripe, but little darker on dorsum on belly.

chub, spring redeye [*Hybopsis harper*]: small, trim, pinkish minnow. Scales along lateral line 30—35; small barbel at base of each maxillary; dorsal fin short (7—8 soft rays). Body only moderately robust on side view; spindle shaped; somewhat compressed. Dark lateral stripe runs along each side from tip of snout to base of tail; above this is a narrow stripe of white and rest of dorsum is pink to pinkish-tan; sides below dark lateral stripe, flesh-colored.

chubsucker, Alabama [*Erimyzon tenuis*]: fish with a suckerlike mouth and without spiny dorsal fin. Mouth suckerlike with fleshy lips; jaws toothless; 11 rays in dorsal fin; no lateral line; 40—42 rows of scales along side of body. Head stout, short. Color variable; young individuals pale with a broad black line down side, adults muddy red in color, darker above than below.

chubsucker, Eastern [*Erimyzon sucetta*]: fish with suckerlike mouth and without spiny dorsal fin; fleshy lips; jaws toothless; 12 rays in dorsal fin; no lateral line; 35-36 rows of scales along side of body. Head stout, short; eye large 4½ times length of head. Coloration variable; young individuals pale with broad black line down sides, adults muddy red in color, darker above than below.

chuck: narrow passage or strait swept by tidal currents; also applied to tidal current itself.

cicatrix: in fossil *Nautiloidea*, a scar on initial shell chamber thought to represent point of attachment of embryonal shell.

cidaroids [sea urchins]: this long-lived order appeared in Devonian times and is common in modern seas. Its members have 2 rows of plates in each ambulacrum and 2 or more in interambulacra. Each interambulacra plate bears one broad tubercle to which large spine is attached, a smooth ring (areole) and circle of small tubercles that carry secondary spines.

C.I.F. [Cost, insurance, and freight]: as used in quoting price of a shipment of goods, indicates insurance and freight charges incidental to delivery of goods are included in price quoted.

cigarfish: carangoid fish (*Decapterus punctatus*) found in Caribbean Sea and southeast U.S. waters, about 1 ft. in length; so called from its cigar-shaped or fusiform appearance. Also called *round robin*.

cilia: 1) hairlike appendages that can move together in a waving motion; used for locomotion in various one-celled animals and to produce a current in a fluid in higher animals or their larvae. 2) in *Foraminifera*, numerous short hairlike processes on surface of cell. Occur in many animals besides protozoans.

ciliated: having cilia or hairlike appendages.

cinereous: ash-gray, color of wood ashes.

cinerite: sedimentary material consisting of volcanic cinders.

cingulum: in dinoflagellates, the horizontal groove around the cell.

ciquatera: intoxication in humans from ingestion of various tropical reef and inshore fishes and possibly certain invertebrates. Most common symptoms are tingling and numbness of lips, tongue, hands and feet, confusion of sensations of head, cold nausea, diarrhea, joint and muscular pain, burning urination, inability to coordinate voluntary muscular movements and difficult breathing.

circle: plane figure bounded by a curved line, all points of which are equidistant from a point within called the *center*.

circular canal: in coelenterate medusae, tube of gastrovascular cavity, lying at periphery of the bell, encircling it and connected to stomach by radial canals.

circulation: flow or motion of fluid in or through given area of volume. General term describing water current flow within large area.

circumnavigate: to sail around; as, *to c. the earth.*

circumoral: surrounding the mouth.

circumpolar: in nautical astronomy, descriptive term for a heavenly body which remains above the horizon throughout its apparent diurnal revolution about the elevated pole; a circumpolar star necessarily has a polar distance *(90°—declination)* of a lesser value than latitude of an observer.

cirri: various slender, flexible appendages found in certain animals ranging from single-celled organisms to fish. The barnacles jointed, curved legs used to catch prey are called cirripedia (cirri feet).

Cirripedia [crustacean larvae]: all cirripeds (barnacles and parasitic *Rhizocephala*) have 6 naupliar stages which can be distinguished from those of other crustaceans by frontolateral horns on carapace. After several moults there is a sudden change to cypris stage which has bivalve shell, compound eye, 6 pairs of thoracic appendages and short abdomen. This stage settles and changes into adult. Rhizocephalan larvae are not common. Naupli of various species can be separated by different sizes.

cirrus: one of appendages of barnacles; one of filamentous respiratory and tactile appendages of annelids; slender, tentaclelike process. In ciliate protozoans a fused group of cilia.

civil time: solar time in a day beginning at midnight.

Cladocera [phylum *Phoronida*]: small branchiopod crustaceans distinguished by bivalve carapace without hinge which is fused to 2 or more of thoracic segments but leaves head free. There are only 4 to 6 trunk limbs of phyllopod type; single compound eye; dorsal cavity below carapace serves as brood pouch. Antenna, although it has few joints, is large, bears plumose bristles and is the main locomotive appendage. Most *Cladocera* live in fresh water.

Cladonema radiatum [phylum *Coelenterata*]: medusa of hydroid of same name. It has branched marginal tentacles which bear clusters of nematocysts; stomach has 5 pouched outgrowths. Fine radial canals may branch to form secondary canals making a total of 8, since some remain unbranched. Celli are very obvious. It is an active medusa and widely distributed.

cladoselachians [sharks]: sharklike fishes did not appear until mid-Devonian times, some 30,000,000 yrs. after bony placoderms became common. First fossils of this group, *Cladodus*, had pointed teeth whose blunt bases rested in cartilaginous jaws. Next came *Cladoselache*, a slender fish 2 to 4 ft. long whose shape and broad heterocercal tail show that it was built for speed. Pectoral fins were broad, but pelvic fins were absent; large eyes were near front of head; skull was merely a brain case to which jaws were attached.

clamm, deep-sea: small grab used to bring up bottom specimens in taking deep-sea soundings, contrived in 1818 by Sir John Ross, British arctic navigator *(1777-1856)*.

clamp [ships]: longitudinal plank connecting beams on inside of hull, just under the deck.

clampshell snapper: bottom-sampling device used to collect small amount (less than 1 pt.) of material from ocean floor. It has metal jaws that snap shut when device touches bottom.

clam [class *Pelecypoda*]: bivalve or 2-shelled mollusk. Mantle divided into 2 lobes, completely enclosing soft-bodied animal, folding over the back and extending over visceral mass, including the foot, on both sides. Each lobe of mantle secretes a shell, becoming enlarged with new successive layers being laid down underneath by outer surface of mantle. A ligament or elastic band holds the 2 shells together. Beneath is the hinge, composed of interlocking teeth (laterals). In clams, openings are prolonged in form of tubes known as siphons. Foot, among bivalve mollusks, is merely a hatchet-shaped ventral prolongation of visceral mass, extending downward on meridian line between 2 pairs of gill flaps, for locomotor or digging purposes.

clam, blunt-nose [*Macoma nasuta*]: delicate, flat shell, rounded at anterior margin; elongated and decidedly bent at posterior edge. Two separate and slender ligaments and 2 teeth in 1 valve and 1 in the other constitute the shell hinge. Extremely thin, fine-wrinkled, gray-brown skin covers the white shell. Seldom grows to more than 2 in. long and 1½ in. wide. Inhabits muddy bays where it lives several inches below surface.

clam, butter [*Saxidomus giganteous*]: average length is 4 in. Shell is solid, broad and heavy, with rather poorly defined concentric lines of growth on surface. Outside of shell is sometimes yellow-brown, but inside is always white. Two valves of shell nearly alike, held together dorsally by hinge ligament made of a tough leathery substance. Umbo or beak of shell is usually twisted or spiral and is oldest part of shell, point on which growth begins.

clam, cockle or heart [*Cerastoderma corbis*]: large, thick, inflated shell with about 37 close set radiating lines with deep grooves between them. Each valve has one prominent tooth near hinge and one on each side at some distance from it. Approximately 2½ to 3 in. long and high and 2 in. in diameter. Cockle is usually yellow-brown, mottled with darker brown spots; beak is lighter in color and nearly free of spots.

clam, cockle or little neck [*Protothaca staminea*]: recognized by distinct lines radiating from beak of shell. Circular and longitudinal lines give shell a rough, checked appearance. Seldom grows to more than 3 in. long. Color variation is from yellow to brown with angular spots. Margins are finely notched. Three hinged teeth are short and ligament is thick and strong.

clam, horseclam [*Schizothaerus nuttalli*]: one of largest clams found on our coasts, 4 to 6 in. long and may weigh 4 lbs. Rather fragile shell is dull white with poorly marked circular lines of growth. Thin, brown epidermis, falling in wrinkles over margin, covers shell. Posterior end, shell is blunt and gapes widely. On anterior edge, shell gapes slightly for protrusion of foot. Teeth on hinge are distinct; beak is high and prominent.

clam, jackknife [*Solen sicarius*]: resembles a jackknife with blade open, when it extends its foot and siphons. Shell forms slightly curved cylinder about 4 times as long as wide. Small terminal beaks and one hinged tooth on each valve; anterior end somewhat rounded, posterior end cut off squarely. Shell is open at both ends; from lower end foot protrudes; from upper end siphons project. A firm, glistening, brown skin covers whole surface of shell.

clam, long or soft [*Mya arenaria*]: has delicate, elongated, smooth white shell covered with thin, grayish-brown skin. Shell somewhat flat and gapes broadly; beak central and bends backwards. At posterior end valve is flatter and more elongated than at anterior end, to allow for extrusion of long, stout siphons. Teeth not well developed on valves. Nearly 2½ in. long, 1½ in. high, ¾ in. thick. Clam's presence indicated at low tide by small hole in sand through which water occasionally squirts.

clam, mud or gaper [*Mya truncata*]: has long shell, 2½ in. in length, 1¾ in. wide and ¾ in. thick. Posterior end narrow, decidedly blunt and gapes broadly. Covering whole surface of shell is brown, papery epidermis which extends some distance beyond margins. Long, united siphons protrude far outside shell at posterior end and small foot projects at other end. It is a burrowing form, inhabiting sand and mud.

clam, razor [*Siliqua patula*]: inhabits either broad, level, sandy ocean beach or one with wide expanse of strong current. Shell is thin and fragile, covered with shiny bottom epidermis. Prominent umbo appears about 1/3 distance from anterior end with well defined lines of growth extending from it. Anterior end rounded, with posterior end somewhat blunt. Approximately 5 in. long and 2 in. wide. Burrows deeply in sand.

clam, rose necklace [*Tellina salmonea*]: common in sand and mud flats, not more than ½ in. in length and breadth; very thin, somewhat triangular shell with umbo at rear. Exterior is clear pink; interior highly polished salmon in color. Valves quite flat and of nearly equal size.

clam, tiny pink [*Macoma inconspicua*]: delicate and beautiful shell, ½ in. in length and breadth, white or pinkish-white both inside and out, and somewhat inflated. Very thin membrane sometimes partially covers shell. It usually lives low on the beach with big clams or where eelgrass is abundant.

clam, white sand [*Macoma secta*]: shell thin and chalky white, partially covered with shiny brown cuticle. Three characteristics which distinguish it are prominent hinge ligament, black, on outside of shell; umbo almost central, about a ¼ in. from left edge, shell bends abruptly downward; left valve is flatter than right. There are 2 adductor muscles and the palliad line is easily seen.

clapotis: French equivalent for type of standing wave. In American usage it is usually associated with standing wave phenomenon caused by reflection of wave train from breakwater, bulkhead or steep beach. Standing wave in which there is no horizontal motion of crests.

clapper: 1) the tongue of a bell. 2) clack-valve in a pump, scupper pipe, etc. A piece of wood fitted between jaws of a gaff to bear against, and hold gaff a constant distance from, the mast; also termed *saddle*, *tongue*, and *tumbler*.

clapper rail: type of marsh bird called a rail that has dull plumage and long bill; common to salt marshes along Atlantic Coast.

Clark-Bumpus quantitative plankton sampler: plankton-collecting device equipped with flowmeter to determine volume of water passed through it in given time interval.

class: division or grouping of vessels according to their size, strength, and/or common characteristics; as, *destroyer class*, *collier class*. Rating given a vessel by a classification society according to her degree of conformity with prescribed standards of structural strength, machinery, equipment, and periodical surveys; the expression *"Al at Lloyd's"* signifies a vessel is assigned highest class in the society's records.

classification: act of placing a vessel in a certain class as prescribed in requirements of classification society concerned.

classification society: corporation or society founded with the aim of establishing certain standards in construction, propelling plant, and equipment of vessels, providing for seaworthiness and safety in connection with marine insurance interests. Such societies maintain watchful concern over all craft registered in their lists; their surveyors supervise construction; test building material as necessary; inspect and control execution of required or recommended repair-work; and determine schedule for periodic inspections or surveys in connection with prescribed procedure in upholding a vessel's "class." While a shipowner is not compelled to build his vessel according to any classification society's requirements, established practice in marine underwriting of quoting a premium based upon the certified classification of a vessel would render the position of an "unclassed" vessel a difficult one in the question of securing a satisfactory rate of insurance. Names of principal societies active at beginning of World War II are:—*American Bureau of Shipping; British Corporation; Bureau Veritas; Germanischer Lloyd; Imperial Japanese Maritime Corporation; Lloyd's Register of British and Foreign Shipping; Nederlandsche Vereeniging van Assuradeuren; Norske Veritas; Registro Navale Italiano; Veritas Austro-Ungarico.*

clean: 1) well shaped; neat; trim; as, *clean lines of a ship*. 2) Free of danger or obstruction; as, *a clean anchorage*. 3) Free of any qualifying or restricting clause; as, a *clean* bill of health, a *clean* bill of lading.

clear: 1) to free from legal detention, as imported goods or a ship, by paying duties or dues and presenting the requisite documents: as, to *clear a cargo*; to *clear a ship* at customhouse. 2) to remove an obstruction.

clearance: in general, any written authority showing that a vessel has conformed to existing customs, naval, or port regulations or laws.

clinid: referring to any member of the blenny family *Clinidae*. Blennies are generally small, shallow-water fish common to temperate and tropical seas all over the world.

clinker: mode of boatbuilding in which planks overlap.

clinker-built [ships]: having external planks overlapping, lower edge of plank overlapping upper edge of the one below it. This is also called "lap-strake."

clino: sloping part of floor of sea which extends from the wave base to deeper parts of sea. Deposits formed in clino-environment are called clino-form.

clinometer: an instrument for measuring angle of a vessel's roll. It usually consists of a suspended metal pointer which indicates direction of the plumb line, as vessel rolls, on a graduated arc of a circle in the athwartship plane; often is a graduated tube of glass containing a liquid in which a bubble marks the degree of roll.

clione: genus of tiny *pteropods* inhabiting Arctic and northern waters in abundance and forming principal food of the Greenland or Arctic right whale.

Clione gracilis [*Gymnosomata*]: body is slender, being no wider than the head; color whitish. As in *Clione limacina*, there are 3 pairs of buccal cones and hook sacs with 30 spines or more. Radula of 18 transverse rows each with median plate and 8 or 9 pairs of teeth.

Clione limacina [*Aporrhaidae*]: this species breeds during summer and lays planktonic gelatinous egg masses which are about 1 mm. long and contain scattered eggs. Newly hatched larva is approximately 0.15 mm. long by 0.1 broad; shell is thin and transparent, attached to larva by longitudinal muscles. After a period of rapid growth the larva sheds the shell which has acquired striations on lip and develops 3 circlets of cilia. Then velum is lost and head cones as well as rudimentary wings appear. When larva reaches about 2 mm. in length, wings are quite large. In 2.8 mm. larva all cilia except the last circlet disappear. In 3 mm. larva all adult organs form and animal is capable of breeding. Head cones and tentacles at this stage are orange-red, wings pink and liver and gonad brownish yellow. This is an Arctic and Boreal species with southern limit at Bay of Biscay and is found in North Sea.

clip [ships]: 4 in. to 6 in. angle bar welded temporarily to floors, plates, webs, etc.; used as holdfast which, with aid of a bolt, pulls objects up close in fitting. Also short lengths of bar, general-ly angle, used to attach and connect various members of ship's structure.

clipper: sailing vessel built with very sharp lines, more or less raking masts and great spread of canvas with a view to speed. First built in Baltimore, hence the name Baltimore Clipper.

clipper schooner: Baltimore-built centerboard fishing schooner used in Cape Cod mackerel fishing in summer and for transporting oysters from Chesapeake Bay to New England ports in winter.

clipper ship: large, sharp-modeled, ship-rigged sailing vessel of great sail-carrying capacity. The "clipper ship" was developed by American ship-builders in response to a growing demand for larger and faster ships.

cloaca: common opening through which digestive remains, excretions and sex products, including eggs and sperm, leave bodies of many vertebrates. There are similar regions in some invertebrates. The cloaca is the animal's one posterior opening, unlike the two possessed by most mammals, the anus and urinogenital apertures.

clone: genetically similar individuals derived by asexual reproduction from one individual or in *Ciliata* from a pair of exconjugants.

close: 1) in immediate proximity. 2) to come near to; to come together, as, to *close* another vessel.

close butt [ships]: joint fitted close by grinding, pulled tight by clips and welded.

closed bay: bay indirectly connected with sea through a narrow pass.

closed sea: that part of ocean enclosed by headlands, within narrow straits, etc.

close ice: ice that covers from 8/10 to 10/10 of sea surface.

close-hauled [ships]: referring to position of ship's sails when sailing as much toward direction from which wind is blowing as vessel's structure and weather will permit. Same as "by the wind."

close-pack ice: sea ice consisting of ice floes that are generally in contact. Their concentration ranges between 7/10 and 9/10.

cloud: 1) a visible collection or mass of vapor, or water or ice particles formed by condensation of vapor, in the atmosphere; fog, mist, or haze suspended in the air. Greatest in altitude in *cirrus* cloud which may reach 18 miles in tropical latitudes, while lowest, *stratus*, may rest on the earth's surface as a fog. Similar cloud formations lie at greater altitudes in the tropics than in high latitudes. Following are the 10 principal clouds as internationally classified. a) **Upper clouds.** *Cirrus (ci.)*—detached; delicate, fibrous appearance; of featherlike structure; generally white, without shading; the sailor's "mares' tails." Average height 31,000 ft. *Cirrostratus (ci. st.)*—thin whitish veil often completely covering sky and giving it a milky appearance; often produces halos around sun and moon. Average height, 29,000 ft. *Cirrocumulus (ci. cu.)*—the "mackerel sky"; small globular masses, without shadows, or white ripple-like flakes arranged in groups and often in lines showing light shadows. Average height, 23,000 ft. **b) Middle clouds.** *Altostratus (a. st.)*—sheet of gray or bluish color, often appearing as thick cirrostratus; causes sun and moon to appear as blurred light spots; sometimes thin and gives rise to solar or lunar coronae; may also form parallel bands as a fibrous veil. Average height, 15,000 ft.; thickness, 1,700 ft. *Altocumulus (a. cu.)*—groups or lines of globular masses, white or grayish and partly shaded; the "woolpack" of sailors' lore. Average height, 12,000 ft.; thickness, 600 ft. **c) Low clouds.** *Stratocumulus (st. cu.)*—heavy globular masses or rolls of soft, gray appearance; may be compact or small openings may disclose blue sky; often wholly compact, dark gray, and covering the whole sky, especially in winter. Average height, 5,000 ft.; thickness, 1,200 ft. *Stratus (st.)*—uniform layer, resembling fog, but not resting on the ground. When close to, or on the surface, termed *fog.* If broken up by wind or summits of mountains, termed *fractostratus (fr. st.)*—the "scud" often observed in a strong wind below the nimbostratus. Average height, 2,000 ft., thickness, 1,000 ft. *Nimbostratus (nb. st.)*—a low, shapeless layer of dark gray color and nearly uniform, from which rain or snow continuously falls. When broken up in stormy weather, also becomes the "scud" of sailors and then termed *fractonimbus.* Average height, about 3,000 ft.; thickness, about 2,000 ft. Common to the front of cyclone areas. *Cumulus (cu.)*—heavy white cloud with vertical development; base appears horizontal and upper surface dome-shaped with outlying protuberances; the "big woolpack." Ragged, detached parts carried along in a breeze are termed fractocumulus. Cumulus is strictly a fine weather cloud. May be 1,000 to 12,000 ft. in altitude and 300 to 8,000 ft. in thickness. *Cumulonimbus (cu. nb.)*—the thundercloud. Heavy masses of great vertical extent; summits rise in form of towers and mountains, often with highest point anvil-shaped; common in rear of cyclones; associated with most summer showers and all thunderstorms. Average height of base, 5,000 ft.; varies in vertical thickness from 7,000 to 30,000 ft. **2)** to become obscured by clouds, as, the sun is clouded over.

clove hitch [ships]: hitch frequently used for securing dock lines to bitts or bollards.

clown fish, marine [*Amphiprion percula*]: color is orange; wide white collar encircles afterpart of head, just behind eye. Second white band begins just behind spiny dorsal fin and widens out to encircle the body behind pectoral and ventral fins. There is a 3rd white band on caudal pedun-

cle. Orange fins are edged with brown with white border on the very edge. Size 4 in. Ranges Indian Ocean.

clown fish, white-tailed [*Amphiprion polymnus*]: grows about 5 in., having white tail and 2 broad white bands running around body. Overall color ranges from deep orange to chocolate brown to black depending upon region from which they come. Ranges throughout tropical Indo-Pacific.

Cl-ratio: amount of any ion or substance per unit weight of chlorinity. It is obtained by dividing the concentration of various ions in grams per kilogram by chlorinity.

club [ships]: spar or boom used in obtaining flat trim on headsail.

club foot [ships]: flattened, broadened after end of stem foot.

club topsail [ships]: triangular topsail used above fore-and-aft mainsail, being bent along its foot and tuff to 2 spars, called clubs, which extend beyond the gaff and topmast.

clutch: 1) forked stanchion. 2) throat of an anchor. 3) mechanism used to connect two shafts and arranged so that one may be stopped or started while the other continues in motion. The two types most in use are called *disc* clutch and *cone* clutch.

cnoidal wave: type of wave profile in shallow water (depth of less than 1/8 to 1/10 the wavelength).

coach roof [ships]: on small boats, the roof of a cabin, often one which extends above deck and provides headroom below deck.

Coal Age: Carboniferous period dominated by lush, swampy forests and development of fossil fuels.

coalsack: conspicuous dark space in the Milky Way caused by an almost complete absence of stars; "Hole in the sky."

coaltitude: complement of the altitude; zenith distance of a heavenly body.

coaming [ships]: the fore-and-aft framing in hatchways and scuttles, while athwartships pieces are called headledges; but the name coaming is commonly applied to all raised framework about deck openings. Coamings prevent water from running below, as well as strengthening deck about the hatches.

coarse sea lace [*Microcladia boreale*]: grows on faces of rocks more or less exposed to surf between 2.5- and 0.5-ft. tide levels. A graceful red alga with many short, stiff, cylindrical to slightly compressed branches arising on one plane only. Erect branches, each of which is divided into 5—6 orders of smaller branches are generally bare for lower 1/3 of length. Much variation in size and attached to substratum by prostrate rhizone-like system of branches.

coast: general region of indefinite width that extends from the sea inland to first major change in terrain features.

coastal area: land of sea area bordering shoreline.

coastal current: relatively uniform drift usually flowing parallel to shore in deeper water adjacent to surf zone. Current may be related to tides, winds or distribution of mass.

coastal grooves [amphibian]: series of vertical grooves along sides of body between fore and hind limbs of most salamanders.

coastal plain: plain which borders sea coast and extends from sea to nearest elevated land.

coastal pressure ridge: ridge formed when floating sea ice is thrust against fast ice.

Coast and Geodetic Survey: in U.S. Department of Commerce, a bureau responsible for topographic and hydrographic survey of the country's Atlantic, Pacific, and Gulf of Mexico coasts and establishing primary triangulation data and precise leveling lines in the interior. It publishes charts, coast pilots, tidal and magnetic information, and currently issues notices to mariners concerning dangers, new charts, changes in water depths, and other information of navigational importance in the coastal field referred to.

coaster: coasting vessel; a person or vessel engaged in the coasting trade.

coasting: 1) act of navigating along a seacoast; in U.S. law, a vessel is coasting when she is navigated in "coastal navigable waters of the United States," or "all portions of the sea within the territorial jurisdiction of the U.S. and all inland waters navigable in fact in which the tide ebbs and flows." 2) configuration of a coast; coastline.

coastlining: surveying of a coastline.

coastwise: by way of, or along, the coast; coastways.

cob: 1) seagull; especially the black-backed gull *(Larus marinus).* Also *cobb.* 2) beating or flogging administered in former days to seamen guilty of dereliction of duty; a *cobbing.*

cobble: rock fragment between 64 and 256 mm. in diameter, larger than a pebble and smaller than a boulder, and rounded or otherwise abraded.

cobblerfish: carangoid fish *(Alectis ciliaris)* found generally in warmer seas, but common in West Indies waters; of the family including the *cavalla, pompano,* and *amberfishes,* it is characterized by filaments extending from some of its fin rays.

Cobb Seamount: favorite trawling grounds off coast of Washington in Northeastern Pacific.

cobia: mackerel-like fish from 4 to 5 feet in length, of dusky appearance and having a long

horizontal black stripe on its sides; found in warmer American waters and East Indies; the *sergeantfish;* sometimes confused with the *robalo.*

coble: small, distinctive open boat of both Durham and Yorkshire, England, 20 to 30 ft. long and 5 to 10 ft. beam. It was designed to be launched from the shore against heavy seas, hence high flaring bow and fine, hollow entrance, running away to clean, flat stern section.

cobre: Dutch fishing craft of early 16th century, similar to the dogger.

coccolith: tiny calcareous concretion, or plate of the *Coccolithophoridae,* often forming a significant part of calcareous marine sediments.

coccolithophore: one of a family *(Coccolithophoridae)* of microscopic, often abundant planktonic algae, cells of which are surrounded by an envelope in which numerous small calcareous discs or rings (coccoliths) are embedded. Large concentrations give the water a milky appearance; this condition is called "white water" by herring fishermen of northern Europe.

cock: small sailboat from 2 to 6 tons burden used in herring fishery out of Brighton, England, in middle 19th century.

cockboat: small dinghy or rowboat used as a tender.

cockle: bivalve (having a shell composed of 2 distinct parts or valves) of mollusc subclass *Lamellibranchiata* with round or elliptical shell prized by shell collectors and gourmets.

cockleshell: any dangerously light craft; a frail boat; a cockboat.

cockpit [ships]: sunken open area in deck toward rear of small vessel from which the boat is usually steered.

coconut crab [*Birgus latro*]: believed to be world's largest land crab. Its body exceeds 12 in. in length and it weighs several pounds. Pinchers and walking legs are firm, hard and strong, covered with spines and bristles; carapace is harder and more calcified than that of most hermit crabs; abdomen, which has become shortened, is of leathery texture. Entire body is a reddish color. This hermit crab has abandoned the ocean and its seashell and has taken up residence upon land. It digs burrows at bases of trees and under logs and usually spends the day hidden away.

cocurrent line: line in a chart passing through places having same tidal current hour.

cod [Atlantic]: dull-colored fish varying in color from gray-green to reddish brown; sides are spotted with yellow or brown; belly is light gray or tan; lateral line is a lighter color than rest of the body. Three approximately equal sized dorsal fins without spines extend from head to tail fin; 2 anal fins of which forward one is slightly larger than the other; small ventral fins are located in front of and below pectoral fins. Average cod is 2 to 3 ft. long and weighs under 10 lbs. Cod are voracious eaters roaming in packs over sea bottom consuming mollusks, sea urchins, starfish, crustaceans, worms and their favorite morsel, herring.

cod [Atlantic tomcod]: more southern fish, olive green, tinged with yellow and marked by dark blotches on the side. Narrow ventral fins have prolonged extension on forward edge. Smaller than Atlantic cod, its average length is 15 in. and its weight rarely more than 2 lbs. Tomcod is a shoal-water fish.

code: system of signals or characters used by ships as a means of communicating with each other or with shore.

codfish: family of coldwater fishes and relatives are elongated fishes with small cycloid scales. The chin bears one barbel, with one exception, the silver hake. Number and shape of dorsal and anal fins are characteristic of cod, tomcod, pollock and haddock. Two dorsal and single anal fin are features of hake and burbot. Cusk has single dorsal and single anal fin. Most of species are bottom dwellers with carnivorous or omnivorous appetites.

codicaria: flat-bottomed boat used in ferrying and general cargo carrying on Tiber River by ancient Romans.

Coelenterata [phylum]: third phylum of animals includes hydroids, corals and jellyfish. These, like sponges, consist essentially of body wall, lacking any internal organs, therefore the name. *Hydra* is simple representative of phylum and particularly class *Hydrozoa*. Corals and sea anemones form another class of this phylum, *Anthozoa* so named because of bright colors and flowerlike symmetry. Coral animal resembles *Hydra* in essentials, but extend from wall part way into central cavity, subdividing it into series of alcoves. *"Coel,"* hollow; *"entron,"* gut; referring to hollow internal cavity of individual. Precambrian to Recent.

coelenterate: 1) one of a phylum *(Coelenterata or Cnidaria)* of two-staged (sessile) and free floating organisms: sessile stage basically is cylindrical and is called a polyp and free swimming stage is disc or bell-shaped and is called a medusa or jellyfish. Many coelenterates, particularly hydrozoans and corals, are colonial, consisting of many polyps united in complex or massive structures. All contain stinging cells or nematocysts and many exhibit bioluminescence and some reportedly scatter sound. 2) member of primitive aquatic phylum distinguished by 2 basic forms: jellyfishlike medusa and polyp, a stalked sedentary creature attached to solid object at one end and having tentacles at other end. Usually marine animals, coelenterates have stinging cells called

nematocysts and simple systems, saclike digestive cavity that is often branched and scattered nervous system. *Coelenterata* have 3 main classes: *Hydrozoa* that includes the Portuguese man-of-war, medusae of *Scyphozoa*, the jellyfish, and polyps of *Anthozoa* which resemble flowers and include corals, sea anemones and sea feathers.

coelenteron [*Coelenterata*]: spacious cavity, enclosed by body wall of coelenterate and opening externally through mouth.

coelom: body cavity lined with mesodermal epithelium, the peritoneum.

coenenchyme: fleshy cellularized mesogloea of alcyonarians, usually traversed by gastral tubes, solenia, connecting gastral cavities of polyps.

coenocyte: tissue in which cytoplasm is continuous rather than divided into individualized cells around each nucleus.

coenosarc: living tissue in hydroid colonies, joining all polyps.

coenosteum: calcareous skeleton of colonial corals; in Bryozoans, vesicular or dense skeletal material between zooecia.

coffin plate [ships]: plate used on enclosed twin bossing, named for its shape. In reality it is an inverted boss plate.

cog: double-ended, bluff-bowed, full-lined vessel in use in 11th to 14th centuries in Northwestern Europe. This clinker-built craft made its appearance in Mediterranean.

Coignet pile: type of reinforced concrete pile similar to so-called Hennebique pile.

col: in meteorology, point of intersection of trough and ridge in pressure pattern of weather map. It is the point of relatively lowest pressure between 2 lows.

colatitude: difference between latitude of a place 90° or its distance in degrees from one of the poles of earth.

cold air mass: air mass that is colder than surface over which it passes. Indicated on weather map by K.

cold pool: body of cold water entirely surrounded by warm water.

cold wall: steep water temperature gradient between Gulf Stream and slope water inshore of Gulf Stream or Labrador Current. It is considered part of Arctic Convergence by most oceanographers.

coliform: referring to the colon bacillus that lives in soil or, especially parasitic sea lice. They are aquatic and may be either free-swimming or live on bodies of larger animals.

collar [ships]: ring used around pipe or mast or a flat plate made to fit around girder or beam passing through a bulkhead. They serve to make various spaces watertight.

collarette: in *Chaetognatha*, thickened ectodermal area in neck region of body.

collector: in underwater optics a device required to fulfill definition of quantity being measured, e.g., Gershun tube in radiance measurements or cosine collector in irradiance measurements.

collier brig: brig used in coral trade on Thames River and English coast in 18th and 19th centuries. Huge single headsail and large topsails were carried.

collimation error: 1) an error in the sight line of a telescope or transit due to faulty adjustment of its parallelism with a plane of reference, as plane of the meridian. 2) an error in a sextant observation caused by line of collimation, or sight line of telescope, not being parallel to plane of the instrument.

collimator: device capable of producing parallel beams of light or forming distant image without distortion.

collision: the striking together, with damage usually resulting, of two vessels, or of one vessel with any fixed structure. In maritime law, it is defined as impact of ship against ship, although usage is increasing scope of the term to include striking of a vessel against any floating body or object.

collision mat [ships]: large mat used to close aperture in vessel's side resulting from collision.

colloblast: adhesive cell in tentacles of *Ctenophora* of class *Tentaculata*; used in capture of prey.

colloid: as size term refers to particles smaller than 0.00024 mm., smaller than clay size.

colonial coral: coral in which individuals are attached together as units and do not exist as separate animals.

colorimeter: instrument used for precise measurement of hue, purity and brightness of color.

colors: ensign or flag flown to indicate a vessel's nationality. In U.S. Navy, a salute to the flag when it is hoisted at 8 a.m. and lowered at sunset.

Columba: southern contellation adjacent to, and southwest of *Canis Major*, containing as its brightest star *Phact (a Columbae)* in 34° 6′ S. declination and 5 hrs. 38 min. right ascension, and of magnitude 2.75; called also *Columba Noachi, Columba Noae,* or *Noah's Dove*.

columella: 1) in *Coelenterata*, longitudinal rod in axis of corallite, formed by inner ends of septa and accessory structures such as tabulae and dissepiments. 2) in *Gastropoda*, medial pillar in spiral shell formed by coalescence of inner walls of whorls. 3) in *Mollusca*, solid or hollow pillar surrounding axis of coiling in most gastropods, formed by inner walls of whorls.

column: 1) formation of a fleet in which ships are placed or proceed one behind another; also

termed *line ahead*. 2) heavy pillar or stanchion supporting a number of deck beams in a hold. Heavy cast iron or steel frames supporting cylinders of an engine.

comb: breaking or curling crest of a wave; a whitecap. A heavy sea or breaker is said to *comb* as its crest rolls over and foams.

comber: 1) deepwater wave whose crest is pushed forward by strong wind and which is much larger than a whitecap. 2) long-period spilling breaker.

comb jellies: common name for members of phylum *Ctenophora;* small jellyfishlike animals which live in surface layers of ocean, usually spheroidal and having comb plates. They are common marine animals, often occurring in enormous concentrations; many species are strongly bioluminescent.

comb plates: flagellated platelets in *Ctenophora* responsible for swimming.

come: word employed in various phrases denoting some current action or maneuver and always with a significant preposition, adverb, or objective phrase; as, to *come away,* to *come in sight*.

commensalism: symbiotic relationship between 2 species in which one species is benefited and the other is not harmed. Relationship between shark and remora or "suckerfish" is an example of commensalism.

commissure [*Brachiopoda*]: junction between edges of valve.

community: integrated, mutually adjusted assemblage of plants and animals inhabiting a natural area. Assemblage may or may not be self-sufficient and is considered to be in state of dynamic equilibrium.

compaction: decrease in volume or thickness of sediment under load through closer crowding of constituent particles and accompanied by decrease in porosity, increase in density and squeezing out of interstitial water.

companion [ships]: covering over top of companionway.

companion ladder [ships]: stairs leading down into cabin.

companionway [ships]: raised hatch or cover; staircase at entrance to ship's cabin or entrance to ladder or stairs leading from upper to lower deck.

compass: device used to determine directions on shipboard. There are 3 main types in use: magnetic compass, employing magnetized metal needle which points to magnetic north, Gyro or Gyroscopic Compass, which points True North through use of electrically-driven gyroscope and radio compass, which is highly directed radio receiver capable of determining direction of origin of known radio signal.

compensating filter: filter used to altar spectral emission of a light source or sensitivity of emulsion to a specified response to different wavelengths.

compensation depth: depth at which photosynthesis equals plant repiration during 24-hour period.

compensation isostatic: theory of equilibrium of earth's crust assuming that columns of rock and water standing on basis of equal area have equal weights, irrespective of elevation and configuration of their upper surface.

compensatorium: in certain *Bryozoa* a water-filled invagination of ectodermal epithelium from which water can be expelled as the animal retracts into its zooecium making room for the retracted body.

composite chart: chart based on data for extending period, usually 5 to 10 days treated as being synoptic.

composite vessel [ships]: vessel with steel frame and wooden hull and decks.

compound shoreline: that shoreline whose essential features combine elements of at least 2 of other shoreline classifications, i.e., emergence, submergence or neutral shoreline.

compound tide: tide constituent with speed equal to sum or difference of speeds of 2 or more basic constituents. Compound tides usually occur in shallow-water regions.

compressibility: change of specific volume and density under hydrostatic pressure.

compressional wave: wave in elastic medium which causes an element of the medium to change its volume without undergoing rotation.

compression factor: coefficient expressing, in lbs. per 100 ft., combined effect of submarine buoyancy of compression of seawater and of ship with increasing depth; always negative in value.

Compton absorption: absorption of x-ray or gamma ray photon in Compton effect. Energy of electromagnetic radiation is not completely absorbed since another photon of lower energy is simultaneously created.

Compton effect: attentuation process observed for x-ray of gamma radiation in which an incident photon interacts with orbital electron of an atom to produce a recoil electron and scattered photon of energy less than incident photon.

Compton scattering: in sea-ice reporting, ratio of area extent of ice present to total area extent of ice and water. Concentrations are usually reported in tenths, and is meaningful to definitions of open water, very open pack ice, open pack ice, close pack ice, very close pack ice.

compulsory pilotage: under law or port regulation in many countries and localities employment of pilots on vessels of certain tonnage and class in specified waters is made compulsory, while in some localities a vessel may elect to proceed without accepting an authorized pilot's services, she nevertheless must pay pilotage, in whole or in part, according to established rate or fee. In U.S. waters, all registered vessels, or, generally, those sailing on foreign voyages, are subject to compulsory pilotage as may be required by state law, while those enrolled or licensed (coasting vessels, war vessels, fishing vessels, yachts, tugs, and other craft) are exempted by federal statute.

concentration factor: expression of relative amount of an element in organism as compared to its relative amount of seawater. Concentration factors as high as 2 million or higher have been reported for some elements in some organisms.

concentration ice: percentage of ice cover in given area of water, usually expressed in tenths.

conceptacle: in brown algae of subclass *Cyclosporeae (Fucales)* a round cavity borne on swollen tip of branched thallus and containing reproductive organs.

conch: large marine mollusks of class *Gastropoda*. Their spiraled shells have long, often beautifully colored opening. Conch's flesh is a delicious seafood and supports a large fishery; shell is used for decoration or as horns.

conchiolin: complex albuminoid organic substance forming outer thin layer of molluscan shells.

concrescent: growing together, coalescent.

concretion: nodular or irregular concentration of material through deposition from solution, usually about a central nucleus, e.g., clay and manganese nodules.

concussion crack: fracture of sea ice produced by impact of one ice cake upon another.

condemned: said of a vessel when pronounced unfit for further service; or of a vessel and her cargo adjudged to be forfeited for cause, or as decreed by a prize court.

condensation: physical process by which vapor becomes liquid or solid; opposite of evaporation. When water vapors condense, heat is released, and surrounding temperature is raised.

condensed deposit: sedimentary material that accumulated very slowly; thin but not interrupted.

conduction: transfer of energy within and through a conductor by means of internal particle or molecular activity, and without any net external motion. Conduction is to be distinguished from convection (of heat) and radiation (of all electromagnetic energy).

cone shell: tropical marine snail of family *Conidae* possessing a venom-injecting apparatus used to subdue prey.

confluent [fish]: not separated; continuous.

conformal projection: map which preserves angles;

i.e., map such that if 2 curves intersect at given angle, images of the 2 curves on map also intersect at the same angles.

confused sea: rough sea where direction and period of sea and/or swell are indeterminate, caused by various overriding wave trains.

conger eel [*Leptocephalus*]: the sea eel growing to 8 ft. in length and about 80 lbs. in weight; back pale brown color and lower part grayish white; common in rocky places on European coasts where it is an important food fish, and sometimes found on American Atlantic coast. The name is locally given to northeast American coast *eelpout* and California *moray*.

conglomerate: rock consisting of gravel, pebbles and sand cemented together.

conglomerated ice: all types of floating ice compacted into one mass; term refers to contents of an ice mass, not concentration.

conic projection: map projection in which surface of sphere is conceived as projected, in geometrical sense, or tangent or second cone, which is then developed on the plane.

Conidae [family]: cone shells are probably, next to cowries, the most beautiful group of gastropod molluscs in the sea, for they exhibit a wide variety of colors to attract the collector's eye. Shells of these molluscs are all conical in shape and have narrower end of cone directed toward front of animal. This inverse conical shape in which body whorls taper toward front is in marked contrast to most other shells of similar design. Spire of these shells is usually low in height and shells themselves are usually heavy and porcellanous. Aperture is long and narrow extending the small anterior end or base. Some species of this family have a poison gland which discharges poison to a slender dart which stings and benumbs prey. Includes more than 500 species most of which make their home in warm waters of tropics.

conjugation: in *Ciliata*, sexual process in which there is a temporary cytoplasmic connection between 2 individuals. While connection lasts there is an exchange of haploid nuclear elements, each of which fuses with corresponding nucleus of the other individual, reconstituting a diploid condition. Then individuals separate. Descendants of pair of exconjugants are all generally alike and constitute a clone.

conjunction: apparent close approach or meeting of 2 heavenly bodies having same right ascension or longitude. When either Mercury or Venus are in that position with the sun, they are said to be in *inferior conjunction*, if between sun and earth, and when on opposite side of the sun, in *superior conjunction;* the other planets, being farther from the sun than Mercury, Venus, or Earth, can be in conjunction with the sun only when in latter position.

connective tissue: supporting tissue which holds other tissues and organs in place.

conning: directing a helmsman in steering or piloting a vessel, especially in narrow waters or in heavy traffic. Also, *cunning.*

conning tower [ships]: protective structure built of armor plates and having various shapes and sizes.

Conrad discontinuity: seismic discontinuity in earth's crust where velocity increased from 6.1 to 6.4—6.7 km. per second; occurs at various depths and is supposed to mark contact of "granitic" and "basaltic" layers.

consecutive mean: smoothed representation of time series derived by replacing each observed value with a mean value computed over selected interval.

consequent stream: river whose course was determined by original slope and irregularities of surface on which it developed.

conservative property: property whose values do not change in course of particular series of events. Properties can be judged conservative only when events (processes) are specified.

consolan: electronic navigation system providing a number of rotating equisignal zones that permit determination of bearings from transmitting station.

consolidated ice: area of sea covered by ice of various origins compacted by wind and currents into firm mass. In sea ice reporting, consolidated ice is term used to describe an area completely devoid of open water and with concentration of 10-tenths. It usually includes some heavier forms of ice.

consolidated pack ice: any large area of drift ice, driven so closely together as to produce complete ice coverage.

consolidated sediments: sediments which have been converted into rocks by compaction, deposition of cement in pore spaces and/or by physical and chemical changes in constituents.

consolidation: reduction in volume of sediment and increase in density in response to increased load through decreases in pore space, void ratio and water content.

consort: vessel sailing in company with another.

constancy of the current: ratio of the magnitude of resultant velocity to mean velocity of current. Constancy is dimensionless and may be expressed as a percentage.

constant plankton: perennial haliplankton in given region.

constellation: one of the many groups or assemblages of stars, or a portion of the heavens occupied by such a group. Many constellations, especially those of northern skies, were named by the early ancients, some mythological hero, goddess, animal, or even inanimate object being so honored, probably because of a fancied resemblance in the groups to the original. In the book of Job, whose lifetime was 1500 B.C. or earlier, we find a remarkable reference to three celestial names in use today. Approximately 90 groups are distinguished by astronomers and, usually beginning with the brightest, with few exceptions each star is designated by a Greek letter, as *a Leonis* (Regulus), 1st star in *Leo;* β *Orionis* (Rigel), 2nd one in *Orion.* (Note the *genitive* form which thus expressed.) Familiar names are also given many constellations or parts of them, as "Dipper," "Plough," and "Charlie's Wagon" applied to *Ursa Major* or the *Great Bear;* "Lady's Chair" for *Cassiopeia;* the "Sickle" as easily recognized in western end of *Leo;* "Seven Sisters" for a small compact group in *Taurus* called by the ancients *Pleiades;* the "Chain-hook," so named by sailors as more appropriate than the classic *Scorpio;* "Cutter's Mainsail" for *Corvus;* etc. Navigators become acquainted with star groups by observing certain triangles, curves, and figures outlined by various bright stars and thus grow capable of recognizing any particular star while many others are obscured in cloudy weather.

constituent: one of harmonic elements in mathematical expression for tide-producing force and in corresponding formulas for tide or tidal current. Each constituent represents periodic change or variation in relative position of earth, moon and sun.

constituent day: duration of earth's daily rotation relative to fictitious star which represents 1 of periodic tide-producing forces; it approximates the length of lunar or solar day and corresponds to period of diurnal constituent of twice the period of semidiurnal constituent.

consumer: organism that feeds on already formed organic matter. All "animals" and a few other forms.

contact chemoreception: capability of some animals' sense organs to receive stimuli upon contact with chemical changes in environment.

contiguous fishing zone: offshore area claimed by a nation for exclusive fishing rights.

continent: large landmass rising abruptly from deep ocean floor, including marginal regions that are shallowly submerged. Continents constitute about 1/3 of earth's surface.

continental borderland: region adjacent to a continent, normally occupied by or bordering continental shelf, that is highly irregular with depths well in excess of those typical of continental shelf.

continental crust: mass of granitic material underlying continents.

continental drift: 1) concept that continents can drift on surface of earth because of weakness of suboceanic crust, such as ice, can drift through water. 2) theory that oceans which now separate continents supposedly were created when continents moved to their present position.

continental glacier: also called ice sheet, massive low-altitude glacier thousands of feet thick, covering huge areas as in Greenland and Antarctica.

continental margin: zone separating emergent continents from deep sea bottom; generally consists of continental shelf, slope and rise.

continental plating: large elevated mass of lithosphere coinciding approximately with a continent and including its continental shelf.

continental rise: gently sloping submerged surface lying to seaward of base of continental slope. An abyssal plane usually lies seaward of continental rise. Part of underwater margin of continent that lies at foot of the slope and curves gently down to ocean basin.

continental shelf: 1) submerged margin of continent generally considered to extend seaward to water depths of about 100 fathoms. Seaward slope of shelf is usually less than 5 ft. per mile. 2) zone adjacent to continent or around an island and extending from low-water line to depth at which there is usually a marked increase of slope to greater depth.

continental slope: relatively steep portion of ocean floor which lies seaward of continental shelf and landward of deep-sea floor. It typically drops from depths of 50 to 100 fathoms to depths to 750 to 1,750 fathoms, at an average slope of 400 ft. per mile.

Continuous Discharge Book: continuous record in book form issued to, and becoming property of, a seaman, by authority of U.S. Coast Guard or similar body in other countries, showing each vessel on which he has successively served, description of voyage, etc. It is in effect a combined certificate of identification and certificate of discharge.

contline: line of space between strands of a rope. Also, space between bilges of casks stowed side by side; casks or barrels are said to be stowed *bilge-and-contline* when successive tiers are laid *in the contlines* of a tier next below. Also written *cantline.*

contour: line on a chart representing points of equal value with relation to datum. It is called an isobath when connecting points of equal depth below sea level.

contour interval: difference in value between 2 adjacent contours.

Contract of Affreightment: provisions of a *bill of lading*. Chartering of a vessel or part of her cargo space while such vessel remains in charge of her owners.

controller: device for checking or holding an anchor cable.

conularians [jellyfish]: early jellyfish, typified by *Conularia*, with pyramidal, horny shell with 4 sides, each with lengthwise groove and many fine cross ridges. Tentacles extended from edge of body, reaching upward while creature was attached, but hanging downward when it became a drifter. Conchopetts departed from norm by building a shell that was low and broad with 4 lobes as in a jellyfish.

conus, conus arteriosus: portion of the heart. In primitive vertebrates it is a small thick-walled chamber which may be lined with several sets of valves; blood passing through the heart enters the conus from the ventricle and leaves the heart.

convection: in general, mass motion within fluid resulting in transport and mixing of properties of that fluid; convection, along with conduction and radiation, is principal means of energy transfer.

convergence: situation whereby waters of different origins come together at a point, or more commonly, along a line known as convergence line. Along such line dense water from one side sinks under lighter water from other side.

convergence zone: region in deep ocean where sound rays, refracted from depths, arrive at surface in successive intervals of 30 to 35 nautical miles.

convergence zone paths: velocity structure of permanent deep sound channels which produces focusing regions at distant intervals from shallow source.

convergency: referred to bearings taken by a *radio compass*, difference between a *great circle bearing*, which is that observed by such compass, and the rhumb or *mercator bearing*; also termed *conversion angle*. For laying off on the commonly used Mercator chart, a radio direction finder *(radio compass)* bearing is corrected for this difference or *convergency* by applying value thereof *toward the equator*. Thus, in *North latitude* given a radio bearing of 250° and convergency 3°, the corresponding rhumb is 247°; with radio bearing 150° we get 153° as the rhumb or Mercator bearing. Radio and Mercator bearings coincide on north and south and, in consequence, no convergency exists on these points, while its greatest values obtain in cases of high and similar latitudes of both ship and station observed.

convolute [*Foraminifera*]: coiled test in which inner portion of last whorl extends to center of the spiral and covers inner whorls.

Copelata [class]: appendicularians, as they are usually called, form a group of small pelagic tunicates, some 6 to 7 mm. long, retaining larval tunicate features of dorsal notochord in trunk region and tail. The animal is surrounded by a transparent "house" through which water is drawn by movements of tail. But the "house" is often damaged or absent in preserved material so that the animal superficially resembles larva of ascidian. There is one distinctive feature which can be used in separation of ascidian larva and appendicularian; while tail of ascidian larva is held in line with longitudinal axis of trunk, that of appendicularian is held at right angles to axis.

copepodid: immature copepod stage occurring between last naupliar stage and mature adult. Copepodids look much like adult copepods but are not sexually mature.

copepods: 1) tiny members of the crustacean subclass *Copepoda*. They are aquatic and live either as free-swimmers (providing a rich source of food for fish and other predators) or as parasites ("sea lice"). 2) these "entomostracan" crustaceans are characterized by small size, body divisible into head, thorax (bearing biramous appendages) and abdomen (devoid of appendages); head and thorax merge smoothly to foramen or fore-body; absence of shell fold or carapace; simple, median or nauplius eye with 3 ocelli. Beyond this it is difficult to make generalizations that would apply to various suborders which comprise *Copepoda*.

coquina: porous limestone composed of shells and shell fragments cemented together.

coracidium: larval stage in certain pseudophyllidean tapeworms in which egg is surrounded by ciliated or flagellated embryophore and swims freely in water.

coracle: primitive bowl-shaped, basketlike craft made of woven grasses or reeds, either oval or round.

coral: 1) hard calcareous skeleton of various anthrozoans and a few hydrozoans (millepores) or stony solidified mass of number of such skeletons. 2) coral belong to *Anthozoa*, a subclass made up of coelenterates that never go through jellyfish stage and have tubelike gullet or stomodeum, that leads from mouth to large central cavity that does work of a stomach. Tentacles are hollow, like those of *Hydra*. One group, sea anemones, have no hard parts; others build horny or strong stony structures that serve as skeletons.

coralgal: carbonate sediment derived from corals and algae.

coral head: massive mushroom or pillar-shaped coral growth.

coralline algae: one of family *(Corallinaceae)* of red algae having bushy or encrusting form and deposits of calcium carbonate either on branches or as crust in the substrate. Certain of encrusting forms, *Lithothamnion* and *Porolithon*, develop massive encrustations or coral reefs.

corallite: skeleton built by one coral animal or polyp whether solitary or part of colony.

corallite wall [*Coelenterata*]: skeletal wall forming sides of corallites and comprising various elements of such as edges of septa, epitheca or accessory deposits.

corallum [*Coelenterata*]: skeleton of colony or solitaire polyp; on latter the corallum and corallite are identical.

coral mariner: *Coelenterata*, solitary and colonial, which form hard external covering of calcium compounds or other materials. Corals which form large reefs are limited to warm shallow waters, while those forming solitary, minute growths may be found in colder waters to great depths.

coral reef: 1) ridge or mass of limestone built of detrital material deposited around framework of skeletal remains of mollusks, colonial coral and massive calcareous algae. Coral may constitute less than half of reef material. 2) calcareous structure formed of skeletons of corals, which live in colonies. Various forms of reefs are atolls, barrier reefs and fringing reefs.

coral shell: low, dome-shaped shell, oval in outline and possessing very wide aperture. Surface of shell is rough and marked with many fine transverse striae. Spire is small and usually not apparent. Outer surface of shell is white while interior is purple or violet. It ranges in length from ½ to 1¼ in. *Rhizochilus madreporarum*.

coral shell [bulb-shaped]: this mollusc bears a shell which is short and bulbous in form and a spire which is comparatively longer than that of *C. neretoidea*. Outer surface is marked by spiral ridges and longitudinal furrows. Aperture is striated within and outer lip is wrinkled. Color of shell is whitish on outside and rose within aperture. It ranges in length from ¾ to 1¼ in. *Coralliophila bulbitemis*.

coral shell [deformed]: this species is short bulbous form with small, sharp spire and very wide aperture. It is spirally striated without and exhibits some longitudinal sculpture; whitish on outside and somewhat reddish within aperture. Measures from 1 to 1½ in. *Coralliophila deformis*.

coral shell [Lamarck's]: shell of this species is elongated, somewhat spindle-shaped and composed of about 3 striated whorls in which suture is concealed. Columella is arched, elongated and bordered by oblique aperture. These molluscs are found imbedded in coral or coralline rocks. *Leptoconchus lamarchii*.

coral shell [Nerita-like]: shell of this species is swollen and bulbous in outline and bears a spire which is comparatively longer than that of *C. veolacea*; white in color without and purplish within aperture. It ranges in length from 1 to 1½ in. *Coralliophila violacea*.

coral shell [*Rapidae*]: shells within this family are mostly bulbous forms with encircling ribs. They live in shallow water and are usually found in crevices, in porous coral rocks or in colonies of living coral. These molluscs are related to *Muricidae* and are sometimes placed within that family.

corange line: line passing through places of equal tide range.

corbita: heavy-built, slow, sailing merchant ship of ancient Rome. Name was derived from Roman *"corbis"* or basket, one of which was carried at masthead to indicate that they carried merchandise and passengers. The corbita was a "round" ship with high curved stern and considerable sheer to raking stem.

cord: any small rope made by laying several strands twisted together; specifically, small hard-laid cotton, silk, or nylon line, such as is used in fishing or netmaking.

cordage: ropes, lines, wires, etc. in a collective sense; ropes constituting hawsers and running rigging of a ship.

cordate: heart-shaped.

cordillera: entire mountain system including all subordinate ranges, interior plateaus and basins.

core: 1) cylindrical sample of soil, ice, snow or rock used for scientific analysis. Usually a hollow tube (corer) is driven into the material, then removed with sample inside of it. 2) vertical cylindrical specimen of bottom sediments from which the nature and stratification of bottom may be ascertained.

core barrel: 1) hollow cylinder attached to specially designed bit and used to obtain and preserve a continuous section of core of rocks and sediments penetrated. 2) tubular section of core sampling device. Bottom sediment samples are collected either directly in core barrel or in plastic liner placed inside it. Barrel diameter may vary from 1½ in. to several inches.

core catcher: mechanical device, placed near bottom of core barrel, used to prevent cohesionless sediments from falling out during core recovery from ocean bottom.

corer: hollow tube driven into ocean floor for purpose of collecting bottom sediment sample.

corer, free fall: weighted metal tube 1.2 meters (3.9 ft.) long and 8 cm. (3.2 in.) in diameter that is allowed to free fall to floor of ocean. Outer core barrel encloses close-fitting plastic sample tube. On top of core barrel are 2 air-filled glass tubes. After core barrel enters sediment, globes are released carrying the core-filled plastic tubes to surface. Outer barrel and weights are abandoned as coring tube and globe rise to surface. The plastic sampler contains a trapdoor and keeps the sample from being disturbed or flushed out by surrounding seawater. One of the globes contains a flashing light, which makes it indispensable for night operations.

corer, gravity and piston: these corers are attached to wire by a chain which an operator lowers to bottom using oceanographic winch. Corer is weighted. At predetermined height above ocean floor, a releasing device is tripped. This allows corer to freefall through water, striking bottom with enough force to drive core barrel into sediment. The barrel has stabilizing fins on top which keeps it vertical during its plunge toward impact. At end of core barrel is a retainer which keeps core sample in the tube, or its liner, while entire device is being retrieved.

corer, hydrostatic: hydrostatic corer which forces the corer into sediment by creating a vacuum over the core. There are also hydrostatic corers that force coring barrel into bottom by pressure difference between the air within sample tube and surrounding water.

corer, impact: impact corers hammer into sediments pneumatically, by movable weights or explosive charges.

core sample: sample of rock, soil, snow or ice obtained by driving hollow tube into the medium and withdrawing it with its contained sample or core.

Corethron [phytoplankton]: cells with rounded ends and numerous spines some of which serve to join up the cells.

coring: taking core or cylindrical samples of soil, ice, snow or rock for scientific analysis. Usually hollow tube is driven into the material, then removed with sample inside it.

coring [rotary drilling technique]: continuous length of pipe made of joined sections, each 9 meters (29.5 ft.) long and 8 cm. (3.2 in.) in diameter is lowered vertically to bottom of sea. This pipe is weighted at the bottom; it rotates, cutting through sediments with diamond-studded drill tip. Twin sliding joints directly above drill act as shock absorbers when corer strikes bottom. Rotary table on board ship or drilling platform turns entire pipe. As drill bit cuts into sediment, drill is cooled by seawater pumped into pipe. To obtain a core, operator releases a 6-meter (19.7-ft.) core cylinder inside the pipe, that plunges to ocean floor. Core cylinder catches sediment internally. As drill bites into ocean bottom, sections of steel casing slide down around

pipe shaft to prevent collapse of surrounding area.

Coriolis force, effect: 1) phenomenon which causes moving object (seawater) to be deflected because of earth's rotation. In Northern Hemisphere, deflection is to right; in Southern Hemisphere, to left. This force has considerable influence on tidal section and major water currents. 2) effect of earth's rotation that causes deflection of moving objects everywhere except at Equator.

corita: large, basketlike "coracle" formerly used by Indians of south central California and lower Colorado River for fording streams with passengers and merchandise.

Cor Leonis: the star Regulus *(Alpha Leonis) (a Leonis)*.

cormidium: in *Siphonophora*, group or colony of individuals borne together on coenosarc of stalk. In some species cormidia are easily detached and usually found separately in plankton hauls.

cormorants [shags]: seabirds comprising this family have long necks, rather bony wings and superficially resemble ducks. Their bills are, however, very different from those of ducks, being slender and cylindrical with sharp hook at tip of upper mandible. Legs are very short and placed far back; large feet have all 4 toes united in a web. Tails are web-shaped, usually rather long and composed of 12 stiff feathers. A region around eye on side of face and small pouch on throat are usually unfeathered and often brightly colored.

cornea: transparent coat covering outside of an eye.

corner boat: skipjack type called "corner boat" at Provincetown, Massachusetts, because topside meets bottom at angle, or chine, forming a corner. It is a compromise between flat-bottom and round-bottom boat.

Cornwall driver: lug-rigged fishing ketch of Cornwall, England, with double headsails.

corona: one or more colored circles sometimes seen close to and around the sun or moon. The phenomenon is produced by diffraction through suspended particles of ice or water droplets at high altitude and often is seen in an intervening *cirrostratus* cloud.

Corona Australis: southern constellation, also called *Corolla*, or *The Wreath*, adjoining and north of *Sagittarius*. It contains no navigational stars.

Corona Borealis: northern constellation adjoining and east of *Bootes*. It contains the bright star *Alphacca (a Coronae Borealis)*, magnitude 2.3; declination 27° n.; right ascension 15 hrs. 32 min.

coronal constriction: in jellyfish of order *Coronatae*, circular constriction of the bell.

coronal pores: in some *Radiolaria*, small pores surrounding the parmal pores.

corposant: ball of light of flamelike appearance sometimes seen running along stays and intermittently flashing or moving about prominent parts of a ship, particularly at the trucks, yardarms, and jibboom end, under certain atmospheric conditions immediately before or during a storm; called also *corpse light, St. Elmo's fire* or *light, dead fire, jack o' lantern*, and *Castor and Pollux.*

corrected establishment: mean high-water interval for all stages of tide.

correction: quantity applied to a given magnitude in order to obtain its exact value, as a *sextant index-error;* a reduction allowance to convert a changing value to that required at a given time, as *an hourly variation in declination of the sun.* Also, procedure involved in application of such errors or allowances, as *correction of an altitude.*

correction for datum: conversion factor used in prediction of tides to resolve the difference between chart datum of reference station.

corresponding speeds: in naval architectural design experiments, speeds at which a model of a proposed hull is towed in observing hull resistance, wave-making, steering, etc. expected in vessel's performance, as considered with questions of requisite economical powering to be installed. Such speeds are proportional to the square roots of linear dimensions of ship and model; thus, a 400-ft. vessel moving at 12 knots is represented by her 25-ft. model at a speed of 3 knots, since $\sqrt{400} : \sqrt{25} = 12:3.$

corrosion: mechanical erosion performed by moving agents such as wear by glacial wind, running water, etc., but is generally restricted to basal rather than lateral excavation.

corsair: referring to pirate or to type of sleek-lined ship much used by pirates because of its speed.

cortical shell: in some *Radiolaria*, portion of skeleton forming outer framework.

corvette: ship common in French navy. It was a "sloop of war" with low freeboard, no high quarter-deck and guns were carried on upper deck.

Corvus: small constellation south of *Virgo* in about 20° south declination and 12¼ hrs. right ascension, often called the *Cutter's Mainsail* from its outline; also called the *Crow* and the *Raven*. A line joining its 2 northern stars and forming the gaff or head of the "Mainsail" extended outward meets, at 10° distance, bright star *Spica* (*a* Virginis).

coryphaena: genus of large fast-swimming acanthopterygian fishes found in tropical and temperate seas, commonly known as *dolphins*. (Not to be confused with a *cetacean* of same name.)

Coscinodiscus [phytoplankton]: simple, disclike cells with curved edges united to form straight chains with ornamentation of roughly hexagonal markings and numerous small chloroplasts.

cosine collector: in underwater optics a light collector which accepts radiant flux in accordance with the cosine law.

cosine-haversine formula: in spherical trigonometry, used to find value of a third side when 2 sides and included angle are known, as in calculating an *altitude* of a heavenly body at a given instant, or a *great circle distance* between 2 geographical points. The formula may be stated thus: Given sides *a* and *b*, with angle *C*, in triangle *ABC:* to find *c*; then,

   hav c = hav (a ↳ b) + hav θ
   [*hav θ = sin a. sin b. hav C*],

θ being an auxiliary arc, and, where *a* and *b* are complements of latitudes or declinations, as in navigational use, *sin a. sin b* becomes *cos(90°-a). cos (90°-b).*

cosmic sediment: particles of extraterrestrial origin identified in deep-sea sediments as black magnetic spherules.

costa: 1) ridge on surface of coral or shell. The costae of shells are radial ridges produced by thickening. 2) external radial ridge on pelecypod shell. 3) in *Gastropoda*, ridge on surface of shell, either parallel to axis of coiling or to border of spiral.

costae [*Brachiopoda*]: ridges on external surface of valve that extend radially from beak. Costae do not involve any folding of inner surface of shell.

cotidal: pertaining to coincidence in time of high water at various places in a coastal area.

cotidal chart: chart of cotidal lines that shows approximate locations of high water at hourly intervals measured from reference meridian, usually Greenwich.

cotidal hour: average interval expressed in solar or lunar hours between moon's passage over meridian of Greenwich and the following high water at specified place.

cotidal lines: lines on a map or chart passing through all points at which high waters occur at same time. Lines show lapse of time, usually in lunar-hour intervals, between moon's transit of Greenwich meridian and occurrence of high water for any point lying along the line.

Coulter's seaweed [*Agardhiella coulteri*]: widely distributed at 1- to 1.5-ft. tide levels in tide pools. This seaweed is conspicuous bright pink to dark red. Its outstanding feature is the neat, smooth surface of the many fleshy branches. Shoots become 12 to 15 or more inches long.

When a number of shoots arise from same holdfast, they form dense clusters. Holdfast is disc-shaped organ growing one to several fleshy roots.

counter: 1) overhang of stern above waterline. 2) special gear box indicating amount of oceanographic wire passed over sheave of meter wheel. The counter may be mounted directly on meter wheel or connected by a flexible cable.

counter [ships]: that part of ship's stern which overhangs sternpost.

countercurrent: secondary current adjacent to and setting in direction opposite to main current.

counter lateral septum [*Coelenterata*]: one of a pair of initial septa next to counter septum. No secondary septa are developed between counter and counter lateral septa.

counterradiation: downward flux of atmospheric radiation passing through given level surface, usually taken as earth's surface and more specifically in oceanography, sea surface.

counter septum [*Coelenterata*]: one of initial septa directly opposite cardinal septum in plane of bilateral symmetry. Distinguished by position of cardinal when that can be determined.

couple, righting: referred to ship stability, the equal and opposing forces of gravity and buoyancy acting, respectively, through extremities of the *righting arm*, or horizontal separation of center of buoyancy from center of gravity, due to a vessel's heel. The moment of force in such couple, tending to restore a vessel to the upright, is equal to her displacement times length of righting arm, expressed in foot-tons.

courache: early Irish "coracle." Oval-shaped, covered with hide, tarred canvas or made of wicker, it carried but one person and was fitted with a pair of oars.

course [ships]: square sail set from lower yard of square-rigged vessel.

course signal: in International Code procedure, a course is expressed in 3 figures denoting degrees from 000 to 359 measured clockwise, and is always considered *true*, unless expressly stated to be otherwise; thus, hoist *E B X*, meaning *"My present course is,"* followed by the numeral hoist *0 1 7*, indicates *"My present course is seventeen degrees true."*

cove: small bay or baylike recess in coast, usually affording anchorage and shelter to small craft.

covert [birds]: one of special small feathers covering base of flight feathers.

cowfish: named for pair of hornlike spines, one over each eye. In addition, 3 large spines on each side of the tail point backward. Cowfish are yellowish with irregular blue horizontal stripes, yellow dorsal and anal fins. Small mouth bears strong teeth capable of crushing coral hiding

places of worms and other small invertebrates. Cowfish swim in slow stately fashion vibrating small rudderlike tail fin much as one sculls a boat with an oar. Pectoral fins act as stabilizers keeping cowfish from being propelled forward as water is ejected from gill opening. Cowfish average 10 to 12 in. in length.

cow pilot: small banded and brilliantly colored coral reef fish found in West Indian waters; also, *cockeye pilot.*

cowrie or cowry: small colored gastropod seashell, tortoise-backed, and having its mouth in the middle and full length of its ventral side. Smaller species of cowries were formerly used as money in many parts of Africa and southern Asia.

cowry, Anna's: some individuals regard this cowry as a broad, heavy, flattened variety of *Cypraea semiplota.* Although it resembles this species in many ways, it differs from *C. semiplota* in shape and to lesser degree in color pattern. Reaches to ½ in. in length.

cowry, Arabian: Arabian cowry is large and heavy shell, somewhat inflated and marginal at base; brownish in color above, marked with light brown areas and wavy interrupted longitudinal lines; white below except at angles of shell and on teeth. It will reach a length of from 1½ to 3 in. *Cypraea arabica.*

cowry, checkered [*Cypraea tesselata*]: checkered cowry has a shell which is thick and heavy, inflated in center and margined about base; yellowish-brown color above and marked on each side by 2 large dark brown spots; brownish in color beneath and teeth are somewhat orange in color. It ranges in length from ¾ to 1¼ in.

cowry, chick pea [*Cypraea cicercula*]: this little cowry is most easily recognized by the fact that extremities are drawn out at both ends to form slender processes; globular in shape with humped appearance and grooved in middle of shell above; glossy yellowish-white above and blotched with brown; the sides are dotted with brown. It ranges from ½ to ¾ in. in length.

cowry, Chinese [*Cypraea chinensis*]: upper surface of this cowry is bluish-white and marked with light orange-brown reticulation; sides are creamy white and marked by round purple spots. Teeth of outer lip extend on to lower surface of shell while teeth of inner lip are limited to aperture. Teeth are white with bright orange interstices. It will reach a length of about 1½ in.

cowry, cylindrical [*Cypraea cylindrica*]: this cylindrical cowry was named for its elongated shape. It is species of medium size with sides and extremities marginal, with large outer teeth and with smaller inner teeth which may extend partway over base of shell. It is bluish above and marked over surface by many fine brownish spots and by large, dark, irregularly-shaped blotch; 2 dark brownish spots at each end of the upper surface; inner surface is white. Reaches length of 1½ in.

cowry [*cypraeid*]: cowries are favorite group with shell collectors because of polished enamel surface and beautiful color patterns. They have solid, firm shells which are of inflated oval-shape above and generally flat below. Aperture is narrow and marginal by teeth on both sides, extends entire length of lower surface and terminates at each end in narrow canal. Mantles of cowries consist of 2 lobes which extend from bottom lip over sides of shell to meet top. This mantle is responsible for beautiful exterior of shell. All cowries have spiral pattern of growth which is more apparent in younger animals. This family is a tropical group and is not found in colder waters; worldwide in distribution.

cowry, eroded [*Cypraea erosa*]: this cowry shell is oval in outline, somewhat flattened and bears a strong margin about base; grayish-brown above and speckled over entire upper surface with small white spots and also by larger and less numerous brown spots. Shell is also marked in side about the middle with large conspicuous dark brownish rectangular spot.

cowry, flesh-colored or carnelian [*Cypraea carneola*]: shell of this cowry is somewhat cylindrical in shape and fairly heavy; flesh-colored above and crossed by 4 or 5 bands of deeper hue. Base and sides of shell are very dull yellowish color; teeth are stained purple. It ranges in length from 1 to 3 in.

cowry, fringed: fringed cowry has small, oval shell with flat base which is somewhat marginal; teeth are quite small and aperture becomes wider anteriorly. It is light bluish above with large central darker area; finely speckled above with brown and marked above with 2 brown spots at each extremity; whitish below. It is ½ to 1 in. long.

cowry, Gaskoin's [*Cypraea gaskoini*]: oval, fairly solid species margined about base and which has strong teeth. It is straw-yellow above and marked over entire upper surface with brown-ringed white spots; sides are dotted with brown; from ½ to ¾ in. long.

cowry, grape or grape shot [*Cypraea staphylaea*]: this cowry is small oval species resembling *C. poraria* in some respects. Specimens which have not developed pustules upon them so closely resemble *C. poraria* that they cannot be easily distinguished from them. Unlike *C. poraria*, teeth of this species extend over base forming grooves and ridges. This is variable species ranging from gray to brown and bears white pustules tipped with reddish brown in varying stages of development and prominence and reaches a length of about 1 in.

cowry, grooved tooth [*Cypraea sulcidentata*]: shell of this mollusc is heavy in texture and swollen in outline bearing narrow aperture with very deep grooves between teeth. It is dull tawny color above and often marked with bands; lighter in color beneath. It measures from 1 to 2 in. in length.

cowry, half-swimmer [*Cypraea semiplota*]: shell of this cowry is small, oval, margined and has narrow aperture. It is olive-brown above and marked over upper surface by many small white spots; light in color below with yellowish aperture. Will reach length of about ¾ in.

cowry, Isabella [*Cypraea isabella*]: Isabella cowry is very light in weight, cylindrical in form with narrow aperture and many teeth. It is bluish above and faintly banded and marked by small black longitudinal spots; marked with deep red at extremities; undersurface is white. Ranges in length from ¾ to 1½ in.

cowry, Jester [*Cypraea scurra*]: jester cowry is of medium size, somewhat cylindrical in form, slightly elongated at ends and bears fine numerous teeth. It is bluish-gray color and covered by reticulated pattern of brown lines; sides are brownish and speckled with black spots.

cowry, Lynx [*Cypraea lynx*]: Lynx cowry has heavy pear-shaped shell with narrow flat base. It is whitish above, but very thickly spotted and covered with brownish, yellowish, and bluish colors; sides and base of shell are white; tinged with red beneath teeth. It varies in length from ¾ to 2½ in.

cowry, Madagascar [*Cypraea granulata*]: Madagascar cowry is flattened, oval in outline and usually bears a margin about base of shell. Upper surface is covered by modules; lower surface is marked by transverse ridges which on outer lip may be alternately larger and smaller. It is brownish and whitish in color. Reaches length of little more than 1 in.

cowry, Mauritius [*Cypraea mauritiana*]: Mauritius cowry is large, heavy species with somewhat angular sides, large teeth and characteristic hump upon upper surface of shell. It is brownish above and marked by light brown spots; entire lower surface is darker in color. It ranges from 2½ in. to 4 in. in length.

cowry, mole [*Cypraea talpa*]: mole cowry is large species with heavy, cylindrical, polished shell. It is pale yellow-brown above and crossed above by 3 light transverse bands; very dark brown or black beneath and marked by white within aperture and between teeth. It ranges in length from 2 to nearly 4 in.

cowry, money [*Cypraea monetal*]: money cowry has shell of medium size which is somewhat flattened and triangular in shape; margins are thick and often bear tubercles at base. It is usually yellowish above and below and often contains white over large areas of shell; it is sometimes marked above by faint red ring. Ranges from ½ to 1½ in.

cowry, nuclear [*Cypraea nucleus*]: this little cowry is oval in outline and has extremities of shell extended as pair of blunt processes. Upper surface is covered by nodules, many of which are connected by narrow ridges; base of shell is covered by transverse ridges. It is whitish and marked with brown; ½ to ¾ in.

cowry, ostergaard [*Cypraea ostergaardi*]: this cowry is small, oval in outline and pitted along margin. Teeth are small and extend only short way onto base. It is whitish and is evenly marked above with brown spots; base is white. It varies in length from ½ to ¾ in.

cowry, porous [*Cypraea poraria*]: this cowry is quite thick, small in size, oval in shape and slightly marginal about base. It is brownish-purple color and is covered over upper surface by small white spots most of which are set within larger brownish spot; sides and much of base are violet color; teeth are white. Reaches 1 in.

cowry, Rashleigh's [*Cypraea rashleighana*]: this cowry is small, somewhat oval, slightly flattened species which bears small margin about base. It is quite oval in outline beneath and exhibits fairly wide aperture and medium-sized teeth. It is light grayish-brown above and marked above with 1, 2, 3 or 4 interrupted brownish bands; marked above margins by small brownish spots; entirely white beneath. It approaches ¾ in. in length.

cowry, red or honey-colored [*Cypraea helvola*]: red cowry is small, oval-flattened, marginal species with large teeth which extend into outer lip. It is brownish above and marked over upper surface by many small white spots and larger brown spots; reddish-brown color over entire undersurface. Reaches ½ to 1½ in.

cowry, reticulated [*Cypraea naculifera*]: reticulated cowry has large, heavy, somewhat inflated shell which is strongly marginal on sides. It is brownish above with many regularly spaced, round light-colored spots; large dark spot is present on inner lip. It ranges from 1½ to 3 in. in length.

cowry, ring [*Cypraea annulata*]: ring cowry is oval in outline and plump in form with smooth surface and with very fine teeth along aperture. It is a whitish ivory color and marked over upper surface by yellowish spots which are encircled by slightly darker colored rings; lower side or base of shell is entirely white. Measures ½ in. long.

cowry, Schilder's: sandy cowry has heavy shell which is oval and flattened in shape; narrow aperture and marginal at edges. It is dusky-blue above

and crossed by 4 reddish bands; sides are ashy-brown; base and teeth are white. It ranges in length from 1 to 1½ in.

cowry, sieve [*Cypraea cribaria*]: this cowry is medium-sized species of light weight and beautiful design. It is yellowish-brown above and marked over entire upper surface with round white spots; entire base, extremities and sides are white. It will reach length of about 1¼ in.

cowry, smooth or tapering [*Cypraea teres*]: this cowry shell is elongated, small in size, depressed at base, marginal in right side and has narrow aperture and small teeth. It is whitish in color and crossed above by 3 poorly defined bands of short, wavy, longitudinal, pale brown lines. It ranges in length from ¾ to 1 in.

cowry, snakehead [*Cypraea caputserpentis*]: snakehead cowry is oval in outline, flattened design and has well developed teeth. It is deep reddish-brown around sides, white on extremities and on teeth and covered over upper surface by large number of white spots of various sizes. Large adult specimens will approach an inch in length.

cowry, tiger [*Cypraea tigris*]: shell of tiger cowry is larger in size, oval in shape, inflated in outline, with flatly concave base and with large teeth. It is highly polished species, white and yellow above and marked with large black spots; base is white. This species, one of largest in family, ranges from 2½ to 5 in.

cowry, york or little calf [*Cypraea vitellus*]: york cowry has thick shell which is oval in outline, large teeth and base which is somewhat rounded. Shell is olive-brown and marked with white spots; pure white beneath. Ranges in length from 1½ to 2½ in.

coxa: in *Arthropoda*, basal segment of one of joined appendages; in biramous appendages, first segment radiole of basipodite.

coxswain [ships]: sailor who has responsibility for ship's boat.

crabber: small open sailboat used in setting out and collecting crabs from "crab pots." Crabbers were 20 to 23 ft. long, with lug or sloop rig, depending on locality.

crab, blood-spotted swimming [*Portunus sanguinolentus*]: this is a large edible, shoreline species. Carapace is smooth, convex and marked at lateral border by very large spine; 4 spines between eyes and 8 spines between eyes and large lateral spine. Rear of carapace is marked by 3 large, conspicuous red spots. Last pair of legs is flattened for swimming.

crab-clar: oceanic lateen sail, resembling claw of crab in shape, made of matting and supported between 2 curved yards.

crab, coconut [*Birgus latro*]: this hermit crab is believed to be world's largest land crab. Its body exceeds 12 in. in length and it weighs several pounds. Pinchers and walking legs are firm, hard and strong and covered with spines and bristles; carapace is harder and more calcified than that of most hermit crabs and abdomen is shortened and of leathery texture. Entire body is reddish color.

crab, convex pebble [*Carpilius convexus*]: very hard and very heavy shell covers body and legs of this pebble crab. Carapace is smooth, convex, oval in outline and without spines; back is marbled and blotched with red and contains lighter areas which are white or gray. Chelipeds are unequal in size. Body is about 3 in. wide.

crab, crenate swimming [*Thalamita crenata*]: this thalamitid crab is one of larger species of the genus and often measures more than 3½ in. across carapace. It can be identified by 6 nearly equal, rounded lobes along anterior margin of carapace between eyes and 5 sharp spines behind eye on each side. Chelipeds or pinchers are quite large and strong. This crab inhabits shallow waters of shoreline where it frequents mouths of rivers and broad muddy flats.

crab, five-toothed swimming [*Lupocyclus quinquidentatus*]: name of this crab is taken from 5 anterolateral spines which border carapace on each side just posterior to eyes. There are also 6 pointed teeth along anterior margin of carapace between eyes. Uppersurface of carapace is almost entirely red and marked with scattered, mottled, lighter areas. Walking legs and swimming legs are banded with alternating red and white; each cheliped is marked with white stripe across pincher. Entire lower surface of body is white.

crab, flat rock [*Percnon planissimum*]: this little crab is very flat in shape and measures little more than 1 in. across carapace. It is green above and marked with a line down middle of back; merus of thigh of walking legs is bordered in front by row of sharp spines.

crab, gemmate hermit [*Dardanus gemmatus*]: gemmate hermit crab gets its name from rough tubercled outer surface of left pincher. Body is marked with yellow and brown in irregular manner; walking legs which are lighter near joints are encircled by darker band between joints. Eyes are somewhat club-shaped and encircled by light band toward end. Body measures from 3 to 6 in. in length. This crustacean lives on outer edge of reef at depths which are usually in excess of 30 or 40 ft.

crab, granular box [*Cyclos granulosa*]: carapace of box crab is somewhat pear-shaped in outline and entire uppersurface is covered with granules and small tubercles. Its length, 1 to 2 in., is somewhat greater than width. Members of genus *Cycloes* lack wide, lateral, winglike extensions of carapace which are found in genus *Calappa*. Cheli-

peds, as in other box crabs, are enlarged and fit together to cover front of body; walking legs are simple and unadorned. Coloration of this animal resembles sandy area in which it lives.

crab, hairy anemone [*Polydectus cupulifer*]: entire body and legs of this crab are covered with thick coat of long, yellowish hair. The body reaches width of at least 1 in. This little crab usually carries a sea anemone in each of its pinchers. These anemones are held firmly by crab and are thought to be used to ward off real or imaginary enemies.

crab, hairy swimming [*Portunus pubescene*]: this crab is so named because body and legs are covered with hairs. Carapace is covered with small, short hairs and edges of walking legs are quite thickly fringed with hair. Front edge of carapace is almost circular in outline, bearing 4 blunt teeth between eyes and 9 spines on each side of eyes of which 8 are almost equal in size and 9th, or last, is a little larger.

crab, hepatic box [*Calappa hepatica*]: in this box crab the carapace is very broad and bears usual winglike projections which extend over legs. Anterior half of carapace is covered with rounded tubercles and posterior half is covered with flattened tubercles and small beady ridges; anterolateral margin of carapace is bordered with 10 or 12 teeth; 4 or 5 teeth on front margin of part of carapace covering legs; rear border of carapace is nearly a continuous curve. Front face of chelipeds is covered with tubercles. Large specimens reach 4 in. in width. It lives on sandy or shelly bottoms, from waters' edges down to depths of at least 150 ft.

crab, horny-eyed ghost [*Ocypode ceratophthalma*]: carapace of this species is rectangular and has beady surface. Chelipeds are unequal in size, quite short and flattened to aid in carrying sand. Body measures nearly 2 in. across carapace. This crab is named for horn at end of eyestalk.

crab, horrid parthenopid [*Parthenope horrida*]: like most parthenopid crabs, surface of this species is rough. It is covered with rough elevations and depressions and with smaller tubercles and pits. Chelipeds are usually unequal in size; walking legs bear spines which grow in such a way that they form a perforated margin along upper edge of leg. Carapace is somewhat 5-sided and 4 in. wide.

crab, Japanese homolid [*Homola parhomola japonica*]: a large, deepwater species. Carapace is pear-shaped in outline, convex above, rough in texture and covered with small spines which become larger toward margin. Walking legs are long and slender; chelipeds are long and slender and tipped with blue-black pinchers; first 3 pairs of walking legs are about equal size; last pair of legs is smaller and placed on upper surface of body at rear of carapace and above fourth pair of legs. Entire body is sandy-colored except for tips of pinchers.

crab, large box [*Calappa calappa*]: has wide, wing-like expansion of carapace extending outward from body on both sides and covering walking legs. Carapace of this crab has surface which is smooth in front and covered in rear with short, horizontal ridges; posterior edge of carapace is one unbroken curve. Chelipeds are held close to front of body and fit together precisely forming complete covering for front of crab; marked on anterior edge by long, longitudinal, wavey ridges. Uppersurface of crab is sandy or cream-colored, while entire underside is white. Has width of at least 6 in.

crab, large, flat, hermit [*Aniculus maximus*]: all species of *Aniculus* have flattened body and carapace. In this species anterior parts of carapace have central area marked out by 4 straight lines, resembling shape of arrowhead; central area has its acute angle pointed forward. This is a very large species with tufts of hair growing from most areas. Legs are ringed by scutes or scales from which many brittle hairs emerge; eyestalks are long and slender. Body of this crab is orange-yellow and tips of legs are black. Carapace reaches as much as 6 in. in length. The home of this crab is on outer edge of reefs at depths below 100 ft.

crab, large red hermit [*Dardanus megistos*]: this hermit crab is one of very largest species in this family. Usually from 6 to 8 in. long, it sometimes reaches total length of over a foot. Body is reddish, and carapace with adjoining areas of legs and abdomen are covered with white circular spots which are ringed with black; legs are covered with black, bristly hairs; pinchers and ends of legs are tipped with black. This large red hermit crab inhabits deep waters on outer side of reefs; rarely caught at less than 50 ft. and most often at greater depths.

crab, left-handed hermit [*Caloinus laevimanus*]: although a small species, this hermit crab is easily identified by its legs: left cheliped is by far the larger, nearly circular in outline and white in color and walking legs are also tipped and banded white. Body of this crab measures from 2 to 3 in. long and is reddish. This crab is found in tropical and subtropical waters and has one or more of these small crabs beneath it.

crab, long-eyed swimming [*Podophthalmus vigil*]: easily identified by astonishing pair of eyes borne upon unusually long eyestalks. These eyes and stalks may be held erect above body or horizontally in groove along front of carapace. Back of carapace is smooth, wider in front than behind

bearing strong spine at its sides. Chelipeds are rather slender and armed with spines. Reaches width of over 5 in. across carapace; brown in color.

crab, long-spined parthenopid: carapace or shell of this crab is covered with tubercles and short spines. Front legs or chelipeds are large and covered with tubercles and spines, of which those along angles of these legs are triangular; walking legs are slender, quite smooth and marked by encircling bands of color. Carapace measures about 2 in. in width.

crab, Pacific mole [*Emerita pacifica*]: bodies of mole crabs are oval in outline, somewhat flattened vertically and are specialized for burrowing backwards through sand. Flattened walking legs are specialized for digging, while first pair of legs is almost straight and lacks pinchers found on most other decapods. Abdomen is small and folded forward under body; end of abdomen or telson is very large, smooth, triangular and ends in a point not far from mouth of crab. Mole crabs live in damp, sandy beaches burrowing in sand just beneath surface at water's edge.

crab pot: nearly cubical cage made of wire mesh. It has several conical funnels through which crabs gain entry in bottom, finer mesh receptacle for bait in center and at top there are 2 more funnels leading to another compartment which confuses and traps the crab. These pots can hold 30 or more crabs.

crab, red frog [*Ranina ranina*]: only known species of this genus. Carapace is broad in front, narrower toward rear, convex in contour and armed with spines along front margin. Back is almost completely covered by large number of small, low, rounded spines; abdomen is small and not hidden beneath carapace. Entire body and legs are adapted for burrowing backwards in sand. This crab is red above and below with large white areas on lower side. Carapace reaches length and width of at least 6 in.

crab, red-legged [*Charybdis erythrodactyla*]: striking color and easily identifiable. Recognized by blue spots upon yellowish-red carapace and bright red legs. Carapace is marked with 6 blunt teeth along margin between eyes. Anterolateral border bears 7 teeth of which 2nd and 4th are very small; 5 larger teeth are sharp and point forward.

crab, red porcelain [*Petrolisthes cinctipes*]: this crab is flat having large flattened chelipeds. Of 4 pairs of walking legs, first 3 pairs are of normal size, while last pair is small and slender and located on uppersurface of body at back of carapace. Carapace is somewhat circular in outline, bluntly pointed at front and marked by short transverse ridges. Legs have spines on anterior margin, but no pairs. Body is red and about ½ in. wide. This species inhabits rocks and old coral beds in shallow water.

crab, sea cucumber [*Lissocarcinus orbicularis*]: this little swimming crab has rather smooth, oval carapace measuring about ½ in. in diameter and bearing 5 lobes upon its anterolateral margin. It is symmetrically mottled above with light and dark areas varying in color from almost black through purple to brown; lighter areas range from light yellow to white. Although this crab belongs in family of swimming crabs *(Portunidae)*, it does not swim and does not have fifth leg flattened as do other members of this family.

crab, serrate swimming [*Seylla serrata*]: carapace of this large active crab is smooth above and bordered along front margin by 4 spines between eyes and by 9 spines on lateral side of each eye. Carapace in large males sometimes measures over 9 in. in width, and in these large crabs chelipeds are enormous. Upperparts of body are brown, while lower surfaces are nearly white.

crab, shining red pebble [*Etisus splendidus*]: carapace of this crab is smooth, oval in outline, variously grooved and furrowed and bordered by spines on lateral margin. There are few spines on chelipeds and walking legs are edged with stiff black hairs. Body is dark red and ends of pinchers are black. Carapace reaches 5 in. in width.

crab, short-eyed hermit [*Dardanus brachyops*]: this beautiful crustacean is second largest hermit crab in Hawaii and one of world's rarest. Upper parts of body are buff and creamy-white, carapace is marked with darker orange areas and lines and undersurface of body and legs is almost white in color. Legs of this crab are covered over upper and outer surfaces with spines and tufts of stiff orange hair; chelipeds are tipped with black; walking legs terminate in black-tipped claw. Antennae are bright orange-red color. Body measures more than 8 in. long. This crab is seldom seen because it inhabits deep water on outside of reefs.

crab, simple spider [*Simocarinus simplex*]: in this species males and females differ from each other in body shape. Males have carapace, triangular in outline and longer rostrum or beak. In females, rostrum is shorter, carapace more rectangular and chelipeds smaller than those of males. Body of this crab is about 1 in. long. Entire body is same brown color as seaweed in which it lives.

crab, sleepy sponge [*Dromidiopsis dormia*]: this sponge crab is a large species which may measure as much as 8 in. across carapace. Entire body is covered with brown fuzz, usually longest on inner surface of chelipeds. Legs are unequal in size and used for different purposes: front pair of legs bears pair of beautiful ivory-white pinchers, 2nd and 3rd pairs of legs are about equal size and used for walking and 4th and 5th pairs are smaller in size and do not touch ground. Eyes are small and beady, black in color. Entire body is brown.

crab, spiny handed box [*Mursia spinimanus*]: box crabs of this genus have oval-shaped carapace bearing large, sharp spine at lateral edge. They lack winglike extension of carapace which covers legs of genus *Calappa*. Back of this species is marked with low tubercles arranged in longitudinal rows and with pair of longitudinal grooves near posterior edge. Long, sharp spine projects outward from lateral joint of chelipeds.

crab, spiny spider [*Hyastenus spinosus*]: body of this spider crab is pear-shaped and bears a few blunt spines. There are 4 blunt spines in midline of back and single, laterally directed spine on each side of carapace just behind widest point. Carapace measures about 1½ in. at widest point. Entire body is brown and usually covered to varying degree with marine growth including sponges, algae and hydroids.

crab, spotted pebble [*Capilius maculatus*]: most distinguishing feature is the very hard and very heavy shell covering entire body and legs. Carapace is convex, smooth, oval in outline and without spines. The species is easily recognized by 11 large round red spots which mark back. Of these spots, 3 form crosswise row in middle of back, 4 form row across rear of carapace and 2 are located behind eyes.

crab, telescope-eyed ghost [*Macrophthalmus telescopicus*]: most remarkable feature of this ghost crab is pair of very long eyestalks. Carapace is oval in shape; chelipeds are small, flat, thin, pointed and channeled on lower sides; walking legs are slender and somewhat pointed. Third and fourth pair of legs are fringed with hair at anterior border, while fifth leg is fringed with hair at both anterior and posterior borders.

crab, tessellated anemone [*Lybia tesselata*]: this anemone crab has carapace which is somewhat hexagonal in shape, smooth and marked with yellow, pink and brown. Back is covered with maze of irregular lines and legs are marked with narrow bands of purple. Body is about 1½ in. wide. This crab has interesting habit of carrying small anemones on its pinchers and using these anemones to ward off crabs and other animals which it fears.

crab, three-toothed frog [*Lyreidus tridentatus*]: this little frog crab has convex carapace with smooth surface and smooth border except for single small spine on each side. Carapace is widest near middle and becomes quite narrow at front with sides almost straight from lateral spine to eye. Entire animal is orange. This is a small species in which carapace seldom measures over 2 in. long. Name of this crab is taken from 3 spines upon each pincher.

crab, tuberculate rock [*Plagusia depressa tuberculata*]: carapace of this grapsoid crab is nearly circular in outline and covered with smooth, low, rounded tubercles; it bears spines along margin lateral to eyes. Pinchers are small, usually unequal in size and carried in front of body. Merus or thigh of each walking leg is flattened and bears spine at forward outer edge. Carapace reaches width of more than 2 in.

crab, two-horned box [*Calappa bicarnis*]: this box crab has very rough carapace, covered with grooves, prominences, depressions and tubercles. Teeth along anterolateral margin of carapace are small and unequal in size; larger tooth is located just lateral to each eye socket. There are 3 spines on front edge of winglike expansion over legs and 4th spine on rear edge. Body is mottled yellow, orange, white and brown; legs are quite uniformly orange in color. Its overall width is about 2½ in.

crab, weak-shelled rock [*Grapus grapsus tenuicrustatus*]: carapace of this crab contains no lobes on margin between eyes. Each eye is protected at lateral edge by sharp spine which projects forward. Pinchers of first pair of legs are small, usually of different sizes and carried in front of body; remaining legs are wide and flattened. Carapace reaches width of 2¾ in.

crack: any fracture or rift in sea ice not sufficiently wide to be described as a lead.

cradle [ships]: framing built up on ways in which ship rests while being launched.

craft: 1) vessel or boat; vessels of any kind, especially smaller types, in a collective sense. **2)** gear or tackle used in catching fish or whaling, especially the latter, collectively.

cran: measure of herrings, amounting to between 900 and 1,300 according to size, average number being about 1,000 herrings.

Crangon allmani [*Crangonidae*]: larvae of this species are larger than those of *C. vulgaris*, being 2.5 mm. long in first and 6.5 mm. in final stage. Chief points of difference between larvae of 2 species are absence of dorsal spine in posterior margin of third abdominal segment in C. allmani and enormous size of lateral spines on fifth abdominal segment.

Crangon vulgaris [*Crangonidae*]: larvae of this species, commonest of shrimp are especially common in spring in inshore plankton. Even first stage zoea is large (2 mm.) and last stage mysis is about 6.5 mm. long. The 3 maxillipeds have natatory exopodites, but remaining thoracic appendages (legs) do not begin to appear until third stage larva and are not all present until fifth stage. Even then third and fourth legs lack natatory exopodite. Inner ramus of antennule is an unjointed spine. Antennal scale is unjointed and

there is a large dorsal spine in posterior margin of third abdominal segment.

craniacea: *Brachiopoda;* aberrant forms in which shell is subcircular, punctate and of calcium carbonate. Fixation by cementing of ventral valve to foreign body; adults lack pedicle foramen; dorsal valve more or less conical.

cranial crest [*amphibian*]: knobby protuberance in top of head of toads.

craniate: animal with braincase of bone or cartilage. Same as vertebrates.

crappie: chunky, basslike fish greenish or olive-brown in color and distinctively barred. In profile, the back slopes down suddenly to head which projects into snout.

crappie, black [calico bass]: small fish usually under 8 in. long and rarely weighing over 2 lbs. Maximum size and weight for this species is 19 in. and 5 lbs. Black crappies are fish of streams and lakes with abundant vegetation. It feeds on insects and their larvae and minnows. Found from Great Lakes south to New Jersey and southwest to Texas.

crappie, white: small size and habits same as black crappie. Light-colored fish with irregular markings; common in streams and lakes from Mississippi River to Rocky Mountains. Have been introduced into California.

craspedote: having a velum, small shelf of tissue forming inward directed ring from edge of bell in hydromedusae.

crater: southern constellation lying to southwest of *Virgo;* also called *the Cup.* It contains no navigational stars.

crawl-a-bottom [*Fladropterus nigrotasciatus*]: slender, trim little fish with 2 dorsal fins. Breast scaled; back with 7 oblique dark saddles; anal spines II, first stiff; anal fin equal to or larger than soft dorsal in size. Eye moderate; mouth rather wide, terminal in position. Olivaceous above, lighter below; dark vertical stripes on sides.

crayer: small coasting vessel of England and Western Europe which preceded the hoy. It was a rotund craft with rounded bow and stern and square sail was carried from single mast. Crayer might be called a small hoy.

creek: small, narrow bay which extends farther inland than a cove and is longer than it is wide.

crenate: with regularly notched edge as of gastropod aperture of pelecypod valves.

crenulate: edge having series of small indentations, giving it a scalloped appearance.

crest: highest part of wave. Narrow rise of more or less irregular longitudinal profile which constitutes top of elevation of sea bottom.

crest of berm: seaward margin of berm.

crest width: length of wave along crest.

Cretaceous: period of Mesozoic era during which much of Europe and North America were submerged and chalk cliffs of England were formed. Reptiles were dominant on land.

crevalle jack: popular food and game fish belonging to family *Carangidae* which includes scads, pompanos and jacks. Although it is not a very large fish, crevalle jack is voracious and speedy predator on other fish and fierce fighter if hooked.

cribbing [ships]: foundations of heavy blocks and timbers for supporting vessel during construction.

cringle [ships]: metal ring or thimble lashed into boltrope of sail which serves as tack or clew when sail is reefed.

Crinoidea: varied and complex group comprising sea lilies and stemless feather stars. Regularly arranged imperforate plates on dorsal side and distinct tegmen that may bear perforate plates in ventral side; arms free and strongly developed. Members are of class *Crinoidea* of phylum *Echinodermata*. Distinguished from other echinoderms by branching arms, disks and stalks (adults of certain species living in shallow water may shed). Abundant remains of stems and flowerlike heads are found in Paleozoic marine sediments. Sea lilies are related to sea urchins and starfishes.

crinoline: framework fitted in a tank of a cable ship to keep each coil sufficiently spread so that kinking of cable will be prevented as it is payed out.

crisp color changer [*Desmarestia aculeata*]: crisp color changer is an early adaptable alga found in upper litoral zone in rather deep water or floating in shallow water. Most noticeable feature of this alga is that it turns bluish-green when removed from water and discolors other plants coming with it. When young the alga is light brown, when mature, dark brown. It has harsh, bare branches growing on one plane with distinct main axis which extends throughout length of the plant. It may reach a length of 6 ft., with alternate branches arising at intervals of 1/8 to 1/4 in.

crisscross network [*Polyneura latissima*]: found between mean low tide and 1.5-ft. tide levels on vertical faces of rocks sheltered from full force of surf. Probably most conspicuous feature of crisscross network is extremely thin blade on one plane which is covered, except in margins, with a network of veins or nerves. The alga is usually 3 to 5 in. tall, but it may reach a height of 10 in. and is half as wide as tall. Lovely deep red or rose color makes this thin seaweed very attractive. It secures itself to a rock either by disc-shaped holdfast or by flattened irregularly divided, ribbonlike branches.

critical tide level: average levels attained by each tide of daily tide cycles during year.

critical velocity: speed at which current can scour the bottom enough to maintain required depth in a channel.

critical volume: volume of unit mass of substance under critical conditions of temperature and pressure.

croaker [*Micropogon undulatus*]: spotted fish with chin whiskers. Barbels present under chin; rays in soft dorsal 28—29; scales along lateral line about 55; body rather elongate, slightly compressed laterally, not strongly arched above. Mouth moderate, subinferior in position; outer teeth in upper jaw somewhat enlarged; cheeks scaly; caudal fin doubly concave. Color tannish above, paler below. About 16 indistinct short, narrow, oblique dark stripes on each side; back and dorsal fins with scattered dark spots.

croaker, Atlantic [hardheads or corona]: silver green or grayish fish with lighter sides marked by pattern of indistinct wavy bars. Dorsal fin is deeply notched between spiny and soft-rayed portions; mouth is on underside of head; lower jaw bears a row of minute barbels. A croaker is usually under 12 in. long and weighs about 1 lb. Like other members of the family it is a bottom feeder on mollusks and crustaceans.

croaker, spotfin: larger fish, weighing up to 5 lbs. found in surf of sandy beaches of California north to San Francisco. This is a bluish species with brassy sides and dusky fins; each pectoral fin has black spot at its base.

croaker, yellow [voncador]: metallic looking fish with dark back and sides marked by lengthwise stripes; belly is rosy; fins are yellow. It grows to length of 12 in. Yellow croaker is fish of sand shores, especially off coast of southern California.

crocodile, American [*Crocodylus acutus*]: huge, rough-backed, lizard-shaped reptile with sharp snout. Recognized by longitudinal anal slit, pointed snout and exposed fourth mandibular tooth. Gray to black above, sometimes mottled; whitish or yellowish below; maximum length between 14 and 16 ft.

crocodilians [phytosaurs]: form a long-lived order including true crocodiles, gavials, alligators, caimans and their fossil relatives. First of these appeared in late Triassic swamps. One ancestral genus, Protoschus, was a reptile about 30 in. long, with relatively short head, large eyes and tail of moderate length. Its back, belly and tail were encased in rectangular plates. Limbs were typically crocodilian and could be used for either swimming or walking. Hind legs were longer than forelegs, a condition that still prevails. It also is one of several features showing that crocodilians are related to ancestors of dinosaurs. Most of this group are inhabitants of fresh waters, but a few became adapted to sea life. Some attain a length of 20 ft.

cromster: popular two-masted vessel used in England and Holland during Elizabethan days. It was rigged as follows: jib; forestaysail extended on a stay running to long bowsprit; hay mainsail; square course and topsail on mainmast; lateen mizzen. Naval cromsters were armed on upper and lower deck.

Cromwell current: countercurrent, deep in Pacific, flowing eastward near equator.

Cromwell undercurrent: eastward-setting subsurface current extending about 1½° north and south of equator and from about 150° E to 92° W. It is 300 km. wide and 0.2 km. thick; at its core speed is 100 to 150 cm. per second.

cross: 1) descriptive combining term indicating across, athwart, from side to side, contrarily, unfavorably. 2) the southern constellation *Crux;* also, sometimes, the 4 stars forming a cross in Cygnus. 3) to send aloft and secure a yard in proper position or, as formerly, a square sail.

crossed royals [ships]: hoisting and fastening the yards to which royals are set.

crossjack [ships]: square sail sometimes hung from lowest yard on mizzenmast of full rigged ship. Another name for "mizzen."

crossopterygians: lobefinned fish which are in direct line of evolution from fish to land-living vertebrates and are now represented by solitary "living fossil," *Latimeria.* In these fish the fin is solid, muscular structure with central axis of bones. They are fishes with fringe fins. Nostrils perforating skull may have been for breathing into a lung; ancestors of amphibians.

cross sea: confused, irregular state of sea occurring where waves from two or more different storms have arrived at a point of observation. Sometimes waves appear to be moving in same direction as one of the original waves; sometimes in between.

cross-spall [ships]: temporary horizontal timber brace to hold a frame in position. Cross-spalls are replaced later by deck beams.

cross tide: tidal current setting in direction approximately 90° from course in navigational usage.

crosstrees [ships]: horizontal members at topmastheads to extend topmast rigging and to afford a standing place for seamen. Horizontal supports at top of mast which spread shrouds or lines laterally supporting the mast.

crosswind: that wind vector component which is perpendicular to course of exposed moving object. Wind blowing in direction approximately 90° from the course.

crown [ships]: term sometimes used denoting roundup or camber of deck. Crown of an anchor is located where arms are welded to shank.

crow's nest [ships]: lookout station attached to or near head of mast.

cruciate [cruciform]: in the form of a cross.

cruising radius: expressed in miles, distance a vessel is capable of covering at normal speed without refueling or restoring; also termed *steaming range.*

crura [*Brachiopoda*]: base portions of calcareous support (brachidium) of lophophore.

crust: that part of earth lying above Mohorovicic Discontinuity. Classified as continental crust or oceanic crust depending on elevation, mineral composition and seismic wave velocities in the layer.

Crustacea: third largest class of phylum *Arthropoda.* Numbering some 25,000 species, crustaceans are mainly aquatic and range in size from miniscule water flea to crabs with leg spans of 9 or 10 ft. Like other arthropods, crustaceans are distinguished by hard external skeletons, segmented bodies and jointed, paired legs; unlike other arthropods, they possess 2 pairs of antennae that usually act as feelers. Crustaceans include water fleas, major portion of ocean's plankton, seed shrimp, barnacles, shrimp, lobsters, crayfish, crabs and fish lice.

crustacean: one of class (*Crustacea*) of arthropods which breathe by means of gills or branchiae; body commonly covered by hard shell or crust. Group includes barnacles, crabs, shrimps and lobsters.

crustacean borer: member of any of 3 families (*Limnoriidae, Sphaeromidae* and *Cheluridae*) of crustaceans which, in first 2 resemble pill or sow bugs and in last, sand fleas.

crutch [ships]: support which keeps boom off deck when it is not in use.

crutches [ships]: same as breasthooks, but fitted at after end.

crux: constellation commonly known as the *Southern Cross,* located in about 60° S. declination and about 40° due south of *Corvus.* Four of its 5 stars, suitable for navigational use, mark the extremities of a well-defined cruciform figure, and, together with 2 brightest stars of *Centaurus* lying west of, and pointing toward, the Cross at 9½° distance, present an imposing sight. *Alpha (a) Crucis,* double star of magnitude 1.05, is brightest in group and marks Cross' foot, or southernmost limit.

cryoclinometer: device for measuring horizontal dimensions of sea ice field from aircraft.

cryology: study of ice and snow or sea ice.

cryoplankton: algae which live on surface of snow and ice in polar regions and on high mountains.

cryptodires [turtles]: "hidden necks." This group tuck both head and neck away by bending the latter into an S between shoulder blades. Fossil cryptodires began as marsh-dwellers that swam well, often sunned themselves on logs or sandbanks and frequently walked on land. Some descendants became aquatic but remained in rivers and swamps, others may have taken to sea.

cryptostoma: flask-shaped cavity in thallus of some large, brown seaweeds, containing hairs which secrete mucilage.

ctenidia: typical gills of most aquatic molluscs.

ctenoid scale: fish scale having tiny spines on posterior edge.

Ctenophora: resemble jellyfish because of gelatinous transparent middle layer (mesenchyme) which fills out entire space between internal cavities and ectoderm. They are distinctly biradially symmetrical and have no nematocysts. They have a transparent muscular structure within mesenchyme; digestive system is branched and forms tubular system instead of stomodeum, as coelenterates. There is also complex sense organ located at end of body, opposite mouth (aboral region). Most conspicuous characteristic is possession of so-called "combplates," 8 rows on external surface passing from aboral sense organ to mouth. Ctenophores are divided into 2 classes: *Tentaculata* (species with tentacles) and *Nuda* (species without tentacles). *Tentaculata* has 4 orders: (1) *Cydippidea*, (2) *Lobata*, (3) *Cestida* and (4) *Platyctenea*.

cubic capacity: as applied to cargo stowage, total space representing a vessel's accommodation for bulky goods; also referred to as *measurement capacity;* and usually expressed in cubic feet. *Bale capacity* is taken as limited by the inward surfaces of cargo battens, or, in absence of these by inward edges of frames; lower edges of deck beams; and, usually, inward edges of bulkhead stiffeners. *Grain capacity* is given as total space within a compartment's bounds.

cubic number: for comparative purposes in naval architectural design of similar type vessels, a numeral equal to one-hundredth the product of length, breadth, and depth.

cucumber, burrowing [*Leptosynapta inhaerens*]: burrows deep in sand or mud, at first sight appears to be a worm. Lives in a tube made of fine grains of sand glued together with adhesive slime; varies from 1¼ to 4 in. long, 1/8 to 1/4 in. wide. Mouth, at anterior end of body, surrounded by 12 feathered tentacles; 5 white lines extend length of body, marking muscle bands; skin covered with little dots, calcareous anchors.

cucumber, creeping pedal [*Psolus chitonoides*]: resembles a chiton; in shape quite different from other cucumbers. Lower side flattened to form a creeping sole. Tube feet appear in rows around edge of sole and extend lengthwise down the center of it. Large calcareous plates, irregular in shape, cover plump dorsal surface. Long cylindrical neck near front of animal bears a profusely branched crown of crimson tentacles, which when extended are nearly as long as body. Upper surface is dull red color with lighter markings; underside flesh-colored. Measures 2 in. long, 1 in. wide. Hides under stones at low-tide mark or in shallow water.

cucumber, large red [*Parastichopus californicus*]: commonly encountered along beach, attains length of 15 in. and diameter of approximately 3 in. Elongated cylindrical animal lying on one flattened side; mouth at one end, anus at the other. Because calcareous plates in body wall are minute, body is not rigid, but has tough warty skin. Some are uniform red-brown, others are dark brown above and pale yellow below. Numerous large tube feet are arranged in rows on underside while prominent conical projections are on dorsal surface. Fifteen tentacles around the mouth are borne on tall columns which end in rosettes of hundreds of tiny branches.

cuddy [ships]: cabin on small boat. Also cookhouse on deck.

culling: act of sorting fish, oysters, crabs, clams, etc., according to size and quality, or marketable value.

culmination: act of culminating or crossing the meridian; said of a heavenly body at *transit* or *meridian passage.* When a body's apparent diurnal path is circumpolar, i.e., its polar distance less than an observer's latitude, both upper and lower culminations take place in the visible heavens. These are separated by an interval of 12 apparent solar hours, if the sun; and 12 sidereal hours in the case of a star (equal to 11 hrs. 58 min. .02 sec. of mean solar time). At upper culmination body attains its greatest altitude; at lower culmination, its least; and at either point its measured altitude provides the basis for determining latitude by simplest means possible.

Cumacea [hyperids]: peracaridans with a carapace covering 3 of 4 thoracic segments, bulging out in front to cover expanded end of exopodite of first thoracic limb. First 3 pairs of thoracic limbs modified to form maxillipeds; slender uropods. In females, second antenna is rudimentary and there are no pleopods. In males, second antenna is large and in all families, except *Nannastacidae*, pleopods are present. Cumaceans are bottom dwellers which may get whirled up and collected with true plankton.

cum sole: with the sun; hence anticyclonic or

clockwise; opposite of contrasolem.

cunner: 1) dugout sailing canoe in oyster fishery of Chesapeake Bay, 25 to 30 ft. long, cat schooner-rigged, with leg-of-mutton sails and sometimes a jib. 2) found from New England to New Jersey, it is an omnivorous fish feeding on seaweeds and small marine invertebrates; most northern member of the family, living on rocky bottoms and water beneath piers and docks. Cunners range in color from dark olive-green to reddish-green or brown depending upon color of surroundings. Common member of inshore fish population. Large individuals reach length of 15 in. and weigh several pounds.

cup and saucer [*Constantinea simplex*]: found short distance below tide mark; after storms, often cast ashore in large quantities. This is an unmistakable species, for it looks like a bright red cup and saucer standing on a pedestal. This effect is produced by the thick, cylindrical stripe which passes through flat, circular blade. Tip forms the cup and the blade the saucer. At first blades are perfectly round, but later they are torn into wedge-shaped segments. Stipes are either solitary or in clusters, arising from disclike base.

cup-and-saucer shell [*Calyptraeidae*]: shells of this group of molluscs are dome-shaped and except for slightly spiral apex, look somewhat like limpets when viewed externally. This group is an unusual one for its members contain an internal plate or cup from which it receives its name. Interior of shells, including cup, is polished and shining. There is no operculum. They live attached to solid objects, including other shells, in water ranging in depth from shallow waters of shoreline to deep water beyond the reef.

cup-and-saucer shell, spiny: this cup-and-saucer shell is a difficult species to identify and to name properly because it varies in form, sculpture and coloration. It may be solid or thin, convex or depressed, circular or oval, etc. Usually marked over external surface by radiating ridges which are quite thickly covered by hollow, tubular, spinelike processes of varying length. Shell varies as widely in color as it does in shape, being white, yellow, blue, purple or even black. This species bears characteristic cup-shaped appendage within shell. This appendage is quite large in size, often laterally compressed and, although usually white in color, may be marked with darker color in center.

cup anemometer: device used to measure wind speed; it consists of 4 vanes with cuplike structures on ends. Wind revolves vanes about central shaft and speed of revolution is proportional to wind speed. Calibrated device is used to measure wind speed.

cup coral: solitary coral generally with cup-shaped depression (calyx) at summit.

cupro nickel: an alloy of 70% copper and 30% nickel used in making condenser tubes and sea-water lines on board ship.

curragh: boat-shaped coracle used by fishermen of west coast of Ireland. Made of light sticks and boards covered with canvas and smeared with pitch.

current: horizontal movement of water.

current base: maximum water depth below which currents are ineffective in moving sediment.

current chart: map of water area depicting current speeds and directions by current roses, vectors or other means.

current cross section: graphic presentation of current shown as vertical plane perpendicular to axis of flow; horizontal distance between surface limits is represented by abscissa and depth is shown by ordinate which increases from surface (zero) down to any depth.

current curve: graphic presentation of speed and duration of tidal current usually shown for areas of reversing tidal currents. The curve is referred to rectangular coordinates; time is represented by abscissa and speed by ordinate. Flood speeds are positive and ebb speeds are negative values measured from slack.

current diagram: graphic presentation showing speed of flood and ebb currents and times of slack and strength over considerable stretch of channel of tidal waterway, time being referred to tide or current phases at some reference station.

current difference: difference between time of slack water or strength of current in any locality and time of corresponding phase of current at reference station for which predictions are given in current tables.

current direction: direction toward which current is flowing, called set of current.

current ellipse: graphic representation of rotary current in which speed and direction of current at different hours of tide cycle are represented by radium vectors and vectorial angles. Line joining extremities of radius vectors will form a curve roughly approximating an ellipse.

current gradient: rate of increase or decrease in speed of current relative to given distance or period of time. Gradient is generally represented by curve.

current hour: mean interval between transit of moon over reference meridian (usually Greenwich) and time of the strength of flood current modified by times of slack water and strength of ebb current.

current meter: any one of numerous devices for measurement of either speed alone or of both direction and speed (set and drift) in flowing water.

current pattern: horizontal distribution of surface or subsurface currents at various levels in specified area.

current pattern, secondary: water movement which differs from prevailing current patterns.

current profile: graphic presentation of current flow from surface to specified depth. Speed of current is generally represented by abscissa and depth by ordinate which increases from surface (zero) downward.

current ripple: type of ripple mark produced by action of current flowing steadily in one direction over a bed of sand. These current ripples have long, gentle slopes toward direction from which current comes and shorter, steeper slopes on lee side.

current rips: small waves formed on sea surface by meeting of opposing currents.

current rose: graphic representation of currents, usually by quadrangles, using arrows for cardinal and intercardinal compass points, to show resulting drift and frequency of set for given period of time.

current speed: rate at which water moves either horizontally or vertically; usually expressed in knots, miles per day, feet per second or centimeters per second.

current tables: tables which give daily prediction of time, speed and directions of currents.

current vector: geometric presentation showing both current direction and speed, generally by an arrow whose length is proportional to speed and whose direction is resolved into points of the compass.

curry comb [*Odonthalia washingtoniensis*]: coarse, brittle species living just below low-tide mark. Average specimen is dark brown or black and reaches height of 10 to 15 in. Curry comb is striking in appearance with each branch and branchlet flattened, distinct, separate and on one plane. Plant arises from small disc-shaped holdfast.

curve: line joining a succession of graphically plotted values and that is straight in no part; a bending without angles, as an *arch*.

curved path theory: method for analysis and plotting of seismic data which allows for curvature of ray paths, resulting from increasing velocities with depth in earth.

curved velocity: rate of motion in which direction as well as speed of flow is considered.

curve fitting: appropriate representation of empirical data by mathematical function, typically with arbitrary constants determined by least squares.

cushion ice: fine fragmented ice found between ice floes. It has effect of cushioning impact of floes on each other.

cusk: dark gray or brown fish, ranging southward from Arctic along Atlantic Coast to Cape Cod. Resembles squirrel hake in general shape, with typical ventral fins, but has only single long, low dorsal fin. Dorsal tail and anal fins are distinctive in their black margins neatly edged in white. Cusk prefers rocky bottoms at depth of over 60 ft. Average individual is 18 to 20 in. long.

cusp [reptiles]: toothlike projection.

cuspate bar: crescent-shaped bar uniting with shore at each end. It may be formed by single spit growing from shore, turning back again to meet the shore, or by 2 spits growing from shore uniting to form a bar of sharply cuspate form.

custom: customs duties, imposts, or tolls, levied by a country on goods or merchandise imported or exported therefrom.

custom of the port: established usage or practice at a particular port, generally with reference to stevedoring costs, mooring, docking, towage, etc. Adherence in fact to an uncommon, but prevailing, custom of a port often carries much weight in cases at law arising from cargo expense claims, charterers' redress, and other maritime contentions.

cut: notch, depression or furrow produced by erosion or excavation of a slope. Many cuts of this type occur on upper or continental shelf.

cuticle: outermost secreted layer of molluscan body.

cut in: surveying term meaning to determine position of distant object for existing or underway survey by direct observation with transit or theodolite (precise instruments for measuring angle between distant objects).

cutlass fish [sea serpents]: attains length of 5 ft. Body is slender and eel-like with long, low dorsal fin; pectoral fins are reduced in size, ventral fins are lacking. It is silvery fish living in warm waters. Name refers to formidable array of many sharp knifelike teeth in large and powerful mouth. Few fishes, even barracuda, have such terrifying armed jaws.

cutter: single-masted sailing vessel with deep underbody, rather narrow beam and heavy keel. Generally, stem is vertical and transom stern is very raking. Rig consists of 4 sails; gaff and boom mainsail, foresail, jib and gaff topsail to topmast. Bowsprit is long.

cutter galley [ships]: small galley about 43 ft. long, with short quarterdeck, 4 gunports and 3 sweep ports to a side. Cutter rigged with square topsails.

cutter rig: type of fore-and-aft sailing rig similar to sloop's but with 1 mast further aft, about 1/3 of boat's length or more from bow.

cuttlefish: marine mollusc of the class *Cephalo-*

poda that has 10 arms including 2 long tentacles it can draw back into body. Cuttlefish is oval-shaped with internal shell that remains after animals die and body disintegrates; this cuttlebone has many commercial uses.

cutwater: 1) Yorkshire, England, for small, sharp-bowed "cable," 18 ft. long and 7 ft. beam. **2)** angular edge of bridge-pier, shaped to lessen resistance it offers to flow of water. **3)** fore part of ship's prow which cuts water.

cycle: one complete and consecutive set of all changes which occur in recurrent action or phenomenon, starting from any point in action and ending with all conditions as they were from start.

cycloidal wave: very steep, symmetrical wave whose crest forms angle of 120°. Wave form is that of a cycloid. Trachoidal wave of maximum steepness.

cyclone: 1) atmospheric cyclonic circulation; closed circulation. Cyclone's direction of rotation (counterclockwise in Northern Hemisphere) is opposite to that of anticyclone. **2)** if H. Piddington had not published the *Sailor's Horn Book* in 1848, he would have been completely forgotten. Listing and analyzing many kinds of winds that seamen experience, he proposed that a general term be adopted for all whirling currents. Borrowing from Greek terms for "coil of a serpent," he coined cyclone to label circular blowing winds. Piddington's description of "these meteors," as he called oceanic winds, was considerably less than accurate. His book made no contribution to geography or to navigation. In spite of its mediocrity the volume launched "cyclone" into the stream of common speech. It has endured so well that the made-up word is the only wind name that can be positively traced to the influence of one person.

cyclonic: having sense of rotation about local vertical, same as that of earth's rotation; i.e., as viewed from above, counterclockwise in Northern Hemisphere, clockwise in Southern Hemisphere, undefined at Equator; opposite of anticyclonic.

cyclonograph or **cyclonoscope:** storm card, or means of graphically determining bearing of a cyclone's center and consequent probable direction of its path of progression, given direction and shift, if any, of wind, and barometric pressure change.

Cyclopoida [copepods]: as in calanoids, fore-body is sharply marked off from urosome. Always first, and sometimes second thoracic segment is fused with head, while last sixth thoracic segment contributes to urosome whose first segment thus bears a rudimentary pair of limbs. There are at most, only four obvious thoracic segments and usually only three in fore-body and movable joint between two main regions of body is between fifth and sixth thoracic segments. Urosome consists of five segments in female and six in male plus a telson, but some unite. Antennules are short and have only a few joints; egg sacs are paired in most species.

cyclostomes: all characterized by absence of several fish characters, paired fins or appendages, true teeth, scales and upper and lower jaws; usually considered very primitive vertebrates in which these structures have not developed. Brain and skull are imperfectly developed; vertebrae column is poorly formed and most supporting structure consists of stiff, rodlike notochord; gills open externally through separate gill-clefts.

Cygnus: northern constellation in the *Milky Way*, adjoining and east of *Lyra*, in 19½ to 21 hours right ascension and 28 to 45 degrees declination. Its five principal stars form a well-defined Latin cross 22° in length, with *Deneb (a Cygni)*, the brightest, of magnitude 1.3, marking the head or northeastern extremity.

cylindrical [*Coelenterata*]: nearly straight corallite which has essentially parallel sides except near base.

cylindrical buoy: one of the can type, appearing above water as round-shaped and having a flat top.

cynosure: anything that strongly attracts attention or admiration; that which serves as a guide; hence, an ancient name for the constellation *Ursa Minor*, or *Little Bear*, containing *Polaris*, the "North Star," which marks its tail end and to which the mariner's eyes customarily were directed; star *Polaris* itself.

cyphonautes larva: planktonic triangular-shaped young of a bryozoan, enclosed in bivalve shell.

cypris larva: stage at which young of barnacles attach.

cyst: resistant wall or shell secreted around organism, or around certain stages in life cycle or organism, to protect it during periods unfavorable to ordinary life activities.

cystoids: means "bladderlike"; had compressed egg-shaped or spherical bodies covered by calyx of plates. Some genera were attached directly to other objects; some had short stalks (columns) made up of round flat sections (columnals) each with central hole through which ran a stalk of flesh. Cystoid mouth lies on upper surface, generally at center of radiating grooves (ambulacra) which must have been lined with cilia that beat to and fro carrying food to mouth.

cytological: referring to study of cells and their function and structure.

cytoplasm: mass of clear, semifluid matter having a colloidal structure and surrounding the nucleus.

D

D: 1) International Code signal flag, "dog," consisting of 3 horizontal stripes of yellow, blue, and yellow, respectively; hoisted singly, indicates "Keep clear of me—I am maneuvering with difficulty." **2)** "d" is often written as an abbreviation for *drizzling* in ships' logbooks. **3)** also corresponds to Greek δ (delta), denoting the 4th star of a constellation in order of magnitude, usually as observed by ancient astronomers.

dace, finescale [*Pfrille neogaeus*]: this species is medium-sized, robust minnow with large, broad, blunt head. It is blackish-bronze with dark lateral bands. Lower parts are crimson in spring males. There are more than 80 scales in lateral line. Teeth in main row are typically 5—4, but sometimes 4—4 or 4—5 or 5—5.

dace, Great Lakes longnose [*Rhinichthys cataractae cataractae*]: body is elongate and cylindrical; snout projects considerably beyond mouth; barbels are present in maxillaries. This dace is rather olivaceous in color with darker splotches. During spring males have considerable red on head, sides and fins. Dorsal fin has 8 rays. Scales are 14—65—8; teeth are 2, 4—4, 2. This species reaches length of 5 in.

dace, northern pearl [*Margariscus margariscus nachtriebi*]: this minnow has heavy body, short head and blunt snout. It is dusky in color and has a faint black lateral stripe. Lateral line contains about 72 scales. Teeth are 2, 4—5, 2.

dace, northern redbelly [*Chrosomus eos*]: this minnow is similar to southern redbelly dace except that jaws and snout are shorter. Mouth is strongly oblique and curved, reaching less than ¼ the length of head. Teeth are 5—5 or 5—4.

dace, redside [*Clinostomus elongatus*]: redside dace is medium-sized minnow with broad, black lateral band, front half of which is bright crimson in spring males. Head is long and pointed; mouth proportionally larger than that of any other minnow. There are less than 80 scales in lateral line.

dace, southern redbelly [*Chrosomus erythrogaster*]: southern redbelly dace is small, brownish-olive minnow with black spots on back, blackish stripe along sides from above eye to tail and another band below running through the eye and ending in black spot at base of caudal fin. Belly and space between bands are usually silvery, but in spring males they are bright scarlet. Dorsal fin has 8 rays; scales are 16—18—10; teeth are 5—5 or 5—4. Mouth is slightly oblique, curved and more than ¼ the length of head.

dace, speckled [*Extrarius aestivalis hyostomus*]: speckled dace is a very slender minnow with long snout projected halfway beyond mouth. It has barbel on each maxillary and about 37 scales in lateral line. Pharyngeal teeth are 4—4. It reaches length of 2½ in.

dace, western blacknose [*Rhinichthys atratulus meleagris*]: this minnow is similar in form to *R. cataractae cataractae*, but snout does not extend far beyond mouth. Barbels are small or absent; dorsal fin has 7 rays. Body is dusky, splotched with black; belly is silvery; breeding males have bright red sides.

dactylozooid: in coelenterates, a modified, mouthless, often rodlike polyp, heavily armed with nematocysts serving to touch and catch prey or to defend colony.

dagger [ships]: piece of timber fastened to poppets of bilgeway and crossing them diagonally to keep them together. Dagger applies to anything that stands in diagonal position.

daggerboard [ships]: on small craft a movable board lowered from bottom of boat to reduce leeway. It is removed when not in use.

dagger plank [ships]: one of planks which unite heads of poppets or stepping up pieces of cradle on which vessel rests on launching.

dahabia: lateen-rigged, long-hulled houseboat used on Nile.

daily rate: referred to a chronometer, denotes amount of gain or loss in 24 hrs., which change in error of a good instrument is nearly constant within ordinary ranges of temperature, and, generally is not more than 2 or 3 seconds.

daily retardation: amount of time by which corresponding tidal phases grow later day by day.

dainty leaf [*Erythroglossum intermedium*]: small, red alga that grows on vertical face of rocks between mean tide and 1.5-ft. levels. Dainty leaf is not more than 2 in. tall with several linear branches 1/16- to 1/4-in. wide, arising from base.

Some plants are wholly erect while others have a prostrate base with some of branches becoming erect; flat blades are irregularly branched once. The dainty leaf is bright rose-red; resembles smaller species of *Delesseria*, of same family.

daisy star: brittle starfish of genus *Ophiopholis*. Daisy star occurs in variety of colors; arms are up to 13 cm. long and disc is about 2 cm. across.

damping: force opposing vibration; damping acts to decrease amplitudes of successive free vibrations.

damselfish: group of species with thin, compressed bodies and circular outlines. Dorsal fin in this family has forward spiny portion continuous with short, pointed posterior portion. Damselfishes have small mouth typical of many reef fishes, suitable for eating only such aquatic organisms as invertebrates and algae. Body is covered with large, ctenoid scales.

damselfish, Beau Grogor: has dark blue back and dorsal fin with golden-yellow sides and belly; same size as yellowtail, but anal fin is yellow instead of black; at posterior portion of dorsal fin it has yellow margin instead of being entirely black. This little damselfish is one of the most aggressive members. Makes home in empty conch shells which it defends against all intruders.

damselfish, Sergeant Major: named for vertical stripes. Schools of this small fish have been seen during explorations of coral reefs. Fins and undersides are pearly-gray while back and upper sides bear broad vertical black and yellow stripes. Sergeant Majors can change color rapidly from dark phase when they are among rocks to light phase when over sandy bottoms. Reach length of 6 in.

damselfish, yellowtail: active little fish about 6 in. long, native to West Indies. Conspicuous color pattern consists of dark blue back and dorsal fin, shading into golden yellow on sides and belly; paired fins and tail fin are yellow. This damselfish feeds chiefly on organic debris that collects among crevices of coral.

dan: *dan-buoy*, or small float for marking position of fishing gear; also used to indicate limits of mine-sweeping operational areas and usually carrying a flag on a light staff. *(England)*

dandy: cutter or sloop-rigged, used in British waters, with mizzenmast abaft. A true "dandy" is lug-rigged, but fore-and-aft mainsail and leg-of-mutton mizzen are now generally used. Term "dandy" is sometimes applied by British fishermen to any ketch or yawl.

dangerous goods: as a cargo term, includes explosives and all substances of inflammable nature which are liable to spontaneous combustion, either in themselves or when stowed adjacent to certain other substances, and which, when mixed with air, are liable to generate explosive gases and so produce tainting of food stuffs, contamination of other cargo, and poisoning or suffocation of persons. Most maritime countries control stowage of such goods by law, and, in general, passenger vessels are forbidden them, excepting under certain conditions as deck cargo, where they may be thrown overboard at a moment's notice.

dapping: notching of wooden pilings for purpose of fastening cross members. Quite acceptable above high tide, dapping of creosoted pilings above high-tide line can produce a break in treated zone, permitting borers to enter softer heartwood.

darter, brown [*Etheostoma edwini*]: slender, trim little brown fish with 2 dorsal fins. Scales along lateral lines 36—41; lateral line somewhat arched above pectorals, infraorbital canal complete; anal fin smaller than soft dorsal. Head and snout somewhat blunt; mouth subterminal in position; caudal fin rounded. Color brownish, with 8 to 9 dark saddles across back; in life somewhat speckled.

darter, Eastern Johnny [*Etheostoma nigrum olmstedi*]: slender, trim little fish with 2 dorsal fins. Single anal spine; lateral line straight; anal fin smaller than soft dorsal. Head slender, rather pointed; mouth rather small for a darter, terminal in position; cheeks and opercle scaly. Olivaceous in color with blotches and zigzag markings along sides; usually with black stripe running downward from eye.

darter, Florida swamp [*Etheostoma barratti*]: slender, trim little fish with 2 dorsal fins. Scales along lateral lines 47—60; lateral line arched above pectorals; infraorbital canal incomplete; anal fin smaller than soft dorsal. Head moderately narrow, tapering to rather sharp snout; gill membranes broadly united. Brownish above, lighter brown below, with 9—12 dark blotches along sides. Length up to about 2 in.

darter, naked sand [*Ammocrypta beani*]: slender, trim little fish with 2 dorsal fins. Body almost naked except for 1 to 3 series of scales along lateral line; anal fin with single flexible spine and equal in size to or larger than soft dorsal fin. Head slender; eye moderate; mouth rather wide, terminal in position; upper jaw slightly protruding. Body rather elongate; somewhat translucent with distinct spots or bars.

darter, Okaloosa [*Etheostoma okaloosae*]: slender, trim little fish with 2 dorsal fins. Gill membranes largely separate and spines II, first heavy and stiff; lateral line straight; anal fin smaller than dorsal fin in size. Head rather long; mouth moderately small, terminal in position; body slender, but slightly compressed; caudal fins rounded. Olivaceous above, light below with a few distinct blotches along sides.

darter, snubnose [*Etheostoma duryi*]: slender, trim little fish with 2 dorsal fins. Gill membrane broadly united; anal spine II, first heavy and stiff; lateral line straight; anal fin smaller than soft dorsal. Head moderate, tapering to a rather pointed snout; caudal fin rounded; olivaceous with generally speckled appearance. Length about 2 in.

darter, speckled [*Etheostoma stigmaeum*]: slender, trim little fish with 2 dorsal fins. Anal spines II, first thin and flexible; lateral line straight; anal fin smaller than soft dorsal. Head moderate, tapering to a rather slender snout; mouth rather small, terminal in position; caudal fin rounded. Color olivaceous, with about 6 dark bars across mid-line of back and with generally speckled appearance.

darter, stargazing [*Hadropterus uranidea*]: slender, trim little fish with 2 dorsal fins. Breast naked or with only one large scale; back with 4 oblique saddles; anal spines II; anal fin equal to or larger in size than soft dorsal. Mouth rather wide, terminal in position; body rather elongate, terete; olivaceous above, lighter below. Four oblique dark saddles along mid-line of back; dark vertical stripes along sides. Reaches several inches in length.

dash [drone antisubmarine helicopter]: operates by remote control from a destroyer. Carries sub-killer homing torpedoes.

date line: usually termed *International Date Line*, fixed by international agreement as joining all places at which each calendar day *first begins*. It roughly follows the 180th meridian, being laid out so that all Asia, with Chatham Island and Tonga Islands of the South Pacific, lie west of it, and all America, including Aleutian Islands, east of it. In order to reconcile both calendar and ship's log with change of date on crossing the *date line*, navigators adhere to the old practical rule: *"When eastward bound, add a day; when westward bound, drop a day."*

datum: any numerical or geometrical quantity or set of such quantities which may serve as reference or base for other quantities.

datum point: any reference point of known or assumed coordinates from which calculations or measurements may be taken.

Davidson Current: coastal countercurrent setting north inshore of California current along West Coast of U.S. (from northern California to Washington to at least 48° N) during winter months.

davits [ships]: one of pair of projecting pieces of wood or iron on side or stern of vessel, used for suspending, lowering and hoisting a small boat or lifeboat by means of sheaves or pulleys. They are set so as to admit to being shipped and unshipped at will, and commonly turn on their axis so that boat can be swung on deck or out over water.

dawn-frogs [*Eoanaura*]: dawn-frogs were creatures about 4 in. long which lived in swampy Coal Age forests of central Illinois. They had blunt heads, large eyes and well developed tails, but skull had already lost some bones, hind legs were longer than forelegs and vertebrae were degenerate.

day's work: account or reckoning of courses and distances run from noon to noon of the nautical day.

deadeye [ships]: round, laterally-flattened wooden blocks encircled by rope or iron band and pierced with 3 holes to receive the lanyards, used to extend shrouds and stays.

dead flat [ships]: flat-surfaced midship section of vessel on sides above bilge, or on bottom below bilge.

deadhead [ships]: partly submerged timber.

deadlight [ships]: formerly heavy metal cover to protect glass of ship's portholes. Now, more frequently, a thick glass permanently set in deck or hull. Shutter placed over cabin window in stormy weather to protect glass against waves.

deadman: log, timber, anchor, etc., placed to advantage on shore as a temporary mooring post.

dead reckoning [ships]: means of navigation without usual sightings on heavenly bodies or other instantaneous means of positioning. Position is estimated using course and speed from last accurately determined position.

deadrise [ships]: onward slope of ship's bottom from keel to bilge. Used to give drainage of oil or water toward center of ship.

deadwater: phenomenon which occurs when ship of low propulsive power negotiates water which has thin layer of fresher water over deeper layer of more sublime water. As ship moves, part of its energy goes into generation of an internal wave which causes noticeable drop in efficient propulsion.

dead weight [ships]: total weight of cargo, fuel, water, stores, passenger and crew and their effects that ship can carry when at her designed, full load draft.

deadwood [ships]: flat, vertical hull material where hull is too narrow to permit framing. Deadwood is usually in after end of hull but may also be found at forefoot.

debacle: rush of water or ice in stream immediately following the breakup.

debouchure: mouth of river. Also point of issuance of underground stream, as from a cave.

debris ice: sea ice which contains soil, stones, shells and other materials.

debris line: line near limit of storm wave uprush marking landward limit of debris deposits.

decade scaler: scaler whose scaling factor is power of ten.

decapod: member of *Decapoda*, order of *Crustacea* including lobsters, crabs, crayfish, shrimp and prawns. Characterized by 10 appendages (including pair of pincers in front), stalked eyes and hard shell or carapace on at least part of back. First 3 pairs of thoracic appendages modified as maxillipeds; 5 pairs of walking legs (pereiopods) with first pair often stout and chelated (cheliped); head and thoracic segments fused together; usually more than one series of gills; first 5 pairs of abdominal appendages modified for swimming but 1 to 2 pairs in male modified as copulatory gonopods; last abdominal appendages (uropods) with telson forming tail fan; terrestrial, freshwater and marine. Cambarus, Palaemonetes, Homarus, Callinectes.

decay area: area of lesser winds through which ocean waves travel often emerging from generating area.

decay constant: rate of spontaneous disintegration of radioactive element, unaffected by heat or pressure.

decay distance: distance between area of wave generation and point of passage of resulting waves outside area.

decay of waves: change that waves undergo after they leave generating area (fetch) and pass through a calm or region of lighter winds. In process of decay, significant wave height decreases and significant wavelength increases.

decibar: unit of pressure. One decibar is 1/10's of a bar, i.e., nearly "one atmosphere," which is 10^6 dyne/cm^2. Pressure in decibars increases almost as geometrical depth increases in meters. Thus the pressure is 100 decibars at depth of 99.4 meters and 1000 decibars at 984.41 meters, difference being about 1 percent.

decinormal calomel electrode: calomel electrode containing decinormal potassium chloride solution.

deck [*Mollusca*]: septum or transverse plate of shelly material.

deck [ships]: covering, or sheltering cover. Approximately horizontal platform or floor extending from side to side of a ship.

deck fitting [ships]: many appurtenances of deck; furnishings and equipment necessary for "working" the ship on or attached to deck.

deckhouse [ships]: small house erected upon deck of ship.

deck stringer [ships]: strip of deck plating that runs along outer edge of deck.

declination: any given location, angle between geographical meridian and magnetic meridian; i.e., angle between true north and magnetic north. Declination is either "east" or "west" as compass needle points to east or west of geographical meridian.

declination of the sun: number of degrees the sun's vertical ray is north or south of equator.

declination reduction: processing of high and low water tide observations or flood and ebb tidal current observations to obtain quantities which result from effect of changes in the declination of moon.

decollation: dropping off of upper whorls of gastropod shell, when animals have ceased to occupy them.

decompression sickness [diving]: 1) condition resulting from formation of gas bubbles in blood or tissues of divers during ascent. Depending on their number, size and location these bubbles may cause wide variety of symptoms including pain, paralysis, unconsciousness and occasionally death. 2) condition that results after a dive or exposure to elevated pressures when nitrogen or other inert gas (such as helium) which was absorbed by blood during exposure to high pressure is not eliminated from body by adequate decompression. This nitrogen or other inert gas forms bubbles in blood and tissues of body and these gas bubbles cause variety of dangerous and harmful symptoms.

decussate: crossed or intersected.

deducted space: in rules for determining *net tonnage*, total, or any single, enclosed space which is deducted from *gross tonnage*.

deductor muscles [*Brachiopoda*]: muscles that open valves; insert on floor of pedicle valve to hinge line that serves to support tooth.

deep: oceanic areas of abyssal depth representing depressions in ocean floor. This term is no longer in general use having been replaced by abyssal plain, e.g., Sohm Deep and Nares Deep of Western Atlantic Ocean have been replaced or renamed from Abyssal Plain and Nares Abyssal Plain.

deepening: in meteorology, a decrease in central pressure of pressure system on constant height chart or an analogous decrease in height on constant pressure chart; opposite of fitting. Term is usually applied to a low rather than to a high, although technically it is acceptable in either case.

deep floor [ships]: term applied to any floor in forward or after end of vessel. Due to converging sides of ships in bow and stern, floors become much deeper in main body.

deep frame [ships]: web frame or frame whose athwartship dimensions is over the general ground.

deep scattering layer: layer or layers often present in ocean waters and consisting of stratified groups of organisms, which can "scatter" or reflect the pulse from echo sounding equipment, thus appearing as "false bottom." Layers move downward during day and up at night and may spread horizontally for miles.

deep-sea anchoring winch [ships]: large-size winch used to anchor an oceanographic-hydrographic ship in deep water. Ordinarily this type uses steel wire rope in lengths of about 20,000 to 35,000 ft. Some types use specially tapered wire particularly when anchoring in great depths, while others use wire of about ½ in. diameter.

deep-sea basin: deep floor of ocean basin from 15,000 to 18,000 ft. deep covering 70% of ocean's total area.

deep-sea deposits: those sediments which accumulate out of reach of ordinary land-derived material; they fall into 2 categories: (1) organic oozes and (2) various muds and clays. In shallower parts of ocean, oozes are composed of hard parts of planktonic organisms embedded in powder arising from their disintegration. In deeper parts silicious organic remains are dominant.

deep-sea lead: lead, or bob used for attachment to leadline measuring beyond 100 fathoms.

deep six: nautical slang for discarding something overboard.

deep tanks [ships]: these usually consist of ordinary hold compartments, but strengthened to carry water ballast. Placed at either or both ends of engine and boiler space.

deep underwater nuclear counter: submersible gamma ray spectrometer used from ships for in situ detection of ocean gamma radiation.

deep water: in wave forecasting, deep water means that depth of water is large compared with wavelength of longest wave generated by wind. In general, waves may be considered deepwater waves when depth of water layer is greater than ½ wavelength.

deep water sailor: of or pertaining to deeper parts of ocean; said of men who went on extensive voyages as opposed to sailing in coasting ships.

deep water wave: surface wave, length of which is less than twice depth of the water. Velocity of deep water waves is independent of depth of water.

deflation: deflation (from Latin "to blow away") is erosion process of wind carrying off unconsolidated material.

deflection of the vertical: angle at point on earth (geoid) between vertical and direction of normal to spheroid of reference through the point.

degaussing: neutralization of strength of magnetic field of ship by means of suitably arranged electric coils permanently installed in ship.

degenerate amphidromic system: system of cotidal lines whose center or nodal (no-tide) point appears to be located on land rather than in open ocean.

degradation: general lowering of surface of land by erosion processes, especially by removal of material through erosion and transportation of flowing water.

degree: unit of angular measure equal to that angle at center of any circle subtended by an arc of 1/360 the circumference; such arc itself. It is divided into 60 *minutes*, each of which contain 60 *seconds;* thus, latitude, longitude, altitude, azimuth, declination, and other values, which may be regarded as either angles or arcs of circles, are written, e.g., $50° \ 22' \ 45''$, or fifty degrees, twenty-two minutes, forty-five seconds. Also, unit or division marked on an instrument, as a thermometer, clinometer, galvanometer, etc.

degree-days of frost: number of degrees that the mean daily air temperature fell below freezing point of fresh or saline waters. Total number of degree-days of frost during specific period is determined by adding deficiency of the mean air temperature from freezing point for each day in the period.

delicate sea lace [*Microcladia coulteri*]: lives on other algae which inhabit lower reaches of tide and extends short distance beyond low-tide mark. Quite abundant and easily recognized, sea lace is deep rose color. It is epiphytic, especially in *Gigartina, Prionitis* and *Grateloupia.* Delicate and lacy, average-sized specimen measures 4 to 10 in. in height, with several orders of rather firm narrow branches extending from central cylindrical or slightly compressed axis.

delphinid: member of family *Delphinidae*, group of toothed whales including almost all dolphins, the killer whales and pilot whales.

Delphinus: 1) small constellation west of *Pegasus* about 10° northeast of bright star *Altair*, containing no navigational stars; the *Dolphin;* also known as *Job's Coffin.* 2) genus of *Cetacea* including the typical *dolphins* and the *beluga* or white whale.

delta: accumulation of sediment where stream empties into a body of quiet water, resulting in building out of shoreline. Alluvial deposit roughly triangular or digitate in shape, formed at mouth of stream or tidal inlet.

delta moraine: glacial deposit in deep water with which delta deposits are associated.

Delta T [△ T]: in diving, term used to express temperature differential between two reference points. (Delta T was 60° F.)

delthyrium [*Brachiopoda*]: opening in pedicle valve adjacent to hinge line; serves for passage of pedicle.

deltidial plate [*Brachiopoda*]: plate of pedicle opening (delthyrium) in pedicle valve that constricts openings or with its mate from opposite side, closes it off completely.

demersal: 1) fishes which live on or near bottom. 2) eggs of certain bony fishes which have hard and smooth or adhesive membrane and sink to bottom. 3) said of swimming organism that prefers to spend most of its time on or very near bottom, e.g., flatfish, octopuses and shrimp.

demersal fish: in zoology, a fish that deposits its eggs on the sea bottom. In British usage, "wet fish," or those taken by trawlers and liners, as cod, haddock, halibut, sole, and turbot; opposed to herring, mackerel, and shellfish.

demurrage: 1) detention of vessel by charterer or his interests beyond period known as *lay days* stipulated in charter party for loading or discharging. 2) rate, allowance, or sum payable to a shipowner in compensation for such detention of his vessel. Unless otherwise agreed upon, demurrage is counted in running days, regardless of Sundays and holidays, upon expiration of lay days, when vessel is said to be *on demurrage*.

dendritic: referring to any branching form that resembles a tree in structure or appearance, especially drainage pattern of this shape.

dendritic drainage pattern: treelike pattern of tributaries of a main stream.

dendrochirote: member of *Dendrochirota*, class of shallow water sea cucumbers with branching tentacles and tube feet.

Dendroidea [graptolites]: most primitive graptolites. Thin thecal bred in groups of 3 and joined by stolons. Characteristically, each colony begins with 1 tubelike theca (sicuta) from whose base a threadlike nema extends. Dendroids bud in groups of 3. Ranged from late Cambrian to Mississippian, but they never became very abundant or attained great variety.

dendrophylliina: *Scleractinia*, simple or compound. Septa laminar of simple trabeculae but generally secondarily thickened, irregularly porous; synapticulae present.

densitometer: device for measuring density of seawater or of bottom sediments.

density: 1) ratio of mass of any substance to volume occupied by it; reciprocal of specific volume. 2) in oceanography density is equivalent to specific gravity and represents ratio at atmospheric pressure, of weight of given volume of seawater to that of equal volume of distilled water at $4.0°$ C ($39.2°$ F).

density current: highly turbid, relatively dense flow of sediment in water or air, by settling of sediment forming layers that grade upward from coarse to fine. Subsurface current heavier (denser) than surrounding water.

density layer: layer of water in which density increases with depth, enough to increase buoyancy of submarine.

denticle: 1) one of small, hard, toothlike structures found on bodies of extinct, primitive vertebrates. Such denticles later developed into teeth and denticles found on shark's skin. 2) in mollusks, small projection resembling a tooth around margin of gastropod aperture or pelecypod valve, especially near hinge.

dentin: hard, bonelike material that is major component of teeth. Mainly composed of type of calcium phosphate, dentin contains tiny tubules leading to soft pulp cavity deep inside tooth where there are nerves and blood vessels.

dentric: having irregular outline resembling tooth marks.

departure: determining position of ship in starting on a voyage.

deperming: process of changing magnetic condition of ship by wrapping large conductor around it a number of times in a vertical plane, athwartships, and energizing the coil thus formed. If single coil is placed horizontally around ship and energized, process is called flashing if coil remains stationary, and wiping if it moves up and down.

deposit: accumulation of solid material on sea bottom which eventually may become compacted and consolidated and form a sedimentary rock.

deposition: as soon as velocity of a stream falls below the point necessary to hold material in suspension the stream begins to deposit its suspended load. Deposition is a selected process. First, the coarsest material is dropped; then as velocity continues to slacken, increasingly finer material settles out.

depression: 1) vertical angular distance of a heavenly body *below* the horizon. 2) altitude of a circumpolar heavenly body at its lower culmination.

depth: vertical distance from specified sea level to sea floor. Charted depth is recorded distance from tidal datum to bottom surface at the point, using an assumed velocity of sound in waters of 800 fathoms per second (U.S.) and with no velocity or slope corrections made.

depth anomaly: graph constructed to determine difference between computed or thermometric depth and ideal or assumed depth of reversal of thermometers attached to Nansen bottle.

depth excess: difference between bottom depth and depth at which sound velocity is equal to either surface velocity, when there is no layer depth, or maximum velocity in surface layer.

depth factor: factor by which apparent depth of water measured stereoscopically is multiplied to give true depth. This factor is a ratio of tangent of incidence angle to tangent of refraction angle.

depth finder: instrument for determining depth of water, particularly an echo sounder.

depth ice: small particles of ice formed below surface of sea when it is churned by wave action.

depth of frictional resistance: depth at which wind-induced current direction is 180° from that of the wind.

depth of hold [ships]: vertical distance from top of keel to top of main deck beams.

depth zones: ocean water depths are usually grouped into 4 zones: littoral, high tide to low tide levels; neritic, low tide to 100 fathoms; bathyal, 100 to 500 fathoms; and abyssal, below 500 fathoms.

derelict: property permanently and voluntarily abandoned, or willfully cast away by its owner, as a vessel abandoned at sea.

derrick [ships]: device consisting of king post, boom, with variable topping lift and necessary rigging for hoisting heavy weights, cargo, etc.

desalination seawater: process by which enough dissolved salts are removed from seawater to render it potable.

desiccation: evaporation of water in unconsolidated sediments, resulting in shrinking and compaction. Tension cracks may form during process.

design wave: in design of harbors, harbor works, etc., type or types of wave selected as having characteristics against which protection is desired.

detritus: organic or inorganic loose matter formed of remains of plants and animals or disintegration of rocks. Detritus constitutes a sediment on ocean floor.

development [ships]: method of drawing the same lines on flat surface which have already been drawn on curved surface. Shapes and lines produced by development are same as though curved surface from which they are taken were a flexible sheet which could be spread out flat without change of area or distortion.

deviation: error in a magnetic compass caused by a ship's magnetism; or, angle at which *compass north* deviates from *magnetic north*, described as + *(plus)*, or easterly, when north point of compass is drawn toward east of magnetic north, and as ‾ *(minus)*, or westerly, when toward west of magnetic north.

deviation clause: 1) that embodied in a charter party stating that ship is permitted to call at other ports beside place at which cargo is to be discharged; **2)** in marine insurance, that indicating penalty for unjustifiable departure from voyage covered in policy.

devilfish [*Manta birostris*]: manta ray; also called "horned ray" because of 2 small fins, one on each side of head, which resemble horns. It is a giant of the sea and may be more than 20 ft. in "wingspread" and weigh as much as a ton and a half. Diet consists of crustaceans and small ocean life; teeth are small and found only on lower jaw. Unlike other rays, mantas live near surface.

Devonian: period of Paleozoic era which began about 400 million years ago and lasted for about 60 million years. Characterized by abundant marine invertebrates and fish and appearance of amphibians.

De wang: two-masted sailing dugout with outrigger used in Sassi Islands in Bismarck Archipelago. Hull has rounded sides and bottoms with ends terminating in sharp beaks, flat on top, usually carved, as are sides of canoe.

dextral: to the right. In gastropods, having aperture of shell on right side when shell apex is upward and aperture is facing observer (on observer's right). Gastropod coiling in which aperture is at the right when shell is held with apex uppermost.

dhow: since time immemorial the dhow has sailed waters of the Red Sea and Indian Ocean, from Rangoon to Zanzibar. General characteristics are sharp bow, with long overhang forward, great beam, raking transom stern, considerable sheer rising to high poop and lateen rig. There is generally a forecastle deck. Poop is often highly ornamented and studded with windows.

diagenesis: chemical and physical changes that sediments undergo after their deposition, compaction, cementation, recrystallization and perhaps replacement, which result in lithification.

diagonal line [ships]: line cutting the body plan diagonally from frames to middle line in loft layout.

Dial lugger: open clinker-built boat used in port of Dial in Southern England since 13th century. It formerly carried 3 lugsails with no jib. Later models discarded mainmast amidships. Small forecastle is built forward and small removable deckhouse amidships.

diameter: in diatoms, greatest width.

diastem: minor interruptions in sedimentation with or without accompanying erosion; if associated with changes in organism, these are judged to lack significant difference in age.

diastrophism: 1) term refers to all processes of earth movement and rock deformation, many of which result in changes of relative position, both vertical and horizontal. **2)** process or processes by which crust of earth is deformed and continents, ocean basins, plateaus and mountains, folds of strata and faults are produced.

diatom: 1) member of class of single-celled or colonial aquatic algae characterized by beautifully patterned siliceous shells. They form large and vital part of ocean's plankton and are source of food for many animals. Skeletons form deep layers of commercially valuable diatomaceous earth. 2) solitary or colonial creatures that build ornate shells or frustules of silica. Each frustule contains 2 parts, one of which partly covers the other, as a lid fits over a box. Oldest marine diatoms are found in late Cretaceous strata; freshwater species appear in lake beds of Tertiary Age. Modern diatoms form large part of sediment that settles on ocean bottoms, especially in arctic and antarctic regions.

diatomaceous earth: earthy siliceous deposit consisting mainly of shells of diatoms.

diatomaceous ooze: pelagic siliceous sediment composed of more than 30% diatom tests, up to 40% calcium carbonate and up to 25% mineral grains. This sediment generally is restricted to high latitudes or areas of upwelling such as Gulf of California.

diatomite: composed principally of accumulated tests of diatoms, which are made of opal. Diatoms have bivalved, siliceous shells in shape of discs, boats, ladders, crests, crescents, needles and many other forms. Many freshwater diatomites are formed from skeletons of small, thick-walled larval-shaped types. Other materials that may be present are clay minerals, detrital quartz, pumice and other rock pieces.

dichotomous: branching into 2 parts of each division.

Dicyemida: order of mesozoans characterized by elongated, symmetric body; single layer of flat cells enclosing a central cell; life cycle consists of sexual and asexual generations in intermediate host.

diffracted wave: wave whose front has been changed in direction by obstacle or other non-homogeneity in medium other than by reflection or refraction.

diffraction: phenomenon whereby waves traveling in straight paths bend around obstacle; bending of waves (sand, water, light, etc.) around obstacles.

diffusion: spreading or scattering of matter under the influence of concentration gradient with movement of stronger to weaker solution.

diffusion coefficient: constant of proportionality between rate of diffusion across a plane area and concentration gradient normal to that plane.

digenetic trematodes: flukes, trematode worms in which sexual adult stage is found in vertebrates and asexual larval stages in molluscs, usually gastropods.

digital disks [amphibians]: round adhesive pads on tips of fingers and toes of some frogs.

digitiform: finger-shaped.

dilatancy: expansion of granular masses such as sand when deformed because of rearrangement of grain.

dilution: reduction in concentration of dissolved or suspended substances by mixing with water of lower concentration.

diluvium: general term for all glacial and fluvio-glacial deposits of continental glaciation.

dimorphic: occurring in 2 forms as differently shaped shells of males and females or minerals identical in composition but having different crystal forms (calcite, aragonite). Sexual dimorphism describes a species in which male and female take 2 distinct, different forms.

dinghi: boat used for transportation on Ganges and Hugli Rivers of India. Open hull is not unlike early Egyptian craft in form, crescentric sheer meeting straight and strongly raking stem and sternpost in a point. Simple square sail hung from horizontal yard, supported by a mast stepped forward of rounded cabin. Sometimes a square topsail is set.

dinghy: small rowboat used as a tender. Popular as small racing craft, they are equipped with sail and outboard rudder.

Dinichthys: genus of huge (to 30 ft.), predatory, arthrodinan fishes; armor-plated, with heads jointed across neck; heavy, piercing teeth. Upper Devonian.

Dinoflagellata [phylum *Protozoa*]: 1) dinoflagellates form an order whose typical members are characterized by having 2 flagella, one trailing along in groove along main axis of cell, the other along transverse groove. Usually the cell is encased in ornamented cellulose theca made of 2 or more plates, but in simpler kinds this is lacking and 2 flagella arise from end of cell. There is often an eye spot or even a simple eye with lens. Nucleus is large and "chromatin" appears to be arranged in beaded filaments. Usually there is a system of vacuoles, probably for the intake of food by means of pseudopodia put out from rentral (longitudinal) groove, for although most dinoflagellates can photosynthesize, most are nixotrophic, that is, they can also ingest solid food. 2) single-celled, usually marine organisms showing either plant or animal characteristics (synthesize food material or eat); usually have 2 flagella, whiplike appendages and cellulose envelopes that are often beautifully sculptured. Some dinoflagellates comprise an important part of plankton. Certain species are luminescent, others form thick concentrations or "red tides" which may kill larger marine organisms.

dioecious: pertaining to organism in which male and female reproductive systems are in different individuals.

Diogenes pugilator [coenobitides]: zoeae of this species are very small; first stage is only 1.3 mm. long and after five stages it reaches only 2.8 mm. In first stage telson is invaginated, but in later stages is straight and there are, by this time, 2 pairs of pleopods. Megalopa is readily distinguished by much larger left chela and by relatively short abdomen which is about same length as carapace. Megalopa rarely exceeds 1.6 mm. in length.

diorite: rock which is chemically similar to andesite but has cooled slowly to coarsely crystalline state and is, therefore, called a Plutonic rock.

Diphda: also called *Deneb Kaitos, Beta (β) Ceti,* brighter of two navigational stars in *Cetus* (the Whale), of magnitude 2.2; Dec. 18¼° S., S.H.A. 349° 40'; located nearly on a line joining the two eastern stars of the Square of Pegasus *(Alpheratz* and *Algenib),* projected southward about 33°; also written *Difda.*

dipleurozoans [jellyfish]: these early Cambrian jellyfish were discovered in South Australia. They were oval in shape with scalloped edges, furrow ran lengthwise through upper surface, which was divided into many segments by diverging grooves. One small tentacle hung from tip of each segment.

diploblastic: formed of two layers of cells, outer epithelium and an inner gastrothelium; grade of construction of simpler coelenterates such as *Hydra.*

diploid: having twice the number of chromosomes normally occurring in mature germ cell.

dipteran: referring to member of *Diptera,* order of insects made up of true flies, e.g., houseflies, horseflies, gnats and mosquitoes.

Dipterus [lungfish]: looked like a fringe-fine until it opened its mouth, then it revealed greatly reduced jaw, nostrils at edge of jaws and broad, ridged teeth which suggest that their owner crushed mussel, snails and other shelled invertebrates. Skull contained many small bones, though some of surrounding ones of brain had degenerated into cartilage. Most significant feature is inferred because teeth and skull bones link it to living sunfish.

Dipurena halterata [phylum *Coelenterata*]: medusa of Coryne-like hydroid bearing same name. It is obviously similar to *Sarsia medusa,* particularly to *S. tubulosa,* from which it differs chiefly in having a swollen mouth region and terminal swelling of nematocysts on each tentacle. Widely distributed but never common species.

direction finding: principle and practice of determining bearing by radio means, using discriminating antenna system and radio receiver, so that direction of arriving wave, ostensibly direction or bearing of distant transmitter, can be determined.

directivity index: measure of sound pressure level in one direction, compared to that in all other directions.

direct tide: gravitational solar or lunar tide in ocean which is in phase with apparent motions of attracting body and consequently has its local maximums directly under the tide-producing body, on opposite side of earth.

discharge: rate of flow of water or ice from a river, fiord or harbor at given instant in terms of volume per unit time, e.g., cubic feet per second.

Discinacea [*Brachiopoda*]: ventral valve flat or concave with longitudinal pedicle slit; dorsal valve conical with eccentric umbo; subcircular. Middle Ordovician to Recent. *Trematis:* pedicle slit extends from posterior margin to umbo; shell surface punctate or pitted. *Orbiculoidea:* pedicle slit restricted by plate called a listrium growing between apex and slit as growth proceeds.

Discinisca lamellosa: found in shallow water or between tidemarks on coast of Peru. Shell differs both in texture and shape from other brachiopods, for it has horny appearance; a quarter of its composition consists of organic matter with remaining three quarters being largely calcium phosphate but with small percentage of calcium carbonate.

discoid [*Coelenterata*]: corallite with very flat, bottomlike form.

discolored water: seawater having color other than blues and greens normally seen; variations of red, yellow, green and brown, as well as black and white, have been reported. Discolorations may appear in patches, streaks or large areas and may be caused by concentrations of inorganic or organic particles or plankton.

Discomedusae: order of *Scyphozoa* comprising active marine forms with 8 or more tentaculocysts; regular alteration of generation occurs.

dismembered river system: drowned stream valley which, as a result of flooding, has its former tributaries enter the sea by separate mouths.

disphotic zone: dimly lighted zone extending from about 250 to 650 or more ft. Little plant production can take place in this zone and plants found here have mostly sunk from layer above.

displacement [ships]: weight in tons of water displaced by ship. This weight is same as total weight of ship when afloat.

displacement volume: volume of fluid displaced by plankton which has been drained of water and which is a measure of planktonic biomass.

display: graphic registration of processed data in easily readable form; analog graphs, lighted numerical readouts, charts showing geographic distribution, etc.

dissected: cut made by erosion into hills, ridges, valleys, etc. May be applied to submarine shelf or slope cut into by submarine canyons or sea valleys.

dissepiment: 1) in *Coelenterata*, small curved plate forming a vesicle. Typically occurs between septa near periphery of corallite with convex surface facing inward and upward. 2) in *Graptolithina*, crossbar uniting adjacent branches (stipes) of dendroid colony.

distal: part of appendage or other structure farthest from point of attachment. Away from point of origin.

distress: referred to a state of danger or necessity, a vessel is said to be *in distress* when in circumstances seriously hindering her continuance of a voyage, as due to fire, stranding, heavy weather change, machinery failure, or provision shortage.

distributary: outflowing branch of river that does not rejoin it. Characteristically occurs on a delta.

distribution graph: in hydrology a statistically derived hydrogen for a storm of specified duration graphically representing percent of total direct runoff passing a point on a stream, as function of time.

Ditylum [phytoplankton]: cells are elongated and at each end there is a pair of (or numerous small) spines and long central one which joins up the cells. There are numerous chloroplasts.

diurnal: 1) tides having period of cycle of approximately one lunar day (24.84 solar hours). Tides and tidal currents are said to be diurnal when single flood and single ebb occur each lunar day. 2) daily, especially pertaining to actions which are completed within 24 hours and which recur every 24 hours; most reference is made to diurnal cycles, variations, ranges, maximums, etc.

diurnal constituent: any tide constituent whose period approximates that of a lunar day (24.84 solar hours).

diurnal cooling: heat lost by surface of body of water during the night. This radiational loss manifests itself in small and transient positive gradient of temperature that is observed near surface in calm weather.

diurnal current: type of tidal current having only one flood and one ebb period in lunar day.

diurnal fluctuations: variations occurring within 24-hour period and related to rotation of earth.

diurnal heating: solar radiation absorbed by body of water during daylight hours. This short-wave radiation, by heating upper layer of water, creates in absence of wind a small and transient surface thermocline.

diurnal inequality: difference in height and/or time of 2 high waters or of 2 low waters of each day; also difference in velocity of either 2 flood currents or 2 ebb currents of each day.

diurnal range: amount of variation between maximum and minimum of any element during 24 hours.

diurnal variation: regular oscillation of compass needle from its mean position during the day, amounting in some places to as much as 12 minutes of arc.

diurnal vertical migration: daily vertical movement of certain members of plankton and nekton. Movement usually is triggered by change in light intensity and influenced by other factors such as temperature and gravity. Migration generally is upward at sunset and downward at sunrise.

divaricate [*Mollusca*]: sculpture consisting of chevrons.

divergence: 1) opposite of convergence; its effect is to create unlike organisms from same or similar ancestors. Thus, from ancient, primitive flesh-eating ancestor came dogs, bears and seals, each adapted to different food and ways of life. 2) horizontal flow of water in different directions, from common center or zone; often associated with upwelling.

divergence loss: part of transmission loss due to spreading of sound rays in accordance with the geometry of situation.

diversity: in zoogeography, an expression that is a function of both number of species present in given region or habitat and also relative proportions of their numbers.

diverted stream: in stream piracy, stream that was diverted from beheaded stream and flows to pirate stream.

diverticulum: saclike projection of tubular organ.

divide: higher land separating 2 adjacent drainage basins.

diving [saturated]: diving techniques in which human body is allowed to reach condition of complete saturation with dissolved gases at pressure encountered in given working depth. Ascent from these depths requires considerable time so that saturated gases can escape gradually and not in large bubbles, causing the bends. To safely dive at these depths saturated divers use large quantities of helium gas which is relatively non-toxic when it saturates the body.

diving bell: watertight working chamber open at bottom, which is lowered into water beneath which excavation or other works are to proceed. Compressed air is used to limit water level inside the bell.

diving trim: condition of submarine which is so compensated that complete flooding of main ballast, safety and low buoyance tanks, will cause it to submerge with neutral buoyancy and zero fore-and-aft trim.

DNA [deoxyribonucleic acid]: essential component of living matter, found in chromosomes and containing genetic code.

dock [ships]: basin for reception of vessels.

doctorfish [surgeon family]: West Indies species, average length of which is 10 in. Doctorfish is brownish with dark vertical bars on sides and oblique stripes across blue and brown dorsal and anal fins. Tail fin is multicolored with vertical striping of yellow and blue.

document: 1) to register, enroll, or license a vessel as required by law; 2) to furnish with necessary documents; 3) to attach cargo shipment papers to a bill of exchange.

dodger: folding hood, like top on convertible car, protecting entry to main companionway of sailboats.

dog [ships]: holdfast; short metal rod or bar fashioned to form clamp or clip and used for holding watertight doors, manholes or pieces of work in place.

dogbody: similar to chebacco boat, but square-sterned, cat schooner-rigged, about 36 ft. long with 11 ft. beam, full rounded bow, little cuddy forward with berth and sometimes fireplace for cooking. Used extensively in cod and mackerel fishing.

dogfish: small marine sharks, family *Squalidae*, found in schools near shore. Although destructive to other fishes and fishing equipment, they are valuable source of oil and fertilizer; considered a delicacy in Scandinavia.

dogger: sturdy two-masted vessel used by Dutch and other nearby peoples for fishing in German seas and on Dogger Banks. On mainmast were set 2 square sails; on mizzenmast was gaff sail and above that a topsail was carried. Dogger also had bowsprit with spritsail and 2 or 3 jibs.

doghouse [ships]: raised after portion of deckhouse or cabin trunk of sailing vessel to afford added protection and even living space at forward end of cockpit.

dogshores [ships]: last supports to be knocked away at launching of ship.

dogwatch [ships]: short watch of 2 hours. There are 2 dogwatches.

doldrums: 1) rainy equatorial belt of low air pressure and rising air. 2) nautical term for equatorial trough, with special reference to light and variable nature of winds. 3) shifting belt of light, variable winds, squalls and calms located near Equator between trade winds of Northern and Southern Hemisphere.

doliolarian larva: short-lived, free-swimming, non-feeding larva of certain shallow water crinoids. *Antedon.*

Doliolidae [*Urochordata*]: doliolids never form permanent colonies and like all thaliacians, have alternation of generations between sexual and asexual phases. Sexual phase (gonozooid) is commonly found in plankton consisting of barrel-shaped body with anterior inhalant branchial aperture and posterior exhalant atrial aperture. Body is encircled by 8 hoops of muscle and test is extremely thin; underlying mantle forms series of lobes around inhalant and exhalant apertures. Branchial sac occupies anterior part of body and communicates with peribranchial cavity by series of slits called stigmata.

Doliolum gegenbauri var. **tritonis** [*Urochordata*]: smallest sexual forms still bear stalk of attachment to asexual oozoid but lose this and soon grow to approximately 17 mm. long. Characteristic feature is that stigmata start on each side of mid-dorsal line behind third muscle band. Most anterior stigmata are round and small but rapidly increase in length posteriorly and join a ventral series which stretches forward only up to halfway between fourth and fifth muscle band. Second characteristic feature is that intestine is very short and wide and curls very sharply ventrally.

dollarfish: silvery, deep-bodied fish, laterally compressed, and round in profile, seldom exceeding six inches in length, plentiful on the U.S. Atlantic coast, and of excellent food value; also called *butterfish, harvestfish,* and *pumpkinseed.* The smaller similarly-shaped *lookdown* or *moonfish* of Atlantic and Pacific coasts of America is sometimes called a *dollarfish.*

dollop: portion of a sea which leaps over the rail and breaks with its fall on deck.

dolomite: sedimentary rock resembling limestone, except it is richer in magnesia.

dolphin: member of cetacean suborder *Odontoceti.* Name is used interchangeably with porpoise by some. More properly it is given to beaked members which have been given the name "whale" such as killer whale and pilot whale; brightly colored fish, blue or green and yellow with deep blue dorsal fin and yellow tail fin. These brilliant colors fade to nondescript grey soon after dolphin is caught. In profile a dolphin has high "forehead" and enlarged forward end to body which tapers gracefully to deeply-forked tail. Found in all seas from Arctic to Antarctica. Most are about 10 ft. long, carnivorous and travel in schools. Most prevalent dolphin is the common dolphin *(Delphinus delphis)* which prefers tropical or temperate waters. It is capable of speeds of 25 knots and can make spectacular leaps out of the water.

dolphin [ships]: term applied to several piles bound together and situated either at corner of pier or cut in the stream and used for docking and warping vessels.

dolphin striker [ships]: 1) short spar projecting downward beneath bowsprit, forming a member of the truss supporting jibboom. 2) metal strut extending down from bowsprit to bobstay to provide extra downward thrust.

Donald Duck effect: human voice assumes higher pitch when diver is subjected to helium-enriched breathing atmosphere. Special electronic "translators" lower pitch to normal levels.

donga: peculiar type of dugout canoe made from trunk of tar palm tree and used by native fishermen of Jessor Bengal, India. Due to shape of tree, prow of canoe has diameter of about 2 ft. 4 in. and stern only 11 in., length being 12 or 13 ft.

donkey engine [ships]: small gas, steam or electric auxiliary engine set on deck and used for lifting, etc.

doppler effect: apparent change in pitch of sound when source and listener are in motion relative to each other. To trained sonarmen, it reveals whether target is approachable or retiring.

Dorado: 1) name for the fish *dolphin;* 2) small star group about 20° east of *Canopus (a Argus)*, also called the *Goldfish* and the *Swordfish*.

dorsal: pertaining to back or upper surface.

dorsal valve: brachial valve of brachiopod.

dorsolateral folds [amphibian]: glandular folds of skin running from behind eye to region of base of hind leg in some frogs.

dory: small, flat-bottomed boat used extensively in fisheries of the U.S., especially in New England. It is open, keelless, clinker-built or rather wide planking; double-ended, both ends raking severely; sharp bows; narrow V-shaped stern. Dory was originated in Newburyport, Mass., about 1800, but it did not become popular in fisheries until middle of last century.

Dosinia sp. [*Heterodonta*]: shell is thicker dorsoventrally, broad end not curving away so steeply from umbo as in other venerids. This results in dorsal edge being longer. Length of shell is normally about 220 μ.

Douarnenez lugger: two-masted, cat-rigged lugger used in mackerel and sardine fisheries out of port of Douarnenez, on west coast of Brittany, France. Bow is high with straight stern, slightly raked; sheer line is almost straight, running to low stern, which is either transom or sharp; carvel-built.

double bottom [ships]: tank whose bottom is formed by bottom plates of ship, used to hold water for ballast, storage of oil, etc. Also term applied to space between inner and outer bottom skins of vessel.

double canoe: craft made up of 2 canoes of equal or nearly equal lengths placed parallel with one another and connected short distance apart by 2 or more transversely placed bows. Hulls were usually dugouts or partial dugouts with planks sewn on to form sides, as in case of the pahi of Tuamotu Archipelago.

double ebb: ebb current having 2 maximums of speed separated by smaller ebb speed.

double-ender: boat with stern shaped like its bow.

double flood: flood current having 2 maximums of speed separated by smaller flood speed.

double tide: high water consisting of 2 maximums of nearly same height separated by relatively small depression or low water consisting of 2 minimums separated by relatively small elevation.

doubling plates [ships]: extra plates (bars or stiffeners) added to strengthen sections where holes have been cut for hawser pipes, machinery, etc.

doublura: in horseshoe crabs, vertical surface of marginal reflected carapace of prosoma.

downdrift: direction of predominant movement of littoral sediment.

down-easter: sturdy 19th century sailing ship from New England to Maritime Province of Canada.

downhaul [ships]: rope by which jib or staysail is hauled down when set.

downward irradiance: radiant flux on infinite element of upper face (0° to 180°) or horizontal surface containing point being considered, divided by area of that element. Unit of measurement is watt per square meter (W/m^2).

drabbler [ships]: additional strip of sailcloth laced to bottom of bonnet to increase area. Common in Middle Ages.

Draco: northern constellation between *Cygnus* and *Ursa Minor*, containing the navigational star *Eltanin* (γ *Draconis*), magnitude 2.4, S.H.A. 91° 07′ and Dec. 51° 30′ N., which may be located at about 20° north and west of, and nearly in line with, the transept outlined in the cross of *Cygnus*.

draft, aft [ships]: draft measured at stern.

draft or draught [ships]: depth of vessel below to lowest part of hull, propellers or other reference point. Depth of a ship below waterline (usually when fully loaded) or depth of water needed to float free of bottom.

draft, extreme [ships]: draft measured to lowest projecting portion of vessel.

draft, forward [ships]: draft measured at bow.

draft, load [ships]: draft at load displacement.

draft marks [ships]: numbers which are placed in

vertical scale at bow and stern of vessel to indicate draft at each point.

draft, mean [ships]: average between draft measured at bow and at stern, or for vessel with straight keel, draft measured at middle length of waterline.

drag [ships]: amount that aft end of keel is below forward end when ship is afloat with stern end down.

dragon: large Viking ship used in warfare. This vessel was elaborately carved and decorated. Sides gleamed with stripes of color and gold, topped off by warriors' shields hung along gunwales.

dragonfish [lionfish, turkeyfish, zebrafish]: scorpaenid related to Mediterranean rockfish and found in tropical waters. Handsome fish with large graceful, diaphanous fins and tail colored in hues of pink and purple, tipped with poisonous spines. Reaches length of about a foot and feeds on crabs, crustaceans and other fishes.

dragon's tail: towed thermistor chain used to measure sea temperature.

drainage basin: drainage basin is entire area from which a stream and its tributaries receive water.

drain well [ships]: chamber where seepage water is collected and pumped by drainage pumps into sea.

draw: 1) to occupy a certain depth of water in floating; as, *ship draws 15 ft.* 2) to pull as a sail trimmed to the wind. 3) that portion of a bridge which may be raised or swung to allow passage of vessels.

dredge: 1) ship designed to remove sediment from channel or dock to maintain draft depths. 2) simple cylindrical or rectangular device for collecting samples of bottom sediment and benthic fauna.

dried ice: ice surface from which water has disappeared after formation of cracks and holes. During period of drying the surface becomes increasingly white.

dried weight: weight of organisms, such as plankton, fouling or benthos, when water has been driven out but which has not been ignited. Term dry weight is more commonly used in study of fouling.

dries: area of reef or other projection from bottom of body of water which periodically is covered and uncovered by water.

drift: 1) effect of velocity of fluid flow upon velocity (relative to fixed external point) of an object moving within fluid; vector difference between velocity of object relative to fluid and its velocity to fixed reference. 2) material deposited by glacier. 3) one of slower movements of oceanic circulation.

drift bottle: bottle of one of various designs which is released into sea for use in studying currents.

drift card: card such as is used in drift bottle, encased in buoyant, waterproof envelope and released in same manner as drift bottle.

drift current: 1) wide, slow-moving ocean current principally caused by winds, e.g., extension of North Atlantic Current (North Atlantic Drift) and West Wind Drift. 2) current determined from differences between dead reckoning and navigational fix.

drift net: any gill net suspended vertically from floats at required depth and free to drift. Used principally in mackerel, herring and sardine fishing, such nets may extend for 1½ miles from vessel.

drill: carnivorous gastropod, such as oyster drill and whelk, which uses its radula to drill a hole through shell of prey.

drive fishing: means of fishing in which fish are "herded" into enclosed area or net.

driver: fishing boat engaged in drift-net fisheries of English waters. Last quarter of a century has seen gradual abandonment of lug-rigged fishing boat and drift, or gill net, in favor of steamers and motorboats equipped with purse seines or trawls.

driver [ships]: similar to "ringtail." Sometimes term driver was used to mean a spanker. Also aftermast on 6-masted schooner.

drogue: 1) sea anchor, usually conically-shaped canvas bag with line from its wide end to ship, to keep bow into seas when hove to or stern to seas when running before wind. 2) current-measuring assembly consisting of weighted parachute and attached surface buoy. Parachute can be placed at any desired depth and current speed and direction can be determined by tracking and timing of surface buoy.

Dromia personatus [brachyurans]: zoeae of this species are heavily pigmented, especially on abdominal segments and telson. There are no spines on abdominal segments but posterolateral margins of carapace are prolonged into long spines. There are 5 stages of which last stage has 4 legs. Of these, only first bears a setose exopodite and other 3 have rudimentary ones. There are 4 pairs of pleopods. First stage is approximately 3 mm. long and fifth stage 6.5 mm.

dromond: large galley of Crusades period of Roman origin, with 2 rows of 25 oars each on either side. Probably three-masted, lateen-rigged. There was a deck above rowers for fighting purposes.

drougher: bluff-modeled vessel in transporting heavy cargoes, as "stone drougher"; also type of West Indian trader.

drowned valley: valley whose lower end has been inundated by the sea and thus converted into bay or estuary.

drum, black [sea drum]: bottom feeder, crushing

mollusks upon which it subsists by means of grinding pharyngeal teeth in throat. The drum is dusky-grey to coppery-black with stout, deep body and cluster of barbels beneath chin; spiny dorsal fin is much higher than soft-rayed dorsal. Black drum is usually under 6 lbs. in weight. With its scraggly "beard" and humped back, it is hardly a beautiful fish.

drum family [*Sciaenidae*]: in this family of fishes body is compressed and somewhat elongated, shaped much like that of a bass. All parts are covered with ctenoid scales, extending over bases of vertical fins. Lateral line is well developed extending across caudal fin; head is large and covered with scales; teeth on jaws; no supplemental maxillary bone in upper jaws, which are somewhat protractile. Pseudobranchiae are well developed; slit behind fourth gill; gill membranes are free from isthmus. Dorsal fin is deeply notched and soft part is much longer than spinous part; spinal fin has 1 or 2 spines; bones are well-developed; air bladder is large. A large family of food and game fishes living in temperate and warm seas.

drum, freshwater [freshwater sheepshead]: species of silty lakes and large rivers where it feeds along bottom in muddy water on snails and mussels, crushed by powerful pharyngeal teeth. Occurs from Great Lakes southward through central U.S. The drum is metallic blue-green with yellowish tints; average size is 15 in. long and 2 lbs. in weight.

drumlin: elongated or oval hill or glacial drift, normally compact and unstratified, usually with longer axis parallel to direction of movement of transporting ice.

drum, red [channel bass or red bass]: metallic bronze or pinkish fish with faint lengthwise brown stripes and black spots at base of tail fin. This drum turns bright red after it is caught. Large individual grows to length of 5 ft. and weighs up to 75 lbs.

drum, sea [*Pogonias cromis*]: humpback fish with chin whiskers, soft dorsals 20—23; scales along lateral line 42—45. Body rather elongate, strongly arched above, not strongly compressed laterally. Mouth moderate; teeth on jaws small and arranged in irregular bands; barbels present under chin; cheeks scaly. Color silvery-grey to dark brown; fins dark; young with 4 or 5 broad, dark vertical bands. Maximum size 146 lbs., but only smaller ones enter fresh water.

drupe shell, brown-lipped [*Drupa brunncolabrum*]: shell of this species is rough externally and crossed by small transverse ridges and rough folds. Tubercles which cover body whorls are larger posteriorly. Reaches about 1 in. in length.

drupe shell, brown scaly [*Drupa fuscoimbricata*]: shell is oval or spindle-shaped and covered with sharp, conical tubercles. In life the shell is reddish-brown; in old shells it is white and red. Reaches length of about 1 in.

drupe shell, bushy [*Drupa species*]: surface of this shell is longitudinally grooved. Row of spots placed in grooves form interrupted brown band which encircles body whorl. Shell is brownish-white without and purplish-grey within inner lip. Reaches length of about ¾ of an inch.

drupe shell, castor bean [*Drupa ricina*]: this mollusc produces a shell which is low and domelike in appearance and covered by short black-tipped spines. Well-developed row of spines borders outer lip; aperture is bordered by teeth in both outer and inner margins. Shell is white both outside and inside, except for spines which are black-tipped.

drupe shell, gooseberry [*Drupa grossularia*]: this drupe shell is compressed in form and has short spire. Outer surface is covered by very small scales and low spiral ridges; these ridges become knobby toward spire and are drawn out beyond lip to form fingerlike processes. Outer surface is whitish or yellowish in color, while aperture is bright orange or yellow; 1½ in. long.

drupe shell, granular [*Drupa granulata*]: surface of this species is covered by very fine revolving ridge and spiral rows of tubercles. Shell is dark brown or black. Aperture is lighter in color usually violet or blue bordered by 2 large teeth. Reaches 1 in. in length.

drupe shell, knobbed [*Drupa nodus*]: surface of this species is covered with rows of tubercles separated by single spiral ridge. Shell is white or orange, tubercles are black and aperture is violet. Reaches length of 1 in.

drupe shell, little basket [*Drupa fiscellum*]: surface of this species is longitudinally and spirally ridged forming recticulated pattern with deep pits. Aperture is purplish and bears whitish teeth within. Measures about ¾ in. in length.

drupe shell, mulberry [*Drupa morum*]: shell of this mollusc is extremely heavy and thick and covered over outer surface by larger, heavy, blunt tubercles. Spire is very short and aperture is toothed on both sides. Outside of shell is dirty whitish color which is black upon tubercles; aperture is violet. Large specimens will measure 1¾ or possibly 2 in. long.

drupe shell, purple-mouthed [*Drupa porphyrostoma*]: this species has shell which is grooved longitudinally and encircled by many fine ridges. It is yellow or white without and usually blue or violet within aperture. Reaches length of nearly 1 in.

drupe shell, showy or brilliant [*Drupa speciosa*]: this mollusc has heavy shell encircled by very fine ridges. It is also grooved and ridged longitudinally with large tubercle placed upon ridges; both outer lip and columella are toothed. Outer surface is yellowish-white, while aperture is rose-colored within and bordered about lip by yellow or yellowish-brown. It varies in length from 1½ to 2½ in.

drupe shell, small: this morula is crossed by longitudinal and transverse ridges which bear nodules. Spire is sharp and aperture is small; whitish in color and nodules are in alternate rows of orange and black. About 1½ in. long.

drupe shell, spiderlike [*Drupa arachnoides*]: drupe shell is low and domelike in appearance and covered over upper surface by black-tipped spines which become longer toward margin. Inner and outer sides of aperture are bordered by teeth. It is white over outer surface except for spines which are marked with black; aperture is bordered by yellow or orange. About 1 in. long.

drupe shell, yellow-mouthed [*Drupa ochrostoma*]: this morula is marked by longitudinal grooves and ridges which bear prominent tubercles where they cross smaller encircling ridges. It varies in color from white through yellowish to chocolate; aperture may be either white or yellowish. About 1 in. long.

dry dock [ships]: dock into which vessel is floated, water then being removed to allow for construction or repair of ships.

dry organic matter: dry plankton less ash after ignition. Most reliable and preferred weighing method in determining biomass.

dry plankton: plankton dried to constant weight by specified method.

duct: layer in ocean or atmosphere where refraction and probably reflection result in trapping of electromagnetic waves or sound waves.

ducting: trapping of sound or electromagnetic waves within layer, resulting in extended ranges.

dugong: aquatic, herbivorous mammal, sometimes referred to as a sea cow, of the order *Sirenia* allied to manatee, but with bilobate tail like that of whale.

dugout: canoe or boat made by hollowing out of a log and shaping it into form of vessel, usually sharp-ended. Dugout was earliest form of hollow water craft and by the Stone Age it had reached well-developed state of efficiency.

dulse or red kale [*Rhodymenia palmata*]: widely distributed, found in tide pools or on rocks at mean low-tide marks where it often forms a distinct zone. May be recognized by dull red, forked, irregularly divided, rosettelike blades which have texture of thin rubber. Numerous blades 5 to 15 in. tall and 1 to 3 in. wide, arise from short, inconspicuous stipe; blades are flat, membranous, sometimes cut into a few segments or

into narrow ribbons. Scientific name (*Rhodymenia palmata*) indicates that the seaweed is shaped like the palm of a hand. Attachment to substratum may be by small disc or by number of root-like hairs or rhizomes.

dum: Dutch fishing boat of Scheveningen, husky and clinker-built, beamy and shallow-draft. It is sloop-rigged with short curved gaff and long boom on mainsail, 1 or 2 headsails and long bowsprit. Outboard rudder is slung from transom stern.

dumped deposit: accumulation of sediment deposited more rapidly than waves and currents are able to redistribute it.

dumping ground: sea area within which material dredged from other areas is deposited.

dundee: name given to large ketches used by Bretons in fisheries off Iceland.

dunnage: 1) pieces of cordwood, boards, slats, etc. appropriately placed under and around cargo in a ship's hold for protection of goods against contact with bilge water, leakage from other cargo, contact with ship's sides or structural parts and condensation therefrom; to chock off and secure cargo from moving, thus preventing chafing; to separate different kinds or consignments of goods; and to provide air passage through certain otherwise closely packed commodities, such as bagged rice, onions, and others requiring ventilation. 2) collective term for working material, such as tools, equipment, and extra building parts found on board ship at a repair yard. 3) baggage of a seaman. 4) equipment carried in a boat or canoe for shore camping, etc.

duration: in terrestrial magnetism it is the time required for completion of magnetic storm, short-period magnetic fluctuations or quiet period; usually expressed in normal time intervals, e.g., 5 days, 2 hours or 150 seconds. Time elapsed from beginning of flood, ebb or slack tides to their culmination.

dutchman [ships]: piece of steel fitted into opening to cover up poor joints or crevices caused by poor workmanship.

dwt: common abbreviation for deadweight tonnage.

dye shell, allied [*Purpura affinis*]: this dye shell is a large and interesting species with straight, thick, heavy spindle-shaped shell which ends in pointed spire. It is covered over outer surface by 2 rows of large, heavy, blunt tubercles between which striations are often visible; aperture is comparatively small in the species; outer lip is toothed on inner margin. Entire outer surface of shell is white; aperture is yellowish-brown within. Reaches length of at least 3 in.

dye shell, harp [*Purpura harpa*]: this shell is covered by revolving ridges which are crossed by oblique longitudinal furrows and ridges. Outer surface of shell is chocolate and spotted with white; shell is bluish within and marked with brown uponlip and on columella. Reaches length of about 1¼ in.

dye shell, intermediate [*Purpura intermedia*]: this shell is heavy and firm, low and domelike in outline and covered over outer surface with low, blunt tubercles. It is yellowish-white and brownish in color and marked over columella and outer lip with brown; aperture is bluish within. It is about 1½ in. long.

dye shell, open [*Purpura aperta*]: this mollusc produces a shell which is large, heavy and domeshaped and covered with short blunt tubercles or spines. It is white or yellowish on outside of the shell; aperture is white within but tinged with yellow about lip and on columella. Reaches 3 in. in length.

dynamically moored [ships]: referring to use of dynamic positioning, maintaining ship in relatively fixed position (with respect to sea floor) without using anchors.

dynamic calculations: procedure based on summation of dynamic depth intervals from surface of ocean to any specified level; dynamic differences between stations are derived and consequently relative speed and direction of currents at different levels.

dynamic height: amount of work done when water particle of unit mass is moved vertically from one level to another; dimensions are those of potential energy per unit mass.

dynamic height anomaly: in oceanography, excess of actual geopotential difference between 2 given isobaric surfaces, over geopotential difference in homogeneous water column of salinity 35 per mille (0/00) and temperature 0° C.

dynamic meter: standard unit of dynamic height expressed as 10 square meters per second per second. Its inclusion in hydrostatic equation eliminates factor of gravity acceleration in dynamic calculations.

dynamic theory: theory considering horizontal tide-producing forces to be most important factor in causing movement of water. Vertical tide-producing forces are simply considered small periodical variations in acceleration of gravity.

dynamic topography: configuration formed by geopotential difference or dynamic height (measured in dynamic meters) between given isobaric surface and reference surface. Topographic chart formed may be used in determining geostrophic currents within oceans. Current along isopleths of dynamic height must be considered to move relative to motion of water at reference surface.

dynamometer: instrument used in bottom sampling or other oceanographic operations to indicate that bottom has been reached. Instrument measures variations in wire tension and is only effective to depths where tension due to weight of sampling device is somewhat greater than tension caused by weight of lowering cable and variable loads produced by ship motion.

E

E: 1) corresponds to Greek leter *epsilon* (ϵ), designating the fifth star (originally in point of brilliancy or magnitude) of a particular group; as ϵ *Orionis*, fifth in the constellation *Orion*. 2) abbreviation for *East* in compass points, as in E by S *(East by South)*; E N E *(East-north-east)*. 3) in International Code of Signals, flag *E*, hoisted singly, indicates *"I am directing my course to starboard"*; in Lloyd's classification system, stands for lowest class; in that of American Bureau of Shipping, an encircled *E* annexed to classification symbols signifies vessel's *equipment* complies with requirements of the Society's rules.

ear shell, chestnut-colored: chestnut-colored ear shell is small conical species with short spire. Smooth polished shell, it is covered in life by a smooth periostracum. Aperture of shell is narrow and bears about 7 teeth on outer lip and about 4 on inner lip. Measures about ½ in. long.

ear shell, closed: this little ear shell is comparatively thin and light in construction and bears an elevated conical spire. Outer surface is marked by encircling lines; aperture is oval in outline and has 3 teeth or folds projecting into it from inner lip. It is light brown, marked by darker brown areas and bands. Each whorl bears a dark central band and anterior end of shell is marked by a dark area. It is about ¼ in. long.

earth current [Telluric Current]: natural electrical currents circulating in crust of earth, constituting worldwide system subject to spasmodic and periodic variations in intensity and direction which are consistently related to changes noted in other cosmic phenomena, such as earth's magnetic field, aurora and solar activity.

earth's magnetic poles: areas in higher latitudes where lines of magnetic force converge.

earth tide: periodic movement of earth's crust caused by tide-producing forces of moon and sun.

east: 1) that one of four cardinal points of the compass lying on one's right hand when facing north; point of the horizon at which the sun rises at the equinoxes; general direction in which sun rises. *The East* connotes Asiatic lands in general; *Near East* comprising Arabia, Asia Minor, Iran, Iraq, Turkey, etc.; *Far East*, China, Indo-China, Japan, Korea, etc. 2) from the east; as *an east wind*.

East Africa Coast Current: seasonal current influenced by monsoon drifts of Indian Ocean. It flows southward along coast of Somalia in Northern Hemisphere winter and northward from about 10° S during Northern Hemisphere summer.

East Australia Current: current formed by parts of Southern Equatorial Current and flows southward along east coast of Australia. East Australia Current turns and joins northeast flow through Tasman Sea.

east by north [E. by N.]: one point or 11¼° north of *east*.

east by south [E. by S.]: one point or 11¼° south of *east*.

East Greenland Current: current setting south along east coast of Greenland and carrying water of low salinity and low temperature. East Greenland Current flows through Denmark Strait between Iceland and Greenland and joins Irminger Current. Greater part of current joins counterclockwise circulation south of Greenland; part curves to right around tip of Greenland and flows northward into Davis Strait as West Greenland Current.

East Ice: sea ice which drifts from Arctic Ocean south along east Greenland coast, around Kap Farrel and up southwest coast of Greenland.

East Indian: large armed cargo-carrying ships that were owned and operated by British East India Company. Also known as Indiamen.

easting: distance eastward from given meridian; distance made by ship on eastern course, expressed in nautical miles.

east-northeast [E.N.E.]: two points or 22½° north of *east*.

east-southeast [E.S.E.]: two points or 22½° south of *east*.

East Wind Drift: west-setting current close to Antarctic Continent caused by polar easterlies.

Ebalia tuberosa [*Leucosiidae*]: zoea is characterized by small size and extreme reduction of lateral spines. Both dorsal and rostral spines are absent.

ebb axis: average direction of tide current at strength of ebb.

ebb current: this tidal current associated with decrease in height of tide. Ebb currents generally set seaward or in opposite direction to tide progression.

ebb interval: interval between transit of moon over meridian of a place and time of strength of following ebb tidal current.

ebb strength: ebb tidal current at time of maximum speed, usually associated with lunar tide phases and spring near perigee and/or maximum river discharge.

ebb tide: outgoing or falling tide.

ebullition: condition of any liquid when bubbles are rapidly forming and rising to surface. Term having same meaning as boiling.

Echinidae [phylum *Echinodermata*]: in this family, test has no depressions or pitlike hollows. Tubercles are smooth; each ambulacral plate has at least 3 pairs of pores. General outline of test is circular; periproct covered with small plates of varying size. There are peristomial gills, situated in shallow indentations of peristome. Pedicellariae are globe-shaped with 1 or 2 teeth on either side of valves. Attachment to stalk is direct, without a neck.

Echinoderidae [phylum *Trochelmia*]: microscopic or submicroscopic animals, not more than 1/8 in. long. Body externally segmented into 13 rings, third and fourth rings being fused. Two bristles terminate anal segment.

Echinodermata [phylum]: 1) echinoderms are peculiarly different from all other animals. This great phylum includes starfishes, echinoids, crinoids, blastoids and cystoids. Bodies are short and commonly globular; almost all have radial and 5-rayed symmetry. Nearly all develop shell in form of limy plates that are secreted in body wall and fit edge-to-edge like pieces in a mosaic. Greek "*echinos*," hedgehog; "*derma*," skin. 2) sea urchins: typical echinoid has globular or bun-shaped body bristling with slender, movable spines, therefore the name. Mouth is at center of lower side and axis of body is vertical. Stripping away spines, body wall of animal is rigid, boxlike shell of polygonal plates arranged in 20 vertical columns. Upon these plates are scattered small rounded nubs, each of which was point for spine. Starfishes are distinguished by star-shaped form, body being depressed and extended at sides into tapering rays. Skeleton is made of small limy plates, articulated by fleshy tissues to permit some flexibility, as in coat of chain mail. Crinoids or sea lilies look more plantlike than animallike for globular bodies are supported by flexible stalks which anchor them to sea floor, mouth upward. Animal consists of three chief parts: stem, body proper and series of branching arms. Blastoids or sea buds form another group of stalked echinoderms. Bodies are globular or bud-shaped and encased in shell of 13 chief plates of which 3 form basal cycle, while 2 suc-

ceeding cycles have 5 plates each. There are no arms, food grooves lying upon surface of body. Cystoids are primitive echinoderms with globular or almond-shaped bodies but differ from both crinoids and blastoids in that plates are irregularly arranged so that body shows up no definite symmetry.

Echinodorella remanei [family *Echinoderidae*]: conspicuous lateral spines present on posterior border of dorsal plates of segments 8 to 11. Mid-dorsal spines of considerable length occur on segments 6 to 10. Close-set fringe of small, even setae present on middle part of segment 4, running around ventral and lateral portions. No eyes are present.

Echinoidea [phylum *Echinodermata*]: echinoderm is enclosed in hard shell made up of immovable plates joined together in regular pattern. Shell may be somewhat globular, or it may be ovoid or flattened to form thin, circular disc. Outside of shell covered with stiff spines, articulating in any direction on tubercles or bosses, in ball-and-socket fashion. Tube feet, in 10 equally spaced bands, radiate from upper center of test or apical pole. Test divided into 10 regular areas. These include sea urchins, cake urchins and sanddollars.

Echiurida [phylum *Annulata*]: these are *Gephyrea* which are peculiar in having solid outgrowth of dorsal portion of head to form long, spoon-shaped or troughlike extension like a proboscis. Grooved or hollow ventral side is ciliated; sinuous digestive tube begins with expanded pharynx and continues through body to posterior end, where anus opens to outside. No special sense organs except proboscis. There are no parapodia or other appendages, except for 2 large setae on ventral side not far from mouth and 2 circlets of setae around anal region. Lie in sand and mud or among stones in shallow water.

echogram: continuous profile of ocean floor produced by echo sounder.

echo ranging: determination of distance by measuring time interval between emission of sonic or ultrasonic signal and return of its echo from bottom. Instrument used for this purpose is called echo sounder.

echo sounder: instrument that determines depth of body of water or object below surface by measuring lapse of time between emission of sound signal and receipt of its reflection from bottom. It may be either sonic or supersonic.

echo sounding: determination of depths based upon speed of sound through water (4800 ft. per second, nearly), essentially consisting of a means of sending out a sound of sufficient intensity from ship's bottom, receiving the echo from sea floor, and accurately indicating depths obtained; also called *sonic* and *acoustic* sounding.

ecology: scientific discipline involving interrelationships among animals, plants and their environment.

ecosystem: ecological system consisting of all living members of biological community and all nonliving factors affecting them.

ectoderm: embryonic cell layer of the Eumetazoa forming outer epithelium lining mouth and various other structures.

ectoparasite: any parasite that lives on outer surface of an animal.

Ectoprocta [*Electra pilosa*]: larva is conical shape with blunt apex which is displaced somewhat posteriorly. Color is opaque yellow-brown; width is approximately 0.5 mm. at widest point of later larva. Larva of this species, sometimes called *Cyphonautes compressus*, constitutes almost half of cyphonautes to be found in plankton.

Ectoprocta [*Membranipora membranacea*]: cyphonautes of this species is distinguished from *E. pilosa* by its transparency and more nearly symmetrical shape. Posterior margin of oral edge bears rounded protuberance. Length of oral edge is 0.7 mm., i.e., much larger than *E. pilosa*. Cyphonautes of *M. membranacea* is dominant cyphonautes larva of summer and reaches its maximum abundance during October and November. It is sometimes referred to as *Cyphonautes balticus*.

E.D.: abbreviation in American and British hydrography for *existence doubtful*, placed near a charted rock, shoal, wreck, or other obstruction, indicating that neither actual presence nor reported nonexistence of such was verified at time of publishing chart.

eddy: circular movement of water usually formed where currents pass obstructions between 2 adjacent currents flowing counter to each other or along edge of permanent current.

eddy-built bar: sediment deposit believed to be formed by rotation action of eddies in tidal lagoon. Ridges surrounding some emerged Carolina bays may have been developed this way.

eddy diffusion: transfer of matter by turbulent eddies in a fluid.

eddy flux: rate of transport (or flux) or fluid properties such as momentum, mass, heat or suspended matter by means of eddies in turbulent motion; rate of turbulent exchange.

eddy heat conduction: transfer of heat by means of eddies in turbulent flow, treated analogously to molecular conduction.

eddy viscosity: turbulent transfer of momentum by eddies, giving rise to internal fluid friction in manner analogous to action of molecular viscosity in laminar flow, but taking place in much larger scale. Value of coefficient of eddy viscosity is of order 10^4 square centimeters per second.

edema: swelling within body tissues or main body cavities caused by accumulation of body fluid due to defective circulation.

edentate, edentulous [*Mollusca*]: without teeth.

edgewater: in oil and gas wells, water that holds oil and gas in higher structural positions. Edgewater usually encroaches on a field after much oil and gas has been recovered and pressure has been greatly reduced.

edge wave: ocean wave traveling parallel to coast with crest normal to coastline. Such a wave, has height that diminishes rapidly seaward and is negligible at distance of one wavelength offshore.

edge zone [*Coelenterata*]: fold of body wall of polyp that extends laterally and/or downward over sides of corallite.

Edman current meter: mechanical device for measuring ocean current velocity. A sensitive impeller is turned by current action and number of turns recorded on attached dial. Speed is measured indirectly from number of impeller revolutions by means of conversion tables.

edrioasters [seated stars]: unique group of echinoderms that appeared in early Cambrian and lived on into Pennsylvanian period. Looks rather like a tiny starfish attached to relatively large button. Actually the button is a calyx made up of overlapping plates that seem to have no special arrangement. Star consists of ambulacra with food grooves from mouth which must have been ciliated and were covered by movable plates.

edta: primitive form of dugout canoes used at Patna, Bengal, India, made from stem of semul tree.

eel: any of the elongated snakelike fishes having no ventral fins, a smooth slimy skin, and often without scales. The *common eel* of Europe and North America, which has minute skin-embedded scales, is considered an excellent food fish. It is remarkable that, although preferring freshwater life, these eels breed only in a warm deep-sea locality, the larvae having been found on coral bottom off Bermuda and the young discovered to have taken up the parents' original habitat.

eel, American: olive-brown fish with yellowish sides; when full grown and ready to return to sea, back becomes a darker color and sides turn silvery. Mature eels are usually 3 to 4 ft. long and weigh up to 5 lbs. They hide among stones and bottom debris of streams and pools by day, with only head visible, and venture forth at night to feed. Eels have small but effective teeth, are voracious carnivores and are also scavengers, eating any kind of food living or dead. Thus they are often found beneath docks and wharves. Eels mature when 5 to 20 yrs. of age, at such time making their way downstream. Seaward migration begins in summer.

eel family [*Anguillidae*]: long, snakelike body of eel is covered with minute, elongated scabs embedded in skin. Some of scales are arranged at right angles to one another. Head is small and conical; bones are much modified from those of typical fish. Preopercle and premaxillary bones are present; maxillaries are absent. Ventral fins are absent; pectoral fins are present; dorsal fin is long and its rays are short.

eelgrass: submergent marine plant with very long narrow leaves.

eelpout: several species of marine fishes, family *Zoarcidae*, resembling blennies; found in shallow to deep bottoms.

eka: clinker-built, flat-bottomed rowing boat used for fishing on small lakes of Sweden. Bottom curves up at ends to narrow, square bow and stern and there is good sheer. Average length is from 15 to 16 ft. with beam of 5 ft. 6 in.

Ekman spiral: theoretical representation of effect that a wind blowing steadily over ocean of unlimited depth and extent and of uniform viscosity would cause surface layer to drift at angle of 45° to right of wind direction in Northern Hemisphere.

elasmobranch: member of fish class *Elasmobranchii* or *Chondrichthyes* that includes shark, rays, skates, chimaeras and various extinct species. They are vertebrates with complete backbones, movable, well-developed jaws and paired fins. Skeletons are formed of cartilage, not bone.

elastic limit [ships]: point beyond which added stress will produce deformation of material.

elbow: sudden turn in a river or coastline. A short pipe fitting or pipe turning at a sharp angle (usually 90°); an *ell*.

electric log: graphic recording of various electrical properties of sediment or rock through which hole has been drilled. Obtained by lowering electrodes into hole.

electric ray: any of family *Torpedinidae* of rays possessing pair of electric organs capable of delivering a strong shock to humans if handled.

electrolysis: act or process of chemical decomposition by an electric current; e.g., that seen in wastage of iron or steel in vicinity of a bronze-bladed propeller, commonly attributed to "galvanic action," or voltaic current, set up through seawater between the bronze and steel. As a means of protection against such action, plates of zinc usually are fitted to both rudder and sternposts. The zinc only then is attached and is from time to time renewed as required.

electron: negatively charged particles forming part of all atoms.

elephanta: south to southeast gale, accompanied by rain, prevalent in September and October, or with ending of the Southwest monsoon, on the southwest coast of Bay of Bengal.

elephant fish: chimeroid fish of about two feet in length found in the South Pacific and vicinity of Cape of Good Hope; so-called from its snout of remarkable proboscis-like appearance.

elevated island: island that rises to few feet above high tide on reef flat and consists either of sand and debris or of solid reef rock.

elevation: vertical distance above or below reference point or surface. Most elevations are measured relative to mean sea level. Average elevation of earth's solid surface is 7,500 ft. below mean sea level.

elk kelp: one of genus *Pelagophycus* of large brown algae consisting of massive holdfast and long stipe terminated by large bulbous pneumatocyst from which single forked lamina-bearing branch radiates. Genus occurs only on Pacific coast of North America from Point Conception, California, southward along coast of California and Baja California. Reaches lengths of 100 ft. or more.

Ellobiidae [family]: ear shells have spirally arranged shell which looks somewhat like cone shells in general appearance. Outer surface of shell is covered by horny periostracum and aperture is elongated and bears teeth or folds along inner lip. Ear shells are family of more than 100 species which are worldwide in warm waters. (Phylum *Mollusca*.)

Elminius modestus [crustacean larvae]: dominant barnacle in southeast waters spreading to other regions. Nauplius is similar to that of *B. balanoides* in shape and in having posterior pair of spines on carapace. Labium is trilobed, large median lobe projecting posteriorly. Stage 2 nauplius is approximately 0.4 mm. long.

El Nino: warm current setting south along coast of Ecuador. It generally develops just after Christmas concurrently with southern shift in tropical rain belt.

elongation: angular distance between a satellite and its primary, or between the sun and planets *Mercury* or *Venus;* greatest distance in azimuth, east or west, of a circumpolar star from the pole.

elops: genus of fishes of the tarpon family which contains the *tenpounder* or *big-eyed herring* found in warmer waters of the Atlantic and Pacific.

elutriator: device for washing or sizing very fine powders in upward current of water.

emarginate [fish]: slightly notched.

embarkation: that which is embarked or placed aboard a ship; act of embarking or going on board a vessel or boat.

embayment: bay or formation resembling a bay.

embryology: branch of biology dealing with development of animals.

emergence: fact that part of ocean floor has become dry land but does not imply whether recession of sea or elevation of land was specific cause.

emergents: algae and sea grasses which are at least partially exposed at lowest low water.

emissarium: floodgate or sluice.

Emplectonematidae [phylum *Nemertea*]: in this family are forms having openings of mouth and proboscis united. Body is long, very slender and contractile; head and body are confluent, without necklike constriction. Cerebral fossae are only slightly developed. Proboscis is quite small and thick.

Encampia [phytoplankton]: cells, concave at each end, united to form very characteristic spiral chains.

encrusting [*Bryozoa*]: colony which forms broad sheet over substrata to which it is attached.

endemic: food only in a given region.

endite: in *Crustacea*, inner lobe or cuticular extension from certain basal segments of appendages; endites of amphipod and isopod thoracic limbs from broad brood pouch in females or gnathobases of appendages of trilobites and of *Limulus* (horseshoe crab).

endoderm: embryonic cell layer from which stomach and its diverticula and glands are formed in *Eumetazoa*.

endogenous detritus: detritus originating in locality where it is found.

endogenous plankton: plankton originating in regions where it is found.

endopodite: in *Crustacea*, inner ramus of biramus appendage. Also endopod.

endopsammon: microscopic fauna of sand and mud.

endoskeleton: skeleton produced within flesh of animal.

endosternite: scleratized process of inner surface of cephalothoracic exoskeleton in certain arthropods for muscle attachment.

endostyle: glandular ciliated groove along ventral side of pharynx in *Urochordata*, *Cephalochordata* and lamprey larvae.

endrol: native term for canoe in Admiralty Islands. The outrigger sailing canoe is a dugout, ends being formed by inserting long blocks of wood into open ends of hollowed log. These blocks are carved and painted to represent a crocodile's head.

energents: algae and sea grasses which are at least partially exposed at lowest low water.

energy coefficient: ratio of energy in wave per unit crest length transmitted forward with wave at point in shallow water to energy in a wave per unit crest length transmitted forward with waves in deep water.

en flute [ships]: describing a ship with guns removed, exposing row of empty gunports.

Enif: 1) *Epsilon* (ϵ) *Pegasi*, a star of magnitude 2.5 and declination 9° 38′ N., having a S.H.A. of 34½°. A line joining the two stars marking south side of *Square of Pegasus*, extended 20° westward, passes close to *Enif*. 2) the transverse of a well-defined cross in *Cygnus*, prolonged south and east for about 25°, will nearly locate the star.

ensign [ships]: flag or banner distinguishing a vessel. In both Navy and Merchant Marine the ensign is national flag; in British Merchant service the ensign has a field of red with union in upper corner, next to staff.

ensonity: penetration of sound into any particular part of sea.

enter: 1) to set down in writing; to record; as an entry in a ship's log. 2) to report to, and supply customs authorities at a port with, required information relating to an arriving or soon departing vessel, her cargo, stores, etc.

Enteropneusta [class]: 1) in *Chordata*, acorn worms. Elongate, wormlike *Hemichordata*, quite common in sand and mud flats. Body is divided into proboscis, collar and trunk region. Proboscis is somewhat cylindrical and tapering to blunt, rounded point at apex, enlarged and rounded at base, connected with the collar by narrow, flexible neck. In species with shorter proboscis, it is somewhat acorn-shaped. Although about 10 genera are known, they are often familiarly called "*Balanoglossus.*" 2) in *Protochordata*, Recent. Solitary; wormlike; collar simple; muscular proboscis. Burrowing; mud strainer.

Entomostraca [phylum *Arthropoda*]: small *Crustacea* in which number of body segments behind head is quite variable. There is often an unpaired eye (nauplius eye) occurring in some species. This subclass belongs to class *Crustacea* which contains *Arthropoda* which breathe by means of gills or branchiae. They are segmented animals with 2 pairs of antennae and provided with segmented appendages, each of which is typically divided into an outer and inner branch.

entrainment: transfer of fluid by friction from one water mass to another, usually occurring between opposing currents. Turbulence between water masses results in mixing. Pickup and movement of sediment as bed load or in suspension by current flow.

entrance [ships]: bow of vessel or form of underbody under load waterline. Opposed to run, which is extreme afterpart of ship's bottom or of hold. Also a report by master of vessel, first in person, then in writing, of arrival at port of call, to chief officer of customs residing there, as prescribed by law.

entrenched meander: 1) streams which have reached advanced stage of one cycle hold their courses in second cycle and cut down in old meanders; result is a meandering stream in young valley. These conditions constitute entrenched meanders. 2) canyon with meandering form, resulting from uplift or rejuvenation of meandering river.

enzyme: complex proteins produced by living cells which act as catalysts. Vital to body metabolism, they can start or speed up reaction but are not destroyed in the process.

Eocene: geological period of Tertiary which began about 60 million years ago and lasted for some 20 to 30 million years. This period was characterized by mild climate all over the earth, species that are ancestors of many modern plants and animals and rapid development of mammals.

eocrinoids: typical "dawn crinoid" has an elongate stalk, vase-shaped calyx whose plates have definite shapes and fine brachioles. The last are either simple or branched and consist of 2 interlocking series of plates. Though eocrinoids never were plentiful, they lived from mid-Cambrian to mid-Ordovician, span of 100 million years. Best-known species are *European*.

eodiscida [trilobites]: these are tiny trilobites 6 to 8 mm. long. Facial sutures are proparian or marginal; eyes are small or more generally are lacking; thoracic segments number only 2 or 3; cephalon and pygidium are relatively large. Some genera are spiny. Eodiscids are limited to early and middle Cambrian deposits.

eolian sands: sediments of sand size or smaller which have been transported by winds. They may be recognized in marine deposits off desert coasts by greater angularity of grains compared with waterborne particles.

eosin: rose-colored dye and acid-base indicator, extracted from coal tar.

Eotovos effect: east-west component of movement of ship, including effect of marine currents, modifies centrifugal force of earth's rotation. It is a vertical force experienced by a body moving in east-west direction on rotating earth. In gravity measurements a positive correction is applied if moving eastward and negative correction applied if moving westward.

epeiric seas: shallow inland seas with restricted communication with open ocean having depths of less than 250 meters (137 fathoms), e.g., Hudson Bay.

epeirogenesis: grander form of diastrophism forming broader features of crustae relief, such as continents and ocean beds.

epeirogenic movement: 1) epeirogenic (Greek *epeiros*, a continent), broad uplift or depression of areas of land or of sea bottom in which strata are not folded or crumpled, but may be tilted or may retain original horizontal attitude. 2) referring to relatively gentle deformations of segments of earth's crust involving upwarp or downwarp or both (by tilting). 3) raising or lowering of land masses of continental magnitude with little, if any, folding.

epeirogeny: broad uplift and subsidence of whole or large portions of continental areas or ocean basins.

ephemeris: tabulation of places of a heavenly body for successive hours or days, with other pertinent data; such as horizontal parallax, semi-diameter, and time of meridian passage, in an *ephemeris of the Moon*. A publication giving computed places and other information concerning the heavenly bodies for each day of the year; an astronomical almanac, as the *American Ephemeris and Nautical Almanac*.

ephyra: earliest free-swimming stage of *scyphozoan medusae* that have been released from polyps or scyphistoma. Also *ephyrula*.

epicenter: in seismology, point on earth's surface directly over focus or theoretical point of origin of an earthquake.

epicone: in dinoflagellates, portion of cell above or anterior to horizontal groove or cingulum.

epicontinental marginal sea: subdivision of ocean generally less than 7,500 ft. deep, overlying continental shelf and a part of continental slope, which is partly enclosed by extensions of land, shallow banks or islands.

epicontinental sea: 1) shallow sea that lies far in upon a continental mass. 2) shallow seas which occupy wide portions of continental shelf or lie in interior of continent.

epidermis: 1) outer layer of skin, which includes hair, fur, feathers or claws of vertebrates. 2) in *Coelenterata*, external layer of cells in body wall. Typically cells are bricklike in form if they are not interconnected to form continuous multinucleat sheet.

epifauna: animals living on surface of firm substrata.

epilimnion: layer of water above thermocline in freshwater lake or pool; distinguished from hypolimnion, layer below the thermocline. In ocean, equivalent is the mixed layer.

epimorphic: having full complement of segments in young.

epipelagic: upper portion of oceanic province, extending from surface to depth of about 100 fathoms (200 meters).

epiphyte: plant growing on another plant; sometimes extended to all organisms growing as sessile forms attached to plants.

epiplankton: plankton occurring near surface in upper 200 meters.

epipodite: laterally directed extension from one of basal segments of arthropod limb.

episome: small bit of nucleic acid in cytoplasm of cell replicating independently of cell's own genome and transferable to another cell of same or closely related type of directed contact.

epitheca: 1) upper or larger half of furstule of diatom or upper plates above cingulum in peridian dinoflagellates. 2) in *Coelenterata*, sheath of skeletal material that forms wall of corallite.

epithelium: cellular tissue covering surfaces and lining body cavities.

epitokous: describing the epitoky, posterior, sexually developed part of body in certain polychaete worms, as opposed to atoke or anterior, sexless portion. Famous edible palolo worm of South Pacific is actually an epitoke which breaks off when it matures and ascends to surface. Rest of worm remains in burrow and grows a new tail end.

epitoky: seasonal modification in posterior part of marine polychaete; posterior part becomes swollen with gonads and eggs or sperm.

epizoon: organism growing attached to external surface of an animal.

epoch: 1) in terrestrial magnetism, period of time over which magnetic elements are considered, usually 10 years. 2) angular retardation of maximum of constituent of observed tide behind corresponding maximum of same constituent of hypothetical equilibrium tide.

equal area projection: map projection on which constant ratio of areas is preserved; i.e., any given part of map on equal area projection bears same relation to area on reference surface which it represents.

equation of continuity: hydrodynamical equation which expresses principle of conservation of mass in a fluid. It equates increase in mass in hypothetical fluid volume to next flow of mass into volume.

equation of motion: Newtonian law of motion states that the product of the mass of elemental volume of fluid and acceleration equals vector sum of forces acting on the volume. In meteorological and oceanographic use, both sides of equation of motion are divided by mass to give force per unit mass. Forces considered in ocean currents are gravity, coriolis force, pressure gradient force and frictional forces.

equator: imaginary great circle on the surface of the earth, sun, planet, or other rotating spherical body, equidistant at all points from the poles of such body; called, in the case of Earth, terrestrial equator, or dividing line between northern and southern hemispheres. Latitude is reckoned north and south from the equator, its own latitude being $0°$.

equatorial: of, or pertaining to, the equator. An astronomical telescope mounted so as to maintain its line of sight in the plane of a celestial body's diurnal circle; rotates on a *polaxis*, or axis parallel to that of the earth, and is elevated or depressed according to position in declination of body observed.

Equatorial convergence: zone along which waters from Northern and Southern Hemisphere converge. This zone generally lies in Northern Hemisphere, except in Indian Ocean.

Equatorial Countercurrent: ocean current flowing eastward near equator. In Atlantic Ocean, it flows east between North and South Equatorial Currents across full width of ocean in northern winter. It eventually becomes the Guinea Current.

equatorial tidal currents: tidal currents occurring approximately every 2 weeks when moon is over equator. At these times, diurnal inequality between successive periods of flood and ebb is at a minimum and currents are most nearly semidiurnal.

equatorial tides: tides that occur approximately every 2 weeks when moon is over equator. At these times, moon produces minimum inequality between two successive high waters and two successive low waters.

equilateral [*Mollusca*]: with posterior and anterior halves of valve equal in size and shape.

equilibrium: in thermodynamics, any state of a system which would not undergo change if system were to be isolated. Processes in isolated system not in equilibrium are irreversible and always in direction of equilibrium.

equilibrium spheroid: shape that earth would attain if it were entirely covered by tideless ocean of constant depth.

equilibrium theory: hypothesis which assumes an ideal earth which has no continental barriers and is uniformly covered with water of considerable depth. It also assumes that water responds instantly to tide-producing forces of moon and sun to form a surface in equilibrium and moves around earth without viscosity or friction.

equilibrium tide: hypothetical tide due to tide-producing forces under equilibrium theory; tide relating to equilibrium theory; tide relating to attractions of celestial bodies, particularly sun and moon.

equinoctial: pertaining to an equinox, the equinoxes, or time or state of equal day and night; also to regions or climate in vicinity of the *equa-*

tor. The celestial equator. Also called *equinoctial line,* because when the sun's place is on it *(declination zero)* day and night are of equal length all over the world.

equinoctial spring tides: those tides occurring near equinoxes when full or new moon and sun have little or low declination and spring tides of greater range than the average occur, particularly if moon is also nearly in perigee.

equinoctial tide: tide occurring when sun is near equinox. During this period, spring tide ranges are greater than average.

equinox: time when sun crosses equator, making night and day of equal length in all parts of earth.

equivalve [*Mollusca*]: with valves equal in size and shape.

erect bryozoan: bryozoan which forms branching upright growths attached basally to underwater surfaces.

erection [ships]: process of hoisting into place and joining various parts of ship's hull, machinery, etc.

eretmocaris stage: postlarval stage in certain decapod crustaceans characterized by possession of long eyestalks.

ergodic: hypothesis asserting statistical equivalence of ensembled averages and time averages when steady state conditions occur.

erichthus: second larval stage in *Stomatopoda.*

Eridanus: long winding constellation extending southward and westward over 53° of declination and 3½ hrs. of right ascension from west side of the *Orion* group. The bright star *Achernar* marks its southern end in 57½° S., or about halfway between, and at 40° distance from, *Canopus* and *Fomalhaut.*

eriographid: referring to members of family *Eriographidae* in phylum *Annulata,* segment worms. They are marine worms with transverse rows of hook-shaped appendages on abdomens; they do not have eyes on their heads, but possess eyespots on last segments of their bodies. They live separately in tubes that are massed together within gelatinous material.

erosion: any or all processes by which soil or rock is broken up and transported from one place to another. It is regarded as including weathering, corrosion and transportation.

erosion ramp: sloping belt of reef rock immediately above reef flat on atoll islet where marine erosion is active.

erosion surface: term refers to area which has been flattened by subaerial or marine erosion to form area of relatively low relief at elevation close to base level (sea level) existing at the time of its formation. Relics of such surfaces may now be found far above sea level, owing to falling base level.

erratic: transported rock fragment different from bedrock on which it lies, either free or as part of sediment.

error: difference between an observed physical quantity or value and the true value; as, *sextant error; heeling error.*

escarpment: elongated and comparatively steep slope of sea floor, separating flat or gently sloping areas.

escolar: mackerel-like food fish attaining a length of 3½ ft., commonly found on the Cuban coast, Canary Islands, Madeira, and occasionally off Nova Scotia, on Grand Banks, and in Mediterranean.

escutcheon [*Mollusca*]: depressed, smooth or otherwise set-off dorsal area behind ligament in pelecypods.

esker: 1) serpentine ridges of gravel and sand. These are taken to mark channels in decaying ice sheet, through which streams washed much of finer drift, leaving coarser gravel between ice walls. Narrow ridge of gravelly or sandy drift deposited by a stream in association with glacier ice. 2) winding ridges of irregularly stratified sand and gravel that occur in area of ground moraine. 3) long, winding ridge of sand and gravel deposited by a stream flowing beneath a glacier.

esnecca: craft of Crusades period, propelled by sweeps and sail. It was, in all probability, huskier and larger model of Viking ship. Esneccas were among ships used by Richard the Lionhearted in his great mass voyage to the Holy Land.

Essex oysterboat: cutter-rigged craft used in oyster fisheries of Burnham, Mersa, Brightlingsea and other ports on Thames estuary. These smart boats somewhat resemble the "bowlegs" except that rig is yachtier in appearance and boom mainsails have loftier cut.

establishment of the port: average interval between upper and lower lunar transits near time of new and full moon and next high water.

ester: compound produced by interaction of acid and alcohol. Esters include fats, oils and waxes. Frequently possessing a very pleasant odor, esters are found naturally in many fruits and flowers and have variety of commercial uses, especially in cosmetics.

estuarine muds: silts, often containing sufficient clay to impart some plasticity and considerable proportion of decomposed organic matter.

estuary: 1) area where river or stream meets ocean; characterized by water whose salt content is between that of fresh and marine environments and by distinct population of animals and plants. 2) tidal bay formed by submergence or drowning of lower portion of nonglaciated river valley and containing measurable quantity of sea salt.

Etamin: *Gamma* (γ) *Draconis*, brightest star in the group *Draco;* magnitude 2.4.

Etaples lugger: two-masted, lug-rigged fishing boat working out of Etaples, France. Higher foremast is set well in bow carrying standing lugsail and jib to bowsprit. Mizzen, set in the stern, is sheeted to a boomkin.

etea: small, light, extremely narrow (10 to 12 in.) dugout canoe used at San Cristobal Island and one or two other islands in Solomon group.

etesian: periodic; annual. Particularly applied to the yearly recurring northerly winds blowing in summer over the Aegean Sea and eastern Mediterranean; *Etesian winds.*

etesian winds: with rare exception mid-May sees the start of strong northerly wind that blows across eastern Mediterranean for about 4 months. Associated with the great low-pressure trough that extends westward from northwest India, it begins and ends with remarkable regularity. Greeks who observed this phenomenon dubbed it *etesios* (annual). Passing through Latin, name for the annual wind entered English in 17th century. Seamen who spend considerable time on Mediterranean often use Turkish *meltemi* as synonym for etesian winds. Their course remains remarkably regular and speed seldom drops below 10 miles per hour. Occasionally they reach a velocity of 40 miles per hour, over long stretches of water. We now know that geographical and thermal features of our planet combine to create a number of "annuals," the yearly blows that were familiar to Greeks in time of Homer.

ethology: scientific discipline dealing with study of animal behavior.

Eucarida [phylum *Arthropoda*]: in this division, carapace is enlarged, covering all thoracic segments and fusing with most of them. Eyes are mounted on eyestalks (peduncles). Heart, as well as gills, is located in thorax. Division is divided into two orders: 1) *Euphausiacea* and 2) *Decapoda.*

Eucrateidae [phylum *Prosopygia*]: colony is erect and branching. Zooecia are trumpet-shaped, often widest at summit. They are arranged in single series or in double series with zooecia back to back. Aperture is obliquely subterminal, but without operculum. There are no avicularia or vibracula.

Euglenida [phylum *Protozoa*]: these are *Mastigophora* without an external shell and with flagella not borne in grooves. Free-swimming marine species of this class comprise 5 orders of which *Euglenida* is one. Species belonging to this order are comparatively large in size. There may be 1 or 2 flagella and a mouth or no mouth at anterior end. There is always a distinct pharynx.

euhalabous: plankton, especially phytoplankton, living in water of $30^\circ/00$ to $50^\circ/00$ salinity.

Eulerian current measurement: direct observation of current speed and/or direction during period of time as it flows past a recording instrument such as Ekman or Robert's current meter.

Eunicidae [phylum *Anulata*]: in the family *Eunicidae*, head is triangular and semioval with lobelike palps more or less united. Only occasionally are there lateral tentacles. Eyes may be 2, 4 or none; body is long, typically wormlike, very often slender and numerous segments ending in 2 or 4 anal cirri.

Euphausiacea [phylum *Arthropoda*]: shrimplike crustaceans with two branched (biramus) appendages, including both pereiopods and pleopods. There are no special maxillipeds, these appendages remaining in original primitive condition as first pair of pereiopods, all of which are walking legs. Transparent bodies are highly luminescent at night; body is colored brilliant red. Millions of these shrimps, in schools, are abundant source of food for whales.

euphotic zone: layer of body of water which receives ample sunlight for photosynthetic process of plants. Depth of this layer varies with water's extinction coefficient, angle of incidence of sunlight, length of day and cloudiness, but it is usually 260 ft. (80 meters) or more.

Euphuridae [*Polyceratidae*, phylum *Mollusca*]: this is of the order *Nudibranchia* (sea slugs). Shell is entirely absent in adult; no ctenidium or branchia proper; nervous system is concentrated; kidney is branched or ramified throughout body; jaws and radula are present; two pairs of tentacles. In this family, body is sluglike and elongate with marginal ridge on each side with prolongations either tubercular or fingerlike. Rhinophores and cerata are not retractile.

euplankton: organisms that spend most or all of their lives as plankton.

Euryalae [phylum *Echinoderma*]: basket stars. This order is characterized by hourglass-shaped surfaces of joints or vertebrae of arms. There is no distinct armature of plates or scales, but both disc and arms are invested with soft skin or with granules. Spines on arms are usually directed downward, often in form of hooks. Genital slits are located vertically on the disc, on either side of base of arms.

eurybathic: tolerant of wide range of depth.

euryhaline: able to tolerate wide range of salinities.

Euryleptidae [phylum *Platyhelminthes*]: flattened, soft-bodied worms without segments. In family *Euryleptidae* mouth is near anterior end of body. Pharynx is tubular; stomach is long and narrow with branches which may be simple or forming a network; ocelli are located on anterior margin of head region and on tentacles when they occur.

eurystomites [nautiloids]: built discordal shells that were light in weight and had long but not large living chambers which finally became almost straight. Body was evidently heavy enough to serve as ballast, but shell must have been so buoyant that aperture pointed obliquely downward. These animals half crawled and half drifted.

eurythermal: able to tolerate wide range of temperatures.

eustatic: 1) pertaining to simultaneous worldwide change in sea level (as from melting of continental glaciers) but not relative change in level resulting from local coastal subsidence or elevation. 2) pertaining to land mass that has not undergone elevation or depression.

eustatism: fluctuation of sea level due to changing capacity of ocean basins or volume of ocean water. Glacio-eustatism causes variations of sea level related to changing volume of glacier ice; sedimento-eustatism is related to rise of sea level due to filling of ocean basins with sediment; tectono-eustatism is due to change in capacity of ocean basins resulting from earth movements such as basin formation which by increasing capacity of ocean receptacles, lowers sea level.

Eutima gracilis [phylum *Coelenterata*]: hydroid is not known with certainty, but probably resembles *Octorchis gegenbauri*. Nearly hemispherical adult has thick mesogloea; only 2, or sometimes 4, marginal tentacles.

eutrophic: pertaining to bodies of water containing abundant nutrient matter.

eutrophic plankton: plankton in areas of especially high productivity.

euxinic deposition: deposition in nearly isolated sea basin where for lack of circulation and mixing, deep waters are deficient in oxygen and toxic to all life but anaerobic bacteria and hydrogen sulfide muds rich in organic matter are produced; e.g., Black Sea, Carioca Basin and some fiords.

evaporite: one of sediments which are deposited from aqueous solution as result of extensive or total evaporation of solvent.

even keel [ships]: when boat rides on even keel, its plane of flotation is either coincident or parallel to designed waterline.

Ewing corer: piston type coring device used to obtain 2½-in. diameter core samples. Sampler consists of weight stand on which removable weights can be placed, core barrel (generally 20 ft. long), core cutter and core catcher.

exceptions clause: in a charter party or bill of lading, a stipulation absolving the carrier from responsibility for loss, damage, or delay in delivery or loading of cargo due to, as in the following quotation, "Act of God, perils of the sea, pirates and public enemies, restraint of princes and rulers, fires, strikes, barratry of master or mariners, strandings and navigation accidents, latent defects in, or accidents to hull and/or machinery and/or boilers, even when occasioned by negligence, default, or error in judgment of pilot, master, mariners, or other persons employed by the carrier, or for whose acts he is responsible, not resulting, however, in any case from want of due diligence by owner of ship, or by ship's husband or manager." Also termed *excepted perils clause*.

excess of hatchways: in tonnage measurement, British and U.S. rules exempt a vessel's aggregate hatchway space, as measured from top of deck beam to underside of hatch covers, from inclusion in gross tonnage to the extent of one-half of one per centum of such gross tonnage, exclusive of tonnage of hatchways. Thus, in a ship of 7000 gross tons whose total hatchway tonnage is 65, *excess of hatchways* is equal to 65 less 35 (.005 x 7000) or 30 tons. The provision apparently was adopted as an encouraging gesture toward supplying ample height of hatch coamings in the interests of seaworthiness and cargo protection, since tonnage taxation generally is based on net tonnage, or freight earning space in a vessel. Suez Canal tonnage rules provide for a similar allowance, while those of Panama Canal give little or no exemption.

exempted space: in measuring a vessel for *tonnage*, such space, or aggregate of space, ordinarily open to the elements or not provided with ready or permanent means of being closed, and in consequence, not included in the gross tonnage.

exogenous plankton: plankton originating in some other locality than where it was found.

exopodite: in *Crustacea*, outer branch or ramus of biramous appendage. Also exopod.

exoskeleton: in arthropods, hardened cuticular covering of body, serving for protection of soft parts and as sites for muscle attachments; laminated crust of 3 layers secreted by skin.

ex quay: in a contract of sale and shipment, indicates that no charges are payable by consignee for transportation or housing of goods up to the stage of delivery from pier or quay.

extinction coefficient: measure of space rate of diminution, or extinction, of any transmitted light; thus, it is attenuation coefficient applied to visible radiation. In oceanography it is a measure of attenuation of downward-directed radiation in sea.

extracapsular cytoplasm: in *Radiolaria*, cytoplasm peripheral to central capsule.

extracellular bioluminescence: light production outside organism resulting from secretion of photogenic material, from special secretory glands. *Cypridina,* an ostracod, extrudes yellow granules of luciferin and small colorless granules of luciferase into seawater. These granules dissolve and react to produce light.

extratropical cyclone: any cyclonic-scale storm that is not a tropical cyclone, usually referring only to migratory frontal cyclones of middle and higher latitudes.

extrusion: lava flows, usually through a fissure onto earth's surface, and resulting formation of extrusive rocks from solidified lava.

exumbrella: top or convex outer surface of medusae. Aboral surface.

eye: in meteorology, usually "eye of the storm" (hurricane, typhoon); i.e., roughly circular area of comparatively light winds and fair weather found at center of severe tropical cyclone. Winds are generally 10 knots or less; no rain occurs; sometimes blue sky may be seen. Eye diameters vary from 4 miles to more than 40 miles.

eyebolt [ships]: bolt having either a head looped to form a worked eye or solid head with hole drilled through it forming a shackle eye. Its use is similar to that of a pad's eye.

eyes [ships]: forward end of space below upper decks of ship which lies next abaft the stern, where sides approach very near to each other. Hawse pipes are usually run down through eyes of a ship.

F

F: abbreviation for fog in logbooks and weather records; for temperature reading by *Fahrenheit* thermometer, as, *50° F.;* and for *forward* in recording draft of ship, as *in 25' 10'' F.* In International Code of Signals, *flag F*, hoisted singly, or by International Morse Code, as a flashing signal, *F* (· · — ·) indicates *"I am disabled. Communicate with me."*

F.A.A.: "Free of all average," as abbreviated in marine insurance policies; indicating coverage is for total loss only.

facies: segregated parts of sedimentary deposit which differ in mineral composition, bedding, fossils, etc., but belong to any genetically related body of sedimentary deposits.

factory ship: wide variety of ships which prepare fishery products for the consumer on board, even canning. Factory ship usually tends fleet of smaller fishing vessels.

Fahrenheit thermometer: by this temperature scale the boiling point of water at sea level is recorded at 212° and the freezing point at 32°, making a difference of 180° between them. To convert Fahrenheit degrees to Centigrade degrees, subtract 32, multiply by 5 and divide by 9.

fair [ships]: to fair a line is to even out curves, sheer lines, deck lines, etc., in drawing and mold loft work.

fairings [ships]: to make fair or beautiful. To adjust; make regular, or smooth; to form in correct shape.

fairlead [ships]: term applied to fittings or devices used in preserving direction of rope, chain or wire, delivering it fairly or on a straight lead to sheave or drum.

fairwater [ships]: plating, in shape of frustrum of a cone, fitted around ends of shaft tubes and struts to prevent an abrupt change in stream lines. Also any casting or plate fitted to hull to preserve smooth flow of water.

fairway: 1) open water in channel or harbor through which traffic normally passes. 2) navigated areas of rivers, channels, bays and harbors.

fair winds or tides: favorable.

fake down a line [ships]: to coil it with each loop overlapping the next so that it is free for running.

Falkland Current: current flowing northward along Argentine Coast. Falkland Current originates from part of West Wind Drift at about 35° S. It is joined by Brazil Current where both turn to flow east across South Atlantic.

fall aft [ships]: sailboat falls off when sailing less close to wind than before.

fall equinox: beginning of fall, about September 23.

fall herring: medium-sized herring which appears in schools during spring along the U.S. Atlantic coast south of Cape Cod.

falling tide: portion of tide cycle between high water and following low water.

fall-off: in underwater sound, decrease in acoustic energy as it travels away from sound source.

falls [ships]: 1) part of rope or tackle to which power is applied in hoisting. 2) lines at davits used to raise and lower the boat.

fall zone: series of falls and rapids occurring where streams flow from harder rock of Piedmont Upland to softer sediments of Atlantic Coastal Plain.

false anticline: structure resembling an anticline produced by compaction of sediment over resistant mass such as buried hill or reef.

false bottom: deep scattering layer.

false ice foot: ice formed along beach terrace just above high water mark, derived from snow melting above beach terrace.

false keel [ships]: extra keel secured to bottom of main keel to give added protection or extra draft.

fan: 1) gently sloping, fan-shaped feature normally located near lower termination of a canyon. 2) detrital material deposited in shape of fan, as an alluvial fan.

fan, alluvial: terrestrial counterpart of delta. These fans are typical of arid and semiarid climates, but may form in almost any climate if conditions are right. A fan marks a sudden decrease in carrying power of stream as it descends from steep gradient to flatter one.

fanfare: towed object used by surface vessels to confuse enemy subs. Fanfare not only keeps ship's exact location in doubt but serves to divert homing torpedoes.

fanglomerate: consolidated gravel and associated sediment deposited as alluvial fan.

fantail [ships]: overhanging stern section of vessel, from sternpost aft.

farlow seaweed [*Farlowia mollis*]: grows abundantly between 0.5 and 1.5 ft. tide levels. As seaweed is rocked by waters, small, dense clusters of bright red to very dark red branches are attractive; soft, loosely arranged branches are occasionally 6—8 in. long; irregularly arranged, either alternate or lying so close together they appear to be opposite; without midribs or veins and are flattened and slimy.

faro: small atoll-shaped reef or coral knoll with lagoons a few feet to about 100 ft. (about 300 meters) deep, forming part of barrier or atoll rim.

F.A.S.: abbreviation in shipping contracts indicating cost of a consignment of goods as delivered to a point within reach of ship's loading tackle, from which point buyer's liability begins: *free alongside ship*.

fascicle: bundle or cluster of threadlike, rodlike or bristlelike structures bound together or arising from same place, as a fascicle of setae.

fascine: referring to mats made of wooden sticks bound together into long bundles and used to help protect dikes or dams.

Fasciolariidae [family]: spindle shells are usually strong, thick, heavy and spindlelike in shape. Spire of their shell is elevated sharply, pointed and without varices; outer lip is not thickened and inner lip is usually marked by a few oblique plaits or plications; operculum is ovate in outline; columella lacks the umbilicus. Spindle shells are a group of slow moving, predatory animals found in tropical seas.

fasciole [*Mollusca*]: spiral band formed by successive margins of a canal (either anterior or posterior) in gastropod shell.

fasiculate [*Coelenterata*]: type of colonial cord skeleton (corallum) in which corallites stand separate though they may be connected by tubules.

fassone: reed or balsa rowing boat of Sardinia. It is made with bundles of reeds fashioned and lashed together to make a boat with curved bow terminating to a point and square stern. It is rowed and wooden outriggers extend outward from sides to carry oarlocks and oars.

fast ice: sea ice that generally remains in position where originally formed and may attain considerable thickness. It is formed along coasts where it is attached to shore or over shoals where it may be held in position by islands, grounded icebergs or grounded polar ice.

fata morgana: complex mirage characterized by multiple distortions of images, generally in the vertical, so that such objects as cliffs and cottages are distorted and magnified into fantastic castles.

fathogram: graphic presentation of bottom profile determined by a Fathometer.

fathom: 1) originally the space reached over or encompassed by extending arms. 2) measurement of depths when sounding, equal to 6 ft. Common unit of depth in ocean for countries using English system of units, equal to 6 ft. (1.83 meters).

Fathometer: type of echo sounder. Device used to determine depth of body of water by measuring time interval between transmission of sonic or ultrasonic signal and return of its echo reflected off bottom.

fault: rock fracturing along which movement or displacement has taken place.

fault coast: straight coast formed by a fault consisting of seaward facing escarpment and downthrown block below sea level.

fault zone: area with a number of faults characterized by rock fracture along which movement or displacement has taken place.

fauna: animal population of particular location, region or period.

faunal province: marine zoogeographic region based on living bottom-dwelling (benthonic) mollusks. American faunal province includes the Aleutian, Californian, Magellanic, Panamic and Peruvian provinces.

fay [ships]: to unite two planks or plates closely, so as to bring surfaces into intimate contact.

feather [ships]: in rowing, an oar is feathered when it is turned parallel to surface on breaking water to eliminate splash and spray.

feather boa [*Egregia menziesii*]: perennial kelp found on surf-swept coasts. From short (2—3 in.) cylindrical stipe, which soon becomes flat and irregular, branches arise, 6—25 main branches, each branch continuing in long narrow stemlike growth. At irregular intervals smaller branches arise from main branches. The feather boa is dark chocolate brown, almost black. It has a compact, cone-shaped, profusely branched holdfast 6—7 in. in diameter, growing around base of stipe.

feather-duster worm: feather-duster worm of Indo-Pacific area is an annelid or segmented sea worm of class *Polychaeta*. It includes variety of species, all of which resemble feather dusters. It is sedentary with tubelike body protruding from sandy bottom and crowded with colorful, featherlike crest. These "feathers" serve as gills and also trap minute organisms on which worm lives. When animals are disturbed, feathers are drawn into tube and down its spiral.

feather stars [*Comatulida*]: crinoid and echinoderm. It has central disc from which radiate 10 arms grouped in pairs. Sexes are distinct and feather star multiplies by means of eggs fertilized in water. There are numerous species of colored feather stars: reds, yellows, oranges. These animals are able to swim by using their arms, but they do not move from place to place; attached to coral or rocks by means of hooked appendages (cirri). They feed on small fauna which they thrust into their mouths by means of minute tentacles on their arms.

fecal pellets, or castings: excrement of marine animals frequently found in sediments. When fossilized they are often called coprolites, which may also connote larger size.

feeder beach: artificially widened beach serving to nourish downdrift beaches by natural littoral currents or forces.

feeder channels: channels parallel to shore along which feeder currents flow before converging to form neck of rip current.

feeder current: current which flows parallel to shore before converging and forming neck of rip current.

feeling bottom: action of deepwater wave upon running into shoal water and beginning to be influenced by bottom.

feldspar: glassy, moderately hard, crystalline mineral composed mainly of aluminum silicates and found in igneous rocks.

felloes [ships]: pieces of wood which form rim of wheel.

felucca: Mediterrean vessel of many varieties, one or two masts, lateen sails, with or without oars. Large "felucca" of former days might have an oposites, galley like, as part of superstructure built above hull, with after part of deck drawn out to tapering, overhanging platform beyond transom stern.

fender [ships]: this term is applied to various devices fastened to or hung over sides of a vessel for purpose of preventing rubbing or chafing.

fend off: to push or hold off, as in keeping a boat from striking or chafing against a wharf.

fenestra: small opening, as in a shell.

Ferrel's Law: winds are deflected to the right in Northern Hemisphere and to left in Southern Hemisphere because of earth's rotation.

ferruginous: color of iron rust.

festoon cloud: *mammatocumulus* cloud, or one having a heavy wool-like appearance with low dark protuberances of various shapes; considered a sign of approaching showery weather.

fetch: effective distance in one direction over which wind acts on water surface. Distance over which generating wind blows in constant direction during wave generation.

fetch length: horizontal distance (in direction of wind) over which wind having constant direction and speed generates a sea.

fiard: Swedish term for glacially-formed, drowned valley with low glaciated sides which occur in lowland regions. Fiards are shorter and shallower than fiords.

fibrous sponge: sponge in which internal skeletal elements are composed of spongin fibers, e.g., commercial sponges.

fid [ships]: wooden pin used in boats to separate strands of rope while splicing.

fiddler fish: shark-like member of the *ray* family found in tropical waters, so named for its shape.

fidley [ships]: framework built around deck hatch ladder, leading below.

fidley deck [ships]: partially raised deck over engine and boiler rooms, usually around smokestack.

fidley hatch [ships]: hatch around smokestack and uptake.

fiducial point: point or line in scale used for reference or comparison purposes. In calibration of oceanographic thermometers, fiducial points are 100° C (212° F) and 0° C (32° F), which correspond to boiling point and ice points at standard pressure (760 mm. of mercury).

field: 1) extent; expanse; as, a *field* of seaweed. 2) space traversed by lines of force; as, a *magnetic field.* 3) area in which a device or drawing is pictured or projected; as, a lion on the *field of a flag; field covered by a chart or map.*

fife rail [ships]: rail for pins around a mast, to which halyards and other lines are belayed.

fifie: 19th century Scotch fishing boat, double-ended, stern and stem straight, the former raked.

filament: threadlike structure.

file bottom: nickname given to early Gloucester fishing schooner because of great dead rise. Afterwards called "sharpshooters." Had low freeboard, raking stem and sternpost, with less rake to latter, deep drag to keel, sharp on waterline and great flare to bow.

filefish: triggerfish and filefish are another unique group, armed with a dorsal weapon consisting of either 3 spines or single larger spine. Family includes 18 species in the U.S. They differ from their reef neighbors in lacking ventral fins; instead this portion of body bears ventral flap of skin that can be erected by means of bony backward projecting bone within the flap. In triggerfish dorsal spines form an ingenious interlocking mechanism. First and largest spine locks into position when erect, thus making an effective weapon. A tendon extends from third spine to base of first spine. Lock which holds forward spine erect can be broken only by depressing third spine. Filefish have only one dorsal spine and lack trigger release mechanism.

filefish, orange: similar in shape and general appearance as the planehead. Orange-yellow body is speckled with irregular areas of small brown spots. An awkward fish, it is often seen head down browsing in algae attached to wharf pilings.

filefish, planehead: filefish are so named because

of the hard rough skin, whose tough scales form sandpaperlike surface. Planehead filefish is a mottled slaty-gray fish capable of quick color changes. When feeding over marine meadows of green seaweed, the young become corresponding bright green protective color. It grows to length of 10 in.

Filibranchia [order]: gills usually W-shaped in cross section with vascular interlamellar junctions, incompletely fused filaments with adjacent filaments attached by ciliary connections (filibranch); muscles unequal with reduced or absent anterior adductor and enlarged posterior adductor; often attached by byssus or cementing substance. *Mytilus, Ostrea, Pecten, Arca.*

filiform: in shape of thread.

filling: in meteorology, an increase in central pressure of pressure system on constant height chart or analogous increase in height on constant pressure chart; opposite of deepening. Term is commonly applied to a low rather than to a high.

filopodium: pseudopodium in form of filamentous projections that may branch but do not anastomose, as in *Amoeba radiosa.*

filter: in ocean wave forecasting, set of formulas that define particular wave frequencies and directions in the fetch which are significant at point of forecast.

filter feeder: animal that obtains food by straining organisms from water passed through some portion of its body; e.g., corals, mussels, sponges and baleen whales.

filtering effect: differential damping of pressure or vertical oscillation of water particles with increase in depth depending upon wave period. Longer waves are damped less than shorter waves at given depth.

filtration method: technique used in quantitative estimation and identification of planktonic organisms. Organisms, usually phytoplankton, are removed from water by filtration and retained on surface of filter. Organisms can then be counted or identified by microscope after suitable preservation and staining of them and subsequent cleaning of filter.

fin [ships]: projecting keel.

finback: one of the rorquals or balaenopterine whales.

finds herself: said of a new vessel, or of one newly rigged or engined, upon having her rigging and/or machinery adjusted to proper working condition; also, of a new iron or steel vessel after divesting herself of a large proportion of magnetism acquired while on the stocks.

fines: silt and clay fraction of sediment.

finfish: true fish as opposed to shellfish.

finger lake: lake occupying long, narrow rock basin or dammed river valley.

fin rays: spiny, supporting elements in fins. There are two types: spines and soft rays.

fins [diving]: semi-rigid, paddlelike extensions worn on feet to increase swimming propulsion.

fiord, fjord: Narrow, deep, steep-walled inlet of sea formed either by submergence of mountainous coast or by entrance of sea into deeply excavated glacial trough after melting away of glacier. Norway is characterized by coastline that includes many long, narrow arms of sea that run between high banks or cliffs. From prehistoric root whose meaning still is not known, Norsemen very early called such a geographical feature a fiord. No known use of the word was made in English before 1674 when Norwegian volume on Lapland was translated for edification of persons interested in that exotic region. Though structure of Norwegian word makes it difficult for tongues only accustomed to English, it filled a gap in our language. So it was adopted without change, just in time for use in exploratory voyages that revealed many fiords in regions far from Norway.

fire ship: generally an old coaster or merchant craft, filled with combustibles, sent out to grapple enemy ships and then set afire. The British built a few special ship sloops which were used as fire ships.

fireworm: luminescent marine worm mainly in Bermuda area. Swarming of this worm during certain phases of moon create luminescent displays.

firn: old snow that has become granular and compacted as result of surface metamorphosis, mainly by melting and refreezing but also by sublimation. Granular snow in intermediate state between newly fallen snow and glacier ice.

fir needle [*Heterochordaria abiefina*]: at or just below low tide mark, fir needles form extensive communities on rocks exposed to moderate surf. Striking features of this seaweed are lobed, crustlike base and short stiff branches surrounding axis of shoots. When young it is light tan, but it becomes dark brown when mature. It has thick covering of mucilage and is slimy to touch. The holdfast of the fir needle is crustlike and many-lobed, sometimes a couple of inches in diameter.

First: British naval lieutenant. A ship might carry as many as 6 lieutenants; they are distinguished as "First," "Second," etc., in order of seniority with rank name omitted.

first ice: first appearance of ice in water at any particular location, whether locally formed (grease ice or young ice) or formed elsewhere (drift ice).

first reduction: name formerly given to high and low water reduction in which quantities sought were mean high and low water intervals, mean high and low water heights and mean range of tide.

firth: long, narrow arm of the sea; especially one opening out from a river; also *frith*.

fish: member of class *Pisces,* which includes true fishes (elasmobranchs excluded) having bony endoskeleton, paired fins and operculum covering gills.

fisherman staysail [ships]: quadrilateral sail set between mainmast and foremast of schooner.

fishery: fishing ground or place where fish or other aquatic animals may be taken regularly; activities embraced in a particular field of the fishing industry, as, *cod fishery, seal fishery, whale fishery;* act or business of catching fish; the right to capture or catch fish within a certain area or in particular waters; fishing season, as, *during the herring fishery.*

fishing cutter: cutter-type of vessel modeled after "Galway hooker" introduced in U.S. from Ireland about 1857 and used extensively by Irish fishermen of Massachusetts Bay.

fistulipora: typical of cyclostomes with massive, irregular zoaria; it is also one of the largest, reaching diameter of 15 in.; upper surface bears shallow pits and rounded elevations; undersurface is covered by wrinkled layer that resembles epitheca of corals and sometimes is given that name. Large, tube-shaped zooecia (autoporis) are separated by much smaller tubes with closely spaced transverse partitions.

fix: relatively accurate position determined without reference to any former position. May be classed as visual, sonic, celestial, electronic, radio, hyperbolic, Loran, radar, etc., depending upon means of establishing it. A pinpoint is a very accurate fix, usually established by passing directly over or near aid to navigation or landmark of small area.

flagella: whiplike appendages found among some of single-celled organisms and other larger invertebrates; used as means of locomotion or sensory organ.

flagellates: organisms of phylum *Protozoa* of class *Flagellata* have flagella which propel them through water environment, e.g., *Euglena. Euglena* has chlorophyll for photosynthesis. Some scientists believe this cone-celled organism may be ancestor of complex plants and animals of today. Other flagellates are similar to *Euglena,* but may lack chlorophyll.

flagfish [*Jordanella floridae*]: little, gray fish an inch or two long with dark blotch on side. Scales along side 25—27; fin with 11—13 soft rays; dorsal fin with single spine and 14—16 soft rays. Body strongly compressed; back strongly arched in profile; teeth flattened, chisel-like; color grayish with large dark spot on each side.

flange: projecting rim which holds a wheel, pipe, rail, etc., in place, giving it strength, guiding it or attaching it to another object.

flare [ships]: spreading out from central vertical plane of body of a ship with increasing rapidity as section rises from waterline to rail.

flashing [ships]: process of reducing amount of permanent magnetism in ship by placing a single coil horizontally around the ship and energizing it. If energized coil is moved up and down along sides of ship, process is called wiping.

flat [ships]: small partial deck, built level, without curvature.

flatfish: member of fish order *Heterosomata.* It swims or lies on one side of its body; sides are greatly flattened and compressed. As young flatfish mature, lower eye "migrates" to upper side so that both eyes are on one side of head. Mainly marine animals, flatfish include such commercially valuable food fish as flounder, sole and halibut.

flatworm: member of phylum *Platyhelminthes.* Lowest of all worms, flatworms generally have soft, flattened, unsegmented bodies. Flukes and tapeworms are parasites.

flaw: sudden gust of wind, often from slightly different direction.

flemish [ships]: to flemish a line on deck is to coil it in tight, flat spiral.

Flemish horse [ships]: short footrope at end of a yard.

flense: to cut away and remove blubber or skin from the carcass of a whale or other cetacean. Formerly, the operation of *flensing* a whale was performed while carcass lay fast alongisde of ship; modern whaling ships haul carcass on board and flense it or otherwise dispose of the whole from the deck.

Flexibilia [crinoids]: joints between plates of both cups and tegmina show that these structures were flexible during life. Lower brachials formed part of cup; interradials ranged from a few to many. Tegmina bore both mouth and open food grooves; arms were uniserial and were not pinnulated. These crinoids supposedly evolved from simple and very ancient members of *Inadunata,* Middle Ordovician to Permian.

flexures [*Mollusca*]: progressive warping or folding of either or both pelecypod valves.

flier [*Centrarhus macropterus*]: bright-marked, circular-looking panfish of medium size. Anal fin nearly as long as dorsal; about 12 spines in dorsal fin. Body ovate, strongly compressed; head small, mouth moderate in size and oblique; fins high; anal fin nearly as long as dorsal. Color greenish or silvery-green; belly yellowish, often with series of dark marks on sides below lateral line. Usually a black spot or ocellus on posterior portion of dorsal fin is very conspicuous in young but fades with age.

FLIP [floating instrument platform]: designed similar to SPAR and used for oceanic research but FLIP is manned and allowed to drift with currents. Can be switched from vertical position to horizontal position at will of crew.

float: air sac or other light structure containing air or gas serving to buoy up body of pelagic animal (e.g., Portuguese man-of-war); pneumatophore.

floating drydock [ships]: U-shaped dock with double skins filled by opening sill cocks. It is allowed to settle so middle section will be lower than keel of ship to be docked. It is then placed under the ship and water is pumped out, raising the ship so that repairs can be made on hull.

floc: small aggregate of tiny sedimentary grains.

flocculate: to aggregate into lumps, as when fine or colloidal clay particles suspended in fresh-water clump together upon contact with salt-water and settle out of suspension; common depositional process in estuaries.

flocculent deposit: aggregate or precipitate of small lumps on sea bottoms.

floe: fragments of ice other than icebergs, with no specific size intended.

floeberg: mass of thick, heavily hummocked sea ice resembling an iceberg or bergy bit.

flood axis: average direction of tidal current at strength of flood.

flood currents: current associated with increase in height of tide. They generally set in same direction as tidal progression and perpendicular to cotidal lines.

flood interval: interval between transit of moon over meridian of a place and time of strength of following flood tidal current.

flood plain: portion of stream valley bordering the channel, built of sediments brought there by stream during time of flood.

flood strength: flood tidal current at time of maximum speed, usually associated with lunar tide phase and/or minimum river discharge at spring near perigee.

flood tide: incoming or rising tide.

floor plan [ships]: horizontal section, showing ship as divided at water or deck line.

floors [ships]: vertical flat plates running transverse of the vessel connecting vertical keel with margin plates or frames to which tank top and bottom shell are fastened.

florescence: rapid reproduction of plankton.

Florida Current: fast current with speeds of 2 to 5 knots that sets through Straits of Florida to a point north of the Grand Bahama Island where it joins Antilles Current to form Gulf Stream.

flotsam [ships]: parts of a wrecked ship and goods lost in shipwreck, both found floating.

flounder: typical member of the *flatfish* family, often known locally in North America as simply *flatfish*. The European *flounder*, called *plaice*; the American *summer flounder*, also called *plaice, southern flounder*, and *winter flounder* are excellent food fishes. Has an oval-shaped body 6 to 8 inches in width and 12 to 14 inches in length. Known also as *fluke*.

flounder, Gulf: very flat fish with both eyes and its color on left side. Scales along lateral line 90—100; rays in dorsal fin 72—80. Mouth large, maxillary extending past eye; body elongate, elliptical, strongly compressed; caudal fin double truncate; pelvic fins thoracic in position. Color of left side brownish to olive-brown with number of more or less pale spots which are sometimes obsolete.

flounder, southern [*Paralichthys lethostigma*]: very flat fish with both eyes and color on left side of body. Anal fin rays 65—73; dorsal fin rays 85—95; mouth large and oblique; mandible heavy and projecting. Body ovate strongly compressed; caudal fin doubly truncate; pelvic fins thoracic in position. Color brownish or olive-brown on left side with a few darker mottlings.

flounder, starry [California flounder]: brownish fish with colorful fins. Dorsal and anal fin are marked by alternate vertical bands of orange with similar horizontal markings on tail fin. Star-shaped tubercles scattered over body give this flounder its common name. This is the species that has not made up its mind as to whether the eyes should be on right side or left. This species attains a weight of 20 lbs., but averages much less. It is often found partly buried in muddy bottom watching for prey with its projecting froglike eyes.

flounder, summer [northern fluke]: left-eyed species, brown or grayish in color and marked with dark spots each surrounded by white margin. It can assume other colors, which seems to indicate an unusual ability to make itself inconspicuous. On red background, summer flounder becomes reddish in color; on blue background, bluish. Average individual is 15 to 20 in. long and weighs under 5 lbs.

flounder, winter [blackjack]: has eyes and pigmentation on right side. This side is dark olive-green or reddish-brown, sometimes spotted with red. It is small with an average size of 15 in. and weight of less than 2 lbs. Its favorite habitat is deep water where it is a popular sport fish as well as valuable food fish.

flounder, witch [gray sole]: grayish brown fish found north of Cape Cod; average length is 24 in. and weighs about 4 lbs. It is usually caught at depths of over 60 ft. but has been brought up from depth of a mile.

flounder, yellowtail [rusty drab]: brown or olive-gray fish tinged with red and marked by scattered reddish-brown spots. On underside, tail is yellowish as are edges of dorsal and anal fins. This flounder occurs at moderate depths and is about the size of witch flounder.

flow: combination of tidal and nontidal current which represents actual water movement.

flower: sailing craft of 8 to 20 tons burden used in herring fishery out of Brighton, England, in middle of 19th century.

flowmeter: device employing propellers, saronious rotors and/or pressure sensors to measure water movement, such as currents, stream flow, etc.

flow noise: noise produced by water movement past transducer or hydrophone array housing and noise produced by breaking waves against hull of moving ship.

fluctuate: changes in water level caused by forces other than tides.

fluctuation: variations of water level height from mean sea level that are not due to tide-producing forces and are not included in predicted heights of tide.

flue: fragments of ice other than icebergs with no specific size intended.

fluid friction: force of friction exerted on object by a fluid (such as air or water) through which it is moving.

fluke: 1) lobe of whale's tail. 2) parasitic flatworm belonging to digenetic trematode.

flushing time: time required to remove or reduce to permissible concentration any dissolved or suspended contaminant in estuary or harbor.

flute: Dutch merchant and trade ship of 17th century. Ship rigged with generous sheer and stable round bow. When armed, guns were carried on upper deck only, lower decks holding cargo. This is the armed "in flute." It was a favorite in Holland.

fluvial: referring to or produced by rivers.

fluviatile: belonging to river or stream.

fluvioglacial: pertaining to streams of glacial melt water or deposits made by them.

fluviomarine: deposits carried into sea from land, resorted and redistributed by waves and currents and mixed with remains of marine animals.

flux: amount of water crossing given area in given time.

fluxoturbidite: strata deposited from turbidity currents later disturbed by sliding or slumping.

flying bar: looped band or spit formed on landward side of an island which remains after island

itself has been eroded to below sea level by wave attack.

flying fish: over 50 species are distributed through warm seas all over the world. Body of flying fish has blunt nose and bears single dorsal fin; tail fin is lobbed unequally, larger, lower lobe being effective in propelling fish along surface water until it becomes airborne. Main support in air comes from extremely large, often semitransparent, pectoral fins that extend outward from anterior part of the fish like airplane wings. As a flying fish taxis over water, body becomes raised at an angle from force of tail's propulsion; fins do not move and flight is a gliding maneuver consisting of series of drops over water.

flying fish, Atlantic: bluish-gray fish with silvery sides, reaching a length of 15 in. It is commonly seen in Gulf Stream from Florida north to Cape Cod.

flying fish, California: 12 to 18 in. long, occurring in great numbers off Catalina Island. It has same coloring and appearance as Atlantic flying fish.

flying gurnard: closely related to sea robin. An olive-green or brown fish 12 in. long with hard bony head and froglike mouth and eyes. Pectoral fins, as in flying fish, are enlarged and serve as wings when fish soars into air; ventral fins are stiff and directed downward, useful to gurnard when it walks along bottom. Another specialization is transformation of first three rays of pectoral fins into feelers to search for food.

flying jib [ships]: 1) outer headsail whose tack is set to jibboom or flying jibboom. 2) on square-rigged vessels, triangular sail set on a stay and extended forward from foremost mast to extension of bowsprit called the flying jibboom.

flying proa: extremely fast, outrigger sailing canoe formerly used in Mariana Islands. Hull was either a dugout or partial dugout with sides of planks built over edges. Assertions have been made that flying proas could travel 20 knots. They have been extinct for over a century.

foam line: front of wave as it advances shoreward after it has broken.

F.O.B.: abbreviation for *free on board*, indicating seller or shipper of merchandise places goods on board carrier without cost to buyer or consignee. Shipper's responsibility ends with delivery of shipment to carrier.

focus: point where earthquake shock is generated. Quakes are classified by amount of energy contained in the seismic disturbance and depth of focus.

fog: hydrometer consists of visible aggregate of minute droplets suspended in atmosphere near earth's surface. According to international definition, fog reduces visibility below one kilometer (0.62 statute mile).

fog bank: fairly well-defined mass of fog observed in the distance, most commonly at sea. This is not applied to patches of shallow fog.

fold [*Mollusca*]: spirally-wound ridge on interior of shell wall.

foliaceous appendage: flat, leaflike subdivided appendage in certain crustaceans.

following wind: generally, same as tailwind. Specifically, wind blowing in direction of ocean-wave advance; opposite of opposing wind.

follow seas: waves moving in general direction of heading.

Fomalhaut: *Alpha (a) Piscis Australis*, only navigational star in the group *Piscis Australis* (or *Austrinus*), or *Southern Fish*; is of magnitude 1.3; its S.H.A. is 16¼°; and has a declination of 29° 52′ S. A line joining *Scheat* and *Markab* (β and *a Pegasi*), two stars marking the western corners of *Square of Pegasus*, will meet *Fomalhaut* if produced 45° southward.

fondo: sea floor exclusive of continental shelf and slope. Sedimentary deposit is the fondoform and rock unit of the fondoform is the fondotherm.

food chain: sequence of living organisms in which members of one level feed on those in level below it and are in turn eaten by those above it. Plants are on lowest level of all. Energy in form of food is transferred along food chain, but a loss of about 90% occurs in each level; e.g., it would take about 1,000 lbs. of plant matter to produce 100 lbs. of even the tiniest of animals.

food cycle: production, consumption and composition of food in the sea, and energy relationships involved in this cycle. Decomposition products are transformed by bacteria into inorganic nutrients suitable for use by producers (marine plants) which directly or indirectly are the food source for all animals in the sea.

food web: group of interrelated food chains.

foot: in ordinary usage, terminal portion of walking appendage that contacts substrata. In molluscs ventral surface of body, variously modified in different groups for creeping or digging or to serve as prehensile arms.

footrope [ships]: boltrope to which lower edge of sail is sewed. Rope extended under a yard and under bowsprit, jibboom and other spars for seamen to stand on while reefing, furling or making sail.

foramen: 1) in *Brachiopoda*, circular opening adjacent to beak of pedicle valve; serves for passage of pedicle. 2) in *Foraminifera*, opening connecting adjacent chambers in test. Typically formed as aperture and enclosed by development of additional chambers.

foramina: among largest of protozoans with shells of various shape. Fossil record dates to close of Devonian period.

Foraminifera [zooplankton]: rhizopods with branching and anastomosing pseudopodia which protrude through and form a network over shell or test. In vast majority test is calcareous and perforated by minute pores. It may be a single shell, but most often is built of many chambers. Most of many-chambered *Foraminifera* occur in two distinct forms: megalospheric with large initial chamber and microspheric with small initial chamber. Contents of microspheric forms undergo repeated divisions to form uninucleate young which are released and secrete initial chamber of megalospheric form, later chambers being added successively. Megalospheric forms undergo repeated division to form swarms of biflagellate gametes which fuse in pairs to form a zygote. Each zygote then secretes initial chamber of microspheric form. They are particularly abundant in warmer seas where tests of dead ones often accumulate on bottom to form deep layers of calcareous ooze.

foraminiferal ooze: pelagic sediment consisting of more than 30% calcium carbonate in form of foraminiferal tests.

forced wave: wave generated and maintained by continuous force, in contrast to free wave.

fore [ships]: part of ship that lies near bow; specifically, forward of midship section; opposed to aft.

fore-and-aft [ships]: applied to objects or fittings in line with keel; opposed to athwartships. Fore-and-aft sails extend from center line of lee side of ship and are generally set on stays or gaffs.

fore-and-after: sailing ship with fore-and-aft rigging in which sails are more or less parallel to length of ship.

fore-and-aft sail [ships]: sail set from vertical mast or stay, normal position being fore and aft or parallel to keel.

forebody [ships]: that part of ship which lies forward of midship section.

forecastle [ships]: short structure at forward end of vessel formed by carrying up ship's shell plating a deck height above the level of uppermost complete deck and fitting a deck over the length of this structure.

foredeep: long, narrow, crusted depression or furrow bordering convex or ocean side of folded organic belt or island arc.

forefoot [ships]: portion of forward section of ship, particularly where keel intersects with stem (main vertical support of bow).

fore, forward [ships]: toward stern; between stern and amidships.

foreland: promontory or cape; point of land extending into water from shoreline.

Forel scale: scale of yellows, greens and blues for recording color of seawater, as seen against white background of Secchi disk.

foremast [ships]: forward mast on ship.

foremast staysail [ships]: jib-shaped sail that sets from foretopmast stay; first headsail forward of foremast.

forepeak [ships]: 1) narrow extremity of vessel's bow. Also, hold space within it. 2) foremost compartments below decks on ship.

forerake [ships]: forward part of bow which overhangs keel.

fore reef: steeply dipping talus slope commonly found on seaward side of organic reef.

forerigging [ships]: all rigging forward of foremast.

forerunner: low, long-peroid, ocean swell which commonly precedes main swell from distant storm, especially a tropical cyclone.

foresail [ships]: 1) on a schooner, fore-and-aft sail set from foremast. 2) on a square-rigger, square sail hung from lowest yard on foremast.

fore-scuttle [ships]: hatch by which forecastle is entered.

fore-set beds: series of inclined layers accumulated as sediment rolls down steep frontal slope of a delta.

foreshore: zone that lies between ordinary high- and low-water marks and is daily traversed by oscillating waterline as tides rise and fall.

fork: junction, or meeting place, of a branch or tributary with a main river, or dividing point in a channel; branch of a river or channel. Throat or separation of parts of a double stay where it forms an eye to lay round a mast, or where its ends separate on each side of a bowsprit, as in a fore stay. A two-pronged fixture for holding a masthead lantern in position.

fork beam [ships]: half beam to support a deck where hatchways occur.

formaldehyde: poisonous, highly reactive organic compound which is a gas with sharp, irritating smell in pure form. In solution with water it is used to preserve biological specimens.

Formalin: clear solution of formaldehyde in water used for fixing and preserving biological specimens held in glass jars.

formation: lithologically distinctive product of essentially continuous sedimentation selected from local succession of strata as a convenient unit for mapping description and reference.

forward [ships]: opposed to aft; toward ship's bow.

forward of the beam [ships]: sailing expression describing direction of wind. When boat is heading into the wind, as long as direction from which wind is blowing is not at right angles to length of boat, wind is said to be "forward of the beam."

forward scattering coefficient: coefficient which relates to forward scatterance. Unit of measurement is m^{-1}.

fossa [*Mollusca*]: groove or spiral depression forming boundary between base of gastropod shell and anterior canal.

fossette: small hollow or pit.

fossils: word fossil (derived from Latin *fodere*, "to dig up") originally referred to anything that was dug from the ground, particularly a mineral or some inexplicable form. Today term "fossil" generally means any direct evidence of past life, e.g., bones of dinosaur, shell of ancient clam. Fossils are usually found in sedimentary rocks, although they are sometimes turned up in igneous and metamorphic rocks. They are most abundant in mudstones, shales and limestones, but are also found in sandstone, dolomite and conglomerate. Fossils account for almost entire volume of certain rocks, such as coquina and limestones formed from ancient reefs.

fossula [*Coelenterata*]: usually wide space between septa caused by failure of one or more septa to develop as rapidly as others; commonly due to abortion of cardinal septum.

foul [ships]: term applied to underwater portion of outside of vessel's shell when it is more or less covered with sea growth or foreign matter.

foul bottom [ships]: hard, uneven, rocky or obstructed bottom having poor holding qualities for anchors or one having rocks or wreckage that would endanger an anchored ship.

fouling: mass of living and nonliving bodies and particles attached to or lying on surface of submerged man-made or introduced object; more commonly considered to be only living or attached bodies. May be plant or animal organisms.

fouling community: assemblage of plants and animals or artificial surface dominated by one or more organisms, such as *Mytilus* (mussel) community.

fouling panel: object of wood, metal, glass or other solid material placed in water to determine various physical and/or biological aspects of fouling; objects may be flat, curved or bent plates or boards and square or rectangular blocks.

found [ships]: ship is well found when it is fully equipped or fitted out.

founder [ships]: to fill and sink.

F.P.A.: abbreviation for *Free of Particular Average*, connoting, in a marine insurance policy, coverage includes only losses through fire, sinking, stranding, or collision.

fracto: combining word employed in cloud nomenclature; as in *fractocumulus; fractonimbus; fractostratus*, indicating a broken condition of *cumulus*, etc.

fracture zone: in geology, zone along which there

has been displacement. In oceans, major fracture zones are found at right angles to mid-ocean ridge system.

Fragilaria [subclass *Pennatae*]: members of this genus form ribbonlike chains and are common in shallow water. There are one or two choroplasts. Cells are very flat and valves are ornamented with dots arranged in rows at right angles to upper and lower surface.

frame head [ships]: section of a frame that rises above deck line.

frame lines [ships]: lines of vessel as laid out in mold loft floor, showing form and position of frames. Also, line of intersection of shell with keel of frame.

frames [ships]: sustaining parts of ship's structure, fitted and joined together. Ribs of ship.

frame spacing [ships]: fore-and-aft distances between frames, heel to heel.

framing: arrangement or system of structural parts constituting framework of a vessel; transverse or longitudinal frames, collectively.

frazil: ice crystals which form in supercooled water that is too turbulent to permit coagulation into sheet ice. Most commonly found in swiftly flowing streams, but also found in turbulent sea (where it is called lolly ice). It may accumulate as anchor ice on submerged objects and obstruct water flow.

free: applied to sailing. To sail somewhat farther from wind than when close-hauled, usually with wind in the beam or quarter.

free air space [diving]: all air spaces in human body that contain air and are normally connected to the atmosphere. Includes pulmonary system, cranial sinuses and middle ear.

freeboard: vertical distance from the projected line of top of deck plating or planking of *freeboard deck* at vessel's side to surface of water at midlength of designed load line. The minimum freeboards assigned a vessel for different seasons, areas navigated, sea or freshwater flotation, are determined by the classification society's rules which take into consideration details of vessel's length, breadth, depth, structural strength and design, extent of superstructure, sheer, and round of beam, as compared with those of a *standard vessel* to which a definite normal or *summer freeboard* has been allotted.

freebooter: 1) pirate. 2) ship which wandered in search of plunder.

free diving [skin diving]: diving, using breath-holding techniques and no life-supporting equipment.

freedom of the seas: recognized law or rule that vessels of all nations are free of any restrictions whatsoever to their right to navigate the high seas; by virtue of which any predatory or un-authorized belligerent acts by persons or vessels against commerce or persons in transportation outside territorial waters of any country are deemed by all maritime nations as acts of a common enemy.

free-flow system [diving]: continuous flow life-support system with flow rate independent of diver's breathing.

freeing ports [ships]: holes in bulwark or rail, which allow deck wash to drain off into sea.

free wave: wave that continues to exist after generating force has ceased to act.

freeze-up: formation of continuous ice cover. Generally freeze-up is restricted to hardening of locally formed young ice, although freezing together of pieces of drift ice can also be called freeze-up.

freezing point: temperature at which a liquid solidifies under any given set of conditions. Pure water under atmospheric pressure freezes at 32° F. (0° C). However, freezing point of water is depressed with increasing salinity; thus seawater with salinity of 35 per mille will freeze at about -1.9° C (28.6° F).

French shallop: large, decked merchant sloop used in Holland and Flanders in 18th century, having one mast and carrying a gaff mainsail, with no boom.

frenum [fish]: broad band of tissue holding two bones together.

freshet: area of comparatively freshwater at or near mouth of a stream flowing into sea.

fresh ice: 1) ice formed on freshwater. 2) young ice of any kind. 3) ice that has been salty but is now free of salt.

fret: to wear away or chafe, as by friction. A wasting, wearing, or chafing.

frictional factor: wave height reduction factor due to friction (along bottom) alone.

frictional layer: layer of ocean which is affected by wind action.

friendly ice: from point of view of submariner, an ice canopy containing many large ice skylights or other features which permit submarine to surface.

frigate birds [*Pelecaniformes*]: large tropical seabirds which constitute this family are the most completely aerial of water birds and perhaps of all birds except swifts. They have very long wings, long forked tails and very short legs. They never settle on water or on level coast and are probably incapable of rising from such situations. In plumage adult frigate birds are either entirely black or black above with white areas below, while young have a white head. They have long, slender bills with sharp hook at end and patch of naked skin between edges of lower mandible on chin. Feet are small and at the base toes are united by a web which extends also to the hind toe.

frigatoon: square-sterned vessel of Venetian days, having mainmast, jigger and bowsprit.

fringing reef: reef attached directly to shore of island or continental land mass. Outer margin is submerged consisting of algal limestone, coral rock and living coral.

Fritillaria borealis [*Fritillariidae*]: trunk is long and narrow, being drawn out post-anally to accommodate testes and ovary. This results in tail appearing to rise from mid-ventral surface of trunk. Tail is short and broad due to presence of broad fin. Length of trunk is approximately 1 mm. There are probably two subspecies. *Fritillaria borealis acuta* is a cosmopolitan cold water form found in polar seas and *Fritillaria borealis truncata* is a warm water derivative that is found in northern seas.

frog crab, three-toothed [*Lyreidus tridentatus*]: this little frog crab has convex carapace with smooth surface and smooth border except for single spine on each side. Carapace is widest near middle and becomes quite narrow at front with sides almost straight from lateral spine to the eye. Last pair of walking legs are small and placed high on body. Entire animal is orange. This is a small species in which carapace seldom measures over 2 in. long. Name is taken from 3 spines on each pincher. Habitat is on sand or muddy bottoms at depths in excess of 100 ft.

frogfish: members of this family are awkward fishes only 3 to 6 in. long with anterior portion of body decorated with numerous appendages. Dorsal, anal and tail fins are large; pectoral and ventral fins resemble miniature limbs. Because of wristlike joint at base of pectoral fin, frogfish can use these fins much as a land animal uses its forelimbs.

frondose [*Bryozoa*]: erect colony consisting of broad flat branches.

front: in meteorology, generally, interface or transition zone between two air masses of different density. Since temperature distribution is most important regulator of atmospheric density, a front almost invariably separates air masses of different temperature.

frontal [reptiles]: single median plate on top of head between eyes.

front bay: large irregular bay connected with sea through passes between barrier islands.

front of the fetch: end of generating area toward which wind is blowing.

frost smoke: foglike clouds, due to contact of cold air with relatively warm seawater, which appear over newly-formed leads (lanes) and pools or leeward of ice-edge.

fruiter: name given the 2- and 3-masted schooners employed in fruit trade from Italy, Malta and other orange growing countries to Europe and England. Vessels were fast and beautifully modeled.

frustule: 1) siliceous shell of diatom, consisting of two valves, one overlapping the other. It is principal constituent of marine diatomaceous ooze. 2) nonciliated planulalike bud that develops into a polyp on some hydrozoans.

fucoid: referring to members of *Fucales*, order of brown algae; typically found attached to rocks of intertidal zone, although some such as *Sargassum* become free floating.

fucoxanthin: brownish xanthin pigment found in seaweeds.

full and by [ships]: sailing close to wind but with all sails fitted and drawing.

full-rigged ship [ships]: sailing ship with at least 3 masts, all square-rigged.

fully developed sea: maximum height to which ocean waves can be generated by given wind force blowing over sufficient fetch, regardless of duration, resulting in all possible wave components of spectrum being present with maximum amount of spectral energy.

fulmar: bird of the Arctic seas, abounding to extreme northern Atlantic waters; of the *petrel* family, similar in size and color to the herring gull, breeds in cliffs of the Orkneys, Shetlands, Iceland, etc., and feeds on fish and floating refuse; said to be particularly fond of whale blubber; much valued for its eggs, feathers, down, and an oil obtained from its stomach which has been a principal product of the lonely isle of St. Kilda off Scotland's west coast. Related species are found in Antarctic and northern Pacific waters and the *giant fulmar* of southern seas and U.S. Pacific coast, also called a *bonebreaker*, is an outstanding bird in that it attains the proportions of a small albatross.

fundamental unit: unit measure of basic physical quantity such as mass, length, time; e.g., 1 gram, 1 centimeter, 1 second, respectively. Other quantities such as force, temperature, etc., may be considered fundamental and each assigned a fundamental unit.

fungus: thallophyte lacking chlorophyll. Many marine fungi have been identified. Some are believed to add to damage caused by marine borers by penetration of wood around burrows of borers.

funicle: ridge of callus spiralling into umbilicus in naticid gastropods.

funnel sea: gulf or bay, narrow at head, wide at mouth and deepening rapidly from head to mouth.

furca: pair of projections at back end of copepod body.

furcilia larva: last larval stages in euphausiids.

furl [ships]: to wrap or roll a sail close to the yard, stay or mast and to fasten it by gasket or cord.

furrow: long narrow depression in the sea floor extending in a direction approximately perpendicular to a coastline. Also termed *shelf-deep*. Such depressions are useful to a navigator when taking a line of soundings, the sudden increase and decrease of depth serving to indicate passage over the charted *furrow*.

fusiform: 1) tapering toward both ends as in many pennate diatoms. 2) in *Foraminifera*, spindle-shaped.

fusulinids: these large *Foraminifera*, with shell rolled in spindle form, are strictly characteristic of Carboniferous and Permian. They lived in open sea and also in whole Mesogean sea. They lived only in open sea of normal salinity and at relatively shallow depths where they built, almost by themselves, purely fusuline limestones.

futtock shrouds: iron rods leading from futtock plates to iron band around topmast or lower mast.

F.W.: freshwater load line mark on ship's side at mid-length, indicating minimum freeboard allowed when floating in river or lake water considered as of density 1000 oz. or 62½ lbs. per cu. ft.; volume of 1 ton of 2240 lbs. being 35.84 cu. ft., 1 cubic meter or kiloliter (approx.), 269 U.S. gallons, or 1000 liters (approx.). *Fresh water* attains greatest density at temperature of 39° F. or 4° C; freezes at 32° F. or 0° C; and 1 cu. ft. of solid ice weighs 57 lbs.

G

G: 1) abbreviation in ships' logbooks and meteorological records for *gloomy* appearance of weather; also for *ground swell.* 2) International Code flag *G*, hoisted singly, signifies "I require a pilot."

gadget [ships]: slang term applied to various fittings.

gadidae: family of fishes which includes several important genera widely used as food, as cod, haddock, pollack, tomcod, and coalfish.

gaff [ships]: spar bent along head of fore-and-aft sail, extending aft from mast. It is hoisted by "throat" halyards at mast and by "peak" halyards at outer end. Kind of rig employing quadrilateral rather than triangular sails on mast. Also spar at top of sail, set at angle to mast.

gaff-headed: quadrilateral sail parallel to length of ship with spar or support called a gaff supporting its upper edge.

gaff-rigged [ships]: describing a ship on which mainsail and perhaps other sails are gaff-headed.

gaff topsail [ships]: triangular sail set from a topmast, clew-sheeted to outer end of gaff of fore-and-aft mainsail or lower sail; sheet from tack leading to deck.

gafter: fishing boat used in drift-net and long-line fisheries at Polperro, Cornwall, England. Hull is carvel-built with square transom and ranges 26 to 30 ft. long.

gag: the *grouper* of southern U.S. coasts, West Indies, and Caribbean waters; considered an excellent food fish.

gage pressure [diving]: pressure above atmospheric pressure indicated by a gage that reads zero pressure at sea level.

gaissa: cargo boat or sailing lighter of Nile River. Bargelike hull has little freeboard and no sheer, except at bow, which curves up strongly, meeting rounded stern in a point. Outboard rudder is slung from short, straight sternpost. These vessels sail upriver and drift down the current.

gal: unit of acceleration equal to 1 centimeter per second per second (1 cm/sec^2) or 1,000 milligals. A milligal is 0.001 gal. The term gal is not an abbreviation. It was invented to honor memory of Galileo.

galactic: pertaining to the *Galaxy* or *Milky Way*, that faintly luminous belt of nebulous masses and myriads of incomprehensibly distant stars appearing as cloudlike masses of light, interrupted in several places but generally following the trend of a great circle in the celestial sphere, or what is known as the *galactic circle.*

Galathea dispersa [anomurans]: first zoeal stage is only 2.5 mm. long and final stage is 6.8 mm., as compared with 7.0 mm. in *G. strigosa*. Lateral spines are lacking from fourth abdominal segment and postero-lateral spines on carapace are relatively shorter than in other species.

Galathea squamifera [anomurans]: first larval stage is smallest of the 3 species mentioned, being only 2.2 mm. long. Fourth or final larva is only 4.8 mm. long. Abdomen bears short lateral spines in segments 4 and 5, shorter than on *G. strigosa*.

Galathea strigosa [anomurans]: first zoea is 3.5 mm. long and second 5 mm. long. As in other *Galathea sp.*, rostral spine and antennal scale are proportionally smaller than in *Munida*. No dorsal spines on posterior margins of abdominal segments; second to fifth abdominal segments are serrated on posterior margins; telson bears 8 spines on all except first stage. Uropods, when they appear, have 9 posteriorly projection spines.

gale: some linguists think the archaic Danish term *galen* (mad, furious) gave birth to the English gale. But connection is doubtful since earliest appearance of the wind is in verse where it rhymes with "sail." Old Norse *gal* (breeze) is most likely source, but when and how this term entered English is uncertain. Even after it was widely used vigorous wind was not clearly defined. Admiral Smyth of British Navy said that it simply implied "what on shore is called a storm." Though it is still in vernacular usage, meteorologists restrict the name to a wind of Force 8 or more on Beaufort Scale, i.e., 35 miles per hour or more. Quite a "breeze," even by standards of hardy Norsemen.

galleass: larger and stronger "galley," used as ship-of-war in late 15th century and through 16th century. Early Venetian galleass carried 3 lateen sails; Mediterranean galleass was lateen-rigged;

used by English in 16th century. Galleass of 400 tons and 20 oars to a side required 5 men at each oar.

galleon: 1) second-class war vessel of 16th and 17th centuries, generally with 3 decks. Forecastle-ended at stern, while long, slim beak projected forward under bowsprit. Galleons carried courses and topsails on main and foremasts and one (sometimes two) lateen-rigged mizzenmast. 2) large, unwieldy, ancient ship, usually having 3 or 4 decks and carrying guns. At one time used largely by Spaniards as treasure ships in trade with South America.

galley [ships]: long single or partially decked vessel of war which depended chiefly on oars or sweeps for propulsion, but had mast and sail for use when wind was favorable.

galley punt: English clinker-built boat which can be sailed or rowed; 21 to 30 ft. long; rigged with long-yarded dipping lugsail on short mast set amidships.

galliot: 18th century Dutch ship of 50 to 300 tons, two-masted, square-rigged on foremast, with several jibs running to rather long bowsprit. Aftermast carried fore-and-aft mizzen sail.

Galofaro: whirlpool in Strait of Messina. Formerly called Charybdis.

Galway hooker: cutter-rigged fishing craft used off Galway coast in Iceland in 19th century. This type was introduced into New England about 1857.

gam: large school of whales. Sperm whales travel about in small parties which sometimes join up to form schools, or gams, of considerable size.

gametangium: in algae, special structure in which gametes are born.

gamete: mature egg or sperm, capable of reproduction after fertilization with sperm or egg from same species.

gametophyte: in sexual generation of algae, male or female plant which produces motile or nonmotile gametes.

gamma ray detector: instrument on ships for identifying and measuring abnormal gamma ray concentrations in ocean areas, as would result from nuclear-powered vessel refuse and nuclear-waste dumping.

ganger: 1) any handy length of chain or rope used to haul a heavy line, cable, anchor, etc., into a required position for making fast. 2) short length of chain attached to anchor as a protective extension to a fiber cable. 3) short wire or chain dropped with a laid-out anchor and buoyed for subsequent connection to a hawser.

ganglia: aggregation of nerve cells.

gangplank [ships]: structure running from ship to dock allowing passengers to board and debark.

Board with cleats, forming bridge reaching from gangway of vessel to wharf.

gangway [ships]: a passage into or out of a ship, or from one part of a ship to another. Plank, bridge, or platform used from the vessel's deck across the intervening space of water between the ship's side and the dock or wharf.

gannets [*Pelecaniformes*]: large, long-winged seabirds with stout, conical, pointed beaks, fairly short necks, stout bodies and long wedge-shaped tails. Legs are short and all toes are connected by webs. On throat they have a small pouch of naked skin and there are also unfeathered areas of naked skin on face.

ganoids: general term for fishes having porcelain-like ganoin, i.e., hard surface on scales. Devonian to Recent. Living species include sturgeon, garpike and bowfin.

gap: steep-sided depression cutting transversely across ridge or rise.

gap coding: in navigation, process of communicating by interrupting transmission of otherwise continuous signal so that interruptions form a telegraphic message.

gape [*Mollusca*]: chink or wider opening between pelecypod valves when in closed position.

gar: widely distributed fish having a much elongated body and long narrow jaws; also known as *gar pike, billfish, needlefish, sea-needle, longnosed gar, shortnosed gar, hornfish,* and *greenbone.* Those of marine habitat, unlike the fresh-water *gars* in general, are good food fishes, *especially* those of the family *Belonidae* found in European, Australian, and Central American waters.

gar, alligator [*Lepisosteus spatula*]: undisputed ruler of Mississippi River and its tributaries living in bayous and swampy ponds of southern U.S. When viewed from front, fish is startingly like an alligator because of huge mouth and numerous daggerlike teeth. This well-armored fish with voracious habits is capable of crushing a 6-ft. alligator with a single bite.

garbling: process of separating, in a consignment of cargo, damaged or inferior goods from those in good order, in view of possible nonpayment or reduction of customs duty; particularly applies to spices, drugs, tobacco, etc. *Garblings* are residue goods after separation from those in satisfactory condition.

garboard [ships]: planking on either side next to keel.

garboard strake [ships]: plank adjacent to keel.

gar family [*Lepisosteidae*]: gars are a remnant of an ancient family. They are all warm water fishes. Distinguished by slender cylindrical bodies and thin, long, snoutlike jaws armed with sharp teeth; teeth are present on vomer and palatines.

Body is clothed with heavy diamond-shaped ganoid scales covered by an enamellike substance, ganoin. Skeleton is partly cartilage and partly bone. Swim bladder is connected with pharynx and may be used as a lung. Tail fin is modified heterocercal type.

gar, Florida spotted [*Lepisosteus platyrhincus*]: dull-colored cylindrical fish with hard scales and long jaws. Mouth extended into a bill-like structure; distance from orbit to edge of opercular membrane more than 2/3 length of snout. Ground color olive-green to muddy; top of head not normally spotted; diffuse spots near base of dorsal, anal and caudal fins.

gar, longnose [*Lepisosteus osseus*]: long or bony gar, widely distributed in sluggish streams and swamps of central and southern states. Name is derived from very long snout, twice as long as rest of head. Longnose gars grow to length of 5 ft. Adult more uniformly muddy-colored with tendency to be spotted particularly about fins.

gar, northern longnose [*Lepisosteus osseus oxyurus*]: longnose gar has very elongate and sub-cylindrical body covered with regular rows of small, hard, enamel plates. Jaws are elongated and both upper and lower jaws are armed with long sharp teeth. It is extremely variable in color, length of snout and body proportions. General color is greenish-olive above, silvery on sides and white beneath; both body and fins are marked with numerous round, black spots. Scales in lateral line number 60—63. In this species snout is more than twice the length of rest of head.

gar, northern spotted [*Lepisosteus productus*]: dully, cylindrical fish with hard scales and long jaws. Usually has 54 to 58 scales in lateral line. Mouth extended into bill-like structure; distance from front of orbit to edge of opercular membrane less than 2/3 length of snout. Ground color olive-green to muddy with spots on top of head and diffuse spots on body, particularly near base of dorsal, anal and caudal fins.

garr: slimy fungus growth on a ship's bottom.

gar, shortnose [*Lepisosteus platostomus*]: shortnose gar is similar to spotted gar except that shortnose gar has no spots on top of its head and has more scales in lateral line. It differs from longnose gar chiefly in length of jaw. Back is short and broad compared to that of *L. osseus oxyurus;* snout is broad and not much longer (about 1.3) than rest of head. Very young fish has short jaws and wide black band on sides. Scales in lateral line usually number 60—64. Shortnose gar seldom exceeds 2 or 3 ft. in length.

garukha: dhow type of Persian Gulf, still in existence. Steering gear is peculiar, having pair of tackles leading from short horizontal spar on each quarter to back of rudder.

gas: state of matter in which molecules are practically unrestricted by cohesive forces. Gas has neither shape nor volume.

gas bladder: gas-filled bladder in fish. Pressure in bladder usually equalizes with depth so that fish does not have to swim against positive or negative buoyancy. These bladders are believed to have developed from lungs of primitive fishes that could sometimes breathe air.

gas chromatography: means of separating gaseous mixture into constituent substances by passing it through a column filled with special absorbent liquid or solid, the constituents become recognizable by their colors.

gas console [diving]: station for monitoring and controlling flow of gas to divers on mixed-gas operations.

gasket [ships]: one of several bands of canvas or small lines (ropes) used to bind sails to yards, gaffs or masts when furled.

gastrodermis [*Coelenterata*]: layer of cells lining body cavity forming inner layer of body wall.

Gastrogaccos sanctus [mysids]: long slender mysid with laterally flattened cephalothorax tapering slightly at front end. Abdomen cylindrical at front but flattened from side to side at level of fifth segment; short carapace with short, blunt rostrum between base of eyestalks. There is a deep hollow in mid-dorsal surface of carapace whose posterior margin is so emarginated as to show last two thoracic segments on dorsal side. Telson narrows distally, shorter than last abdominal segment and bears 6 spines on lateral margin of which last is longest.

gastrolith: one of small rocks used to help break up food in stomach of various animals such as lobsters; stones which have been transported in stomach of marine animals such as walruses.

gastropod: Greek "*gaster*," belly, "*podos*," foot. From the class *Gastropoda*, early Cambrian to Recent. Organism has distinct head with mouth, tentacles and eyes. Tip of spiral shell points backwards and opening into largest, last-formed turn of shell is in forward position, directed downwards. They inhabit marine and freshwater environments and in these are found as benthonic, sessile and vagrant and planktonic forms. They exist as herbivores, parasites and scavangers and include snails, periwinkles, nudibranchs, abalone, limpets and sea hares.

gastrovascular cavity: central cavity found in *Cnidaria* and *Ctenophora*.

gastrozooid: 1) feeding zooid of siphonophore colony. 2) in *Siphonophora* and in *Doliolidae*, individual of colony specialized for feeding.

gat: natural or artificial passage or channel extending inland through shoals or steep banks.

G.A.T.: navigators' abbreviation for *Greenwich*

Apparent Time; that indicated by the true sun at the Prime Meridian. Reckoned from midnight to midnight, 0 hours to 24 hours of each day, it is equal to 12 hours *minus* the true sun's easterly hour angle or 12 hours *plus* true sun's westerly hour angle (time from noon) from upper transit of that body, i.e., apparent noon; thus, two hours before apparent sun arrives at the meridian of Greenwich, G.A.T. is 10 hrs. 00 min. 00 sec.; while two hours after that event becomes 14 hrs. 00 min. 00 sec.

gata: kind of shark found in West Indies waters; attains a length of 7 feet.

gateway: 1) passage for vessels through an opened section of a protective submarine net, a harbor boom, etc. 2) any narrow waterway, channel, port entrance, etc., used for navigation.

gatewood system: modification of the *Isherwood,* or longitudinal, method of framing used in shipbuilding.

Gaussian error: as observed on a sharp change of course, a temporary component of deviation caused by magnetism induced by earth's magnetic field in soft iron during a period in which vessel lies in one direction only. *Especially* in the old iron ships, this error often amounted to 8 or 10 degrees upon a broad change of course after steering in an easterly or westerly direction for some days, as, e.g., in an eastbound trans-Atlantic vessel upon hauling up through Straits of Dover. Its amount and subsiding period normally were constant on such passages in individual ships, found by observation, and allowed for. The rule for *Gaussian error* effect is that it *always carries vessel toward direction of her last course;* the eastbound vessel in example, accordingly, being required to allow for an *easterly* error or deviation.

Gaussian wave packet: isolated group of waves, with infinitely long crests in direction perpendicular to direction of propagation and with constant wavelength in direction of propagation, of sine wave form, which is modulated mathematically according to normal probability curve (Gaussian curve).

G.C.T. [Greenwich Civil Time]: mean solar time of the meridian passing through *Greenwich Observatory* (London, England), or *prime meridian,* from which terrestrial longitude is reckoned. Ephemerides of heavenly bodies are given in the *Nautical Almanac* for this time, also known as *Greenwich Mean Time,* and by some astronomers as *Universal Time.* It is reckoned from midnight to midnight, or 0 hours to 24 hours, of each day.

gear [ships]: ropes, blocks, etc., belonging to any particular sail or spar. Broadly, all working parts or appliances on ship. Also personal effects of people on board.

gehazi: local name of Arab dhow of same type as sambuk with high pooped hull. Employed on African Coast as far south as Zanzibar.

geleira: "canoe" of Amazon delta which carries ice on fishing trips to prevent spoilage of fish.

Gelidium: genus of red algae with much branched cartilaginous fronds, including *G. cartilagineum,* source of agar-agar.

Gemini: northern zodiacal constellation containing the navigational stars Castor *(a Geminorum)* and Pollux *(β Geminorum),* of magnitude 1.6 and 1.2 respectively. Castor lies north of and is nearly 4° distant from its mate.

genera [genus]: one of taxonomic or scientific classifications of plants and animals. Groups of similar species belong to same genus and related genera form families. First of two names comprising organism's scientific name is the genus. For animals, in descending order, the system is kingdom, phylum, class, order, family, genus, species. Thus man would be *Animal, Chordata, Mammalia, Primate, Hominidae, Homo, sapiens.*

generation of waves: creation of waves by natural or mechanical means. Creation and growth of waves caused by wind blowing over water surface for certain period of time. Area involved is called generating area or fetch.

genes: units found at specific points on chromosomes. They transmit hereditary characteristics and consist primarily of DNA and protein.

geniculate: elbowed, with kneelike bend, as in antennae of various isopods and other *Crustacea.*

genital somite or segment: in copepods, the somite or fused pair of somites bearing genital openings, usually first segment of urosome.

Genoa jib [ships]: large, triangular headsail which overlaps mainsail. It is a reaching jib used in racing yachts.

genome: one complete haploid set of chromosomes of an organism.

genotype: type of genes possessed by organism or group of organisms; genetic makeup of an individual.

geo: Icelandic term for narrow inlet walled in by steep cliffs.

geodesic line: line of shortest distance between any two points on any mathematically defined surface.

geodesy: scientific measurement and determination of various dimensions of earth, including density, weight, shape and gravitational and magnetic variations. It especially refers to surveying of areas that are so large an allowance must be made for earth's curvature.

geodetic datum: datum consisting of 5 quantities; latitude and longitude of initial point, azimuth of line from this point and 2 constants necessary to define terrestrial spheroid. It forms basis for computation of horizontal control surveys in which curvature of earth is considered.

geoid: figure of earth considered as mean sea level surface extending continuously through continents. Actual geoid is an equipotential surface to which, at every point, plumb line (direction in which gravity acts) is perpendicular.

geological oceanography: study of floors and margins of oceans, including descriptions of submarine relief, features, chemical and physical composition of bottom materials, interaction of sediments and rocks with air and seawater and action of various forms of wave energy in submarine crust of earth.

Geomagnetic Electrokinetograph [GEK]: shipboard current measuring device used in depths greater than 100 fathoms. It is dependent upon the principle that electrolyte moving through magnetic field (earth) will generate an electric current. Current is measured by means of electrodes towed behind ship.

geomagnetic equator: great circle on earth's surface that is everywhere equidistant from geomagnetic poles; i.e., equator in system of geomagnetic coordinates.

geomagnetic pole: point where axis of centered dipole, that most nearly duplicates earth's magnetic field, would intersect surface of earth. Earth's geomagnetic poles are located approximately $78.5°$ N, $69.0°$ W and $78.5°$ S, $111.0°$ E.

geomagnetism: magnetic phenomenon, collectively considered, exhibited by earth and its atmosphere.

geometric: period of ancient Greek art, especially pottery, extending from 11th or 10th century B.C. to about 700 B.C. Pottery style is distinguished by extensive use of geometric forms and extremely stylized animals, if they appear at all.

geomorphology: that branch of both geography and geology which deals with the form of the earth, general configuration of its surface and changes that take place in evolution of land forms.

GEON [Gyro Erected Optical Navigation]: system of celestial navigation which employs a meridian gyrocompass as level reference plane instead of present method of using natural horizon. It allows ship's position to be determined from single sight on single celestial body.

geonavigation: as distinguished from *celonavigation*, or determining ship's position and checking course by observations of heavenly bodies, navigation performed by piloting, compass or radio bearings of terrestrial objects, soundings, radar, or dead reckoning.

Geophilomorpha: order of arthropods with slender body specialized for burrowing; pair of lateral spiracles on each segment, except first and last; mouthparts variable; intraspecific variability of trunk segments; segments up to 183; epimorphic; cosmopolitan. *Geophilus.*

geophones: detector, transducer placed on or in ground in seismic work responding to ground motion at point of its location.

geosphere: "solid" portion of earth, including water masses; lithosphere plus hydrosphere.

geostrophic: current or wind resulting from effect of Coriolis force on pressure gradient force, resulting in movement parallel to isobars and proportional to their spacing, itself related to pressure gradient force. Hence from spacing of isobars velocity can be determined.

geostrophic current: current defined by assuming that exact balance exists between horizontal pressure gradient and Coriolis force.

geosyncline: 1) elongated trough in which sediments accumulate to considerable thickness (up to 40,000 ft.) where they are available from neighboring land masses by erosion. Buckling of geosyncline involving intense folding and transportation along thrust-planes is believed to be prime cause of mountain building. 2) large, generally linear subsident trough in which many thousands of feet of sediment are accumulating or have accumulated. Deep oceanic trenches paralleling island arcs are considered to be developing geosynclines.

geothermal gradient: change in temperature of earth with depth expressed either in degrees per unit depth or in units of depth per degree.

geotome: instrument used for taking soil samples without disturbing surrounding soil.

Germanischer Lloyd: German classification society established in 1867.

germ cell: cell from which new organism can develop.

gharawa: Arab dugout with outriggers on both sides. About 17 ft. long, 2 ft. 6 in. beam. Upper strake is pegged in.

ghobong: long, narrow dugout canoe used on rivers and streams of Borneo by natives. It has long, tapering, graceful, overhanging ends, which terminate in small upfacing square, sharp-edged on forward side. Bow and stern alike. Paddles are used for propulsion.

ghobun: native name for canoe in Astrolabe Bay district of Mandated Territory of New Guinea. Outrigger canoe with long, pointed, solid ends and decorated washstrokes and high breakwaters above hull. Canoes in this district are employed mainly in pottery trade.

ghost crab, horn-eyed [*Ocypode ceratophtalma*]: carapace of this species is rectangular and has beady surface. Chelipeds are unequal in size, quite short and flattened to aid in carrying sand.

Body measures nearly 2 in. across carapace. This crab is named for horn at end of eyestalk. It inhabits sandy beaches above waterline.

ghost crab, telescope-eyed [*Macrophthalmus telescopicus*]: most remarkable feature is pair of very long eyestalks which usually measure an inch or more in length and extend far beyond edge of carapace. Carapace is oval and about 1½ in. in width in larger individuals; chelipeds are small, flat, thin, pointed and channeled on their lower side; walking legs are slender and somewhat pointed; third and fourth pair of legs are fringed with hair at both anterior and posterior borders. This crab inhabits shallow areas along shoreline.

giant clam [*Tridacna*]: one of genus (*Tridacna*) of large bivalves inhabiting coral reefs in Indo-Pacific region. It is the largest of bivalve mollusks; diameter of shell may exceed 3½ ft. It is a fixed animal living within coral reefs. When its shell is ajar, one can see a blue, fleshy mantle with central line of emerald green. Clam's mantle contains number of transparent cells which focus light onto animal's tissue inside the shell. When that light is interrupted by shadow of an object, shell snaps shut. These same cells and light they transmit contribute to development of minute algae, which live in symbiosis with the clam. Algae dispose of wastes of clam and at same time provide oxygen by means of photosynthesis.

giant kelp: one of genus (*Macrocystis*) of large vinelike brown algae, which grows attached to sea bottom by massive holdfast and reaches lengths to 150 ft. Members of this genus are the largest algae in existence.

giant squid: these animals inhabit the mid-depths in oceanic regions but may surface at night normally or by accident. It is food for the sperm whale but often may give battle.

gib [ships]: metal fitting that holds a member in place or presses two members together.

gibbous: said of the moon's appearance during period between first and last quarter, or when having a rounded periphery; as in the *gibbous phase*; opposed to the *crescent* phase.

gibstaff: rod used for sounding or to pole a boat in shallow water.

gig [ships]: small boat formerly carried on shipboard and meant for use when in port. Generally the captain's boat.

giglio trawler: Italian fishing craft, single-masted, lateen mainsail and large jib carried on bowsprit; clipper bow and outboard rudder.

gill: 1) general term for special structure evolved for underwater respiration. 2) platelike or filamentous outgrowth; respiratory organ of aquatic animals. 3) in *Mollusca*, leaf-shaped structure lying in posterior portion of mantle cavity and used in respiration. Typically occurs in pairs, one mounted on either side of body.

gill arch: tissue of pharynx which supports gills; it is usually supported by cartilage or bone in fish, between gill slits.

gill net: net which is set upright in water. Gills of fish become entangled in its meshes.

gill raker: one of small, bony structures on inside edge of fish's gill arches which support gills; they prevent solid particles from injuring gills and stop food from escaping with the water which flows in through fish's mouth, over gills and out again through opening in animal's skin.

gilthead: any of several small food fishes so named for their brilliant colors; the *wrasse* or *cunner* of Britain.

gimbals [ships]: contrivance (usually two movable hoops or rings, one within the other, moving on horizontal pivots) for securing free motion in suspension so that an object such as a lamp, compass, chronometer or barometer may keep a constant position in equilibrium regardless of motion of ship.

girdle: connecting bands of two halves of diatom frustules.

girellid fish: any member of family *Girellidae*, group of plant-eating marine fish.

girt: said of a vessel moored with an upstream and a downstream anchor when she lies against her lee cable because of both cables being hove too taut. Vessel is also said to be *girt with her cable* when it leads under her bottom to its anchor.

girth [ships]: distance measured in any frame line, from intersection of upper deck with the side, around body of vessel to corresponding point on opposite side. Half girth is taken from center line of keel to upper deck beam end.

girth band [ships]: strip of canvas, from fore-leech or luft to clew ring, sewed across a jib or staysail to strengthen it.

gizzard shad [family *Clupeidae*]: silver in color, with bluish back. Belly is sharply serrated or keeled. This species is easily distinguishable by last ray of dorsal fin, which is very long. Teeth are absent in adult, though present in young; stomach is very muscular or gizzardlike and intestine is long and coiled. Gill rakers are long and extremely fine reaching a length of over 15 in.

glabella: median part of head of trilobite and some others.

glabrous: having a smooth surface.

glacial: 1) pertaining to presence, size and composition or activity of extensive masses of land ice. 2) pertaining to characteristic of, produced or deposited by or derived from a glacier.

glacial cirque: all mountain systems which are or have been centers of local glaciation exhibit numerous examples of a type of alpine valley which terminates at their heads in rocky amphitheaters known as "glacial cirques."

glacial drift [glacial alluvium]: rock debris which has been transported by glaciers and deposited as ice melts or carried some distance by accompanying melt water before deposition.

glacial epoch: Pleistocene epoch; earlier of two divisions of geologic time included in Quarternary period; characterized by continental glaciers which covered extensive regions now free from ice.

glacial lobe: tonguelike extension of glacial ice sheet.

glacial milk: melt water from glaciers, colored by suspended particles of clay and silt.

glacial striae: glacial scratches on smoothed rock surfaces.

glacial trough: U-shaped valley, excavated by glacier either on land or sea bottom.

glaciated coast: coast whose features indicate that it has been covered by continental glaciers of Pleistocene epoch or coast covered by glaciers of present time.

glacier: field or stream of ice formed by accumulation of snow, moving down a slope and spreading by its own weight; birthplace of icebergs.

glacier, alpine: valley glaciers that are nourished on flanks of high mountains and flow down mountain sides.

glacier berg: mass of glacier ice that has broken away from parent formation on coast and either floats, generally at least 5 meters (16.4 ft.) above sea level, or is stranded on a shoal.

glacier, continental: usually reserved for great ice sheets that obscure mountains and plains of large sections of a continent, such as those of Greenland and Antarctica.

glacier ice: any ice floating on sea, such as iceberg, which originated from a glacier.

glacier iceberg: iceberg derived from a glacier as distinguished from tabular icebergs derived from shelf ice.

glaciers, Piedmont: form when glaciers emerge from their valleys and spread out to form apron of moving ice on plains below.

glacier table: large block of stone supported by column of ice on surface of a glacier.

glacier tongue: projecting seaward extension of a glacier, usually afloat. In Antarctic, glacier tongue may extend over many tens of kilometers.

glaciology: study of snow and ice on earth's surface with specific concentration on regime of active glaciers.

glacon: fragment of sea ice, ranging in size from brash to a medium floe.

glance: 1) sudden change in direction of motion due to contact with an obstructing object; as, *the glance of the colliding vessels caused both to heel outward.* 2) to polish or give a lustre to; as, to glance the brightwork. 3) to move swiftly and elegantly in sailing; as, *the yacht glances along.*

glare ice: any highly reflective sheet of ice on water, land or glacier.

glass-minnow, freshwater [*Menidia beryllina*]: silvery-greenish, streamlined little fish. Scales along side to 37 to 39 with 16 to 18 soft rays; 2 dorsal fins. Body very slender, fusiform; mouth terminal and oblique, lower jaw short and weak; sides of head scaly. Color greenish, narrow lateral strip of silver. Length up to about 4 in.

glass sponges [*Hyalospongiae*]: these sponges have siliceous spicules with 6 rays, one of which may be so much longer than the others that it looks like a wisp of spun glass. Glass sponges were present in early Cambrian seas and rare in Ordovician and Silurian formations, but are preserved in enormous numbers in late Devonian formations of western New York. These sponges are principally inhabitants of deep water to depths as great as 16,400 ft. (5,000 meters).

glauconite: green mineral, closely related to micas and essentially a hydrous potassium iron silicate. Occurs in sediments of marine origin and is produced by alteration of various other minerals in marine reducing or anaerobic environment.

glaze: smooth, transparent or translucent coating of ice deposited by heavy fall of freezing rain; sleet.

glimmer ice: ice newly formed in cracks, holes or puddles on surface of old ice.

glitter: spots of light reflected from a point source by surface of sea.

Globigerina: genus of globular *Foraminifera* now most common; globigerina ooze constitutes upper part (12,000 to 18,000 ft.) of deep sea deposits with consistency of thick soup. One-celled animals whose shells form calcareous deep-sea ooze.

globigerina ooze: 1) deep-sea deposit covering large part of ocean floor (one-quarter of surface of globe) consisting chiefly of minute calcareous shells of foraminifers. 2) pelagic sediment consisting of more than 30% calcium carbonate in form of foraminiferal tests of which *Globigerina* is dominant genus.

glochidium: bivalve larval stage in freshwater mussels.

glomeruli: small clumps of capillaries in kidneys which filter out water, wastes and food materials from blood and pass than on as urine to be excreted.

Gloucester fishing schooner: schooner developed in and sailed out of Gloucester and other Massachusetts Bay ports. This type of vessel is designed for market fishing, offshore fishing and service on the Great Banks.

glowing ball luminescence: display of biological light appearing as distinct and separate flashes or blobs of light of various diameters, commonly having disc or globular shape, and originating either at or below surface of sea. Organisms responsible for this type of display include jellyfish, ctenophores and tunicates. Glowing ball displays are seen more frequently in warmer waters.

Glycymeris: shell is circular in outline and lenticular in shape; valves are symmetrical to one another and very nearly symmetrical in themselves. External surface is marked by radial and concentric lines; latter are always very slightly marked. Beneath umbo and above hingeline there is an obtusely triangular cardinal area which in fossil shell is seen to be bounded above by lightly raised margin and to bear number of ridges arranged like a set of chevrons or inverted V's, one within the other uniting the two valves, conchiolin.

G.M.: in ship stability, vertical distance of metacenter from center of gravity.

G.M.T. [Greenwich Mean Time]: as used by navigators, time shown by chronometer corrected for error, or that indicating *mean solar time* at Greenwich.

gnathobase: basal process on appendages of certain arachnids; usually for crushing or handling food.

gnathochilarium: appendage of united second maxillae or lower lip of millipedes.

gnomonic chart: used for navigation in high latitudes or in great circle sailing, chart in which arcs of great circles appear as straight lines.

gnomonic projection: perspective map projection upon a tangent plane with point from which projecting lines are drawn situated at center of sphere. Projection is neither conformal nor equal area. It is the only projection on which great circles in spheres are represented as straight lines.

gnotobiotic: literally "known biology," said of culture grown in chemically defined medium without other organisms or with only known organisms present in culture.

goby: small fish of family *Gobiidae* with no commercial value. Freshwater as well as marine, gobies have pelvic fins that are often joined together into suckerlike structure to help them hold on to bottom.

goby, crested [*Lophogobius*]: 2-in.-long fish with big head and high fins. Soft rays in anal fin 9 or 10; scales along sides 25 to 30. Head long, snout short, blunt, about as long as eye; mouth very oblique, gape slightly curved; front of upper lip of level of lower border of eye; profile convex. Body short and deep, little compressed; dorsal fins separate; caudal fin rounded. Head naked but body scaled; color greenish-black.

goby, darting [*Gobionellus boleosoma*]: tiny

(about 2 in.), slender, extremely active fish with 2 dorsal fins and ventral sucking disk. Pelvic fins fused at base to form sucking disk; head naked but body scaled; 12 soft rays in dorsal fin; upper rays of pectoral fin not silky. Head moderate, but not very blunt; snout as short as or shorter than eye; mouth not large, horizontal in profile. Color light to dark olive-green mottled with darker; fins usually tinged with orange.

goby, large-mouth [*Microgobius gulosus*]: small goby with large mouth. Pelvic fins fused at base to form sucking disk; head largely naked; body scaled. Head large and long; mouth big, oblique; lower jaws strongly projecting; maxillary extending to line of eye. Body rather slender; dorsal fins separate; caudal fin about as long as head, pointed. Coloration grayish-olive with mottlings of darker on body; pale blue stripe on each side of head above jaw.

goby, naked [*Gobiosoma bosci*]: small fish with big mouth and no scales. Pelvic fins fused at base to form sucking disk; head broad, mouth terminal; body rather short and stocky. Caudal fin rounded; anal fin usually with 11 soft rays; pelvic fin thoracic in position. Color brownish or blackish, usually with about 9 whitish crossbars on body.

goby, river [*Awaous tajasica*]: large goby with tiny scales and white belly. Pelvic fins fused at base to form sucking disk; head naked but body scaled; 60 to 70 scales along side of body. Head broader than deep; mouth large, horizontal. Caudal fin rounded, shorter than head; anal fin with 11 soft rays; pelvic fins thoracic in position. Color olivaceous with dark blotches along sides and dark streaks radiating around eyes.

goe: Scottish term for small sea-cut gorge eroded into a cliffed coast.

goldeye [*Hiodon alosoides*]: goldeye is bluish above; sides and belly are silvery, with more or less golden luster forward. It is distinguished from common mooneye by sharp ridge or carina on belly anterior to ventral fins and by number of rays in dorsal fin. Dorsal fin has only 9 developed rays and anal fin has 30. Anterior margin of dorsal fin is inserted just above or slightly behind anterior margin of anal fin. Maxillary reaches past middle of the orbit. Lateral line is incomplete and has 56 to 58 scales. Goldeye reaches length of over 12 in.

goldfish: relative of carp and native of Asia. In wild state, it is greenish-brown lacking barbels of the carp but possessing same elongated dorsal fin. Because of having been bred by Chinese for centuries, many strange varieties of goldfish have been produced.

gonad: sexual gland that produces gametes (sperm or eggs) and in some animals, also secretes hormones.

gonangium: in hydroids, modified polyp from which medusa buds are developed.

gondola: 1) double-ended Venetian craft with high ornamental posts in bow and stern, propelled by one or two oarsmen, each with single oar or sweep. It is used in canals of Venice, more or less as taxicab is used in our streets. 2) flat-bottomed, double-ended vessel, 40 to 60 ft. long, cutter-sloop or hoy-rigged, with deep bulwarks and gunports. Used in American Revolution on Lake Champlain.

gong buoy: modification of the *bell buoy*, in which a *gong*, or two or more gongs differing in tone, are sounded by being struck by suspended hammers during motion of buoy in surface waves.

Goniaulax [phytoplankton]: species of *Goniaulax* are widely distributed. Some are luminescent. Together with some species of *Gymnodinium*, *Goniaulax* is one of best known examples of organisms causing "toxic bloom" which may be so dense and virulent as to poison all organisms in food chain which depend on plankton. *G. catanella*, for example, is one such and colors the sea red off California coast.

gonimoblast filament: special filament produced during fertilization in some groups of algae. It bears sporangia containing carpospores.

Gonioceras [nautiloids]: "angle horn" of Ordovician. Its shell was very wide and low with moderately convex central portion and "wings" which thinned to sharp edges that explain the name. Under surface was almost flat; siphuncle was not very heavy; during adult life aperture narrowed until lateral wings were closed.

goniometer: instrument for measuring angles; a marine direction finder.

gonodendron: in *Siphonophora*, processes in gonophores bearing sex cells.

gonophore: asexual bud of polyp or polypoid colony in certain hydroids, produces medusae or gametes.

gonopods: modified appendages used to transfer sperm from male to female.

gonotheca: vaselike sheath around blastostyle of certain coelenterates.

gonozooid: polyp specialized for reproduction in certain hydrozoans.

gooney: gooney or albatross, large seabird.

goose barnacle: barnacle with bony stalk of subclass *Cirripedia* in class *Crustacea*. It lives attached to objects floating on ocean surface with its legs extended from shells to catch food.

goosefish: angler fish, *Lophius americanus*, found in Europe, Asia and America. This large fish has very big head and mouth; it lies partly buried in sand and catches prey by moving a tentacle on its head which resembles a lure.

gooseneck [ships]: return, or 180° bend, having one leg shorter than other. An iron swivel making up fastenings between boom and mast. It consists of pintle and eyebolt or clamp.

gorce: 1) obstruction in a river preventing passage of vessels. 2) a whirlpool.

gorgonian: member of coelenterate order *Gorgonacea* of subclass *Alcyonaria* in class *Anthozoa*. *Gorgonacea* include horny corals such as valuable red coral, sea whips and sea fans. The term "gorgonian" is usually used to refer to plantlike lacy sea fans.

Gorleston lifeboat: sailing "beach yawl" used in lifesaving service out of Gorleston, England. Two lugsails are used.

gouge [ships]: tool with a half-round cutting edge used to cut grooves.

grab: instrument in which jaws enclose portion of bottom for retrieval and study. Sample may be unrepresentative in coarse sediments where jaws may be propped open by gravel or stones permitting part of sample to wash out.

graben: geological structure, usually long section of earth's crust depressed between two faults.

graceful coral [*Corallina chilensis*]: common rocks between 0.5- and 1.5-ft. tide levels. Like rocks exposed to strong surf. Graceful corals are calcified, hard and brittle, through deposit of lime salts within segments of thallus. Portion between segments is not calcified, however, so that species have erect shoots with joined flexible branches. They are purple-red to deep purple. When exposed to light, they bleach to white or pink.

graded bedding: type of stratification in which each stratum displays graduation in grain size from coarse below to finer above.

graded shoreline: shoreline that has been straightened by building of bar across embayment and by cutting back of headlands.

graded stream: stream in which long profile is in equilibrium. It neither degrades nor aggrades.

gradient: 1) slope of stream bed, usually expressed in feet per mile. 2) any departure from horizontal. 3) ratio of elevation of two points and distance between them. 4) rate of decrease of one quantity with respect to another, e.g., rate of decrease of temperature with depth.

gradient current: current defined by assuming that horizontal pressure gradient in sea is balanced by sum of Coriolis forces and bottom frictional forces. At some distance from bottom, effect of friction becomes negligible, and above this, gradient and geostrophic currents are equivalent.

gradient wind: when isobars are not straight, curvature causes centrifugal force to deflect a moving particle. Gradient wind is geostrophic wind adjusted to curvature of isobars and can be obtained from spacing of isobars. In most instances it is not substantially different from geostrophic wind and is approximately equal to wind at 2,000 ft. altitude.

Graf Sea Gravimeter: balance-type gravity meter (heavily overdamped to attentuate shipboard vertical accelerations) consisting of mass at end of horizontal arm that is supported by torsion spring rotational axis. Mass rises and falls with gravity variation, but is restored to near its null position by horizontal reading spring, tensioned with micrometer screw. Difference between actual beam position and null position gives indication of gravity value after micrometer screw position has been taken into account.

grail: coarse or medium-sized sediment particles, i.e., gravel or sand.

grains: individual particles which form a sediment ranging in size from smaller than 0.0039 mm. (clay particles) to larger than 256.0 mm. (boulders).

gram: cgs unit of mass; originally defined as mass of 1 cubic centimeter of water at 4° C; but now taken as one-thousandth part of standard kilogram.

grampus: cetacean of the family *Delphinidae* found in northern hemisphere seas; attains a length of 15 feet; allied to the *blackfish* (caaing whale or pilot whale), to which the term is often erroneously applied; differs from the latter in having teeth in lower jaw only, its head being distinctly flatter and more uniformly rounded than that of the blackfish. Also called *orc*, not to be confused with the *Orca*, or much larger *killer whale*.

granite: light-colored, igneous rock composed primarily of quartz and potassium, sodium-rich feldspars, in which mineral grains are visible to naked eye (phaneritic texture).

granny [ships]: false reef knot. Kind of square knot average landlubber ties on a package. Hard to unfasten.

granular ice: ice composed of many tiny, opaque, white or milky pellets or grains frozen together and presenting a rough surface. This is the type of ice deposited as rime and compacted as neve.

granule: rock fragments of overall gravel size larger than very coarse sand (2.0 mm.) but smaller than pebbles (4.0 mm.).

granulometric facies: cumulative curves representing sedimentary grain size analysis; subdivided into linear, parabolic, logarithmic and hyperbolic facies depending upon shape of curve.

grapestone: cluster of small calcareous pellets, resembling grapes, stuck together by incipient cementation shortly after deposition.

grapestone [*Gigartina*]: common to all species of *Gigartina* are prominent outgrowths, resembling grape seeds that almost cover surface of thallus.

Blades are variously divided: entire, forked, leaflike and irregular. Some species are quite large, up to 15 in. long and 6 to 8 in. wide, but most species are comparatively small, 2 to 5 in. with many divided blades, which are 1/8 to 1 in. wide. Color is variable; sometimes it is clear dark red, but usually black, with heavy, leathery texture. Almost all species become black and shrink considerably when out of water.

grapnel [ships]: anchor for small boats having 6 prongs or hooks at one end instead of flukes. Also used in dragging for objects on bottom.

grapsoid crab: any member of *Grapsidae*, family of crabs numbering more than 300 species. Its members are primarily marine, but include some land and freshwater species as well.

graptolite: extinct marine colonial invertebrate with chitinous hard parts, now classed as *Hemichordata;* especially common in many Ordovician and Silurian dark-colored shales.

Graptolithina [class]: phylum: *Protochordata.* Cambrian to Mississippian. Branching colonial; chitinoid skeleton; soft parts largely unknown; *Sicula.* Planktonic and/or sessile, benthonic.

Graptolitoidea [graptolites]: this advanced order had lost its special budding zooids and retained only one type of open cup or tube. Any zooid, therefore, was able to bud and build up its colony as well as to reproduce sexually. Stolons also disappeared and thecae opened into one long interval cavity or canal. In many genera there were two canals and two rows of thecae, one on each side of threadlike nema. Graptoloids are limited to Ordovician and Silurian formations.

grassboat: a grass boat made of bundles of reeds lashed together; 3 bundles are used; center one is about 1/3 the length of two outer ones. Used by Mexican Seri Indians on Gulf of California.

graticule: network of lines representing parallels and meridians on map, chart or plotting sheet.

grating [ships]: open iron latticework used for covering hatchways and platforms.

gravel: loose detrital material ranging in size from 2 to 256 mm.

gravimeter: gravity-measuring instrument. Instrument for measuring variations in magnitude of earth's gravitational field.

gravimetry: measurement of gravity, attracting force between two bodies.

graving docks [ships]: dry dock. Vessel is floated in and gates at entrance are closed when tide is at ebb. Remaining water is then pumped out and vessel's bottom is graved or cleaned.

gravity corer: any type of corer that achieves bottom penetration solely as a result of gravitational force acting upon its mass.

gravity meter: device used to measure differences in gravity. It consists of weight of constant mass which is moved from reference station where gravitational acceleration is known to location where it is to be determined.

gravity wave: wave whose velocity of propagation is controlled primarily by gravity. Water waves of a length greater than 2 in. are considered gravity waves.

gray ice: Russian term for sea ice 10 to 30 cm. (4 to 12 in.) thick. It is roughly comparable to medium water ice.

gray mud: deep-sea deposit of grayish color which is intermediate in composition between red clay and globigerina ooze.

gray whale [*Eschrichtius glaucus*]: whalebone whale found in North Pacific and distinguished by many white spots.

grazing: feeding of zooplanktonic organisms upon phytoplanktonic organisms. Generally in reference to feeding of copepods upon diatoms.

grazing angle: angle that sound ray path forms with reflecting surface; usually applies to sound rays reflected from bottom; conventionally, angle is measured from horizontal.

grease ice: sludge of ice crystals in sea that give sea surface a greasy appearance.

great circle: curve on surface of a sphere traced by intersection of sphere and a plane containing center of sphere.

great diurnal range: average difference in height between all mean higher high waters and all mean lower low waters measured over 19-year period, or its computed equivalent.

greater ebb: stronger of two ebb currents occurring during tidal day, usually associated with tidal currents of mixed characteristics.

greater flood: stronger of two flood tidal currents occurring during tidal day, usually associated with tidal currents of mixed characteristics.

greater tropic range: average difference in height between all tropic high waters and all tropic low waters which occur twice monthly when moon's north and south declination is greatest.

Great Lakes bloater [*Leucichthys hoyi*]: this bloater has an elliptical shape and is small, ranging from 6 to 8 in. in length. Lower jaw is longer than upper and more or less hooked; gill rakers of first branchial arch usually number more than 40. It resembles *L. kiyi* but differs from it in usually having less than 75 scales in lateral line, whereas *L. kiyi* has more than that number. Lives in deep water.

green alga: one of division or phylum *(Chlorophyta)* of grass-green, single-celled, filamentous, membranous or branching plants. Green algae are cosmopolitan in upper littoral zone but are most abundant in warmer waters.

greenball [*Cladophora trichotoma*]: grows between 3 ft. and mean low tide level. Most con-

spicuous features of this seaweed are bright green color, ball shape and fact that it is buried in sand. It is about size of a lime or small lemon. When attached it is ball-shaped. Plant body is made of profusely branched barrel cells, containing hundreds of tiny branches which divide 3 or 4 times, with 3 to 6 cells branching. In center of body mass is a cavity filled with air. This gives seaweed its ball-like shape.

green confetti [*Enteromorpha compressa*]: it is widely distributed from Bering Sea to Lower California. It lives rather high on the beach, rarely extending below low-tide mark. It frequently attaches itself to retaining walls along the beach or is found on rocky shores where freshwater escapes from cliffs. Distinctive feature is flattened tubular thallus (plant body) from which great numbers of lateral threadlike branches arise. It is transparent yellowish-green with single layer of cells embedded in gelatinous substance; usually attached to a rock or other algae by rhizoidal outgrowth from basal cells. Holdfast is perennial, but thallus disintegrates at end of each season, reappearing next spring.

green flash: at sunset or sunrise, very brief green coloration of sun just before it completely sinks below or rises above horizon; refraction in atmosphere causes this strange phenomenon.

greenhouse effect: 1) in ocean, where layer of low salinity water overlies layer or more of dense water, short wavelength radiation of sun is absorbed in deeper layers. Radiation given off by water is in far infrared, and since this cannot radiate through low salinity layer, a temperature rise results in deeper layers. 2) ability of air to absorb long heat waves from earth after allowing sun's short waves to pass through it.

greenling: this small family with 7 American species is found only on Pacific Coast. It is a cold-water group of fishes; lingcod and kelp greenling are common representatives. They have large mouth, protruding lower jaw and sharp teeth both in jaws and in roof of mouth.

greenling, kelp: small fish about 18 in. long; grayish-brown or coppery, variously spotted and blotched. Like the lingcod, it has a deep notch between two portions of dorsal fin. As name indicates, it is commonly caught near kelp beds.

green mud: fine-grained terrigenous mud or oceanic ooze found near edge of continental shelf similar to other terrigenous muds except for greenish color and in some cases less organic matter. It occurs in depths of 300 to 7,500 ft. (91 to 2,286 meters).

green rope [*Spongomorpha coalita*]: grows on rocks or other algae at 1- and 1.5-ft. tide levels. Distinguishing feature is bright green, ropelike appearance, rope being branched and much frayed. Plant body grows 6 to 8 in. long and ¼ in. wide. Individual filaments or branches are threadlike, but they begin to entangle almost immediately upon rising from holdfast. Grows in well aerated waters. When old, green rope becomes dull yellowish-green.

green string lettuce [*Ulva Linza* (Linnaeus)]: grows on rocks or other seaweed from 2-ft.-tide level to average low-tide mark. This species of *Ulva* is easily recognized by transparent bright green color, long slender blades, ruffled margins and swirled appearance. The blade, from 6 in. to 2 ft. long and from ½ to 1 in. wide, tapers gradually to short, hollow stipe.

Greenwich: site of astronomical observatory in England through which passes prime meridian or 0° longitude. For navigational purposes times are reckoned from "Greenwich mean time."

Greenwich epoch: phase difference between tidal constituent and its equilibrium argument referenced to corresponding Greenwich equilibrium argument.

Greenwich interval: interval referred to as transit of moon over meridian of Greenwich as distinguished from local interval which is referred to as moon's transit over local meridian.

gregale: during classical times international rivalry often led people to credit their enemies with anything unpleasant. In south-central Mediterranean area, strong wind often blows from northwest or northeast. Seamen and merchants of north African cities called this air current *graecus* (Greek). In one of the strange cases where obscure word survives for centuries with little change, *graecus* entered modern speech as grecale and was soon modified to gregale. It first appeared in print in 1804. Before end of century it had won space in major reference works. Not yet Americanized, name of "the Greek wind" is sufficiently well established to be familiar to Mediterranean travelers and to be included in geographical and meteorological dictionaries.

Greta Garbo: nickname given to quadrilateral jib with two clews and two sheets. Present-day sail used on racing yachts.

Griffith seaweed [*Griffithsia pacifica*]: grows on rocks between 0.5- and 1.5-ft.-tide levels; not a common seaweed. It is small, clear, reddish pink, threadlike species with branches which spread out into fanlike pattern. Branches, 2 in. long, remain distinct from one another and are naked, without branchlets or outgrowths of any kind. Gelatinous envelope encases entire thallus. Texture is rather harsh. Strong rhizoids which develop from basal threads fasten this seaweed to substratum.

gripe [ships]: sharp forward end of dished keel on which stem is fixed.

groin: low artificial wall-like structure of durable material extending from land to seaward for particular purpose such as to protect coast or to force a current to scour a channel.

grommet [ships]: 1) ring of fiber usually soaked in red lead or some other packing material, used under the heads of bolts and nuts to preserve tightness. 2) short piece of rope, with knot at one end and eye in the other, for temporarily confining ropes or small spars.

gross: entire; total; whole; opposed to *net;* as, *gross freight; gross weight; gross tonnage.*

gross production: total of organic matter being produced in given unit of time in system studied, without any correction for respiration or catabolism.

grounded hummock: hummock which has stranded on bottom, either during its formation or later upon drifting into shallow water. Grounded hummocks appear either singly or in lines.

grounded motion: displacement of ground caused by passage of elastic waves, arising from earthquakes, explosives, seismic shots, machinery, wind, traffic and other causes.

ground fish: fish that live on sea bottom, including many of important food fishes such as cod and flounder.

ground swell: 1) wide deep swell. 2) long high ocean swell; long, low waters produced by distant winds and storms; height decreases as they travel further from point of origin.

ground tackle [ships]: group term for all gear used in anchoring ship.

ground water: subsurface water occurring in rocks or unconsolidated sedimentary deposits within zone of saturation.

ground-water level: upper surface of zone within earth below which openings in rocks are filled with water.

ground wave: sound (seismic) wave whose path is partially through water and partially within sediments or rocks, beneath ocean bottom.

groundways [ships]: large pieces of timber laid across ways on which keel blocks are placed. Also large blocks and planks supporting cradle on which ship is launched.

groupers: stout, often clumsy-looking fish whose bodies are covered by small ctenoid scales deeply embedded in skin. Other characteristics of these members of sea bass family are large mouth, ventral fins set far forward beneath pectorals, strong spines on gill cover and rounded margin on tail fin. Groupers get their name as a result of their habit of hovering in small groups.

groupers, black [Warsaw grouper]: common fish off Florida Gulf Coast. It has changeable color but usually is dusky reddish-gray with horizontal black markings. Black groupers are usually under

3 ft. long and weigh less than 10 lbs. This species prefers to stay on offshore banks and reefs where it feeds on mullets and other small fishes.

groupers, Nassau [rockfish]: West Indian species that is found northward to Florida coast. It has numerous color phases and can change from one to the other rapidly, usually matching color to that of environment. Sometimes it is gray with vertical brown bars; at other times it is white, tan or brown and may be mottled or blotched in a blending of these colors. Nassau grouper is large fish 2 to 3 ft. long and weighing up to 50 lbs.

groupers, red [red-bellied snapper]: more northern species found as far up Atlantic Coast as Virginia. Its usual color is warm mottled brown, but color ranges from reddish-tan to a solid black. Red groupers are smaller than the Nassau being about 24 in. long and weighing under 25 lbs. They are bottom feeders, hiding among submarine caverns and hollows where they feed on shrimp, other crustaceans and octopus.

group velocity: velocity of wave disturbance as a whole, i.e., of entire group of component simple harmonic waves. For water-surface waves, group velocity of deepwater waves is equal to ½ velocity of individual waves in the group; for shallow-water waves, it is same as their velocity.

grow: 1) to lead, tend, lie, or stretch out in a direction indicated; as, *the cable grows to leeward.* **2)** to increase, as size of sea or swell; as, *an easterly swell is growing.* **3)** also, growe.

growler: piece of ice smaller than bergy bit, which often appears greenish in color and barely shows above water. It may originate from sea ice and glacier ice.

growth line [*Brachiopoda*]: series of fine to coarse ridges or beaks on outer surface of shell; subparallel to edges of valves and concentric about beak.

grunt: many of common inhabitants of coral gardens are members of grunt family; chunky fishes with elevated backs and short deep bodies, related to snappers. Name grunt comes from peculiar sounds made by grinding pharyngeal teeth together. They are spiny-rayed fishes, with spiny portion of dorsal fin continuous with soft-rayed portion; tail fin is deeply forked and ventral fins are placed far forward beneath pectoral fins. Mouth has startling bright red interior displayed effectively as grunts charge each other with open mouth. Most species are 12 to 18 in. long and rarely weigh over 3 lbs.

grunt, French [yellow grunt]: West Indies fish. It is brightly colored with horizontal stripes of alternating blue and yellow and with bright yellow fins.

grunt, white: largest of grunts, common member of coral reef community; it reaches weight of 4 lbs. It is brassy blue with many small somewhat horizontal stripes and blue markings in head region. This fish can change color to match surroundings, being dusky as it swims among coral shadows and turning straw-colored when over sandy bottom.

Grus: southern constellation lying immediately southward of *Pisces;* contains the navigational stars *a* and *β Gruis,* each of magnitude 2.2, east and west of each other about 6° apart. *β Gruis* is located east of its mate and about 17° nearly due south of the bright star *Fomalhaut,* in 47° 08′ south declination and having a S.H.A. of 20°.

guano: deposits of substance primarily composed of excrement of seabirds and commercially valuable as rich fertilizer for plants.

gudgeons [ships]: metal fittings on sternpost with cast or bored eyes, to receive pintles in which rudder hangs.

guffa: bow-shaped craft or coracle of Bagdad, made of woven switches and lined with bitumen. Giffs have been in use on Tigris River since antiquity and are still employed commercially.

Guiana Current: current flowing northwestward along northeast coast of South America (Guiana region). Guiana Current is extension of South Equatorial Current. Eventually it joins North Equatorial Current and sets through Lesser Antilles to become Caribbean Current.

guillemots [*Charadriiformes*]: members of this family are very small seabirds with comparatively short necks, small, narrow wings and very short tails of 12 to 18 feathers. Legs are short and placed very far back near tail; they have only 3 toes which are connected by webs. Various species differ remarkably in form of their bills. Some are fairly long and slender, but most are comparatively short and considerably compressed.

Guinea Current: current flowing eastward along south coast of northwest Africa into Gulf of Guinea. Guinea Current originates from Equatorial Countercurrent which flows east across equatorial Atlantic.

gul: outrigger dugout sailing canoe of islands lying in Torres Straits, between Queensland, Australia, and New Guinea. Some canoes had double outriggers, some simple. The rig was peculiar. Two high oblong mat sails were carried on arrangement of masts and straits in bow. Backstays were carried to outrigger booms. This rig is now extinct, being supplanted by western fore-and-aft sails.

gulf: to ever-poetic and always romantic Greeks, a bay of water partly surrounded by gently sloping land, seemed to have much in common with a woman's breast. So ancient sailors used kolphos to designate geographical as well as feminine anatomical features. Sir John Mandeville (fictitious name assumed by unknown compiler of travelers' tales) borrowed from ancient lore and wrote of Adriatic Sea as "the Goulfe of Verrope." Before end of 15th century, the word was firmly established in English. Even today distinctions between "bay" and "gulf" are not always precise, although a gulf is usually larger. But when winds are high, waters of gulf really do seem to heave like a living woman's bosom.

gulf ice: winter ice formed in gulf or bay; rare.

Gulf Stream: warm, well-defined, swift and relatively narrow ocean current which originates north of the Grand Bahama Island where Florida and Antilles Currents meet. Gulf Stream extends to Grand Banks at about 40° N, 50° W where it meets cold Labrador Current and two flow eastward as North Atlantic Current. Florida Current, Gulf Stream and North Atlantic Current together form Gulf Stream system.

gull [*Charadriiformes*]: members of this family are long-winged seabirds of moderate or fairly large size, ranging in length of body from 1 ft. to 2 ft. 6 in. They have short necks and rather short legs with webbed feet, which are somewhat hidden in feathers when they are flying, but more often carried under tail. Bills are slender and tapering in smaller forms, but in some of larger species they are stout and wedge-shaped, upper mandible being almost hooked at tip and lower mandible having conspicuous blunt angle, often marked with red spot near tip. Nostrils open on sides of upper mandible nearly halfway to tip, openings being oval slits without any covering. Tails of most species of gulls are nearly square at end. In adult plumage nearly all gulls have white body and tail and gray or black wings and back.

gull, aden [*Larus hemprichi*]: head, nape and throat coffee-brown in summer, in winter pale brown mottled with whitish eyelids; neck white all around in summer, grey in winter; mantle grayish-brown; primaries blackish-brown; secondaries and posterior primaries tipped with white; edge of wing white; breast pale brown, mottled with white in winter; abdomen, tail coverts and tail white; bill greenish, with subterminal black crossbar and red tip; feet yellowish; length 17.5 to 18.5 in.

gull, California [*Larus californicus*]: similar to herring gull in plumage; bill yellow, with red spot at the angle, usually with dusky subterminal band; feet greenish-yellow; length 20 in.

gull, dusky [*Larus fuliginosus*]: head black, eyelids white; mantle dark leaden-gray; underparts, rump and tail gray, almost white on abdomen; tips of secondaries almost white; bill red, feet black; length 15 to 17 in.

gullery: breeding place for gulls or similar birds, usually on rocky cliffs.

gull, glaucous [*Larus hyperboreus*]: head and neck white in summer, in winter streaked with gray; underparts, rump and tail white; mantle pale gray; primaries and secondaries pale gray with whitish ends; bill yellow with red spot at the angle; feet pinkish-flesh color; length 28 in.

gull, glaucous-winged [*Larus glaucescens*]: similar to herring gull but mantle somewhat paler; primaries dark gray subterminally with white tips, outermost also with white subterminal spot; secondaries gray with white tips; bill yellow with red spot; flesh-colored feet; length 25 to 26 in.

gull, gray [*Larus modestus*]: head white in summer, pale brown in winter; mantle lead-colored; wings dull black; secondaries broadly tipped with white; tail gray with broad, black band; rest of upper and underparts gray; gill and feet reddish-black; length 18 in.

gull, great black-backed [*Larus marinus*]: head and neck white in summer, streaked with gray in winter; mantle sooty black; underparts and tail white; wing-gills sooty and white tips; bill yellow with red spot at the angle; feet pale flesh color; length 27 to 30 in.

gull, great black-headed [*Larus ichthyaetus*]: head deep black in summer, in winter white with dusky streaks; small crescentric patches above and below eye white; mantle gray; primaries mainly white, outer ones with subterminal black bands and white tips, inner ones and secondaries gray with broad white tips; underparts and tail white; bill very stout towards tip, yellow with subterminal black band; feet greenish-yellow; length 27 to 29 in.

gull, Heerman's [*Larus heermanni*]: head and upper neck grayish-brown in winter; mouth slate-colored; lower neck, underparts and upper tail coverts pale gray; tail dull black, tipped with white; wing quills mostly with white tips, undersurface of wings grayish-brown; bill red; feet black; length 17 in.

gull, herring [*Larus argentatus*]: head and neck white in summer, in winter streaked with dusky gray; underparts, rump and tail white; mantle gray; primaries black with white tips, outermost also with white subterminal spot; secondaries with white tips; bill yellow with red spot at the angle; feet pinkish-flesh color; length 22 to 24 in.

gull, Iceland [*Larus leucopterus*]: similar to glaucous gull but considerably smaller with proportionally longer wings; length 22 in.

gull, Japanese [*Larus crassirostris*]: head white in summer, grayish-brown in winter; mantle slate-gray; first two primaries gray, rest black; all primaries and secondaries with white tips; tail white with black band near end of central feathers; bill yellowish with black crossband and red tip; feet yellowish; length 19 in.

gull, lesser black-backed [*Larus fucus*]: head,

neck, underparts and tail white; mantle sooty-black and slate-gray; wing quills black; first primary with white spot near tip, secondaries and tertials with broad white tips; bill yellow with red spot at the angle; feet yellow; length 20 to 24 in.

gull, magellan [*Gabianus scoresbye*]: head pale gray in summer, dusky in winter; neck and underparts pale gray; mantle slaty-black; undersurface of wings dark gray; wing quills with white tips; tail white; bill and feet red; length 18 in.

gull, Pacific [*Gabianus pacificus*]: head, neck and underparts white; mantle black; primaries black with small apical white spots except on first two; secondaries black with broad white tips; tail white with subterminal black band, broadest on central feathers; bill compressed, very deep, yellow with red spot at the angles; feet yellow; length 25 in.

gull, slaty-backed [*Larus schistisagus*]: head and neck white in summer, streaked with gray in winter; underparts and tail white; mantle dark slate color; wing quills black, outer primaries with white spots; inner primaries, secondaries and tertials with broad white tips; bill yellow with red spot at the angle; feet pinkish-flesh color; length 24 to 25 in.

gull, southern black-backed [*Larus dominicanus*]: head, neck, underparts and tail white; mantle sooty-black; wing quills, except first primaries, with white tips; bill yellow with red spot at the angle; feet yellowish; length 23 in.

gull, swallow-tailed [*Creagus furcatus*]: head and neck dark gray in summer with white stripe on each side of forehead; in winter whitish with ill-defined gray collar and grayish-black rings around eyes; eyelids crimson; mantle smoky-gray with white line on each side of back; outer webs of outer primaries black; inner primaries and adjacent secondaries gray and white; inner secondaries and wing coverts white; throat and breast rosy-white; abdomen, upper tail coverts and tail white; bill greenish-gray with pale tip; feet pinkish-red; length 20 in.

gull, western [*Larus occidentalis*]: head and neck white, sometimes slightly streaked with gray in winter; underparts and tail white; mantle leaden-gray; wing quills gray with white tips; first 4 primaries with black outer webs and first with white subterminal spot; bill yellow with red spot at the angle; feet flesh-colored; length 22 in.

gully: 1) trough or lengthy, comparatively narrow, depression in the sea floor, extending into a continental shelf, or toward a seacoast. 2) any channel worn by flow of water, as in a gap or rift in a high coastline.

gull, yellow-legged [*Larus cachinnans*]: similar to herring gull in plumage but mantle slightly darker gray; bill yellow; length 22 to 26 in.

gundalow: also called Merrimac gundalow. River barge used on Merrimac and other rivers of New England in 18th century. Short mast carried lateen sail with counterbalance on lower end of yard.

gunwale [ships]: 1) upper portion of vessel's side. 2) top edge of small boat's sheer. 3) top of any rail of boat or vessel.

gunwale bar [ships]: term applied to bar connecting stringer plate on weather deck to sheer strake.

gurdy: roller fixed on a boat's gunwale, providing a frictionless bearing over which lines or trawls are hauled in fishing.

gusset: 1) also called *gore, gusle,* and *gusset-plate,* a piece of plate, usually triangular in shape, fitted to distribute a strength connection between two structural members; as, at ends of panting-beams, where wide end of gusset is secured to a panting-stringer; at union of a margin-plate bracket with a tank top; or as a knee connection for a light deck beam with a frame. 2) loosely applied to any connecting plate; as a *diamond plate,* or one spreading the union of two crossing members.

gusset plate [ships]: tie plate, used for fastening posts, frames, beams, etc., to other objects.

gust: Old Norse *giosa* (to gush) is most likely source of our modern name for rushing or driving wind that rises suddenly and dies abruptly. Term may have been long transmitted by word of mouth, for it did not enter English until comparatively recently. William Shakespeare, famous for having accumulated a vast vocabulary of obscure but expressive words, is first writer known to have paid literary tribute to the power of a gust. Whether his influence was sufficient to establish the word or whether he simply gave literary expression to oral usage, no one knows. But since Shakespeare first employed it in 1588 "gust" has become a household word naming a sudden blast.

gut: narrow channel or strait.

gutter ledge [ships]: bar laid across hatchway to support hatches.

gutterway [ships]: sunken trough in shelter deck outer edge which disposes of water from deck wash.

guyot: flat-topped submarine mountain, rising at least 1,000 meters above surrounding sea floor; thought to represent a volcano.

guys [ships]: wire or hemp rope or chain to support booms, davits, etc., laterally. Guys are employed in pairs. Where span is fitted between two booms, for example, one pair only is required for the two.

Gymnodinium breve: microscopic form of sea life, which, under certain set of conditions, will trigger fish-killing "red tide."

gyral: swirling systems of clockwise-flowing sea

currents, combined results of wind, earth's rotation, gravity and other forces.

gyre: closed circulatory system, but larger than whirlpool or eddy.

gyro: short for gyroscope; combining term for mechanical instrument, functioning of which is effected basically by applied gyroscopic principles.

gyroscope: heavy steel-mounted wheel so suspended that it is balanced and can rotate rapidly about axis. Since it resists any force applied to orientation of its axis of rotation, it is useful in stabilization, navigation and guidance mechanisms.

H

H: hoisted singly, *International Code* flag *H ("how")* indicates *"I have a pilot on board."* As an abbreviation in nautical astronomy, *h* = hour; *h* or *H* = altitude or elevation; *H* = hack watch. In compass magnetism, *H* = horizontal component of earth's total magnetic force. In logbooks and weather recording, *H* = heavy sea; *h* = hail. *H-bar, H-beam, H-girder, H-iron* signify structural metal of H-shaped cross section; also *I-bar, I-beam,* etc.

H.A.: abbreviation commonly used in nautical astronomy for *hour angle*. Letter *t* is also employed, *especially* when angle is noted in degrees, as *westerly*, from 0 up to 360.

haak: large Dutch sailing lighter. Average length about 120 ft. by 20 ft. beam. Considerable sheer at ends with very little freeboard amidships; flat-bottomed and square-rigged.

haar: wet sea fog which sometimes invades eastern Scotland and parts of eastern England, especially during summer.

hacha: Spanish name for member of genus *Pinna* of large clams with thin triangular shells.

hachures: 1) short lines on topographic or nautical charts to indicate slope of ground or submarine bottom. They usually follow direction of slope. 2) inward-pointing short lines or "ticks" around circumference of closed contour indicating depression or minimum.

hackleback [shovelnose sturgeon]: readily distinguished from lake sturgeon by longer snout and absence of spiracle. It rarely exceeds length of 3 ft. or weight of 5 or 6 lbs. Body of this species is more slender than that of lake sturgeons. Large caudal fin terminates in long filament nearly if not equally the rest of fin. It also differs from young rock sturgeon of corresponding size in that small bony shields completely cover tail, which is flattened from above. Snout is broad, flat and shovel-shaped.

hadal: pertaining to greatest depths of ocean.

haddock: important food fish. Haddock differ from cod in being dark gray with silvery sides and belly and in having conspicuous black lateral line and high first dorsal fin. Specimen of average size weighs 3 to 4 lbs.; maximum length is about 3 ft. and weighs 24 lbs.

Hadley's quadrant: named for *John Hadley, English astronomer (1682-1744),* the original of our present marine sextant and employing the same optical principles therein. Had an arc of 45° and measured angles up to 90°. Though *Hadley* is credited with invention of the instrument, it also is claimed that *Thomas Godfrey, American mathematician (1704-1749)* brought out a similar quadrant subsequently known as *Godfrey's bow,* at about the same time, or circa 1730, independently of Hadley's innovation; also called *Hadley's octant.*

Hague Convention: meeting of delegates of 44 countries at The Hague, 1907, for purpose of agreement in recognition of status, certain rights and immunities, and employment as vessels of war, of merchant ships in time of war, with other pertinent questions of international law. It was the outgrowth of the *Hague Tribunal* established by the *International Peace Conference, 1899,* for the settlement of international disputes. In 1921, what are known as *Hague Rules* were drawn up by a similar meeting for purposes of universal agreement in defining various rights, risks, and liabilities of shipowners, charterers, and shippers in connection with carriage of goods by sea.

hair rail [ships]: top member of two or three curved timbers, extending from either side of figurehead to bow or cathead, to brace head or projecting stem; used on old-time ships.

hake, Pacific: iron-gray fish with silvery sides; similar habits to those of eastern silver hake.

hake, silver [whiting]: differs from Pacific hake by having only two dorsal fins and single anal fin. Second dorsal fin is very long, about half the length of body; anal fin is equally long. Silver hake is brownish with silvery glint to entire body; chin lacks barbel type of other members of cod family. Pikelike head terminates in large mouth armed with strong teeth. Average length is 12 to 20 in. and weight under 5 lbs. Silver hake is voracious eater, preying on smaller fish.

hake, squirrel: also known as red hake or ling. Back and upper sides are brown or olive-gray; lower sides are silvery. Like silver hake it has two dorsal fins; second dorsal is extremely long and low; anterior dorsal fin has elongated and tapering forward ray. Another distinctive feature is shape of ventral fins which are long and slender, tapering to threadlike extremities. Squirrel hake is usually under 30 in. long and weighs less than 8 lbs.

half: as used in designating compass direction, marking midway between any two points; as, *N ½ E; NE ½ N; SW by W ½; WNW ½ W.* In sounding by hand lead, indicating an intermediate half-fathom depth, as called out by leadsman; thus, *a half five* (=5½ fathoms); a *half less ten* (=9½ fathoms).

half-breadth plan [ships]: plan or top view of half of ship divided longitudinally. It shows waterlines, bow and buttock lines and diagonal lines of construction.

half-clipper: this type of merchant vessel was designed to have greater cargo-carrying capacity than extreme clipper ships of 1850's and therefore were not quite as fast. "Half-clippers" were used in 70's and 80's and superseded extreme clippers, which were unprofitable to operate because of their uneconomical design and lower freight rates.

half deck [ships]: short deck below main deck.

half-meter plankton net: qualitative-type filtering net with half-meter opening tapering to detachable bucket of a few inches in diameter. The net is usually some grade of silk bolting cloth numbered 0000 to 25 depending upon number of meshes per linear inch.

half ring [*Graptolithina*]: one of series of chitinous half rings that form inner wall of graptolite tube.

half-round or **turtleback** [ships]: convex, moulded outboard portion of poop deck; intended as protection against damage from heavy seas breaking on board and to better shed water.

half tide: condition or time of tide when at level midway between any given high tide and following or preceding low tide.

half-tide level: plane midway between mean high water and mean low water.

half time [diving]: time required to reach 50% saturation for specific partial pressure.

halibut, Atlantic: species of northern seas. This is a right-eyed flounder with dark gray or olive-brown upper sides and white lower side. Atlantic halibut has a single long continuous dorsal fin and bony anal fin; small ventral fins are located actually in front of pectoral fins. It lives in deep water, from several hundred to several thousand feet below surface. Average individuals are 4 to 6 ft. long, weighing 50 to 200 lbs.

halide: compound of a halogen (flourine, chlorine, iodine, etc.) with another element or a radical.

haliplankton: marine or inland saltwater plankton.

halmyrolysis: chemical rearrangement, replacement and weathering which occurs in sediment or rocks on sea floor.

halocline: well-defined vertical gradient of salinity which is usually positive.

halogen: any of 4 elements (chlorine, bromine, iodine and fluorine) found as ions in seawater.

Halosphaeria: genus of green, single-celled marine phytoplankton of class *Xanthophyceae.* It occurs in both warm and temperate waters and has been reported to be very abundant at times in antarctic waters.

halyard [ships]: rope used to hoist or lower yards, sails and flags.

halysites [coral]: resembles *Catenipora* in general appearance but has a small angular corallites between those that are oval in section. Tabulae are well developed, but septa are absent.

Hamal: *a Arietis,* brighter of two navigational stars lying about 4° apart in *Aries;* of magnitude 2.2 and having declination of 23¼° N. and S.H.A. of 329°, may be located about 20° east of the *Square of Pegasus. Sheratan (β Arietis)* is his near-by companion.

Hamilton group: highest division of middle Devonian rocks of North America consisting of marine sandy shale and sandstone.

Hampton boat: small type of small, centerboard fishing boat used in certain sections of New England coast. It has two small masts and carries spritsails.

handiness: quality or degree of satisfactory maneuverability exhibited by a vessel under action of propeller or in sailing.

handlining: fishing with hooks and line that fisherman watches and brings up if fish are biting, rather than setting the line, leaving it and returning later to examine his catch.

handsaw fish: 1) large voracious fish of the deeper waters of Pacific; has a long high dorsal fin and long lancet-like teeth from which it gets its name. 2) a small fish having an almost round profile, long dorsal and anal spiny fringes, and lancelike spines on each side of base of tail; chiefly found in East Indian seas; called also *tang, barberfish, doctorfish,* and *surgeonfish.*

hand-sectioning: technique of cutting thin sections of material by hand for microscopic study, as opposed to instrumental sectioning accomplished with a microtome.

handy billy [ships]: pair of blocks and tackle of general utility purpose on deck where extra purchase is needed.

hank [ships]: ring of wood, rope or iron fastened around fore-and-aft stay and having the head of a jib or staysail seized to it. Iron hanks are used in wire and wooden ones on rope stays.

haploid: having full number of chromosomes normally occurring in mature germ cell or half the number of usual animal somatic cells.

haptic: clinging tightly, as *Gnathostomulida* which are strongly haptic, clinging to sand grains.

harbor oscillation: nontidal vertical water movement in harbor or bay. Usually vertical motions are low, but when oscillations are excited by a tsunami or storm surge they may be quite large. Variable winds, air oscillations or surf beat also may cause oscillations.

harbor volume: volumetric water content of harbor or port measured at given datum.

hard: to full extent, as in helm order, *"Hard left!"*; *"Hard alee!"*; extreme in direction or contact, as, *hard aft, hard against the pier*; sharply defined and ominous, as, *hard edge of a cloudbank*. A firm foreshore or beach used as a landing place.

hard bottom: sea floor not covered by unconsolidated sediment.

hard patch [ships]: plate riveted over another plate to cover hole or break.

hardtack: large, coarse, hard biscuit baked without salt or leaven, then kiln-dried; formerly much used on ships in place of bread.

Hardy continuous plankton recorder: plankton sampler designed to collect specimens of plankton during normal passage of ship. Device consists of towed container enclosing continuously moving strip of silk gauze (about 60 meshes per inch) which filters and stores plankton passing into orifices of container. Knowing speed of travel of gauze and course and speed of ship, it is then possible to determine distribution of plankton along ship's route.

Hardy recorder: plankton net stretched across narrow tunnel of fine gauze, which has numbered divisions for quantitive analysis.

harmonic analysis: 1) statistical method for determining amplitude and period of certain harmonic or wave components in set of data with aid of Fourier series. 2) process of splitting a complex curve into its harmonic or sine curve constituent, which will differ in period and amplitude.

harmonic constant: amplitude and epoch of any harmonic constituent of the tide or tidal current at any locality.

harmonic function: 1) any solution of Laplace equation. 2) in tide and tidal current predictions, quantity that varies as cosine of an angle that increases uniformly with time.

harmonic prediction: method of predicting tides and tidal currents by combining harmonic constituents into single tide curve.

Harpacticoida [copepods]: although by far vast majority of harpacticoids are benthonic, some are truly planktonic and in shallow seas with sandy or muddy floor many get swept up so as to be taken in plankton samples. Most obvious features are minute size (most being less than 1 mm. long) and lack of obvious divisions between main regions of body. Egg sacs may be single or paired and antennules are short, usually with less than 6 points.

Harpidae [family]: harp shells are small but beautiful group of molluscs. They are nearly all of fairly large size and are longitudinally ribbed over outer surface. Body whorl is large and broad and opens through large aperture; aperture is bordered on outside by lip which is thickened at margin and on inside by a broad and highly polished columella; no operculum. The family is found in tropical waters of Pacific and Indian Oceans; less than 12 species are known.

harping [ships]: fore parts of walls of vessel which encompass bows and are fastened to stem, thickened to withstand plunging.

hatch [ships]: formerly, cover for hatchway but now it usually refers to opening from deck to interior of vessel. Forward hatch opens into forecastle of a yacht.

hatch bars [ships]: bars by which hatches are fastened down.

hatch-boat: fishing and commercial vessel from 7 to 10 tons used on lower Thames River in 18th and 19th centuries. Hatches covered a portion or all of deck.

hatchway [ships]: one of large square openings in deck of ship through which freight is hoisted in and out. There are 4 pieces called head ledges which rest on beams and carlines extending between beams.

haul [ships]: 1) to pull or draw by force. To haul down is to bring down any object from rigging, particularly yards and sails. 2) when wind shifts in clockwise direction, it is said to haul. When it shifts counterclockwise, it veers.

hauling part [ships]: part of line in tackle to which power is applied in order to move an object.

Havre pilot boat: cutter-rigged, keel sailing vessel used in piloting out of Havre, France, before powerboats came into use.

Havre trawler: lug-rigged French "trawler" used in vicinity of Havre. It was double-ended with straight stem and sternpost, two or three masts and single headsail to long bowsprit. Gaff topsail was sometimes carried.

hawker: round-sterned merchant craft of 17th and 18th centuries, used by Dutch and other northern nations in Europe. It was relative of buss and dogger, having two masts and ranging in size from 50 to 200 tons. Rig varied according to locality and period.

hawse [ships]: part of ship's bow in which are hawseholes for anchor chain.

hawsehole [ships]: cylindrical hole in bow of ship through which cable is passed. Hawsepipe, iron lining of hawsehole, prevents anchor chain from wearing out wood of hole. To come through the hawsehole is to commence seaman's life as a common sailor; used in contradistinction to "come through the cabin window," i.e., to begin as an officer.

hawsepipe [pipe]: tube lining or hawsehole in ship's bow.

hawse plug or block [ships]: stopper used to prevent water from entering hawsehole in heavy weather.

hawser: thick rope (either wire, fiber or synthetic) used for mooring or towing vessel.

hawsing [ships]: chalking planking with oakum with large maul or bevel and wedge-shaped iron.

hay barge: Thames barge built for carrying hay from east coast towns of England. Hull is a barge type but of shallow draft so that it may enter little creeks and inlets of Thames estuary.

haycock: isolated conical pile of ice thrown up above surface of land ice and shelf ice, resulting from pressure or ice movement.

head: 1) in hydraulics, vertical distance between surface of liquid and another point in column; thus, measure of force exerted at lower point by weight of column. 2) part of rip current that has widened out seaward of breakers. 3) precipitous cape or promontory extending into large body of water. 4) ship's toilet. 5) in *Mollusca*, anterior dorsal portion of body. Bears mouth, sensory organs and major nerve ganglia. May be more or less distinct from foot and visceral hump.

headbit [ships]: bitt on bow of ship.

headgear [ships]: stays, ropes, blocks, etc., belonging to head of ship, between foremast, bow and jibboom of sailing ship.

heading [ships]: direction toward which ship is oriented. Heading is often designated as true, magnetic, compass or grid north, respectively.

headland: high, steep-faced promontory extending into sea. Usually called head when coupled with specific name.

head on [ships]: with head directly or in a right line toward some object, as "the ship struck head on."

headsails [ships]: sails carried forward of mast, including jibs, staysails, yankees, genoas.

head sea: sea driving toward head of bow of ship at anchor or when hove to. Sea coming in opposite direction of ship's movement when under way.

head stay [ships]: stay which helps support foremast.

head up [ships]: to point a sailboat higher into wind.

headway [ships]: motion ahead or forward; force or amount of such motion; rate of ship's progress.

heart [*Mollusca*]: enlarged portion of median dorsal tube that pumps blood through body.

heat conducting [diving]: transfer of heat from one point of body to another, or from one body to another in physical contact with it without displacement of the particle of the body.

heat transport: process by which heat is carried past a fixed point or across a fixed plane; thus, warm current such as Gulf Stream represents a poleward flux of heat.

heat trap: temperature increase just above thermocline; winter phenomenon due to surface cooling in areas of warm water advection.

heave: 1) motion imparted to floating body by wave action. It includes both vertical rise and fall and horizontal transport. 2) up-and-down motion of center of gravity of ship. 3) to throw, as to heave a line.

heave to [ships]: vessel is said to be hove to in a storm when there is no forward progress, but carrying a sea anchor or just enough power or canvas to hold position in seas.

heaving line [ships]: light line weighted at one end and attached to heavier line on the other; weighted end is thrown to ship or dock, then heavier line can be pulled in.

heavy minerals: accessory detrital minerals of high specific gravity 2.8 or more, in rock or sediments, e.g., magnetic ilmenite.

heavy sea: sea in which waves run high.

hectocotylus: modified arm in certain molluscs for use as copulatory organ.

heel [ships]: 1) to tilt, incline or cant over from vertical position, as "the ship gave a heel to port." Ship is said to be heeling when due to action of wind on sails, inclining it to lee side. 2) convex intersecting point or corner of web and flange of a bar.

heeling [ships]: causing ship to roll by mechanical means so as to enable it to gain headway when working in ice.

heel tapper: local name for fishing schooner of Massachusetts coast in 1820's having square stern and short, high quarterdeck. They were rarely over 50 ft. long.

height [*Mollusca*]: greatest vertical dimensions; in gastropods, parallel to axis of coiling in pelecypods through beak at right angle to a line bisecting adductor muscle scars.

height [ships]: vertical distance between two decks or vertical distance measured from base line to any waterline.

height of the tide: vertical distance from chart datum to surface water level of or at any stage of tide usually measured in feet; predetermined reference plane.

hekistoplankton: flagellated nannoplankton.

helical [*Mollusca*]: coiling formed by expanding tube, with each volution attached below suture of previous one.

heliotrope: instrument used in geodetic surveying for making long distance observations; consists of a mirror adjusted by clockwork so that, at a pre-arranged hour, sun's rays may be reflected directly to a particular station; *heliograph;* also the term for a similar instrument employed in signalling by flashes, as by *Morse Code. U.S. Coast Guard* regulations require ocean vessels' lifeboats to include in their equipment two *signalling mirrors* of approved type. During World War II many instances of timely rescues were recorded through aircraft being attracted to men adrift at sea by this simple means of throwing sun's rays in a direction desired.

heliox diving [diving]: mixed-gas diving using oxygen with helium as inert dilutant.

helix: coiled spiral, as in gastropod shells.

helm [ships]: term applied to tiller wheel, steering gear and also rudder.

helmet [diving]: protective enclosure for entire head that forms part of diver's life-support system.

helmet shells [*Cassididae*]: helmet shells are nearly all large, thick, heavy shells which are triangular on outer side. Spire is short and aperture is usually long and leads into anterior canal which in some species is curved backward and upward; operculum is small and horny; outer lip is thickened and usually toothed on inner margin. They live on sandy bottoms in tropical waters where they crawl along in search of other molluscs on which they feed. This family includes more than 25 species.

helmet shells, horned: this helmet shell is very large and heavy and marked over outer surface with 3 rows of spiral tubercles, of which posterior row is by far the largest. Surface of shell has honeycombed pattern which may be obscured by marine growth. Shell is creamy white above, orange-brown in aperture and has white teeth. It will reach a length of 8 to 12 in. *Cassis cornuta.*

helmet shells, ponderous [*Casmarea ponderosa*]: this little helmet shell is smooth over outer surface. Whorls are angled at shoulder and possess a spiral row of low tubercles extending anteriorly as folds onto body whorls; outer lip is wide and thick, bearing a row of small, sharp tubercles along outer and lower margin. Shell is white and marked about the sutures by brown spots; upper side of outer lip is marked by series of rectangu-

lar brown spots. It will reach a length of about 1½ in.

helmet shells, striped [*Casmarea erinaceus*]: this helmet shell is globular in shape, smooth within and without and has thickened outer lip. It is white or brownish-white and marked with faint longitudinal stripes and brown bands. Lips are marked with dark brown spots. Varies from 1 to 3 in. in length.

helmet shells, strongly grooved [*Semicassis tortisulcate*]: this helmet shell is spherical, thin, small in size and has external surface evenly marked by deep spiral grooves. It is white and faintly blotched with brown. Ranges in length from 1 to 2 in.

helm port [ships]: hole in counter of a vessel through which rudder stock passes.

helmsman [ships]: man at helm or wheel and steers the ship.

hemibranch: fish's gill arch in which there are gill filaments on one side of arch instead of on both sides, which is the usual case.

Hemichordata [*Chordata*]: with axial structure and other characters lacking in higher chordates.

Hemimysis lamornae [mysid]: rather short and small mysid. Carapace has short triangular rostrum and emarginated posterior border leaves last two thoracic segments exposed dorsally; bright orange or red.

hemipelagic abyssal sediments: deep-sea deposits which contain terrestrial material.

hemiplankton: organisms spending only part of their lives in plankton; meroplankton.

hemmema: Swedish armed-craft of latter 18th century; combination of "galley" and "man-of-war." It was armed with 26 guns, with sweeps in pairs between guns; 3-masted and square-rigged.

hengst: Dutch pleasure craft similar to hoogar but with less overhang forward and stubbier in appearance.

Henry's Law: states that amount of gas which dissolves in liquid is proportional to pressure of gas above.

hermaphrodite: 1) two-masted vessel, square-rigged on foremast, fore-and-aft rigged on mainmast. 2) animal or plant possessing both male and female reproductive organs. An unusual condition in higher vertebrates, it is common in many worms and some molluscs and echinoderms.

hermatolith: reef rock, also called hermatobiolith to indicate organic origin.

hermit crab [*Dardanus gemmatus*]: gemmate hermit crab gets its name from rough, tubercled outer surface of left cheliped. Body is marked with yellow and brown irregularly; walking legs, which are light near joints, are encircled by darker band between joints; eyes are somewhat club-shaped and encircled by light band toward their end. Body measures from 3 to 6 in. long. This crustacean lives on outer edge of reef at depths which are usually in excess of 30 or 40 ft.

hermit crab, large flat [*Aniculus maximus*]: all have flattened body and carapace. In this species anterior part of carapace has central area which is marked out by 4 straight lines, resembling shape of an arrowhead; central area has acute angle pointing forward; tufts of hair grow from most areas. Legs are ringed by scutes or scales from which many bristly hairs emerge; eyestalks are long and slender. Body of this crab is orange-yellow and tips of legs are black. This is a large species in which carapace reaches as much as 6 in. in length. Habitat is on outer side or edge of reef at depths below 100 ft.

hermit crab, large red [*Dardanus megistos*]: one of very largest species in this family. It is usually from 6 to 8 in. long, but it sometimes reaches a total length of over a foot. Body is reddish; carapace and adjoining areas of legs and abdomen are covered with white circular spots which are ringed with black; legs are covered with black, bristly hairs; pincers and ends of legs are tipped with black. Inhabits deeper water on outer side of reef.

hermit crab, left-handed [*Calcinus laevimanus*]: small species easily identified by its legs. Left cheliped is by far the larger, nearly circular in outline and white in color; walking legs are tipped and banded with white. Body of this crab measures from 2 to 3 in. long and is reddish color. Almost every boulder in shallow water has one or more of these small crabs beneath it.

hermit crab, short-eyed [*Dardanus brachyops*]: one of world's rarest. Upper parts of body are buff or creamy-white in color; carapace is marked with dark orange areas and lines; undersurface of body and legs is almost white. Legs are covered over upper and outer surface with spines and tufts of stiff orange hair; chelipeds are tipped with black; antennae are bright orange-red color. Body measures more than 8 in. long. This crab is seldom seen because it inhabits deeper water on outside of reefs.

herring: members of this family are small streamlined fishes whose bodies are covered with small cycloid scales. Single dorsal fin, without spines, is situated in middle of back; tail fin is deeply forked; special row of spiny scales along midline of belly gives underside saw-toothed appearance. Pointed head terminates in large mouth that is either toothless or armed with very small teeth. Herring obtains most of its food swimming through water with open mouth sucking in minute plankton organisms that are in its path.

herring, Atlantic: most plentiful fish in the sea. It is a greenish or steely-blue fish with gleaming sil-

very sides often tinted with gold. One-year-old herring 3 to 5 in. long are marketed as sardines. At 4 years, herring reach length of 10 in. Atlantic herring are found in cold waters from New England and Canada to north Atlantic and Great Britain. Herring swim in tremendous schools, sometimes near surface. All members of school are usually of same size and age.

herring, blue [*Alosa aestivalis*]: moderately-sized, laterally compressed, silvery fish. Lining of body cavity black; head short, about as deep as long; lower jaw protruding; eye ¼ length of head; peritoneum black. It is bluish above, silvery on sides and below; dark spot behind opercle; faint dark stripes along scale rows. May attain length slightly in excess of 6 in.

herringbone cross-lamination: thin layers of sand cross-laminated in opposite directions in alternating layers by frequently shifting currents in shallow water.

heterocercal tail [*fish*]: unsymmetrical tail, upper lobe of which is often longer than lower. Backbone may extend into upper lobe or merely curve upward before reaching it as in mudfish.

Heterocorallia: simple corals. Septa inserted within "bifurcated" outer ends of 4 original septa (cardinal counter and alars); tabulae formed of fibrous calcium carbonate. Range Carboniferous only.

heterogamous: having differentiated gametes, sperm and egg cells.

heteropods [*zooplankton*]: this is a group of permanently pelagic gastropods further adapted for this mode of life than *Janthinidae*. Shell is greatly reduced and animal is of gelatinous consistency; foot is drawn out into lobes. As in *Janthinidae*, most species of these animals float upside down from surface film and possess pair of tentacles with eyes at base as well as proboscis containing a radula and bearing a terminal mouth. Eggs are aggregated into gelatinous masses which float on surface of water.

heterostrophic [*Mollusca*]: coiling in which initial or nuclear whorls seem to be coiled in opposite direction to that of later whorls. Actually coiling may be dextral but with whorls attaches successively above suture instead of below (ultra-dextral) with sudden change to normal dextral in post-apical whorls.

heterotrophic: mode of nutrition of organisms that cannot synthesize new organic matter from inorganic substrates. Requiring already formed organic matter. This includes all animals and most bacteria.

heterotrophic nutrition: that process by which organism utilizes only preformed organic compounds for nutrition.

Hexameroceras [*nautiloids*]: were not so narrow

or so abruptly coiled. They almost certainly drifted and shape of living chamber suggests that the place where eyes and arms emerge was lower than funnel. It too gave forward motion, though shell was relatively wider than that of *Phragmoceras*.

hexocoral: coral distinguished by hexameral symmetry; scleractinian.

high: in meteorology, "area of high pressure" referring to maximum of atmosphere pressure in two dimensions (closed isobars) in synoptic surface chart or maximum of height (closed contours) on constant-pressure chart.

high energy environment: region characterized by considerable wave and current action which prevents settling and accumulation of fine-grained sediment smaller than sand size.

higher high water [HHW]: higher of two high waters occurring during tidal day where tide exhibits mixed characteristics.

higher high water interval [HHWI]: interval of time between transit (upper or lower) of moon over local or Greenwich meridian and next higher high water. This expression is used when there is considerable diurnal inequality.

higher low water [HLW]: higher of two waters of tidal day where tide exhibits mixed characteristics.

higher low water interval [HLWI]: interval of time between transit (upper or lower) of moon over local or Greenwich meridian and next higher low water. This expression is used when there is considerable diurnal inequality.

highly stratified estuary: estuary in which salinity increases significantly from head to mouth and surface to bottom; characterized by density discontinuity separating surface river flow and bottom seawater.

high speed layer: layer in which compressional wave velocity is greater than in at least one adjacent layer.

high water [HW]: also called high tide. Highest limit of surface water level reached by rising tide. High water is caused by astronomic tide-producing forces and/or effects of meteorological conditions.

high-water line: intersecting of plane of high water with shore; varies daily with changing lunar phases and meteorological conditions.

high-water mark: established reference mark on structure or natural object which indicates maximum observed stage of tide.

high-water stand: condition at high tide when there is no change in height of water level.

hinge crack: crack in sea ice running parallel and adjacent to pressure ridge.

hinge joint: in *Copepoda*, major articulation between prosoma and urosome.

hinge line: 1) line marking position of articulation between two shells of bivalve invertebrates (pelecypods, ostrocodes, etc.) generally dorsal but may be posterior. 2) edge of any bivalve shell along which its two parts are held together.

hinge plate: 1) in *Brachiopoda*, simple or divided plate that lies along hinge line in interior of brachial valve. Nearly parallel to plane between valves, it bears hinge sockets and is joined to base of crura. 2) in *Mollusca*, infolded dorsal margin, carrying hinge teeth.

hinter deep: deep-sea trough on convex side of island arc.

hinter surf beds: littoral, lagoonal, deltaic and tidal flat deposits which form continental shelf.

hippagi: Roman house barge.

Hippolytidae prodeauxiana [carideans]: larvae have fine lateral spines on carapace and those on fifth abdominal segment are long. First stage zoeae of this species are about 1.6 mm. long, i.e., like those of *H. varians* they are rather small.

Hippolytidae varians [carideans]: this has five larval stages in each of which there is a small lateral spine on each side of fifth abdominal segment; 3 spines on each side of carapace. Conspicuous rostrum is pointed and 3 pairs of maxillipeds of first zoeal stage form main swimming organs; compound eyes are covered by carapace until second zoeal stage is reached. First stage zoea is 1.25 mm. long.

histological: referring to histology, branch of anatomy which is the study of animal and plant tissues with microscope.

H.M.S.: 1) official abbreviation for His (or Her) Majesty's Ship, or Station, applied to all names of British naval vessels and shore stations; as, *H.M.S. Drake*. 2) *H.M.S. Excellent*, training station at Portsmouth, England; also known as *Whale Island*.

H.O.: letters, followed by a number, by which *U.S. Hydrographic Office* charts and other publications are catalogued; as, *H.O.20*.

hoarfrost: white, frozen dew on ground, leaves, etc.; rime.

hodograph: in general mathematics, locus of one end of variable vector as other end remains fixed. Common hodograph in oceanography represents tidal current or component of tidal current for a complete tide cycle. Current speed is shown by length of arrow; change in time is shown by the different directions of arrow from common center.

hog [ships]: scrub-broom for scraping ship's bottom under water.

hogfish: tropical member of reef fishes living around Key West, Florida. It is reddish-brown or gray with projecting front teeth and very ornate fins. First 3 dorsal spines form long streamers and anal fin and posterior dorsal fin extend tapering tips. Hogfish reach a weight of 12 to 15 lbs.

hog frame [ships]: fore-and-aft frame, forming truss for main frames of vessel to prevent bending.

hogged [ships]: ship that is damaged or strained so that bottom curves upward in middle; opposite of sagged.

hoggie: fishing craft peculiar to Brighton, England, up to 1850's. It was great of beam, clinker-built, flat-floored and rounded-ended. It carried a gaff or sprit mainsail and often a spit or lug-mizzen, with large jib set to bowsprit.

hog sheer [ships]: curve of deck on vessel constructed so that middle is higher than ends.

hold [ships]: interior part of ship in which cargo is stored. Various main compartments are distinguished as main, forward and after holds.

hold beams [ships]: beams that support lower deck in cargo vessel.

holdfast: 1) rootlike base of alga by which it attaches to substrate. 2) basal attachment structure of algae, ranging in complexity from simple or modified cells of filamentous algae to massive rootlike structures of kelp.

holdfast [ships]: dog or brace to hold objects rigidly in place.

holding ground: sea bottom of anchorage designated as good or poor, depending upon whether anchor holds, catches or drags. Mud or silt usually is good holding ground. Rock, gravel or hard-packed sand often is poor holding ground since anchor often will drag, snag or become fouled.

hole: 1) abrupt hollow in ground or ocean floor. 2) opening through piece of sea ice or open space between ice cakes. 3) small bay, particularly in New England.

holectypoids [sea urchins]: most primitive order of irregular echinoids. They have lanterns, some *Irregularia* do not; ambulacra run from oculogenital ring to peristome and generally contain compound plates. Holectypoids range from early Jurassic to Recent, but are larger and more plentiful in Europe than in America.

holiday [ships]: parts of ship's surface which have been accidentally missed by coat of paint or other protective preparation.

holoblastic cleavage: complete and nearly equal cleavage of cells in early embryology.

Holocene [Recent]: referring to present geological epoch, dating back to end of Pleistocene or "Ice Age" about 11,000 years ago when last great glaciers began to retreat.

holopelagic: pelagic throughout entire life cycle.

holophytic: having plantlike nutrition, synthesizing new organic matter from inorganic substrata. Photosynthetic.

holophytic nutrition: type of nutrition by which green plants are able to make food from simple inorganic substances.

holoplankton: organisms that are planktonic throughout entire life cycle.

Holoptychius [bony fishes]: late Devonian genus that apparently ranged around the world. Some species reached lengths of 30 in.; they had deep bodies, large rounded scales and long narrow pectoral fins. *Rhizodus* of Mississippian age apparently reached lengths of 15 to 18 ft.

Holostei: fish which had heavy scales but more symmetrical tails, fins supported by flexible rays and relatively more bone in skeletons.

Holothuroidea: holothurians have number of larval stages before adult form is attained. In family *Synaptidae* there is a typical auricularia larva, but in *Dendrochirota* and also in *Leptosynapta inhaerens* auricularia stage is omitted, and larva en townelet (barrel-like) is formed. This resembles doliolaria stage which follows auricularia in typical development sequence. Both doliolaria and larva en townelet develop into final larval stage, pentacula, which finally settles on substratum reaching adult stage.

holozoic: having animal-like nutrition. Fed by ingestion or organisms of other organic matter.

holozoic nutrition: that process by which organism ingests solid food and digests it internally; typical of free-living animals.

homing torpedo: torpedo with special devise which guides it to particular target.

homocercal tail [fish]: type of fish tail in which vertebrae are not markedly graduated in size and end at base of caudal fin, lobes of which are about equal.

homogenous fluid: fluid with uniform density.

homolid crab, Japanese [*Homola; parhomola japonica*]: this crab is a large, deepwater species. Carapace is pear-shaped, convex above, rough in texture and covered with small spines which become larger toward margin. Walking legs are long and slender; chelipeds are long and slender and tipped with blue-black pinchers. First 3 pairs of walking legs are about equal size; last pair of legs is smaller and placed on upper surface of body at rear of carapace above fourth pair of legs. Entire body is sandy colored except for tips of pinchers.

homopycnal: sediment-laden stream enters basin filled with water of comparable density, as when stream enters freshwater lake. Resulting delta is classical type with top-fore and bottomset beds.

homosphere: part of atmosphere, from surface to about 50 miles up, which is a uniform mixture of gases.

honeycomb coral: tabulate coral with small polygonal corallites.

honeycombing: process of partial melting that leaves piece of ice filled with pockets of water. Occurs during final disintegration of floating ice. Honeycombed ice is generally soft and spongy, floating low in water.

honey wave [*Alaria valida*]: perennial kelp often washed ashore; widely distributed; forms large beds in rough water 15 to 25 ft. deep. Single large blade with conspicuous midrib and number of small blades (sporophylls) are outstanding features of *Alaria*. Short, cylindrical stipe (2 to 8 in.) is perennial, the blade annual. Honey wave is clear, almost transparent yellow-brown with textures of medium-weight rubber. Holdfast is circular, wide-spreading mass (3 to 4 in.) made up of many short, solid fibers.

hood [ships]: covering for companion hatch, scuttle or skylight.

hooding end [ships]: endmost plate of complete strake. Hooding ends fit into stem or sternpost.

hoof shell [*Amal theidae*]: hoof shells are nearly all small molluscs with thick conical shells in which apex is directed backwards. They are grayish-white, rough in texture over outer portion of shell and smooth within. Hoof shells form base beneath them by secreting a plate upon object to which they are attached, so that they are resting upon their own shell.

hoof shell, conical: southern hoof shell is oval or nearly circular in outline and marked over outer surface with flat radiating ribs which are separated by narrow grooves. Circular growth lines found in some hoof shells are not apparent in this species. Prominent apex of shell is situated posteriorly and inclines to point in posterior direction. Outside of shell is white, often with brownish markings in grooves; interior is also tinged with brownish markings. It will reach a length of about ¾ in.

hoof shell, Dillwyn's: this mollusc bears a shell which resembles cup-and-saucer shells *(Calyptraeidae)* but it differs from them in having basal plate beneath it. In general this species is circular in outline and of varying convexity. It is marked upon upper surface by fine radiating ribs which are usually more obscure toward apex and which become more prominent toward margin; margin is sometimes minutely crenulated. Central appendages or lamina, which are thickened basally and attached at apex or opening in front, bears winglike extensions upon sides. Shell is usually white or yellowish in color. Reaches about 1½ in. in diameter.

hoof shell, hairy: this hoof shell is oval or circular in outline, somewhat depressed and has apex of shell placed well toward back end of shell. It is marked above by radial and concentric lines; upper surface covered by brown pilose epidermis; apex is usually smooth, while lines and epidermis become increasingly apparent toward periphery of shell; margin of aperture is smooth. Shell is white without and brownish within. Large specimens will reach ¾ in. in length. *(Pilosabia pilosa)*.

hoogar: sloop of Dutch design used mainly for pleasure purposes in Holland and Belgium. Hull is flat-bottomed, keelless, decked with cabin top and cockpit and has generous sheer.

hook: spit or narrow cape of sand or gravel whose outer end bends sharply landward.

hooked bay: open bay or bight having only one headland.

hooked skein or rope [*Antithamnion pacificum*]: attached in large masses to stipes and air bladders of *Nereocystis* and *Macrocystis*. They are found wherever these kelps are washed ashore. Distinguishing features of these seaweeds are attachments in conspicuous masses to big kelps, bright colors and delicacy. In both species individual branches and brachlets are as fine as the most delicate thread but when these are massed together the hooked rope gives impression of a frayed rope, while hooked skein looks like skein of thin silk floating in water. Both species are uniform, dark red.

hooked trades: winds that change direction as they cross equator.

hooker: contemptuous slang for boat of any kind. Also a small fishing craft local to Polperio, Cornell, England, used for long-line fishing.

horizon: one of several lines or planes used as reference for observation and measurement relative to given location.

horizontal haul: towing of one or more nets for predetermined periods at selected depth or depths. In this type of haul, attempts are made to minimize sampling from other levels.

Hornbaek boat: sailing boat used in place fishery of Hornbaek, Denmark. Average size was about 36 ft. long, 13 ft. 8 in. beam, by 5 ft. draft. Clinker built, with stem and stern alike, considerable sheer, flaring bow and quarters.

hornblende: blackish-green or dark brown silicate of calcium and magnesium found in granite and other igneous rocks.

horn coral: 1) belonging to subclass *Rugosa*, so called because surface is commonly marked by wrinkles. *Rugosa* corals are common in Paleozoic formations all over the world, but species of Silurian and later ages are products of long continued evolution. 2) conical solitary coral, straight or curved, shaped like horn.

horning [ships]: setting frames of vessel square to keel after proper inclination to vertical due to declinity of keel has been given.

horns: arms of cleat.

horn shell [*Cerithiidae*]: horn shells are elongated in shape and composed of many whorls, surfaces of which are covered with tubercles. Apertures are small and oblique, bear short anterior canal and are covered by horny operculum. Horn shells are large family consisting of more than 200 species which live on rocks and on marine vegetation in comparatively shallow water in tropical and sub-tropical countries; difficult group to classify.

horn shell, banded [*Cerithium baeticum*]: this horn shell is thin and spirally encircled by shallow grooves and low ridges. It is longitudinally ribbed and covered by pattern of beads and tubercles; whorls are constricted at sutures; aperture is oval and anterior canal is comparatively short. Shell is whitish to yellowish in color and encircled by wide brown line anterior to suture and by other smaller and finer spiral lines. It will reach a length of about ½ in.

horn shell, black-margined [*Conocerithium atro-marginatum*]: short, stout species which is spirally grooved and ridged and which is covered over outside by heads or tubercles. Aperture is oval; outer lip is spotted and thickened; anterior canal is short. It is light in color and mottled and clouded with various shades of brown. It will reach a length of about ½ in.

horn shell, Chinese [*Cerithium sinense*]: this shell is encircled by spiral ribs bearing tubercles and by 9 granular lines. Anterior whorl bears prominent lateral varix and canal at anterior end of aperture is curved upward. The shell is whitish to yellowish in color and decorated with brownish markings. It will reach 2½ in. in length.

horn shell, columnar [*Cerithium columna*]: this shell is moderately long and presents rough surface, encircling spiral ridges and angular whorls which are marked by quite large low longitudinal ribs. It has short anterior canal and widely expanded lip. It is white to grayish in color and marked with encircling brownish or blackish lines. It will reach 1½ in.

horn shell, Hawaiian [*Cerithium hawaiiensis*]: Hawaiian horn shell is moderately slender species which is longitudinally ribbed and grooved. Surface is faintly spirally grooved to form reticulated pattern of short longitudinal ridges or tubercles. It is creamy white and encircled by about 3 narrow lines per whorl. It ranges in length from ½ to 7/8 in.

horn shell, island: this is short species which is encircled by alternating larger and smaller ridges. It is white and marked with faint brown spots below sutures. It will reach a length of about ¾ in.

horn shell, pharos [*Cerithium pharos*]: Pharos horn shell is elongated, narrow species in which posterior half of each whorl is longitudinally ribbed. It has curved anterior canal, oblique aperture, fluted outer lip and columella which is thickened and bears single plate. It is whitish in color and variously marked with brown, usually as interrupted bands. It will reach a length of about 2 in.

horn shell, prickly [*Cerithium echinatum*]: this shell is fairly robust in outline, of heavy construction and presents rough exterior. It is encircled by spiral grooves and by ridges bearing somewhat pointed tubercles. Outer lip is crenulated and marked with purplish-brown spots upon inner surface. Shell is light mottled brown and bears darker brown blotches. It will reach a length of 1½ in.

horn shell, Thaanum's: somewhat slender species in which whorls are encircled by ridges bearing beads. Aperture is nearly circular and lip is somewhat flaring. It will reach a length of more than ½ in.

horse latitudes: belts of latitudes over oceans at approximately 30° to 35° N and S where winds are predominantly calm or very light and weather is hot and dry. These latitudes mark normal axis of subtropical highs and move north and south by about 5° following the sun. The two calm belts are known as calms of Cancer and calms of Capricorn in Northern and Southern Hemisphere respectively. In North Atlantic Ocean these are latitudes of Sargasso Sea.

horses [ships]: footropes. Also an iron rod secured to the deck, on which a sheet block travels.

horseshoe crab: arthropod of subphylum *Chelicerata*. Characterized by 3 body divisions, i.e., prosoma, unsegmented abdomen and spikelike tail. Cephalothorax is horseshoe-shaped carapace, convex above and concave below. Usually found in shallow, brackish water.

horseshoe plate [ships]: small, light plate fitted on counter around rudder stock for purpose of preventing water from backing up into rudder trunk. Frequently it is made in 2 pieces.

horsetails: modern horsetails live in both wet and very dry places. Their straight, slender stems are jointed and are made gritty by large amounts of silica. Calamites, chief Pennsylvanian genus, grew 2 or 3 to as much as 40 ft. high, with stems that were smooth or had lengthwise ridges. Upright, woody stems grew from rootstock and were supported by roots that came from lowermost joints like prop roots of corn. Clusters of slender leaves also grew from nodes, especially in young branches, though they often remained on good-sized stems.

hostile ice: from point of view of submariner, an ice canopy containing no large ice skylights or other features which permit submarine to surface.

hot-water suit [diving]: loose-fitting wet suit

through which hot water is circulated to maintain thermal equilibrium in extreme cold-water exposure.

houario: small vessel with two masts and bowsprit, sometimes used as coasting vessel or pleasure boat in inlets and rivers of Mediterranean in 18th century.

hounding [ships]: portion of mast between deck and hounds.

hounds [ships]: masthead projections supporting trestletrees and top. Also applied in vessels without trestletrees to that portion at which houndband, for attaching shrouds, is fitted.

houndshark: dogfish or houndfish, a small dark shark common on North Atlantic coasts; also, *dog shark.*

hour: sixty minutes, or one twenty-fourth of a *mean solar day* (common clock time, as referred to a standard meridian) or of a *sidereal day* (interval between two successive transits of a fixed star). Angular unit of 15 degrees used in indicating *right ascension* of an observer's meridian (or sidereal time) or of a heavenly body. One hour of *mean time* (mean solar time) = 60 min. and 9.856 sec. of *sidereal time;* one hour of *sidereal time* = 59 min. and 50.170 sec. of *mean time.*

hourly difference: *Nautical Almanac* term indicating hourly change in tabulated ephemerides of sun, moon, and planets.

housing [ships]: portion of mast below surface of upper deck.

hove aboard [ships]: heaved or lifted aboard.

Hoveller: term used in Southern England for lug-rigged sailing craft on lookout for shipping and hauling jobs. Also a term applied colloquially to vagrants which formerly plied English coast in bad weather looking for plunder from wrecks.

hove to [ships]: ship is hove to when kept almost stationary in heavy wind and sea by bracing yards up with just enough sail to steady her. In fine weather yards may be reversed. This maneuver puts the ship "in stays."

hoy: coasting vessel in which much of freight was carried between English ports and those of the Continent in 16th, 17th and 18th centuries. Rig was usually that of fore-and-aft spritsail with single post.

hoy sail [ships]: tall high-peaked spritsail used on English barges of 17th century. Vangs were often used.

hulk: body or hull of a dismantled, disabled, or old vessel unfit for further sea service but used as a depot, store, or training ship; also, a vessel built for special use other than for seagoing, as, formerly in Europe, a prison. In a disparaging sense, a heavy vessel of clumsy appearance.

hulk [ships]: round-sterned, square-tucked, high-pooped vessel of 18th century ranging in size from 100 to 800 tons. Square-rigged on main and foremasts, lateen-rigged on mizzenmast.

hull [ships]: frame or body of ship exclusive of decks, masts, yards and rigging.

hull down [ships]: ship at sea on horizon with hull below the line and only masts showing.

Humber keel: flat-bottomed sailing barge or keel, typical to Humber River in England. Rig consists of single mast with large square sail and small square topsail.

Humboldt Current: also called *Chilean* or *Peruvian* Current.

humeral scale [fish]: body scale above base of pectoral fin and immediately behind opercle.

humic acids: various organic acids derived from humus, the organic portion of soil formed of partly decomposed animal and plant matter.

hummock: mound or hill in pressure ice; corresponding submerged portion is called a hummock.

hummocked ice: pressure ice, characterized by haphazardly arranged mounds or hillocks (hummocks). This has less definite form and shows effects of greater pressure than either rafted ice or tented ice, but in fact may develop from either of those.

humpback: 1) the *humpbacked whale.* 2) also, the *humpbacked salmon,* a small fish of that species found on both sides of North Pacific waters; so called because the male has a swelling or hump anterior to his dorsal fin during breeding season.

hurdy-gurdy: a kind of hand windlass used by fishermen for hauling in trawl lines when working in deeper water, as in taking halibut. It is fixed to topside of boat or dory at the bows and one man turns crank while another hands in and stows trawl.

huronian: simple type of coelenterate, some of which secrete calcareous hard parts; prevailing marine.

hurricane: 1) composed of destructive circular winds which always originate over ocean waters of 80° F or more. It has low-pressure center with surrounding winds in excess of 64 knots (75 mph). Hurricane has no fronts, but central core of calm winds, called the eye. Typhoon is name for similar storm in Eastern Hemisphere. 2) tropical cyclones that develop over oceans near West Indies. 3) severe tropical cyclone in North Atlantic Ocean, Caribbean Sea, Gulf of Mexico and eastern North Pacific off coast of Mexico.

hurricane [history]: Carib Indians, for whom Caribbean Sea is named, were accustomed to violent storms, but their Spanish conquerors had never seen anything like the winds of the West Indies. These winds sometimes blow 140 mph in vast circular pattern. Adapting native term for this disturbance, Spanish called it *huracan*. Contact between sailors caused the word to go international very early. Portuguese adapted it to *furacaco*, French to *ouragan*, Germans to *orkan*. However, the English changed the borrowed word most. During 16th century it appeared in colorful spellings that ranged from *haurachana* to *hurry cane*. Sometimes used on the theory that its title stemmed from frequent destruction of sugarcane plantations, it was "hurry-cane," and fanciful as the term was, that shaped hurricane. Any wind of force 12 on Beaufort Scale falls into this category of a hurricane. But in popular speech the term is reserved for tropical cyclones of West Indies that still destroy much of the sugarcane regularly.

hurricane delta: deposit formed in lagoon by sand carried by storm waves washing across reef.

hurricane surge: waves produced by hurricane that cause marked increase in water level.

hurricane wave: sudden rise in level of sea on islands and along shore associated with a hurricane. In low latitudes, hurricane wave appears to occur in proximity of storm's center.

husband, ship's: person responsible for management of vessels on behalf of owners and having authority as a managing owner at port or ports visited by ships concerned, other than at the home port. Generally, he is empowered to appoint agents in chartering or freight contracting, in addition to engaging crews, contracting for dry-docking, repairs, supplies, towing, etc. *Husbandage* is term used for commissions and other payments made to a *ship's husband* for services rendered.

Huygen's principle: very general principle applying to all forms of wave motions stating that every point on instantaneous position of advancing phase front (wave front) may be regarded as source of secondary spherical "wavelets." Position of phase front a moment later is then determined as envelope of all secondary wavelets.

hvalorbaad: spritsail-rigged, deck craft of Southern Norway formerly used extensively as pilot boat. Very broad, bluff and deep, it was a fine sea boat; clinker-built, double-ended, with curved stem and sternpost, outboard rudder.

H.W.: abbreviation for high water.

H.W.F. & C.: abbreviation for high water at full and change of moon.

Hyades: also, *Hyads*, a V-shaped group of stars in *Taurus*, in which is included *Aldebaran* (a Tauri).

hyaline: anything transparent or semitransparent with glassy or gelatinous consistency.

Hybocodon prolifer [phylum *Coelenterata*]: medusa of hydroid of same name. It has from 1 to 3 marginal tentacles arising close together on bell margin. There are fine meridional tracks of nema-

tocysts on exumbrellar surface; stomach is short and broad; widely distributed.

hybodonts [sharks]: resembled modern sharks in shape and reached lengths of 7 to 8 ft. Many species had sharp teeth at front of mouth, but low-crowned plates at back. Several late Paleozoic hybodonts developed remarkable series of teeth in midline of both upper and lower jaws.

Hydatinidae [family]: shells of these molluscs are oval and very light and thin in texture. They have body whorl which is very large, low or nearly inconspicuous spire and are usually marked with beautiful pattern of colored stripes. Animal which inhabits the shell is large and possesses a gigantic foot. Head of animal has characteristic pair of folds developed from it which extend over portion of shell. Green bubble shells make up a family of less than 12 species which are found in tropical Indo-Pacific and Atlantic Oceans.

Hydra: small freshwater polyp of coelenterate class *Hydrozoa*. It can reproduce either sexually or asexually but has no medusa form.

hydranth: individual polyp in hydrozoan colonies. Polyp is slender, stalklike coelenterate attached at one end with circle of tentacles surrounding mouth at other end. This hydrozoan may have either colonial or solitary polyps, or jellyfishlike medusae. Some species may take both forms, usually in alternating generations. Hydrozoans are usually marine and include Hydra and dangerous Portuguese man-of-war.

hydrate: compound formed by intimate union of water with molecule of some other substance, molecular structure of which is represented as actually containing water. Hydroxide, such as calcium hydrate, is a hydrate from which water may be separated by simple readjustment of molecular structure.

hydraulic current: gravity flow through channel that results from difference between water levels at two ends of channel because of difference in phase or range of tide.

hydraulic gradient: 1) energy that causes underground water to flow is derived from gravity. Gravity draws water downward to water table, from there it flows through ground to point of discharge in stream, lake or spring. Just as surface water needs a slope to flow on, so must there be a slope for flow of ground water. This is slope of the water table, hydraulic gradient. It is measured by dividing length of flow (from point of intake to point of discharge) into vertical distance between two points called a head. 2) slope of profile of static level for hydraulic system. In open channel flow, hydraulic gradient is slope of water surface taken parallel to flow.

hydraulic jump: steady state, finite-amplitude disturbance in a channel, in which water passes turbulently from region (uniform) of low depth and high velocity to region of (uniform) high depth and low velocity. When applied to hydraulic jumps, usual hydraulic formulas governing relations of velocity and depth do not conserve energy.

hydraulic radius: quotient of cross-sectional area of a channel (below water surface) divided by wetted perimeter.

hydraulic tidal stream: tidal stream due to difference in level caused by different tidal range or time of high water at either end of strait.

hydrocarbon: 1) in ocean, hydrocarbon is derived mainly from phytoplankton, being organic compound of carbon. It represents minor proportion of organic material in sea sediment, partly susceptible to solution and other chemical processes; oxidation is most impoartant factor. 2) one of group of organic compounds of carbon and hydrogen, including methane or "marsh gas" and benzene. They can be found in coral, petroleum and natural gas.

hydrocoel: embryonic coelomic vesicle in echinoderms and in tornaria larvae of *Hemichordata*, communicating to outside of water pore.

hydrocoral: *Hydrocorallina* or hydrocorals are of class *Hydrozoa*. Belong to genus *Millepora* and are distinct from madreporarian corals, which they resemble with squat or branched forms. Along with madreporarians they build coral "massifs" or "banks." But they are not themselves scleractinians.

hydroecium: in *Siphonophora*, extended part of swimming bell, covering proximal part of stem of colony.

hydrofoils: 1) "stilted" craft that are lifted out of water by ski-like foils as speed increases. 2) any surface, such as a wing or rudder, designed to obtain reaction upon it from water through which it moves. Also connotes a ship equipped with planes which provide lift when ship is propelled forward.

hydrograph: graphical representation of stage or discharge and a point on a stream as function of time. Most common type, observed hydrograph, represents river gage readings plotted at time of observations.

hydrographer: one who measures and charts physical aspects of sea floor and other bodies of water, usually for navigational purposes.

hydrographic: of, or pertaining to, *hydrography*, or that branch of surveying in which contour of sea bottom, depths of water, position of channels, shoals, rocks, details of coastlines, etc., are determined and shown on charts drawn to appropriate scale, together with other data of interest to navigators, including magnetic variation, tide and current information, description of lights,

signal stations, etc. An expert in this work is called a *hydrographer*.

hydrographic data: observations of temperature and salinity, in particular, from which ocean movements can be computed.

hydrographic station: fixed location where vessel remains so that certain hydrographic observations and measurements can be taken over period of time.

hydrographic survey: survey of water area and any adjacent land, with particular reference to submarine relief.

hydrography: hydrography is that science which deals with measurement and description of physical features of oceans, seas, lakes, rivers and other waters, and their adjoining coastal areas, with particular reference to use for navigational purposes.

Hydroida [phylum *Coelenterata*]: 1) fixed, bottom-dwelling or hydroid stages are usually polymorphic and colonial. Most release pelagic reproductive zooids called medusae, which bear male and female gonads. In many, however, medusoid stages are retained on parent colony as gonophores. 2) polyp form of coelenterate class *Hydrozoa*. Usually colonial hydrozoans may also take form of jellyfishlike medusa. Some species may take both forms at different stages of their lives. Hydrozoans include *Hydra*; siphonophores, such as Portuguese man-of-war and sea fir.

hydrologic cycle: water cycle in which water is evaporated from sea, then precipitated from atmosphere to surface of land, and finally returned to sea by rivers and streams.

hydrologist: a scientist who specializes in hydrology.

hydrology: scientific study of waters of earth, especially with relation to effects of precipitation and evaporation upon occurrence and character of water in streams, lakes and on or below land surface.

hydrolysis: chemical reaction in which water acts upon another substance to form one or more entirely new substances, e.g., conversion of starch to glucose by water in presence of suitable catalyst.

hydrolyzed: describing a substance subjected to hydrolysis.

hydromedusae: medusae or jellyfishlike offspring produced by budding from hydroid polyp. It sexually reproduces new polyps. This reproductive alternation of generation is called metagenesis.

hydrometer: instrument for measuring density of water.

hydronauts: name applies to sea pioneers, particularly those who go in for deep-sea exploration.

hydrophone: underwater microphone for receiving

sound transmitted through water. It receives sound waves and sends out equivalent electrical waves that are amplified and then made audible with a loudspeaker.

hydrophotometer: instrument used to measure extinction coefficient or transmission of light in water. Consists of constant light source placed at specific distance from a photocell. When placed in water, electrical output of the photocell is proportional to amount of light striking the cell, which in turn, depends upon transparency of water.

hydrophyte: plant which lives on surface of, or submerged in water.

hydroplane: fast, powered, flat-bottomed boat designed to glide on, rather than to part, the water. As speed increases, forward end of boat rises clear of water in "planing" effect desired, for which reason some boats are made with two or more "steps" or breaks in their bottom surface continuity corresponding to different speeds. Upper, or forward, step gives initial gliding effect at a lower speed; next step, at a higher speed, etc., that part of boat forward of step indicated rising clear of water. A horizontal *rudder* of a submarine is sometimes also termed an *hydroplane*.

hydroponics: science of growing vegetables without soil.

hydropsis: part of oceanography concerned with continuous observations, data collecting and reporting of oceanographic phenomenon on regular and prompt basis with the aim of supplying to those using seas, particularly in commercial fishing, current information.

hydrosol: colloidal solution in water.

hydrosphere: 1) water portion of earth as distinguished from solid part or lithosphere, and from gaseous outer envelope or atmosphere. 2) water spheres of earth, including surface and subsurface waters.

hydrostatic: branch of physics dealing with science of equilibrium and pressure of water and other fluids at rest.

hydrostatic equilibrium: state of a fluid whose surfaces of constant pressure and constant mass (or density) coincide and are horizontal throughout. Complete balance exists between force of gravity and pressure force. Relation between pressure and geometric height is given by hydrostatic equation.

hydrostatic pressure: pressure caused by water depths, commonly measured in pounds per square inch.

hydrotheca: in *Hydrozoa*, cuplike extension of perisarc around feeding polyp, into which it can withdraw. Present in members of the suborder *Calyptoblastea.*

hydrothermal: pertaining to or resulting from activity of hot aqueous solutions originating from magma or other source deep in earth.

hydrothermal metamorphism: kind of change in mineral composition and texture of a rock which was effected by water under conditions involving high temperatures.

hydrothermal solutions: hot waters originating within earth carrying mineral substances in solution.

hydrotroilite: black, finely divided colloidal material (FeS) reported in many muds and clays.

Hydrozoa [phylum *Coelenterata*]: 1) most familiar hydrozoans are polymorphic coelenterates which form colonies of zooids. These may be either of medusoid or polypsoid type of individual or both. Some hydrozoans occur solely in hydroid or medusoid phase. 2) delicate marine animals, usually in clusters or colonies; individual polyps are encased in gelatinous cups and often secrete coral as supporting structure. Related to jellyfishes (coelenterates). Highly branched polyp or hydroid stage of many members is important component of fouling. 3) hydrozoan jellyfish range from early Cambrian to Recent but are unusual fossils. Some Recent forms produce eggs that develop into new jellyfish, but offspring of others settle down and become bottom-dwelling hydrozoans such as millepores. These jellyfish have central mouth on underside of body, which is not divided into lobes. Tentacles hang down from edge of body and may be either shallow, saucerlike or bell-shaped.

hyetograph [Greek *hyetos*, rain]: instrument which collects, measures and records rain.

hygropetrical fauna: animals living in thin film of water surrounding stones not truly submerged.

Hymenocaris [arthropods]: ranges from British Columbia to Europe, has two pairs of antennae, jointed thorax that bears 11 pairs of legs and abdominal region that lacks them. Thorax is covered by thin, smooth bivalve shell which is common Burgess fossil. It can be readily distinguished from *Tuzoia*, which is larger, has reticulate surface and straight upper margin and generally possesses spines.

hyomandibular: upper portion of one of fish's bony or cartilaginous gill arches which is usually modified into support for jaw.

hyperbaric: condition of increased pressure above atmospheric pressure. High-pressure hyperbaric chambers in which pressure can be varied for experimental purposes are used for pressure tests on equipment and for work and therapeutics of diving.

Hyperiidea: family and suborder of *Amphipoda* with very large head and eyes; 5 abdominal segments; 7 pairs of thoracic legs.

hyperoxia [diving]: partial pressure of oxygen in

body above the normal at sea level.

hyperpycnal: sediment-laden water flowing down side of a basin and then along bottom as a turbidity current, with vertical mixing inhibited because of dense water seeking to remain at lowest possible level.

hypersaline: abnormally high in salinity.

hyperstrophic [*Gastropoda*]: rare shell type in which whorls are coiled in inverted cone so that apex points forward rather than back, not easily distinguished from orthostropic unless shown siphon pointed in same direction as apex.

hyperventilation [diving]: 1) practice of "blowing off" normal carbon dioxide level in body, by ventilating lungs through series of deep inhalations and exhalations. 2) repeated forced exhalation leading to abnormally low partial pressure of carbon dioxide in body.

hyphalomyraplankton: plankton of brackish water.

hypocapnia [diving]: low partial pressure of carbon dioxide in body.

hypolimnion: layer of water below thermocline in freshwater lake or pool, distinguished from epilimnion, layer above thermocline.

hypoplankton: demersal plankton; plankton taken close to bottom.

hypotheca: in diatoms, smaller or lower valve of shell; in armored dinoflagellates lower plates below or back of cingulum.

hypothermia [diving]: low body temperature caused by exposure and thermal stress.

hypsographic chart: chart, or part of chart, showing land or submarine bottom relief in terms of height above datum; also hypsometric chart showing gradients by means of tints.

hypsography: science of measuring or describing elevations above a datum.

I

I: 1) in International Code of Signals, flag *I* hoisted singly indicates *"I am directing my course to port."* 2) in mechanics, a symbol for *moment of inertia.* 3) descriptive of structural steel, iron, or other metal having cross-sectional shape resembling letter *I*, such as is used in ship construction; as, *I-bar; I-beam; I-iron; I-rail;* sometimes, also, when flanges are deeper, called *H-iron*, etc.

I.C.: *Index correction;* that quantity required to be applied to readings of a gage, scale, or other measuring indicator, to determine true reading; especially, to angles as read off on arc of a sextant.

ice: water frozen or turned to the solid state by cold. Fresh water congeals at a temperature of 32° F. (0° Centigrade); seawater at 27° F. (-3° C.); and seawater ice is *fresh*. Specific gravity of ordinary ice being .92 and that of seawater 1.025, 89.7% of a mass of floating ice is submerged, 10.3% showing above water. Submerged part of an *iceberg* is, therefore, nine times (nearly) greater than its emerged volume.

Ice Age: when capitalized, this term refers to last, or Pleistocene, glacial epoch. It involves several glacial advances and retreats in Northern Hemisphere. There were several earlier ice ages.

ice bar: ice edge consisting of ice floes compacted by wind, sea and swell; difficult to penetrate.

ice basin lake: lake, pond or pool on sea or glacier ice.

ice bay: 1) baylike recess on edge of large ice floe or ice shelf. 2) inward bend of edge or limit of pack ice, formed either by wind or current.

iceberg: large mass of detached land-ice floating in sea or stranded in shallow water. Irregular icebergs generally calved from glaciers whereas tabular icebergs and ice islands are usually formed from shelf ice.

ice blink: relatively bright, usually yellowish-white glare on underside of low cloud layer, produced by light reflected from distant ice-covered surface such as pack ice.

ice boulder: large fragment of sea ice stranded on shore which has been shaped by ice and wave action into nearly spherical form.

icebreaker: ship specially designed for breaking channels through floating ice.

ice breccia: ice pieces of different age frozen together.

ice cake: ice floe smaller than 10 meters (32.8 ft.) across.

ice canopy: pack ice and its enclosed water areas from point of view of submariner.

ice cap: perennial cover of ice and snow over extreme portion of earth's land surface. Most important of existing ice caps are those on Antarctica and Greenland.

ice cluster: concentration of sea ice covering hundreds of square miles which is found in same region every summer.

ice day: in climatology, day on which maximum air temperature in thermometer shelter does not rise above 32° F and ice on surface of water does not thaw.

ice edge: boundary at any given time between open sea and sea ice of any kind, whether drifting or fast.

ice flowers: 1) formation of ice crystals on surface of quiet, slowly freezing body of water. 2) delicate tufts of hoarfrost that occasionally form in great abundance on ice or snow surface (surface hoar).

ice fog: type of fog, composed of suspended particles of ice, partly ice crystals 20 to 100 microns in diameter but chiefly, especially when dense, droxtals (crystals) 12 to 20 microns in diameter. It occurs at very low temperatures and usually in clear, calm weather in high latitudes. Sun is usually visible and may cause halo phenomena.

ice foot: fringe of ice frozen to shore along coasts of polar seas.

ice island: large tabular fragment of shelf ice found in Arctic Ocean.

Icelandic low: low-pressure center located near Iceland (mainly between Iceland and southern Greenland) in mean charts of sea level pressure. It is principal center of action in atmospheric circulation of Northern Hemisphere.

ice limit: average position of ice edge in any given month or period, based on observations over number of years.

ice piedmont: ice covering a coast strip of low-lying land backed by mountains. Surface of ice piedmont slopes gently seaward, may range from width of about 150 meters (164 ft.) to 50 kilometers (27 n. miles) and fringes long stretches of coastline with ice cliffs.

ice point: true freezing point of water; temperature at which a mixture of air-saturated pure water and pure ice may exist in equilibrium at pressure of one standard atmosphere.

ice rafting: transportation of rock fragments of all sizes by floating ice.

ice rampart: ridge of sand, gravel and boulders that parallel a lake shore. Results from expanding ice overriding low shore zone.

ice rind: thin elastic, shining crust of ice, formed by freezing of ice slush or sludge on quiet sea surface.

ice sheets: broad, moundlike masses of glacier ice that tend to spread radially under their own weight. Vatva Glacier of Iceland is small sheet of ice, 750 ft. thick, measuring about 75 miles by 100 miles.

ice shelf: thick ice formation with fairly level surface formed along polar coast and in shallow bays and inlets, where it is fastened to shore and often reaches bottom.

ice tongue: any narrow extension of glacier or ice shelf, such as projection floating on sea or outlet glacier of ice cap.

ichthyological: pertaining to ichthyology, scientific study of fish.

Ichthyostega [fish]: body flattened from top to bottom rather than from side to side. Long slender tail bears low fins rather than expanded ones; vertebrae are large, heavy and closely articulated, and except for those in tail, each bears pair of ribs. In place of paired fins are legs articulated with broad plates, peloric and pectoral girdles, on sides of body. Some of palatal bones bear large teeth, but these are never in radial rows as they are in lungfish. As in the fish, nostrils open extending into mouth.

ideal sea level: theoretical sea surface which is everywhere normal to plumb line. Reference of all depth soundings to this level would make them all comparable.

igneous rock: rock formed from molten state, i.e., lava which spilled on surface or solidified quickly.

Illaenus [trilobites]: opisthoparians were much larger, with smooth pygidia, cephalons and compound eyes that were carried well above rubbish and mud. They probably were crawlers that plowed into bottom only when they were feeding. If pygidium was thrust into mud, it provided leverage for thrusting movements of thorax and cephalon.

illite: group of clay minerals composed of interlayered mica and montmorillonite and intermediate between muscovite and montmorillonite.

ilmenite: mineral, $FeTiO_3$, principal ore of titanium. Sometimes mined from beach and shallow-water sand deposits.

imbricate: overlapping, like shingles, as in scales of fish and reptiles.

impunctate brachiopods: without minute pits.

Inachus dorsettenis [*Maiidae*]: this is not a very common crab. It has larvae occurring in late summer and autumn plankton. Zoea is distinctive with only a dorsal spine on carapace, rostral and lateral spines being absent on telson. There are only two zoeal stages, first being about 2.5 mm. long and second 2.9 mm. Megalopa is smaller, only 1.6 mm. long. It has two large spines near base of rostrum as well as a number of spines on dorsal surface of carapace.

Inadunata [crinoids]: relatively simple crinoids including oldest known members of the class. Plates of calyx are firmly fastened together; tegmen covers mouth and lower food grooves; interradial plates appear on only one side of cup. Arms are uniserial or biserial and nonpinnulate or pinnulate; in most genera they are free above radial plates. Early Ordovician to late Permian.

Inarticulata: class of brachiopods having unhinged valves held together by muscles. Shells which are usually chitino-phosphatic have no teeth or sockets.

inboard [ships]: 1) interior of ship or boat; being within hull or hold. Opposed to outboard, not projecting over the side. 2) ship at sea, on horizon, hull below the line and only the mast showing.

inboard profile [ships]: plan representing a longitudinal section through center of vessel, showing heights of deck, assignment of various spaces and all machinery, etc., located on center or between center and shell on port side.

inch-trim moment: usually abbreviated I.T.M., moment to change a vessel's trim, i.e., to increase or decrease difference in draft at stem from that at stern by 1 in.

incident radiation: direct radiation of sun's energy into water from the sun as opposed to radiation that is reflected; together the two affect the equation for net radiation.

incised: pertaining to steep-sided trench or notch cut into plane surface or slope by current erosion, as sea valley or submarine canyon cut into continental shelf or slope.

incised [*Mollusca*]: sculptured with one or more sharply cut grooves.

inclination: in terrestrial magnetism, angle which total magnetic field vector makes with its horizontal component.

inclining test: that carried out to determine a vessel's *metacentric height* in a test of her initial stability.

inclinometer: instrument used to measure slopes (angles of inclination); used by oceanographers to measure wire angle on cables suspended from ship.

increment lines [molluscs]: faint concentric lines resulting from growth of shell.

independent piece: timber in the stem of wooden vessels.

Indian header: Gloucester fishing schooner, built with round stem, known by name locally to Gloucester and Salem neighborhoods after introduction of this type of stern in late 1890's as first ones built had Indian names.

Indian Ocean: that ocean area bounded on north by southern limits of Arabian Sea, Laccadive Sea, Bay of Bengal, limits of East Indian Archipelago and Great Australian Bight; on east from South East Cape (southern point of Tasmania) down meridian to Antarctic Continent; on west from Cape Agulhas southward to Antarctic Continent.

Indian spring water: approximate mean water level determined from all lower low waters at spring tide. It is also computed plane located below mean sea level by amount equal to sum of amplitudes of harmonic constants.

Indian tide-plane: also termed *harmonic tide-plane*, reference level used on British charts for soundings in coastal areas where diurnal inequality is considerable. It corresponds, very closely, to level of lowest possible low water, or the mean of lower low waters. Thus, charted soundings in such localities indicate, in ordinary conditions, absolute minimum depths of water.

indicator species: species of marine plankton characterized by certain water mass to which it is restricted, so that with proper precautions, its presence can be taken as indication of presence of water of that origin. Species of medusae, chaetognaths, euphausiids, pteropods and tunicates, among others have been shown to be indicator species.

induration: hardening of sediments through cementation, pressure, heat or other processes.

Indus: small southern constellation between *Grus* and *Pavo*. Its brightest star, *a Indi*, of magnitude 3.21, is located in Dec. 47½° S. and S.H.A. 51½°.

inequilateral [*Mollusca*]: with anterior and posterior section of valve dissimilar in shape and size.

inequivalve [*Mollusca*]: pelecypods in which valves are dissimilar in shape or size.

inert gas [diving]: that part of breathing medium that serves as transport for oxygen and is not used by body as life-support agent. Also known as carrier gas or dilutant gas.

inert gas narcosis [diving]: narcotic effect of inert gas on body at elevated partial pressures.

inertia current: currents resulting after cessation of wind in generating area or after water movement has left generating area.

infauna: animals living in and on soft bottom.

inferior: 1) descriptive of a planet less distant from the sun than is the earth; as, *inferior planets Mercury* and *Venus*. 2) of *conjunction* of such when either is on same side of sun as the earth.

influent stream: stream or reach of a stream is influent with respect to ground water if it contributes water to zone of saturation.

infraorbital canal [fish]: sensory canal below orbit.

infrared radiation: electromagnetic radiation of long wavelengths outside the range of normal vision, it includes thermal radiation.

infrared radiometer: instrument that detects and measures infrared radiation. Infrared radiometer on a ship or especially in air can accumulate great amounts of temperature data about large expanses of water.

infrared thermometry: measurement of object's temperature by determination of its infrared radiation. Infrared radiation (including thermal radiation) comprises long wavelengths that lie outside range of normal vision.

inherent vice: in cargo stowage parlance denotes an innate tendency of certain goods to self-damage through spontaneous heating, wasting, rotting, fermentation, etc., with sequential injury to other merchandise stowed in same compartment. Copra, certain nuts and seeds, dyestuffs, onions, molasses, green hemp, and some kinds of bituminous coal are included in goods known to possess this fault. It is the shipper's lawful duty to inform carrier of any knowledge he may possess regarding a particular cargo's *inherent vice* and the treatment such cargo requires, in order to lessen or prevent any damage arising from this source.

injection organ: in certain burrowing polychaetes, such as *Opheliidae*, a muscular sac back of prostomium that withdraws or injects coelomic fluid of head coelom.

injection probe: thermistor installed in ship's sea-water injection intake pipe (engine room).

injection temperature: temperature of seawater as measured at seawater intakes in engine room of ship.

ink sac: in some cephalopods, diverticulum of intestine located near anus. It secretes dark fluid of melanin pigment.

inland sea: sea surrounded by land connected with

ocean or another sea by one or more narrow straits. Examples are Mediterranean and Baltic Seas.

inlet: 1) short, narrow waterway connecting bay or lagoon with sea. When it is a natural inlet maintained by tidal currents, the name tidal inlet or tidal outlet is applied. 2) from earliest times, experienced ship's master was careful to avoid waters in which receding tides might leave his vessel stranded. At least as early as 13th century, an exit or channel of egress took a special name; a very early scroll reports that a vessel spent a period in Dorset "Bi thare see in ore out-lete" (by the sea in an outlet). In a probable reversal of the old word for a way to move the sea, inlet came to mean any narrow opening by which water penetrates land. Though thousands of inlets are now marked on world maps, this special title for "a small arm of the sea" did not appear in writing until about 1570. Earliest known reference insists that in England's County Kent (notorious as a haven for smugglers) "an indraught or inlet of water into the lande" was "a thing yet well knowne."

inner bottom [ships]: tank top.

inner jib [ships]: headsail first formed from fore-topmast staysail.

inner lip [*Gastropoda*]: inner border of aperture; portion adjacent to last whorl and to columella.

inner space: nickname given to area involved in modern marine research, especially in regard to underwater exploration.

inquilinism: special kind of commensalism in which one organism lives with another, usually in digestive tract or respiratory chamber, without being harmful to host.

inshore: 1) region shoreward of certain depth of water, usually either of 3- or 5-fathom isobath. 2) in beach terminology, zone of variable width between shoreface and seaward limit of breaker zone.

inshore currents: movement of water inside surf zone, including longshore rip currents.

insolation: adsorption of solar energy by the ocean.

insonification: penetration of sound into any particular part of sea.

insurance, marine: act of insuring, assuring, or securing against damage or loss to a vessel and/or her cargo and/or freight from causes usually fully specified for a stipulated sum called the *premium;* written contract in which one party called the *insurer, assurer,* or *underwriter,* agrees to indemnify another called the *insured,* or *assured* against loss to subject matter insured in a sum of money agreed upon, if such loss is caused by peril or perils, called the *risk,* enumerated and set forth in such document, known as the *policy.* In laws governing insurance, a person having an *insurable interest* in a marine venture usually is defined as one who would suffer damage, detriment, or prejudice in event of loss insured against.

integument: animal's external covering or layer; especially refers to skin of vertebrates.

intensity: magnetic force, measured in oersteds or gammas, exerted upon a unit magnetic pole located at given point.

interaction: so-termed effect produced in shallow areas by motion of water displaced by moving vessels in close proximity, in which vessels either are drawn toward or repelled from each other. That phase of the phenomenon, or, properly, resultant of forces causing such, which has been rendered more noticeable because of actual collisions attributed thereto, has been called *suction* and may be defined as return of displaced water toward a vessel's stern, both laterally and following her wake. Danger of collision from this cause is present in case of a vessel overtaking another in a narrow channel, because of the indraft which may carry overtaking ship's bows against the quarter of her slower neighbor; and this, generally, is the one real peril that may be assigned to *suction effect.* Where, as vessels meeting in a canal, the laterally displaced water from bows of each tend to throw ships away from each other, combined forces thus brought into action are of but momentary duration and hence seldom have serious results; similarly, the temporary indraft on passing of vessels' sterns usually is effectively countered by the helm.

interarea [*Brachiopoda*]: plane or curved surface between back and hinge line on either valve; distinguished by sharp break in angle from remainder of valve and by absence of costae, plications or coarse growth lines.

intercardinal points: four compass-points, *Northeast, Northwest, Southeast,* and *Southwest;* also called quadrantal or semi-cardinal points, each being halfway between two cardinals; as, Northeast between North and East, etc. Abbreviated *NE, NW, SE, SW.*

intercept: in nautical astronomy, difference between true altitude of a heavenly body, as obtained by sextant observation, and that determined by calculation as occurring at same instant in an assumed position, as by dead reckoning, given the ship. Value of the intercept gives location of point through which may be drawn a *line of position,* at some point on which vessel is located at time of observation.

intercoastal: as used chiefly in U.S. shipping parlance, of, or pertaining to, trade or traffic between domestic ports located in different coastal regions, as that between Atlantic and Pacific ports.

intercostals [ships]: 1) plates which fit between floors to stiffen double bottom of ship. Intercostal comes from Latin words *inter-* meaning between, and *costa*, meaning rib. 2) any girder or other structural unit composed of short members running between and secured to continuous members.

interface: surface separating two media across which there is a discontinuity of some property.

interface unit: electronic complex forming boundary between two systems; such a unit manipulates information from sensors so that it is comparable with computer system it will feed.

intermediate waves: waves under conditions where relative depth (ratio of water depth to wavelength) lies between 0.5 and 0.04.

intermittent stream: stream that flows only part of the time. One that has not cut its valley below water table.

internal waves: waves occurring within a fluid whose density changes with depth, either abruptly at sharp surface discontinuity (interface) or gradually. Their amplitude is greatest at density discontinuity or in case of gradual density change somewhere in the interior of fluid media and not at free upper surface where surface waves have effects.

internasal [reptile]: one or two scales on top of head just behind rostral.

international low water [ILW]: plane of reference below mean sea level (msl) by following amount; half range between mean lower low water (mllw) and mean higher high water (mhhw), multiplied by 1.5.

interparietal [reptile]: single median scale on head behind frontal.

interpolate: to determine an intermediate value, as in use of navigational tables, according to rate or variation indicated in a series; e.g., sine of $40°$ $10'$ being .64501 and that of $40°$ $11'$, .64524; by interpolation, value of sine of $40°$ $10'$ $20'' = .64501 + 20/60 (.64524 - .64501) = .64509$.

interradial: in medusae, portion midway between primary radial (perradial) canals of gastrovascular cavity.

intersecting waves: one of component waves which, when superimposed on others, produces cross swells.

interseptal ridge [Coelenterata]: longitudinal ridge on outer surface of corallite wall. Occurs between position of septa on inner surface.

interspaces [Mollusca]: channels between ribs.

interstitial: 1) in biology, living between spaces or crevices of another substance. 2) in crystalline structure, referring to space between crystal atoms or ions.

interstitial water: water contained in pore space between grains in rock and sediment.

interstitial zone: generally considered to be zone between mean high water and mean low water levels.

intertidal zone: shore area bounded by levels of low and high tide.

intestinal spiral valve: fold in intestine of fish, especially elasmobranchii, which, because of its many spiraled turns, delays passage of food and increases surface area available for it to be absorbed.

intracellular bioluminescence: widespread form of biological light production usually associated with special luminous organism or organs (photophores) or luminous cells which contain photogenic granules. In some organisms intracellular light may be produced by luminous bacteria with special sacs or organs. In all organisms, light emitted is internal below body surface.

intrainment force: motion induced in water in physical contact with region of relatively high velocity.

intramarginals [reptile]: short rows of laminae between plastrals and marginals in turtle shell.

inverse estuary: estuary in which evaporation exceeds land drainage plus precipitations, with resulting mixtures of high salinity estuarine water and seawater.

inversion layer: layer of water in which temperature increases with depth.

invertebrate: any animal without backbone or spinal column.

inverting telescope: as used with a marine sextant, a glass of higher power than the ordinary *direct telescope*. Arrangement of its lenses has for its object sacrifice of a minimum of light, but thus causes objects to appear *inverted*. Although requiring much practice to become proficient in its use, some navigators prefer an inverting glass for all celestial work.

involute [Mollusca]: with last whorl enveloping earlier whorls so that height of aperture is greatest vertical dimension.

ion: atom or group of atoms with net positive or negative electrical charge. Ions frequently appear in solution; solution called an electrolyte can conduct electricity by ionic exchange of charge.

ionic solution: solution containing ions. Ion movements in ionic solution can conduct electricity.

ionosphere: layer of atmosphere beginning about 25 miles above earth's surface and extending outward for over 25 miles. Gaseous particles in this region become electrically charged by various kinds of radiation from sun. Resulting highly variable band of ionized (charged) particles is vitally important to terrestrial communication because it can reflect radio waves back to distant sections of globe.

iridescent seaweed [*Iridophycus*]: number of species of *Iridophycus* are found on beach attached to rocks exposed to heavy surf. Most striking feature is iridescence. When in water *Iridophycus* is brilliantly colored. As light falls from different directions, it exhibits a succession of bright metallic hues of blue-green and purple. It is also characterized by single large, flat blade that is thin with rubberlike texture and bright red to dark purple. Sizes and shapes for this seaweed vary with specimen whose thallus is 3 to 4 in. long to those 6 ft. long, depending upon species.

Irish moss: one of several species of red algae, but particularly *Chondrus crispus,* having short busy form and often forming a carpet on rocks in lower intertidal zone. Carrageen or carragheen is prepared from this algae.

Irish pennant: loose end of line, especially one dangling over side.

Irminger Current: ocean current that is one of terminal branches of Gulf Stream system and part of northern branch of North Atlantic Current; flows west off south coast of Iceland. Small part of Irminger Current turns clockwise around west coast of Iceland but greater amount turns southwest and joins East Greenland Current.

irons [ships]: sailboat is said to be "up in irons" when coming into wind and losing way, unable to fall off on either tack.

irradiance: at point of surface; radiant flux incident on an infinitesimal element of surface containing point under consideration, divided by area of that element. Unit of measurement is watt per square meter (W/m^2).

irradiance ratio: ratio of upward to downward irradiance at a depth in sea.

Isaac-Kidd midwater trawl: device designed to collect actively swimming marine organisms from subsurface ocean layers. Midwater trawl consists essentially of towing bridle, net and inclined plane surface placed in front of net to act as depressor. When streamed the trawl is shaped like an asymmetrical cone with large pentagonal mouth opening on one end and small perforated collecting can on other.

isabelita: an angelfish of good food value found in Caribbean Sea and adjoining waters; about 12 in. in length, brightly colored in orange, blue and golden; has deep compressed body with wide rear dorsal and ventral fins, in profile appearing as pointed spreading wings above and below the tail.

isallotherm: lines connecting points in which equal temperature variation is observed within definite interval.

isanomal: line connecting points of equal variations from normal value.

Ise Fjord fishing boat: Danish craft, similar to "Hornbaek" boat, but with beamier and shallower hull. Used in fishing grounds of Kattegat.

isentropic: of equal or constant entropy with respect to either space or time.

Isherwood system [ships]: method of framing a vessel which employs closely spaced longitudinals, with extra heavy floors spaced further apart.

island arc: occurring in areas of volcanic unrest. On concave side of island arc are rows of volcanoes. On convex side, ocean floor makes sharp down-bend resulting in deep, V-shaped trenches.

isoballast lines: set of lines on submarine bathythermograph chart, starting from set of selected points on temperature scale and passing through all points for which net change in buoyancy, resulting from changes in water temperature and depth, is zero for submarine of given compression.

isobaric surface: surface where pressure is same everywhere.

isobars: curves relating quantities measured at same pressures. Lines drawn on map through places having same atmospheric pressure; as in weather map.

isobath: contour line connecting points of equal depths on chart.

isobathymetric: pertaining to equal depths; especially, deep-sea surroundings.

isobathytherm: line or surface showing depths in oceans or lakes at which points have same temperature. Isobathytherms are usually drawn to show cross sections of water mass.

isobune: rowboat used in fishery and on coast of Japan; about 20 ft. long.

isochasm: line connecting points having same average frequency of auroras.

isochrone: line drawn on chart connecting all points having same time of occurrence of particular phenomenon or of particular value of a quantity, e.g., a line representing all points having same time difference in reception of segments from two radio stations such as master and slave stations of Loran radar.

isoclinic: pertaining to or indicating equal *dip* or *inclination* of the magnetic needle from the horizontal; isoclinal.

isoclinic line: line drawn through all points on earth's surface having same magnetic inclination. Particular isoclinic line drawn through points of zero inclination is given special name of aclinic line.

isodisperse: dispersing in solutions having same pH value.

isodynamic: line connecting points of equal magnitude of any force.

isodynamic lines: lines on magnetic map which

pass through points having equal strengths of earth's magnetic field.

isoelectric point: pH value at which charge of colloid is zero. It may also be considered as pH value at which ionization of ampholyte (an amphoteric electrolyte) is at maximum. It has definite value for each amino acid and protein.

isogal: contour lines of equal values on surface of earth.

isogamous: having gametes that show no obvious differentiation into distinctive male and female gametes. Gametes that look alike.

isogenic line: imaginary line drawn through points on earth's surface where magnetic deviation is equal.

isogonic: pertaining to, or having equal angles.

isohaline: of equal or constant salinity. Line on a chart connecting all points of equal salinity; isopleth of salinity.

isohyet: 1) line drawn through geographical points recording equal amounts of precipitation during given time period or for particular storm. 2) line which connects places with equal average total precipitation.

isolume: theoretical warped plane or level in water connecting points with equal light intensity.

isomegathy: chart showing distribution of sediments in terms of median grain size. Isomegathies are lines connecting points of equal median grain size.

isopach: contour line on chart drawn through points of equal thickness of sedimentary layer.

isopag: line connecting points where ice is present for same number of days per year.

isopectic: line connecting points at which ice begins to form at same time each winter.

isopiestic: term denoting equal or constant pressure.

isopleth: line of equal or constant value of given quantity with respect to either space or time.

isopod: crustacean of order *Isopoda* that includes some 4,000 species such as water slaters, woodlice, sowbugs, pill bugs and many parasites. They lack hard outer skeletons and stalked eyes but do possess oval, usually flattened bodies divided into 7 segments, each with a pair of broad, flat abdominal appendages.

isopor: line sometimes found on magnetic charts showing points of equal annual change.

isopycnic: 1) of equal or constant density, with respect to either space or time; equivalent to iso-

stere. 2) line on chart connecting all points of equal or constant density; isopleth of density.

isopycnic surface: surface of constant density. Particle of water of certain density moves along an isopycnic surface or, if forced away from this surface, will seek to return to it.

isostasy: condition of approximate equilibrium in outer part of earth, such that gravitation effect of masses extending above surface of the geoid in continental areas is approximately counterbalanced by deficiency of density in material beneath those masses, while effect of deficiency of density in ocean waters is counterbalanced by excess of density of material under oceans.

isostatic adjustment: balancing process of earth's surface whereby disparity of levels is equalized, i.e., when meteors hit and dig out a basin, isostatic adjustment tends to restore normal surface.

isostere: line of equal or constant specific volume. It is equivalent to an isopycnic.

isotac: line connecting points at which ice melts at same time each spring.

isotach: line connecting points of equal rates of speed, e.g., flow of currents.

isotherm: line drawn on map through places having same atmospheric temperature at given time.

isothermal: of equal or constant temperature, with respect to either space or time.

isotope: different form of chemical element. Element and its isotope have same atomic number (number of protons or positive electrical charges in the nucleus) but possess different numbers of neutrons or neutral charges in nucleus of atom. Frequently unstable, isotopes tend to stabilize through release of energy or radioactivity.

isotopic species: various animals or plants that live in same locality.

isotropic: having equal properties in all directions or dimensions.

isovelocity: having equal values of sound velocity in all parts of given water column. No change in sound velocity with depth.

isthmus: narrow strip of land, bordered on both sides by water that connects two larger bodies of land.

isthmus [fish]: ventral part of throat and breast between gill opening.

Italian lateener: this type could be called a lateen-rigged yawl with square maintopsail. Single broad jib is carried to a spike bowsprit. Hull has low transom stem with sheer line rising to higher bow having curved stem.

J

J: in International Code is called the *semaphore flag* which, hoisted either singly or inferior to a group of signal letters, signifies *"I am going to send a message by semaphore."* It is kept flying while message is being made and hauled down on completion of message.

jack: 1) name applied to common seaman or sailor. 2) small flag used as signal or to designate nationality. 3) union jack (flag). 4) large family of warm water fishes represented in United States by over 30 species found off Atlantic and Pacific coasts. Most members of the family have two separate dorsal fins, although in some species spiny dorsal is close to soft-rayed portion and in other species it is reduced to small separate spines. Posterior dorsal and anal fins are low and long, after reaching to tail fin. Some species have unique keel along posterior part of lateral line, strengthening narrow tail. The family includes many popular game and food fishes: amberjack, crevalle jack, rudderfish, pompano. 5) device for raising heavy weights, as by turning or pumping a lever by hand; a screw jack or hydraulic jack. 6) Newfoundland fishing schooner of 15 to 20 tons and full body build; of simple rig, rarely carries more than one headsail, sometimes a maintopmast staysail; now nearly obsolete, was once called a *jackass*. 7) one of a pair of bars, usually of iron, at topgallant masthead for spreading royalmast shrouds; also, *jack crosstrees*.

jackass: 1) a plug for a mooring- or hawsepipe. 2) kind of fishing schooner. 3) combining term connoting, often derisively, an extraordinary departure from a particular class or rig; as, jackass brig; jackass rig.

jack, crevalle: small fish weighing less than 10 lbs. and with more compact body than amberjack and high sloping forehead; pectoral fins are long and gracefully tapering. It is golden yellow with lavender tint to silvery side. The jack occurs in schools along Atlantic Coast north to Cape Cod.

jack ladder [ships]: ladder with wooden steps and side ropes.

jackmariddle: the chiro or tenpounder; or any closely allied fish.

jack staff [ships]: forward flagstaff or bow staff which carries the jack when flown.

jackstay [ships]: rod along top of a yard to which sails are bent.

Jacob's ladder [ships]: ship's ladder generally made of rope with wooden rungs, which hangs over side.

jaegers: large dark-colored birds, with some resemblance to immature gulls but characterized by stout, hooked beaks. Upper mandible is sharply curved downward at tip and basal portion is covered by separate horny plate (cere), front of which partly overhangs nostrils. Wings and legs are long; webbed feet rather stout. Jaegers in America have rather long wedge-shaped tails, two central feathers being elongated in the adult.

jaegt: Norwegian craft of former days used in coastwise trade. Single-masted, with a course and small topsail; course was reefed by means of bonnets along front. Foretopsail was sometimes used. Hull was heavy, beamy and of generous sheer. Pole mast was stayed by 4 shrouds on each side.

jalor: open, double-endless, keelless dugout canoe of Jahore. Used by natives for fishing with small net. Long raking ends; bottom curved up at each end; sharp floor; moderate sheer. Average length about 20 ft. with 1/5 the beam.

Jamaica sloop: sharp-modeled sloop developed in Jamaica, West Indies, popular previous to 1700. It had much dead rise, raking stem and sternpost, low freeboard and was very fast. The mast raked aft considerably.

Jamie Green: sail on clipper ships, set beneath bowsprit and jibboom. It was used mainly when sailing to windward. Halyard hauled sail to end of jibboom and tack led to lower end of martingale boom or dolphin striker. It was sheeted by means of a pendant to fore-rigging and a whip to forecastle head. It was cut the same as topgallant studding sail, but was longer on hoist.

jangada: raftlike boat or catamaran which is used in certain parts of South America, mainly Brazil and Peru. Natives around Bahia, Brazil, employ the jangada for offshore fishing.

Jansen Clause: in a marine insurance policy, stipulates agreement is "free of particular average on ship under 3 per centum, whether stranded, sunk, or burned"; i.e., shipowner must bear first 3 per centum of loss claimed.

Japan Current: north and northeast flowing current offshore from Japan, also called Kuroshio Current.

Javanese prau: native outrigger sailing craft, or "prau" of island of Java, rigged similarly to "Madura prau" except that tack of foresail is supported by a bowsprit. Hull is generally built of teak, double-ended with little sheer, strong rake to stern and less to sternpost, from which rudder is hung.

Jaxea nocturna [*Thalassinidea*]: larva is type of zoea called a trachelifer. It has an unmistakably slender appearance due to great length of region immediately behind eyes. Rostrum is small, telson lacks median spine; there are only two maxillipeds in first larva and third develops later. There are 6 larval stages, each of which is not uncommon in inshore plankton.

jellyfish: 1) jellyfish of all species have certain characteristics in common: generally umbrella-shaped, transparent and tentacled. They belong to classes *Scyphozoa* and *Hydrozoa* of phylum *Cnidaria*. They are best known for tentacles which trail below jellyfish, are numbered in the dozens and are armed with stinging cells. Tentacles enable jellyfish to capture small animals for food. In some colonial hydrozoans, e.g., Portuguese man-of-war, these stings are powerful enough to paralyze a man, at least temporarily. A marine invertebrate, the jellyfish is related to coral polyps and sea anemone; most species pass through medusa and hydroid (or polyp) stage. 2) any various free-swimming coelenterates having disc or bell-shaped body of jellylike consistency. Many have long tentacles with nematocysts (stinging cells). Some are capable of producing flowing ball luminescence.

Jessor boat: rowing or paddling boat built of teak, used for fishing and other purposes in vicinity of Jessor on Bengal Coast, India. It is carvel-built, planks being fastened together with staples clenched over opposite side.

jetsam: goods or cargo thrown overboard, or jettisoned, to lighten a vessel in distress, or otherwise for safety of ship and cargo; often applied specifially to such goods when washed ashore.

jet stream: narrow band of very strong westerly winds at high levels in middle latitudes. Usually at heights of 30,000 to 40,000 ft.

jettison [ships]: throwing overboard of objects, especially to lighten a craft in distress. Jettisoned objects that float are termed flotsams; those that sink, jetsam.

jetty: structure such as a wharf or pier, so located as to influence current or project the entrance to harbor or river. Jetty extending into sea to protect coast from erosion is called a groin.

jewfish: also known as black grouper, a tropical fish ranging northwest into Florida waters. This clumsy but harmless giant is mottled black and has very large head. Average individual weighs about 50 lbs. Jewfish live along rocky shores and under wharves feeding on smaller fishes.

jib [ships]: 1) triangular sail extending forward from foremast to bowsprit or extension of bowsprit. 2) triangular headsail. 3) triangular fore-and-aft sail set upon a stay extending from foremast to jibboom.

jibboom [ships]: spar extending beyond bowsprit to take outer headsails. Also spar or boom bent to foot of jib.

jibe: to bring wind from one side of sailboat to the other from astern. Opposite of tacking.

jib hanks [ships]: rings that secure jib to a stay so that it may freely travel on the stay.

jib-headed rig [ships]: rig in which all sails are triangular.

jib-o-jib [ships]: jib set on fore-topgallant or fore-royal stay. Sometimes set as a jib topsail.

jibstay [ships]: stay (a heavy rope, today usually of wire) that supports the jib, a triangular sail between a ship's bowsprit and the foremast mast.

jib-topsail [ships]: jib set on outer head stay, tack being well above bowsprit or jibboom; usually smaller than other headsails.

jig: fishing device with one or more hooks that, as it is drawn through water, serves as spinning bright lure to attract fish.

jigger: fishing schooner of Massachusetts developed from "chebacco boat," but carrying bowsprit and jib. First known about 1820 and later called "pink" or "pinky." Length ranged from 40 to 50 ft.

jigging: 1) act of taking fish with a jig or jigger. 2) taking short pulls or *swaying up* on a rope or tackle fall.

jingle shell: one of family (*Anomiidae*) of rounded bivalves with asymmetrical, thin almost transparent valves. Individuals are attached to firm surfaces by calcified byssus projecting through hole in lower smaller valve. These organisms are abundant foulers in some regions.

joggle [ships]: to lap a joint by keeping one edge straight and bending the other, in order to leave both surfaces even on one side.

Jog-log: towed electrode that can detect ocean electric current induced by magnetic disturbance.

john doree: food fish of European coasts, *Zeus faber* of the family Zeidae, usually called *John Dory* in England, of bright yellow or golden color with silvery reflections, having a dark spot on each side; oval in profile, its compressed body about 10 inches in length, has long spiny appendages on dorsal fin and an extended ventral fin, with upper and lower fringing anterior to tail.

joint chasms: deep indentations formed along coasts where joints have been quarried out by waves.

jolly balance: very delicate spring balance used to determine densities by method of weighing in water and in air; determines specific gravity of minerals.

jolly boat: boat similar to dinghy; also workboat carried by merchantman, usually at stern of schooner.

journal [ships]: that portion of shaft or other revolving member which transmits weight directly to and is in immediate contact with the bearing in which it turns.

jugum [*Brachiopoda*]: simple or complex skeletal connection between right and left halves of the brachidium.

jumping the ship [ships]: deserting the ship before completion of voyage.

junk: sailing vessel used through ages by Chinese and other Mongolian people for trading, transportation of goods and humans, fishing, warfare, pirating, etc. Even today it is common on eastern seas and rivers. Though ungainly in appearance, it is remarkably seaworthy. Junks are carvel- or clinker-built, or combination of both; round or flat-bottomed and frequently keelless.

Jupiter: largest planet and fifth of major planets in order from the sun and next to Venus in brightness. Its mean distance from sun is 483,327,000 statute mi. and completes one revolution in its orbit in 11.86 yrs.; has an equatorial diameter of 88,698 mi. and polar diameter of 82,789 mi., angular diameter attaining a maximum of 45″ at its closest approach to the earth; and inclination of its orbit to ecliptic is 1°18′21″, showing its range of declination closely approximates that of the sun. The planet is attended by at least 8 moons or satellites and, for 4 of these, their eclipses by the parent body are timed to the nearest tenth of a minute in the *Nautical Almanac*, thus often presenting a handy means, with a good ship's telescope, of obtaining a check on chronometer time.

Jurassic: period of Mesozoic era characterized by appearance of first birds.

jury [ships]: term applied to temporary structures, such as masts, rudders, etc., used in an emergency.

jury rig [ships]: temporary rig set up when permanent masts have been disabled or carried away in a storm.

jutty: structure projecting from a shore, river bank, breastwork, etc.; as, a mole, small wharf, or revetment; a jetty.

juvenile: coming to surface for first time; fresh, new in origin; applied chiefly to gases and waters.

juvenile water: water which enters hydrological cycle for very first time, coming directly from magma inside earth.

juvenile wave platform: shoal near shore bottom consisting of rock, jagged reefs, cobbles and boulders and having little material easily movable by waves. It represents stage before planation by wave erosion.

K

K: 1) denotes, as a single-letter flag hoist or Morse code flashing signal, in International Code: *"You should stop your vessel instantly."* **2)** in lower case letter, abbreviation for *knots* in expressing speed of vessel; as, *14 k.*

kaep: outrigger sailing canoe of Palau Archipelago, which lies eastward of Mindanau, Philippine Islands.

kaiki: small sailing craft of Greece, high-ended of great sheer and having very little freeboard amidships, necessitating use of weather cloths. Single lateen sail and jib set to steered bowsprit comprise the rig. It is generally steered with oar or paddle.

Kakap Jeram: fishing canoe of Malayan east coast and Selanger. Stem and sternpost are high and ornamented with considerable rake. Single lugsail carried.

kambou: an edible brown seaweed gathered and used extensively on Japanese and northern neighboring coasts and islands.

kames: mounds of stratified drift deposited by glacial meltwater.

karyotic: having nucleated cells.

katabatic wind: any wind blowing down an incline. If wind is warm it is called a foehn; if cold, it may be a fall wind or gravity wind.

kawasaki: flat-bottomed, keelless sailing boat with long sharp bow, used in trawl-line cod fishery of northern Japan. Average size is about 40 ft. in length, with ¼ the beam.

kayak: skin canoe with single manhole used extensively by Eskimos of Arctic regions of North America. It is made by covering a light wooden frame with skin sewed together with sinews and stretched while "green."

kealema: very heavy surf breaking on Guinea Coast of Africa during winter.

kedge [ships]: to move by being pulled along with aid of an anchor. In the process, the kedge anchor is taken some distance away in small boat and dropped overboard. Then ship's crew haul on the hawser and in so doing move the ship. It is extremely slow procedure, but is used sometimes in emergencies.

keel [ships]: **1)** longitudinal timber or built-up timbers, extending along center line of bottom, which forms backbone of the hull of a vessel and from which rise frames, or ribs, stem and sternpost. **2)** flat-bottomed, sailing cargo barge of Durham and Yorkshire, England, used mostly for inland navigation. Hull is blunt, bow and stern alike with low freeboard and outboard rudder. **3)** in *Foraminifera*, keel-like ridge on outer margin of test. **4)** in *Mollusca*, a carina, or outstanding rib usually marking abrupt change of slope in shell outline.

keel blocks [ships]: blocks on which keel of vessel rests when being built, or when in dry dock.

keel bracket [ships]: bracket, usually triangular plate, connecting vertical keel and flat keel plates between frames or floors of ship.

keel-docking [ships]: in dry-docking, weight of ship is carried almost entirely on keel and bilge blocks. Keel and keelson provide means of distributing pressure on center line and docking keels composed of doubling strips of plate or built up girders are sometimes fitted on bottom at a distance from center line corresponding to best position for bilge block. Docking keels are fitted in fore-and-aft direction, generally parallel or nearly so to keel.

keelhauling [ships]: means of punishing or inflicting injury by tying victim to ropes and then pulling or "hauling" him under ship's keel from bow to stern.

keel rider [ships]: plate running along top of floors and connecting to vertical keel.

keelson [ships]: large I-beam placed above vertical keel in rider plate for reinforcing the keel. Term may be also applied to bottom fore-and-aft girders on sides or at bilge.

keep: 1) combining verb usually confined to expressions concerned with sailing or maneuvering, in the sense of to place in, maintain, and/or continue in a position or course of action indicated. **2)** a term for a protecting cover, as that fitted for a deck instrument, such as a telegraph, sounding-machine, binnacle, etc.

keeper: any locking or securing device; as, a locknut; sliding link on a slip or pelican hook; small lug or plate for securing a compass-bowl in its gimbals; mousing on a hook; key-pin; etc.

keg: small cask of about 10 gal. capacity.

kelp: 1) one of order *Laminariales* usually large blade-shaped or vinelike brown algae. Representing species are the giant kelp *(Macrocystis pyrifera)*, bull kelp *(Nereocystis luetkeana* or *Durvillea antarctica)*, elk kelp *(Pelagophycus porra)* and laminarian (species of *Laminaria*). 2) general name for large seaweed. Kelp typically grows on rock or stony bottoms. Brown algae of order *Laminariales*, including largest known algae. Kelp typically grows to greater size in cold waters, with lengths as great as 100 ft. and blades 4 or more feet wide.

Kelvin temperature scale: absolute temperature scale independent of thermometric properties of working substance. For convenience Kelvin degree is identified with Celsius degree (0° K = 273.16° C). Therefore the ice point on Kelvin scale is 273.16° K.

Kelvin wave: in oceanography/oceanology, tidal system in which tidal range is increased on right-hand side of narrow channel and decreased on left-hand side in Northern Hemisphere, if progressive wave is traveling in the direction observer is facing.

kentledge [ships]: pig iron used either as temporary weight for inclining a vessel or as permanent ballast.

Kepler's Laws: three laws to which the planets adhere in their orbital motion, discovered by Johannes Kepler, German astronomer (1571-1630), viz.: 1) orbit of each planet is an ellipse having the sun in one of its foci. 2) radius vector of each planet sweeps over equal areas in equal times. 3) squares of periodic times of planets vary as cubes of their mean distances from the sun.

ketch: literally, "ship" with foremast. Modern ketch is fore-and-aft rigged, with mainmast forward and shorter mizzenmast stepped ahead of the helmsman.

kettle bottom [ships]: vessel with unusual depth, considerable tumble home, making less beam on deck, full bow, little sheer, heavy square stern and long flat floor.

kettle holes: 1) when kames occur in groups, depressions between them are called kettles. Term kettle or kettle hole is also applied to circular depressions found in terminal moraines and outwash plains. Kettles are formed when moraine or outwash deposits surround and bury large blocks of ice left by slight glacial recession. When blocks melt they leave the kettle hole. 2) sometimes a block of stagnant ice becomes isolated from receding glacier during wastage and is partially or completely buried in till or outwash before it finally melts. When it disappears it leaves a kettle, a pit or depression in the drift.

kettle topography: as glacier ice wastes away, remaining topography of irregular knobs and hollows is called kettle topography. Hollows are kettle holes formed when ice block had been partially or completely buried.

key: low island or reef.

kick: first outward sweep or throw of a vessel's stern from her line of advance upon putting helm hard over. As ship settles down to her *turning circle*, angle her keel makes with line of advance decreases to a constant *angle of drift,* or that which keel makes with tangent to turning circle.

kid [ships]: small tub or vessel in which sailors receive food.

kidney [*Mollusca*]: excretory organ, it filters metabolic wastes, etc., from body fluids. Typically one or more pairs, one pair on either side of body cavity.

Kiffa Australia; Kiffa Borealis: the two navigational stars in *Libra,* respectively catalogued as a^2 *Librae and* β Librae, of magnitudes 2.9 and 2.7 a^2 Librae, or *Kiffa Australis,* a binary star, lies nearly in a line drawn from the bright star *Spica (a Virginis)* to northernmost one (β *Scorpii*) in the handle of the "Chain-hook," or *Scorpio,* a little more than halfway toward the latter. β Librae, or *Kiffa Borealis,* is located about 9° N.N.E. of his companion and a line joining the two forms base of a neat isosceles triangle having its apex at β *Scorpii to the S.E.*

kill: to suppress, or deprive of an active quality; as, to *kill the sea,* or cause heavy waves to subside as by a heavy rainfall or by storm-oil slowly poured from ship's wastepipes, etc. A vessel's way, or speed, is said to be *killed* by presence of thick barnacle-growth on her bottom; by a heavy head sea; by much top hamper, as that in a steamer against a head wind; by steaming through oozy bottom, as in the Rio de la Plata estuary; by heavy cables often attached to drags, as when launching; etc.

killer whale: largest member (Orcinus orca) of dolphin family (Delphinidae) having worldwide distribution. It is the most voracious and spectacular member of the family. It is usually black-olive and white below, marked by white spot behind eye. Many reach a length of 30 ft. or more and weigh over a ton. Its dorsal fin may be as high as 10 ft.; largest number of teeth found in any mammal. Killer whales prey on seals, walruses, seabirds and other whales, in addition to standard diet of fish, squid, etc. They travel in schools.

killifish [*Cyprinodontidae*]: fishes of this family have somewhat elongated bodies, compressed posteriorly. Head is considerably depressed; cycloid scales are rather large; lateral line is very imperfect; mouth is small. Lower jaw is projecting and upper jaw protractile in all American species; teeth are in the jaws and sometimes on the vomer. Gill membranes are free from isthmus; gill rakers are short; branchiostegal rays number 4 to 6; pseudobranchiae are not developed. Dorsal fin, composed of soft rays, is single and usually inserted far back; caudal fin is not forked; ventral fins are inserted on abdomen. Air bladder is sometimes absent.

killifish, banded: silvery species with dark vertical stripes; average is only 2 or 3 in. in length. It lives in quiet bays as well as streams of central and eastern U.S.

killifish, black stripe topminnow: about 2 in. long, it is a colorful member of the family, inhabiting quiet lakes and ponds of central U.S. It is yellowish with silvery belly and sides marked by conspicuous dark brown stripe extending from mouth to tail.

killifish, common: small fish under 5 in. long, but surprisingly voracious for its size. It lives in weedy and muddy ponds from New England to Gulf of Mexico. Females are brownish-green with lighter sides and underparts; males are silvery on sides with yellowish belly and fins. Both sexes are marked by narrow vertical bars. This is a hardy species capable of surviving in stagnant and polluted water; like carp, it buries itself in mud for winter.

killifish, diamond [*Adinia xenica*]: small, compressed fish, somewhat diamond-shaped in profile. Anal fin rays 11 to 12; scale rows about 25; body compressed. Head pointed, mouth small, teeth all pointed, small and arranged in bands; livery-green, little minnow with numerous pearly vertical bars on sides.

killifish, Florida gold-spotted [*Floridichthys carpio carpio*]: chubby little fish with yellowish or orange spots on sides. No lateral line; anterior margin of dorsal fin in front of anterior margin of anal fin; scales along sides about 24. Body compressed; back rather arched; head large. Color silvery to olive with golden or orange spots or blotches on the sides except in young individuals.

killifish, Gulf [*Fundulus grandis grandis*]: heavyset, freckled little fish with small mouth. No lateral line; scale rows along side 33 to 36; freckled pattern; dorsal rays 11. Body thick-set, short and deep; head short and blunt, broad and flat on top. Lower jaw projecting beyond upper; teeth pointed in several series; eye moderate. Dorsal color olivaceous to dull dark green, pale to yellowish-orange below. Most scales have little spots or light centers which give the fish a freckled appearance.

killifish, Lake Eustis Sheepshead [*Cyprinodon hubbsi*]: laterally compressed little fish about an inch long. Anal fin rays 11; scale rows about 25; body slightly compressed, not deep; back not strongly arched. Teeth in single series, wedge-shaped with two notches in each, making them

trifid. Color pale with about 8 vertical dark olivaceous bars on sides.

killifish, least [*Heterandria formosa*]: tiniest of fishes, with a spot on the dorsal fin. Scales along side 24 to 28; anal rays 6 to 0; anterior margin of anal fin below or slightly in advance or origin of dorsal fin. Body short, slightly compressed; back slightly arched; teeth small and pointed, in single series. Ground color olive-brown with darker stripe down each side and traces of vertical bars superimposed on dark lateral stripe; dark spot on dorsal fin of males, and on dorsal and anal fins of females. Maximum size about 1 inch.

killifish, long-nosed [*Fundulus similis*]: greenish, rather heavy-bodied little fish with indistinct vertical bars on side and long nose. No lateral line; about 33 scales along side; dorsal rays 11 to 13. Body oblong, little arched and a little compressed; head somewhat elongate and narrow; mouth small, terminal; teeth tiny, pointed, arranged in several series. Olive-green above; pale to bronze-colored below; about 10 to 15 indistinct narrow vertical bars on sides. Length up to 6 in.

killifish, ocellated [*Leptolucania ommata*]: tiny, greenish fish with dark, eyelike spot on base of tail. Anal rays 9 to 10; scale rows 26 to 28; teeth pointed. Body fusiform, slender, slightly compressed; head moderate; mouth very small. Cleft almost vertical; teeth very tiny, pointed and arranged in a single row. Greenish to straw-colored fish with dark ocellus on base of tail.

killifish, rainwater [*Lucania parva*]: small, insipid looking fish 1 or 2 in. long. Anal fin rays 9 to 10; dorsal fin rays 10 to 12; scales along side 25 or 26; body compressed; back somewhat arched; head narrow, compressed, tapering to vertically rounded snout. Mouth small; teeth pointed. Color grayish with each scale marginal with darker pigment.

killifish, red-finned [*Lucania goodei*]: tiny fish with dark stripe along side from eye to tail. Scale rows along side 29 to 32; dorsal rays 9; origin of dorsal fin well in advance of origin of anal fin. Body tiny, rather elongate, not strongly compressed; base of caudal fin red in life in males.

killifish, southern common [*Fundulus heteroclitus heteroclitus*]: heavy-set, speckled little fish with small mouth. No lateral line; scale rows along side 35 to 38; dorsal fin rays 11. Body thick-set, short and deep; head short and blunt, broad and flat on top. Dorsal color olivaceous to dull dark green, pale to yellowish-orange below. Most of scales have light spots or light centers, which gives the fish a freckled appearance.

killifish, southern sheepshead [*Cyprinodon variegatus variegatus*]: small chunky, strongly compressed fish with mottled pattern. Dorsal fin with 11 rays; anal fin with 10 rays. Body strongly compressed; back strongly arched on profile;

head rather small; teeth in single series, wedge-shaped with two notches in each, which makes them three-pronged. Greenish or bluish-gray, often with vertical blotches on the sides; brassy orange about head and often with orange shading on sides.

killifish, spotfin [*Fundulus confluentus confluentus*]: fish 3 or 4 in. long. No lateral line; scales along side about 35 to 37; dorsal fin with 10 to 11 rays; often eyelike spot on posterior margin of dorsal fin. Body moderately slender, not compressed; head short and relatively narrow. Olive-brownish above, pale yellowish to golden below; usually with about 15 dark, narrow vertical bars on each side.

killifish, striped: larger fish, up to 8 in. long, is found in bays and river mouths along Atlantic Coast from southern New England to Florida. This species reveals a difference in appearance of sexes: in male belly and fins are yellow and sides are vertically barred and in female underparts are more silvery and sides are marked by longitudinal stripes.

killifish, striped [*Fundulus majalis*]: rather heavy-bodied fish with narrow bars on sides. No lateral line; about 36 scales along side; dorsal fin ray 12. Body oblong, little arched and little compressed; mouth small, terminal and oblique. Color olivaceous above, pale to yellowish-orange below, with either 12 narrow vertical bars on sides or 1 or 2 narrow horizontal stripes along sides. Length up to about 6 in.

kilo: prefix denoting 1,000; used in metric system.

kilometer: unit of distance measurement in metric system equal to 0.62 statute mile or 0.54 nautical mile. Statute mile equals 1.61 kilometers; nautical mile equals 1.85 kilometers.

kinetosome: small body or basal granules underlying cilium or flagellum and capable of self-reproduction; may be involved in controlling motion of flagellum or cilium.

kingfish, California [white croaker]: found from San Francisco southward. It is a small silvery-brown fish with yellowish fins and oblique wavy markings on upper sides.

kingfish, Northern [whiting]: elongated fish with gray and silver coloring, marked by irregular oblique bars on upper sides; spiny dorsal fin is higher than soft-rayed dorsal. Conspicuous barbel hangs from chin and tail fin has S-shaped margin. Kingfish is of modest size usually 12 to 17 in. long and weighs about 3 lbs. It is unusual in having no air bladder and in being very sensitive to weather changes.

kingfish, Southern: silvery-gray and white, lacking prolonged dorsal spines of its northern relative. This species is same size as northern whiting and is most common south of Chesapeake Bay.

king plank [ships]: center plank of deck.

king posts [ships]: main center pillar posts of ship. May be used as synonym for samson post.

King's cutter: bluff-bowed, cutter-rigged vessel used in Revenue Service of England during late 18th and early 19th centuries. Rigged with fore-and-aft mainsail, two square topsails, staysail and jib.

king spoke [ships]: when rudder is exactly amidships, upper spoke of wheel is usually scored or wrapped with something to make it readily identifiable for steering in the dark.

Kirklandia jellyfish: hydrozoan jellyfish of early Cretaceous age from Texas. Crucimedusina from the Pennsylvanian of Nebraska had a quadrangular body that was bluntly parallel.

kittiwake: 1) the kittiwake-gull, or white gull. 2) the red-legged kittiwake.

kluge line [diving]: auxiliary gas line used in conjunction with a pneumofathometer for diver depth measurement.

kneaded gravel: gravel or conglomerate transported by mud flows.

knee [ships]: 1) plate connecting a boat's supporting structures where they join at right angles. 2) timber with right-angled grain used to connect hull frames with deck beams.

kneophoplankton: plankton found between 30 and 500 meters depth.

knightheads [ships]: upright timbers found inside and on either side of stem; bowsprit sets between them.

knobby snail shell [*Aplodonidae*]: these snails produce somewhat flat, top-shaped shell in which whorls are grooved and covered with tubercles. Columella in this family terminates in a tooth; small narrow umbilicus is also present. This family is a small group of less than 10 species all of which live in warm water.

knobby snail shell [*Aplodon tectus*]: this knobby snail is top-shaped in outline and exhibits a small, depressed spire covered with spiral lines and rounded tubercles. Columella bears a tooth which projects into aperture. Shell is whitish and spotted with brown. It reaches a length of about 1 inch.

knockabout: sloop or schooner having no bowsprit.

knoll: elevation rising less than 500 fathoms (100 meters) from sea floor and of limited extent across the summit.

knorr: large Viking ship, essentially sailing ship, but oars were also used. Used in ocean trading and overseas warfare. Some were capable of carrying 150 men.

knot: division of log line, so called from series of pieces of string stuck through strands and knotted at equal distance on the line, being the space between any consecutive two of such knots. Also a unit of speed, not of distance, equivalent to 1 nautical mile per hour (6080.2 ft. per hour). One knot is equal to a velocity of 1.689 per second.

knuckle [ships]: abrupt change in direction of plating, frames, keel, deck or other structure of vessel. Most frequently used with reference to lines at apex of angle dividing upper and lower part of stern or counter.

knuckle line [ships]: line on stern of ship, on cant frames, which divides upper and lower parts of stern.

Kochab: star β *Ursae Minoris,* one of the *Guards* in *Ursa Minor* or "Little Dipper." Of magnitude 2.2, is nearest bright star to *Polaris* (North Star), which marks tail end of the group. It lies 16½° from *Polaris.*

koff: similar to "galliot" but having no leeboards. Either schooner or ketch-rigged.

koff-tjalk: "koff" with leeboards.

Kogia: genus of sperm whales belonging to subfamily *Physeterinae;* commonly called *pygmy sperm whale* or *pygmy cachalot.* Has from 9 to 12 lower teeth and 2 upper teeth, if any; is from 8 to 12 ft. in length; has a head of more moderate proportions than his 60-ft. cousin; and is found in warmer southern seas.

koleh: Malay racing canoe, *koleh* being the Malayan term for canoe. Hull is narrow in proportion to length and transversely the second is V-shaped with round flaring sides. Smaller canoes are about 18 ft. long, while larger ones range up to 45 ft. They are extremely fast, but they cannot come about.

kolek: seagoing canoe of Singapore with odd-shaped spritsail and jib. It is double-ended with outboard rudder. If a forward "hornbill" projection is used, the natives call the type a "parahu buaya." Half-decked kolek is a "katop luan."

k₁ constituent: lunisolar diurnal constituent of theoretical tide-producing forces.

Kornephorus: β *Herculis,* star of magnitude 2.8 in constellation *Hercules.* It may be located at 10° to southeast of *Alphacca,* brightest star in *Corona Borealis,* the Northern Crown.

kort nozzle: named for its originator, a cylindrical-shaped "shroud" or tunnel built to encase the propeller in shallow-draft vessels, *especially* those encountering a high slip ratio, as towboats and steam trawlers. Has advantage of allowing a larger disc diameter of screw in such vessels, thus generally producing greater efficiency because of confining effect on the thrust column by such means. Experiments have shown average merchant ship would benefit little more than 1% by this sleeve or nozzle, while smaller hard-working craft, principally tugs, have shown increase of propeller efficiency up to 15% when so fitted.

kotia: two-masted Indian dhow of Malabar coast. Large lateen mainsail is carried on forward raked mast stepped amidships; also a small lateen mizzen and triangular jib. Distinctive mark of all kotias is parrot beak at stem head.

kreng: remains of a whale after baleen, blubber, oil, and all commercial products are removed; also, *crang; krang.*

krill: 1) Norwegian name for principal food of whalebone whales; planktonic creatures. *Euphausiacea.* 2) shoals of *Euphausiidae,* which serve as whale food; in antarctic waters especially, red *Euphausia superba.*

k₂ constituent: lunisolar semidiurnal constituent of theoretical tide-producing forces.

Kullenberg corer: coring device (piston or gravity fall) used to obtain 2-in. diameter core samples. Sampler consists of weight stand on which removable weights can be placed, core barrel (generally of 12-ft. lengths), core cutter, core catcher and tripping arm if used with piston.

Kuroshio Current: 1) fast ocean current (2 to 4 knots) flowing northeastward from Taiwan to Ryukya Islands and close to coast of Japan to about 150° E. The Kuroshio originates from greater part of North Equatorial Current, which divides east of Philippines. Beyond 150° E, it widens to form slower moving North Pacific Current. 2) major warm northeasterly current off shores of Japan, sometimes termed Japan's Current. Counterpart of Gulf Stream in western Pacific. It flows north.

Kuroshio extension: general term for warm eastward transitional flow that connects Kuroshio and North Pacific Current.

Kuroshio system: system of ocean currents which includes part of North Equatorial Current, Tsushima Current and Kuroshio about the Kuroshio extension.

kurran kahn: type of small, open fishing boat off coast of Lithuania, named for the net it operates; "kahn" means boat.

K value: reciprocal of difference between coefficient of thermal expansion of mercury and that of the type of glass used in thermometers.

kymatology: science of waves and wave motion.

L

L: 1) as an International Code signal, flag *L*, hoisted singly, or flashed by Morse Code (· — · ·), denotes *"You should stop. I have something important to communicate."* 2) in logbooks and weather recording, capital *L* usually signifies *long, rolling sea* and sometimes *latitude;* a small *l* = lightning. 3) abbreviation on charts for *lake, loch, or lough.* 4) on board ship denotes *lower,* as in *L.H.* (lower hold); *L.T.D.* (lower 'tween deck); *L.M.R.* (lower mail room). 5) in load line marks for timber-carrying ships, as in *L.F.; L.S.; L.T.; L.W.*

labial grooves [fish]: narrow grooves extending anteriorly from each corner of the mouth in some sharks.

labials [reptiles]: upper and lower scales bordering jaw.

labor [ships]: vessel labors in high seas when headway is slow and pitches and rolls excessively.

Labrador Current: current that flows southward from Baffin Bay, through Davis Strait, and southeastward along Labrador and Newfoundland coasts. East of Grand Banks of Newfoundland the Labrador Current meets Gulf Stream and the two flow eastward as North Atlantic Current.

Labridae: large family of spiny-finned fishes comprising the *wrasses,* of which the *cunner* and *tautog* are American species. Usually ranging from 10 to 15 in. in length, often brilliantly colored, and generally a good food fish, many species are found in tropical Pacific and Indian Oceans, but probably best typified in genus *Labrus* comprising the European wrasses.

labrum: fleshy upper lip of mouth in insects and in some barnacles.

Lacazella mediterranea: small living brachiopod with very thick shell. It has no pedicle, but is found cemented to other shells by its ventral umbo. Long and narrow delthyrium occupies middle of a large interarea and is completely closed, not by a pair of plates, but by a single one (deltidium).

Laccadive Islands canoe: crude dugout canoe used in lagoons of Laccadive Islands, which lie west of India in Indian Ocean. Large settee sail is used on mast which rakes forward strongly and is stepped amidships.

Lacerta: constellation in the *Milky Way,* north of *Pegasus.* It contains no navigational stars, brightest being of 4th magnitude.

lacustrine: produced by or belonging to lakes.

lacrustrine planes: lake plains, formed by emergence of lake floor by either uplift or drainage.

ladder network: transmission network constructed from number of equal symmetrical filter elements.

Laevicardium crassum [eulamellibranch]: larva of this species is large, but the valves are not so convex and are truncated posteriorly. Smallest veliger is 200γ, reaching 450γ in length at metamorphosis. Common in spring and summer plankton.

lagan: jettisoned goods or cargo sunk at sea and marked by a buoy for subsequent recovery; also *ligan.*

lagging of the tide: periodic retardation in time occurrence of high and low water due to changes in relative positions of moon and sun. Opposite effect is called priming of the tides.

lag gravel: residual accumulations of coarse particles for which fine material has been winnowed by currents unable to move the coarse material.

lagoon: 1) area of quiet, shallow water between a bar and mainland. Shallow sound, pond or lake, generally separated from open sea. 2) *lacuna,* early Latin term for a pool of fresh- or saltwater passed into Spanish as *laguna.* Adopted by French sailors as *lagune,* the word gradually came to be reserved for area of salt or brackish water separated from the sea by low banks. Such areas were common in the region near Venice, but were seldom found in British waters. But when English explorers began to penetrate the New World and to map Pacific atolls, they found themselves in need of a specific term for an almost landlocked body of brackish water. Borrowing from the French the word that has been transmitted from South European speech, lagoon was adopted into 17th century English in a form remarkably close to Latin original.

lagoon beach: lagoonward facing beach of reef islands.

lagoon channel: properly refers to navigational channel or pass through a reef and into and through the lagoon.

lagoon floor: undulating to nearly level floor of lagoon.

lagoon reef margin: lagoonward margin of reef or island in an atoll.

Lagrongian current measurement: direction observation of current speed and/or direction by recording device, such as a parachute drogue which follows movement of a water mass through the ocean.

laguna: shallow coastal sound, channel or lake connected with sea.

laid: generally, a combining word connoting a setting, condition, state, or form, as in *laid* the keel; *was laid* on the other tack; *cable-laid; laid up.*

laid aback [ships]: when ship's sails are placed in same position as when taken aback in order to effect immediate stoppage or to give the ship sternway, so as to avoid some frontal danger. Term also refers to position a ship is placed in when taking on a pilot while at sea or when launching lifeboat to rescue a sailor lost overboard.

laid down [ships]: put or set down; thus, ship's course is laid down on the chart, ship's hull lines are laid down on plans.

lakatoi: picturesque sailing raft of Port Moresby, Papua, British New Guinea, used by Motu natives for transporting cargoes of earthware pots and ornaments from the port and adjacent villages to settlements at mouth of rivers in Papuan Gulf.

lake plains: plains formed by emergence (all or part) of lake floor. This may happen when waters of a lake run or evaporate, or when lake floor rises. Greatest lake plain in North America extends over more than 100,000 square miles of North Dakota, Minnesota and Canadian province of Manitoba. This region was once the floor of great Ice Age lake called Lake Agassiz.

Lake Superior Cisco [*Leucichthys artedii arcturus*]: Lake Superior cisco, or herring is large, reaching length of 12 in. or more. Body shape is elongate; lower jaw is either equal to or slightly shorter than upper; usually more than 43 gill rakers; lateral line scales seldom number less than 80. Frequently confused with common whitefish but can readily be distinguished by absence of overhanging snout and upper jaw characteristic of whitefish and some other coregonids.

Lambeophyllum corals: cumbersome term for exoskeleton of one small coral, also termed a corallite or slightly curved cone of calcite containing a cup, or calyx, in which body rested. Cone is covered by outer layer of epitheca, marked by growth lines and lengthwise grooves that correspond to internal partitions called septa. Half of these septa are short and half are so long that they reach center of calyx.

lamellae [reptiles]: plates forming pads on feet of some lizards.

Lamellaria perspicua [*Lamellaridae*]: this species of mesogastropods spawn from January to May and larva, called echinospira, has coiled shell some 44 mm. long.

lamellar layer: 1) calcareous shell or ostracum of pelecypod is commonly divided into two or more layers of unlike structure. Two most common types of lamellar structure are nacreous or pearly structure and crossed lamellar structure, ordinarily of microscopic lamella of calcite or aragonite separated by equally thin layers of conchiolin. 2) in *Graptolithina*, outer layer of graptolite tubes consisting of concentric laminae.

lamellibranch: bivalve member of mollusk class *Lamellibranchiata* or *Pelecypoda*, which includes familiar mussels, oysters, clams and scallops. A bivalve has shell composed of two distinct parts, one on each side of body. Lamellibranchs are aquatic and commercially valuable as source of food and such products as pearls and mother-of-pearl. Like other mollusks, they lack distinct heads and live by straining organisms from seawater that is pumped through their bodies by incurrent tubes.

lamelliform: flat and leaf-shaped.

lamina: sediment or sedimentary rock layer less than 1 cm. thick visually separable from material above and below. Lamination refers to the alternation of such layers which differ in grain size or composition.

laminae [reptile]: scales of turtle shell.

laminar flow: flow in which fluid moves smoothly in streamline in parallel layers or sheets; nonturbulent flow.

laminate: formed of thin layers.

lamination: thin layers of stratified rock deposit.

Lamnidae: family of voracious deep-water sharks of which the *porbeagle (Lamna cornubica)* is typical. Commonly known as the *mackerel sharks* from their form, have stout body, high dorsal fin at about mid-length and one of small size just forward of tail, wide mouth, large teeth, and, unlike most sharks, upper lobe of tail differs little, if any, in size from lower one.

lamprey: an eel-like vertebrate of 2 to 3 feet in length, widely distributed in temperate waters, and often esteemed as food. Some species live in fresh water only; those of marine habitat always spawn in fresh water streams. Some larger lampreys take their prey vampire fashion, or by attaching themselves to fish by their large circular suction-powered mouth, while gnawing at the victim with their hard conical teeth. The ugly creature is of the family *Petromyzonidae* of the *Cyclostomata* class.

lamprey, American brook [*Entosphenus lamottenii*]: brook lamprey is small and very slender, seldom reaching length of over 8 in. Funnellike buccal cavity is small, diameter being only slightly more than that of body. Most of teeth are blunt and small; 3 large bicuspid teeth are located on each side of mouth. Dorsal fin of adult consists of anterior and posterior portion separated by slight notch or narrow space.

lamprey, chestnut [*Ichthyomyzon castaneus*]: chestnut lamprey is small, slender eellike animal, 8 to 16 in. long, with large funnel-shaped buccal cavity which when expanded is greater in diameter than the body. Circumoral teeth are partly bicuspid. Dorsal and caudal fin are continuous.

lamprey family: lampreys or lamper eels are characterized by circular funnellike "mouth," or buccal cavity, armed with toothlike horny spines. They are without scales or paired fins and possess a single nostril. Skeleton is wholly of cartilage and consists of imperfect skull and poorly developed vertebra column supported by unconstricted notochord, 7 pairs of external gill-openings are present; gills are supported by arrangement of cartilage known as branchial basket. Buccal cavity or buccal funnel contains horny, toothlike spines; those immediately surrounding mouth opening are commonly called circumoral teeth.

lamprey, Michigan brook [*Ichthyomyzon fossor*]: body form of Michigan brook lamprey is similar to that of silver lamprey except that funnellike buccal cavity is much smaller. Adults after metamorphosis have degenerate digestive tracts and do not feed.

lamprey, sea: mottled brownish or greenish fish reaching length of 3 ft. and a weight of several pounds. Sea lamprey attaches itself to body of larger fish by means of its sucker-mouth. Horny tongue rasps the flesh enabling lamprey to feed on blood of the unfortunate host. When mature, sea lampreys migrate up coastal streams to spawn. It is elongate, eellike animal without paired fins or scales and with permanently open mouth. Single nasal opening on top of head; 7 nearly circular gill openings behind eye; mouth without jaws; no paired fins; dorsal fins distinctly separated into anterior and posterior portions; pattern of regular mottling; 64 or more body segments between last gill opening and anus.

lamprey, silver [*Ichthyomyzon unicuspis*]: small, slender, eellike animal 8 to 16 in. long, with large, funnel-shaped buccal cavity greater in diameter than body. Circumoral teeth are entirely unicupoid. This lamprey is parasitic on fishes and very destructive.

lamprey, southern brook [*Ichthyomyzon gagei*]: elongate, eellike animal without paired fins or scales and with permanently open mouth. Single nasal opening on top of head; 7 nearly circular gill openings behind eyes; mouth without jaws; no paired fins; dorsal fin with slight notch but not divided into 2 separate fins; 61 to 64 body segments between last gill opening and anus.

lamp shell: brachiopod, especially terebratuloid shells that resemble a Roman lamp.

L.A.N.: usual abbreviation in nautical astronomy for *local apparent noon*, or instant at which the true, or apparent, sun's center passes the meridian of any place.

lancet fish: the surgeon, barber, or doctor fish.

lancha: Malay seagoing craft with two lugsails of equal size. Spars are raked. Hull has extended clipper stem, which acts as a bowsprit for tack of foresail. Stern gallery extends over straight sternpost.

lanchang to-aru: Malay vessel similar to lancha, but it is fore-and-aft rigged and carries long topmasts.

land breeze: light wind blowing from land over a lake or sea because of unequal cooling of land and water areas.

landfall: approach or coming to land either in the course or at end of voyage.

landfast ice: all types of ice, either broken or unbroken, attached to shore, beached or stranded in shallow water; also called fast ice.

landing [ships]: spaced distance from edge of a bar or plate to center of rivet holes.

landlubber: person who, from want of experience, is awkward or lubberly on board ship. A green seaman. Anyone unacquainted with ways of the sea. Term of reproach or ridicule among sailors.

land sky: relatively dark appearance of underside of cloud layer when it is over land that is not snow covered. Term is used largely in polar regions with reference to sky map; land sky is brighter than water sky, but is much darker than ice blink or snow blink.

lane: prescribed track or route on the high seas; a lead or clear passage through an ice field.

lane route: trans-ocean track followed by vessels of a regular line, or that agreed upon by maritime nations to be adhered to by their merchant shipping.

Langmiur circulation: system of cells of convergence and divergence that forms in open water at right angles to direction of prevailing wind. If water is flowing at different angles, small rips or zones of convergence formed may not be directly crosswind in direction.

langoustier: craft used in crab fishery off Land's End at Scilly Islands by Breton fishermen. Larger boats are ketch-rigged, of great beam, decked, with high bow, counter stern, steep draft and about 50 ft. long.

langskip: Viking "long ship"; fighting ship.

Lanon: type of Malay craft formerly used by native pirates of Johore, at southern tip of Malay peninsula, for attacking merchant vessels. Hull was junklike with sharp and very hollow bow having a recurved stem, over which was a projecting platform; square, heavily carved stern.

lantern [echinoids]: intricate complex of calcareous plates and muscles that is fitted for seizing and chewing food. Consists of 5 jaws, each with pointed tooth that projects into mouth region.

lantern fish: one of small, usually deep sea fish belonging to family *Myctophidae*. They owe their name to many luminescent spots on their bodies.

lanyard or laniard [ships]: small rope or cord used for certain purposes on board ship. Specifically, a rope rove in deadeyes of rigging, for settling up and tightening shrouds, backstays, etc.

Laodicea undulata [phylum *Coelenterata*]: medusa of species of *Cuspidella*. Distinguishing features are broad velum, 4-sided stomach, mouth with 4 lips with folded margins, hundreds of hollow marginal tentacles some of which bear small ocelli and cordyli between each pair of tentacles. It may attain diameter of 155 mm.

lap: distance one piece of material lies over another, as in strakes of planking or plating in sides of a boat or in a ship's outside plating; a lap joint. In a reciprocating engine, distance a slide-valve overlaps a steam port, when at piston's half stroke. To place or fit anything to partly lie over another, as in a clinker-built boat's planking system.

lapil [lepalepa]: "lapil" is term of "canoe" on Tumelo (Tamara) Island and "lepalepa" on Angle, Ali and adjacent islands in Aitape (Berlen Harbor) district off north coast of Northwest New Guinea. Large dugout sailing canoe from these islands is used for trading purposes, transporting pots to mainland in exchange for sago. Canoes range up to 50 ft. long, 30 in. wide and are capable of carrying up to 2 tons.

lapilli: volcanic ejecta ranging from 4 to 32 mm. in diameter.

lapstrake [ships]: applies to boats on clinker system in which strakes overlap each other. Top strakes always lap on outside of strake underneath.

larboard [ships]: old term for port or left side of vessel, facing forward.

largemouth bass [*Huro salmoidea*]: differs from smallmouth largely in position of angle of jaw, which reaches back to below hind margin of eye, and in number of scales on cheek. It differs also in absence of vertical bars and dark mottlings on sides. A faint dark, horizontal stripe may be present on sides. In fingerlings and young this stripe is very distinct.

larva: early stage of an animal after embryo form but still not resembling adult.

larvacean: member of class of tunicates. These very small marine animals are free swimmers. They have primitive backbone or notochord and resemble larvae of immature forms of tunicates.

lash [ships]: to secure or fasten by cordage. To lash a sail to mast or yard; to lash things on deck. Hence lashings are ropes or cords for binding or making fast one thing or another.

L.A.T.: local apparent time; hour angle of true sun measured at a particular place. It is time shown by a sun dial.

lateen heat of evaporation: that amount of heat required to change one gram of water into water vapor without a change in temperature.

lateen-rigged: describing a ship with heavy lateen rigging characterized by short masts and common in Mediterranean.

lateen sail: triangular sail extended by long yard hung from mast; used chiefly on Mediterranean craft and also on ships such as caravel, etc. Yard is in two or more parts, according to length, and is spliced together. It is hoisted by a halyard, usually in port side, which passes in two parts through double block at masthead. Fourfold block is secured to, and some distance above, the deck and just abaft the mast.

latent defect: in maritime legal parlance, a fault not apparent or visible, such as a hidden flaw in a machinery part or in a vessel's steering gear, to which might be attributed cause for loss or damage to ship or cargo, in event of failure of such equipment. One clause of *Carriage of Goods by Sea Act, 1936 (46 U.S.C. 1304)* provides that neither vessel nor carrier shall be responsible for damage or loss arising or resulting from *"latent defects* not discoverable by due diligence."

lateral: of or pertaining to the side; at, toward, or from the side of anything; sidewise; as, *lateral stresses in a ship's hull.*

lateral [fish]: pertaining to sides.

lateral line: 1) structures on heads and sides of many fishes and some amphibians. Often marked by different scales, the lines include sensory organs that detect low frequency vibrations. 2) system of sense organs possessed by fishes, usually arranged in single series along sides of body, functioning in part to detect low frequency vibrations such as those produced by local disturbances in water.

lateral moraine: moraine built along edge of valley glacier and composed of angular rock fragments that had fallen on glacier from valley wall.

laterals [reptile]: row of enlarged laminae on each side of centrals in turtle's shell.

lateral shift: offset of position of peak of an anomaly with mass of magnetization or gravitation.

lateral teeth [*Mollusca*]: hinge teeth in heterodont pelecypod anterior or posterior to cardinal teeth.

latitude: distance in degrees north or south of Equator and measured by parallels. Latitude of Equator is zero degrees written as 0°. Points farthest from Equator are two poles of the earth,

North Pole and South Pole. Since the poles are located one quarter of circular distance around the earth from Equator, then their latitudes are 90s,e N and 90° S respectively.

latitude correction: amount of adjustment of observed gravity values to arbitrary chosen latitude.

Lauderia [phytoplankton]: short cylindrical cells united in straight chains with very little space between cells. Sometimes spiny. Numerous chloroplasts.

launch [ships]: sliding of boat or vessel's hull from land or builder's ways into water.

launching: process of putting north or south of Equator.

Laurasia: northern member of two supercontinents supposed to have existed prior to Tertiary time, composed of what is now North America, Greenland and northern Eurasia.

lava delta: deltalike body of lava formed where a lava flow enters the sea. Coast consisting of such deltas formed by recent lava flows has convex shoreline and is called a lava flow coast.

laver: green alga, *Ulva*, dried and sold for food.

law of constancy of relative proportions: regardless of absolute concentration of total dissolved solids in seawater, the ratios between more abundant substances are virtually constant in world's oceans.

law of relative proportions: ratios among more abundant elements of seawater tend to be constant, i.e., if amount of chlorine in water sample is known, then same amount of most other elements can be determined from the ratio established. The law allows working with only three basic parameters: salinity, temperature and pressure of ocean water.

Law of Universal Gravitation: Newton's law of gravitation. Gravitation is directly proportional to product of masses of two bodies and universely proportional to square of distance between them.

lay [ships]: to move or go, as "lay below" or "lay forward." On a sailboat to "lay off" is to sail a little farther off the wind.

layer depth: in oceanography, thickness of mix layer or depth of top of thermocline.

layer depth effect: weakening of sound beam owing to abnormal spreading as it passes from isothermal or positive gradient layer to underlying negative layer.

layer of no motion: layer assumed to be at rest at some depth in ocean. This implies that isobaric surfaces within the layer are level, hence they may be used as reference surfaces for computation of absolute gradient currents.

layout: 1) extent of, or stretch occupied by, a setline or trawl, as in long-line fishing; area dragged over by a seine. 2) plan of an area occupied by, or an assembly of, anchors, cables, tugs, etc., in a salvage operation. 3) *laying-out* or planning.

lazaret [ships]: below-deck storage space in stern.

lazy guy [ships]: light rope or tackle by which boom is prevented from swinging around.

lazy jacks [ships]: ropes leading down vertically from topping left to boom to hold sail when taking it in.

leach [ships]: after edge of sail. Leachline is line that tightens the leach.

lead: long, narrow, but navigable water passage in pack ice. Lead may be covered by thin ice.

lead [lead line]: sounding device consisting of lead weight with marked line affixed to top and hollowed base which may be filled with grease or wax to determine character of bottom.

leader: 1) fence or barrier, as of stakes, brush, stones, etc., extending from shore for *leading* fish into a weir or fixed net. 2) snell, or snood, of fine line to which one of the hooks is attached on a long-line or trawl; piece of fine line next to hook on any fishing line. 3) foremost vessel in a line formation of ships, as a naval fleet or a convoy. 4) *fairlead*.

leaf coral [*Bossea manza*]: this unusual alga, which varies from 1 to 6 in. in height, attaches itself to rocks or shells between mean low tide and 1.5-ft. tide levels. Characteristics of genus are calcification, many erect, jointed shoots, forked branches, thick, broadly rounded branchlets and brittleness. It varies in color from pinkish-white to deep purple, variation due to bleaching of exposed plants. Leaf coral has crustlike, lobed base from which shoots arise.

lecithotrophic: said of larvae that are nourished from nutrients in egg rather than by feeding on plankton.

lee [ships]: side opposite that from which wind is coming. When sailboat is on starboard tack, wind is coming from starboard side which is the weather side. Port side is the lee side. Lee shore is one onto which wind is blowing.

leeboard: section of metal or flat board lowered into water on lee side of sailing craft to lessen drift to that side.

leech [ships]: perpendicular or sloping edge of square sail. In fore-and-aft sails only after edge is called the leech, forward edge being called the luff.

leeward: toward the lee; that part toward which wind blows; opposed to windward.

leeward side: side opposite to that from which wind blows; sheltered side.

leeward tidal current: tidal current setting in same direction as that in which wind is blowing.

leeway: sidewise motion through water to leeward, caused by pressure of wind and waves.

left gill [*Gastropoda*]: in all recent snails left gill is rotated so it lies in right anterior side of body. In dextral individual it is typically smaller than the right or absent.

left longitudinal nerve cord [*Gastropoda*]: in recent gastropods, torsion of viscera loop to left cord over to right side of body.

leg-of-mutton [ships]: triangular mainsail used usually on small boats, upper corner hoisting.

lembus: ancient boat with sharp bow and fine lines used by Illyrians east of Adriatic Sea at time of early Romans.

lemmeraak: Dutch pleasure craft of Lemster district of Holland similar to boeier, but having somewhat straight lines and finer stern. It is usually built of steel.

length [*Mollusca*]: in pelecypods, greatest horizontal dimension parallel to line bisecting adductor muscle scars and at a right angle to height; in gastropods and scaphopods, same as height in chitons greatest dimensions parallel to axis of symmetry.

length over all, LOA [ships]: distance from foremost of stern to aftermost part of stern. "Length between perpendiculars." Distance from fore part of stern to after part of sternpost where they intersect to top of upper deck beams.

lens: transparent structure inside an eye that focuses light rays, usually onto retina.

lens, fresnel: named for *Augustin Jean Fresnel, French optician* and *geometer (1788-1827)*, a lens originally designed for lighthouses and now also extensively fitted in signal lanterns—particularly in those prescribed in Regulations for Prevention of Collisions. By its means light is sent out in horizontal parallel rays and thus may be seen at comparatively great distance. A lantern thus equipped is often termed a *Fresnel lantern*.

Lepidocentroida [sea urchins]: early types, from late Ordovician of Europe, characterized by spheroidal crowns, two rows of plates in each ambulacrum, and interambulacral plates with overlapping edges and no uniformity of arrangement. Though most lepidocentroids are extinct, two genera survive in both deep and shallow waters. Their crowns reach diameters of 6 in. and are covered with short but poisonous spines.

leptaena rhomboidalis: of Wenlock Limestone, broad shell with quadrate or semi-elliptical outline, the straight hinge-line forming greatest breadth of shell. Early (posterior) part of shell is flat, but after growing to length of about 2 cm., a sudden change takes place and surface of ventral valve becomes bent at about right angles making that valve in adult highly convex externally while dorsal valve is correspondingly concave, so that

change does not result in great increase in thickness.

Leptocephalus: small, elongate, transparent, planktonic larva of eel.

Leptomedusae [phylum *Coelenterata*]: these are medusae of calyptoblast hydroids which have polyps fully retractile into hydrothecae. Although sometimes bell-shaped, medusae are usually more flattened or saucerlike than *Anthomedusae* and moreover, have gonads situated on radial canal (not on manubrium). There are usually numerous marginal tentacles which increase in number throughout life. Sense organs are marginal vesicles or statocysts, not ocelli. Marginal cordyli replace vesicles or ocelli in *Laodiceidae*, while in *Melicertidae* and *Dipleurosommidae* sense organs are lacking from margin of bell.

Leptomysis gracilis: slender mysid whose carapace has pointed rostrum and concave posterior border, which leaves last three thoracic segments visible in dorsal view. Its anterior margin has sharp point on each side; cuticle is covered by minute oblong scales. This species is common near bottom in inshore waters and being euryhaline and eurythermic, often swarms in estuaries.

leptopel: large organic molecules and aggregates of molecules of approximately colloidal size dissolved or suspended in water.

Lernaeopodoida [order]: body segmentation reduced or absent; thoracic appendages usually lacking in female; male with modified head appendages for clinging to female; ectoparasites of fish; freshwater and marine. *Salmincola, Lernaea.*

lesser ebb: weaker of two ebb tidal currents occurring during tidal day, usually associated with tidal currents of mixed characteristics.

lesser flood: weaker of two flood tidal currents occurring during tidal day, usually associated with tidal currents of mixed characteristics.

Leuckartiara octona [phylum *Coelenterata*]: medusa of hydroid of same name, formerly known as *Perigonimus repens*. It is very common and may reach a height of 4 mm. It can be regarded as a summer and early autumn species.

leucocyte: one of white blood corpuscles which fight infection in vertebrate body. Eosinophilic leucocytes are capable of being strained with a biological dye called eosin.

levee: embankment bordering one or both sides of sea channel or the low gradient seaward part of canyon or valley.

level surface: surface which at every point is perpendicular to plumb line of direction in which gravity acts.

leviathan: 1) huge and formidable aquatic animal referred to in ancient writings; probably the crocodile or the whale. Description of such occupies entire chapter 41 of *Book of Job* in which *Levia-*

than is seen to typify *Satan* and his powers of darkness. 2) figuratively, a large oceangoing vessel, as one of transAtlantic greyhounds.

lewis bolt: deck eyebolt enlarged in diameter at its lower end and set in a socket of similar shape. A wedging piece inserted against its side, or molten lead set around bolt withstands upward pull by jamming against sides of socket. Also called *movable eyebolt*, used in wood decks of yachts and passenger vessels.

Libra: southern constellation lying to northwest of *Scorpio* and which the sun passes through in November. It contains two navigational stars: *Kiffa Australis* and *Kiffa Borealis*.

Licmorphora [phytoplankton]: triangular cells attached by pointed ends to algae, hydroids or even to planktonic crustacea. Belongs to subclass *Pennatae*.

lie: combined with an adverb, preposition, or phrase, almost exclusively connotes a vessel's position with relation to some object, or as being in a certain trim, heading, or condition. While *lay* and *lie* are often used synonymously, as in, to *lay,* or *lie, along the shore,* former is preferable word in that it really signifies to *lay ship along the shore,* or *sail along,* etc. As compared with *lie,* which implies position, *lay* generally is connected with the idea of motion; hence, to *lie up* a vessel is better usage than to *lay up,* although both expressions are commonly employed.

lifeboat: open boat especially designed for seaworthiness and heavy weather such as those used by Coast Guard and steamers.

lifelines [ships]: lines along rail of ship, usually supported by stanchions, to provide safety for crew when moving about deck. Also called life rail.

life preservers: cloth jackets made with pads of buoyant material to sustain a person in water.

lift [ships]: part of standing rigging on square-rigged ship used to help support yards when not raised.

ligament [*Mollusca*]: band of tough, elastic fibers uniting two valves of pelecypod variously situated along dorsal margin, its major portion posterior to beaks, externally; it may or may not be supplemented by cartilage.

light bottle: container used for measuring photosynthetic activity of primary producers.

lightening hole [ships]: hole cut out of a plate to make it lighter and yet not reduce strength and to make a passage through the plate.

lighter: 1) small vessel used for loading and unloading larger vessels lying in open roadstead. 2) full-bodied heavily built craft, usually not self-propelled, used in bringing merchandise or cargo alongside or in transferring same from a vessel.

light, fixed [ships]: thick glass, usually circular, fitted in a frame fixed in opening in ship's side, deckhouse or bulkhead to provide access for light. Fixed light is not hinged.

light load line [ships]: waterline when ship rides empty.

light saturation: amount of light at which given kind of plant cell will carry out photosynthesis most actively.

lightweight gear [diving]: all diving systems less complex than standard dress, particularly shallow-water diving gear.

lily: the traditional *fleur-de-lis* commonly marking the North point of a magnetic compass card.

lily pad ice: pancake ice when cakes are not more than about 18 in. in diameter.

lima coast: alluvial coast usually characterized by many lagoons.

Limacomorpha: order of phylum *Arthropoda.* Body usually of 22 segments; male gonopods present on last segment; 36 pairs of legs; not ball-rolling. *Glomeridesmus.*

liman: shallow coastal lagoon or embayment with mud or slime deposit near stream mouth.

Liman Current: cold flowing current in western North Pacific.

limb: designated part of extreme edge of apparent disc of sun, moon, or a planet; as, *sun's lower limb; moon's eastern limb.* Graduated arc or other indicating part of an angle measuring instrument; as, *limb of a sextant.*

limber chains [ships]: chains passing through limber holes of vessel, by which they may be cleaned of dirt.

limber hole [ships]: hole or slot in floor timbers or frames at bottom of a ship to permit water to drain to lowest part of bilge, where it is then pumped out.

limbers: originally, space along each side of keelson, including the *limber holes* cut in lower edges of floor timbers, which allows accumulated bilge water to flow to the pump well. Now, also such gutterway along outer sides, or margin plates, of double-bottom tanks, usually termed the *bilges,* designed to drain water to nearest *bilge-suction,* or in larger ships, to a *bilge-well.*

lime-juicer: nickname for British vessel. British law requires a daily ration of lime juice to prevent scurvy, hence the name.

limestone: sedimentary rock composed of calcium carbonate.

liming: solution of lime and water swabbed on a wood deck and allowed to dry for bleaching purposes.

liminology: physics and chemistry of freshwater bodies and of classification, biology and ecology of organisms living in them.

limited form wave: deformation of waves by formation of sharp crest followed by propagation with bubbling of water on the front face until final breaking into a roller.

limiting ray: sound ray which becomes tangent at depth where sound velocity is at maximum.

Limnomedusae [phylum *Coelenterata*]: these are *Hydromedusae* having either gonads on wall of manubrium or along radial canals and in which marginal vesicles may or may not be present. In a few, gonads may occur both on manubrium and on radial canals. From this it is apparent that characters of *Limnomedusae* overlap those of enclosed sensory clubs and in this respect *Limnomedusae* resemble *Trachymedusae*. Fortunately there are only a few marine *Limnomedusae*, most being freshwater.

limpet, black-mouthed: this limpet shell is tall and conical with nearly circular base and with steeply sloping sides which are nearly straight in outline. Side of shell bears well-developed, rounded, radiating ribs which are occasionally crossed by fine lines. It is more usual however to find entire outer surface of shell somewhat eroded. It is usually white or buff and is often marked or spotted with black. Entire interior of shell is white or silvery except for central callus which is nearly black. It will reach about 2½ in. in diameter.

limpet, Hawaiian: individual limpets of this species vary considerably in shape and markings. In general they are conical in shape, oval at base and have apex of the shell placed just anterior to center. Surface of shell is sculptured by between 38 and 48 radiating ribs and by intervening smaller ribs. Shell is black above; ribs are usually darker than intervening areas; underside of shell is bluish-lead silvery color through which markings of ribs are visible; blackish in center, often bordered by lighter area and this in turn is surrounded by pattern of radiating lines. It will reach 2 in. in diameter.

limpet, keyhole: like tiny volcanoes these limpets live clinging to their rocky perch. Their "keyhole" is used to expel used water and waste products. Usually shells are decorated with numerous ribs. In most species shell covers entire animal, but in some, like giant keyhole, the animal is much larger than shell. Tough teeth, as in other snails and chitons, located on the tongue help wear away beach rocks.

limpet, Patellidae: these limpets inhabit shoreline of temperate and tropical seas. Commonly found clinging to smooth places upon tides. They are valued by inhabitants of many localities who pry them off rocks for food which they offer. Limpets are simple, conical shells with spiral design in young stages; apex of shell is slightly anterior to middle and, unlike keyhole limpets *(Fissurellidae)*, is closed from this apex. Ribs radiate out to cover entire upper surface of shell. Limpets lack operculum which is found in many gastropod molluscs.

limpets: 1) primitive gastropods similar to snails that are found in both ocean and fresh water and have low, cone-shaped shells. 2) one of several suborders *(Docoglossa, Petellacea, Fissurellidae or Zygobranchia)* of flattened cone-shaped gastropods in which spiral of shell is absent or not apparent.

limpets, true: cap-shaped shells found on rocky beaches around the world. They hang tightly onto their rocky home but move around after dark grazing on minute algae or seaweeds. Shape is adapted to stem or "leaf" of host plant.

limpet, talc: this limpet is a large species with shell which is oval at base and which presents a conical outline when viewed from side. Apex of shell is placed anterior to center; surface, which is convex, is covered by unequal radiating ribs. It is brownish-coppery color on outside; interior of shell is marked by large white central callus which is bordered by duller area; outer area of lower surface is usually a glistening silvery color through which radiating pattern of ribs show. It will reach about 4 in. in length.

line: general term for a length of cordage, particular size of which usually being understood by its use as indicated in a combining word: as, *fishing line, heaving line, lead line, gant line, leechline, life line, mooring line, tow line.* Use of a *line* in fishing is indicated in *long line* or *great line fishing;* often shortened to *lining.* A series of lengths of pipe constituting a *pipeline;* as, *steam line, ballast line, fire line.* Ship operating business or firm, or number of vessels managed by such, engaged in regular transportation service between certain ports; as, *Cunard Line, American-South African Line.*

linear: line, as in an end-to-end arrangement of objects. In graphic representations, usually taken to mean forming straight line on graph rather than curve.

liner: strip of plate, tapered or otherwise, filling space between a raised plate and a frame or other structural part, to ensure solid riveting work. A person or vessel engaged in line fishing at sea. Merchant vessel on a regular run or belonging to a line of vessels; as, a *cargo line; Cunard line, express line, passenger line, transpacific line.*

ling: North Atlantic gadoid fish in length about 1¼ times that of the true cod and having dorsal and ventral fringelike fins extending half-body length to tail. An important food fish, it is often salted and dried. The *white* and *squirrel hakes* of U.S. coast south of Cape Hatteras are also called *ling,* and various similarly shaped fishes are locally so named, as the *buffalo cod* of U.S. Pacific coast, the American *burbot,* and the *sergeant fish.*

lingcod: mottled brown or gray fish often spotted with blue or red. Long dorsal fin has deep notch between spiny and soft rayed portions; tail fin is square cut; pectoral fins are unusually broad. In this species female is much larger than male, weighing as much as 70 lbs. while male rarely weighs more than 30.

lingual ribbon: radula in molluscs.

Lingula unguis: brachiopod which burrows umbones downward in sea bottom in shallow water. It has very long pedicle which it pushes into sediment and uses to withdraw itself from surface into its burrow if necessary. Horny shell is about one-half phosphatic in composition and organic matter and phosphate are in alternating layers and not uniformly admixed.

Lingulidae: *Brachiopoda*, elongated in form, biconvex, burrowing with thin shell and long pedicle. Lower Cambrian to Recent. This genus survives to present time, and so is one of longest lived of all genera. In later Paleozoic and younger deposits, *Lingulidae* tend to occur in poorly aerated brackish water deposits commonly to exclusion of other fossils.

lining: 1) act of fishing by means of lines; as, *hand lining; long lining.* 2) process of marking lines on a plate or other structural part preparatory to fitting, boring holes, cutting, etc.; *lining out.* 3) interior covering of wood, or *cleading,* as over steel structural parts in a cabin, lockers, storerooms, etc. 4) covering as protection from chafing, as an extra piece or cloth of canvas sewed on a sail. 5) temporary wood sheathing over an unceiled tank top to prevent contact of cargo with metal, as in carrying bulk grain. 6) insulating mixture of thick paint and granulated cork covering exposed steel in crew accommodation, cabins, storerooms, etc., for minimizing condensation during cold weather.

link confetti [*Enteromorpha intestinalis*]: has long, tubular, bright green, paper-thin, bladelike branches (thalli). This species is attached to rocks or other algae between 3 ft. and mean low-tide marks. It is held firmly to substratum by means of rhizoids which are outgrowths of basal area. The seaweed has fragile, tubular structure only one layer in thickness. At intervals branches are compressed and constricted. Common and variable species, almost worldwide in distribution.

lionfish [scorpionfish family]: small member of family, only 8 in. long. It is warm-water species, common in Florida. Lionfish has shaggy head because of many fleshy tabs and tubercles. Polynesian relative of this fish is armed with poisonous dorsal spines. Each spine is grooved from tip to base, where poison gland is located. Venom flows along grooves in spine into wounds made by the fin.

lipid: chemical term designating simple, compound or derived substances of fats and soaps.

liquid: state of matter in which molecules are relatively free to change positions with respect to each other but restricted by cohesive forces so as to maintain a relatively fixed volume.

lisi: plank-built "mon" type canoe of southeastern Solomon Islands. Upturned peaks at ends are formed by washboards. They are often highly decorated and carved. No outrigger is employed.

list [ships]: lean of a vessel to one side or another due to weight on board rather than to pressure of wind or wave.

Lithistida: spicules united into continuous skeleton: *Siphonia*, pear-shaped, stalked; *Doryderna*, cylindrical, branched; *Verruculina*, cup-shaped or irregular, with short stalk.

lithocyst: cystlike hydrostatic organ in margin of disc in coelenterate medusae.

lithodesma [*Mollusca*]: calcareous reinforcement of internal ligament or resilium.

Lithodidae [paguridans]: there are two zoeal stages which are characterized by large number of spines (8 or 9 pairs) on the telson and the concave posterior margins of telson. Longitudinal diameter of eye is shorter than in *Paguridea* and is less than width of abdomen. There are no uropods and length of first zoea is 7.6 mm. reaching 7.9 mm. in final (second) stage. Megalopa has no uropods and is very spiny. As in the zoea, there are small pleopods on 6th abdominal segment. Length about 4.5 mm.

lithofraction: fragmentation of rocks by wave action on beaches.

lithoid tufa: gray algal reeflike material forming beds and the core of reef domes.

Lithophaga [clams]: date clam attaches itself with cluster of threads and is said to secrete acid that dissolves rock into which the creature bores. Periostracum is very thick, protecting shell's layers.

lithosphere: moderately strong and rigid layer of earth which generally includes continental crust, oceanic crust and mantle to depth of approximately 70 km. (44 miles).

lithostyle: sensory club or tentaculocyst on free margin of disc of a jellyfish usually containing calcareous concretion with cushion of sensory cilia. Lithocysts are modified form of lithostyles.

Lithothamnion: red, crusting alga whose thallus is permeated with limestone. *Lithothamnion* is found on rocks where it forms a mauve-colored, wavy or lobed, overhang. It absorbs and assimilates calcium carbonate from water and in tropical seas, plays a part in bonding madreporarians together. It is found in Mediterranean as well as in tropics. Similar limestone alga is *Lithophyllum*.

Lithothamnion ridge: ridge composed of calcium

carbonate secretions of *Lithothamnion* and other red calcareous algae, which rises about 3 ft. above sea level at seaward edge of reef flat. Secretions of *Lithothamnion* and related genera may comprise 50% or more of coral reef.

lithotope: area and environment of uniform sedimentation. Layer or deposit of uniform or uniformly heterogeneous composition and texture produced in lithotope is called lithostrome.

little dove shell, lined [*Columbella lineolata*]: variable species in which whorls are longitudinally ribbed. It is white or marked with brown spots. Measures from ½ to 2/3 in. long.

little dove shell, pretty [*Pyrene bella*]: spindle-shaped with long pointed spire. It is yellowish-white and marked by light brownish areas and spots. It measures about ½ in. long.

little dove shell, turtle [*Columbella turturina*]: shell is short and thick with enlarged and swollen body whorl. It is white and often marked with yellowish-brown. It will reach about 2/3 in. long.

little dove shell, variable [*Pyrene bella*]: somewhat oval in shape with short spire. Exterior surface is usually smooth, although it is often spirally grooved and bears longitudinal ribs in varying degrees of prominence. Aperture is narrowed posteriorly; outer lip is angled and toothed within. This species is white with variable markings. It may range from almost pure white to nearly pure brown but it is usually marked with interrupted brown bands. Columella is always brown-tipped at aperture and white within. It ranges in length from ¼ to ½ inch.

little dove shell, zebra [*Columbella zebra*]: somewhat spindle-shaped with spire which is larger than most members of this group. Body whorl may be smooth or may have posterior portion longitudinally folded, but almost always spirally striated at anterior end. Aperture is broad; lip is slightly thickened and feebly toothed within. It is white and marked longitudinally with zig-zag zebralike, brownish markings; aperture is faintly violet within. Reaches length of about ½ inch.

littoral: 1) coastline including both land and nearshore waters, particularly that portion between extreme high and low tide; intertidal zone. 2) benthic zone between high and low water marks. 3) coastal region; of or pertaining to a shore. Shore areas between low and high tide.

littoral current: current, caused by wave action, that sets parallel to shore; usually in nearshore region within breaker zone.

littoral deposits: deposits of littoral drift, i.e., sand, gravel and other minerals which move along shore between high and low water marks. Also refers to longshore movement or littoral transport of such material by longshore currents.

littoral drift: 1) movement of material produced by waves and currents in intertidal zone. 2) material moved in littoral zone under influence of waves and currents.

littoral transport: movement of material along shore in littoral zone by waves and currents.

littoral zone: 1) coastline including both land and nearshore water, particularly intertidal zone between extreme high and low tide. 2) living on, or pertaining to shore, especially seashore; marine environment influenced by land mass; coastal region.

Littorina litorea [mesogastropods]: eggs are extremely common in inshore plankton. Egg capsules are 0.96 mm. across, i.e., much larger than those of *L. neritoides*. Each capsule contains up to 9 eggs but normally there are only 2 or 3 eggs per capsule. Larvae hatch after 5 days as veligers with one and a half whorled shells and are characterized by presence of two dark pigmented patches, one on each velar lobe. These show through shell when animal has retracted into it. Length of larval shell before metamorphosis varies but may reach 0.6 mm. Larvae are in plankton for two weeks before settling.

Littorina neritoides [mesogastropods]: egg capsules are present in inshore plankton during winter and spring. Capsules are approximately 0.16 mm. across and 0.09 mm. high and contain a single egg. Veliger is shelled and bears spiral strias and dots as in some rissoids.

littorine: referring to littoral or intertidal zone.

live: to float, in the sense of surviving a danger; as in: *we thought no boat could live in such a breaking sea.*

Lizzia blondina [phylum *Coelenterata*]: this is the medusa of an unknown hydroid. Despite wide occurrence of the hydroid, medusa is seldom recorded in northern waters. It seems to be mainly a summer and southern species. Distinguishing feature is presence of 4 branches or branched tentacles around mouth.

Lloyd's: an association of underwriters in London, England, incorporated by Act of Parliament in 1871. As a corporation, does not undertake insurance business, but is conducted solely by its members on their own account, subject to the society's rules. Briefly, it is a great market for every kind of insurance excepting that of human life, and *Lloyd's Committee* may be said to be the umpire body in conduct of insurance activities.

load: quantity of material being transported by current of water, wind or glacial ice.

load [ship construction]: in reference to ship's structure, load denotes total force that vessel or part of vessel must withstand when floating in given condition.

load waterline [ships]: waterline when ship is loaded.

loam: soil composed of clay, silt, sand and organic matter. Term is occasionally used to describe marine sediment.

lobster, Antarctic slipper [*Parribacus antarficcis*]: body is extremely flat and wide, especially at anterior end. Antennae also are very flat and wide and bordered with short spines; back of carapace is rough and covered with tubercles; eyes are set on orbits on edge of carapace. There are no chelipeds except for small pair on fifth and last pair of legs in female. Body is mottled reddish-brown and resembles rocks on which it lives; measures about 8 in. in length. This lobster lives on rocks of coral reef where it is very difficult to observe because of its shape and color.

lobster boat: class of small, sloop-rigged boats with centerboard; in general use in lobster fishery of New England. It varies somewhat according to locality. Average size is about 25 ft. long, with a beam from 8 to 10 ft.

lobster, Japanese spiny [*Panulirus japonicus*]: body is nearly cylindrical in front but becomes increasingly flattened toward tail. Carapace is covered with spines which point forward; spines about head and eyes are particularly large, strong and sharp; large pair of spines protect eyes. Antennae are large, long, rounded and covered with spines which also point forward. Fifth pair of legs on female ends in small pinchers. Body of this lobster may be as long as 16 in. These crustaceans inhabit rocks and crevices of coral reefs. They feed upon algae and various kinds of animal food.

lobster, long-handed spiny [*Justitia longimanus*]: this rare and unusual lobster measures about 6 in. long. Carapace is rough and armed with spines at anterior end; base of antennae are heavy and also have spines. This lobster bears unusual pair of front legs which are long and large, ending in pinchers. Alternating red and white bands encircle lip and antennae and are vaguely evident on body. It lives on shoreline waters on outer edge of reef at depths below 100 ft. It is a species which is rare to both fishermen and scientists.

lobster, regal slipper [*Arctides regalis*]: lobsters of this group are all flattened in shape to fit their manner of life in crevices of reef. Carapace is flat, rough and covered with tubercles and bears eyes in orbits along antero-lateral margin; antennae are likewise very flat and broad and often bear spines along outer edge. There are no chelipeds upon first pair of legs, although 5th pair of legs on female is tipped with small pair of pinchers. In this species back of abdomen is marked with pattern of rosettes upon each segment. Body is pink and reddish and measures from 3 to 6 in. long. It lives at depths of about 150 ft. or more on outer edge of reefs.

lobster, scaly slipper [*Scyllarides squammouse*]: this is one of larger species of slipper lobsters that reaches length of about 12 in. Body is covered by small tubercles and is mottled reddish-brown; antennae are very flat and broad; eyes are set in orbits in outer edge of carapace. Chelipeds are absent in male, but female has small pair at end of 5th pair of legs. They inhabit rocky areas of coral reef, hide away in crevices during the daytime and come out at night to search for food.

lobster, timid slipper [*Scyllarus timidus*]: this slipper lobster is somewhat scaly in appearance and armed with forward projecting spines along lateral border and midline of back. Segments of abdomen bear rosettelike decorations similar to those of other members of this group; legs are marked with encircling bands. This is a small species measuring about 2 in. long.

lobster, tufted spiny [*Panulirus penicillatus*]: body is cylindrical in front and becomes increasingly flattened toward abdomen and tail. Carapace is rough and spiny; spines are largest and strongest about head and eyes and all point in forward direction; large pair of spines project forward above eyes. Antennae are large, long and rounded and covered with spines. Fifth pair of legs of female end in small pinchers.

lobster, western [*Enoplometopus occidentalis*]: this lobster is a brilliant salmon red and body is marked with round white spots which are bordered by ring of deeper red color. Body is covered with hairs; carapace bears a groove on midline extending backward and bordered by ridge on both sides. Chelipeds are large and heavy and covered with hairs. Body is about 8 in. long. This is a rare and uncommon species in shoreline waters. It appears to live commonly at depths of 100 ft. or more on outer side of reef.

local moon: moment when sun crosses meridian of particular locality.

local winds: winds which, over small area, differ from those which would be appropriate to general pressure distribution or which possess some other peculiarity.

loch: inlet or arm of sea, often nearly landlocked.

lockage: toll charged for passing through a lock or series of locks, as in a canal. Process of moving a vessel through a lock. Amount of elevation or descent, or both, covered in a system of locks, as in a canal.

locker [ships]: storage compartment on shipboard.

lodsbaad: Norwegian pilot boat, fore-and-aft rigged, with staysail, jib and loose footed mainsail. Topsail is often carried.

loftsman [ships]: man who lays out ship's line in mold loft and makes the molds or templates therefrom.

log: device used to measure speed of moving ship or current. It consists of block and line that is let out from a reel. The block spins, thus turning the line and actuating a meter on ship.

logarithm: exponential power to which base number, usually 10, is raised to give desired number.

logarithmic amplifer: device for increasing strength of signal so that amplified output is logarithmic multiple of input.

logarithmic scale: opposed to equally spaced arithmetic scale in plotting paper, logarithmic scale is based on logarithms or numbered values rather than on numbers).

logbook [ships]: official record of proceedings on board ship. Journal of important happenings on entire voyage.

logged: 1) said of a crew member when note of an offense committed by him is entered in ship's *official log*, with statement of any admonition, fine or forfeiture imposed, or punishment inflicted; as, *Jones was logged for insubordination; logged a day's pay for failure to work;* etc. 2) also said of any occurrence of phenomenon noted in any log; as, *the after draft was logged* as 24 feet; *we logged the gale as N.W., force 10.*

log line: part of device used to measure speed of moving ship or current. Taffrail log consists of rotating brass body on a line that is let out from stern. Receiving device on taffrail automatically records rotations which correspond to speed of vessel.

lolly: term used chiefly on northeast U.S. and Canadian coasts for slushy or granulated ice formed by grinding together of floating ice, as in a floe.

Lomonosov ridge: one of 3 submarine ridges which divides Arctic Ocean into series of basins or deeps.

longcrested wave: wave, crest width of which is long compared to wavelength.

longfin madtom [*Schilbeodes funebris*]: tiny, muddy brown catfish with a large broadly rounded tail fin. Adipose fin fused to caudal fin; caudal fin rounded; form robust; pattern uniform; spine of dorsal fin exceeding ½ height of dorsal fin. Eight barbels on head. Coloration muddy brown, lighter ventrally, with no definite pattern.

longitude: 1) distance in degrees east or west of prime meridian and measured by meridians. Meridians are semicircles that are drawn around earth from North Pole to South Pole. Longitude degrees are also divided into minutes ($-1°$ longitude = 60 min. longitude). 2) distance east or west on earth's surface, measured by angle which meridian through a place makes with some standard meridian as that of Greenwich or Paris.

longitudinal: 1) of, or pertaining to, longitude, length, or the lengthwise dimension; laid or running fore-and-aft or lengthwise, as distinguished from athwartship or transverse; fore-and-aft. 2)

one of the structural members or girders laid parallel with keel in a ship's bottom; a side keelson.

longitudinal framing [ship construction]: includes parts of structural framework which runs in fore-and-aft direction. Function is to supply longitudinal strength.

longitudinal wave: also known as primary wave, pressure wave, compressed wave, dilatational wave, and irrotational wave. Elastic wave in which displacement is in direction of wave propagation.

long line fishing: fishing with long lines or trawl lines. Hooks used on lines are small and spaced at short intervals. Usually ¼ to 2 miles long.

long period constituent: tide or tidal current constituent with a period that is independent of rotation of earth but which depends upon orbital movement of moon or earth. Period is usually longer than a day and, in general, half a month or more.

longshore current: inshore current moving essentially parallel to shore, usually generated by waves breaking at angle to shoreline.

longshore drift: sediment transported by currents parallel to shore.

long waves: 1) in oceanography, same as shallow-water waves. 2) waves in which distance between two crests is much greater than ocean depth at that location; examples are tides and tsunamis or "tidal waves."

lookdown: member of jack family whose body is about as deep as it is long with high, sloping "forehead." It is small fish under 12 in. long and weighs less than 1 lb. In color it is light blue-green with iridescent silvery sides; first rays of posterior dorsal and anal fins are prolonged into tapering tips. Lookdown is an Atlantic Coast species most common south of Chesapeake Bay.

lookout [ships]: watching for occurrence or appearance of anything. As to "keep a good lookout." Place where watch is kept.

loom: 1) loom of light is the glare seen above horizon when the light itself is not yet visible. 2) loom of an oar in rowboat is the inboard portion.

loop: 1) part of standing wave or clapotes where vertical motion is greatest and horizontal velocities are least. Loops are associated with clapotes and with seiche action resulting from resonant wave reflections in harbor or bay. 2) in *Brachiopoda*, brachidium consisting of pair of simply curved or doubly bent longitudinal "arms" and relatively simple jugum connecting the anterior edges of these arms.

loop bar: bar formed by junction of the ends of two spits on mainland side of offshore island undergoing wave erosion.

loop-tuning error: error in bearing given by direction finder, if loop is improperly tuned.

loose color changer [*Desmarestia intermedia*]: although loose color changer grows commonly on rocks below tide mark it prefers deep water in cold latitudes. It has bare, untidy arranged branches borne on axis extending the length of plant. Young plants are light brown; older ones are dark brown. Each plant has short stipe (1 to 2 in.) and each branch short stipe. Alternate branches divide and redivide until those at ends are fine threads. This species is attached to substratum by a disc, 1/16 in. in diameter.

lop: condition of sea surface characterized by short choppy or lumpy waves, or such as result from a cross sea. It is caused by a breeze against a current, meeting of currents, or change of wind direction after regular sea has been set up by a former breeze. *Loppy* is a synonym for choppy.

lophophore: horseshoe- or double-shaped ridge of tissue and supporting structures surrounding mouth and bearing ciliated tentacles in *Bryozoa*, *Brachiopoda* and *Phoronidea*.

lorac: acronymn for Long Range Accuracy radar system. Navigation system which determines a position fix by intersection of lines of position. Each line is defined by phase angle between 2 heterodyne beat frequency waves.

LORAN [Long Range Navigation]: radio navigation system that enables navigator of vessel at sea to determine position by means of pulsed signals broadcast by 2 or more fixed transmitters at predetermined points.

Loran C: low frequency, long baseline hyperbolic radio system for fixing precise positions over large areas of ocean surface. Systems are operated by U.S. Coast Guard.

lorcha: sailing vessel, typical to Bangkok, Siam. Hull is that of western model, with vertical stem and overhanging transom stern. Rig is that of Chinese lug, with 1, 2 or 3 masts. Sometimes bowsprit and jib are carried.

lore: region between eye and bill of bird, also corresponding region in fishes and reptiles.

loreal [reptiles]: small scale between nasal and preocular.

lorhumb line: in navigation, a course line in lattice; deviation of one coordinate from the other is always equal to ratio of difference between coordinates at beginning and ending of course line.

lorica: secreted noncellular protective case, as in *Tintinnidae*.

lorilabials [reptiles]: irregular group of scales arranged longitudinally between loreal and labial or posteriorly between subocular and loreals.

Loriolaster [starfish]: had small mouth and well-developed ambulacra that did form arms, though rest of body was encased in skin. Like *Cheiropsteraster* and several other unusual starfish, this

genus is found in hard Devonian shales of Bundenbach, Germany.

lotic fauna: animals living in running waters, such as rivers or streams.

Louisiana pirogue: dugout canoe, made from cypress log, used for fishing and transportation in bayous and swamps south of New Orleans, Louisiana. It is open, keelless, flat-bottomed canoe with sharp bow, which is straight, vertical above waterline and curved below. Stern resembles bow. Paddles or oars are used.

louver [ships]: small opening to permit passage of air for purpose of ventilation which may be partially or completely closed by operation of overlapping shutters.

love wave [Q-wave]: in seismic investigation, surface wave in which components of elastic medium vibrate transverse to direction of wave's travel, with no vertical component.

low: 1) cyclone or area of low atmospheric pressure. 2) submarine depression of any size or shape; also called bathymetric low.

low energy environment: region characterized by general lack of waves or current motion, permitting settling and accumulation of very fine-grained sediment (silt and clay).

lower high water: lower of two high waters of any tidal day where tide exhibits mixed characteristics.

lower high water interval: interval of time between transit (upper or lower) of moon over local or Greenwich meridian and next lower high water. This expression is used when there is considerable diurnal inequality.

lower low water: lower of two low waters of any tidal day where tide exhibits mixed characteristics.

lower low water interval: interval of time between transit (upper or lower) of moon over local or Greenwich meridian and next lower low water. This expression is used when there is considerable diurnal inequality.

lowest low water: plane of reference whose depressions below mean level correspond with level of lowest low water of any normal tide.

lowest normal tide: plane of reference lower than mean sea level by half maximum range.

Lowestoft smack: ketch-rigged trawler typical to Norfolk, England. Formerly lug-rigged but with fore-and-aft sails and two headsails, as well as mizzen staysail. Bonnets are often used to reef main and mizzen sails. Powerful hull is carvel-built.

low velocity layer: any layer found on both sides by layers of higher velocity. Such a layer can act as efficient channel for propagation of elastic waves to great distances.

low water [LW]: minimum height reached by tide.

Height may be caused by periodic tidal forces or it may have superimposed upon it effects of meteorological conditions.

low water datum: approximation of mean low water which has been adopted as standard datum for specific area although it may differ slightly from later determination.

low water equinoctial springs: low water springs near time of equinoxes.

low water line: intersection of plane of low water with shore; it varies daily with changing lunar phases and meteorological conditions.

low water stand: condition at low tides when there is no change in height of water level.

loxodograph: instrument for registering course or courses steered; a course recorder.

loxodrome: 1) loxodromic curve or line drawn on the globe shown as a spiral, intersecting in its course all meridians at a constant oblique angle and, theoretically, never reaching the pole while closely approaching it. 2) also called a *rhumb line*, it is a ship's true course as represented by a straight line on a Mercator chart, other than one in direction of the cardinal points.

L S; L T; L F; L T F; L W; L W A: letters designating the various freeboard, or load line, marks assigned a powered vessel which carries or may carry a *timber deck cargo*, or any vessel carrying a complete timber cargo. The *L* presumably indicating *lumber* and chosen rather than *T*, the letter indicating *Tropical Zone*, above letters read, in order given: Summer, Tropical, Fresh (water), Tropical Fresh, Winter, Winter North Atlantic.

L.S.T.: usual abbreviation for *local sidereal time*.

lubber line [ships]: mark in compass indicating fore-and-aft line of ship.

Lucida: brightest star in a particular group; as, *Polaris* is the *lucida* of *Ursa Minor*.

luciferase: enzyme which is heat labile, has protein characteristics and catalyzes oxidation of luciferin in bioluminescence.

luciferin: group of heat stable compounds containing amino acids and showing properties of polypeptides. Bioluminescence is produced when these compounds are oxidized by catalytic action of luciferase.

luff [ships]: forward edge of fore-and-aft sail. To luff a vessel is to bring her up toward direction of wind.

lug sail [ships]: form of fore-and-aft sail bent to yard or gaff which is slung from 1/4 to 1/3 of its length forward of mast. End of the halyard is usually fastened to iron hoop or traveler which keeps yard to mast.

lug topsail [ships]: quadrilateral sail set above mainsail of lug-rigged vessel with gaff along head, hoisted to topmast. Gaff extends short distance forward of topmast, as in case of lug mainsail.

lumachelle: shell conglomerate formed of mollusk shells which have been consolidated into cemented aggregate.

luminance: in photometry, measure of intrinsic luminous intensity emitted by source in given direction. It may be defined as illuminance produced by light from source upon a unit surface area oriented normal to line of sight at any distance from source divided by solid angle subtended by source at receiving surface.

lumpfish: common, shallow-water marine fish. *Cyclopterus lumpus* is found along New England Coast.

lunar day: interval between two successive upper transits of moon over local meridian. Period of mean lunar day, approximately 24.84 solar hours, is derived from rotation of earth on its axis relative to movement of moon about the earth.

lunar declination: angular distance of moon expressed in degrees north or south of celestial equator; it is indicated as positive when north and negative when south of equator. Maximum declination is about $28\frac{1}{2}°$ and minimum declination about $18\frac{1}{2}°$, depending on longitude of moon's node. Moon's declinational cycle of $27\frac{1}{2}$ days is called a tropical month.

lunar interval: time difference between moon's transit of Greenwich meridian and a local meridian.

lunar tide: that part of tide caused solely by tide-producing forces of moon as distinguished from that part caused by forces of the sun.

lunate: half-moon-shaped or crescent-shaped.

lunation: period during which moon completes all its phases from one new moon to next new moon, approximately 29.5 days.

lungfish: primitive fish belonging to order *Dipneusti* capable of living out of water because of lunglike bladder. Once common, millions of years ago, lungfish are now confined to 3 genera found in tropical areas of South America, Africa and Australia.

lunicurrent interval: interval between moon's transit (upper or lower) over local or Greenwich meridian and specified phase of tidal current following the transit, such as strength of flood and ebb of slack water.

lunitidal interval: interval between moon's transit (upper or lower) over local or Greenwich meridian and following high or low water. Average of all high water intervals for all phases of moon. Mean high water lunitidal interval is abbreviated to high water interval. Similarly, mean low water lunitidal interval is abbreviated to low water interval.

lunule [*Mollusca*]: heart-shaped area set off by difference of sculpture in front of beaks in bivalve shell.

lunuled: describing portion of animal's body bearing crescent-shaped markings.

lurker: rowboat used in pilchard fisheries of England from which skipper gives his orders and superintends manipulation of seine net.

lutite: 1) red clay, covering roughly 1/3 of ocean bottom. Grain size is less than 4 microns. 2) sediments or sedimentary rock composed of mud silt and/or clays.

L.W.: 1) usual abbreviation for *low water*. 2) L W designates *winter season* line in freeboard, or load line, marks cut and painted on sides of vessels carrying timber cargoes.

L.W.L.: load waterline, as indicated in sheer plan of a vessel; sometimes L.W.P., or *load water plane*.

L.W.O.S.T.: *low water ordinary spring tides.*

Lyall's seaweed [*Prionitis lyallii*]: abundant on every exposed beach between mean low tide and 1.5-ft. tide levels on rocks exposed to heavy surf. Surface of flattened branches is smooth, soft and gelatinous. Arising from holdfast are one or more shoots which begin to flatten out into main stem when about ½ in. long. From this arise many irregularly arranged flattened branches, all approximately same breadth.

lymphoid tissue: tissue in lymphatic system which circulates lymph (fluid similar to blood plasma and containing white blood corpuscles) through tissues and then into veins.

Lyomeri: order of neopterygil comprising black, scaleless, abyssal marine forms with very large mouth and distensible stomach. Animals are able to swallow prey larger than themselves.

Lyra: named for the *Lyre of Orpheus* in Greek mythology, a small northern constellation on west side of *Cygnus* (the Swan). It contains the navigational star *Vega*, or *a Lyrae*, magnitude 0.1; sidereal hour angle 81° 10′ and declination 38¾° N., and which, with *Deneb (a Cygni)* and *Altair (a Aquilae),* marks out a neat triangle, nearly right-angled at its brightest corner, or that occupied by *Vega* itself.

L-Z graph: graph used to determine in situ depths of oceanographic observations by wire depth means versus thermometric depth method.

M

M: in International Code of Signals, *M* flag, hoisted singly, denotes *"I have a doctor on board."* In form *M* or *m*, signifies *moderate* sea or swell and misty in ships' logbooks or weather observation records; *main*, as in *main hatch, main topmast*, etc.; and *minute* of time, as in *"clocks advanced 17m."* In navigation, *M* is often used to denote *meridional* parts; *m* for *meridional difference*; while on charts, *m* also indicates *mud* sea bottom.

mackerel: about 60 widespread species ranging high seas all over the world in both temperate and tropical waters. Members of the family are typically cigar-shaped fishes built for speed. Body is covered with minute cycloid scales; forward end tapers to large mouth which is armed with sharp teeth. Fins of some species can fold and fit snugly into grooves, thus being out of the way when fish is swimming. Unusual feature is presence of small finlets between tail fin and dorsal and anal fins. Tail, except in common mackerel, has keels along each side and terminates in deeply forked tail fin. This family includes several kinds of mackerel, tuna, albacore and wahoo.

mackerel, Atlantic [Boston mackerel]: blue-green fish with silvery sides marked by irregular dark bars. It is usually about 12 in. long and weighs 1 lb. Atlantic mackerel is a cold-water fish found from Labrador to mid-Atlantic states. Schools of mackerel approach shore in spring, move out to deeper waters in winter.

mackerel, Pacific: found from California to Alaska, it is metallic green fish with silvery sides whose upper portion is marked by oblique bars, small, 12 in. long and weighing under 2 lbs.

mackerel, Spanish: southern mackerel living in warmer waters of Atlantic from Carolinas to Florida. It differs from northern species in having a keel on each side of tail. Dark blue back and silvery sides are sometimes marked by orange or red spots. Long low spiny portion and higher soft-rayed portion of almost continuous dorsal fin are also distinctive features. Average weight is 2 lbs. Spanish mackerel is also an oceanic wanderer but at times forms large schools near shore.

macrobenthos: larger organisms of benthos, more than 1 mm. long.

macronucleus: larger vegetative nucleus in ciliate *Protozoa* which does not undergo mitosis during division nor participate in nuclear exchange during conjugation.

macroplankton: plankton organism ranging in size from 1 mm. to 1 cm. Sometimes referred to as mesoplankton.

Macrura: division of decapod (ten-legged) crustaceans including the lobster, crawfish or spiny lobster, prawn, shrimp, and many others of less importance. Macrurous meaning long-tailed.

Mactracea [*Heterodonta*]: provinculum of all species belonging to this superfamily, except *Mactra corallina*, is characterized by series of rectangular teeth of which one on posterior end of right valve is especially prominent, being enhanced by suppression of other teeth in some species. Prominence of this tooth is a diagnostic and readily recognizable feature of *Mactracea*.

Mactra corallina [*Mactracea, Heterodonta*]: broad end of shell is truncated and whole shell is yellowish color. Umbones are characteristically indistinct and valves are crossed by fine concentric striations and occasional coarser lines. Shell is about 200μ long. Provinculum is not toothed as in other members of the superfamily.

MAD [Magnetic Anomaly Detection]: detection device which notes changes in earth's magnetic field caused by submerged submarine. Advantage as enemy submarine detector is that it is invulnerable to jamming; its limitation, so far, is shortness of range.

made fast [ships]: secured permanently to some object as "the sails are made fast to the yards."

Madrepora: genus of hard branching corals common to all tropical seas, where its amazing formation of myriads of adhering calcareous skeletons is chiefly responsible for building the nuclei of coral reefs; also termed *Acropora*.

madrepore: branching or staghorn coral; also any perforated coral.

madreporite: sievelike porous plate (usually on surface) which enables fluid to pass in and out of water vascular system in echinoderms.

madtom, Gulf [*Schilbeodes leptacanthus*]: tiny, slender catfish with rounded tail and pale brown or yellow ground color, usually with mottling of dark gray along sides. Adipose fin fused to caudal fin; caudal fin rounded; form slender; mottled pattern. Spine of dorsal fin less than ½ height of dorsal fin.

Madura prau: native sailing craft used in Madura, island near eastern end of Java. It is built of teak and no frames are employed in its construction, hull being held together with transverse timbers secured to sides. Edges of the planks are doweled together.

maelstrom: confused and often destructive current usually caused by combined effects of high wind generated waves and strong opposing tidal current; rapid flows may follow eddying patterns or circular paths with whirlpool characteristics.

magma: molten rock deep in earth, from which igneous rock is formed.

magnetic anomaly: 1) reversal in direction of magnetic orientation in rocks or sediments, indicating reversal of polarity of earth's magnetic field. 2) distortion of regular pattern of earth's magnetic field due to local concentrations of ferromagnetic minerals.

magnetic declination: at any point, angle between direction of horizontal component of earth's magnetic field and true north.

magnetic deviation: angle between magnetic meridian and axis of compass card, expressed in degrees east or west to indicate deviation in which northern end of the compass card is offset from magnetic north. Deviation is caused by disturbing magnetic influences in immediate vicinity of compass, as within the craft.

magnetic dip: angle which magnetic lines of force make with plane of horizon.

magnetic disturbance: irregular, large amplitude, rapid time changes of earth's magnetic field which occur at approximately same time all over earth.

magnetic diurnal variation: oscillations of earth's magnetic field which have periodicity of about a day and that depends to close approximation only on local time and geographic latitude.

magnetic equator: imaginary line on earth's surface where magnetic inclination is 0°, i.e., magnetic field is horizontal.

magnetic field intensity: magnetic force exerted on imaginary unit magnetic pole placed at any specified point of space. It is a vector quantity. Its direction is taken as direction toward which north magnetic pole would tend to move under influence of the field.

magnetic inclination: angle that magnetic needle makes with surface of earth.

magnetic latitude: at any point on earth's surface angle whose tangent is ½ the tangent of magnetic dip at that point.

magnetic meridian: at any point, direction of horizontal component of earth's magnetic field.

magnetic moment: quantity obtained by multiplying distance between two magnetic poles by average strength of poles.

magnetic north: direction north at any point as determined by earth's magnetic line of force.

magnetic pole: north magnetic pole is point on earth's surface where north-seeking end of magnetic needle, free to move in space, points directly down. At south magnetic pole same needle points directly up. These poles are also known as dip poles.

magnetic variation or declination: angle by which compass needle varies from true north.

magnetic variometer: instrument for measuring differences in magnetic field with respect to space or time.

magnetite: important iron ore. When magnetized, it is called loadstone.

magnetometer: all electronic instrument for measuring magnetic intensity. It may measure total intensity or portions of ambient magnetic fields. Apparatus is widely used in oceanographic and dry land type of geophysical explorations.

magnitude: as met with in the term *stellar magnitude*, degree of brightness of a celestial body, especially a star, as expressed in *first, second, third, etc., magnitude, sixth* being faintest to unaided eye. Scale used by astronomers gives a body *magnitude* numerically *less* by 1 when it is 2.512 times brighter than one with which it is compared; thus star *Capella* of *magnitude* 0.2 is 1 *magnitude* brighter than *Pollux* with his 1.2 *magnitude*. Generally, however, stars of *magnitude*—1.5 to 1.4 are classed of *first magnitude;* those 1.5 to 2.4 as *second magnitude;* 2.5 to 3.4 as *third magnitude;* and so on. Stars of lesser *magnitude* than third are seldom used in navigation.

mahona: Turkish equivalent of Venetian "galleass." Present-day types are fishing and cargo boats of Bosphorus. Hulls have generous sheer, good lines and carry sprit mainsail or lateen rig, with one or two jibs.

Maia squinado [*Maiidae*]: larvae of spiny spider crab mainly in late summer plankton. Protozoeae are about 2.5 mm. long and soon change into first zoea stage which has greenish color because it has yellow and black chromatophores. Lateral spines are short, dorsal and rostral spines curved. First zoeal stage is unusual in having flagellum to antenna as well as having pleopods. There are 6 abdominal segments even in first zoea. Lateral spines are present on second to fifth abdominal segments and those of third and fifth increase in length until second (last) zoeal stage which has long pleopods but small walking legs.

main: 1) even persons who have never been near a

coast would like to go adventuring "over the bounding main." But how did the ocean gain such a title? In old English speech *maegen* was roughly equivalent to "great." The modernized adjective was applied to chief or greatest member of any group of persons or things. Since open ocean or "high sea" was obviously greater than bodies of coastal water, it became customary to speak of the "main sea." But the term was cumbersome and eventually was abbreviated in common speech. In a 16th century translation of Plutarch's famous *Parallel Lives*, a description of a shipboard incident is rendered, "The winds stoode full against them coming from the maine." Though it has no organic ties with the sea, the abbreviated term came into common use as a poetic equivalent for "ocean." 2) as mainmast and mainsail, principal mast or sail on ship.

mainbeam [ships]: main longitudinal beam on ship, running down center line and supported as a rule by king posts.

mainbody [ships]: hull exclusive of all deck erections, spars, stocks, etc.; naked hull.

main deck [ships]: 1) portion of ship's upper deck that lies between poop and forecastle. 2) highest complete deck on ship; highest deck which runs full length of ship.

mainmast [ships]: principal mast of ship or other vessel. In three-masted ship it is the middle mast.

mainsail: excepting in more recent square and fore-and-aft rigged vessels having more than three masts, largest sail carried and perhaps earliest so named, evidence in Old Norse history indicating that even the single square sail spread by the Vikings was called *megin segl*. It is always set on the *mainmast*.

major articulation: in copepods, articulation between prosoma and the urosome.

major constituents: those chemical elements present in seawater which together make up over 99.9% of known dissolved solid constituents of seawater. These include following ions: chloride, sulfate, bicarbonate, bromide, fluoride, boric acid, sodium, magnesium, calcium, potassium, and strontium.

major septum [*Coelenterata*]: one of initial or secondary septa. Typically major septa are of subequal length and extend most of distance from wall to axis.

make: 1) to arrive at, or sight, a place or position steered for; as, to *make the cape; we made the lightship right ahead*. 2) to work to windward or fall off to leeward; as, *she makes weatherly courses; she makes too much leeway*. 3) to act, move, or produce a certain effect; as, to *make* a tack; to *make* sternway; to *make* bad weather of it. 4) to perform something or accomplish a purpose; as, to *make* fast; to *make* good a course

steered. 5) to *make* a seam (in calking). 6) to grow or increase in appearance or fact; as, *bad weather is making; ship is making water*. 7) to indicate or observe an occurrence; as, to *make* sunset (by formally lowering the colors); to *make* eight bells (by striking ship's bell as so ordered). 8) to unfurl sails when getting under way, either when leaving port or from any temporary stopping; as to *make sail*.

Malacostraca [*Copepoda*]: this huge subclass includes all larger and more obvious crustaceans, as well as many smaller and less known ones. In short, malacostracans are distinguishable by having rigid pattern of segmentation: 6 segments in head, 8 in thorax and 6 in abdomen (except in *Leptostraca*, which have 7). Thoracic limbs differ sharply in structure from those of abdomen and from 1 to 3 pairs may assist in feeding (multipeds); carapace over thorax; compound eyes (often borne on stalks); scalelike exopodite on 2nd antenna; biramous antennules; abdomen which can be flexed under thorax and tail fan borne in last (6th) abdominal segment.

malar panshi: primitive Bengal boat. Hull is dugout or built on dugout frame. There is high steering platform aft with fixed steering oar; one or two square sails on single mast.

Malay outrigger canoe: fast, outrigger sailing canoe used by natives on Straits of Malacca. Canoe is double-ended, long and extremely narrow, a 25-footer being about 9 in. wide.

Maldive Islands trader: large, three-masted, decked trading vessel of 100 tons or more of Maldive Islands, which lie southwest of India in Indian Ocean. Hull and rig resemble 15th century *Santa Maria* of Columbus' time, with poop and overhanging forecastle.

malleation [*Mollusca*]: sculpture resembling hammered surface.

Malpighian tubule: excretory, blind tubular glands opening into anterior part of hind gut of many terrestrial arthropods.

Malus: the *mast* in constellation *Argo*.

Mammalia [class]: phylum *Chordata*, latest Triassic to Recent. Hair; mammary glands; endothermal. Most bear young partly developed; some have marsupium; others have inguina embryonic development with placenta. Terrestrial, aerial and aquatic. Predators and herbivores.

mammatocumulus: cumulus cloud having dark nipple-like lower protuberances; also called *festoon cloud*.

manatee: any of 3 species of sea cow which constitutes genus *Trichechus*. All 3 are confined to shallow tropical marine waters, estuaries and rivers on both sides of Atlantic Ocean. Tail is broad and rounded, not whalelike as in dugong.

Mandaloceras [nautiloids]: Ordovician to Devonian age. Their shells became both short and wide, with scarcely a trace of curvature and Y- or T-shaped apertures. Crossbars of Y or T accommodated eyes, and the rear (ventral) extension provided opening for funnel, with arms emerging between.

mandible [reptiles]: lower jaw.

Mandibulata [subphylum]: phylum *Arthropoda*, body of 2 or 3 divisions: cephalothorax-abdomen, head and trunk, or head-thorax-abdomen; antennae of 1 or 2 pairs; mandible or jaws paired; maxillae 1 or 2 pairs; walking legs 3 or more pairs; respiration by gills or tracheae; excretion by glands or Malpighian tubules; sexes usually separate; development usually with larval stages; terrestrial, freshwater or marine.

maneuver: 1) tactical operation in seamanship; especially, any orderly change made in a formation of naval ships with view of obtaining an advantage at scene of hostilities. In *plural*, exercises of a fleet in operations of changing formation, lines of advance, etc., with view of theoretically obtaining advantage in attack or defense. 2) to perform such naval operational tactics; to sail a vessel with different changes of courses, trimming of sail, use of anchors, etc., in order to arrive at a certain position or point of vantage.

manger [ships]: perforated elevated bottom of chain locker which prevents chains from touching main locker bottom and allows seepage water to flow to drains.

Mangilia nebula [*Turridae*]: shell of newly hatched larvae is approximately 0.3 mm. high and bilobed velum bears number of orange spots (usually 12). In later veliger foot develops a pair of small ciliated lobes and large median one. Orange spots fuse to form border or spot at corner of each velar lobe and velum becomes enormous and covers shell and animal. Shell is tuberculate and striated near aperture while dark foot is characteristically truncated at anterior end.

mangrove: one of several genera of tropical trees or shrubs which produce many prop roots and grow along low-lying coasts into shallow water.

manhole [ships]: hole in a tank, boiler or compartment in ship, designed to allow entrance of man for examination, cleaning and repairs.

manifest: list of shipments contained in a cargo, showing terms, amount, or quantities of goods, identifying marks and numbers, names of shippers and consignees, and, sometimes, corresponding number of bills of lading and weight or measurement of goods. The document is of special interest to ship's agents at port or ports of destination, to customs officers at port of departure, and to consular representative of countries to which goods are consigned.

manifold [ships]: casting or chest containing sev-

eral valves. Suction or discharge pipes from or to various compartments; tanks and pumps are led to it making it possible for several pumps to draw from or deliver to a given place through one pipeline.

manrope [ships]: handrope. Short span or rope along ship's ladder used as aid in ascending or descending steps.

manta, Atlantic [devilfish]: batlike ray that grows to width of 20 ft. and may weigh as much as 3,000 lbs. Huge pectoral fins are expanded to form undulating "wings" and additional set of fleshy outgrowths known as cephalic fins form pair of "horns" on either side of snout. Body, covered with tiny tubercles, is dark brown or black and contrasting white on underparts. Corners of pectoral fins are pointed like wings of bird; cephalic fins form scoop that funnels prey into huge mouth. Lobes made of leathery muscle tissue resemble animated horns as manta swims gracefully through water.

Manta birostris: devilfish. Genus of rays containing the devilfish of West Indies and Gulf of Mexico; also, *Mobula*. The ugly fellow's tough and leathery skin is valued among Mexicans for shoemaking and his liver for oil and food.

manta ray: species of ray-form fishes (genus *Manta*) that are very large, and heavy and live in warm seas. They produce live young. Like other rays, they have flattened bodies with mouth and gills on lower surface and eyes on upper. Mantas and other rays have large pectoral or side fins, cartilaginous skeletons and usually long slender tails.

man the windlass [ships]: term "to man" means literally to supply with sufficient complement of men to do the job effectively.

mantle: 1) in biology, portion of body wall in mollusks that lines shell and contains shell-secreting glands. 2) in geology, portion of earth's interior between mainly molten core and comparatively thin surface crust, about 4½ km. (20 miles) thick under continental land masses. Mantle extends down to discontinuity that is 2,900 km. (1,800 miles) under surface. 3) in *Brachiopoda*, two folds of body wall that lie respectively above and below viscera and line the inner surface of each valve.

mantle canal [*Brachiopoda*]: canal within mantle that connects coelomic cavity of body.

mantle cavity: space containing respiratory organs between mantle and body of a mollusk or brachiopod.

mantle convection: theory that new crust (of earth) may emerge from plant's mantle, overriding some crustal areas while giving fresh exposure to others.

manubrium: in jellyfish, ectodermally lined protrusion from surface of subumbrella, bearing mouth.

maota: outrigger canoe of island of Napuka, one of northernmost of atolls of Tuamotu Archipelago. These canoes are formed of single dugout without end pieces, keel or thwarts. Often washboard is sewed on above each side.

mapo [*Bathygobius soporator*]: small, slender fish seldom same color. Pelvic fins fused at base to form sucking disk; head naked but body sealed; 9 to 10 soft rays in dorsal fin. Upper rays in pectoral fin soft and silky. Head broad, low, rounded in profile; mouth large, oblique; lips thick. Caudal fin short, pelvic fin thoracic in position, united at base to form sucking disk. Color extremely variable but dorsal and caudal fins usually dusky while anal is usually clear. Size from 3 to 6 in.

Marconi rig: modern rig with lofty triangular mainsail, short boom and 1 or 2 headsails. It is descended from leg-of-mutton Bermuda rig.

Marcq St. Hilaire Method: first introduced by *Commandant M. St. Hilaire* of French navy, about 1885, an important improvement in determination of the *line of position*, called *New Navigation* for a probationary period of something like 30 years. Its marked departure from prevailing practice lay in a short cut offered by the solution of spherical trigonometrical problem involved for value of a heavenly body's altitude at ship's estimated position at instant corresponding to an altitude of same body observed by sextant; and in using the difference between such calculated and observed altitudes, called the *intercept*, for laying off position line on chart. Thus, if observed altitude exceeded the calculated altitude by 5′, a distance of 5 miles is laid off on chart from ship's estimated or assumed position in direction of azimuth of body observed; conversely, away from body, if observed altitude were less. Position line is drawn through point thus plotted at right angles to, or 90° from, the body's true azimuth. The method has been greatly simplified by comparatively recent tables of *Ageton, Dreisonstock, Weems, H.O. 214*, and others. Those named may be obtained from U.S. Hydrographic Office, Washington, D.C., or its agencies at principal seaports of U.S.

Mare: the sea. *Mare clausum*, as sometimes used in legal phrasing, is a sea subject only to jurisdiction of a particular nation and, as such nation decrees, may be a *closed sea* in the sense of prohibiting certain or all vessels from sailing in such area; opposed to *Mare liberum*, or high seas, on which all vessels have equal rights.

mares' tails: long, featherlike streamers appearing in *cirrus* cloud formation; accompanied by *cirrocumulus*, presages bad weather.

margate: pearly-gray fish with several widely spaced lengthwise stripes on upper side; when distributed it turns a greenish hue. Fins are light olive-green; lips are yellowish; open mouth reveals vermilion interior. Reaches length of 24 in. and weight of 10 lbs. Margates live among rocks and submerged wrecks as well as on coral reefs; food consists of algae, mollusks, crustaceans and small fish.

margate, black [pompon]: pearly-gray in color with dusky fins; often there is dark band beneath pectoral fins; black margate grows to considerable size, reaching length of 36 in. It hides by day in holes and grottoes among coral, emerging at night to feed on small aquatic invertebrates.

marginal conglomerate: coarse pebble deposits along shore which form landward margins or facies of other types of sediments into which they grade.

marginals [reptiles]: laminae forming edge of turtle's shell.

marginal seas: semi-enclosed seas adjacent to, wide open to and connected with oceans at surface but bounded at depth by submarine ridges, e.g., Yellow Sea. When shallow (less than about 150 fathoms) they are called shelf seas, e.g., Hudson Bay.

marginal trench: deep furrow paralleling trend of continental margin between base of continental slope and abyssal plain; usually about 1,000 fathoms deeper than general level of neighboring sea floor. Trenches are common in Pacific Ocean but less so in north or south Atlantic Oceans.

marginal zone: outer seaward ridge and generally highest portion of coral reef.

margin plates [ships]: longitudinal plate which closes off ends of floors along midship section.

mariculture: aquaculture, controlled cultivation of marine plants or animals.

marigram: graphic record of rise and fall of tide in form of a curve which shows time of any stage of tide represented by abscissas and height in feet by ordinates.

marigraph: instrument by means of which a continuous record of duration of rise and fall and, also, times of high and low water, is graphically indicated at a selected station. Record thus obtained is called a *marigram* or *tidal curve* and is used in connection with predictions of times and heights of high and low water.

marine abrasion: erosion of bedrock surface by wave movement of sand and gravel.

marine bench: small wave-eroded terrace along shore which is level or gently inclined seaward.

marine biogeography: description of distribution of marine animals and plants, and analysis of those factors which determine distribution and abundance of given species.

marine biology: study of plants and animals living in sea.

marine borer: any marine invertebrate that excavates tunnels, holes or depressions in one or more of variety of materials by abrasive, chewing or chemical action. Marine borers exist in several phyla, including sponges, annelids, arthropods, mollusks and echinoderms.

marine-built terrace: terrace seaward of marine-cut terrace, shore platform or plain of marine abrasion consisting of material eroded from marine-cut terrace.

marine cliff: cliff or slope marking inshore limit of beach erosion. It may vary from inconspicuous slope to escarpment hundreds of feet high.

marine climate: regional climate which is under predominant influence of sea, i.e., climate characterized by oceanicity; antithesis of continental climate.

marine-cut plain: nearly flat surface carved by sea waves or current scour.

marine-cut terrace: level or gently sloping submerged shelf formed along seacoast by erosive action of waves and currents.

marine denudation: erosive and sweeping action of sea, as evidenced by geological records to be found in ancient shorelines.

marine ecology: science which embraces all aspects of interrelations of marine organisms and their environment and interrelations between organisms themselves.

marine humus: less digestible organic residues that accumulate in solution or suspension in seas.

marine meteorology: that part of meteorology which deals mainly with oceanic areas, including island and coastal regions.

marine plains: ocean plains formed by emergence of shallow parts of ocean floors. Largest plains in the world originated in this way. Marine plains may be either coastal or interior plains, depending on locations. Atlantic Coastal Plain, running along Atlantic Coast from Long Island, New York, to Florida, is a coastal plain, as is Gulf Coastal Plain along Gulf of Mexico. Both of these were formed by emergence of continental shelves. Marine plains in Europe include coastal plains of northern France, southeastern England and western Scandinavia, as well as great interior plains of central Europe and Russian Ukraine.

mariner: seaman or sailor; one whose vocation is that of sailing or navigating vessels, or in any way assisting in such occupation. The word usually is confined to legal use in which it is defined as "every person, male or female, employed in whatever capacity on board ship and whose labor contributes in any way to the accomplishment of ship's voyage."

mariner's measure:

6 feet	=	1 fathom[1]
100 fathoms	=	1 cable[2]
10 cables	=	1 mile
6080 feet	=	1 mile[3]
3 miles	=	1 league

marine salina: body of salt water separated from sea by sand or gravel barrier through which seawater percolates. Marine salinas are found along arid coasts where little or no inflow of fresh water occurs.

marine terrace: flat, platformlike area showing position of former beach or area cut back by sea.

maritime: situated or living near, or bordering on the sea; as, a maritime plant; a maritime country. Pertaining to or connected with the sea in respect to commerce, navigation, or shipping; as, maritime law; maritime belt; maritime lien. In many instances synonymous with *marine*. Nautical; seamanlike.

maritime air: type of air whose characteristics are developed over extensive water surface and which, therefore, has basic maritime quality of high moisture content in at least its lower level.

maritime air mass: air mass that originates over water areas and is relatively moist.

mark: 1) line, notch, groove, etc., for indicating a limit, measure, or position of something; as, *freeboard* or *Plimsoll mark; lead line mark; highwater mark.* 2) indicated depth by hand lead line when one of its *marks* is at water surface is reported, *"By the mark, 5,"* etc.

Markab: *a Pegasi,* a star of magnitude 2.57 situated at S.W. corner of *Square of Pegasus.* In 1953 its sidereal hour angle is given as 14° 23′ and declination 14° 58′ N. A line from *Scheat,* or β *Pegasi,* his neighbor at N.W. corner of the Square, drawn through *Markab* and produced 45° southward passes very close to *Fomlhaut (a Piscis Australis).* (*Markab* should not be confused with *Markeb,* a 3rd magnitude star in *Argo* and catalogued by astronomers as k *Velorum* or k *Argus,* having a S.H.A. of 219° 50′ and declination 54¾° S.)

marker: 1) short-range, local automatic radio beacon fixed on a dolphin, pier end, buoy, etc., for indicating a channel entrance or turning point, a pier, mouth of a small harbor, etc. 2) a marking pin, or piece of small pipe used for marking intended rivet holes on plates or templates; dipped in light paint and carefully laid on end at each required hole, thus leaving a small circular mark; used by the workman called a *marker off, liner off,* or *marking off plater* in a shipyard.

market fisherman: fishing craft which markets fish as soon as catch is made. Fast vessels are used in order to reach marketing port quickly to prevent spoilage of fish.

marl: general term for very fine-grained rock, either clay or loam, with mixture of calcium carbonate.

marlin [ships]: tarred cord about 1/8 in. in diameter made of hemp.

marlin, blue: larger species than white marlin. It has same dark blue back and long dorsal fin, but forward edge of latter rises to sharper point. Coppery color often tints upper sides which also reveal faint vertical stripes. Blue marlin is a popular game fish of southern Atlantic waters. Average individual weighs about 200 lbs.

marline spike [ships]: pointed metal pinlike device used on boats to separate strands of rope while splicing it.

marlin, striped: Pacific Coast species usually caught in California waters. It is same color and has same dorsal and ventral fin characteristics as other marlins, but it has shorter spear and is marked by pale lavender stripes that extend from back to belly. This species reaches weight of 250 lbs.

marlin, white: dark blue back and long dorsal fin; latter extends from head almost to tail, with bluntly rounded forward edge. Ventral fins, situated below pectorals are reduced to slender and elongated appendages. This is a rather small marlin, usually weighing 50 to 100 lbs.

marlstone: indurated mixture of calcium carbonate and clay of which clay comprises 25 to 75 percent.

Marrella [arthropods]: lace crab has very narrow thorax, 4 very large spines and many gill-bearing legs. It has been regarded as newly molted trilobite, but this interpretation seems to be ruled out by two pairs of feathery antennae. Despite its delicate, lacy appearance, *Marrella* also are common in Burgess shale.

marry [ships]: to join two rope ends so that joint will run through block; also, to place two ropes alongside each other so that both may be hauled in at same time.

Mars: named for ancient Romans' god of war. Fourth planet from the sun and next outside the earth, easily recognized by its steady reddish light; mean distance from sun about 141,000,000 statute miles; its orbit from that of Earth, 35,000,000 miles; has a diameter of 4,216 miles which gives an angular measure of 18″ at his nearest approach to earth; completes a revolution around sun in 687 days; has two small satellites; and plane of his orbit is inclined 1° 51′ from that of earth (the ecliptic). For navigators' use, planet's declination, Greenwich hour angle and time of transit are given in the *Nautical Almanac*.

Marsden chart: system introduced by Marsden early in 19th century for showing distribution of meteorological data on chart especially over oceans. Mercator map projection is used; world between 90° N and 80° S being divided into Marsden "squares" each of 10° latitude by 10° longitude. Squares are systematically numbered to indicate position. Each square may be divided into quarter squares or into 100 one-degree subsquares numbered from 00 to 99 to give position to nearest degree.

marsh: area of soft wetland. Flat land periodically flooded by saltwater is called salt marsh.

marsh gas: volatile odorless and colorless gas which comes from marshes and swamps where vegetation is in process of decay. When found in petroleum it is called methane. When purified it is known as benzine. In coal mines it is called black damp where it presents ever-present danger of causing damaging and fatal explosions. Simplest paraffin hydrocarbon.

marsillian: Mediterranean vessel of 16th century, similar to "huk."

marsupium: pouch.

martingale [ships]: short spar extending perpendicularly downward from cap of bowsprit, and serving to support jibboom by means of martingale stays.

martingale boom: a dolphin striker.

martite: hematite pseudomorphous after magnetite.

Maru: part of name given each Japanese merchant vessel, as in *"Midori Maru," "Toyo Kuni Maru,"* etc., said to carry the idea of rounded out perfection or completeness in accord with original symbolic meaning attached to a circle or a sphere.

mash-huf: open boat used by farers of Southern Iraq. It is similar to "tarada" but is wider and undecorated.

mashwa: term employed on East African coast to any round-sterned vessel, originally meaning fishing boat.

massive [*Bryozoa*]: colony form consisting of thick zoarium, generally hemispherical or subglobular in shape.

mass movement: unit movement or slippage of mass of sediment down a slope, such as in submarine canyon, which often initiates a turbidity current.

mass transport: transfer of water in direction of wave propagation in deep water. In shallow water, mass transport varies in depth.

mast [ships]: 1) spar of wood or steel usually circular in section, which is erected vertically on center line of ship to sustain yards, sails, etc. 2) spar or hollow steel pipe tapering smaller at top, placed in center line of ship with a light after rake. Masts support yards and gaffs. On cargo vessels they support cargo booms.

mast collar [ships]: piece of canvas lashed to mast and fastened to deck to keep water from entering.

mast hole [ships]: hole in deck to receive mast. Diameter of hole is larger than mast for purpose of receiving two rows of forwarded wedges to hold mast in place.

Mastigophora [order *Diniferida*]: order includes all dinoflagellates considered as typical, i.e., from present point of view all those most likely to be met with in plankton. Even here there are wide differences in organization.

masting: arrangement of masts in a vessel; the mast collectively. Disposition of masts in a sailing vessel with regard to their function in spreading a balanced sail area and so providing craft with satisfactory steering qualities with particular rig considered. Special attention is given to position of hull's *center of lateral resistance* and, depending upon vessel's underbody lines, *masting* is so planned that center of gravity of ordinary sail area lies slightly forward of center of lateral resistance.

masts, pair [ships]: pair of cargo masts stepped on either side of center line with heads connected by spars.

mast step [ships]: fitting on ship into which bottom of mast is set when it is installed or stepped.

mast table [ships]: structure built up around mast as support for cargo boom pivots.

mast tang [ships]: metal fitting on mast to which standing rigging may be attached.

masula: light, wide, flat-bottomed scow used for conveying passengers and cargo through surf to and from ships on Madras Coast. They range from 28 to 35 ft. long and 1/3 the beam; rowed by 12 men with 2 steersmen.

mate [ships]: ship's officer whose duty it is to oversee execution of orders of the master, or immediate superior.

mathaea: light open boat used on northeast coast of Africa. It is primitive canoe-type with single square sail. It is employed by Somalians for fishing and general use.

mature wave platform: platform of marine abrasion which has abundance of rocky debris not yet reduced to pebble size by wave action.

maxilla: 1) in vertebrates, important portion of bone on upper jaw. Premaxillae are a pair of bones between and in front of the 2 maxillae. 2) head appendage (1 or 2 pairs) modified in various ways for food handling in many arthropods. 3) in *Crustacea*, there are 2 pairs of maxillae immediately back of jaws or mandibles. First pair are often termed maxillulae, term maxillae being used for 2nd pair.

maxillaries [fish]: outer bones of upper jaw.

maxillary [reptiles]: pertaining to upper jaw.

maxillipeds: in *Crustacea*, first 2 or 3 pairs of thoracic appendages back of maxillae, when turned forward and modified to aid in handling of food.

maximum ebb: greatest speed of ebb tidal current.

maximum flood: greatest speed of flood tidal current.

Mayday: corresponding to French pronunciation of *"m'aider,"* the spoken word prescribed by International Code of Signals to be used by *radio-telephony* in case of aircraft in distress and requiring assistance. *International Conference on Safety of Life at Sea, 1948*, revised *Article 31* of International Regulations for Preventing Collision at Sea to include, as *Rule 31(e)*, the above signa among other distress signals prescribed for *"a vessel or sea-plane on the water."*

meagre: European food fish of the *Sciaenidae* family *(Sciaena aquila)* similar in appearance to the *red drumfish* of southeastern U.S. coast and member of same family, which also includes the *croaker, grunt, drum* and others noted for their croaking or grunting habits—a characteristic of the entire tribe. The *meagre* attains a length of 5 to 6 feet, is well-proportioned and has a long dorsal fringe extending almost to the tail from an anterior distinctive dorsal fin.

mean chart: any chart on which isopleths of mean value of given oceanographic element are drawn.

mean current: current speed and direction determined to be average of total number of observations for specified area.

meander: 1) one of series of looplike bends in course of a stream. 2) deviation of flow pattern of current.

mean diurnal high water inequality [DHQ]: half average difference between heights of two high waters of each tidal day over 19-year period, obtained by subtracting mean of all high waters from mean of higher high waters.

mean diurnal low water inequality [DLQ]: half average difference between heights of two low waters of each tidal day over 19-year period obtained by subtracting mean of lower low waters from mean of all low waters.

mean higher high water [MHHW]: average height of all daily higher high waters recorded over 19-year period, or computed equivalent period.

mean high water [MHW]: average height of all high waters recorded over 19-year period, or computed equivalent period.

mean high water neaps [MHWN]: average height of all high waters recorded during quadrature over 19-year period, or computed equivalent period.

mean lower low water [MLLW]: average height of all lower low waters over 19-year period, or computed equivalent period. It is usually associated with tide exhibiting mixed characteristics.

mean low water [MLW]: average height of all low waters recorded over 19-year period, or computed equivalent period.

mean low water neaps [MLWN]: average height of all low waters recorded during quadrature over 19-year period, or computed equivalent period.

mean neap range [Np]: average semidiurnal range occurring at time of quadrature. It is smaller than mean range where type of tide is either semidiurnal or mixed and is not of practical significance where type of tide is diurnal.

mean neap rise: height of mean high water neaps above chart datum.

mean range: difference in height between mean high water and mean low water over 19-year period.

mean rise: height of mean high water above chart datum.

mean sea level [MSL]: mean surface water level determined by averaging heights at all stages of tide over 19-year period. Mean sea level is usually determined from hourly height readings measured from fixed predetermined reference level (chart datum).

mean sounding velocity: mean values for velocity of sound through vertical water column of specific depths based on different velocities of sound in different sections of column.

mean sphere depth: uniform depth to which water would cover earth if solid surface were smoothed off and were parallel to surface of geoid. Depth would be about 8,000 ft. (2,440 meters).

mean tide level: reference plane midway between mean high water and mean low water.

mean water level [MWL]: mean surface level determined by averaging height of water at equal intervals of time, usually at hourly intervals, over considerable period of time.

median septum [*Brachiopoda*]: calcareous ridge built along midline of interior valve.

medimarimeter: instrument for measuring mean sea level.

mediterranean: large body of salt water or inland sea surrounded by land, which may have one or more narrow openings to ocean or another sea.

medregal: amberfish of the *Carangidae* family, classified as *Seriola fasciata*, found in West Indian and other tropical waters. Also, *madregal, amberjack*.

medullary shell: in *Radiolaria*, part of shell forming inner framework.

medusa: free-swimming, sexually mature form of coelenterates. Umbrella- or bell-shaped, medusa swims by pulsations of its body; tentacles and sense organs are located at edge of bell. Medusae reproduce sexually by discharging fertilized eggs into seawater instead of budding, asexual reproduction of other coelenterates called polyps.

medusoid [*Coelenterata*]: type of coelenterate of free-living jellyfish form; inverted bowllike form with mouth and tentacles downward.

meeting vessels: those proceeding on such courses as to involve risk of collision; especially in an end on situation, or when approaching each other *head to head*, or nearly so.

megalops: larval stage just before adult stage of marine crabs.

megalospheric: foraminiferal shell with relatively large initial chamber (proloculus) formed by asexual reproduction.

Meganyctiphanes [euphausiids]: in this genus only 8th leg is rudimentary, 6th and 7th legs have indopodites in both sexes. *M. norvegica* is large species reaching 40 mm. in length. Front end of carapace has convex curve but no rostral spines; prominent pair of spines occur on each laterofrontal border and smaller one about halfway along each lateral margin of carapace. First antennular segment has dorsal backwardly directed leaflet.

megaplankton: plankton organisms larger than 1 cm. in length or diameter.

megaripple: large, wavelike sediment feature in very shallow water composed of sand. Wavelength may reach 100 meters and amplitude is about 0.5 meters.

megascopic: observable with unaided eyes.

meiobenthos: small benthic organisms that will pass through 1 mm. mesh sieve but be retained by a 0.1 mm. mesh.

melanin: black or dark brown pigment in animals or plants.

Melicertum octocostatum [phylum *Coelenterata*]: medusa of hydroid of same name. Three to 7 tracts of nematocysts in exumbrellar surface are important characters. There are no marginal sense organs but 64 to 72 marginal tentacles in adult, which may reach diameter of 14 mm. Although it has wide distribution, it is mainly northern species.

melon: in toothed whales, mass of oily blubber between blowhole and end of snout.

melon seed: small, wide, shallow-draft, centerboard boat used for hunting ducks and other sea fowl in shallow waters of New Jersey coast. It is decked except for cockpit.

Melosira [phytoplankton]: cylindrical cells each containing numerous chloroplasts; frustules, with sculpturing of fine dots. Cells unite to form chains like a string of beads.

membranelle: in ciliates, group of cilia fused together to form vibratile plate or membrane.

menhaden: silvery fish of variable coloring: green, blue, gray or brown. It is a more chunky fish than herring and marked by large spot behind upper margin of gill cover. Menhaden are usually under 12 in. long but may reach a maximum of 20 in. Menhaden are commonly found in schools near shore along the entire coast. This species is so rich in oil that it is unfit for use as food.

Menkalinan: star of magnitude 2.07 in *Auriga*, located about 8° east of *Capella*, the second brightest in the northern sky. Usually catalogued as β *Aurigae*, it has a sidereal hour angle of 271° and declination of nearly 45°, lying 37½° due north of the red *Betelguese* in *Orion's* group, or roughly halfway from that star toward *Polaris*.

Menkar: *a Ceti*, a star of magnitude 2.82 lying somewhat isolated at about 40° W. by N. of *Orion's belt*. Only member of consequence in *Cetus*, it makes a tolerable western corner for an equilateral triangle formed by *Aldebaran* to the N.E. and *Rigel* toward the S.E. Its S.H.A. is about 315°; declination 4° N.

Merak: one of the *pointers* in *Ursa Major*, the *Great Bear*, or *Big Dipper*, star at lower corner of the *bowl* and farthest from *handle of Dipper*. Listed as β *Ursae Majoris*, has a magnitude of 2.44, S.H.A. of 195¼°, and declination 56½° N.

Mercator, Gerhard: flemish geographer (1521-1594) credited with introducing a projection of earth's surface subsequently found second to none for mariners' use in latitudes up to about 75°.

Mercator projection: a map projection in which the meridians and parallels of latitude appear as lines crossing at right angles and in which areas appear greater farther from the equator.

Mergui pearling vessel: small craft (sailing) used in pearl fishery of Mergui Archipelago in Indian Ocean just off lower Burma Coast. In general, it is Malayan in character with slipper bow and overhanging counter. It is decked, of shallow draft and larger pearlers have cabin house between helm and mainmast.

meridian: north-south reference line, through geographical poles of earth from which longitudes and azimuths are measured.

meridional flow: that flow which moves in north-south along meridians.

Mero: large members of the grouper family—*black jewfish, guasa,* and *red grouper*—that are found in warmer seas.

meroplankton: chiefly, floating development stage (eggs and larvae) of benthos and nekton. These forms are especially abundant in neritic waters.

merostome: type of chelicerate arthropod, includes king crab *(Limulus)*, eurypteroids.

Mersey lighter: sailing barge or lighter used on Mersey River, England. It is similar to "keel" except that fore-and-aft rig is employed.

merus: in *Crustacea*, third segment of leg in thoracic legs.

mesenchyme: more or less loosely formed tissue between ectoderm and endoderm.

mesentery: 1) supporting membrane. 2) in *Coelenterata*, one of several radial sheets of soft tissue that partitions internal body cavity.

meshalobous: phytoplankton or plankton in general, living in brackish water with salinity ranges of 5 to 20 percent.

mesoderm: middle germ layer between ectoderm and endoderm.

Mesogastropoda [gastropod larvae]: this group includes vast majority of common intertidal *Prosobranchia*. Eggs of nonviviparous forms are always encased singly or in clumps in gelatinous material and are normally attached to substratum. Rarely, as in *Littorina litorea* and *L. neritoides*, eggs occur in plankton. First free-living stage is veliger. This is characterized by possession of lobed velum. Number of lobes varies; it is usually 2 or, in newly hatched larvae, may increase to 4 or 6 in later larvae. Whorls are continuously added during larval life and may be as many as 8 before metamorphosis.

Mesogean seaway: greatest of all geosynclinal belts, extended halfway around world, almost parallel with equator, it is occupied territory that is now within and adjacent to Mediterranean Sea and great east-west mountain systems of Europe and Asia. This belt was occupied by succession of shifting seas, coal-forming swamps, lakes and sandy lowlands, which received a great variety of sediments. Like geosynclinal areas in general, area was geologically active. By contrast, most of central and southern Africa and Baltic and Angara shields remained stable and above water. Beginning with the Carboniferous a huge sea is clearly outlined, stretching out parallel to the equator and occupying all mountainous areas of Southern Asia (Himalayas) and Mediterranean chain (Alps). Sea is today reduced to western remnant which has become the Mediterranean. Therefore it is called the Great Mediterranean or Mesogean sea. It was bounded on north by North Asiatic and North European (north Atlantic) continents, temporarily and imperfectly separated, up to middle Permian by arm of Russian sea. To south extended another continental mass, continent of Gondwana, including, especially, Australia, Peninsular India, Arabia and central Africa.

mesoglea: amorphous jellylike material between epidermis and gastrodermis in sponges and coelenterates; when it has cells and fibers, it is considered a third germ layer (mesoderm).

mesogloea: gelatinous noncellular or secondarily cellular material between outer epithelium and gastrothelium in many coelenterates. It is particularly well developed in medusae of *Hydrozoa* and *Scyphozoa*.

mesopelagic: intermediate depths below euphotic zone but above completely aphotic zone. Dysphotic depths. Organisms are found in these depths. That portion of oceanic province extending from about 100 fathoms (200 meters) down to depth of about 500 fathoms (1,000 meters).

mesoplankton: planktonic organisms between 0.5 and 1 mm. in size.

mesopodopsis slabber [mysids]: long slender mysid with narrow cephalothorax and short carapace which leaves last two thoracic segments exposed. Anterior margins of carapace are rounded; prominent spine on antero-lateral margins and posterior margin is nearly straight. Peduncle of antennule is very long and antennal scale longer and slender. Eyestalks are also exceptionally long, perhaps most obvious feature of this species. Exopodites of uropods are long and slender, third longer than indopodites; telson short. It is euryhaline and flourishes in brackish waters.

mesosphere: lower mantle below asthenosphere; at present time it does not play an active part in deformation processes that produce geologic features.

mesozoans: wormlike animals that are parasites in bodies of certain marine invertebrates, such as brittle stars and clams.

messenger: cylindrical metal weight approximately 3 in. long and 1 inch in diameter; it is usually hinged with latch and attached around oceanographic wire and sent down to actuate tripping mechanism on oceanographic devices such as Nansen bottles and current meters after they have been lowered to desired depth.

messroom [ships]: space or compartment where members of crew eat meals; dining room.

metabolite: product of metabolism that supports physical and chemical processes within living cells and converts energy forms, maintaining the body.

metacecaria: larval stage in trematodes in which larva loses its tail and becomes encysted on intermediate host.

metacenter: in ship stability, the *transverse metacenter* is that point of intersection of a vertical line through vessel's center of buoyancy, when she is floating upright, with a vertical line through the new center of buoyancy upon being inclined, no change in displacement taking place. *Positive* initial stability is present when *metacenter* occurs *above* vessel's center of gravity; *neutral,* if coincident with *metacenter;* and a *capsizing force* obtains where *metacenter* is *below* center of gravity. Similarly, the *longitudinal metacenter* is point of intersection of a vertical through ship's centers of gravity and buoyancy, when she is on an even keel, with a vertical through new center of buoyancy upon vessel being depressed at either end. *Positive* longitudinal stability is always present since that point of intersection always is located at a great height—generally about vessel's length—above the hull.

metacentric height: vertical distance of *metacenter* from center of gravity of vessel and all weights on board, and usually is referred to or indicated in a stability diagram as *G M.* Unless otherwise specified, it is vessel's transverse *G M,* the *L G M* being usual notation for *longitudinal metacentric height* which, ordinarily, is not considered in questions of stability. The *G M,* or *metacentric height* for small angles of heel (up to about 12°) is very nearly constant and, mathematically, is a function of vessel's initial dynamic stability or righting power, expressed as a moment in foot-tons and equal to *G M x sine of angle of heel x displacement,* G M times sine of heel angle being the *righting arm* (or *lever*), or horizontal distance between center of gravity of the mass and a vertical line indicating upward thrust of total buoyancy (considered as concentrated in center of buoyancy.

metagenesis: alternation of sexual and asexual generations, as in many hydroids.

metamorphism [rock]: changes in rocks due to heat and pressure acting in rocks below immediate surface.

metamorphosis: physical change occurring in development of various animals; change in form, structure or function.

metanauplius: in *Euphausiacea,* post nauplilar larval stage in which appendages in addition to original 3 pairs of naupliar limbs are present but before metamorphosis to calyptopis stage has occurred.

metanephridium: type of nephridium with open inner ends; inner end called nephrostome and external opening the nephridiopore; common in annelids, mollusks and others.

metapleural folds: in *Cephalochordata,* ventrolateral fin folds in pharyngeal region of body. Probably metapleural folds of early *Chordata* gave rise to paired fins of fish.

metasoma: in *Copepoda,* thoracic somites behind cephalosome and in front of major articulation.

metazoan: any animals beside one-celled protozoans and sponges. Adult metozoans have numerous cells organized into tissue and organs, nervous system and usually digestive system.

meteorological: of or pertaining to meteorology, or science treating of the atmosphere and its phenomena, including winds, storms, precipitation, variations of heat and moisture, and predictions of changes in weather conditions over specified areas of land or sea; or, as pertaining to *ocean meteorology*, also including, by extension, wind drift currents, origin and paths of tropical cyclones, sea temperatures, trade winds, waterspouts, and other hydrographic phenomena.

meteorological tide: change in water level due to meteorological conditions, such as wind and barometric pressure.

meter: basic unit of length of metric system, equal to 1,650,763.71 wavelengths of Kr^{86} orange-red radiation.

meter wheel: special block used to support oceanographic wire payed out over side of ship. Attached to or connected by means of speedometer cable is a gear box to measure length of wire.

methane: flammable hydrocarbon gas used as fuel. It is major component of natural gas and marsh gas.

metonic cycle: period of approximately 19 years, occurring during all phase relationships between moon, sun and earth. During any cycle, new and full moon will reach approximately same day of same year.

metric system: decimal system of measures and weights which originated in France about 1800 and subsequently made law in many countries. It is based on the *meter* (or *metre*), which is one ten-millionth of the distance measured at sea level on a meridian between the equator and pole, equal to 3.281 feet or 39.37 inches. Primary units are the *are* equals 100 square meters; the cubic meter, or *stere;* the *liter* equals volume of a cube having sides one-tenth meter in depth; and the *gram* (or *gramme*) equals weight of a cube of distilled water at 4° *Centigrade* having sides one-hundredth of a meter in depth. Multiples of these are designated in increasing order by Greek prefixes *deca-, hecto-, kilo-, myria-,* as in decameter, hectometer, kilometer, myriameter, or 10, 100, 1000, and 10,000 meters, respectively, in measures of *distance;* decaliter, hectoliter, kiloliter (or *stere*), or 10, 100, and 1000 liters as measures of *capacity;* and decagram, hectogram, kilogram, and myriagram, or 10, 100, 1000, and 10,000 grams, respectively, as measures of *weight*. Parts of the primary units are designated successively by Latin prefixes *deci-, centi-, milli-,* as, in measures of *distance*, decimeter, centimeter, millimeter, or one-tenth, one-hundredth, and one-thousandth of a *meter*, respectively; in *capacity*, as, deciliter, centiliter, milliliter, or one-tenth, etc., of a *liter;* and in *weight*, decigram, centigram, milligram, or one-tenth, one-hundredth, etc., of a *gram*. In surface measure, the *are* is multiplied in the *hectare* to 10,000 square meters, while divided in the *centare* to one square meter. *Decimeter*, unit often used in marking stem and stern drafts on vessels of nations employing the *metric system*, is equivalent to 3.937 inches. For English *feet*, multiply *decimeters* by 23 and divide by 70. *Gram*, weight of a cubic centimeter of distilled water at greatest density, or 15.432 grains *avoirdupois*, or .035 of an ounce. *Kilogram*, usually shortened to *kilo*, 1000 grams or 2.2046 lbs. *avoirdupois*. To convert *kilos* to pounds, very nearly, multiply by 11 and divide by 5. *Kilometer*, a distance of 1000 meters, equivalent to 3280.8 feet or .54 of a nautical mile, very nearly, or about 5/8 of a statute mile. For *nautical miles*, multiply *kilometers* by 41 and divide by 76. *Liter*, capacity measure of 1 cubic decimeter, equals 61.02 cubic inches, equals 1.0567 U.S. liquid quarts or .908 dry quart. *Meter*, also especially in British use, *metre*. To convert meters to *feet*, multiply by 3.28; to *fathoms*, multiply by 6 and divide by 11. *Metric ton*, also termed *tonneau* and *millier*, weight of a cubic meter of distilled water at 4° *Centigrade* (39° *Fahrenheit*), or 1,000 kilograms (or *kilos*), equivalent to 2,204.6 lbs. In converting kilos to tons, as sometimes required in handling heavy cases, machinery, etc., for shipment, a close approximation to the 2,240-lb. ton (as used in shipping) is obtained by dividing by 1,000; thus, a piece of cargo weighing 4,015 kilos is only about a hundredweight less than 4 long tons. An exact result here may be found by multiplying the 4.015 *metric tons* (represented in 4,015 kilos) by .984, which gives 3.95 *long tons*, or 112 lbs. short of the former method. *Millimeter*, frequently used in scientific work, refined gauge or instrument readings, etc., 1/1,000 of a meter, or .03937 inch; also *millimetre*. *Quintal*, weight of 100 kilos, or 220.46 lbs. Confined to the *metric system*, not to be confused with British and U.S. hundredweight, also called *quintal* in certain trades, or a few other weights of the name in different countries. *Stere*, measure of volume equal to the *cubic meter* or 35.34 cubic feet. It is the space which 1 metric ton (2,204.6 lbs.) of distilled water at 4° *Centigrade* would occupy.

Miaplacidus: star of magnitude 1.8 in *Argo*, catalogued as either β *Argus* or β *Carinae*, having a S.H.A. of 221°50′ and declination 69½° S. Southernmost of all stars suitable in magnitude for navigational observation, it may be located S 71° W and distant about 20° from *Acrux*, the star marking lower extremity, or "foot" of the *Southern Cross*, at that group's upper transit.

mica: any of group of complex silicates that crystallize in thin, easily separated layers; resistant to heat and electricity.

Michigan kiyi: kiyi, or chub, has ovate shape and is small, reaching 6 or 8 in. in length. Lower jaw is longer than upper and more or less hooked. Fish resembles *L. hoyi*, but scales in lateral line number more than 75. Lives in deep water.

microatoll: circular growth of coral with central depression and breadth of only a few feet.

microbenthos: benthic organisms small enough to pass through a sieve with 0.1 mm. mesh.

microcoquina: partially cemented, sand-size (2 mm. and smaller) shell fragments.

micron: 0.001 of a millimeter.

micronucleus: in *Ciliata*, small nucleus (or nuclei), which is comparable to nucleus of other cells. It undergoes mitosis during cell division and undergoes reduction division to haploid state prior to conjugation.

microphagous: feeding on microorganisms.

microplankton: plankton within the size range of 60 microns to 1 mm. Most phytoplankton forms are included in this group and nannoplankton.

microseisms: minute earth tremors. Period of microseisms is half than the waves causing them. Origin of microseisms may be due to fluctuations of pressure in sea or waves on shore.

microspheric [*Foraminifera*]: test with relatively small initial chamber. Constructed by individual formed from asexual union of two cells.

microtome: machine used to cut processed plant or animal tissue into thin pieces or sections which will be viewed under microscope.

middle body [ships]: that part of ship adjacent to middle section.

middle ground: bar deposits formed by ebb and flood tides in middle of channel at entrance and exit of strait.

middle passage: route across Melville Bugt which is direct course from Upernavik to Kap York, Greenland.

mid-extreme tide: level midway between extreme high water and extreme low water occurring at a place.

mid-ocean canyon: canyon-type continuous depression traversing abyssal plain. Thought to have been formed by turbidity current erosion, canyons may be up to 5 miles wide and 600 ft. deep.

mid-oceanic islands: isolated volcanic islands rising from deep sea floor, composed of basaltic lava or limestone reefs on base of volcanic rock.

mid-oceanic ridge: 1) submarine mountain chain 40,000 miles long. Chain runs through Atlantic, Indian and South Pacific oceans. 2) great median arch or sea bottom swell extending length of an ocean basin and roughly paralleling continental margins.

mid-ocean ridge: system of rifts and parallel mountain ranges or hills found in all major oceans, thought to be sites of upwelling of new ocean floor material from earth's mantle, from which ocean floors are gradually spreading out laterally.

mid-ocean rift: deep cleft valley, about 15 to 30 miles wide, found to exist almost continuously along crest of mid-ocean ridges. Gulf of Aden, Red Sea, Dead Sea, Jordan Valley, Icelandic graben and the rift valley system of East African Plateau are all considered to be landward extensions of mid-ocean rift system.

mid-ocean sofar: proposed sound fixing and ranging (sofar) system installed in mid-ocean area. Designed for sonar-type navigation, apparatus affords taking of bearings of triangulation.

midship beam [ships]: longest beam, transverse or longitudinal, or midship of vessel.

midship frame [ships]: frame at midships which is largest on vessel.

midships [ships]: same as amidships, indicating center of vessel.

midwater trawl: large net, having 10- to 155-ft. mouth for collecting marine biological specimens. Operates at depth of 100 ft.

migrating inlet: tidal inlet, such as one connecting coastal lagoon with open sea, which shifts its position in direction of longshore current flow.

mile: geographical, nautical or sea mile varies from 6,045.95 ft. at equator to 6,107.85 at poles. U.S. Coast Survey has adopted value of 6,080.27 ft. which is very nearly the value of admiralty knot (6,080) adopted by British Hydrographic Office.

milkfish: silvery fish of the herring family found in tropical Pacific waters. It attains a length of 2½ feet.

millepores [hydrocorallines]: millipores are colonial hydrozoans that build up limy parts. Each colony contains two basic types of animals or zooids. One type (gastrozooids) captures food and swallows it; second type is mouthless and therefore gets nourishment secondhand from gastrozooids. Fossil millepores appear in Cretaceous rocks and continue into Recent deposits. Some are massive but many branch their surfaces and show large pores that once housed gastrozooids and smaller pores that contain dactylozooids.

millibar: internationally adopted unit of atmospheric pressure in scientific use, equal to .02953 inch of the mercury column. The *bar*, or 1000 *mb.* or *millibars*, is the equivalent of 29.5306 inches (750.076 millimeters) at 32° Fahrenheit (0° Centigrade) at sea level in latitude 45°. A barometric reading of 30.00 inches equals one of 1016 *millibars*.

millilambert: 0.001 of a lambert. Very small unit of illumination in expressing bioluminescence of some planktons.

minimum current: phase of tidal current when speed is least; usually referenced in knots and in hours or after low and high water.

minimum duration: time necessary for steady state wave condition to develop for given wind velocity over given fetch length.

minimum ebb: lowest speed of continuously outflowing current during period of ebb tidal current, usually in river or estuary; where currents are solely tidal, lowest speed of ebb current is at or near slack water.

minimum flood: where currents are solely tidal, lowest speed of flood current is at or near slack water.

minisub: small, free-flooded submersible operated by two scuba-equipped men using foot pedals or electric motor. Can cover 6 miles underwater in 1½ hours.

minnow: any small fish is considered a minnow. True minnows however are particular species belonging to minnow family. This is one of largest groups of fishes, with about 200 species in U.S. alone. Its representatives live in various kinds of freshwater habitats throughout north temperate zones. Minnows are soft-rayed fishes with cycloid scales, single dorsal fin and forked tail fin. Jaws are toothless but pharyngeal teeth in throat assist in grinding and masticating food, which consists mainly of small aquatic animals such as insects and larvae, crustaceans and mollusks. Many members of the family are small and some exhibit rainbow variety of colors. Common aquarium goldfish is a minnow, as are much larger foodfish and squawfish.

minnow, common: silver shiner is very familiar species found throughout eastern and central U.S. Size ranges from 2 to 5 in. During spawning season male develops rosy tints on belly and lower fins and small spiny outgrowths on head. Chief use of minnows is for bait.

minnow, cutlip: has peculiar 3-lobed lower lip. It is sluggish and fairly large, growing to length of 8 in., olive green in color with dusky bar behind gill cover. Cutlip minnows live in streams of eastern U.S. Male constructs nest of carefully selected pebbles that he moves to the site, usually beneath overhanging rock.

minnow, fallfish [silver chub]: one of larger members of minnow family, growing to length of 18 in. It is found in swift streams and clear lakes from New England to Virginia. Fallfish is silvery species with bluish back and small barbel on upper lip. It feeds on algae, crayfish, insects and small fishes.

minnow, mud [*Umbra pygmaea*]: small, big-mouthed, muddy-colored minnow. Posterior angle of jaw extending to below middle of eye; tail rounded; mouth not produced into beak. Lower jaw black; head large, flattened above; mouth moderate. Color dark greenish with about 12 narrow longitudinal pale stripes; dark bar at base of caudal fin.

minnow, pugnose [*Opsopoeodus emiliae*]: small, graceful minnow with scarcely any mouth; rays in anal fin 7 to 9; no barbel at base of maxillary; dorsal fin with 9 rays. Head moderate; body

rather elongate, somewhat compressed not elevated. Color yellowish above, silvery below; rather narrow indistinctly defined dark stripe along each side from snout to base of tail. Size 1½ to 2 in.

minnow, red [*Notropis maculatus*]: graceful, often reddish little minnow with spot on base of tail. Lateral line incomplete; rays in anal fin 7 to 8. Head flattened above; snout rounded. Pinkish red above, paler below. Fairly prominent dark lateral stripe from tip of snout to base of caudal fin where it terminates in distinct oval dark spot about size of an eye.

minnow, redbelly dace: small species only a few inches in length, it is rated as most handsome of all minnow species. It is brownish with black spots on back, two dark stripes along side and bright red belly.

minnow, redside dace: about 4 in. long, it is a colorful minnow found in clear streams throughout southeastern U.S. In spring male becomes bright crimson in forward portion of body and also develops many small tubercles. Redside dace is often sold as aquarium fish.

minnow, silverjaw [*Ericymba buccata*]: small, silvery minnow with pocket face. Sides of head pitted with numerous cavernous chambers; dorsal fin with 8 rays; lips thin; no barbel at base of maxillary. Head rather long, somewhat depressed above; muzzle broad and prominent but mouth small, subinferior in position. Color is pale olive above, silvery on sides and below.

minor constituents: those chemical elements present in seawater which together comprise approximately 0.1% of total known dissolved solid constituents. Nearly all of elements occur in seawater, although most are present in extremely small amounts.

minor septum [*Coelenterata*]: one of a third cycle of septa formed between initial and secondary septa and much shorter than they.

Mintaka: westernmost star of the three comprising the belt of *Orion* and catalogued as δ *Orionis*. A double star of magnitude 2.48, has a S.H.A. of 277° 35' and declination 0° 20' S.

minute: one-sixtieth of a degree of angular measure; 1/21600 of a circle; or 60 seconds (60''). Expressed by the symbol ('), as in 0° 15', in a circle the radii limiting an arc of 1' are inclined to each other at an angle of 1'. In a *great circle* described on the earth's surface, 1' is practically equal to 1 geographical or nautical mile; thus, a place in Lat. 20°N. is 20 x 60, or 1200', or *miles*, north of the equator; and a *great circle* distance of 18° 10', as computed between two points, is 18 x 60 + 10' equals 1090', or miles, very nearly. The *minute* of arc in a *small circle*, as a parallel of latitude, however, varies in length with distance from the equator, or very nearly as cosine of the latitude, being in Lat. 60° for example, half the length of a minute of the equator, considering our planet a perfect sphere. As a measure of *time,* the *minute* is 1/60 of an hour, and expressed as a difference in longitude of two places, is equal to 15 minutes of arc (15′).

Miocene: geological period of Tertiary about 25 million years ago characterized by manlike apes, highly developed primates and relatively modern plants and animals, especially mammals.

Mirach: β *Andromedae,* a star of magnitude 2.37 lying 25° nearly due south of *Cassiopeia's* middle star (γ *Cassiopeiae*) and easily recognized, when the *Square of Pegasus* is on the meridian, at about 14° E.N.E. of *Alpheratz,* star marking N.E. corner of *Square. Mirach* (or *Mirac*) is central in the group representing, according to ancient Greek mythological lore, the lovely *Andromeda* who was chained to a cliff for no fault of her own and rescued from a devouring monster by brave *Perseus,* hero of the adjoining constellation of that name. The star has a S.H.A. of 343° 12′ and declination 35° 23′ N.

miracidium: larval stage that emerges from egg in digenetic trematodes and carries infection to molluscan host.

Mississippian: epoch in Carboniferous period of Paleozoic era, preceding Pennsylvania and similar to it.

mitosis: method of cell division characterized by threadlike nuclear chromatin breaking into segments or chromosomes that are then split lengthwise; halves come together in 2 sets, each forming nucleus for new cell.

mitraria larva: modified trochophore larva of some annelid tube worms, having two bundles of very long setae extending below larva.

Mitridae [family]: miter shells are usually thick, heavy, spindle-shaped shells with sharp tapering spines. Aperture of shells are small, narrow and notched in front; outer lip is usually thin and quite often toothed along inner margin; columella also bears several plaits; epidermis is usually very thin or absent. This family is limited to warm seas of the world.

mixed gas [diving]: breathing medium consisting of oxygen and one or more inert gases synthetically mixed.

mixed layer: layer of water which is mixed through wave action or thermohaline convection.

mixed tide: type of tide in which presence of diurnal wave produces large inequality in either high or low water heights with two high waters and two low waters usually occurring each tidal day. This term is applied to tides intermediate to those predominantly semidiurnal and those predominantly diurnal.

mixotrophic: 1) able to exist by either autotrophic or heterotrophic nutrition, as conditions necessitate. 2) process by which organism obtains flood by both autotrophic and heterotrophic modes.

Mizar: second star in tail of the Great Bear *(Ursa Major),* or handle of the Big Dipper, listed by astronomers as ζ^1 *Ursae Majoris,* S.H.A. 159° 29′ and Dec. 55° 11′ N. It is a binary star of magnitude 2.40 and lies exactly opposite the pole and about same distance from it as δ *Cassiopeiae (Ruchbah).* The faint close companion of this star is called *Alcor,* from an Arabic word meaning the *weak one.*

mizzen [ships]: sail carried on aftermast of yawl or ketch or third mast of ship.

mizzen course: in 18th century fore-and-aft sail suspended either from lateen yard or gaff on mizzenmast of a ship. It has no boom.

mizzenmast [ships]: hindmost mast of three-masted vessel.

mizzen staysail [ships]: lower staysail (3- or 4-sided, supported by stay) on mizzenmast. Mizzenmast is aftermast in two-masted fore-and-aft-rigged sailing vessel or on three-masted ship. On ship with more than 3 masts, mizzenmast is third mast.

moat: annular depression that may not be continuous, located at base of many seamounts or islands.

Modiolus modiolus [*Anisomyaria*]: shell is about same size as that of *Mytilus edulis* but more massive and with more pronounced umbo. Ribs and coloration are also more obvious. Shape is also different from that of *M. edulis;* in *M. modiolus* broad end drops ventrally.

modular: composed of readily interchangeable units or modules that contain electronic components, especially ones that may be readily plugged in or detached from computer system.

modulation techniques: various means of "modulating" or changing electromagnetic wave (carrier) to create intelligence-bearing signal such as radio or television.

Mohorovicic discontinuity [Moho]: boundary surface between planet's crust and mantle. Moho is usually encountered 22 miles below under the continent. In the Moho, primary seismic waves suddenly increase to speed of about 8.1 km/sec. It has been suggested that Moho and phenomena associated therewith may only indicate change of state rather than of material.

Mohr-Knudsen: chemical method for estimating chlorinity of seawater. In this method, volume of silver nitrate necessary to precipitate sample in relation to volume of silver nitrate necessary to precipitate normal water is determined by titration using potassium chromate as indicator.

mojarra [*Eucinostomus argenteus*]: vertically flattened, silvery fish with long dorsal fin. Anal spines, 2; second not particularly enlarged; second dorsal spine 3 or 4 times length of first; last dorsal spine contained in first ray of soft dorsal. Body elliptical, strongly compressed, back moderately arched; mouth small; caudal fin forked. Buffy above, silvery on sides and below.

mold: impression of exterior (external mold) or interior (internal mold) of shell or other organisms; may be natural or artificial. Impressions left on surrounding rock by shell or other organic structure.

molded breadth [ships]: greatest breadth of vessel, measured from heel of frame on one side to heel of frame on other side.

molded depth [ships]: extreme height of vessel amidships from top of keel to tip of upper deck beam.

molded line [ships]: datum line from which exact location of various parts of ship is determined.

mold, external: mold showing form and markings of outer part of original shell or organisms.

molding edge [ships]: edge of ship's frame which comes in contact with skin, is represented in drawings.

mold, internal: mold showing forms and markings of inner surfaces of shell or organisms.

mold, loft [ships]: large enclosed floor where lines of vessel are laid out and molds or templates made.

mole: 1) large structure built of masonry and used as breakwater and/or pier. 2) massive, solidly filled near-shore structure of earth, masonry or large stone, which may serve as either breakwater or pier.

moleta: fishing boat of Tagus, Portugal. Mainmast stepped amidships. It carried lateen mainsail, and short forward raking mast in bow had small square sail. Jib-shaped sail led from boomkin to upper part of lateen yard and other kites were hoisted here and there wherever possible when weather was moderate.

Mollusca [phylum]: 1) this great phylum includes bivalves, snails, octopuses, squids, pearly nautilus and extinct ammonoids. These commonly possess solid, limy external shells, and are generally known as "shellfish." The phylum is enormous, with probably no fewer than 50,000 species now living. Latin *"mollis,"* soft, referring to typical forms with soft unsegmented bodies. Members typically show almost complete lack of segmentation, elongate form, bilateral symmetry of body organization and development of head and foot regions. Inhabits marine water, freshwater and terrestrial environments. 2) in *Gastropoda*, body generally asymmetrical, with single cap-shaped or spirally-coiled shell not divided into chambers. Mostly marine but common in fresh water and on land.

mollusc or mollusk: member of large phylum of animals, including some of most highly developed, various and familiar of invertebrates, e.g., snails, octopuses, squids, mussels, chitons, nautiluses, clams and oysters. Molluscs have soft, bilaterally symmetrical, unsegmented bodies, frequently covered by shell secreted by fold of body wall, the mantle. Many have large muscular "foot." Some molluscs are important as food source and such products as pearls and mother-of-pearl.

momentum: that property of a particle which is given by product of its mass with its velocity.

mon: plank-built canoe, without outrigger, used in central portion of Solomon Islands and in New Ireland in Bismarck Archipelago. Mon canoes are highly decorated with carving and inlay.

monkaryon: nucleus with only one centriole.

monkey fist [ships]: round knot at end of heaving line to make it heavier for more accurate throwing.

monkey tail [ships]: curved bar fitted to upper, after end of rudder, and used as attachment for rubber pendants.

MONOB [Mobile Noise Barge]: research data ship equipped with acoustical equipment whose mission is to measure radiated noise from ships.

monomyarian: in bivalve molluscs, having only one adductor muscle.

monsoon: 1) wind that changes direction with change of season, particularly in Asia. 2) name for seasonal winds (derived from Arabic *"mausion"*); season. 3) Arabic-speaking peoples of eastern Asia used sun and moon to mark season before they adopted formal calendars. Their verb "to mark" *(wasama)* came to be general term for fixed or "marked" season. No seasons were more important than those in which systems of prevailing winds abruptly reversed direction. Early Dutch navigators, awed by this phenomenon, went home clumsily talking of the strange *wasama*. They quickly slurred the word, monssoemi, later. English seafarers adopted it as monsoon. Contrary to popular opinions, not all monsoons are alike. Famous southwest monsoon of early summer, heavily laden with moisture, brings with it a first rain called the burst of the monsoon. Northeast monsoons of autumn are cold and dry. But whatever its character and direction, the monsoon marks distinctive season of the year.

monsoon current: seasonal wind-driven current in northern part of Indian Ocean and northwest Pacific Ocean.

monsoon junk: type of Chinese junk, making but one voyage a year from Canton during favorable direction of "monsoon" or eastern trade winds.

Monstrilloida [order]: second antennae and

mouthparts lacking; cephalic segment fused with first thoracic; legs usually long with spines; larval stages in marine invertebrates; marine. *Monstrilla.*

montaria: open canoe used by Brazilians of Amazon delta. It had dugout bottom with boards forming flaring sides, which connect to V-shaped end pieces that form raking bow and stern. When canoe is about size of a dory, it is termed *"montario fundo de casco"* or simply *"casco."*

montycat: small, cat-rigged racing boat about 15 ft. long.

mooneye [family *Hiodontidae*]: mooneyes are silvery fishes with deeply compressed bodies, small heads, feeble mouths and large eyes. They reach a length of over 12 in. Dorsal and anal fins are without spines; mouth is medium-sized, obliquely set and has equal jaws and tongue; vomer, palatines and pterygoids are well developed. Gill membranes are free from isthmus; 8 to 10 branchiostegal rays and straight lateral line; the few gill rakers are short and thick. Stomach is horseshoe-shaped and has one pyloric caecum. Mooneyes have large air bladder; scales are large and cycloid; head is naked, with blunt snout.

mooneye, toothed herring [*Hiodon tergisus*]: mooneye is silvery fish with pale olive-buff back. It can be distinguished from goldeye or northern mooneye by keel or ridge on belly, which is developed only between ventral and anal fins. Eye is contained 3 times in the head; maxillary reaches to center of orbit. Dorsal fin contains 11 or 12 developed rays, anal fin 28; anterior margin of dorsal fin is inserted considerably in front of anterior margin of anal fin. Lateral line is complete and contains about 55 scales. Mooneye reaches length of over 12 in.

moonfish, Atlantic: similar fish to lookdown, of same size and range, but profile is not quite so high and fins lack tapering tips.

moon jelly: flat jellyfish, phylum *Coelenterata*, blue or white in color, found along North American coasts.

moonraker: triangular sail set from truck and to yardarms of highest yard. A "raffee."

moonsail [ships]: sail sometimes carried above skysail on square-rigged ship.

moon shell [*Naticidae*]: moon shells or shark's eyes are usually smooth and polished and have very wide apertures. Molluscs which inhabit these shells burrow along sand with aid of very large foot looking for shellfish on which they feed. Group is worldwide in warm waters.

moon shell, arrow [*Natica sagittata*]: this moon shell is somewhat oval in shape and bears large aperture and wide and deep umbilicus which is nearly filled with large callosity. Exterior of shell is smooth or polished and marked with row of fine spirally-directed wrinkles just anterior to

suture. Color of this species is variable and may range from gray to yellow, brown or red. It may be uniform in color, with light or dark, and may be marked by encircling bands and closely set longitudinal lines. Often a white band follows suture. It ranges in length from ¾ to 1½ in.

moon shell, arrow [*Natica sagittifera*]: this moon shell is regarded by some individuals as simply a color variety of *Natica sagitata*. It differs from *N. sagitata*, however, in many details. It is light in color and marked over outer surface by wavy longitudinal lines which form two spinal rows of darker arrow-shaped markings. Shell in the plate measures about ½ in. long.

moon shell, opaque [*Polinices opacus*]: this moon shell is pointed and bears small spire; outer surface of shell is smooth and marked by fine spiral lines. Operculum is thin, corneous and pliable. This species varies widely in color; it is usually white or flesh colored, but is often spirally banded with light brown areas. Umbilicus and columella are always dark chocolate or black. It will reach a length of 1½ in.

moon shell, pear-shaped [*Polinices pyriformiz*]: this moon shell, also known as *Polinices mamilla* is oval and conical in shape, slightly flattened and has smooth, polished surface. Umbilicus is covered over by thick, heavy callosity and operculum is thin, corneous and pliable. Color is beautiful, pure, shining white. It measures from ½ to 2½ in. long.

mooring [ships]: among pleasure craft, mooring consists of anchor embedded in bottom of chain, from it to buoy to vessel, usually with pickup can or buoy to facilitate getting the pennant on board.

mooring line [ships]: cable or hawse line used to tie up ship.

mooring pipe [ships]: opening through which hawse lines pass.

moraine: rock debris, deposited chiefly by direct glacial action, and having various constructional topographic features independent of control by underlying preglacial surface.

moraine bar: bar rising from deep water on both sides, composed of glacial detritus including large boulders. It is deposited as terminal moraine by valley glacier and extends across a fiord.

moray, green: large and ferocious eel attaining length of 6 ft. Large specimens may weigh 25 lbs. or more. Armed with sharp teeth, pugnacious and savage, this moray is a dangerous predator in tropical paradise. It is usually brilliant green but may be slaty brown or mottled. Cause of green color is rather unusual. If scraped off, mucus coating of skin is seen to be yellow while skin beneath is bluish-gray; combination of the two results in green color.

morays: moray family includes eels without pectoral or pelvic fins. Thick leathery skin is entirely devoid of scales. Morays are largest of all eels and possess powerful jaws armed with vicious teeth. These marine carnivores hide amid rocks and coral, turning their long bodies into crevices and striking like rattlesnakes at passing prey.

moray, spotted: ever-present inhabitant of coral reefs, it is common from West Indies to Florida. It reaches length of over 3 ft. and has mottled yellow and black body covered with small and large round spots. Coloring is excellent camouflage as moray hides among coral grottoes. Back bears long low dorsal fin along its ridge.

morbihan lugger: two-masted, lug-rigged fishing boat typical of coast of Brittany, France. It is rigged with curious tall narrow lugsails, almost rectangular in shape. Boats are fast and seaworthy.

morphology: external structure and features of both nonliving and living objects.

Morse: to signal by *Morse* code, as by means of a flashing lamp or ship's whistle; *Morse code* signaling. According to signaling procedure prescribed in the *International Code of Signals*, use of *Morse code* now is limited to flashing and sound signals. Formerly its use was extended to signaling by short and long strokes made in waving a flag.

mortar line: lifesaving or other small line fired from a *line throwing gun* or *mortar*.

mosquitofish, Eastern [*Gambusia affinis holbrooki*]: little white-bellied, pregnant-looking fish. Scales rows 30 to 32; dorsal rays 8; body not strongly compressed, more fusiform; back not strongly arched in profile. Mouth small and terminal; teeth in broad villiform bands. Color grayish above, whitish below, female with black pregnancy spot; vertical fins speckled; melanistic individuals common.

mosquitofish, mangrove [*Gambusia* species]: little-bellied, pregnant-looking minnow. Scales 28 to 31; dorsal rays 7 to 9. Body compressed; back not strongly arched in profile; mouth small and terminal; teeth in broad villiform bands; scale of belly about 9. Color grayish above, whitish below, with longitudinal rows of black spots on sides of body; vertical fins speckled.

motor sailer: combination of powerboat and sailboat, usually roomier and with more power than sailboat, but with mast or masts and complement of sails.

moulded breadth [ships]: measurement over frame at greatest breadth (not to outside of planking or plates).

moulded depth [ships]: vertical distance from top of keel to top of upper deck beams at side of a vessel (taken at middle of the length). This applies to ships with 1, 2 or 3 decks. In the case of spar-decked ship, distance is to top of main deck beam.

Mountis Bay driver: Cornish fishing boat, ketch-rigged without bowsprit, gaff-topsail carried on mizzenmast, which is controlled from a long after boomkin. Hull has high freeboard, straight stem and wide rubbing strakes.

Mousehole lugger: lug-rigged fishing boat working out of Mousehole, Cornwall, England. Majority are (or were) 30 to 33 ft. long on deck, beam 1/3 the length, straight stem and transom stern.

mousing [ships]: winding small stuff around hook between its end and its shank to keep whatever is hanging from hook from slipping or flying off or out.

mouth: 1) place of discharge of stream into ocean or entrance to bay from ocean. 2) in *Coelenterata*, external opening of body cavity serving in coelenterates for discharge of indigestable materials as well as intake of food.

Mozambique Current: part of South Equatorial Current that turns and flows along African Coast in Mozambique Channel. It is considered part of Agulhas Current.

mtepi: East African dugout canoe with single square matting sail. Hull is sharp-ended and useless bowsprit is carried, which is decorated with fringe of grass or reed. Upper and lower yards are used on sail. It is used in Lamu Islands off coast of Kenya.

muchra: this peculiar craft, used by fishermen in vicinity of Bombay, India, is one of most distinctive types of fishing boats in the world. It is reputed to be fastest boat of the Orient excluding certain outrigger canoes. It is open, carvel-built, commonly built of teak, having long, sharp overhanging bow with strongly raking stem.

mucro: short, sharp point that projects from certain parts and organs.

mud: pelagic or terrigenous detrital material consisting mostly of silt and clay-sized particles (less than 0.06 mm.) but often containing varying amounts of sand and/or organic materials. It is general term applied to any sticky fine-grained sediment whose exact size classification has not been determined.

mudfish, bowfin [*Amia calva*]: dark fish with very long soft dorsal fin extending for most of length of back, broad head and big mouth. Tail heterocercal, though not apparently so; mouth large but not extended into bill-like structure; dorsal fin very elongated, exceeding ½ length of body. Color black to dark olive; male with conspicuous ocellus of black orange at base of caudal fin.

mud flat: muddy or sandy coastal strip usually submerged by high tide.

mudminnow family [*Umbridae*]: mudminnows are soft-rayed fishes with rather heavy bodies, compressed posteriorly. Large head is flattened above; mouth is medium-sized with teeth on jaws, vomer and palatine bones. Upper jaw is not protractile; maxillary bones form posterior part of margin of upper jaw. Gill rakes are well developed; branchiostegal rays number 6 to 9; pseudobranchia are not well developed. Cycloid scales cover the head and body; no lateral line is present.

mud pickerel [*Esox vermiculatus*]: small pickerel rarely reaching length of over 12 in. Body is olive-green and marked with dark, wormlike wavy bars. Branchiostegals usually number 11 to 13; about 105 scales in lateral line; opercle is entirely scaled.

mudstone: rock consisting of indefinite mixture of clay, silt and sand particles, proportions varying from place to place.

mud volcano: cone-shaped, clay mound composed of clay and usually formed by eruption of sulfurous and bituminous mud from central orifice or vent. There are both land and submarine forms.

mule: fast, ketch-rigged trawler working out of Bixham, England, of less than 40 tons displacement. Those above this tonnage are called "smacks" locally.

muletta: small Portuguese fishing boat, now quite scarce. Mainmast was stepped about amidships, raking forward and carrying lateen sail and also staysail suspended from top of yard to stern of boat and sheeted to long boomkin extending aft from stern.

mullet: 1) small family of 6 American species occurring for most part along Atlantic Coast. Small spiny dorsal fin is set far forward from equally small soft-rayed fin. Elongated body terminates in small head and mouth. Because of abundance of fat in broad rounded back, some mullets are known as fatbacks. 2) various marine and freshwater fishes, often silvery-colored and fairly large in size. Mullets, family *Mugilidae*, ordinarily live near coast; some species are invaluable food fish.

mullet, fantail [*Mugil trichodon*]: fish with two dorsal fins and suckerlike mouth. Scales extending onto base of soft dorsal and anal fins, scale rows 32 to 34; adipose eyelid. Body rather robust, not much compressed; sides of head scaly. Bluish-olive above, silver below, no dusky streaks along sides; dark blotch at base of pectoral fins.

mullet, mountain [*Agonostomus monticola*]: fish with two dorsal fins and suckerlike mouth. Lower lip thick and fleshy, upper lip thin; no adipose eyelid. Body moderately stout, not much compressed; head standard length, tapering to small mouth, which has lateral cleft extending posteriorly to level of margin of eye. Color pale brownish above, whitish below; yellow around base of caudal fin.

mullet, striped [*Mugil cephalus*]: fish with two dorsal fins and suckerlike mouth. Scales not extending onto soft dorsal and anal fins; scales 40 to 42; adipose eyelid. Body moderately elongate, not much compressed; sides of head scaly. Color bluish-gray above, whitish below. Many scales along back; sides have dusky centers, thus forming dark streaks along sides.

mullet, white [*Mugil curema*]: fish with two dorsal fins and suckerlike mouth. Scales extending onto base of soft dorsal and anal fins; adipose eyelid. Body moderately elongate, not much compressed; sides of head scaly; caudal fin forked. Color bluish-olive above, whiter below; no conspicuous dusky streaks along sides. Attains weight of only 1 or 2 lbs.

mullion: vertical bar dividing light in window.

multiple tide staff: succession of tide staffs placed on sloping shore so that vertical graduations on several staffs form continuous scale with reference to same datum.

mumble-bee: English cutter-rigged trawler, typical of southern coast, whose mast is stepped well aft. Beamy boat from 15 to 30 tons, with full, high bow, straight keel and raking sternpost.

Munida bamftica [*Anomura*]: first larval stage is about 6 mm. long. Spiny tip to antennal scale is unique among galatheid larvae. All abdominal segments bear paired dorsal spines while 4th and 5th have lateral spines in addition.

mural pore [*Coelenterata*]: circular or oval hole in wall between corallites.

Muricidae [family]: rock shells are miscellaneous assemblage of variously shaped shells. They are, in general, thick, heavy, solid shells of spiral design in which whorls are usually covered by varices, nodules or spines all of which add to weight and thickness of shell. Aperture is usually roundish in outline, covered by horny operculum and terminates in straight anterior canal or notch. Members of this group are active and carnivorous in habits and are most commonly found in shallow water in rocky areas. They are large group which occur in all of oceans of the world, but are most numerous in tropics.

Musca: small constellation located immediately south of the *Southern Cross*. Its brightest star is *a Muscae*, of magnitude 2.94 which lies 6° about S by E from *Acrux (a Crucis)*, southernmost and brightest of the *Cross*.

muscovite: common, light-colored mica.

mushroom [ships]: kind of anchor, like an inverted mushroom, used for permanent moorings. Wide, rounded base sinks into mud and/or sand and has great holding power.

muskellunge [great pike]: found in Great Lakes and Canada. Muskellunge is one of largest freshwater game fishes with length ranging from 30 to

50 in. and weight up to 50 lbs. It is olive or brownish fish with faint vertical markings on sides and spotted fins. "Muskies" lead solitary lives in cool, clear water where they prey on other fishes, snakes or frogs.

mussel: bivalve mollusc of class *Lamellibranchiata* found in salt and fresh waters, attached to substrates by byssal threads. Dark, horny layer covers long shell, which is commercially valuable for manufacture of buttons. Mussels are also sought as food and source of pearls.

muttonfish: also known as mutton snapper; large member of the family growing to length of 27 in. and weighing up to 25 lbs. It is very colorful with olive-tinted back, light red sides, rose-red belly, brick-red paired fins and yellow dorsal fin.

mutualism: symbiotic relationship between two species in which both benefit. Example in which both benefit is attachment of certain sponges and coelenterates to shells of crabs. Attached animal is carried about to fresh feeding areas and crab is camouflaged by animal on its back and thus may be protected from enemies.

myctophid: one of family *(Myctophidae)* of small oceanic fishes which normally live at depths between 100 and 2,000 fathoms (2,000 and 4,000 meters). They characteristically have numerous small photophores on side of body. Many species undergo extensive diurnal vertical migrations and are thought to contribute to sound-scattering layers in the sea.

Myodocopa [order]: shell, when closed, has notch for extension of second pair of antennae; second antennae are only organs of locomotion; 3 pairs of thoracic legs; cosmopolitan and marine. *Philomedes.*

myoparo: ship of about 200 A.D. used by Mediterranean pirates.

myophore [*Mollusca*]: same as apophysis; process projecting into cavity of bivalve shell for attachment of foot muscle.

mysid: marine animal belonging to family *Mysidae* is crustacean order *Mysidacea.* They are small, shrimplike animals with stalked eyes, 6 pairs of appendages and tail fin. Mysids are vital source of food for many fish and whales, and they constitute large portion of plankton.

Mysidacea [mysids]: shrimplike *Peracarida* with shieldlike carapace, which covers but does not fuse with most or all of thorax. Stalked eyes are present in all except where they have become vestigial; swimming thoracic limbs with many jointed exopodites; brood-pouch formed of up to 7 oostegites on thoracic limbs, one pair of which is modified as maxillipeds. Most mysids have obvious statocyst on each indopodite of last abdominal appendages (uropods), but some deep water forms, belonging to families *Lophogastrida,* and *Eucopidae,* have none. Most mysids live near or on bottom and are particularly abundant, but seasonal, in inshore and estuarine waters. They migrate to surface at night and many are euryhaline.

mysis stage: larval stage of certain crustaceans resembling the schizopod, *Mysis.*

Mystacocarida, subclass [phylum *Arthropoda*]: body wormlike; microscopic; antennae long with bristles; labrum large; maxillipeds on thoracic segment separate from head; 4 thoracic segments with platelike appendages; abdominal segments (6) without appendages; caudal rami large; restricted intertidal sandy beaches. Recent. *Derocheilocaris.*

Mytilidae [*Anisomyaria*]: provinculum is long and extends beyond limits of straight hingeline region of shell margin. Teeth are well marked and distinguish *Mytilidae* from all other groups. Two most common genera are *Mytilus* and *Modiolus* which are distinguishable by texture of shell as well as by shape.

Mytilus edulis [*Mytilidae*]: shell is transparent and about 200 to 250 μ across. Shape is ovoid, important difference from *Modiolus.* Larvae occur from May to June.

myxosphyceae: blue-green algae. They appear to have no sexuality, no zoospore; propagate mainly by vegetative means. There are many freshwater and marine species.

N

N: in International Code, denoted by square flag *"Negat,"* having four horizontal rows of alternate blue and white squares. Hoisted singly, signifies "No" *(negative);* as initial letter in radio call signs of civil aircraft indicates nationality as of *United States of America,* which 5-letter call is painted on lower surface of a plane and on each side of its fuselage, the *N,* or *nationality mark* in this case, being separated from rest of the group by a hyphen. As an abbreviation *N* stands for *Navy; Nimbus* (cloud); *Noon; North* or *Northern.* It is signified in Morse code by — · *(dash dot).*

N.A.: abbreviation for *Nautical Almanac.*

na-ak: term for canoe in Atchin Island, which lies off northeast coast of Malekula in New Hebrides group. There were two kinds of canoes used in Atchin Island, large seagoing canoe (now extinct) and small coastal canoe, which is still in use.

nabby: open sailing skiff used on Firth of Clyde and Loch Fyne on west coast of Scotland, from 32 to 34 ft. long, carrying single lugsail and jib on raking mast. It dates from 1880. This type of boat was and is, to a lesser extent, used in herring and "longline" fisheries.

nacreous: pearly; with iridescent luster and special shell structure.

nacreous layer: innermost lustrous layer of mollusk shell.

nadir: 1) shallow draft Malay fishing boat of Malacca coast. Hull is about 24 ft. long, carvel-built with straight stem and sternpost; rig is single lug. 2) point on celestial sphere vertically below observer, or 180° from zenith.

naggar: cargo boat of upper Nile with sharp-bowed hull and large outboard rudder. Rig is simple balance lugsail, set obliquely with boom along foot parallel with head.

nail brush [*Endocladia muricata*]: extremely abundant, often forming an algal zone at uppermost reach of seaweeds. This seaweed is bushy, dark or blackish-brown with stiff, short branches. Dense branches are 1 to 2 in. long and 1/16 in. in diameter. Covering surface of cylindrical branches are harsh brushlike spines 1/32 to 1/16 in. long. Holdfast is small strong disc from which number of thalli arise.

naked: said of a wooden vessel's hull when not sheathed below about light load line; having no bottom *sheathing.*

naked dinoflagellates: members of suborder Gymnodinioidea that do not have protective plates on cell surface.

namatak: isolated mountain peak which projects through ice sheet or glacier.

nameboard: board or surface on which a vessel displays her name. U.S. law requires that every documented vessel shall have her name marked on each bow and upon the stern and also her home port marked on the stern, in roman letters, smallest of which shall be not less in size than four inches; to be in light color on a dark ground or dark on a light ground and to be distinctly visible; and every machinery-propelled vessel shall, in addition to her name shown on her stern, have same displayed in distinct plain letters not less than six inches in length on each outer side of her pilothouse and, also, if a paddle steamer, on outer sides of her paddle-boxes. *(46 U.S.C. 46, 493)*

nannoplankton: very small plankton organism in size range from 5″ to 60″. Plankton organisms too small to be retained by plankton net.

Nansen bottle: device used by oceanographers to obtain subsurface samples of seawater. The "bottle" is lowered by wire, its valves are open at both ends. It is then closed in situ by allowing a weight (called a messenger) to slide down wire and strike reversing mechanism. This causes the bottle to turn upside down, closing valves and reversing thermometer which are mounted on special thermometer case on it.

nao: generic term for medium-sized sailing vessels of Middle Ages, more heavily built than "caravels" but smaller than "carracks."

Napier's circular parts: used in solution of right-angled and quadrantal spherical triangles according to *Napier's Rules,* as in many computations in navigation and nautical astronomy. Named for their originator, *Lord John Napier (1550-1617),* a Scottish mathematician, who is also credited with invention of *Napierian logarithms.* (See any good work on spherical trigonometry.)

Naples trawler: double-ended boat employed in fisheries of Bay of Naples. Typical Naples trawler has single lateen-rigged mast, with 2 or 3 auxiliary sails hung about in moderate weather, as is customary with Tuscan and Portuguese craft.

Narcomedusae [phylum *Coelenterata*]: these are medusae with firm, glassy bells and thin sides. Their margins present scalloped appearance because of thickened ridges of ectoderm from inner surface of tentacle extending on to exumbrellar surface and joining thick circumferential tract of nematocysts. Radial canals so characteristic of most hydromedusans are absent, as is also the manubrium which is confined to interior of bell, while mouth opens directly into it. Gonads lie on stomach wall. Solid tentacles arise a little way above margin of bell and sense organs are solid clublike structures.

nares [amphibians]: nostrils.

nasal [reptiles]: scale in which nostrils lie.

naso-labial groove [amphibian]: groove running from nostril to edge of upper lip on each side in some salamanders.

Nassariidae [*Nassidae alectrionidae*]: members of this group are all of small or moderate size and usually of oval or conical shape. Outer surface of these shells varies among species. They may be ridged, covered with tubercles, smooth or even polished, but they never have varices upon them. Inner lip of shell is usually spread over columella; outer lip is thickened and usually bears teeth. These creatures are usually sand-dwelling forms and burrow about in search for bivalves and other molluscs on which to feed.

Nassarius incrassatus [*Nassariidae*]: confined to inshore plankton. Newly hatched larva is approximately 0.2 mm. across shell and has colorless bilobed velum which later becomes 4-lobed and develops pigment spot at the tip of each lobe. After larval life of at least 8 weeks, shell is about 0.6 mm. long and has characteristic tooth on outer lip.

Nassarius reticulatus [*Nassariidae*]: shell of newly hatched larva is about 0.3 mm. long, smooth and transparent. There is a siphonal canal and characteristic peglike process on outer lip of shell. Larvae of this species are to be found in both inshore and offshore plankton and may be dominant pelagic gastropod larva of the area. Velum is bilobed at first but soon becomes 4-lobed at border and develops continuous band of brownish pigment. After about 8 weeks in the plankton, larva is 0.75 mm. long and settles. At this stage foot is darkly pigmented.

natatory: adapted for swimming.

Natica alderi [*Naticidae*]: larvae of this species are common in both inshore and offshore plankton. Veliger is larger than that of *N. catena*, reaching 0.8 mm. in length before metamorphosis and having shell with 3½ whorls. Dark spot develops at end of each lobe of 4-lobed velum which becomes very large. Veliger resembles that of *Nassarius incrassatus* but latter has shell siphon and peg on outer lip of shell.

Natica catena [*Naticidae*]: larvae are confined to coastal plankton during spring and summer. First larva has smooth shell of 1½ whorls and velum is bilobed and colorless. Later, a wide umbilicus develops in shell and border of velum becomes purple or brown. Shell of late larva is approximately 0.5 mm. long and has 2½ whorls. Larva closely resembles that of *Nassarius reticulatus* but latter has shell siphon and bears toothlike process on outer lip of shell.

Naticidae [*Gastropoda*]: family whose shells are globose and flattened with short spire; umbilicus open or closed by callus; very large foot; small tentacles; several hundred species.

natural frequency: characteristic frequency, i.e., number of vibrations or oscillations per unit time of a body controlled by its physical characteristics (dimensions, density, etc.). In harbor, natural frequency gives rise to waves called seiches, which have periods and amplitudes dependent on physical characteristics of harbor.

natural scale: ratio between linear dimensions of chart, drawing, etc., and actual dimensions represented, expressed as proportion.

nauplius: larval stage in many of lower groups of *Crustacea*, having only 3 pairs of appendages and single median eye.

nauplius eye: unpaired median eye of crustaceans.

Nauri: "dhow" of Baluchistan, exceptionally fast. It has ornamented stem head and is steered by a wheel.

nautical mile: 1) 1/6 of a degree of latitude; distance varying with latitude; length of minute of arc, 1/21,600 of average circumference of earth. Generally, 1 minute of latitude is considered equal to 1 nautical mile. In England, the Admiralty measured mile is 6,080.20 ft., approximately 1.15 times as long as statute mile of 5,280 ft. 2) in general, unit used in marine navigation equal to a minute of arc of a great circle on a sphere. Depending upon radius of sphere, various lengths of nautical miles have been defined.

Nautilidae [family]: nautiloids belong to group of cephalopods which have 4 gills. They were once a large and important group in seas of ancient times, but today only a few species remain. Although the group includes animals with both straight and coiled shells, only those with coiled shells remain today, the others having perished in ancient times. Shells of these molluscs are of conical spiral design and are coiled upon single plane.

They are smooth externally, or very nearly so, and have interior of shell divided into series of chambers by single, simple, curved septa of which last chamber or open end of shell builds new and larger chambers as it continues to grow. Various species inhabit open ocean of all tropical seas. Family contains a single genus. There are at least 6 living species.

Nautiloidea, subclass [*Tetrabranchia*]: shell external, coiled in one plane in existing species, and chambered; simple sutures; retractile tentacles suckerless; funnel of 2 separate folds; 2 pairs of gills; 2 pairs of kidneys; eyes without cornea or lens; marine *Nautilus*. Any of large group of marine invertebrate organisms constituting division of class *Cephalopoda* of phylum *Mollusca*. They range from Cambrian to present with maximum development in Silurian.

nautilus: 1) small cephalopod mollusc that is common fossil. Found in Pacific and Indian Oceans, this pearly or chambered nautilus has many small arms and lives in outermost chamber of beautiful spiral, chamber shell. 2) nautili have ivory-white and reddish-brown shells, eyes with pinholes that focus light and about 90 soft arms that are used in crawling or stretched out to capture food. Their name, which means "headfoot," makes sense when we realize that arms actually are elongate sections of highly specialized foot. It and the head come together so that arms lie in front of eyes and cluster around mouth.

nautilus, paper: egg case of "shell" of the argonaut is very light, thin and frail in construction. It is flat and covered over sides of exterior by radiating ribs, which divide as they proceed from the center. Keels of the shell are marked by a row of numerous, small markings upon keel and measures from 6 to 10 in. in diameter. This species is worldwide in warm waters.

nautilus, pearly or chambered: shell of this nautilus is nearly circular with smooth exterior and interior and with umbilicus covered by callous deposit. It is white or whitish in color and marked in radial fashion by red or red-brown. This species is known from Polynesia and waters of tropical Pacific Ocean.

navicello [balancelle]: two-masted Italian coasting vessel rigged with fore-and-aft mainsail, with short hoist and long gaff, maintopsail, forward-raking foremast, stepped well up in bow, with staysail set in much same manner as rig on present-day "staysail-rigged" schooner yachts and triangular jib to long bowsprit.

Navicula [phytoplankton]: subclass *Pennatae*, cells creep about in characteristic jerky fashion. A few are truly planktonic and some, e.g., *N. membranacea*, are common in most coastal waters. Cells of this species join to form chains.

navigable: having sufficient width and depth to provide passage for vessels; said of a river or other stretch of water. In a technical sense, as determining the right of public use of certain waters as a highway, it is accepted generally that to be *navigable in fact* the body of water, or considered part of such body, must be customarily used, or may be used in its natural state if required, as a highway for commerce or traffic. In Great Britain, however, any river or other body of water is considered navigable only to the limits of ebb and flow of tide, unless otherwise prescribed by law.

navigate: 1) to manage or direct in sailing; as, *the brig is navigated by a blue-water seaman.* 2) to use or traverse a body of water as in sailing; as, *"across the Atlantic the Norsemen navigated in deckless vessels."* 3) to sail over or across; as, to *navigate* the Gulf. 4) to steer, manage, sail, or direct a vessel; as, "among the ice our skippers *navigate* their steamers with unusual care."

navigation: 1) act of navigating; art or science of conducting a vessel from one place to another, as by use of a compass and sails or other means of propulsion, embracing, more especially, determination of ship's position by celestial observations or bearings of points or places on shore, shaping the course and checking of compass error by observations, and generally keeping account of vessel's progress along the desired track. 2) passing of shipping over a waterway or body of water.

navigator: one who navigates; one skilled in the art of navigation; specifically, an officer of a war vessel, usually ranking next below the executive officer, or third in order of command, who is charged with navigation of the ship and has under his immediate care all navigational instruments, charts, and matters pertaining to navigation in general. In merchant vessels, particularly those of liner type, the *navigator*, or *navigating officer*, usually is a senior watch officer third or fourth in line of command. As a point of interest, the word *navvy*, in England denoting a laborer who digs canals, ditches, etc., or similarly is engaged with pick and shovel, is a shortened form of *navigator*, meaning one employed at digging a canal, or a *navigation*, as an artificial waterway has been called.

ndrua: large, finely constructed double canoe of Fiji Islands. Dugout hulls, usually of unequal length, had "U" section (transversely) with some tumble home and deep washstrakes above. This type of canoe is no longer in existence.

neap: neap tide; designating a tide of least rise and fall from mean sea level, or that usually occurring twice in a lunar month, one or two days following first and third quarters of the moon. A tide is said to *neap* when diminishing in range after advent of *spring tide*, and a vessel is said to be *neaped* (older form *beneaped*) after stranding at high water on a spring tide, in the sense that a decreasing tidal rise delays prospect of refloating until recurrence of usual two weekly springs.

neap tidal currents: tidal currents of decreased speed occurring at time of neap tides.

neap tide: 1) tide that has least rise and fall. 2) tide of small range occurring at quarter phase of moon. 3) tide of decreased range which occurs about every two weeks when moon is in quadrature.

nearshore current system: current system caused by wave action in and near surf zone.

nearshore zone: pertaining to zone extending seaward from shore to indefinite distance beyond surf zone.

Nebaliacea [order]: thorax and part of abdomen covered by bivalved shell; adductor muscle joining the 2 valves; head appendages well developed; thoracic limbs foliaceous; last abdominal segment without appendages; first 4 pairs of abdominal appendages biramous, others uniramous. *Nebalia*.

neck: narrow band of water flowing swiftly seaward through surf.

nectocalyx: in Siphonophora, one of members of colony modified as a swimming organ.

nectochaeta: 1) type of free-swimming larva in some *Polychaeta*. 2) stage of young of certain annelids, more advanced than polytrocular larva, in which muscle-powered parapodia provide swimming power.

nectophore: swimming, bell-shaped medusa of siphonophore colony.

needle: 1) sharp-pointed steel instrument used in sewing; as, a *sail needle*. 2) one of the slender bar magnets giving directive force to a compass card; *compass needle*. 3) sharp pinnacle of rock on a coast.

needlefish, northern [*Strongylura marina*]: skinny, green fish with long, pointed beak; pelvic fins closer to anal fin than to pectorals; caudal fin shallow-forked. Eye large; jaws about twice as long as rest of head, with numerous tiny sharp teeth; dorsal fin above anal fin in position. Color is green above, lighter on sides and pale below.

negative: opposed to affirmative: as in a *negative signal;* or to positive: as, *negative pole* of a magnet. Of or having an indicated value or condition less than, below, or opposite a definite standard, parity, or mark; as, *negative slip; negative stability; negative angle.*

negative gradient: layer of water where temperature decreases with depth.

negative pressure duration: length of time bottom pressure is affected by passage of the trough of a

wave. It is approximately equal to one half the wave period.

negative pressure response: maximum amount (in inches or feet of water) of bottom pressure is reduced by passage of the trough of a wave.

negligence clause: 1) in a marine insurance policy, a clause generally disclaiming the carrier's responsibility in case of loss or damage to cargo for negligence of master, crew, or pilots. 2) latent defects in machinery or hull. 3) damage by accidents to loading or unloading gear. 4) other hidden causes over which carrier has no control; where it can be shown that he has exercised due diligence in providing a vessel to the best of his knowledge seaworthy in every respect.

Nehlis gland: cluster of unicellular glands surrounding ootype in some trematodes and cestodes; formerly called shell gland.

nekton: 1) aquatic, free-swimming organisms whose swimming activity largely determines direction and speed of their movement, including fish, cephalopods, some larger crustaceans, etc. 2) pelagic animals that are active free-swimmers, relatively unaffected by waves and currents, such as marine mammals, adult fishes, octopuses and squids.

nektonic: pertaining to marine swimming animals.

N.E.L. spade core: cylindrical sample (core) of sediment or soil taken with shallow water corer that Naval Electronics Laboratory developed from modified box corer.

nema [*Graptolithina*]: delicate tube to which base of graptolite colony is attached.

nematocyst: stinging mechanism of coelenterates, consisting of chitinous sac filled with venom and elongated at one end into long narrow pointed hollow thread, which normally lies inverted and coiled up within the sac, but can be exerted by mechanical or chemical stimuli.

nematode: member of class *Nematoda* in phylum comprising roundworms. Nematodes may live on land or in water and are often parasites in man, other animals or plants; they include the familiar hookworm.

nematogen: individual dicyemid mesozoan found in young cephalopods; gives rise to vermiform larvae.

Neogastropoda [order]: snails with highly concentrated nervous system; shell with siphon, reversible proboscis, and large bipectinate osphradium; many species carnivorous, some with poison glands; radula often with a few large teeth in each row; veliger larva mostly suppressed with intracapsular embryos; strictly marine. *Urosalpinx* (oyster drill), *Busycon, Buccinum* (whelks), *Terebra* (auger shell), *Murex* (rock shell).

Neomysis integer [mysids]: carapace bears anteriorly a triangular plate and spine on each antero-lateral border. Antennae scale is long and narrow; eyestalks are about 1½ times longer than broad; telson is long, narrow and triangular with 20 to 24 spines along margins. A fully euryhaline species is rarely, if ever, found in waters with salinity above 18%.

Neotremata: inarticulate brachiopod in which one valve acquires a more conical form and pedicle becomes surrounded by ventral valve and comes to emerge close to umbo and at a distance from margin. In all superfamilies, except *Craneacea*, shell is horny.

nepheloid zone: suspension of fine organic matter and clay-sized sediment particles in seawater which forms a zone about 200 to 1,000 meters thick near bottom of continental slope and rises in western North Atlantic.

nephridium: tubular organ for excretion and osmoregulation in annelids, mollusks, arthropods and other invertebrates.

Neptune: in Roman mythology, god of the waters; identified with *Poseidon* of the Greeks; distinguished for his unfailing attention to initiation of new arrivals at *Latitude Zero*.

neritic: 1) of or pertaining to marine environment which extends from low tide to depth of 600 ft. or lower limit of effective penetration of radiant energy of sun. 2) pertaining to that part of continental shelf between low tide and depths of about 600 ft., including both bottom and water.

neritic zone: region between low-tide level and depth of 600 ft. in which marine invertebrate life flourishes; depth to which sunlight can penetrate.

Neritidae: sea snails are group of molluscs whose shells are usually globular and which have depressed spires and very large body whorls. Columella is broad and toothed, outer lip is simple and may be toothed and aperture is covered by calcareous operculum.

neritina, decayed: this mollusc is compact and humped in appearance with winglike structures extending laterally from lips. Columellar area is very large and columella bears a few very fine teeth along center and one large tooth at posterior side. Color of shell is dark brown or black and flecked over outer surface with very small yellow spots; aperture is bluish or sometimes yellowish. It reaches a length of about 1 inch. This species is known from Hawaiian Islands.

neritina, grained: this mollusc has shell that is low and dome-shaped, triangular in outline and superficially resembles a hoof. Lips of aperture are extended laterally to form broad winglike expansion which extends around 3 sides of shell. Entire upper surface of shell is covered by low rounded tubercles. Shell is black; aperture is bluish-white and speckled with darker spots; columellar area is white, yellow or orange and becomes darker to-

ward apex of spire. It will reach a length of nearly 2 in. This species is known from Hawaiian Islands where it lives attached to stones on freshwater streams.

neritina, Tahitian: this shell is flat and bears large winglike expansions on each side. It is thin and corneous in appearance and texture. Columellar area is large but aperture is small. It is light olive-brown and without markups. It will reach a length of about 1 inch. This mollusc is brackish water species and lives attached to stones in mouth of streams. This species is found in Hawaiian Islands, Samoan Islands and Society Islands.

net: 1) remaining after deduction of space, charges, losses, etc.; as, *net tonnage; net freight.* 2) free and clear of tare, waste, or that which is allowed for; as, *net weight; net load.* 3) an open fabric of thread, twine, cord, etc., woven or worked in meshes as a *fishing net.* 4) network or netting, as that between a ship's open rail and the deck or forming the sides of a receptacle for stowage of hammocks, etc.; a *net sling* or *cargo net.*

net primary production: total amount of organic matter produced by photosynthetic organisms, minus amount consumed by these organisms in respiratory processes.

net production: gross production minus amount lost in same time by catabolic processes.

nettlefish: jellyfish; so-called from the stinging quality of its hair-like tentacles being likened to that of the *nettle plants.* Also, *sea nettle.*

neuston: group of organisms living in association with surface film; majority are freshwater forms, since ocean surface generally is too rough to support such a group. Marine strider, Halobates, and surface floaters such as Portuguese man-of-war may be considered to be neuston forms.

neutral shoreline: that shoreline whose essential features do not depend on either submergence of former land surface or emergence of former subaqueous surface.

neve: snow converted into granular ice. Also called snow firn or firn.

neve iceberg: similar in appearance and color to an iceberg, but composed of neve (firn).

new ice: general term which includes frazil ice, sludge, medium winter ice, pancake ice and ice rind.

New Orleans lugger: single-masted, shallow-draft, lug-rigged boat used in coast fisheries in vicinity of New Orleans, La. on Gulf of Mexico. Of European origin, it is ususlly manned by southern Europeans. It is carvel-built, halfdecked, with centerboard with coaming around elliptical-shaped cockpit and covered hatch forward.

newt, Florida [*Diemictylus rividescens piaropecola*]: small, reddish-brown to blackish salamander. No costal grooves; red marking on back restricted to a few minute red dots, or absent; belly with numerous small black dots. Head wide at eyes, slightly converging posteriorly, anteriorly tapering to rather blunt snout; no well developed cranial ridges; body slender, slightly compound.

newt, Louisiana [*Diemictylus viridesceus louisianensis*]: small, greenish to brownish salamander. No costal grooves; red markings on back restricted to a few minute red dots, or absent; belly with but a few scattered small black spots. Head widest at eyes converging posteriorly, anteriorly tapering to rather blunt snout; no well developed cranial ridges; legs slender; 4 toes on front foot, 5 toes on hind foot.

newt, red-spotted [*Diemictylus viridescence viridescens*]: small, greenish to brownish salamander with row of separate red spots down each side of back. No costal grooves; red dots usually encircled with black; belly with a few scattered small black dots.

newt, striped [*Diemictylus perstriatus*]: small, reddish-brown salamander with bright red stripe down each side of back. No costal grooves; red markings on back composed of bright red stripe on each side from above eye to base of tail. Head widest at eyes, slightly converging posteriorly, anteriorly tapering to rather blunt snout.

nickey: double-ended, two-masted fishing boat of Isle of Man, England. Present-day types are lug-rigged without headsails, gaff topsail being carried on mizzenmast.

nidamental: referring to production of protective covering for egg or egg mass.

nilas: Russian term for gray or dark-colored ice that forms in a sheet on calm sea.

nip: cut made by waves in shoreline of emergence.

nipped: pertaining to ship which is icebound and subjected to pressure from ice, sometimes to the extent that ship is damaged and even sunk.

nipping: closing of ice around ship so that ship is beset and subjected to pressure from ice.

nitrate nitrogen: most abundant and readily assimilable form of nitrogen for marine organisms. Like phosphate, it is essential nutrient.

nitrogen cycle: series of chemical changes that nitrogen undergoes in its use by plants and animals. Inorganic nitrogenous compounds (nitrate, nitrites and ammonium) and to small extent, organic nitrogenous compounds in sea are utilized by marine plants, which form other nitrogenous compounds such as amino acids.

nitrogen narcosis: narcosis caused in divers because of greater amount of nitrogen gas in high-pressure air they are breathing. This narcosis can produce a dangerous state of euphoria or "rapture of the deep." Usually the effect first becomes noticeable at depth of 100 ft. or more, although individuals vary in susceptibility.

Nitzschia [subclass *Pennatae*]: *N. closterium* is most common species. Its spindle-shaped cells have long spine at each end. They can move but do not join up as do those of some other species.

nobbie: dandy-rigged of Holylake, England, descended from and similar to "Manx nickey." Average size about 40 ft. by 12 ft. by 6 ft. draft.

no-bottom: notation appearing on nautical charts indicating that sounding did not reach bottom.

Noctiluca: genus of usually pale pink luminescent dinoflagellates large enough to be seen by unaided eye. This particular organism is responsible for much of sheet type luminescence noted in coastal waters of various parts of ocean world. Green form occurring in coastal regions of Far East is not luminescent.

nodal line: in tide area, line about which tide oscilates and where there is little or no rise and fall of tide.

noddies [terns]: long-winged seabirds of rather small size with tapering pointed bills, straight or slightly curved at tip. Legs are very short; webbed feet are small. Majority of species have long, forked tails; outer tail feathers are exceptionally elongated in some marine species. Mainly birds of coasts of warmer parts of world, but number of species migrate into north temperate regions during summer to breed.

node: that part of standing wave or clapotis where vertical motion is least and horizontal velocities are greatest. Nodes are associated with clapotis and with seiche action resulting from resonant wave reflections in harbor or bay.

node cycle: time required for regression of moon's nodes (points where plane of moon's orbit intersects the ecliptic) to complete a circuit of 360° of longitude; period of approximately 18.6 years. It is accompanied by corresponding cycle of changing inclination of moon's orbit relative to plane of earth's equator, with resulting inequalities in rise and fall of tide and speed of tidal current.

nodule: in pennate diatoms, part of complex system, including raphe and nodules, that enables them to move.

nodules: lumps of manganese, cobalt, iron and nickel found in various regions on ocean floor.

noise level: comparison of sound intensity usually measured in decibels, to reference level.

no joint juice [diving]: pain in joints; common during rapid compression to depths greater than 500 ft.

nonemergents: algae and sea grasses which are not exposed at lowest low water or chart datum.

nonharmonic constant: tidal constant such as lunitidal interval, range or inequality which may be derived directly from high- and low-water observations without regard to harmonic constituents of tide.

nonlinear waves: waves in relatively shallow waters, with no superimposition of motion.

nonmagnetic: describing a ship specially built to measure earth's magnetism. It contains very little steel or iron that would affect measurements and is constructed of wood with copper fastenings.

nontidal current: any current that is caused by other than tide-producing forces; this includes all permanently established oceanic currents as well as all temporary ocean currents caused by winds.

noon: middle of the day; 12 o'clock in the day by standard local time; time of sun's upper transit. It is customary at sea to reckon the day's run, fuel consumption, and work done by engines from *noon* to *noon*. Astronomical time, prior to 1925, also was thus reckoned.

Nordlands Cod-boat: double-ended open boat used in cod fishery on west coast of Norway, similar in line to old Viking "long ship." Clinker-built with side planks (15 to 16 in.); great sheer at ends with high stem and sternpost; straight keel; low freeboard amidships and outside rudder.

normal gravity: value of gravity at sea level according to theoretical formula which assumes earth to be spherical or of some similar, regular shape.

normal water: standard seawater preparation, chlorinity of which lies between 19.30 and 19.50 per mile and has been determined to within ±0.001 per mile. Normal water is used as convenient comparison standard for chlorinity measurement of seawater samples by titration.

Norske Veritas: shipping classification society of national importance in Norway, instituted in 1864 and patterned after *Lloyd's*.

north: one of the four cardinal points of the compass; specifically, that point of a true compass indicating direction of *true*, or *geographical*, *north*, or direction of the geographical *North Pole*; direction of intersecting point of horizon and meridian, or that point of an observer's horizon vertically below the elevated celestial pole in any northern latitude. The *compass north*, or *north* point on a compass card, usually denoted by an ornamental design such as a *fleur de lis*. The *magnetic north*, or direction indicated by a freely suspended bar magnet's north-seeking, red, or positive pole; or by *north* point on a compass card where no deviation is present. Northern, or designating something lying toward, relative to, from, or toward, the *north*; as, *north coast of Ireland*; a *north course*; a *north wind* (from the *north*); a *north* (or northerly) *set of current* (toward the *north*). Usually abbreviated *N.* in designating compass points from *West* through *N.* to *East*; as in *N by E, NNE, NW, WNW, etc.*

North-About-Route: coastal route through Melville Bugt from Upernavik to Kap York, Green-

land, by going along Greenland coastal fast ice or floe leads. This passage usually offers earliest route to Thule and "North Open Water" and can generally be effected before end of August, even in worst season.

North Atlantic Current: wide, slow-moving continuation of Gulf Stream originating in region east of Grand Banks of Newfoundland at about 40°N and 50°W.

North Atlantic Drift: weak, sluggish, northeast part of North Atlantic Current that is easily influenced by winds; currents have been observed to change speeds and direction frequently and at times reverse direction.

North Cape Current: warm current flowing northeastward around northern Norway and curving into Barents Sea. North Cape Current is continuation of Norway Current.

northeast: usually abbreviated *N.E.* or *NE*, point of the compass or the horizon lying midway between *north* and *east;* in a direction toward both *north* and *east*. Pertaining to the northeast; as a *N.E. gale*.

North Equatorial Current: ocean currents driven by northeast trade winds blowing over tropical oceans of Northern Hemisphere. In Atlantic Ocean it is known as Atlantic North Equatorial Current and flows west between Atlantic Equatorial Countercurrent and Sargasso Sea. In Pacific Ocean it is known as Pacific North Equatorial Current and flows westward between 10° and 20°N. East of Philippines it divides, part turning south to join Equatorial Countercurrent and part going north to form Kuroshio.

northern carpsucker: back moderately compressed and slightly arched; snout is not rounded. Nostrils are slightly posterior to tip of lower lip. Longest dorsal ray is 2/3 to 3/5 the length of base of fin and is never filamentous; dorsal rays range from 23 to 27. Lips are thin and silvery-white in life, and halves of lower lip meet at wide angle. Color is dull silver, sometimes brassy; often some of scales are brownish at base. Sometimes attains weight of 10 lbs.

northern rock bass [*Ambloplites rupestris rupestris*]: body of rock bass is thicker than body of crappie or sunfish. Rock bass is more or less oblong, back is considerably elevated and forehead is considerably rounded. Back and sides are ordinarily olive-brown and each scale has dark spot; eye is more or less red. Young fishes may be readily recognized by broad, irregular, black vertical bars on sides. Rock bass can change color with great rapidity; in a few minutes it can change from silver to almost solid black or to silver with black splotches. It reaches length of 8 to 10 in.

northern, smallmouth bass [*Micropterus dolomieui dolomieui*]: mouth is moderate size, maxillary not extending beyond eye. Young are more or less barred or spotted and never have black lateral band; caudal fin has yellow or orange base, black center and white tip; very young fry are jet black. Color of adult varies above from dark green flecked with gold to pale olive-brown; it is white below. Body is sometimes uniform in color, but often it is mottled with vermiculations of darker olive-green; mottling is most often noted after smallmouth bass has been landed; eyes are more or less reddish.

North Open Water: considerable area of open navigable water in northern Baffin Bay, roughly oval in shape, with major axis oriented north to south. It is bounded by fast ice of Smith Sound to the north and by Baffin Bay pack to the south. Its southern boundary is usually a little north of 75th parallel.

North Pacific Current: warm branch of Kuroshio extension flowing eastward across Pacific Ocean.

North River Sloop: large shoal-draft, centerboard, used on Hudson River for carrying passengers and freight before advent of steam. These sloops were 70 to 90 ft. long on deck, fast and fine weather boats. Square topsail was replaced by triangular topsail after War of 1812.

northwest: that point of the horizon or the compass lying midway between N. and W.; situated in, directed toward, or coming from, the *northwest* (or *N.W.*); as, the *NW entrance; a NW gale; a NW set of current.*

Norway Current: continuation of North Atlantic drift, which flows northward along coast of Norway.

nose: stem or extreme forward end of a vessel. A prominent point or seaward-projecting part of a cliff or bold shore. To point, or head, a vessel into a narrow or congested area; as, to *nose* into a berth; she *nosed* through a fleet of trawlers.

Nostoc: genus of blue-green freshwater algae; found in most places and made up of filaments united into jellylike spherical or lobed colony.

notch: deep, narrow cut in base of sea cliff made by breaking waves.

notochord: in *Chordata*, stiff rod of turgid vacuolated cells extending longitudinally dorsal to digestive tract, between it and dorsal nerve cord, and serving as axial skeletal support. In adults of most vertebrates, it is replaced by centrum of vertebral column.

Notodelphyoida [order]: body mostly with uniform segmentation; thorax humped or swollen in female for brood chamber; trunk appendages small; articulation between 4th and 5th thoracic segments in male; often commensal in tunicates; marine. *Notodelphys, Doropygus.*

notothyrium [*Brachiopoda*]: opening in brachial valve adjacent to and outside hinge line. Forms part of opening for pedicle.

Nova: a blaze star, or one observed to glow or to almost suddenly burst into brilliance for a brief period and return to its former magnitude or into obscurity. Such stars are named by astronomers according to constellation in which appearing; as *Nova Andromedae; Nova Cygni.* Of the few more recent important phenomena of this kind was that appearing in *Perseus*, February 22, 1901, which for the night of February 23 became brightest star in the sky. It then slowly diminished in lustre until it disappeared in July of same year. It was called *Nova Persei.*

N_2 constituent: larger lunar elliptic semidiurnal constituent of theoretical tide-producing forces.

nucleic acid: macromolecules characteristic of all living things, containing coded information by which their genetic characteristics are determined.

nucleus [*Foraminifera*]: dense body suspended in interior of living cell. Bears most of hereditary material and controls most of cellular activity.

nucleus nuclear shells [*Mollusca*]: protoconch or initial whorls in gastropod; prodissoconch in pelecypod.

nudibranch [sea slug]: 1) one of order *Nudibranchia* of gastropods in which shell is entirely absent in adult. Body bears projections which vary in color and complexities among species. 2) sea slugs, member of mollusc class *Gastropoda.* Nudibranch is soft-bodied, often brightly colored animal with 2 pairs of tentacles.

nun buoy: red or red-striped buoy of conical shape.

nutation: slow libratory or oscillatory movement of the earth's axis as observed in the wavering of our celestial poles in their gradual sweep and around the poles of the ecliptic in the phenomenon termed *precession.* It may be likened to the staggering motion of a spinning top as it slowly swings, axially inclined, about its bearing center. The movement produces a small variation in position among the stars of the equinoctial points, modifying displacement of these due alone to westward motion in precession of about 50″ annually. This wobbling of our planet is attributed to unequal forces of attraction, chiefly of sun and moon, on the earth's mass due to her departure from spherical form in a "big waistline," or bulging with an excess of equatorial diameter.

nutrient: in the ocean any one of number of inorganic or organic compounds or ions used primarily in nutrition of primary producers. Nitrogen and phosphorous compounds are essential nutrients. Silicates are essential for growth and development of diatoms. Vitamins such as B_{12} are essential to many algae.

nyctipelagic: found in surface waters of ocean at night only.

O

O: square flag, in color diagonally halved in red and yellow, hoisted singly, or Morse flashing signal (— — —), denoting letter *O*, indicates *"Man overboard"* in International Code of Signals. The symbol *o*, as that occurring in German and Scandinavian alphabets, in visual and sound signaling by use of International Morse Code, is indicated by (— — — ·). *Overcast sky*, in ships' logbooks and weather records, usually is indicated by *O* or *o*.

oakum [ships]: material made of tarred rope fibers obtained from scrap rope, used for calking seams in wooden deck. It is also used for calking around pipes.

oarfish: name refers to slender, long ventral spines that terminate in small oarlike blades. Oarfish is elusive; few have ever seen a living specimen. One oarfish encountered by a scientist in South Pacific was 11 ft. long, yet only 3 in. thick and about 12 in. deep. Blue and silvery body was adorned with crest of scarlet dorsal spines 3 ft. long and ventral fins transformed into long slender streamers with oarlike tips.

oarlock [ships]: device on small boat's gunwale in or on which the oar rests and swings freely in rowing.

oarweed: British term for blade-shaped brown alga.

Obelia [phylum *Coelenterata*]: these are medusae of hydroids of genus *Obelia*. They are well known and characterized by having very flat bell; rounded gonads on each of four radial canals; numerous solid marginal tentacles; short manubrium; absence of ocelli; right adradial marginal vesicles. Although numerous species of hydroids are distinguished, their medusa are difficult to identify down to species.

obelisk shell [*Eulimidae*]: member of large group of small, usually highly polished shells with long spires which in some species are bent toward one side. Many members of group are parasitic in echinoderms and spend their life within tissues of starfishes and sea urchins. Here they may be observed or often felt as a lump beneath surface of these sea creatures. Most members of this family live within the tropics.

obelisk shell, Mittres [*Balais cumingii*]: this shell has spire which is almost straight and contains about 13 whorls. Varices upon shell are irregular and not always visible. Shell is white opaque color and will reach a length of about 1½ in.

obelisk shell, Thaanum's [*Balcis thaanumi*]: rather solid species with ovate aperture and with spine which is usually slightly curved in 2 directions. Whorls of shell are slightly convex and each bears opaque varix which together unite somewhat to form a line ascending spire on right side and back making in this ascent between ¼ and ½ turns to right. It is glistening white with somewhat transparent appearance. It will reach a length of about 1 in.

oblate spheroid: spheroid, flattened or depressed at poles. Shape of earth.

oblique haul: retrieval of open plankton net from certain depth at certain rate while ship is under way.

Obolacea: brachiopods, rounded and lenticular in form, with short pedicle and thick shell; probably fixed to seaweed. These lived in older Paleozoic era and were formerly believed to include supposed brachiopods. *Fermoria* and *Protabolella* of Vindhyan of India.

occlude: to take in and retain in pores or other openings; to absorb; used particularly with respect to absorbing of gases by certain substances which do not lose characteristic properties, as charcoal, iron, etc.

occluded front: front formed when cold front overtakes warm front.

occulation: disappearance of a heavenly body due to intervention of another; especially, the sudden obscuring of a star or planet by the moon due to her orbital advance, or that of a planet's satellite behind its primary. The term often is applied loosely to an *eclipse*, or phenomenon in which a darkened body obscures a luminary, wholly or in part.

216

ocean: before time of Homer, who may have lived as early as 1200 B.C., Greeks had devised an elaborate cosmology. Major feature of it was "the great river," or *akeanos*, that was conceived as encompassing the flat disc of the earth. Mariners of later periods abandoned the concept of ever-flowing global stream. But they retained its name to designate the boundless body of water, quite different from the land-rimmed Mediterranean, that washed the whole world with its waves. Until middle of 17th century, English seafarers commonly referred to this vast expanse as "the ocean sea." Abbreviated to ocean, name gradually came to indicate any large body of water. Even today there is no universal agreement concerning number of oceans on our planet. Through evaporation and condensation each feeds the continuous cycle that evoked Homer's wonder at the fact that rivers never run dry.

ocean area of earth: ocean waters cover exactly 71% of globe's surface.

ocean basin: that part of floor of ocean that is more than 100 fathoms below sea level.

ocean current: movement of ocean characterized by regularity, either by cyclic nature or more commonly as continuous stream flowing along definable path.

ocean depths: greatest depth (over 10,400 meters) lies in Pacific. Depths over 8,500 meters and 7,000 meters have been recorded in Atlantic and Indian Oceans, respectively.

oceanic: that portion of pelagic division seaward from approximate edge of continental shelf.

oceanic crust: mass of gabroic material approximately 5 km. thick which lies under ocean bottom and may be more or less continuous beneath continental crust.

oceanicity: degree to which point on earth's surface is, in all respects, subject to influence of sea; opposite of continentality. Oceanicity usually refers to climate and its effects.

oceanic lateen: lateen sail made of matting or other material laced between 2 yards. It is used in certain Pacific Islands.

oceanic plankton: plankton characteristic of open sea beyond continental shelves.

oceanic spritsail: sail of various shapes made of matting, etc., supported between sprits, used on canoes in a number of Pacific Islands.

oceanogenic sedimentation: sediments, exclusively marine, siliceous, chemical or organic in origin, which accumulate in abyssal depths far from land.

oceanographic analysis: science of manual or automatic production of charts of oceanographic parameters in which isopleths are drawn to indicate data by some rational theory.

oceanographic equator: zone of maximum sea surface temperature located near geographic equator. It generally lies north of this line, but crosses during southern summer in Indian Ocean, western Pacific Ocean and western Atlantic Ocean.

oceanographic forecasting: production by automatic or manual means of charts showing forecasted values of oceanographic parameters, similar to weather charts.

oceanographic model: theoretical representation of marine environment. Generally, a pattern or expression which relates known with derived oceanographic properties. These oceanographic properties may be physical, chemical, geological and/or biological.

oceanographic slide rule: specially designed slide rule used for calculating correction of thermal expansion of deep-sea reversing thermometer.

oceanographic station: term used to designate oceanographic observations taken at geographic location from a ship that is lying to or anchored at sea.

oceanographic tracer: foreign substance introduced into ocean by natural or artificial means which enables determination of ocean water movement through measurement of distribution and location of substance at same time.

oceanography: study of the sea. In its technical research methods, this science embraces practically all scientific disciplines known to man. Study of the sea embraces and integrates all knowledge pertaining to sea's physical boundaries, chemistry and physics of seawater and marine biology.

ocean sunfish: this mammoth fish lives in open ocean but occasionally becomes stranded on beach or is harpooned as a curiosity. It is absurd looking seeming to be all head and no body and covered with thick leathery skin. Truncated posterior suggests that rest of fish was chopped off behind the tall dorsal and anal fins. Body is circular, dusky gray on back, silvery gray on sides and white on belly. Is so named from habit of basking near surface. Average individuals measure 4 ft. deep.

ocean temperatures: mean surface temperature of Atlantic and Pacific Oceans is 17° C; that of Indian Ocean 18° C. Maximum temperatures are, respectively, 30° C, 32° C and 35° C.

Oceanus: one of the Titans; ancient Greek god of great river "Ocean" that surrounded the world, father of ocean nymphs, Oceanids and all rivers.

Oceanus Procellarium [Ocean of Storms]: largest "sea" on the moon, with area almost twice that of Mediterranean Sea. It lies near northeastern limb.

ocean water: water having physical and chemical characteristics of open sea, where continental influences are minimum. Average salinity is 35°/oo.

ocellated [fish]: having appearance of an eye; rounded and surrounded by ring of another color.

ocellus: in *Arthropoda*, a simple eye. Also used for light-sensitive pigmented structures in other groups, as in medusae.

Octocorallia [*Alcyonaria*]: exclusively colonial (compound) mesenteries in multiples of 8. Skeleton in most cases consisting of loose calcareous spicules only but continuous in modern *Tubipora* (organ-pipe corals). Alcyonarian spicules have been found in Cretaceous and Tertiary deposits and forms allied to *Tubipora* in some formations.

octopod: having 8 arms, feet or tentacles.

Octopoda, order [*Octopus, Argonauta* (paper nautilus)]: body globose, usually without fins; 8 arms with 1 to 3 rows of sessile suckers; mantle forms muscular sac around viscera; internal shell lacking; some with special egg case secreted by dorsal arms; 3rd arm of male may be modified as copulatory organ (hectocotylus); ink sac present.

octopus: one of family *(Octopodidae)* of cephalopods with round or saclike bodies, 8 arms, no shell and, generally, without fins.

odograph: an instrument which records courses steered and distances (or time intervals) run on each course; a course recorder.

oecia: in colonial Bryozoa, special reproductive zooids containing egg cells.

oersted: unit of magnetic intensity in metric system, usually expressed in centimeters—gram—second.

oesophagus: gullet; division of digestive canal leading from pharynx to stomach.

offlap: in geology, situation where terrestrial deposits are laid down over marine deposits, as when sea level becomes lower relative to land in given region.

offset: vertical changes in position of rock layers due to faulting.

offshore: comparatively flat zone of variable width which extends from outer margin of rather steeply sloping shoreface to edge of continental shelf.

offshore bar: sandbar running parallel to coastline.

offshore currents: 1) nontidal currents outside surf zone which are not affected by shoaling and river discharge. 2) prevailing nontidal current usually setting parallel to shore outside surf zone.

offshore water: water adjacent to land in which physical properties are slightly influenced by continental conditions.

offshore winds [land breeze]: winds blowing seaward from coast.

off the wind: ship's distance from shore.

ogee [ships]: molding with concave and convex outline like an S.

oikoplast: in *Larvacea* such as *Oikopleura*, cell or cells that secrete gelatinous house.

Oikopleura dioica [*Oikopleuridae*]: tail is narrow, being 2 to 4 mm. long and about 0.3 to 0.6 mm. at widest point. It bears pair of characteristic large subchordal cells about 2/3 along its length on right side which are readily distinguishable even in unstained material. Ovoid trunk is between 0.5 and 1 mm. long and bears either ovary or testes posteriorly.

Oikopleura fusiformis [*Oikopleuridae*]: tail is relatively long, being about 4 times length of trunk, with narrower muscles than *O. labradorensis* and with no subchordal cells. There is single ovary and paired testes which extend over each side of alimentary canal.

Oikopleura labradorensis [*Oikopleuridae*]: this species is of similar general appearance to *O. dioica* but can be immediately recognized by presence of numerous large subchordal cells near tip of tail on right side. Unlike *O. dioica* which is dioecious, *O. labradorensis* has single ovary and paired testes in posterior trunk region.

oiler: vessel used for transportation of oil; especially, one built for supplying a naval fleet with fuel oil. A member of engineering department in a merchant vessel.

oilskins: cloth of cotton or silk prepared with oil to make it waterproof. Also garment of oilskin worn by seamen.

old man [ships]: piece of heavy iron bar bent to form a Z.

old salts [ships]: older men in crew before the masts, also called "sea dogs."

oligotrophic plankton: plankton of seas with low level of nutrients, where light penetrates deeply into clear, relatively barren water.

olivine [rock]: common in meteorites; ranges in color from green to light gray to brown; transparent to translucent.

onlap: in geology, condition where marine sediments are deposited over terrestrial sediments, as when sea level becomes higher than before, relative to land in the region.

ooblast: connecting filament through which zygote nucleus moves from carpogonium to auxiliary cell.

oolite: limestone composed of small grains of carbonate of lime in layer of sedimentary rock.

oostegites: flat plates extending medially from thoracic appendage of certain crustaceans.

ootype: thickened portion of oviduct in trematodes and cestodes; formerly considered place where shell is formed.

oozooid: a sexually produced compound tunicate

larva that by budding gives rise to blastozooids.

open center [*diving*]: hydraulic system in which oil is continuously cycled.

open current [*diving*]: diving life-support system in which diver's exhalation is completely vented to water.

operculum: plate closing an opening or covering some other structure.

Ophiuchus: an equatorial constellation lying immediately north of *Scorpio*.

ophiuroid: member of echinoderm class *Ophiuroidea* that includes brittle stars and basket stars. Unlike true brittle stars, ophiuroids have long, slender, jointed arms distinctly separated from bodies. These flexible limbs have remarkable power of regeneration.

opposition: situation of a celestial body when differing from another by 180° in longitude or 12 hours in right ascension; especially, that of a planet with respect to the sun; as expressed in *Mars is now in opposition to the sun.* Our *moon* is in that situation when at the *full*.

oral disks [*Coelenterata*]: fleshy wall closing off upper end of cylindrical column, that forms polyp's sides.

ordinary seaman [*ships*]: crew member subordinate to able seaman but who has learned part of usual deck duties.

Ordovician: period of Paleozoic era before Cambrian period. More than half of continent of North America was under water. Earliest known vertebrates appeared in this period; cephalopods were common.

organ-pipe coral [*Tubipora*]: belonging to order *Stolonifera*; cylindrical and thin-walled polyps arise singly and connect together by solenial tubes of stolons and by crossbars; calcareous spicules of skeleton are fused into tubes.

orthostropic [*Gastropoda*]: common shell type in which whorls are coiled on erect cone so that apex points back rather than forward. If notch for siphon is in aperture it will be opposite direction of apex.

oscla: plural of osculum, opening in sponge's body through which water enters for oxygen and food exits carrying animal's waste products.

osmotically: referring to osmosis, diffusion of fluid through semipermeable membrane until equilibrium is reached between concentrations of fluids on either side of membrane; e.g., food reaches tissues from blood through osmosis.

Osteichthyes [*class*]: phylum *Chordata*, Devonian to Recent. Body skeleton; notochord reduced; jaws variously attached to skull; 2 pairs of paired appendages. Marine and freshwater, nektonic; predators and herbivores.

otter trawl: baglike fishing net with mouth kept open by two large structures called otter boards, on each side of net.

outcrop: naturally protruding, erosionally exposed or part of rock bed or formation, most of which is covered by overlying material.

outer: on the outside; external; farther or farthest from a given position or chosen starting point; opposed to *inner*; as, *outer jib; outer planking; outer buntline; outer bottom.*

outer lip [*Gastropoda*]: lateral border of aperture.

outrigger: frameworks extending beyond ship's rail, e.g., oarlock base, log to prevent canoe from tipping; a canoe.

ovicell: greatly modified zooecium serving as brood pouch for early embryo in certain marine *Bryozoa*.

oviduct: tube in which female's eggs are carried from ovary to exterior or to uterus where they develop as embryos.

oviparous: producing eggs that hatch outside mother's body.

ovisac: egg receptacle.

ovoviviparous: reproductive pattern in which eggs develop within mother's body without nutritive aid from mother.

oxidation: induction of chemical reaction or reactions in which oxygen is added to substance.

oxyarc burning: process for cutting ferrous metal using electrode and stream of oxygen.

oxygen high pressure [OHP]: in diving, higher than normal partial pressure of oxygen within body.

oxygen low pressure [OLP]: in diving, lower than normal partial pressure of oxygen within body.

oxygen toxicity [*diving*]: condition of elevated partial pressure of oxygen in body causing undesirable reactions. Extremely dangerous in diving operations because it can result in loss of consciousness and subsequent drowning.

Oyashio Current: cold current from Arctic, in western North Pacific.

oyster: well-known bivalve mollusk those species of which found on coasts of North America and Europe are most important as food. Growing on hard bottom, it attaches itself to rocks, old shells, etc., in bays and at or near mouths of rivers, only in water of more or less salty content. Oysters are gathered by means of *tongs* or *rakes*, which may be likened to a pair of long-handled large sized garden rakes worked scissors fashion, so that the catch is taken between the rakes' meeting teeth. A more elaborate device for this purpose is a heavy toothed *drag*, hauled over the bottom (*oyster bed*) by an *oyster dredger*, as craft using this method are called. Vessels engaged in taking oysters, or *oyster fishing*, locally are termed *oyster sloops, oyster schooners, oyster scows*, etc., according to rig. Laws limiting season for oyster fishing and size of the mollusk captured are in force in U.S. and Canada, both countries including in their programs for maintaining propagation of oyster life the yearly replenishing of beds with seed oysters produced by laboratories devoted to the work.

oyster rock: among fishermen in the Chesapeake Bay region of the industry, natural *oyster bed*, or hard bottom consisting of a more or less compacted mass of dead and broken shells, on which the oysters grow.

P

P: in International Code, a square blue flag with a white square in its center, popularly known as the *Blue Peter* (a corruption of *blue repeater*, as used in a former British naval code). Hoisted singly at the fore, denotes, "All persons are to repair on board as the vessel is about to proceed to sea." As a Morse Code flashing signal at sea (· — — ·), denotes, "Your lights are out or burning bad." Also, as a towing signal, or that between a towing vessel and her tow, flag *P* held in the hand or shown by hoisting to an appropriate position, or Morse *P* at night, by *ship towing*, signifies, "I must get shelter or anchor as soon as possible"; by *ship towed*, "Bring me to shelter or to anchor as soon as possible." As a symbol in a logbook or weather record, *p = passing showers;* also, in nautical astronomy, often denoting *polar distance*, and in navigation, *departure*.

P.A.: abbreviation used on American and British charts *for position approximate*, as indicated with reference to a shoal or rock.

Pacific: largest of the oceans, so named by *Magellan* from fine weather conditions he experienced as first European navigator of that expanse. About 70,000,000 miles in area, extends from Bering Strait to Antarctic Circle, but usually divided in cartography as North and South Pacific, or respective areas north and south of the equator. From America it extends westward to Japan Islands, Philippines, New Guinea, and to longitude of southwest extremity of Australia (about 114° E.).

Pacific high: nearly permanent subtropical high of North Pacific Ocean, centered in the mean at 30° to 40° N and 140° to 150° W.

Pacific Ocean: ocean area bounded on east by western limits of coastal waters of southwest Alaska and British Columbia, southern limits of Gulf of California and from Atlantic Ocean by meridian of Cape Horn to Antarctica; on north by southern limits of Bering Strait and Gulf of Alaska; on west by easterly limits of Sea of Okhotsk, Japan Sea, Philippine Sea, East Indian Archipelago from Luzon Island to New Guinea, Bismarck Sea, Solomon Sea, Coral Sea, Tasman Sea and from Indian Ocean by line from Southeast Cape, down meridian to Antarctic Continent.

packers [ships]: men who fit lampwicking, tarred felt or other material between parts of structure to insure water- or oiltightness.

packet: dispatch vessel or ship employed to convey letters from one country to another, hence, vessel starting on regular days and at appointed time.

packet ship: passenger ship of period from 1816 to 1860's when sailing vessel made way for steamship. Early packets were small, three-masted, square-rigged ships, from 300 to 500 tons register, but size increased until they were over 1,000 tons.

pack ice: floating ice blocks driven closely together in irregular ridges and covering large area. Term is used to denote any area of sea ice other than fast ice no matter what form it takes or how disposed.

padda boat: open, square-ended, flat-bottomed canal boat of Ceylon used for transporting freight, with sharply raking ends, having graceful sheer, roofed over with rattan or bamboo frame. Paddles.

paddlefish, American: also known as spoonbill cat and shovelnose cat; lives in silty lakes and ponds of central and southern U.S. It is gray and grows to length of 6 ft. weighing as much as 150 lbs. It is a filter-feeder, maintaining its huge bulk on diet of plankton that is strained from water by sievelike gill rakers in throat.

paddlefish family: paddlefishes belong to ancient group of fossil fishes which are known by several fossils representing two species. Two modern species are living today. One is the paddlefish found in Mississippi River system and the other is *Psephurus gladius* found in Yangtze River in China. *P. gladius* is said to reach length of 20 ft. Paddlefishes are smooth-skinned fishes with snout prolonged into long, thin, paddle-shaped projection, which is somewhat flexible.

paddlefish, spoonbill cat: primitive fish having

skeleton composed chiefly of cartilage. It has long, thin, paddlelike snout, extending almost 1/3 length of body. Mouth is broad and subterminal; skin is smooth without scales, though traces of rhomboid scales are found in upper lobe of caudal fin. Gills are covered by large, peculiar soft opercle reaching to base of ventral fin and ending posteriorly in a point. Spiracle is present; tail is heterocercal; color is uniform leaden gray. Internally paddlefish has swim bladder like that found in most higher fishes. It has a peculiar intestine of spiral-valve type usually found in sharks. It attains length of over 6 ft. and maximum weight of 184 lbs.

pad eye [ships]: fitting having an eye integral with plate or base in order to distribute strain over greater area and to provide ample means of securing. Pad may have either "worked" or "shackle" eye, or more than one of either or both. Principal use of such a fitting is that it affords means of attaching rigging, stoppers, blocks and other movable or portable objects.

padow: large trading "dhow" of India, north of Bombay, generally having painted parts under the poop.

Paguridae [family]: there are 4 zoeal stages in which eyes are characteristically longer anteroposteriorly than width of abdomen. Uropods are present in last two zoeal stages and telson, which is only slightly concave posteriorly, bears 6 or 7 pairs of spines.

Paguridea [tribe]: *Pagurus* is commonest genus containing all common hermit crabs. There are 4 larval stages and post-larval one, once thought to be separate genus and still termed *Glaucothoe*. Early larvae resemble those of the galatheids. There are similar projections from carapace, 2 at rear and 1 at front, but never any serrations on lateral margins of carapace. Endopodite of uropods is so small as to be called vestigial in pagurid larvae. There are two families, *Paguridae* and *Lithodidae*, and their larvae are easily distinguishable.

Pagurus bernhardus [paguridans]: zoea have long straight antennal spire which is at least 6 times as long as broad. Rostrum projects beyond spine on antennal scale; 5th abdominal segment bears pair of small lateral spines; characteristic feature is that longest spine on telson is more than half the greatest width of telson. First zoea is about 3.5 mm. and final stage reaches 8 mm. Megalopa of all species belonging to this genus possess 4 pairs of functional pleopods; chelae of *P. bernhardus* have smooth propodus; antennae reach as far as tip of chaelae; eyestalks are about twice as long as broad.

Pagurus cuanensis [paguridans]: zoeae of this species differ from those of *P. bernhardus* and *P. pubescences* in that antennal scale is curved and only 4 times as long as it is broad. Longest telson spine is less than ½ the greatest width of telson; 5th abdominal segment bears prominent lateral spines. Paired yellow chromatophores are present on carapace in stage 1 and 2 and also on abdominal segments 5 and 6. First zoea is approximately 2.7 mm. long and final stage rarely exceeds 4 mm. in length.

Pagurus prideauxi [paguridans]: zoeae are similar to those of *P. cuanensis* but paired yellow chromatophores are present in 5th abdominal segment only. Additional features are orange chromatophores on each side of carapace and presence of small mid-dorsal spine on posterior margin of 6th abdominal segment. Largest spine on telson of 1st and 2nd zoeal stage is just less than 1/3 the greatest width of telson. Length is from 3.5 to 6 mm., i.e., much larger than those of *P. cuanensis*.

Pagurus pubescens [paguridans]: zoeae of this species are similar to that of *P. bernhardus* but 5th abdominal segment has large lateral spines and rostrum is somewhat shorter, reaching only tip of spine on antennal scale. First zoea is approximately 3 mm. and in final zoea, attains length of 5.5 mm.

pahi: term applied by Tahitians to any large seagoing double canoes formerly used by natives of Tuamotu Archipelago and Tahiti.

painter: 1) rope attached to bow of small boat, used to fasten it to stake or ship; any short rope used in similar manner. 2) fog frequently experienced on coast of Peru. Brownish deposit which it often leaves upon exposed surfaces is sometimes called Peruvian paint.

paired terraces: terraces that face each other across stream at same elevation.

palacca: Italian "palacca" with 3 pole masts, foremast being lateen-rigged, main square-rigged with topsail and mizzen lateen-rigged with square topsail.

Palaeosmilia regia: compound, massive coral found in one of highest zones of Carboniferous limestone. Each corallite is bounded by distinct wall. There is no columella. Tabulae are very flat domes, and break up marginally into more convex tubellae; dissepiments are numerous, regular, small and globose; keyhole fossula at outer part of tabularium. Individual corallites may be as large as 50 mm. in diameter or as small as 15 mm.

Palaeotremata [brachiopods]: though all articulates have hinges, teeth and sockets are poorly developed in this early Cambrian order. It contains only a few rare genera from Vermont, Pennsylvania and the West.

palatine: pair of bones between and behind maxillae.

Palau Archipelago: group of islands in Pacific, between Mindanao and Caroline Islands.

pale [ships]: one of interior shores for steadying beams of ship while building.

paleocrystic ice: old sea ice, generally considered to be at least 10 years old; it is nearly always a form of pressure ice, and often is found in floebergs and in pack ice of central Arctic Ocean.

paleomagnetism: study of earth's ancient magnetic field properties as recorded in rocks. Remanent magnetism produced by earth's field when material was initially found.

paleontologist: scientist who studies historical geology of earth, especially fossil plants and animals and their development in relation to modern species.

Paleozoic: major era of geologic history that began over 600 million years ago with Cambrian period and lasted over 350 million years; particularly noted for inundation of much of present-day continents by sea and many marine invertebrate fossils dating from this era.

pallets [*Mollusca*]: pair of simple or compound calcareous structures at syphonal end of certain woodboring pelecypods, used to close burrow when siphons are withdrawn.

pallial line [*Mollusca*]: linear impression connecting adductor muscle scars, marking attachment of mantle margin to shell.

pallial sinus [*Mollusca*]: curved embayment in pallial line.

palm [ships]: flat inner surface of fluke of an anchor; device used in sewing canvas, consisting of leather strap fitting around hand and containing indented piece of metal for pressure against needle.

palmately: flat and having branches radiating from central point, resembling a hand.

palmella: stage in life cycle of many flagellates involving aggregation of numerous individuals, simulating a colony.

palolo worm: species *(Eunice viridis)* of polychaete worms which spawn in vast, free-swimming swarms over reefs of Samoan and Fiji Islands during last quarter of moon; at lowest tide during October and November.

palp: in arthropods, exopodite of mouthpart appendages, sensory in function.

palpon: in *Siphonophora*, simple mouthless zooid serving as accessory digestive zooid.

paludal: pertaining to swamps or marshes and to material deposited in swamp environment.

pancake ice: pieces of newly formed ice, approximately circular about 30 cm. (12 in.) to 3 meters (10 ft.) across with raised rims caused by striking together of pieces as result of wind and swell.

Pandalidae [carideans]: as in all other decapods except peneids, nauplius stage is omitted and first larva is a protozoea in which main segments are already delimited and carapace and compound eyes are present. Pandalid zoeae always have rostrum which, in later stages, becomes toothed. Antennal scale (exopodite) is segmented; of 5 thoracic limbs behind the 3 which form maxillipeds all except the 5th have exopodites. Endopodites of 2nd pair are chelate in later stages. Caridean larvae always have 2 pairs of chelate walking legs in contrast to peneids and stenopids which have 3 pairs.

pandanus: common tropical tree resembling the palm whose leaf fibers are suitable for weaving mats and similar articles.

panga: flat-bottomed rowboat of Central America.

panting [ships]: pulsation in and out of bow and stern plating as ship alternately rises and plunges deep into water.

panting beams [ships]: transverse beams that tie panting frames together.

panting frames [ships]: frames in forepeak usually extra heavy to withstand panting action of shell plating.

pantomictic plankton: plankton not dominated by any particular species.

papers [ships]: documents required to be carried on board. A merchant vessel's papers include: articles of agreement between master and crew; bills of health; bills of lading; certificates of classification, inspection, and registry; cargo manifest; consular invoice; customs clearance; charter party; freeboard or load line certificate; fumigation certificate; logbook; passenger manifest; receipts for tonnage tax; and tonnage certificates for Panama and Suez Canals.

papulae: dermal branchiae or skin gills in echinoderms.

parachal: open circular-shaped coracle used in Bowani River, Coimbatore, India. Made by covering rattan frame with oilcloth.

parachute spinnaker [ships]: large spinnaker with short boom which inflates like a balloon.

paraharpes [trilobites]: small hypoparians whose broad fringes spread far beyond rest of body when they were unrolled. When feeding they apparently plowed through mud and rubbish, with fringes pushing both sides much as snowplow moves snow.

paralia [phytoplankton]: short, disk-shaped cells with curved edges united to form straight chains. Ornamentation of roughly hexagonal markings. Numerous small chloroplasts.

parallax: tidal term referring to angle at center of earth and line tangent to earth's surface; ratio of mean radius of earth to distance of tide-producing body. Term is usually applied to inequalities in tide which result from continually changing distance of principal tide-producing body, the moon.

parallax inequality: variation in change of tide or in speed of tidal currents because of continual change in distance of moon from earth. Range of tide and speed of tidal currents tend to increase as moon approaches perigee and to decrease as it approaches apogee.

parallax of a star: angle formed by 2 lines from star to sun and to one end of earth's orbit.

parallel: surfaces, planes, or lines lying in same direction at equal distances apart, however far extended, are said to be *parallel*. Such *lines*, as those running east and west indicating latitude on a chart, map, or globe, are called *parallels*.

parallelism of axis: each position of earth's axis is parallel to every other position during revolution.

parallel of latitude: circle or approximation of circle on surface of earth parallel to equator, and connecting points of equal latitude.

parallels: east-west circles around earth parallel to equator.

paralytic shellfish poisoning: intoxication in humans resulting from ingestion of marine mollusks, usually mussels or soft clams, that become toxic during periods of high concentrations of certain dinoflagellates. Effects range from mild discomfort to fatal respiratory paralysis, with symptoms including tingling or burning of lips, gums, tongue and face, followed by numbness of extremities, general feeling of weakness and dizziness, inability to coordinate muscular movements and respiratory distress.

parameter: 1) constant by which population or environment is defined. 2) in general, any quantity of a problem that is not independent variable.

Paramysis areonosa [mysid]: small, robust mysid with carapace bearing small or short, blunt rostrum and concave posterior margin. Eyes are short and thick; long apex on antennal scale. Coastal species.

paranzello: Italian 2-masted trawler with large lateen mainsail on mast, or "trunchetto," stepped about amidships, small lateen mizzen and 2 headsails.

parapodium: paired lateral locomotive structure on body segments of polychaetes.

parapyle: in *Radiolaria* of order *Phaeodaria*, 2 lateral pore fields in central capsule.

parasitic nutrition: process by which organism absorbs organic food directly from body of host.

parasitic sea laurel [Janczewski gardner]: since alga is parasitic on sea laurel, its habitat and range are same as those of its host. Noticeable feature of this seaweed is that it does not look at all like seaweed. It grows on host plant with irregularly-shaped, cushionlike patches covered with limelike, modular outgrowths. Cushion is solid compact tissue composed of short, thin-walled cells with diameter of 1/8 to 1/4 in. and height of 1/8 in., which grows from tips of cells buried in pits of *Laurencia*. Parasitic sea laurel is neutral yellow-beige or pale pink.

parasitism: relationship between 2 species in which one lives on or in body of host and obtains food from its tissue.

Parasmilia centralis: simple coral found in White Chalk of England. It is attached to molluscan or echinoid shells by spreading base from which rises short cylindrical perpendicular portion soon expanding into conical form which may attain length of 25 mm. and diameter of 12 mm. Calice is nearly circular, showing prominent columella. Vertical section shows lumen to have very few tabulae and dissepiments; surface of septa bears little tubercles. Columella is not a solid pillar but irregular network of trabeculae.

parasphenoid teeth [amphibian]: teeth in roof of mouth of some salamanders, usually well behind internal nares and arranged in longitudinal series.

paravane [ships]: water plane with protecting wing placed on bottom forward end of keel stern. Also special type of water kite which, when towed with wire rope from fitting on forefoot of vessel, operates to ride out from the ship's side and deflect mines which are moored in path of vessel, and to cut them adrift so that they will rise to surface where they may be seen and destroyed.

parcelling [ships]: winding strips of canvas which lay around rope, preparatory to serving.

pardo: vessel used in 17th and 18th centuries in China Seas for trade and war. It was not so large as a "junk" but was similar, except that sails were slackly laced by one side to masts instead of being suspended by yard.

parietal [*Mollusca*]: based area in helically-coiled gastropod shell, just inside and outside aperture; i.e., inner lip area.

parmal pores: in some *Radiolaria*, primary pores through shell, surrounding each radial spine.

parotoid glands: rounded or oval glandular protuberance on back of head in toads.

parrel [ships]: ring around mast secured to middle of yard by which latter is held to mast.

parrotfish: some of brilliantly colored fishes hovering close to coral seeming to browse along its surface as rabbits nibble grass. Closer look reveals that they are suitably named because of beaklike mouth formed by the fusion of front teeth. They scour rock and corals snipping off attached algae and sedentary invertebrates, and also feed on calcareous algae that constitute large part of coral massifs. Parrotfish travel and graze in schools. In Red Sea there is variety of parrotfish characterized by prominent lump on forehead; lump grows as fish ages. Size of parrotfish varies widely according to species.

parrotfish, rainbow: oblong body is covered with large cycloid scales. Blunt head terminates in greenish-blue beak strong enough to bite through fish hook. It is one of most brilliantly colored of reef fishes and also one of largest, often 36 in. long. Body is mixture of green and gold with rosy-red breast; pectoral fins are green; other fins red with blue margins. Dorsal fin is long and low with very little separation between spiny and soft-rayed portions.

parthenopid crab, horrid [*Parthenope horrida*]: surface of this species is rough. It is covered with rough elevations and depressions and with smaller tubercles and pits. Chelipeds are usually unequal in size; walking legs bear spines which grow in such a way that they form perforated margin along upper edge of leg. Carapace is somewhat 5-sided and 4 in. wide. This species is reported to live on bottoms of mud or broken shells from shallow water to depths in excess of 300 ft.

parthenopid crab, long-spined: carapace or shell of this crab is covered with tubercles and short spines. Front legs or chelipeds are large and covered with tubercles and spines, of which those along angles of these legs are triangular in shape; walking legs are slender, quite smooth, and marked by encircling bands of color. Carapace measures about 2 in. in width. This rare crab has been retrieved from rocky bottoms at depths of about 100 ft.

partial pressure [diving]: that portion of total pressure exerted by specific constituent of gas mixture.

partial tide: one of harmonic components comprising the tide at any point. Periods of partial tides are derived from various combinations of angular velocities of earth, sun, moon and stars relative to each other.

particle velocity: in ocean wave studies, instantaneous velocity of water particle undergoing orbital motion. At the crest, its direction is same as direction of progress of wave, and at the trough it is in the opposite direction.

partners [ships]: similar pieces of steel plates, angles or wood timbers used to strengthen and support the mast where it passes through deck, or placed between deck beams under machinery bed plates for added support.

Pascal's law: pressure exerted at any point upon confined liquid is transmitted undiminished in all directions.

pass: narrow connecting channel between 2 bodies of water; also inlet through barrier reef atoll or sandbar or navigable channel at river's mouth.

passage: narrow navigable pass or channel between 2 landmasses or shoals.

patache: southern European vessel, popular previous to 19th century. It resembled the brigantine. Mainmast was a pole without topmast, rigged with large fore-and-aft sail without boom. Foremast consisted of 3 sections each with square sail.

patani: Malay craft with 2-masted Chinese lug rig; sharp bow and stern with overhanging counter and curved stern.

patch: 1) collection of pack ice, less than 10 km. (5.4 nautical miles) across. 2) irregular cluster of floating sea ice fragments of any concentration.

patellate [*Coelenterata*]: corallite with angle of about 120° between sides expanding from apex.

Paterinacea: ventral valve with high interarea "delthyrium" closed by homeodeltidium, apparently no pedicel opening. Confined to lower and middle Cambrian.

pater noster lakes: chain of lakes resembling a string of beads along glaciated valley where ice plucking and gouging have scooped out a series of basins.

pattamar: large 2- or 3-masted dhow of India. Hull is sharp forward, long stem severely raking in dhow manner; stern is square without poop deck. There is generous sheer.

Pavo: small southern constellation containing a single navigational star—*Peacock*, of magnitude 2.12 and located in declination 57°, right ascension 20 hours, 22 minutes.

pawl [ships]: metal cog used inside winches and capstans to prevent teeth from slipping back.

pay [ships]: 1) to cover a seam with tar, pitch or glue. Also to slack away a rope or chain. 2) to slack away or allow to run out (usually with *away* or *out*); to pass out; as, to *pay away* a line; to *pay out* cable. A vessel under sail is said to *pay off* when she swings to leeward of her course or original heading, or to *play round*, as when forced by backing head sail in *casting*. (In above uses of the word, preterit and past participle form is *payed*). 3) to *pay off* a crew is to discharge and settle all payments due each man, as at end of a voyage. Compensation, payment, or salary for one's services; as, *port pay; sea pay; half pay.*

payang: native fishing craft of east coast of Malay Peninsula. Hull has rounded sections; bow and stern alike; some sheer; shallow draft; hardwood frames and planking; carvel-built. Keel is V-shaped in section and parallel longitudinally to gunwale. Hull is painted in various color schemes.

pay off [ships]: 1) to steer or so position ship's sail so that course changes and heading is more away from direction from which wind is blowing. 2) to fall to leeward, said of head of ship.

P.D.: abbreviation for *position doubtful*, as printed on American and British charts to denote that the geographical position of a shoal, reef, rock, or other isolated danger, or of a place at which comparatively shallow water is reported to exist, is indicated with uncertainty or has not been satisfactorily established.

Peacock: navigational star in constellation *Pavo*. It lies about 30° SE by E of the *Scorpion's tail*.

peak [ships]: top after-corner of gaff sail. Also forepeak and afterpeak are extreme ends inside vessel.

peak tank [ships]: tanks in forward and after ends of vessel. Principal use of peak tanks is in trimming ship.

Pea pod: open, double-ended, clinker-built boat used in general fisheries off coast of Maine; 15 ft. long with 4½ ft. beam; good sheer, cat-rigged with single sail.

pebble crab, convex [*Carpilius convexus*]: very hard, very heavy shell covers body and legs. Back or carapace is smooth, convex, oval in outline and without spines. Back is marbled and blotched with red with lighter areas that are whitish or grayish in color. Chelipeds are unequal in size. Body is about 3 in. wide. This is shallow-water species which inhabits reef from shoreline to depths of over 100 ft.

pebble crab, shining red [*Etisus splendidus*]: carapace of this crab is smooth, oval in outline, variously grooved and furrowed and bordered by spines on lateral margin. There are a few spines on chelipeds; walking legs are edged with stiff black hairs. Body is dark red; ends of pinchers are black. Carapace reaches 5 in. in width. This is an uncommon shoreline species which lives on outer edge of reef. It appears to inhabit depths beyond 50 ft.

pectin: complex carbohydrate produced in plants.

Pectinibranchia, order [phylum *Mollusca*]: *Mesogastropoda, Monotocardia*. Snails with organs of postorsional right side lost; with only one ctenidium, one auricle and one nephridium; ctenidium with only one row of filaments (pectinibranch); eversible proboscis in some; nervous system partially concentrated; operculum often present; larva often a veliger; terrestrial, freshwater and marine. *Littorina* (periwinkle), *Crepidula* (slipper or boat shell), *Strombus* (conch), *Campeloma, Cypraea* (cowrie).

Pectinidae [*Anisomyaria*]: this contains genera *Chlamys* and *Pecten* as well as *Lima*. Provinculum is similar to that of Mytilidae but teeth are extremely small in middle region.

pectoral: pertaining to anterior or upper thoracic region, as pectoral fins of fish; in chest region.

pedal ganglion [*Mollusca*]: one of pair of large nerve centers which supplies nerve connections to muscles of foot.

pedalium: in certain jellyfish, expanded gelatinous peduncle bearing one or more marginal tentacles or sense organs.

pedal muscles [*Mollusca*]: paired muscles connecting foot to interior surface of shell.

pedicellariae: 1) minute pincerlike structures around spines and dermal branchiae or dermal gills of certain echinoderms for keeping surface of body free from debris. 2) one of minute pincerlike appendages of sea urchins and some starfishes borne abundantly in test between spines, and consisting of three movable jaws mounted on a stalk.

pedicle [*Brachiopoda*]: muscular and/or fibrous stalk which is attached to inner surface of pedicle valve and which passes out posteriorly to attach to substrata.

pedicle opening [*Brachiopoda*]: opening adjacent to or along hinge line that serves for passage of pedicle; located in pedicle valve only or in both pedicle and brachial valves.

pedicle valve [*Brachiopoda*]: valve to which pedicle is attached by connecting ventral in position.

pedigree mud: descriptive term for high chemical content rotary mud, which includes barium, sulfate, caustic soda, soda ash, sodium bicarbonate, phosphates, etc.

pediwak: decked, keel sailing craft of northern Celebes. It is 30 to 35 ft. long, wide and deep. Bow is hollow and sharp and much lower than main part of hull; raking curved stern; sharp aft with large square, vertical stern; high poop.

peduncle: 1) in some jellyfish, extension of central part of the subumbrella, bearing manubrium at its end. 2) any stalklike structure supporting another structure.

Pegasus: northern constellation, three principal stars of which, with a fourth *(Alpheratz)* in the group *Andromeda*, form the *Square of Pegasus*. A line from *Polaris* through the eastern member of Cassiopeia *(Caph)*, when latter is above the pole, extended southward for 30° passes through *a Andromedae* (Alpheratz) and 14° farther on meets *γPegasi* (Algenib). The two last named form the eastern side of *Square*. Its western side has *Scheat* (β Pegasi) at the N.W. corner and *Markab* (a Pegasi) at S.W. corner. *Algenib*, at the S.E. angle, is closest navigational star to the *vernal equinoctial point*, being about 15° nearly due north of it.

pelagic: 1) free-swimming (nektonic) or floating (planktonic) organisms of sea, not living in the bottom (benthonic), but pertaining to open sea. Term usually refers to wide-ranging aquatic animals. 2) pertaining to open sea, when used in connection with sediment type; it also refers to fish which do not spend their whole life on bottom, although they may remain fairly near shore, such as herring or sardines.

pelagic-abyssal sediments: deep-sea sediments that are free of terrestrial material except for small proportion of very fine clay.

pelagic deposit: material formed in deep ocean and deposited there; e.g., ooze.

pelagic division: primary division of the sea which includes whole mass of water. Division is made up of neritic province which includes water shallower than 100 fathoms (220 meters) and oceanic province which includes water deeper than 100 fathoms.

pelagic environment: open waters of sea far from land. Epipelagic is upper oceanic waters between 40 and 100 fathoms deep; beneath this layer is bathypelagic region containing strange deep-sea fishes and numerous species of highly modified invertebrates with lower limit from 1,000 to 2,000 fathoms. Everything below this in great ocean deeps is known as abyssopelagic.

pelagic limestone: rock formed principally of calcareous tests of pelagic foraminiferans. It usually is deposited in deep water.

Pelecypoda: class of bivalved mollusks inhabiting both marine and freshwater ranging in size from a few millimeters to 2 meters in length, largest being *Tridacna*, giant clam of South Seas. They are generally free-moving creatures which plow through soft bottom sediments. Pelecypods are grouped into 3 categories: burrowing, such as *Teredo*, the shipworm and rock-burrowing oyster *Pholadidea;* mobile types which include clams; sedentary types which include oysters attached throughout their lives to some hard object. Altogether, pelecypods include clams, oysters, pectenoids and mussels from Cambrian to Recent.

pelican [*Pelecaniformes*]: pelicans are very large waterbirds with heavy bodies, broad rounded wings and fairly long necks. Bills are extremely large with great distensible pouch suspended from lower mandible; legs are short and feet large with all 4 toes connected by a web. Tails are rather short and rounded and usually composed of 22 feathers, but some species have 20 or 24.

pelican hook [ships]: 1) ready releasing hook with metal securing ring now chiefly used to break life rail for boarding or leaving ship. 2) fastening used where security and great speed of removal are required.

pelite: clastic sediments composed of clay, minute particles of quartz, rock flour or volcanic ash (pelitic tuff). It may be calcareous.

Pelmatozoa [*Echinodermata*]: sessile, generally attached by stalk composed of slightly movable superimposed disks.

pelorus: navigational instrument similar to compass but without a needle, used for taking bearings relative to ship's heading. Taking a bearing with pelorus is a 2-man job since 0° in the pelor-

us is always in line with vessel's bow. A man takes pelorus bearing on distant object called "mark" and helmsman notes ship's compass heading at that instant. From these two figures, true bearing of object is calculated.

Penchalang: craft used for transportation purposes at Johore, average size 30 to 35 ft. long, 7- to 7½-ft. beam; mast 15 to 18 ft. high above gunwale is stepped in forward thrust and carries lugsail with yard on the foot; sharp, hollow bow and stern; raking, curved stern and sternpost; 4 or 5 thwarts; no sheer; steered with a paddle.

pendant [ships]: length of rope, usually having thimble or block spliced into lower end for hooking on tackle.

peneplane: in large region of old rivers, low rolling surface produced by erosion is so nearly flat that it is called a peneplane. Pene means almost plane, flat surface. Broad, regional, gently sloping, eroded surface approaching elevation of sea level.

penguins [*Sphenisciformes*]: this family is composed of flightless seabirds inhabiting southern hemisphere. They differ from all other birds in having no specially developed quill feathers on wings. Flippers, as wings of penguins are usually termed, are covered with small scalelike feathers and used only for swimming. Penguins are stout-bodied, short-necked birds of moderate or large size with short, flat webbed feet, set very far back, so that when on land they stand upright. Bills are stout and covered with several separate horny plates, somewhat as in albatrosses, instead of single sheath on each mandible as in most birds. Tails are usually very short, composed of from 12 to 20 feathers, according to species.

peninsula: body of land nearly surrounded by water and connected with large body by neck or isthmus; also any piece of land jutting out into water.

Penjajap: Malay trading vessel, rigged with 2 dies which are combination of square sail and dipping lug, common on native Malay craft. Hull is low, sharp, long, of small beam, generous sheer with raised overhanging poop.

pennant: special flag, variously shaped, but usually having a greater length or "fly" than its breadth or "hoist." A blue triangular flag flown by a U.S. naval vessel to denote ship carries the senior officer of force or squadron present. Any small flag of peculiar color, design, or shape exhibited by a government vessel to denote a department to which she is attached. Older form *pennon* designated a triangular streamer or swallow-tailed tapering flag.

pennate: diatom with valves bilaterally or asymmetrically arranged on longitudinal axis. Members of order *Pennales*.

Pennsylvanian: epoch in Carboniferous period of Paleozoic era characterized by deltaic depositions and dominance of lower vascular plants.

penteconter: early galley, having 25 oars to side.

Penzance lugger: lug-rigged fishing boats out of and registered in Penzance, England.

Peracarida, order [zooplankton]: *Malacostraca* which incubate eggs in ventral brood pouch formed by plates (oostegites) borne on endopodites of thoracic limbs. Carapace if present, is not fused to last 4 thoracic segments.

peracilis [*Gymnosomata*]: calcareous shell is coiled into a spiral and columella is produced anteriorly into twisted process, the rostrum. Fins are thick and proboscis short in all species.

perch: 1) pole or staff on which is mounted a distinguishing mark, such as a ball, cylindrical cage, cross, or board bearing a letter or number, and so constituting a beacon indicating a shoal, edge of a channel, rock, or reef; also, a similar mark surmounting a buoy; especially, in U.S. buoyage system, in which it indicates a turning-point in a channel. 2) sea perch, any of several spiny-finned fishes resembling the familiar perch of U.S. lakes and rivers; as, *American sea bass; European bass; black perch; white perch; rosefish;* and *morwong.*

perch family [*Percidae*]: perch family includes perch, walleye, sauger and numerous species of darters. Body is more or less elongated or elliptical; lateral line is complete; mouth may be terminal or inferior; palatines, sharp pharyngeal teeth are present; opercle ends in flat spine. Seven branchiostegals are present; gill membranes are free from isthmus; slit occurs behind 4th gill-arch; gill rakers are slender and toothed. Dorsal fin is completely divided, anterior usually containing about 13 spines.

perch, Iowa darter: colorful fish, common in Great Lakes region. Dorsal fin is orange and black, underside is yellowish and conspicuous brown streak extends along side.

perch, mud [*Acantharchus pomotis*]: small, heavy-set panfish with stripes along sides. Anal fin shorter than dorsal; 4 or 6 spines in anal fin; tail rounded. Body oblong, not strongly compressed; head and jaw moderately stout; mouth oblique; caudal fin rounded. Color tan or olive-brown with 5 to 8 dark longitudinal stripes along side of body and about 4 dark longitudinal stripes along side of head. Length up to 5 in.

perch, mud darter: common along Atlantic and Gulf Coasts, it is species of slow-flowing and muddy streams. It lacks an air bladder and as a result spends life resting on bottom among water weeds. This species and its relatives have the habit of suddenly darting out after prey.

perch, pirate [*Aphredoderus sayanus*]: hump-backed little fish with anus under throat. Vent

jugular in position. Body oblong; back arched at origin of dorsal fin; body compressed posteriorly. Mouth large, terminal; lower jaw slightly projecting. Sides of head scaly. Color dark olive with occasionally a lavender tinge; narrow dark ventral bar at base of tail.

perch, pumpkinseed: also known as redbelly and pond perch, inhabits weedy ponds and streams throughout eastern U.S. and western states. Brightly colored fish with mottled yellow and brown sides, it has bright blue stripe across cheek. It is usually 7 to 10 in. long and rarely weighs as much as 1 lb. Its food consists of bottom-dwelling crustaceans, insects and snails.

perch, redbreast [yellowbelly]: thrives in lakes with dense bottom vegetation; although found from Maine to Florida, it prefers warmer lakes south of New York. Has red belly, is slightly longer than pumpkinseed and elongated earflap is entirely black.

perch, Sacramento: native to Sacramento River region of California; only member of the family native to Pacific Coast. Sacramento perch varies in color from silvery white to black; average size ranges from 8 to 12 in. Unlike its relatives, this species exhibits no nest-building activity and no care of young.

perch, sauger [sand pike]: long and slender fish, with olive-green coloring and yellowish sides. Markings are irregular dark blotches rather than vertical bars; dorsal fin is also spotted. The sauger is ordinarily under 12 in. in length and rarely weighs as much as 2 lbs.

perch, silver [sand perch]: greenish or bluish-gray fish with silvery sides, is found from New York to Texas. Chin lacks barbels; front of gill cover is edged with spines. Although silver perch grows to length of 12 in., young fish about 6 in. long make up average catch along mid-Atlantic Coast. Members of drum family are sometimes confused with white perch but differ in having 2 anal fins instead of 3 and in lateral line extending into tail fin.

perch, speckled crappie: greenish, black-speckled, big-mouthed, compressed panfish with long anal fin. Anal fin nearly as long as dorsal; about 7 spines in dorsal fin. Body compressed, oblong; head long, mouth large; fins high; 6 rows of scales in cheeks; anal fin nearly as long as dorsal. Ground color of both sexes overlaid with speckles or spots of black.

perch, striped: this surf perch is colorful with dusky back, olive-green fins and numerous lengthwise stripes of blue and red. Its length is same as that of barred surf perch. Striped perch lurk around piers and docks feeding on shrimp, worms and other small aquatic animals.

perch, walleye: yellow pike perch or walleyed pike

is common Great Lakes fish. This is largest member of perch family, averaging 10 to 20 in. long. Walleye is olive-green and yellowish with indistinct dark markings. Lower jaw is armed with long front teeth, lacking in yellow perch. They live in deep clear lakes and are powerful and swift swimmers capable of catching bass and perch as well as sunfishes and minnows.

perch, yellow: also known as red perch or striped perch, familiar fish of central and eastern U.S.; it has been introduced on Pacific Coast. First dorsal fin bears very strong spines. Viewed from side, head is somewhat concave above eyes; body is humped in front of dorsal fin. Yellow perch is yellowish-green; there are several dark vertical bars on sides; back is dark green; pectoral fins have yellow tinge. As in sunfish family, ventral fins are located almost directly beneath pectorals. Yellow perch is usually 8 to 14 in. long and weighs less than 2 lbs.; 4 lbs. is maximum size. This species prefers quiet streams and ponds.

percolation: process by which water is forced by wave action through interstices of bottom sediment and has tendency to reduce wave heights.

percolation factor: quantity by which wave heights are reduced through percolation alone.

pereion: in *Crustacea*, the thorax.

pereiopods: thoracic appendages in *Crustacea*.

perennial kelp [*Macrocystis integritolie*]: perennial kelp, worldwide seaweed is found on ocean beaches. It is a plant of outer shores exposed to strong wave action and seen on beaches only when it has been torn loose from its holdfast, for it lives far from shore in water 35 to 50 ft. deep. Here it forms great beds several miles in area. Its great length is brought about by asymmetrical splitting of the terminal blade from base to apex. Air bladders suspend kelp at surface of water. Single blade, 1 to 2 ft. long and 3 to 5 in. wide, will extend from each air bladder. Holdfast is either conical mass or forked rhizoid from which extend densely matted branches.

perforate: 1) to provide with holes or pores. 2) in *Foraminifera*, test with many small openings in chamber walls.

Peridinium [phytoplankton]: true peridinians belong here. They are one of commonest of all genera of dinoflagellates and are very important in productivity of sea. All are more or less top-shaped cells which sometimes bear projecting horns, but these are never as long as in species of *Ceratium*.

periga: small lateen-rigged vessel of Mediterranean.

perigean range [Pn]: average of all monthly tide ranges occurring at time of perigee. It is larger than mean range, where type of tide is either semidiurnal or mixed, and is of no practical significance where type of tide is diurnal.

perigean tidal currents: tidal currents of increased speed occurring at time of perigean tides.

perigean tides: tides of increased range occurring monthly near time of moon's perigee.

perigee: point in orbit of moon (or any other earth satellite) nearest to earth; opposite to apogee.

perihelion: point in earth's orbit nearest to sun.

period [wave]: time needed for one full wavelength to pass given point.

periodic plankton: organisms that regularly appear in plankton only at certain times, as at dusk.

periostracum [*Mollusca*]: outermost layer of mollusc shell, composed of conchiolin in various textures; erroneously called epidermis.

periphery: 1) in *Foraminifera*, outer margin of coiled test. 2) in *Gastropoda*, portion of whorl lateral to axis of coiling. 3) in *Mollusca*, part of any gastropod shell or of any whorl that is farthest from axis.

periproct [sea urchins]: circular membrane bearing embedded endoskeletal plates with small spines and pedicellariae.

perisarc: cuticular outer covering of hydroid.

periscope depth range [PDR]: maximum range at which active sonar echo ranging contact can be made with submarine operating at periscope depth.

peristome: 1) in *Bryozoa*, elevated rim surrounding aperture. 2) in *Mollusca*, margin of aperture in gastropod said to be entire or complete when it is not interrupted by parietal area of body whorl.

peritoneum [fish]: shiny membrane that lines body cavity.

periwinkle: small gastropod mollusk of family *Littorinidae* with thick, spiral, conical shells. Numbering several hundred species, periwinkles usually live in shallow ocean water, often intertidal zone; however, they also exist in brackish and freshwater. Periwinkles often live in thick masses, encrusting rocks. They are widely distributed throughout the world.

periwinkle [*Littorina pintade*]: this periwinkle is globular and bears short, sharp spire. Surface is spirally striate and rather smooth; columella is broadly excavated. It is grayish or bluish-white and minutely dotted with purple red dots. It ranges in length from ¼ to ¾ of an inch. This species occurs in Hawaii and elsewhere in Pacific.

periwinkle [*L. horindae*]: periwinkles are fairly heavy shells with only a few whorls; these whorls may be either spiral, turbinate or globular in shape. Aperture, which may be either oval or circular, is entire along margin and covered by heavy operculum. Outer lip is simple and columella is thickened, flattened and without umbilicus. Members of this group usually live among rocks in shallow water or along shoreline. Family name suggests that they are littoral or shore-dwelling forms. Periwinkles are large family including well over 150 species which are distributed around the world.

periwinkle [*Tectarius pictus*]: this periwinkle is turbinate and bears a well-developed spire with sharp apex. Whorls are convex, sometimes granulated and minutely striated. Shell is often encircled about the middle by rough, spiral ribs. It is brownish and marbled with white; aperture is purple within. It will reach a length of about ¾ in. This species occurs in Hawaiian Islands. *Littorina picta philippi*.

periwinkle, rough [*L. horina scabra* (Linnaeus)]: shell of this periwinkle is globular, moderately thin, spirally ridged and possesses sharp spire. Whorls are convex and slanting and sutures between them are channeled. It is brown and obliquely streaked with interrupted lines; it is often yellowish or rose-colored. It will exceed more than 1 in. in length. This is an Indo-Pacific species ranging from Hawaiian Islands southward to Polynesia, westward across entire tropical Pacific Ocean to coast of China, through the East Indies and across Indian Ocean to coast of Africa. It has been reported from west coast of Africa and from west coast of Mexico.

periwinkle, wavy [*Littorina undulata* (Gray)]: this periwinkle has firm and solid shell which may be either smooth or spirally striated. Color pattern is extremely variable and of little help in identifying species. It is yellowish or whitish in color and most often marked with brown lines, checks, spots or in clouded patterns. Columella is always violet. It will reach a length of 1 inch. Species is distributed from Hawaiian Islands southward, westward through entire tropical Pacific to Philippine Islands, through East Indies and across Indian Ocean.

permanent current: current such as Kuroshio, which flows continuously and whose speed and direction is little changed by tide and meteorological factors. Permanent current also includes continuous outflow of fresh river water discharge.

permeable rock: rock having a texture that permits water to move through it.

Permian: last period in Paleozoic era characterized by large glaciers, salt deposits in Germany, earliest cycads and conifers and primitive reptiles.

per mille: symbol°/oo. Per thousand or 10^{-3}; used in same way as percent (%, per hundred, or 10^{-2}). Per mile (by weight) common term used in oceanography for salinity and chlorinity; e.g., a salinity of 0.03452 (3.452 percent) is commonly stated as 34.52 per mile (parts per thousand).

perpendicular: in connection with ship measurements, a line drawn perpendicular to the base line, or keel, for purpose of providing, at its intersection with a deck line or waterline, a point of reference, as in defining vessel's *registered length* or *length between perpendiculars*.

perpendicular, after [ships]: line perpendicular to keel line, drawn tangent to after contour of stern.

perpendicular, forward [ships]: line perpendicular to keel line, intersecting forward side of stem at designed load waterline.

perpendicular, mid or midships [ships]: line perpendicular to keel line taken midway between forward and after perpendicular.

perradius: in jellyfish, axes of disc in which primary radial canals lie.

Perseus: northern constellation lying southeast of the *Cassiopeia* group and northeast of *Andromeda*. It contains two navigational stars: *Mirfak* or *Marfak* (α Persei) of magnitude 1.9; and *Algol* (β Persei), remarkable for its periodic changes in brilliance from magnitude 2.2 to 3.5. A line from *Algol* westward to the bright *Capella* forms the base of an isosceles triangle having its apex at reddish *Aldebaran* 30° to SE. *Mirfak* lies 9½° N by E ½ E from *Algol*.

person: in colonial coelenterates, urochordates, etc., one of individuals of colony.

personal equation: also termed *personal error*, a consistent error in taking observations, as with a sextant, which is characteristic of an individual observer. Such error is determined and allowed for in astronomical work, such as observing transits of stars, and among navigators takes the form of measuring angles as greater or smaller than their true values, usually by a very small amount. Elimination of effect of such error in sextant observations, especially when an artificial horizon is used and a high degree of accuracy is desired, is effected by taking the mean of altitudes of stars lying nearly opposite each other in azimuth.

Peru Current: cold ocean current flowing north along coasts of Chile and Peru. Peru Current originates from West Wind Drift in subantarctic Pacific Ocean. Northern limit of current can be placed a little south of the equator, where flow turns toward the west, joining South Equatorial Current.

Peter boat: small, sturdy, beamy, open fishing boat. Double-ended, rounded stem and stern alike, very shallow keel, clinker-built, with outboard rudder. Single spritsail and jib carried. This type was used in lower Thames in England for centuries and was descended from Vikings.

Petersen grab: type of bottom sampler consisting of two hinged semicylindrical buckets held apart by locking device. On striking bottom locking device is released so that, on hauling, buckets revolve and come together, enclosing a sample of the bottom.

petrel [*Procellariiformes*]: seabirds which constitute this large family exhibit great diversity in size and coloring, though comparatively uniform in habits. Apart from various skeletal characters almost only distinguishing feature is the bill, which is hooked at tip, somewhat compressed at base with 2 nostrils opening together at end of double tube on upper mandible. In coloring, petrels are black, brown, gray or white or some combination of these colors and, even then, bills and feet are usually not very brightly colored, though sometimes bluish or pink.

petrel, ashy storm [*Oceanodroma homochroa*]: sooty black, edges of wing coverts paler, underwing coverts edged with white; tail forked; length 7.5 in.

petrel, black [*Procellaria parkinsoni*]: sooty black; shafts of primaries white beneath; bill yellowish horn-color with black tip; feet black; length 18 in.

petrel, black storm [*Loomelania melania*]: sooty black; underparts somewhat paler; upper wing coverts pale grayish, sooty brown; tail strongly forked; length 9 in.

petrel, Bulwer's [*Bulweria bulwerii*]: sooty black, rather pale on chin and edges of greater wing coverts; tail long, wedge-shaped; bill black, flesh-colored, outer toe and webs black; length 10.5 in.

petrel, giant [*Macronectes giganteus*]: dark grey with light or white head usually more or less spotted with dark brown; bill large, pale straw-color or grayish-green; feet silvery brown or sooty black; length 33 to 36 in.

petrel, great-winged [*Pterodroma macroptera*]: dark brown; patch around bill; throat, gray; wing quills and tail, black; bill and feet, black; length 15 to 16.3 in.

petrel, Jamaica [*Pterodroma caribbaea*]: sooty brown, dark on back, pale on undersurface, gray on forehead and throat; upper tail coverts whitish; tail sooty black, outer feather whitish at base (dark phase), light phase, which is grayer, also occurs; feet black; length 14 in.

petrel, Kerguelen [*Pterodroma brexirostris*]: slaty-gray, pale on face and throat, dark on wings and tail; bill and feet black; length 13 in.

petrel, least storm [*Halocyptena microsoma*]: dark sooty black, undersurface brown, greater wing coverts paler; tail wedge-shaped; length 5.5 to 6 in.; smallest of petrels.

petrel, Murphy's [*Pterodroma ultima*]: above and below blackish brown, brownest on crown and nape, paler and slightly slate-colored on back, scapulars and coverts; dark patch before and under eye; narrow white infraorbital line; feathers of forehead with grayish or whitish margins; throat mottled with white; inner webs of primaries and secondaries gray; bill black; feet fleshy or bluish-white margined with black.

petrel, reunion [*Pterodroma aterrima*]: dark grayish-brown; bill very stout, black; feet dark reddish-flesh color, outer toe and webs black; length 14 in.

petrel, Samoan storm [*Nesofregetta moestissima*]: sooty black; wings and tail rather blacker; tail deeply forked; length 9.5 in.

petrel, Solander's [*Pterodroma solandri*]: upper parts slate gray, inclining to dark brown on head, wings and tail; forehead and throat whitish; black patch before eye; underparts brownish-gray; base of primaries beneath and some of underwing coverts white forming white patch in center of undersurface of wings; bill black; feet, flesh color, black outer toes; length 16 in.

petrel, sooty storm [*Oceanodroma markhami*]: sooty brown; face, wing coverts, lower rump and undersurface of wings somewhat paler; wing quills sooty black; tail deeply forked; length 9 to 10 in.

petrel, storm: storm petrels are smallest of seabirds. Characterized by rather slender hooked beaks on upper surface of which nostrils open with single median tube. Slender legs are frequently very long in proportion to size of bird; toes are united by webs. Wings are fairly long but so narrow in proportion to those of larger petrels and albatrosses; tails are usually either square or forked. Most of them are dusky colored, a few gray; many have patch of white at base of tail and some have white areas on undersurface. All species have black bill and legs, but in a few webs are partly yellow.

petrel, Swinhoe's storm [*Oceanodroma monorhis*]: upper parts sooty brown, forehead and upper wing coverts paler, upper tail coverts in American race, gray, lateral ones frequently white; underparts, including undersurface of wings, sooty gray; tail forked; length 6.8 to 7.6 in. Asiatic form appears always to have upper tail coverts dark, but in American form they are light and lateral ones are often white.

petrel, white-chinned [*Procellaria aequinoctialis*]: sooty black, tendency to chocolate-brown on mantle and underparts; chin white, white sometimes extending to sides of face and crown, sometimes entirely absent; bill greenish-white, marked with black; feet black; length 21.5 in.

Petricola pholadiformis [*Heterodonta, Eulamellibranchia*]: larva has a thicker shell than those of other venerids and possesses strong provincular projection. Valves are more strongly colored than in other venerids. Length is usually about 170μ.

petrography: division of geology concerning mineral makeup of rocks.

pevalar axis: in diatoms, axis through center of valves or through length of diatom cell.

pH: measure of acidity and alkalinity (hydrogen ion concentration) based on 0 to 14 scale. Seven is pH of pure water and represents neutrality. Below 7, acidity increases as hydrogen ions increase; above 7, alkalinity increases as ions decrease.

Phact: star of magnitude 2.75 of the small southern group *Columba*. Catalogued as a *Columbae*, it is located in right ascension 5 hrs. 38 min. and declination 34°06′ S., or 32° nearly due south of *Alnilam*, middle star of the three in *Orion's Belt*.

Phaeocystis: genus of brown, unicellular and colonial marine plankton (phytoplankton) of class *Chrysophyceae*. Colonies surrounded by large gelatinous sheaths. This alga appears in vast concentration at times, especially in neritic parts of North Atlantic, coloring water brown and imparting offensive odor to it.

phaeoplankton: plankton of upper 30 meters.

phalarope [*Charadriiformes*]: small seabird that looks like the sandpiper. It generally lives along shore but is sometimes found in huge flocks out at sea. Toes have broad fringing webs, somewhat like those of coots and grebes, usually lobed or scalloped. Legs (tarsi) are also very much compressed so that they offer little resistance to water when bird is swimming. Underplumage is thick like that of gulls, and they have heavy underdown like ducks.

pharology: art or science which treats of directing the course of vessels and warning them of presence of dangers to navigation by means of light signals, as from lighthouses, lightships, beacons, and buoys.

pharyngeal teeth: specialized dentition on various gill arch elements in fishes; in some species these teeth are used in sound production.

pharynx: portion of digestive tract between mouth and esophagus; passage leading to stomach. In water-breathing vertebrates, pharynx contains gill slits; in adult, air-breathing vertebrates, it gives rise to the passage leading to lungs.

phase: state of aggregation of a substance, e.g., solid (ice), liquid (water), or gas (vapor).

phase inequality: variations in tide or tidal currents associated with changes in phase of the moon. At new or full moon (springs) tide-producing forces of sun and moon act in conjunction, resulting in greater than average tide and tidal currents. At first and last quarters of moon (neaps) tide-producing forces oppose each other resulting in smaller than average tide and tidal currents.

phase reduction: procession of high- and low-water observations to obtain quantities such as spring and neap tide ranges and tidal currents, which are associated with changing phases of moon.

phases of the moon: apparent shape of moon or planet at given time; phases of moon are: new moon, first quarter, full moon, last quarter.

phase velocity: 1) velocity of electromagnetic propagation of any one phase state, such as point of zero instantaneous field, in steady train of sinusoidal waves. 2) velocity measured over short time interval, at which particular (water) wave crest is propagated through water or rock media.

Phecda: star γ *Ursae Majoris*, or that marking the lower inner corner of the "bowl" in the *Big Dipper*, or *Plough*—the group *Ursa Major*. It has a sidereal hour angle of 182° and declination of nearly 54°N., and magnitude 2.54.

phenology: study of organisms in relation to climate; study of quality and quantity of seasonal changes in plankton.

Phialella quadrata [*Coelenterata*]: medusa of the hydroid of same name, formerly known as *Campanulina repens*. Bell is nearly hemispherical and has, around margins, up to 32 tentacles. There are no ocelli but there are 8 marginal vesicles in adradial position. Bell may reach diameter of 13 mm.

Phialidium hemisphericum [phylum *Coelenterata*]: medusa of *Clytia johnstoni* is very common. It may attain 32 or so marginal tentacles. Up to 3 marginal vesicles are to be found between each pair of tentacles.

Philocheras fasciatus [*Crangonidae*]: larvae closely resemble those of 2 proceeding species but differ in having 2 spines on posterior margin of 3rd and 4th abdominal segments. Peduncles of antennules are proportionately longer and may be twice the length of rostrum. Animal has distinctive dark coloration and is much smaller than corresponding larvae of *Crangon vulgaris* and *C. albmani*, final stage larvae being only 3.5 mm. long.

Phi scale: scale used in expressing relative sizes of particles.

Phleger corer: gravity sampling tube used to obtain 1½ in. diameter samples up to 4 ft. long. Sample consists of tailfin assembly with attached weight, core barrel with plastic liner inside it, core cutter and core catcher. When fully rigged, corer weighs about 100 lbs.

Phoenix: small constellation in about 45° S. declination, between *Grus* and *Eridanus*. It contains one navigational star, *a Phoenicis*. Located in right ascension 0 hrs. 24 min. and declination 42° 35′ S., and of magnitude 2.44. The star is "in range" with east side of the *Square of Pegasus* at 57½° to the southward.

Pholadidae [clams]: fastens suckerlike foot to some firm surface and then moves shell up and down. Forward portion is covered with ridges that scrape away surrounding clay or stone. Some members of family keep on boring and growing throughout their lives. Others reach full size, cover sucker foot with shell and spend rest of their lives feeding and reproducing.

Phoronidia [phylum]: small, gregarious, wormlike animals with U-shaped gut, inhabiting tubes attached to stones. Mouth is surrounded by horseshoe-shaped lophophore bearing ciliated feeding tentacles. There is a blood vascular system with red blood corpuscles, a true coelom and a pair of metanephridia. Most are hermaphrodile and fertilized egg develops into planktotrophic larva called actinotrocha. After cataclysmic metamorphosis this settles on bottom to form adult. Phoronids are widely distributed.

phosphate phosphorus: ionic form of phosphorus occurring in nature; essential nutrient for marine organisms. Estimates of primary productivity have been made by determining phosphate concentrations in water column during different seasons.

phosphorescence: property of emitting light without sensible heat, luminescence. Bioluminescence is preferred sea term.

phosphorescent wheel: phenomenon which when fully developed gives appearance of wheel of light revolving around a point source of just beneath sea surface. Vast majority of wheels have been observed in oceans bordering southern Asia and in Indonesian Archipelago.

photocondria: granules occurring in cytoplasm of luminous cell or animalcule.

photogenic: capable of generating light, as photogenic tissue in luminescent organs.

photometer: instrument for measuring flux per unit area from sunlight plus skylight (reflected and diffused from sky) above water surface, below surface and at all desired depths to instrument's limit.

photon: quantum of electromagnetic energy having no charge or mass but possessing momentum. Light energy and X rays are carried by photons.

photophore: luminous organ, resembling an eye; within, light is produced either by chemical reaction controlled by organisms or by luminous bacteria living within cells. Photophores occur most commonly in marine organisms inhabiting mid-depths.

photoreceptor: light-sensitive sense organ.

photosynthesis: production of plant tissue in green plants. Process essentially requires carbon dioxide, water, sunlight and chlorophyll. It is a basic support system for life on earth by returning oxygen to atmosphere and removing carbon dioxide. Animals use oxygen and give out carbon dioxide as waste product.

phototactic: referring to phototaxis, reflex movements of animal, especially one of simpler animals, in response to source of light.

photothermograph: Soviet terminology for instrument that provides time history of temperature at selected depth by photographic, mercurial thermometer at time intervals chosen by research group.

phototropism: positive phototaxis; attraction toward light.

phragmocone: in extinct cephalopods of group *Belemnoidea*, chambered portion of shell.

phycologist: botanist who studies algae, term describing great variety of spore-producing plants.

Phylactolaemata: differs from other bryozoans in having horseshoe- or U-shaped lophophore, lip that overhangs mouth and body cavities that run together instead of remaining separate. Some zoaria are chains or mats of leathery tubes; others are wormlike gelatinous masses that reach lengths of 8 to 10 in. and are provided with flattened soles on which colonies crawl.

phyllopods: some branchiopods with flat, leaflike appendages.

phyllosoma larva: modified, free-swimming schizopod stage of spring lobsters; it is planktonic, paper thin and transparent.

phylogenetic: referring to evolutionary history and relationships of organisms or groups of organisms.

phylum: basic scientific groupings of plants and animals. System in descending order is kingdom (animal or plant), phylum, class, order, family, genus, and species.

physical properties: physical properties or characteristics of seawater; e.g., temperature, salinity, density, sound, velocity, electrical conductivity and transparency.

Physophorida [phylum *Coelenterata*]: colony has apical float, but apart from this feature colonies are so variable as to warrant considerable taxonomic subdivision. By some, chondrophorids, like *Velella* are put into separate suborders. *Physalia*, well-known Portuguese man-of-war.

phytoplankton: plant form of plankton, such as diatoms. They are vital as food source for other organisms and are basic food supply in ocean. They are basic synthesizers of organic matter (by photosynthesis) in pelagic division.

phytoplankton bottle: container for taking up sample of water at desired depth in order to obtain quantitative sample of phytoplankton by filtration in laboratory.

picaroon: corsair's or pirate's craft. A term used usually in Caribbean.

pickerel, chain [*Esox niger*]: jack fish. Elongate fish with mouth like a duck's beak. Pectoral fins low on body; about 125 rows of scales along side of body; branchiostegal rays 14 to 16; jaws with sharp needlelike teeth. Color, greenish-golden with streaks and lines along sides, giving reticulated appearance. Fins plain, not pinkish.

pickerel, Eastern: also known as chain pickerel. It is 15 to 24 in. long and reaches weight of 9 lbs. It is a golden-green fish marked by network of dark lines. Eastern pickerel inhabits clear, grassy ponds and lakes from northern New England to Florida. This species is greedy eater of frogs and small fishes.

pickerel, redfin [*Esox americanus*]: pike. Elongate fish with mouth like that of a duck's beak. Pectoral fins on body; less than 110 rows of scales along side of body; branchiostegal rays 11 to 13; jaws with sharp teeth. Ground color greenish, sometimes with series of faint curved bars along sides, blackish bar below eye; fins usually reddish or pinkish. Size about 12 in.

picket boat: outpost scouting or guard boat.

Piedmont: plateau between Atlantic coast and Appalachian mountains.

Piedmont glacier: glacier formed by coalescence of valley glaciers and spreading over plains at foot of mountains from which valley glaciers came.

pigfish: bluish-purple grunt with silvery sides and golden stripes along back. Dorsal fin is spotted with bronze; paired fins and base of tail are yellow. Sides are marked above lateral line by lengthwise stripes. Pigfish is found not only in warm reef waters but also at times as far as New York.

pike: this is group of Arctic fishes common to northern Europe and North America. Pikes and relatives, pickerels and muskellunge, have long slender bodies terminating in sharply pointed head; large mouth is well armed with teeth in jaws, in roof of mouth and on tongue. Short dorsal fin is set far back on body above ventral fins; body is covered with cycloid scales that have deeply scalloped margins. They are all voracious carnivores. They devour not only other fishes but also muskrats, mice, frogs and even ducklings. Using submerged vegetation and stumps as lurking places, they dart out suddenly to capture prey.

pike, northern: great northern pickerel is olivegreen fish with horizontal markings of lighter color and yellowish or white belly. Head when viewed from above bears remarkable resemblance to duck's bill. Northern pike lives in sluggish streams and weedy lakes from New England across continent to Alaska. Average individual ranges in length from 20 to 40 in. and maximum weight is 40 lbs.

pile [pilings]: spars driven into bottom with tops projecting above waterline.

pilidium larva: helmet-shaped planktonic larva of some nemertans.

pillars [ships]: vertical columns supporting decks. Also called stanchions.

pilot [ships]: one who conducts ship out of or into harbor.

pilotage: 1) act or business of piloting; pilotship. 2) fee or compensation for a pilot's services.

pilot boat: American pilot boats were fast schooner-rigged vessels. Of prime consideration in pilot boat design were speed, sail-carrying capacity, seaworthiness and ability to roll easily in seaway.

Pilot Chart: chart of major ocean areas published for benefit of mariners by U.S. Naval Oceanographic Office in cooperation with U.S. Weather Bureau. These charts contain information required for safe navigation including ocean currents, ice at sea, wind roses, storm tracks, isotherms, magnetic variations, great circle routes, limits of trade winds, etc.

pilot cutter: cutter-rigged vessel used in pilot service in Bristol Channel before steam was employed about 1912. Fast and able ship, easy in seaway, with cutter bow, short counter and long keel with deep drag. Mast was set well back from bow and supported by three shrouds without bobstay.

pilotfish: similar to rudderfish in following boats, but is found in deeper offshore waters than rudderfish. Pilotfish is bluish with indistinct vertical bars; it lacks spiny dorsal fin. It grows to length of 24 in.; inhabits waters off southeastern coast.

piloting: chiefly in U.S. usage, that branch of navigation, or practice of such, by which a vessel's position is determined by soundings, shore fog signals, or bearings of visible landmarks. Act of conducting a vessel through a channel, strait, etc., as by direction of a *pilot*.

Pilumnus hirtellus [*Xanthidae*]: this species is often abundant and larvae may occur in vast numbers in inshore plankton. Zoeae are smaller than those of other crabs and have short dorsal and rostral spines. There are 3 lateral spines on telson; megalopa has no spines on carapace and rostrum points downward. Protozoea is about 1 mm. long and metamorphoses in about 3 hours into first zoea which is brownish in color with lateral spines on second and fifth abdominal segments. Second zoeal stage is about 1.8 mm. long and at this time pleopods appear, while lateral spines appear in first abdominal segments.

pinching [ships]: sailing too close to the wind so that sailboat's progress is slowed below maximum efficiency.

pinfish [*Lagodon rhomboides*]: strongly compressed fish with protuberant teeth, spot on shoulder and 3 or 4 vertical dark stripes on sides. Scales along lateral line 65 to 70; teeth incisorlike; body elongate, elliptical, laterally compressed and markedly arched above; mouth small, terminal. Color olivaceous to yellowish with distinct round dark spot on each shoulder and about 4 vertical dark bands on each side. Length about 6 in.

pinfish, spottail [*Diplodus holbrooki*]: strongly compressed fish with protuberant teeth and black saddle across base of tail. Scales along lateral line 55 to 57; body elliptical, laterally compressed and markedly arched above; mouth small, terminal. Dorsal fin long and low; caudal fin forked. Color darkish above, fading to silvery below.

ping: acoustic pulse signal projected by underwater transducer.

pinger: battery-powered acoustic device equipped with transducer that transmits sound waves. When pinger is attached to wire and lowered into water, direct and bottom reflected sound can be monitored with listening device. Difference between arrival time of direct and reflected waves is used to compute distance of pinger from ocean bottom.

pingo: hill or mountain completely covered by ice sheet, but revealing its presence by surface indications.

pink [ships]: term applied to different kinds of hulls and rigs. The "pink" is characterized by upper part of stern, which is narrowed and projects the hull proper, planking underneath curving sharply to sternpost. This is called "pink stern."

Pinky: pink-sterned schooner-rigged vessel used extensively in cod and mackerel fisheries in New England from 1820 until middle of century, although until recently a few could be found here and there on Maine Coast.

pinnacle: sharp pyramidal or cone-shaped rock partly or completely covered by water. Also small coral spire which lies near water surface in lagoon.

pinnacled iceberg: iceberg formed and weathered in such manner as to produce spires or pinnacles.

pinniped: marine mammal of order *Pinnipedia*, which comprises seals, sea lions and walruses.

pinnulate: any of lateral branches of arm of a crinoid.

pintle [ships]: metal pin secured to rudder which is hooked downward into gudgeons on sternpost, and affords axis of oscillation as rudder is moved from side to side for steering.

pip: echo trace on electronic indicator screen.

pipefish: includes sea horse as well as pipefish. In this family body is armored with small plates instead of being clotted in scales; bony snout terminates in small sucking mouth; gill opening is reduced to small pore. In pipefishes, lengthwise axis of body continues through head; in sea horse, heart is at right angle to rest of body. Pipefish have normal tail terminated by tail fin,

but in sea horses there is no tail fin and tail is used to grasp objects.

pipefish, bay: grows to length of 12 in. It changes so rapidly from green to brown that this species is another "chameleon of the sea."

pipefish, dusky: slightly smaller species with brown-speckled side and silvery belly; found from Virginia southward along Atlantic Coast.

pipefish, northern: slender fish that grows to length of 12 in. It is green, brown or red depending upon surroundings. This pipefish lives among seaweeds and on sandy bottoms in brackish or saltwater where it feeds on small crustaceans.

pipefish, Scovell's [*Syngnathus scovelli*]: odd little creature that looks more like slender piece of dead weed stem than fish. Body very elongated and encased in body armor; snout long and tubular. Bony rings on truck 21 or less; on caudal part of body 20 to 34. Brownish or brownish-green in color; several inches in length.

piracy: diversion of upper part of stream by headward growth of another stream.

piragua: piragua is usually used by Carib Indians of British Guiana. It is made by hollowing out section of tree trunk until sides are thin. Each open end is filled in with V-shaped piece. These piraguas are crude affairs, but they are made to comparatively large sizes.

pirate perch family [*Aphredoderidae*]: body of pirate perch is considerably compressed, back somewhat elevated and head flattened above. Mouth is of medium size and rather oblique with lower jaw projecting beyond upper. Jaws, vomer, palatines and pterygoids bear teeth; upper jaw is not protractile; maxillary bones are well developed. Edges of the preopercle and preorbital are toothed or serrated; spine on opercle; no pseudobranchia; 6 branchiostegal rays; no lateral spine. In adults vent is located just back of lower jaw. Air bladder is simple; pyloric caeca number 12.

pirate perch, Western [*Aphredoderus sayanus gibbosos*]: very dark, purplish fish. Caudal fin has 2 black bars at base with lighter bar between. This species becomes somewhat iridescent and yellow-bellied in spawning season. Body is oblong, rather heavy anteriorly and compressed posteriorly; back is somewhat elevated in region of dorsal fin. Dorsal fin is rather high and has 2 spines and 6 soft rays; ventral fins have 1 spine and 7 soft rays. Scales are ctenoid, varying from 45 to 60 in direct line from opercle to base of caudal fin. This fish reaches length of about 5 in.

pirogue: old West Indian name for dugout canoe.

Pisces: constellation southward and eastward of the *Square of Pegasus*, containing no navigational stars. The so-called *First Point of Aries*, or *vernal equinoctial point*, is located in this group.

Piscis Australis: southern constellation, also sometimes called *Piscis Austrinus*, containing the navigational star *Fomalhaut (a Piscis Australis* or *a Piscis Austrini)* of magnitude 1.29.

pisolites: rounded, granule-sized concretions larger than oolites found in land and marine deposits. They form pisolitic limestone when cemented together.

piston corer: 1) device for underwater drilling. Piston inside core tube provides "suction" that helps overcome friction between sample and inside wall of core tube. 2) pipes or tubes used to sample ocean bottom sediments up to 60 ft. long. Tube is driven into sediments due to free-fall type inertia and by suitable weight. Piston is used to remove residual water from inside of coring tube as sample is procured in situ.

pistonphone: apparatus in which rigid piston is vibrated, so that, by measurement of its motion, acoustic velocities and pressures can be calculated.

pitch [ships]: 1) motion of ship plunging with alternate fall and rise of bow and stern, when passing over waves. Motion is most marked when running into head sea. 2) measure of angle of propeller blade; distance propeller will travel forward in one revolution if there were no slip.

pitching [ships]: alternate rising and falling motion of vessel's bow in nearly vertical plane as crests and troughs of waves are met.

pitchpole: boat is said to pitchpole, or to take a pitchpole tumble, in capsizing end over end, as in running before a heavy breaking sea or a surf.

Pitometer log: log consisting essentially of Pitat tube projecting into water with suitable registering devices.

pitted plain: glacial outwash plain with numerous small kettle holes.

pituitary: vital gland located at base of brain which secretes different hormones through body via bloodstream.

placer: deposit containing valuable minerals (especially gold) found in streambeds and ocean or left by glaciers.

Placodermi [class]: phylum *Chordata,* Silurian to Mississippian. Notochord large; gill chambers generally reduced; elongate, fishlike; bony or cartilaginous jaws of paired appendages. Freshwater, marine and nektonic; predators and herbivores. Plate-skinned fishes including three principal orders that are easily distinguished; acanthodians, arthodires (armored fishes) and antisarchs. Acanthodians have rhomboid scales and sharp, paired fin spines. General shape is sharklike, but internal structures differ from anything possessed by sharks or their close relatives. They appeared at about beginning of Devonian and became extinct at end of Paleozoic.

plagioclase: rock-forming minerals found in igneous rock.

plain: flat, gentle sloping or nearly level region of sea floor.

planform: outline or shape of body of water as determined by still-water level.

planisphere: representation on a plane of the circles of a sphere; especially, a polar projection of the heavens for use in locating positions of stars and planets, with adjustable appendages for indicating part of celestial sphere visible in any given latitude, time of meridian passage, rising, and setting of stars, etc.

planispiral: 1) having shell coiled in one place. 2) in *Foraminifera,* coiled test with whorls of cell in single plane. 3) in *Gastropoda,* shell type formed by spiral coiled in single plane and symmetrical in that plane. Very rare in *Gastropoda* though many genera approach planispiral.

planking [ships]: boards used on sides and decks of wooden ship.

plankter: 1) planktonic organism. 2) single organism in plankton.

planktobiont: organism living solely in plankton. Holoplanktonic organism.

plankton: 1) drifting or slowly swimming animal and plant life found in water. Usually comprising small organisms, term also includes such creatures as large jellyfish. 2) animals and plants floating in waters of aquatic environment, as distinct from animals which are attached to, or crawl upon the bottom; especially very small plants and animals which travel with water movement.

plankton bloom: 1) rapid growth and multiplication of plankton (usually plant forms), producing obvious change in physical appearance of sea surface, such as coloration or slicks; also called sea bloom. 2) enormous concentration of plankton in an area, caused either by explosive or gradual multiplication of organisms (sometimes of single species) and usually producing obvious change in physical appearance of seawater, such as discoloration. Blooms consisting of millions of cells per liter often have been reported.

plankton centrifuge: device for separating plankton from water samples by centrifugal force.

plankton equivalent: relationship between various chemical constituents or characteristics of plankton whereby measurement of one characteristic can be used to derive quantity of other characteristics.

plankton pulse: periodic variation in congregation and abundance of plankton in any particular area, caused by various ecological factors. Also called plankton bloom and sea bloom.

plankton spectrum: qualitative and quantitative

composition of plankton population at given time and place.

planktophile: living mainly as plankton, although able to live otherwise.

planktoxene: only occasionally in plankton.

planoblast: free swimming medusa.

planoeboid [*Mollusca*]: planispiral coiling in single plane.

planulae: free-swimming, ciliated (having hairlike appendage) larvae of coelenterates. They take one of two basic forms, either medusa (such as jellyfish) or polyp (such as sea anemone or coral, colonial animal composed of many polyps).

plasmolysis: removal of water from cell by osmotic methods, with resultant shrinking.

plastic flow: denotes phenomena whereby bottom sediments under pressure of an object's weight flows out from under the object, allowing partial or complete burial.

plastic zone: lower and slower part of glacier beneath rigid zone.

plastids: small, specialized structures outside of nucleus in cells or organisms. One type, chloroplasts, contain chlorophyll of green plants; all act as organelles.

plastron [reptiles]: lower shell of turtle.

plat: small, flat-bottomed, square-sterned rowboat, about 5 ft. long, used as dinghy by Briton fishermen.

plate [ships]: bar; band of sheet iron; buttock plates, channel plates, etc. Metal which forms part of strake on ship's side.

plateau: comparatively flat-topped elevation of sea floor of considerable extent across the summit and usually rising more than 100 fathoms (200 meters) on all sides.

plate, furnaced [ships]: plate that requires heating in order to shape it as required.

platform [ships]: partial deck.

platform reef: organic reef with flat upper surface.

plating [ships]: steel plates which form shell or skin of vessel.

playa: flat-floored center of undrained desert basin; dried-up lake basin in arid region.

playa lake: flat-floored, shallow desert basin containing temporary lake.

Pleistocene: so-called "Ice Age" which began some million years ago and includes 4 cycles of glacial advance and retreat. Some geologists believe the Pleistocene ended with beginning of the Recent age about 10,000 years ago, while others think we are in between glacial advances now.

pleon: in *Crustacea*, the abdomen.

pleopod: one of paired abdominal appendages among some crustaceans; pleopods may be used in swimming, fanning water, respiration or reproduction (decapod females carry eggs on pleopods).

plesiosaurs: turtlelike marine reptiles with broad bodies, long flippers and short tails; to 50 ft. long. Descendants of nothosaurs, meaning "like lizards," but few creatures were less lizardlike in appearance and habits. Plesiosaurs were marine reptiles adapted to life in open sea. One group of these reptiles had short, flattened heads, long neck and plump oval bodies strengthened by mats of abdominal ribs. Tails, though fairly long, were finless; they swam by means of legs and feet that had grown into oarlike paddles. Bones of hips and shoulders were broad, providing attachment for powerful muscles which brought paddles down and backward. Second group of plesiosaurs were similar in body, paddles and tail but skulls were extended by long slender jaws. Necks were also short. Triassic to end of Cretaceous.

pleuracanths [sharks]: descendants of cladoselachian sharks characterized by slender body, dorsal fin that ran almost the length of back, homocercal tail that tapered to a point with fins both above and below, paired fins with central axis and rays that branched off to either side. There was also a long spine behind head. Most surprising of all is that pleuracanths left the sea and took up life in fresh water, where their remains were covered by deposits of late Devonian to Triassic.

pleurodires [turtles]: possess some primitive features, but they swing their long necks sidewise and so tuck their heads under for shelter. Fossils which date back to Cretaceous, are surprisingly like forms that still live in Southern Hemisphere. All surviving turtles of Australia belong to this "side-necked" group.

Pleurosigma [subclass *Pennatae*]: although true bottom-dwellers, they are able to creep about and never form chains, some species are found in inshore plankton samples, particularly after rough weather which stirs up the bottom.

pleuston: community of macroorganisms floating on surface of sea, e.g., siphonophores, barnacles, isopods, gastropods, etc.

plica [*Brachiopoda*]: radial ridges and depressions that involve entire thickness of shell and appear as corrugations on inner as well as outer surfaces; distinguished from fold and sulcus by small amplitude and by occurrence to side of midline.

plicate [*Mollusca*]: folded or twisted.

plication [*Mollusca*]: plait or fold, especially in gastropod columella.

plimsoll mark [ships]: mark stencilled in and painted on ship's side, designated by circle and horizontal lines to mark highest permissible load waterlines under different conditions.

plot: to mark or delineate, as ship's position, a course, or a bearing, on a chart.

Plow or Plough: constellation *Ursa Major;* also called *Charlie's Wagon* or *Wain* and *Big Dipper.*

plucking [glacier]: when a glacier flows across fractured or jointed stretch of bedrock, it may lift up large blocks of stones and move them. This process is known as plucking or quarrying.

plum duff [ships]: stiff kind of flour pudding containing raisins, usually boiled in a bag. Favorite sea dish, considered great delicacy by sailors in old wind ships.

plumed chenille [*Dasyopsis plumosa*]: usually attached to wharf pilings, may be dredged from depths of 30 to 35 ft., but is more often found in deep water in tropical seas. Most striking characteristics of plumed chenilles are soft, chenillelike texture and clear, bright red color. When unbroken may be 2 ft. long with branches 1 ft. wide at lower end. Characteristic of *Dasyopsis* is sympodial growth, i.e., branch continues growth in direction of axis, and axis continues growth as lateral branch.

plumularian: member of genus *Plumularia*, group of fernlike colonial hydroids.

plunge point: 1) for a plunging wave, point at which wave curls over the falls. 2) final breaking point of waves just before they rush up on beach.

pluteus: free-swimming larva of sea urchins and brittle stars, forming resemblance to upturned easel.

pluteus larva: ciliated planktonic larva of sea urchins and other *Echinoidea.*

plutonic rock: igneous rock which has cooled some distance below the surface and usually possesses coarse-grained texture.

plutonite: all rocks occurring in major (plutonic) intrusions; igneous rock which has cooled some distance below the surface.

pluviometer: rain gauge.

pneumatocyst: air or gas bladder or float; found in siphonophores and in several species of brown algae.

pneumatophore: in certain organisms gas-filled, saclike structure, such as float of Portuguese man-of-war, which generally serves as buoyant mechanism.

Pneumodermopsis ciliata [*Gymosomata*]: this animal is 12 mm. long and has pale violet tinge. There are cephalic appendages which, apart from size of animal, distinguish it from *Clione limacina;* North Atlantic species.

pneumofathometer [diving]: diver depth-indicating system based on air pressure necessary to reach steady flow condition in open tube terminating at diver's equipment.

pocket or oyster thief [*Colpomenia sinuosa*]: strange alga that is either epiphytic on another alga or attached to mollusc shell at 0.5 and 1.5-ft. tide levels. Easy to identify. It is olive-brown balloon; 1½ to 2 in. in diameter. When young, seaweed is a globular sac filled with water or gas which acts as a float. Walls of seaweed are composed of two layers: inner layer of large, rounded, colorless cells and outer layer of small, club-shaped cells. Large sac arises as result of extensive surface growths by repeated crosswise division of outer layer of cells.

pod: number of animals (as seals or whales) closely clustered together.

podobranch: in *Crustacea*, gill attached to base segment of one of thoracic legs.

Podocopa, order [phylum *Arthropoda*]: carapace without notch; antennae for locomotion; mandible with palp and setae; 4 pairs of postoral appendages; freshwater and marine. *Darwinula, Cypris.*

Poggendorff compensation method: method of measuring unknown emf by finding point at which it just opposes steady drop of potential along a wire, etc.

point: extreme end of a cape; other end of any protrusion into water, usually less prominent than a cape.

pointed lynx [*Grateloupia pinnata*]: grows profusely on rocks in littoral zone or at 1.5 ft. tide level. It is also found in tide pools, in polluted areas or where fresh water enters sea. Most noticeable characteristics are featherlike leaflets (proliferations) that extend edges of flat blades, 5 to 7 in. long and 1/16 in. wide, all lying on same plane. With color range from bright red to olive-purple, seaweed is striking in appearance. Holdfast is disc-shaped organ with several shoots growing from it.

points: "points" is angular unit, 11¼° (1/8 of a right angle), being an angle between adjacent "points" of the compass, the card of face of which has 32 divisions, or "points," beginning with North, and continuing North by East, North Northeast, Northeast by North, etc. Word "points" is used to define location of object (or wind) observed from ship forward or abaft a line drawn at right angles to keel at midship section on both starboard and port sides.

pojama: Swedish galley-type, armed naval vessel of 19th century with two heavy guns at each end. It was two-masted, with fore-and-aft mizzen and square-rigged in mainmast. Hull was built much heavier than that of the galley. There were ports for sweeps.

polacre: sharp-bowed Mediterranean vessel. This type still exists. It usually carried 3 pole masts without crosstrees or caps and one-piece bowsprit. Cleats were put on masts as stops for shrouds and stays. It was square-rigged.

polacre-settee: similar to polacre, but with mainmast square-rigged and lateen-rigged on fore and mizzenmast. Also called "polacre corvette."

polar: of or pertaining to the poles of the earth, of the celestial sphere, or those of a magnetic field. Proceeding from or found in vicinity of either of the earth's geographical poles; as, *polar winds; polar ice.*

polar air: type of air whose characteristics are developed over high latitudes, especially within subpolar highs. Continental polar air (cP) has low surface temperatures, low moisture content and, especially in its source region, has great stability in lower layers. It is shallow in comparison with arctic air. Maritime polar air (mP) initially possesses similar properties to those of continental polar air.

polar convergence: line along which cold polar intermediate water sinks under warmer subpolar water in its movement toward lower latitudes. It is marked by sharp change in surface temperatures, particularly in Southern Hemisphere.

polar creep: slow movement of cold water along ocean bottom from Poles to Equator.

polar easterlies: winds that blow out of polar highs toward subpolar lows.

polar front: semipermanent, low-pressure area around 60° north. Polar cell is to north of this, with subsiding southerly winds aloft.

polar ice: sea ice that is more than 1 year old (in contrast to winter ice). It is usually thickest form of sea ice, at times exceeding thickness of 10 ft.

polarimeter: instrument for measuring amount of polarized light or extent of polarization in light received from given source.

Polaris: star *a Ursae Minoris,* or brightest in *Ursa Minor,* or the *Little Bear,* a constellation also known as the *Little Dipper,* extremity of the "handle" of which is marked by this star; also called *Polestar* and *North Star,* from its close proximity to the north pole of the heavens. Due to its slow apparent diurnal motion, *Polaris* has long been a favorite with navigators for determining latitude by its altitude; in lower latitudes for compass observations; and as a ready reference point for showing direction at night. On January 1, 1950, as given in the *Nautical Almanac,* declination of the star was 89° 02′ N. and its magnitude, 2.12.

polarization: confinement of oscillation of light waves or other radiating energy waves to certain plane.

polar siderostat: optical instrument designed on same principle as coelostat to reflect portion of sky in fixed direction; in this case, however, observer looks down polar axis to a mirror.

polder: piece of low-lying land reclaimed from water.

pole: 1) either extremity of the axis of a sphere; north or south extremity of the earth's axis: *north pole* or *south pole.* One of two points of apparent flux or concentration of force, as in a magnetic field; distinguished as *positive* and *negative poles* or, *respectively,* N. and S. *poles.* 2) part of a mast above uppermost shrouds or standing rigging. 3) flagstaff. 4) portion of lower jaw of a sperm whale which contains the teeth (whaling cant).

pollack: food fish of the cod family found on Atlantic coasts of Europe and North America; also called *coalfish,* from its dark back. The name is also applied to the *greenling* or *rock trout* of Alaskan waters.

pollock: bluish or greenish-brown fish with yellow-gray side and lighter gray underparts. Lateral line is conspicuously white; tail is more distinctly forked than in either cod or haddock. Average weight is between 4 and 12 lbs.; larger individuals reach length of 4 ft. and weigh as much as 40 lbs. Pollock is a gluttonous bottom-feeder especially destructive of young cod.

Pollux: β *Geminorum,* brighter of two navigational stars in *Gemini* (the Twins). It lies 23° due north of the bright *Procyon* and 4½° SE by S of his younger brother *Castor.*

polly pacific [*Polysiphonia pacifica*]: grows on rocks between 2- and 1.5-ft. tide levels. Distinguishing feature is presence of dense clusters of delicate plants which grow from wide rhizoidal base. In its central range this alga may be 5 to 6 in. tall, with branches so narrow and matted that individual branches are scarcely discernible. Texture is soft and lax; color is reddish-brown to black.

polychaete: member of class *Polychaeta* of *Annelida,* phylum of segmented worms. Well developed, with many setae, polychaetes are mostly marine and usually have distinct head with sensory organ. They include many tube dwellers as well as other free-swimming and burrowing species. Palbo worms, sea mice, scaleworms, nereids, rockworms, lugworms and clamworms are all polychaetes.

polyclad: wide, often brightly colored member of *Polycladida,* order of marine flatworms. They may live in rocks or along shore among plants or permanently attached to animals. Some species have many eyes or tentacles. Bodies are sometimes leaf-shaped; all species have multibranched gut.

poly collins or polly hendry [*Polysiphonia*]: P. *collinsii* grows on rocks and *P. hendryi* grows on other seaweed. Grows in midlittoral zone, roughly from 3.5- to 1.5-ft. tide levels. Like all species of *Polysiphonia,* these two are characterized by many siphons, cells arranged in tiers with 4 to 24 cells surrounding central layer and by unlimited growth of erect branches. Plants of both species usually grow in reddish-brown matted tufts so heavily encrusted with diatoms that one can scarcely see the plant itself. Great numbers of thalli grow from rhizoids.

polyconic projection: projection where latitude curves are developed as series of tangent cones. Scale is chosen to be true along selected central meridian. This projection is neither conformal nor equal area.

Polykrikos [phytoplankton]: dinoflagellates with thin pellicle but united to form permanent colonies, each member of which is rather like *Gymonodinium* so that composite dinoflagellate with several nuclei is formed.

polymictic plankton: with several species present in great numbers.

polynya: 1) water area enclosed in ice, generally fast; this water area remains constant and usually has oblong shape; sometimes limited to one side by coast. 2) any enclosed seawater area in pack ice other than a lead, not large enough to be called open water.

polyp: 1) in *Coelenterata*, stage commonly developing from planula larva. In *Hydrozoa* and *Scyphozoa*, polyp is usually sessile in form and multiplying asexually, whereas sexual form is commonly free-swimming medusa or attached, reduced medusoid. In *Anthrozoa* there is no medusa stage and gonads are borne on mesenteries on polyp. 2) slender, stalklike coelenterate, either colonial or single animal, attached at one end and with circle of tentacles surrounding mouth at other end.

polypide [*Bryozoa*]: living portion, soft parts of individual bryozoan (zooid).

Polyplacophra, subclass [phylum *Mollusca*]: body elliptic or oval with shell of 8 transverse plates; broad ventral foot; shell bordered by scaly girdle or mantle; gills vary from few to many and located in groove around foot; separate sexes; single median gonad; trochophore larva; marine coastal waters. *Chiton, Lepidopleurus.*

polythalamous: many-chambered, as in shells of some *Foraminifera*.

polytroch: having several ciliated bands, as in some trochophore larvae.

polytrocular larva: advanced stage of plankton young of certain annelids, in which several segments, each bearing ring of cilia, are present.

polyzoans: *Polyzo* or *Bryozoa* ("moss animals") are tiny animals that live, for the most part, in fixed colonies comprising large numbers of individuals. Often resemble either little shrubs, shrubby trees or plates. Individuals measure about 1/25 of an inch and possess "houses" with a hole that allows the animal or zooid to spread beyond it. Individual has shape of an annelid and

head is topped with tentacles that protrude from the hole of its domicile. Bryozoans reproduce eggs, which in turn produce larvae. Larvae fix themselves on bottom and become first section of a colony. This section buds and soon after individuals are added. All zooids of a colony share common nervous system.

pomacentrid: member of family of brightly colored, small marine fishes with 2 spines in anal fins and single nostrils on each side of heads. These are damselfishes so common on coral reefs.

pompano: belong to family *Carangidae* which is related to *Scombridae* (tuna and mackerel); seafood delicacy and shallow water game fish. It is light colored with blue back and silvery sides tinted with yellow; tail fin is blue and yellow. In pompano the spiny dorsal fin is reduced to series of very small spines. Pompano lack teeth and feed on invertebrates and small fishes. Average individual is 18 in. or less in length and weighs under 2 lbs. This species is common along Atlantic Coast south of the Carolinas.

pompon: lives in extensive beds well below tide mark. It is partial to deep crevices in rocks where waves beat hard. The pompon looks like a pompom waved at football games. Age is determined by annual rings on stipe. Stipe is about 2½ ft. long and 1 to 2 in. wide, woody, exceedingly stout, erect, unbranched, cylindrical at lower end and flattened at upper end. Arising laterally from upper edges on each side of stipes are large number (up to 40) of streamers called sporophylls. Both stipe and streamers are covered with mucilage ducts and are dark brown, becoming black when dry.

ponto: Roman vessel, circa 200 A.D., rigged with square mainsail and small antenon, latter being supported by shrouds. Tye yard and sail were kept stowed until required.

pontoon: low, flat-bottomed vessel resembling a barge and utilized for many purposes such as being used to support temporary bridges or landings.

pookhaun: double-ended Scandinavian yawl-type, lug-rigged craft of Galway, Ireland.

pool: any enclosed, relatively small, sea area in pack ice other than a lead or lane.

poop: 1) raised deck abaft mizzenmast, generally over a cabin. 2) stern or aftermast part of ship. Deck above ordinary deck in aftermost part of ship. To break heavily over the stern or quarter of a ship. 3) In old sailing ships, high enclosed superstructure on stern, extending from side to side and usually containing captain's and officer's quarters.

poop deck [ships]: raised deck on after part of ship.

popo: "flying proa" or outrigger sailing canoe used

for sea voyages and interisland travel in Caroline Islands. Like most of Micronesian seagoing canoes, this canoe has flattened side of the hull. The latter is usually built of planking above dugout base. Ends are elongated and carved to represent head of a bird. Hulls are painted in varying designs of red, black and white.

poppets [ships]: those pieces of timber which are fixed perpendicularly between ship's bottom and bilgeways at foremost and aftermost parts of ship, to support her in launching.

porbeagle: small rapacious shark of North Atlantic and North Pacific Oceans, classified as *Lamna cornubica*. It has a pointed nose and both tail lobes of about equal length; attains a length of about 8 ft.

Porcellana platycheles [anomurans]: this species is distinguished from *P. longecornes* by relative lengths of rostral and posterior spines of carapace. In *P. platycheles*, posterior spines are half the length of rostral spine.

Porcellanidae longicornis [anomurans]: much more widely distributed species. Posterior spines are only 1/3 the length of rostral spine. Common in inshore plankton but also found in offshore water.

porcupine fish: fifteen species of porcupine fish of family *Diodontidae*, all found in temperate and tropical seas; related to puffers. Like puffers, porcupine fish have very large, fan-shaped pectoral fins, no ventral fins, single, small dorsal fin and small anal fin. Scales are modified into long sharp spines similar in appearance to porcupine quills, these can be folded close to body and pointed backward when fish is swimming. The largest grow to length of 3 ft. Porcupine fish are noted for ability, when frightened, to swell up to a sphere. They have additional protection of very tough body covering and very sharp spines which protrude when body is distended.

pore canal: in echinoderms and hemichordate larvae, canal from hydrocoel to exterior.

pore field: in *Radiolaria*, area on central capsule bearing spores.

porgy: small family of fishes with large heads and high backs; of 15 species found in U.S. all but one is confined to Atlantic Coast. As in many families of marine fishes, eggs are buoyant and float near surface.

porgy, grass: more colorful, southern species living amid eelgrass off Florida Coast. It is small, olive-hued fish with dark bars and spots, spotted fins and yellow spots along lateral line.

Porifera [phylum]: 1) *Porifera* or sponges are multicellular animals in which there is little specialization of tissues. Essential features are better displayed by very simple sponge. Such an individual has form of slender vase; there is nothing to it but living wall surrounding large, hollow space. Wall is made up of 3 layers: outer layer is formed of protective cells (ectoderm), inner layer feeding cells (endoderm) and middle layer of noncellular jellylike substance (mesoglea). Endodermal cells feed as do protozoans, each capturing and swallowing other microscopic organisms; ectodermal cells do not take food but absorb what is needed from nearly endodermal cells. Thus no digestive or circulatory organs are required. Latin *"porus,"* passage or pore; *"ferre,"* to bear, referring to fact that wall of sponge is perforated by simple pores or complicated passages. Older Precambrian to Recent. Phylum represents evolutionary "dead end." Although *Porifera* developed from *Protozoa*, no other group evolved from *Porifera*. 2) phylum of *Parazoa* composed of sessile and aquatic animals with single cavity in the body lined, in whole or in part, by choanocytes.

Porites: important genus of reef-building coral.

porkfish: conspicuous and common species of coral reef community. It has blue and gold horizontal stripes, golden yellow fins and conspicuous black vertical bars in head region; one extends from mouth through eye to top of head, another from pectoral fin to forward edge of dorsal fin. Average weight is 1 lb. Like the other grunts, porkfish are nocturnal, feeding on shrimp, crab and other small marine invertebrates.

porosity: 1) percentage of pore space on material. 2) percentage of pore space on total volume of dry bottom sediment sample. This percentage expresses volume that can be occupied by water.

porpoise: small to moderate-sized member of cetacean suborder *Odontoceti*. Name is used interchangeably with dolphin by some. More properly it is given to small and beakless members of family *Delphinidae*, which have triangular dorsal fin and spade-shaped teeth.

port: 1) harbor. 2) left-hand side of ship looking from aft to bow; at night marked with red light.

port flange [ships]: protruding flange above a port to keep drip from entering.

port gangway [ships]: opening in side plating, planking or bulwarks for purpose of providing access through which people may board or leave ship or through which cargo may be handled.

porthole [ships]: aperture in ship's side fitted with glass for admitting light.

port lid [ships]: shutter for closing porthole in stormy weather. It is hung by top hinges.

Portpatrick line boat: two-masted, open, fishing skiff about 16 ft. long, 7 ft. beam, used in "long line" cod fishery at Portpatrick, Scotland. Foremast is set well up in bow and aftermast stepped amidships.

port side [ships]: left-hand side of ship looking forward.

Portunus puber [*brachyurans*]: zoeae are often abundant in April and megalopae reach peak in July. First zoea is about 1.8 mm. long with long dorsal and rostral spines on carapace as well as short lateral ones. Pleopods appear as small knobs in 3rd zoeal stage at which time lateral spines become apparent on abdomen. Black and orange carapace bears lateral bristles. In later zoeal stages, flagellum of antenna grows much longer and pleopods branch. Final zoeal stage is about 4 mm. long and has 2, instead of 3, spines on telson by which time first walking leg has become chelate. Megalopa stage is somewhat smaller than last zoea.

positive estuary: estuary in which there is a measurable dilution of seawater by land drainage.

positive gradient: positive rate of change with depth.

post: pillar, stanchion, mooring bitt, pawl bitt, or other upright piece of timber or metal used as a prop, support, to withstand lateral pressure, etc. In old sailing navy days, rank attained by a captain who was appointed to a vessel of at least 20 guns; to appoint an officer to command such vessel. To list or publish, as at *Lloyd's*, the fact of a mishap to a vessel; as, *the "Waratah" is posted as missing.*

posterior: 1) in *Brachiopoda*, direction defined by position of hinge line and/or pedicle opening. 2) in *Gastropoda*, direction opposite head along middle axis. In nearly all shells, spical direction.

post-femoral [amphibian]: back of thigh.

postlabials [reptiles]: scales behind and in line with upper labials.

postlarva: in *Crustacea*, young individual of essentially adult morphology but not yet sexually mature.

postnasal [reptiles]: one or two scales just behind nasal.

postoculars [reptiles]: one or more small scales directly behind eye.

post-ship: in British Navy, ships carrying less than 24 and more than 18 guns. They were lowest class of ships a captain could command.

potential density: density that parcel of water would have raised adiabatically to surface, i.e., if determined from parcel's in situ salinity and potential temperature.

potential energy: energy resulting from elevation or depression of water surface from undisturbed level. This energy advances with wave form.

potential temperature: in oceanography, temperature that water sample would attain if raised adiabatically to sea surface. For deepest points of ocean, which are just over 10,000 meters, adiabatic cooling would be less than $1.5°$ C.

potentiometric recorder: recorder using potentiometer, device for varying electric potential (difference in electrical force between two points in a circuit).

potrero: accretionary ridge separated from coast by lagoon and barrier island, as along Texas coast.

potted: instruments, connections or fittings encapsulated in waterproof plastic material.

pottery seaweed [*Ceramium pacificum*]: widely distributed, epiphytic alga attached to shells, rocks or other seaweed either in tide pools or in deeper water. It is found in almost every part of the world. Color varies from clear dark red to brown or purple, depending on habitat. Probably most noticeable features are transverse bandings on young parts of plants and widely diverging hairlike branches, which are forked 5 to 6 times. It grows in sprawling, loose tufts, 4 to 6 in. high, with branches as fine as hairs. Pottery seaweed is fragile and dainty; point of attachment is almost invisible.

pounding: act of coming down heavily upon sea waves, as bows of a light vessel in a head or cross sea; distinguished from *plunging* in that vessel's bottom strikes the sea with a resounding thud felt throughout the hull.

power block: hydraulic-powered block with large, V-shaped sheave (pulley) used to haul in purse nets.

PPI [Plan Position Indicator]: radarscope on which spots of light, representing reflections of radar waves, indicate range and bearing of objects.

praam: Norwegian sailing lighter.

prahu [prau]: Malay term for boat. Malay pirate prahu known by sailors as "flying prau," was a type of rowing and sailing vessel of East Indies, formerly used by Malay pirates to attack merchant vessels when becalmed. It is carvel-built with sharp, hollow bow at stern; raking, curved stern with long, oddly-shaped head, straight raking sternpost and high square stern; easy run.

prahu pelet: Malay, lug-rigged pilot boat.

pratique: term in general use by most maritime nations for permission of persons to land from, or to board, any merchant vessel, fishing vessel, yacht, or other vessel, usually excepting naval craft, arriving from a foreign port, upon compliance by such vessel with quarantine regulations or presentation of a clean *bill* (or bills) *of health.* A *certificate of pratique* or *quarantine clearance* usually is granted vessel's master where port officials are satisfied no contagious disease exists or is likely to arise amongst crew and/or passengers. Vessel is then said to be *granted pratique* or *admitted to pratique.* If pratique is not obtainable, vessel is placed in *quarantine.* Excepting naval vessels generally, all others arriving from a foreign port are required to display International Code flag Q, denoting *"My vessel is healthy and I* *request free pratique.''* Presence of contagious or infectious cases on board should be announced by appropriate signal indicated in Code Book under *Quarantine.* Also written *pratic* and *pratick.*

prau bugis: two-masted cargo boat of East Indies. Hull is of ancient model, not unlike that of a junk, having overhanging poop roofed over with matting supported by bamboo poles. Usually built of teak.

Praumus flexuosos [mysid]: large slender mysid with narrow carapace with pointed antero-lateral regions and rounded rostrum. Emarginated posterior margin of carapace leaves part of 7th and whole of last thoracic segment visible in dorsal view. There is a long and stout abdomen sharply curved downward in region of 2nd to 4th segments and upwards beyond this.

prau nadi: keelless dugout used by natives of Jahore, Malay States with V-shaped raking ends. Floor rises sharply and there is sharp turn to bilges; no sheer. It is sometimes partially covered with a deck of bamboo. Average length 20 to 25 ft. with beam about 1/5.

prawn: crustacean of order *Decapoda.* Prawns are often mistaken for shrimp but abdomens are more slender. They are caught and sold as food in U.S. and in other countries.

prawner: small sailing vessel engaged in trawling for prawns (pink shrimp) off English coast. Beam trawl is used, beam being about 20 ft. long.

prawn, painted [*Hymenocera picta*]: very few prawns or shrimps are more beautiful and delicate than this little species. It is light pink over body and marked by large purple spots which are bordered by yellow. First pair of legs is small, but 2nd pair carries large pair of pinchers which are broad, decorated with large spots and carried in horizontal position; remaining legs are naked and unadorned except for alternating bands. Antennae are slender and almost touch the tail. Body measures about 2 in. long; inhabits quiet inshore waters of coral reef.

prawn, spiny [*Stenopus hispidus*]: this little prawn is brightly colored. Chelipeds are marked with about 4 alternating red and white bands; body is marked with 3 red areas; chelipeds and body are covered with fine, curved spines. There are 6 long feelers extending from head. Bodies of these shrimps are usually a little more than 2 in. long. Almost worldwide in warm water; live in calm, shallow water crawling about over coral reef.

precentral [reptiles]: single lamina preceding centrals.

precipitate: solid substance that becomes separated from liquid solution.

prefrontals [reptiles]: one or two pairs of scales on top of head in front of frontal.

prehensor: grasping organ, e.g., in centipedes, one of paired maxillipeds.

premaxillae [fish]: most anterior bones of upper jaw.

preocular [reptile]: one or more small scales in front of eye.

preopercle [fish]: anterior part of bony covering of gill chamber.

pressure fluctuations: oscillation about static water pressure caused by wave action.

pressure gage: tide gage that is operated at bottom of body of water and which records tide heights by change in pressure due to rise and fall of tide.

pressure ice: sea ice (river or lake ice) which has been deformed or layered by lateral stresses of any combination of wind, water currents, tides, waves and surfs.

pressure ice foot: ice foot formed along shore by freezing together of stranded pressure ice.

pressure proof [diving]: able to structurally resist ambient pressure without leakage.

pressure ridge: ridge or wall of hummocks where one ice floe has been pressed against another. Ridges may be several miles long and up to 100 ft. high. Corresponding ridge may also occur on underside of ice canopy (ice keel).

prevailing current: flow most frequently observed during given period, usually a month, season or year.

prevailing westerlies: winds that originate in horse latitude highs and blows toward subpolar lows.

prevalent plankton: species that constitutes more than half the plankton in given place.

preventer: wire or rope line used as stay or support for extra safety.

prevent stays [ships]: additional ropes or chains employed to support any other stay when latter suffers unusual strain.

Priapulida [worms]: small group of marine worms characterized by wrinkled body, straight digestive system and proboscis that is covered with spines. They are variously ranked as a phylum, as one class in phylum called *Gephyrea* and as annelids. Small number of modern species seem to be remnants of ancient group that includes several fossils from Burgess shale as well as others from Silurian of Illinois.

Price-Gurley current meter: battery-powered, electromechanical current meter which measures current speed only.

primaries: bird's outermost feathers. They are principally used in flight and usually number 9 or 10.

primary consumers: organisms that eat plants; herbivores.

primary film: thin, slimy layer that usually forms

initially on surface placed in seawater; composed of bacteria, diatoms or both; believed by some to be necessary precursor to attachment of larger fouling organisms.

primary lows and highs: areas of air pressure that result from movements of air caused by unequal heating. Also called semipermanent lows and highs.

primary production: amount of organic matter synthesized by organisms from inorganic substances in unit time in unit volume of water or in column of water of unit area cross section and extending from surface to bottom.

primary productivity: synthesis of organic matter by marine plants from inorganic materials.

primary tide station: place at which continuous tide observations are made over number of years.

primary waves: first waves of earthquake, having speed of 3.4 to 8.5 miles per second; one of two body waves.

prime meridian: meridian of longitude 0° used as origin for measurements of longitudes. Meridian of Greenwich, England, is internationally accepted prime meridian on most charts.

priming of the tides: periodic acceleration in time of occurrence of high and low water because of changes in relative positions of moon and sun. Opposite effect is called lagging of the tides.

primitive period: primitive period of periodic quantity is smallest increment of independent variable for which function repeats itself.

principal rays [fish]: branched, soft rays reaching to margin of fin.

proa: narrow, double-ended dugout sailing canoe of Micronesian Islands and Malay Archipelago. Outstanding feature is flattened lee side of hull. Rig consists of oceanic lateen sail on raking mast.

probe: measuring device or sensor inserted into environment to be measured. As applied to oceanography, term is used for devices which are lowered into sea for in situ measurements.

proboscis: elongated or protruding organ or tubelike structure located on mouth region of many animals. Commonly used in feeding, it sometimes has other functions.

Processidae [carideans]: processid larvae can be distinguished only with great difficulty from those of pandalids, sole clear feature being that exopodite or scale of antenna has no sign of segmentation whereas in pandalids and hypolytids it is clearly jointed. Absence of rostrum in stage one processid larvae also serves to separate them from some pandalids, as does presence of pair of small dorsalateral spines in 5th abdominal segment. Adult processids are rarer than would perhaps be suggested by abundance of larvae from spring to autumn inshore waters.

Procyon: star of magnitude 0.48 in the *Canis Minor* (Little Dog) group situated next to and east of *Orion*. It has a declination of 5° 21½' N. and right ascension 7 hrs. 36½ min. Lines joining the bright *Sirius*, ruddy *Betelguese* of *Orion*, and *Procyon* form an almost perfect equilateral triangle.

production: sum of organic matter produced by living organisms in given area or volume in given time, inclusive of such organisms which might have developed and disappeared in given time.

profile: chiefly applied to drawings of vessels, showing the longitudinal structure arrangement, transverse framing, waterlines, bulkheads, decks, houses, etc., as viewed at right angles to fore-and-aft line; side elevation or longitudinal view of a vessel.

profile drag: dimensional drag of a body, excluding that due to life; sum of friction and form drag. Improperly designed magnetometer housings, towed behind ship are subject to this.

pro-frogs [*Eoanura*]: similar to "dawn frogs" except they had lost still more bones in skull but kept primitive salamanderlike body. Pro-frogs probably crept through moist shady Triassic forests, eating insects and wriggling into water when danger threatened on land.

progressive wave: wave which is manifested by progressive movement of wave form.

projection: in cartography, the representation on a plane of part or whole of the earth's surface so that all points and areas thereon, with their directions of bearing from each other, conform to those existing in nature. Since it obviously is impossible to depict a considerable area of the globe without some degree of distortion taking place, a projection suited to navigators' use must be such that a direction or a course line may be plotted thereon as a straight line. Hence, the necessity that all points and areas, no matter to what degree such depiction may be distorted, must lie in same relative direction to each other as on the earth itself. Of the several projections in use two only are necessary for navigation in any latitude.

proloculum: in *Foraminifera*, initial, or first chamber of test. Typically at small end of series or at center of coil.

promontory: high point of land extending into body of water.

promotumedusae [*Coelenterata*]: primitive, free-swimming cnidarians with prominent radial pouches.

proostracum: in extinct cephalopods of group *Belemnoida*, dorsal platelike portion of shell.

propagation anomaly: in underwater acoustics, difference between actual propagation loss for given length of water path and nominal value of propagation loss identified with distance covered by that path.

propagation loss: transmission loss associated with any given length of ray path in water.

proportional dividers: mechanical drawing device consisting of many equally spaced, pointed legs. It is used to divide lines, drawn to any scale, into equal parts.

proprietary absorbent: absorbent manufactured by private firm; its exact chemical composition is not disclosed to the public.

Prorocentrum, phylum Protozoa [phytoplankton]: *Prorocentrum micans* is widely distributed, particularly common in neritic and estuarine waters. *P. scutellum* is somewhat familiar.

Prosobranchia [gastropod larvae]: there are 3 main periods in the year during which prosobranch larvae become common in plankton; spring, summer and autumn, majority of species occurring in summer plankton. Roughly 60% of these larvae have long pelagic phase, about 4/5 of them being derived from epifaunal parents. Most *Prosobranchia* encase their eggs in gelatinous or horny masses which are attached to substratum so that eggs of prosobranchs are rarely found in plankton.

prosogyrate [*Mollusca*]: turned forward, as of pelecypod beaks that are anteriorly directed.

prosoma: in *Copepoda*, forepart of body in front of major articulation.

prostomium: anterior portion of head of annelids.

prosumia: Roman vessel, circa 200 A.D., similar to ponto.

proteolytic: capable of degrading proteins. Said of enzymes that digest proteins.

proteolytic enzyme: complex catalyst within the body that helps break down proteins into less complex substances.

Proterozoic: era, beginning about 550 million years ago and characterized by earliest known ice age and rise of invertebrates.

Protochordata [phylum]: Cambrian to Recent. Coelomate; level of organization approximates that of annelids. Possesses some traces of notochords and gill slits; nonsegmented; distinguished by muscular collar that may bear tentacles. Marine; burrowing, benthonic or planktonic.

protoconch: larval shell of gastropod:

protoecium [*Bryozoa*]: skeleton of larva formed when it is attached to substrata; consists of 2 chitinous valves of free-living larva cemented to substrata.

proton magnetometer: device that measures magnetic intensity.

Protophragmoceras [nautiloids]: had living chambers that were compressed but open. Shell expanded rapidly to large but greatly compressed living chamber; aperture also is constricted, but irregularly, until it is roughly I-shaped or even more elaborate. Apparently crawled most of the time, with eyes and arms projecting from large part of aperture and funnel at rear.

protoplasm: basic matter of living cells in which all essential life processes take place. It is a grayish, fluid, complex substance containing water and organic and inorganic components, such as hydrogen, nitrogen, carbon, oxygen, phosphorus, potassium, iodine, sulphur, calcium, iron and magnesium.

protoplast: protoplasm within cell wall; protoplasm of cell.

prototroch: in trochophore larvae, ciliated band in preoral position.

Protozoa [phylum]: so-called single-celled animals constitute phylum *Protozoa*. Although widely distributed, protozoans are numerous and nearly all microscopic and therefore seldom seen. Each protozoan is tiny droplet of fluid, living matter enclosed in a membrane. Unlike higher animals, it has no special visceral organs for digestion, circulation, reproduction, etc. Some lack mouth and take food through temporary rupture in cell wall, and later void indigestible residue by same means. When fully grown, the tiny animal reproduces by simply splitting into two or more young, each of which is like the parent but smaller. Since parent passes completely into its offspring, there is no death in normal course of events for these simple creatures. Greek "*protos,*" first; "*soon,*" animal, e.g., members of this phylum are first among animals in simplicity. Older Cambrian to Recent.

protozoans: 1) simplest of all animals, one-celled organisms. They vary in form and live in multitude of environments; often parasitic (causing many diseases). 2) minute, one-celled animals occurring in surface layers of sea. Several genera capable of producing bioluminescence.

protractor: instrument for laying off or measuring angles on paper, as a chart. It consists of a semicircular disk, often of transparent material, having its arc graduated to degrees and is used in conjunction with a ruler, as to find inclination or angle latter makes with a meridian; hence, a course or bearing expressed in degrees. It is often called a *course protractor*.

proud of the bottom: resting on surface of bottom, not imbedded in bottom.

province: region composed of group of similar bathymetric features whose characteristics are markedly in contrast with surrounding areas.

provision: 1) store of needed material for a voyage; especially, a stock of food for use of crew and passengers. 2) to supply a vessel with a store or stock of eatables.

prow [ships]: part of bow from load waterline to top of bow.

proximal: toward origin of appendage.

P.S.C.: *Per standard compass;* indicating a given course or bearing according to ship's standard compass.

pseudobranch: gill-like structure on inner surface of gill cover of fish near its upper edge.

pseudochitinous: superficially like chiton but chemically different.

pseudocoelom: body space, as in the *Aschelminthes*, between the gut and body wall, not lined by peritoneum and derived from the blastocoel rather than from an internal split in the mesoderm.

pseudodeltidium [*Brachiopoda*]: single plate covering all or part of pedicle opening in pedicle valve.

Pseudophyllidea: order of tape worms in phylum *Platyhelminthes* that are parasitic in all classes of vertebrates.

pseudoplanispiral [*Gastropoda*]: shell coiled in one plane but whorls not symmetrical in that plane.

pseudoplankton: organisms not normally planktonic, carried into plankton by turbulence.

pseudopod [*Foraminifera*]: lobate or threadlike extension of cell periphery that changes in shape, character and position with activity of cell.

pseudopodium: retractile locomotory processes in certain protozoans.

pseudopunctate [*Brachiopoda*]: shell microstructure characterized by structureless rods of calcite in prismatic layer perpendicular to shell surface. Many weather out in fossil shells, leaving tiny openings as those in punctate shells.

pseudozoea: larva of certain stomatopods, e.g., *Squilla;* not comparable to or derived from zoea stage of decapod crustaceans.

psychoid: applied to inexplicable regulating elements of developing embryo; morphaesthetic.

psychrometer: hygrometer, or instrument for measuring the aqueous content, or humidity, of the atmosphere.

pteropod: 1) member of group of small gastropod molluscs which swims near surface by means of modified foot with winglike appendages. Many pteropods lack gills and shells. 2) small, free-swimming, shelled mollusks, related distantly to oysters and mussels. One of marine organisms believed to cause "Deep Scattering Layer." 3) some pteropods are as bare and soft as nudibranchs, but others have coiled or conical shells. Head has become indistinct but foot is spread; with pair of winglike fins, animals swim. Fossil pteropods are thin-shelled and slender.

pteropod ooze: 1) pelagic sediment containing at least 30% calcium carbonate in form of tests of marine animals, dominant form being pteropods. 2) calcareous deep-sea ooze dominated by remains of minute molluscs of group *Pteropoda*.

pterygoid: bone in skull with winglike shape.

puffer: puffers are clumsy, thickset fish whose scales have been transformed into armor of prickles. Puffers are able to swell their bodies to 3 times normal size when frightened or handled. They do this by gulping water or air and so inflating a saclike portion of gullet through functioning of special breathing valves. Increase in body size makes prickles stick out like thorns in a cactus resulting in appearance that undoubtedly discourages predators. Most species are very toxic due to strong nerve poison (neurotoxin). Live mainly in tropical waters.

puffer, northern: dusky brown fish with yellowish-green or orange side and white belly; it grows to length of 10 in. This is inshore species found over sand bottoms where it searches for crustaceans and molluscs. Puffer can bury itself in sand by using its collarbones as shovels, moving them easily beneath loose baggy skin. Thus it lies hidden with only eyes and top of head visible.

puffins [*Charadriiformes*]: members of this family are rather small, or very small seabirds with comparatively short necks, small narrow wings and very short tails of 12 to 18 feathers. Legs are short and placed very far back near tail; they have only 3 toes connected by webs. Various species differ remarkably in form of their bills. In some, they are comparatively short and considerably compressed.

pu hoe: outrigger, dugout, paddling canoe of Society Islands. On large sizes a washstrake is usually added. Undecked hull ranges in size from 15 to 28 ft. long, 16 to 20 in. wide, 12 to 18 in. deep, and has rounded bottom, vertical, slightly concave stem, pointed stern. Long outrigger float is on portside and connected with hull by 2 asymmetric booms.

pulwar: native sailing craft of Bengal, India, similar to malar panshi with larger single, square sail.

pumice: light, porous, volcanic rock used to remove stains, to polish and to smooth.

pumpkinseed: dinghy of wide beam.

pumpkinseed [*Lepomis gibbosus*]: pumpkinseed, or common sunfish, is characterized by very deep, compressed body with bright orange belly. Back is usually raised or humped more than in other sunfishes; distinguished from bluegill by bright orange spot on long opercular lobe. Yellow bellies of young aid in distinguishing them from young bluefishes or bluegills. Body may be covered with orange spots; bars may be absent from sides. Wavy bright blue bars are sometimes present on lower sides of head.

punctae [*Foraminifera*]: small to large holes in external walls of chambers.

punctate: 1) in *Brachiopoda*, shell microstructure characterized by small canal extending perpendicularly from inner to outer surface of shell, appearing under lens as closely spaced pores. 2) in *Mollusca*, with minute pits.

pungy: two-masted, keel schooner which was employed extensively in dredging of oysters in Chesapeake Bay. It is built on the lines of Baltimore clipper. Hull is carvel-built, with moderately flaring bow and strongly raking curved stem; masts are tall and raking in Baltimore manner, bowsprit long and sails high and narrow. Heyday of pungy was from about 1845 to 1900. It is purely a local type.

punt: small, flat-bottomed open boat for rowing or sculling. Term used at sea for broad, beamy dinghy. Also, large type of deep-ballasted, half-decked boat of Falmouth, England.

punter: small pleasure craft of Netherlands, combination of hoogar and dory of New England. There is narrow transom at stern; bow has long raking stem of the latter. Usually has leg-of-mutton mainsail and jib to short bowsprit.

puppet shell, Thaanum's: this species is fairly solid shell, oval in outline with well developed acute, conical spire; it is encircled by many fine grooves. Shell is whitish and marked with irregular pinkish or reddish-brown spots which tend to form themselves into spiral rows. It will reach about 1/2 in. in length.

purchase [ships]: mechanical advantage such as offered by tackle for increasing power applied.

purge button [diving]: mechanism for clearing mouthpiece of diving regulator by replacing water with compressed air.

purse seiner: fishing boat with large net drawn around school of fish by smaller boat. When school is encircled, bottom of net is closed.

purse seines: large nets used in commercial fisheries, placed in circle around school of fish and drawn together.

pursing gear: purse line, brail lines, etc., by means of which a *purse seine* or any *purse net* is closed in capturing fish.

pustule: vacuolelike structure in dinoflagellates.

pygidium: terminal body segment in many invertebrates; anal segment in annelids.

Pyramidellidae [family]: molluscs of this family bear shells which are small, slender, conical or pyramidal-shaped, and consist of many whorls. In this family columella is usually plicated with one or two folds; aperture is entire and covered by horny operculum. They are usually white and highly polished. These molluscs are found on sandy bottoms in tropical and temperate seas.

Pyrenidae [*Columbellidae*]: little dove shells are group of small, solid species with protruding spires. They vary greatly in shape and include shells which are triangular, spindle-shaped and ellipsoid in outline. Anterior canal is short; columella is arched and tuberculated below. Outer lip is thickened, curved at middle and toothed on inner border. Horny operculum is present and epidermis covers shell.

pyrenoid: structure in plastids of plant concerned with synthesis of starch.

pyrheliometer: general term for class of activmeters which measure intensity of direct solar radiation. In oceanography, this instrument measures total sun and sky radiation received on horizontal surface.

pyroclastic: solid material ejected from volcano.

pyrolysis: decomposition of substance by heat.

pyrosome: one of genus *Pyrosoma* of luminescent, pelagic, colonial tunicates. Individuals form thimble-shaped colonies, commonly 3 or 4 in. long but reaching length of at least 2 ft. They occur only in warm waters and produce brilliant luminescence resembling long incandescent gas mantles.

pyroxenes: water free, silicate mineral usually found in fine grained igneous rocks.

Q

Q: denoted in *International Code of Signals* by a square yellow flag or by flashing or sound signal *(International Morse Code)* — — · — *(dash dash dot dash).* Flag *Q* hoisted singly by a vessel arriving from a foreign port—in some countries required of a foreign vessel arriving from *any* port—signifies *"My vessel is healthy and I request free pratique."* Also, as a towing signal, displayed by vessel towing, denotes *"Shall we anchor at once?"* or by towed vessel, *"I wish to anchor at once."* Such towing signal may be made at night by flashing *(Morse).* Abbreviation *Q* or *q*, in ships' logbooks and weather records, is used for *squalls* or *squally weather.*

Q factor: pressure coefficient of unprotected thermometer expressed in ° C.

quadrant: 1) fitting to the rudder, shaped like sector of a circle. Steering cable is affixed to this and controls the rudder through it. 2) specific area marked off on sea floor and used by biologists for long-term animal counts.

quadrate [*Mollusca*]: squarish or rectangular in outline.

quadrature: position in phase cycle when 2 principal tide-producing bodies (moon and sun) are nearly at right angle to earth; moon is then in quadrature in its first quarter or last quarter.

quadrature spectrum: spectral decomposition of the 90° out-of-phase components of covariance of the function of time.

quaiche: French term for ketch.

qualitative plankton sampler: sampler that sieves out organisms from water but does not measure volume of water filtered.

quantitative: test to show amounts of constituents present in compound or mixture.

quantitative plankton sampler: sampler that sieves out organisms from water and measures volume of water filtered.

quar ice: Labrador term for ice formed in spring from melt-water draining on to beach, ice foot or fast ice, where it refreezes.

quarter [ships]: 1) side of a ship aft, between main midships frames and stern. 2) on the quarter; strictly speaking, 45° abaft the beam; used to designate position between abeam and astern.

quarter boats: boats swinging from davits at quarters of vessel.

quarter deck [ships]: term applied to after portion of weather deck. In warship, that portion allotted for use by officers.

quarter-diurnal tide: shallow-water type of tide, which has 4 high waters and 4 low waters during one day. It originates as result of distortion of normal tidal curve in shallow water.

quartering: 1) coming toward the quarter, or from a direction well abaft the beam; said of the sea or wind; as, *a moderate quartering sea;* synonymous with *quarterly;* as, *a heavy quartering* or *quarterly* gale. 2) procedure of sailing with wind on alternate *quarters,* as in a fore-and-aft rigged vessel having a breeze from opposite direction to course to be made good. Vessel is thus maneuvered in order to more effectively spread her sail area and so make better speed than if sailed directly before the wind.

quartermaster: in merchant vessels, particularly those of liner type, one of a number—from 4 to 8, depending on size and class of ship—of able seamen who steer, keep navigating bridge and equipment, wheelhouse, chart room, etc., clean and in order, stand gangway watch in port, attend to flags displayed, and generally assist in matters pertaining directly to safe navigation of vessel. In naval ships generally, a petty officer whose duties include care and operation of signals, sounding gear and apparatus, steering ship, receiving and transmitting orders over telephone system, etc., under supervision of officer of the watch.

quartz: form of silicon dioxide. Most common inorganic constituent of marine sediments.

quasi-synoptic: nearly simultaneous, environmental measurements.

Quaternary: period in Cenozoic era characterized by 4 major glacial advances. Also known as Age of Man.

quay: artificial wall or bank, usually of stone,

made toward sea at side of harbor or river for convenience in loading and unloading vessels.

quay punt: sailing craft of Falmouth, England, used for fishing, carrying stores to ships, pleasure boating, etc. This type of boat has deep keel, straight stern, transom stern and large open cockpit. It is high-sided and deep-hulled.

queche: Portuguese name or term for ketch.

quenching: great reduction in underwater sound transmission or reception resulting from absorption and scattering of sound energy by air bubbles entrapped around sonar dome. Roll and pitch of ship in relatively rough water is primary cause of air bubble entrapment.

quench/ping ratio: in sound ranging, measure of sound lost from quenching. Based on ratio of number of echoes received (quench) to number of pulses emitted (ping).

quick: sediment or clay to sand size which by absorption or admixture of water becomes a loose, incoherent, unstable, liquid or semiliquid and capable of flowing usually under load or by force of gravity. Quick clay of glacial or marine origin becomes metastable of "quick" as result of leaching out of salts and their replacements by water. Any shock may cause reorientation of grain structure with squeezing out of interstitial water and conversion of clay into plaster or semiliquid state in which clay will flow and fail under load.

quicken: in boat and ship construction, to shorten the radius of, or sharpen, a curved line in the structure; as, to *quicken the flare* (of the bows), the *turn of the quarter*, the *sheer*, etc.

quicksand: sand supersaturated with water and easily movable or "quick." Will not support heavy object.

quillback [*Carpiodes cyprinus*]: heavily built fish with very long, soft dorsal fin. Elongate, soft dorsal line with anterior rays very long; mouth conical and projecting, suckerlike with thick, fleshy lips. Head moderate; muzzle conical, projecting, obtusely pointed. Color silvery to dusky. Length not exceeding 12 in.

quinquereme: term applied sometimes to galley having 5 banks of oars, but more correctly designating number of men per oar; in this case, 5 men per oar.

quintant: an instrument similar in construction to that of the *sextant*, but capable of measuring angles up to about 140°; so named from its arc of 72°, or *fifth* part of a circle. It is used chiefly in hydrographic surveying for boat work, where measurement of horizontal angles by a theodolite is impracticable.

quoddy: type of open-keel boat used in fisheries off coast of Maine, sloop- or cat-rigged, 20 to 35 ft. long. Cuddy was placed just aft of mast. Stem and sternpost raked; rudder was hung outside.

R

R: as an abbreviation in ships' logbooks and weather observation records, R or r denotes *rain;* also, *rough sea.* In U.S. navy, abbreviation R, in records of enlisted men signifies *deserted.* International Code flag R (indicated orally as *Roger*) is a yellow Greek cross on a square red ground; International Morse Code R = *dot-dash-dot* (. — .). Flag R, hoisted singly, or Morse Code R, by flashing, means *"The way is off my ship; you may feel your way past me."* Also, as a towing signal, as above, means, when shown by ship towed, *"Go slower";* by towing ship, *"I will go slower."*

R.A.: in nautical astronomy, abbreviation for *right ascension;* in naval records, often used for *Rear Admiral.*

rabbit [ships]: 1) longitudinal recess cut in face of timber to receive planking, as along top of keel and inside of stem and sternpost. 2) groove or slot in one section to receive complementary fitting or tongue of another section and afford smooth, well mated juncture.

racks [ships]: grating or open framework fastened about top of galley stove and saloon table to prevent cooking utensils and table service from sliding off in rough weather.

radar: coined from initial letters of *"radio direction and range."* Electronic device developed in World War II for detecting the presence of objects, as vessels, buoys, a coastline, etc., by means of radio waves sent out on a narrow beam which sweeps the horizon or is otherwise directed as desired. The radio waves rebound as echoes from objects in path of the beam and outline of such objects or coastline is shown instantaneously on the oscilloscope, or *scope,* as it is familiarly called, with *bearing* (relative to ship's fore-and-aft line or true, as required) and *distance* from vessel (or *range*) indicated. With promise of further development and simplification, the *radar* system appears destined to become an outstanding anticollision device and means for successfully navigating in narrow waters during thick weather, apart from its use as a detector of surfaced submarines or other enemy craft in the dark hours

or other period of shortened visibility for which it primarily was designed.

radeau: square-ended scow, fitted with deep bulwarks, sweeps, gun ports; rigged as schooner, brig ketch or even a ship; 40 to 95 ft. long. They were very fast running before the wind. Used for harbor defense in Revolutionary War.

radial [*Mollusca*]: sculpture radiating in relatively unbroken lines from beaks of pelecypods, apex of gastropods or mucro of chitons.

radial canals: in coelenterate medusae, tubes of gastrovascular system passing from centrally located stomach to periphery of the disc.

Radiata: invertebrates that are radially or circularly symmetrical about central axis, e.g., echinoderms, coelenterates and ctenophores.

radiated noise: underwater sound energy emitted by ships, submarines and torpedoes.

radio-facsimile recorder: instrument used to printout still pictures transmitted over radio link; commonly used for recording weather maps.

radioisotope: radioactive isotope of an element that is normally nonradioactive. It is created artificially.

radioisotopic oceanography: that oceanographic discipline dealing with measurement and distributional analysis of oceanborne radioisotopes.

Radiolaria [zooplankton]: rhizopods with rather stiff radiating pseudopodia and with cytoplasm of body composed of central mass (enclosed in perforated capsule) and more peripheral extracapsular layer. Skeleton formed of silica, which may be merely radiating spicules but which may be a complicated latticework, is usually present. Often considered as separate group, *Acantharia* are distinguished from other radiolarians mainly by having spicules of strontium sulphate. There is no perforated membrane between central and peripheral cytoplasm. Radiolarians thrive in colder seas and skeletons often form siliceous ooze on sea bed. Typical radiolarian consists of spherical or compressed body supported by shell of glass silica that may contain several netlike layers and is commonly studded with spines. Another porous capsule lies in jellyfish flesh, or proto-plasm, and divides into 2 regions: outer one sends out raylike pseudopods and digests food and inner one contains one or more nuclei and carries on reproduction.

radiolarian ooze: deposits of siliceous sediments distinguished by large proportions of minute opa-line silica shells (tests) or radiolarians. Water depths between about 13,000 and 25,000 ft. are most favorable for preservation of radiolarian tests. Siliceous deep-sea ooze dominated by deli-cate and complex hard parts of minute marine protozoa called *Radiolaria*.

radiolarite: consists of opaline skeletons of *Radio-laria*, usually spherical or elongated, with lattice-work structures, spines and other ornamenta-tions. Other constituents are diatom shells, sponges, spicules, detrital clay, quartz, feldspar, augite, hornblende and magnetite, some calcite and fragments of pumice and other volcanic rocks.

radiole: 1) semicircular, feathered gill that pro-trudes from tube in which annelid worms, such as *Myxicola* live. 2) spines of sea urchins. One of crown of pinnate tentacles in certain poly-chaetes.

radiosonde: large, unmanned sounding instrument, towed by balloon equipped with elements for determining temperature, pressure and relative humidity. It automatically transmits measure-ment by radio.

radula: 1) movable chitinous band found in nearly all molluscs except bivalves. Radula's many small, sharp teeth are used to scrape off particles of food. 2) in *Mollusca*, strip of horny material bearing teeth like those of a file. It can be pro-truded out through mouth from its position in floor of digestive canal.

radux: long-distance, low-frequency, navigational system which provides hyperbolic lines of posi-tion. It is continuous wave, phase-comparison type.

raffled ice: pressure ice in which the ice floe over-rides another.

rafting: transporting of sediment, rocks, silt and other material or matter of land origin out to sea by ice, logs, etc., with subsequent deposition of rafted matter when carrying matter disintegrates.

rail [ships]: upper edge of bulwarks.

raise: 1) to give rise to; originate; or start; as, *this breeze will raise a choppy sea.* 2) to cause to rise; to lift; or elevate; as, *salvors were sent to raise the wreck; anchor was raised at dawn;* and, as in the order *"Raise tacks and sheets!"*, preparatory to coming about or wearing ship. 3) to cause the land or other object to appear above the horizon by approaching it; as, *we shall soon raise Boston Light.* 4) to lift or cause to be lifted, in the sense

of cessation; as, *a northwest wind will raise this fog; blockade of the port was raised at noon.* 5) to rig or prepare a lifting device, tackle, etc.; as, *to raise a purchase;* to *raise a boom.*

rake [ships]: 1) to incline from perpendicular or horizontal, as masts of ship. 2) angle of mast. 3) forward pitch of stem; backward slope of stern.

rakit: "Malacca catamaran." Crude, primitive raft used in shallow waters of Malay Peninsula. Aver-age size about 40 ft. long.

ram: underwater ice projection from iceberg or hummock ice floe. Its formation is usually due to more intensive melting of unsubmerged part of floe.

ramp: accumulation of snow that forms an in-clined plane between land or land ice elements and sea ice or shelf ice.

ram schooner: schooner carrying no topmasts, but tall pole masts.

ram's-head boat: large "chebacco boat." Charac-terized by high stem, generally painted red, around which mooring hawser was put.

ramus: branch; in *Crustacea*, one of branches of biramus appendage.

range beacon: one of a pair of beacons which pro-vide line of position to ships entering channel. If ship keeps both in straight line with bow, there will be no problem maintaining course through channel.

range of tide: vertical distance between consecu-tive high- and low-water levels at a place.

range-positioning buoy: floating buoy used for navigational fixes. Some range-positioning buoys send out radio signals that can be detected with radio direction finders.

ranges [ships]: to lay out anchor chain evenly in preparation for running or painting. Also, range consists of 2 lights or beacons affording a bearing to be used in piloting.

Rangoon lighter: cargo vessel of India with sharp-sterned hull, having high freeboard and built en-tirely of teak. Rig consists of square-headed lug-sail on foremast, stepped well forward, and small-er leg-of-mutton mizzen. No shrouds are used and sheets are single lines with no purchase.

raphe: longitudinal slit in side of pennate diatoms.

raptorial: pertaining to structures such as claws or pinchers used to seize prey or enemies. Term is also used to describe organisms that actively seize their prey, as raptorial birds.

Ras-Al-Hague: *a Ophiuchi*, brightest star (magni-tude 2.14) in the group named by the ancients *Ophiuchus* (Gr. = serpent-holder), located in 12° 35′ N. declination and 17 hrs. 32½ min. right ascension. A line from this star to *Spica* forms the hypotenuse of an isosceles triangle having its right-angled apex at the ruddy *Antares*. It also lies at the western corner of a nearly isosceles triangle having its apex in *Vega*, with *Altair* at eastern angle.

rate: 1) quantity or amount measured or estimated in a given unit of time; as *loading proceeded at rate of 100 tons per hour.* 2) class or order to which war vessel belongs, according to size, type, armament, etc., as, *first rate, second rate,* etc. Formerly found only in descriptive term, *first-rate warship,* meaning a *ship of the line.* Class of a merchant vessel as an insurance risk, considered according to standards required in structural strength and equipment by *classification* society concerned; as, *an A1-at-Lloyd's rate was given the barque.* 3) to fix relative class, position, rank, etc., of a vessel or a seaman; as, *ship is rated 100A1 in A.B.S.; our stowaway was rated as ordinary seaman.* 4) to merit or deserve, as by reason of rank or grade; as, *this officer rates a single-berth cabin.* 5) to determine number of seconds a chronometer gains or loses per day; as, to *rate* the time-piece by radio signals. To arrange for carriage of goods via a certain route or vessel; as, *a shipment was rated to London by the Cunard Line.*

Rathkea octopunctata [phylum *Coelenterata*]: medusa of minute hydroid of same generic name which has been identified so far only from specimens reared in the lab; i.e., it has not been found occurring in nature. It reproduces by asexual budding from wall of manubrium which has a mouth bounded by 4 lips bearing clusters of nematocysts. There are 8 groups of marginal tentacles with no ocelli at bases. There are 4 radial canals and the gonads completely surround stomach. Number of marginal tentacles increases with age until there are 5 in preradial positions and 3 in each interradial position. Medusa reaches height of 4 mm.

rattee [ships]: triangular sail hung from truck and bent to yardarms of highest yard.

ray: marine elasmobranch member of fish order *Rajiformes.* Ray has flat body with mouth and gills on lower surface and eyes on upper; large pectoral on side fins; usually long slender tail that may have poisonous spines. Like other elasmobranchs, rays have skeletons made of cartilage.

ray-fins [teleosts]: most recent of all bony fishes, latest products of evolutionary changes made during 150,000,000 years. Teleosts appeared in early Jurassic seas and varied widely during Cretaceous times. They have fully ossified internal skeletons in which long established structures are often supplemented by variety of new spines and bones. Tail is homocercal, i.e., backbone stops short, letting fin-rays grow out from end. Scales are thin, with no trace of ganoid layer. They normally overlap like shingles.

Rayleigh wave: type of surface-seismic wave in which oscillation is partly in direction of propagation and partly vertical; particle motion is retrograde elliptical.

ray pattern: graphic presentation of paths of sound rays in relation to depth and range.

ray theory: method for determining part of transmitted underwater sound based on Snell's law.

razee: in American Navy, "razee" was very heavy frigate which had been cut down from ship-of-the-line. The *Independence* was a "razee" and was 188 ft. long.

reach: arm of sea extending into land.

reach boat: clinker-built, open-keel boat employed in fisheries off coast of Maine. It is from 14 to 22 ft. long with curved stem, straight sternpost and both ends sharp; cat-rigged with single spritsail and one pair of oars.

reaching jib [ships]: large, triangular head sail of light material used on yachts and "fishermen" in light weather, when wind is just forward of abeam.

recall: 1) any prearranged signal, as by flag, flashlight, or whistle, denoting that boat addressed is ordered to return to ship. 2) in yacht racing, a flag showing the number of one of the competitors who must return to the starting line because of having sailed past it before starting signal was given. It usually is accompanied by a sound signal, as from a horn or a gun. 3) to call back from a distance, as a vessel on a cruise or voyage.

receptaculitids: commonly called "sunflower corals." Their fossils generally are shaped like saucers or bowls, but these contain only lower portion of creatures that actually resembled beets or broad turnips turned upside down. Most fossils also are hardened fittings or external molds and so are solid where creatures were soft and have pits in place of original skeleton.

recession: continuous landward movement of shoreline. Net landward movement of shoreline over specified time.

recessional moraine: 1) ridgelike accumulation of drift deposited by glacier along outer margin, back from position of its maximum advance. 2) marginal glacial deposits marking halt of ice front during its retreat.

reckoning: calculated or estimated position of a vessel; especially, that arrived at according to course and distance made good from a reliable *fix,* as that obtained from celestial observations or from bearings of shore objects.

recompression [diving]: increasing ambient pressure on diver for primary purpose of medical treatment.

reconstructed glacier: ice blocks that have cascaded or fallen from a hanging valley and reunited to form glacier at base of plunge.

recurved [*Mollusca*]: hooked or bent, as siphonal canal in gastropods, which may be turned backward far enough so that it cannot be seen when shell is held with aperture at right.

recurved spit: shoal developed when end of spit is turned toward shore by current deflection or by opposing action of 2 or more currents.

red alga: one of division or phylum (*Rhodophyta*) of reddish, filamentous, membranous, encrusting or complexly branched plants in which color is imparted by predominance of r-phycoerythrin over chlorophylls and other pigments. Some notable members of group are sources of agar-agar, such as *Gelidium*, *Gracilaria* and *Eucheuma*, Irish moss, *Chondrus* and encrusting calcareous *Lithothamnion* of coral reefs. Red algae are worldwide in distribution, being more abundant in temperate waters and ranging to greater depths than other algae.

redbreast [*Lepomis auritus*]: panfish with red or orange breast and no bright-colored margin on opercular spot. Tail emarginate; pectoral fin short and rounded; opercular spot uniformly dark; scales on breast much smaller than those on sides. Body ovate, moderately compressed; cheek scales in about 6 rows; palatine teeth present. Color olive to brownish-gray above, paler below; breast region from bright orange to red. Adult size up to 8 in.

red eyelet silk [*Rhodymenia pertusa*]: usually found near or below low-tide mark, but may also be dredged from depths of 30 to 50 ft. A subarctic, sublittoral species, it is a striking seaweed with large, single, flat, bright red thallus dotted with holes of more or less uniform size which suggests common name, red eyelet silk. Short stipe arises from minute, disclike holdfast. Blade when fully grown may be 12 to 20 in. long and 5 to 10 in. wide. Usually, markings on blade are the perforations. Blade is as thin as tissue paper.

redfin [*Notropis lutrensis lutrensis*]: this minnow is deep-bodied and has small eye. Fins are distinctly reddish; body is olivacous above with greenish-gray and silver side; spring males are brightly colored with orange and red on body and head. Teeth usually number 4—4; scales are 6, 34—37, 3—4; dorsal fin has 8 rays, anal fin usually 9. Redfin is similar to *Notropis spilopterus* but does not have black spot on dorsal fin.

red fringe [*Porphyra naiadum*]: on sandy beaches, red fringe hangs from edges of eelgrass and other seed-bearing marine plants like a delicate fringe. Fringe is purplish-red to deep purple, while blades of host eelgrass are dark green. Three to 5 blades of each alga are about ½ to 1 in. long and ½ in. wide at upper end, narrowing at base until they become stipelike. Because red fringe has only one layer of cells, it is fragile as thinnest tissue paper.

red frog crab [*Ranina ranina*]: this astonishing crab is only known species in this genus. Its carapace is broad in front, narrower toward rear, convex in contour and armed with spines along front margin. Back is almost completely covered by large number of small, low, rounded spines. Abdomen is small and is not hidden beneath carapace. Chelipeds, which are flattened vertically and open medially, are large and bear 7 or 8 teeth. Other legs are flattened and pointed for movement through sand. Entire body and legs are adapted for burrowing backwards in sand. This crab is red above and below with large white areas on lower side. It inhabits sandy bottoms on outer side of reef from depths of about 30 ft. to those in excess of 150 ft.

redhorse, black tail [*Moxostoma poecilurum*]: fish with suckerlike mouth and no spiny dorsal fin. Jaws toothless; 12 rays in dorsal fin; lateral line usually incomplete; 42—44 scales along lateral line. Head moderate; mouth subinferior, lips full and fleshy; body elongate, moderately compressed, somewhat elevated anteriorly. Ground color muddy brown; all fins except caudal reddish; caudal fin with upper lobe reddish and lower lobe black with distinct white margin along lower side.

redhorse, golden [*Moxostoma erythrurum*]: this species is similar to *M. rubregues* but smaller. Halves of lower lip meet at sharp angle. Eye is more than 1/4th the length of the head in young, and more than 1/7th the length of the head, in adults. Scales number 38—44.

redhorse, greater [*Moxostoma rubregues*]: large fish reaching length of over 2 ft. In general shape it is similar to *M. anisurum* but is usually not as deep. Least depth of caudal peduncle is more than 2/3rds its length. Halves of lower lip meet at sharp angle; mouth is rather large. Head is longer than in *M. aureolum* and squarish when seen from side, top or front. In adults head is contained 3.7 to 4.4 times the length. Scales have dark spots or crescents on scale bases. Caudal fin is bright red; in adults tip of dorsal fin is whitish near margin.

redhorse, northern [*Moxostoma aureolum*]: very much like *M. anisurum*, but tail as well as lower fins is always red. Caudal lobes are subequal; dorsal fin is rather low with 12—14 developed rays. Mouth is small; halves of lower lip meet in straight line in adults, at obtuse angle in young. Head is bluntly subconical and short. Scales in lateral line number about 45. It attains length of 2 ft. with weight of 8 or 10 lbs.

redhorse, northern black [*Moxostoma duquesnei duquesnei*]: rather large fish reaching length of over 2 ft. In general form it resembles other species of *Moxostoma*. Eye is usually small, less than 2/5ths the snout in adults; mouth is large; scales number 42—49 but typically 44—47. Rays of pelvic fin usually number 10.

redhorse, silver [*Moxostoma anisurum*]: silver redhorse is pale in color; caudal fin is smokey gray with upper lobe narrower and longer than lower; lower fins are red in spawning season. It is distinguished by large dorsal fin, which has 14 to 17 developed rays. Eye is large, more than 1/7th the length of head in adults. Scales number 38—44, usually 40—42. Halves of lower lip meet at rather sharp angle. Fish reaches length of 2 ft.

redingskoite: sailing lifeboat used on west coast of Norway. It was carvel built, with extremely heavy hull and gear; yawl- or ketch-rigged.

red jabot laver [*Porphyra lanceolota*]: beautiful seaweed. As thin, ruffled, spirally twisted red blades undulate with quietly moving waters on sandy beach, it looks like a frilly jabot such as women used to wear on their blouses. May be 3 to 9 ft. long and 6 to 12 in. wide. There is only one layer of cells in red jabot which is gelatinous and elastic with satiny sheen. Sheen and red color are retained when plant is dry. Red jabot has beautiful iridescence, shades of green, blue and purple, as sun plays upon it.

red laver [*Porphyra perforata*]: common everywhere between 3 to 5- and 2-ft. tide levels. When floating on water red laver is beautiful, the single flattened blades with ruffled margins swaying on restless waters. When out of water, it is dull and slimy. When plant is young, it is bright red, blade narrow and tapering with deeply ruffled margins; when older it becomes grayish-purple, blades broad, deeply slashed and torn. Both shape and size vary greatly depending upon climatic conditions.

red mud: reddish-brown terrigenous, deep-sea mud containing up to 25% calcium carbonate which accumulates on sea floor near deserts and off mouth of large rivers.

red porcelain crab [*Petrolisthes coccineus*]: this crab has flattened body and large flattened chelipeds. Of 4 pairs of walking legs, first 3 pairs are of normal size, while last pair is small and slender and located in upper surface of body at back of carapace. Carapace is somewhat circular in outline, bluntly pointed at front and marked by short transverse ridges. Legs have spines on anterior margins, but no hairs. Body is red and about ½ in. wide. This species inhabits rocks and old coral heads in shallow water.

red rock crust: appears as stony encrustation on rocks or shells between 0.5- and 1.5-ft. tide levels. Rock crust resembles thick blotch of red paint spilled on a rock. It usually has roughly circular shape 1 to 4 in. in diameter, either smooth, covered with small knoblike outgrowths or with raised plates extending across surface. Outgrowths may be 1/16 to 1/8 in. high. Color varies from whitish-pink to deep purple. These seaweeds are perennial, sometimes living many years.

red sea fan [*Callophyllis edentata*]: found attached to rocks below mean low-tide levels. Uniform, clear, dark red blade is fan-shaped. Average size plant is 4 to 8 in. tall with maximum width of fan 5 to 6 in. For distance of about 1 inch, blade is narrow and undivided, then suddenly it divides 4 to 6 times.

red serving fork [*Sarcodiotheca furcata*]: most conspicuous feature is flat, single, bright red, forked blade. Rather narrow, cylindrical stipe, arising from small, disclike holdfast, gradually widens and flattens into the blade which begins to fork when 1 to 2 in. wide. Overall height of seaweed may be 7 to 8 in. with spread of 4 to 5 in. Texture of seaweed is firm and rubberlike.

red tide: red or reddish-brown discoloration of surface waters most frequently in coastal regions, caused by concentrations of certain microscopic organisms, particularly dinoflagellates. Toxins produced by dinoflagellates can cause mass kills of fishes and other marine animals. Airborne particles which are optic and respiratory irritants to humans and animals may be carried from red tide areas overland. Red tides may develop rapidly, apparently as a result of abrupt change in one or more environmental factors. In some regions at least, notably off west coast of Florida, onset of red tide appears to follow increased rainwater runoff from land.

reducers: organisms such as bacteria whose life activities result in mineralization of organic matter.

reduction: 1) act or process of converting a value to its equivalent in a different denomination; as, reduction of longitude in degrees of arc to longitude in time. 2) act of correcting a changing value to that corresponding to a given instant; as, reduction of declination, hour angle, etc., of a heavenly body to a certain *Universal* or *Greenwich Mean Time*. 3) application of a determined correction to a given quantity, for comparison with a standard value; as, reduction of soundings. 4) change of speed, as in a system of gears, in which a given wheel meshes in a larger and thus *reduces* velocity in the latter; thus, reduction being usually expressed as a ratio of circumferences of such wheels, if one wheel is five times that of the other in circumference, reduction is said to be 5 to 1, or speed varies inversely as circumference of meshing gears.

red wing [*Ptilota filicina*]: found between mean-low and 1.5-ft. tide levels. Often it is epiphytic on other algae, especially on coralline algae. Probably the strong central axis, 4 to 10 in. long with closely set alternate branches which become 2 to 3 in. long, is the most conspicuous feature of this algae. Its branches are compressed, harsh, brittle and covered with a cortex. Leaflets are sickle-shaped with both edges toothed like a saw, teeth turning toward apex. This seaweed is deep, bright red.

reef: 1) to reduce sail by folding part of it and tying reefing points to secure it along a boom or rolling up part of it around a boom. 2) chain or range of rocks or coral, at or near surface of water, in depths less than 6 fathoms. 3) thick lenticular limestone mass surrounded by distinctly different sedimentary formations. 4) rounded or ridgelike elevations of sea bottom reaching close to sea level; also rock mass composing a reef.

reef atoll: ring-shaped coral reef enclosing body of water.

reef band: strong strip of canvas extending across sail with eyelet holes at regular intervals for reef points which secure sail when reefed.

reef complex: solid reef core and all contiguous detrital limestone and coral and genetically related, sedimentary rocks.

reef flat: flat expanse of dead reef rock which is partly or entirely dry at low tide. Shallow pools, potholes, gullies and patches of coral debris and sand are features of reef flat.

reef front: upper seaward face of reef, extending above dwindle point of abundant living coral and coralline algae to reef edge. Zone commonly includes shelf bench or terrace that slopes to 8 to 15 fathoms as well as living wave-breaking face of reef.

reefing point [ships]: when sail is reefed, short pieces of rope called reefing points attached to band of canvas across sail may be used to secure sail.

reef knot: square knot used in making fast reef points.

reef patch: term for all coral growths that have grown up independently in lagoons of barriers and atolls. They vary in extent from expanses measuring several kilometers across to coral pillars or even mushroom-shaped growths consisting of single large colony. Smaller representatives are called coral knolls or coral heads.

reef tackle patch [ships]: reinforcing piece of canvas sewed about or upon leech of sails.

reef talus: massive, inclined beds of debris derived principally from reef and deposited along seaward margin of living reef.

reeve: to pass end of rope or chain through opening.

reference level: in underwater sound, standard to which other sound levels can be related. Two reference levels commonly used are 1 dyne per square centimeter and 0.0002 dyne per square centimeter.

reference station: place where tide or tidal current constants have been determined from observations and which is used as standard for observations at subordinate station. It is also a place for which independent daily predictions are given in tide or tidal current tables.

reflectance: ratio of light given off by object to amount of light striking object, expressed as percentage.

reflectance function: ratio of upwelling irradiance at same depth.

reflected wave: wave that is returned seaward when a wave impinges upon very steep beach, barrier or other reflecting surface.

reflection profiler: electroacoustic device that produces continuous graphic profile of geologic reflections beneath ocean bottom by transmission of acoustic signals and reception of their echoes.

refraction: 1) in a homogeneous medium, sound waves travel in a straight line. Sound waves are bent if velocity of propagation is not the same at all points. Thus, when sound wave passes obliquely from medium of one velocity to medium of another velocity, sound will be bent toward medium of lower velocity. This phenomenon is called refraction. 2) process in which direction of energy propagation is changed as result of change in density within propagation medium, or as energy passes through interface representing density discontinuity between 2 media.

refraction coefficient: in wave hydrodynamics, square root of ratio of spacing between adjacent orthogonals in deep water to that at selected point in shallow water. When multiplied by shoaling coefficient or ratio of refracted wave height at any point to deep-water wave height. Also square root of energy coefficient.

refraction diagram: drawing showing positions of wave crests and/or orthogonals in given area for specific deep-water wave period and direction.

refraction loss: that part of transmission loss due to refraction resulting from nonuniformity of medium.

refraction of water waves: process by which direction of wave moving in shallow water at angle to contours is changed. That part of wave advancing in shallower water moves more slowly than other part still advancing in deeper water, causing wave crest to bend toward alignment with underwater contours.

register: 1) a written record or account; especially, an official book containing particulars of persons, property, transactions, ships, etc.; as, *register of seamen; Lloyd's Register.* 2) a document serving as evidence of nationality and ownership of a vessel, also termed *certificate of registry,* issued by Collector of Customs at vessel's hailing port to her owners, who usually are required by law to be bona fide citizens of country concerned, especially so in U.S.A. Register is issued in accordance with sworn particulars presented by builders and owners of ship concerned, which, generally, must have been built or rebuilt under certain conditions in, seized by, or forfeited to the government of, country in question; contains vessel's name, origin, date built, owner's name, port of registry, type, tonnage, power, principal dimensions, and other identifying information. In U.S., vessel is then said to be *documented.* The master's name must be endorsed on the register before the Customs officer concerned or by a Consul at a foreign port. The document usually must be produced by ship's master in entering at customs at any port during course of a foreign voyage and in any transaction in which the fact of authorized title to ownership of vessel is required. In U.S., registration or documentation is denoted by three terms, *viz.,* vessels in foreign trade are *registered;* those in coastwise or inland trade are *enrolled;* those of smaller tonnage engaged in coastwise trade, whale fishery, cod fishery, etc., and yachts under certain conditions are *licensed.* A document combining the last two registration forms, term *Certificate of License and Enrollment* may be granted certain domestic vessels. (*Cf. Documentation of Vessels* in *Navigation Laws of the United States,* issued by U.S. Government Printing Office, Washington, D.C.)

registered: officially certified and recorded, as certain data concerning a vessel appearing in the *certificate of registry* or the *tonnage certificate.*

regressive: applied to bodies of water and sediments deposited therein during withdrawal of water and/or emergence of land.

regressive reef: one of series of reefs or bioherms close to and generally parallel to shore as result of retreating sea or rising landmass.

regular reflection factor: ratio which luminous flux regularly transmitted through surface bears to total luminous flux falling on surface.

rejuvenated stream: one which has become more active in erosion because of uplift in land.

relative current: current which is function of dynamic slope of isobaric surface and which is determined from assumed layer of no motion. Current flows along contours of dynamic topography; surface slopes upward to right of current in Northern Hemisphere and to left in Southern Hemisphere.

relative current speed: speed determined by spacing of dynamic contours drawn at equal intervals of dynamic height anomaly; speed is inversely proportional to distance between contours.

relative visibility factor: ratio of parent brightness of monochromatic source to that of source of wavelength, 550 angstroms having same energy.

relief: vertical distance between top and bottom of some topographic features. Relief of oceanographic topography is usually expressed in meters or fathoms.

remetalling: act of renewing the copper sheathing on bottom planking of a vessel.

remora: fishes in this family have typical streamlined bodies of ordinary fish. Although capable of swimming by themselves, they prefer to travel attached to body of larger fish. This is accomplished by unique sucker disk considered to be modified dorsal fin and located on top of head. It consists of series of cross partitions that can open and shut like slats of a shutter. When remora comes in contact with larger fish, commonly a shark or swordfish, shutter opens and creates a vacuum that holds it fast to its carrier. Remora are not parasites and do not harm obliging carriers. They feed on fragments of food discarded or overlooked by larger predator.

remora, Atlantic: also known as shark sucker, it is a slaty brown or gray fish with conspicuous broad, dark stripe and anal fin and small pectoral and ventral fins. It reaches length of 3 ft., yet weighs less than 2 lbs.

remose [*Bryozoa*]: colony form consisting of erect, round or moderately flattened branches.

render: 1) to ease or lighten up a line through a block, sheave, deadeye, thimble, etc.; to assist in slacking a rope, chain, etc., through or around an aperture or object; as, to render the fall through a set of blocks; to render turns around the capstan. 2) in older usage, to coil or flake down a line for clear running, as a halyard or a brace. A line is said to render when passing through a block, fairlead, etc., without obstruction; or, when under stress, is forced to pay out.

Rennell's Current: relatively strong (1.0 to 1.5 knots) nonpermanent current that sets northward across western approaches to English Channel. It appears to be independent of North Atlantic Drift or local winds and occurs most frequently during winter.

repeater: frigate stationed behind each of the van, center, and rear naval squadrons when in action. Its purpose was to remain out of the smoke where it could be clearly seen and repeat signals from Admiral's flagship.

reptant [*Bryozoa*]: colony form consisting of largely separate zooecial tubes which lies attached to substrata.

Reptilia [class]: phylum *Chordata.* Pennsylvanian to Recent. Well developed limbs and limb girdles; vertebrae bony and well articulated; gill slits absent in adult; eggs laid on land with protective shell and membranes. Marine, freshwater, terrestrial and aerial; predators and herbivores.

resilifer [*Mollusca*]: socketlike structure (fossette

or chondrophore, depending upon shape) that supports internal ligament or cartilage in certain bivalves.

resilium [*Mollusca*]: ligamental portion of bivalve hinge; it may be made up of 2 parts, ligament proper (external) and cartilage (internal).

resonance: occurs when natural period of oscillation of water body, which depends on its length and depth, approximates to the period of one of tide-producing forces.

resonance, tidal: resonance occurs when natural period of oscillation of body of water, which depends on its depth and length, approximates period of tide forces. Mediterranean, e.g., has no tidal resonance, since tidal range rarely exceeds 2 ft.

respiration: oxidation-reduction process by which chemically bound energy in food is transformed to other kinds of energy upon which certain processes in all living cells are dependent. Measurement of carbon dioxide as product of respiratory activity in marine phytoplankton is essential in determining net productivity.

resultant current: vectorial average of all current observations for specified area, usually for specified period of time.

resurgence: continued rising and falling of bay or semienclosed water body many hours after passage of severe storm.

retained magnetism: transient magnetism received by induction from earth's magnetic field and temporarily retained in an iron or steel vessel while steering for some days in about one direction. Also, *retentive magnetism*.

retardation: amount of time by which corresponding tidal phases grow later day by day (average approximately 50 minutes).

reticulated bars: bars with crisscross pattern, with both sets diagonal to shoreline.

reticulopod: pseudopodia forming anastomosing network, as in *Foraminifera*.

reticulum: a network.

retina: membrane at rear of eye that receives visual image and transmits it to brain via optic nerve.

retrograde: moving in a backward direction. Astronomically, appearing to move from east to west; contrary to general planetary motion, whether apparent or real; decreasing in right ascension or celestial longitude; as, *retrograde motion*. Rotating in a reverse direction. To go, or appear to go, backward; as a planet in decreasing its right ascension, when it is said to be in *retrogradation*.

reverberation: in sonar, result of large number of very weak echoes arising from small bodies (air bubbles), suspended solid matter, etc., in soundwave propagation path. These tiny bodies scatter part of sound energy as it passes. Some of scat-

tered sound energy will return to listening apparatus; in turn it is heard as a reverberation.

reversed tide: gravitational tide, which is completely out of phase with apparent motions of principal attracting body; last height is directly under tide producing body on opposite sides of earth.

reverse frame [ships]: angle bar placed with its heel against another angle to give other angle additional strength. Flanges of deck stiffeners always face outboard.

reversing current: tidal current that flows alternately in approximately opposite directions, with period of slack water at each reversal of direction. Reversing currents usually occur in rivers and straits where flow is restricted. When flow is toward shore, current is flooding; when in opposite direction, it is ebbing.

reversing thermometer: mercury-in-glass thermometer that records temperature upon being inverted and thereafter retains its reading until returned to first position.

revolver: in the procedure of finding a vessel's position by two horizontal angles measured between a central charted object and two others at either side of such object, or by what is called the *three-point problem*, the indeterminate condition, in which vessel is found to occupy a place afloat on any part of the circle passing through all three charted objects, is called a *revolver*. Source of the term probably lies in the fact that the *station pointer* may be "revolved" through the seaward arc of circle referred to, while its arms remain in coincidence with the selected objects. (A revolver occurs only when middle object lies on the landward side of a line joining the other two.)

rhabdolith: minute calcareous bodies contained in deep-sea ooze, classed as protozoans by some investigators and as algae by others.

rheology: study of elasticity, viscosity and plasticity; science of flow matter.

rheotactic: pertaining to sense organs that can detect water currents.

Rhizocephala: order of crustaceans. Mantle present but shell lacking; no appendages or digestive system; mostly parasitic on decapod crustaceans.

rhizoid: unicellular or uniseriate rootlike filament serving for attachment of algae.

rhizome: rootlike filament that creeps just below surface of bottom, bearing at nodes erect stems or leaves and one or more roots.

rhobdosome [*Graptolithina*]: entire graptolite colony.

rhodamine B dye: synthetic red or pink dye sometimes used as tracer in studies of flow of water, turbulence, pollution, etc., in rivers, estuaries and oceans.

rhopaloneme: type of nematocyst found only in *Siphonophora*.

rhumb line: curve which crosses all meridians at constant angle.

Rhynchonelloidea: shell fibrous, impunctate, except for *Rhynchoporacea* which are punctate. Pedicle functional; deltidial plates more or less embracing foramen, which is small, often elliptical and does not encroach on umbo. Typical form is short and stout with short curved hinge line, usually with fold on dorsal valve and sinus on ventral.

rhyolite [rock]: fine-grained volcanic rock with a granite mineral assemblage sometimes characterized by flow lines that show speed and viscosity of lava flow.

ria: any broad river opening into ocean. Not necessarily a submerged river mouth or open valley in mountainous coast.

ria coast: coast having drowned river valleys characterized by long fiordlike bays having few branches. Bays differ from fiords in origin and are shorter, shallower and more funnel-shaped, broader and deeper seaward.

ria shoreline: shoreline formed by partial submergence of land mass dissected by numerous river valleys.

ribband [ships]: longitudinal strip of timber following curvature of vessel and bolted to its ribs to hold them in position and give stability to skeleton while building.

rice boat: distinctive type of craft used for carrying rice on Irrawadi and other Burmese rivers. Hull is canoe-shaped, usually with clipper bow and rounded up ends, shallow draft, heel and forefront often out of water. Sail and topsails are braided to mast when furled and hauled out along yard when set.

rider frame [ships]: any frame riveted or welded on another frame for purpose of stiffening it.

rider plates [ships]: bed plates set on top of center keelson, if fitted for pillars to rest on.

ridge: long, narrow elevation of sea floor with steep sides and irregular topography.

ridged ice: pressure ice having readily observed surface roughness in the form of ridge or many ridges.

ridging: process that leads to formation of ridged ice.

riding light [ships]: anchor light. A 32-point white light shown at anchor after dark.

rig [ships]: 1) arrangement of sails and masts. 2) to set up rigging.

Rigel: brightest star of the *Orion* group; has a magnitude of 0.34; declination 8¼° S.; right ascension 5 hrs. 12 min.

rigger: one whose occupation is to prepare, fit, and install the various pieces of rigging in a vessel; particularly, the fitting and setting up of stays, shrouds, backstays, and other *standing rigging* units; a *ship-rigger*. In a shipyard, an employee who oversees the hoisting into place of heavy structural parts or units, such as stern frame, stempost, rudder, masts and booms, large ventilator cowls, machinery, boilers, etc. The term in Great Britain is applied to one of a number of men engaged in shifting vessels about a harbor at such times as a crew is not attached to the vessel thus handled.

rigging [ships]: collective term for various lines and stays used in supporting and operating masts and booms. Standing rigging is not readily removable. Running rigging can be adjusted while sailing.

right [ships]: to come back to normal position, as "the ship righted herself." To set straight, as to "right the helm"; to put helm amidships or in line with keel.

right gill [*Gastropoda*]: in all recent snails right gill is rotated to left anterior position. In dextral individuals it is the larger gill; in sinistral, the smaller.

righting: act of returning or being restored to a natural or normal position; specifically, the act of returning, or return, by whatever means, of a heeled or listing vessel to her normal upright position.

right longitudinal nerve cord [*Gastropoda*]: torsion of gastropod viscera loops right cord to left side of body.

right whale: whalebone whale without teeth or dorsal fin.

rigid zone: upper, faster moving layer of brittle ice in structure of glacier.

Rigil Kentaurus: *a Centauri*, or brightest star in the *Centaurus* group. Easily recognized as the brighter of a conspicuous couple 4½° apart called the *pointers*, because in line with about the middle of near-by *Crux*, the *Southern Cross*, to the westward. It is a binary star, or one of a pair revolving about a common center of gravity and appearing as a single star to the unaided eye. Astronomers now list this luminary's place as that of a^2 *Centauri*, which is somewhat brighter than his close-sticking brother a^1.

rill mark: small groove, furrow or channel made in mud or sand on a beach by tiny streams following outflowing tide.

rime: white, icy coating formed on grass, leaves, etc., from atmospheric moisture; hoarfrost.

ringbolt [ships]: metal bolt with eye to which is fitted a ring.

ringtail [ships]: addition to after side of "spanker." Used extensively on clipper ship. When the "spanker" was a trysail, the ringtail or driver was a triangular sail placed above the former.

rip: turbulent water produced by conflicting tides of current; generally, vertical oscillation.

rip current: 1) return flow of water piled up on shore by incoming waves and wind; strong narrow surface current flowing away from shore. Rip current consists of 3 parts-feeder current flowing parallel to shore inside breakers; neck where feeder currents converge and flow through breakers in narrow band or "rip"; and head where current widens and slackens outside breaker line. 2) narrow seaward-moving water currents which return to deep water the water carried landward by waves. Rip currents are almost universally associated with larger breakers on exposed coast.

ripple: ruffling of surface of water; little curling wave or undulation.

ripple marks: undulating surface features of various shapes produced in unconsolidated sediments by wave or current action. Compound ripples are characterized by systematically offset crests and are produced by simultaneous interference of wave oscillation with current action. Metaripples are asymmetrical sand ripples. As size increases, ripples grade into sand waves, sand ridges, sand dunes and migratory sandbanks or shoals.

riprap: foundation or support made by simply piling stones together.

rips: turbulent agitation of water generally caused by intersection of currents and wind; in nearshore regions, rips may also be caused by currents flowing swiftly over irregular bottom.

rise: long, broad elevation that rises gently and generally smoothly from sea floor.

rise of the tide: height of tide measured above chart datum.

risers: in a ladder, vertical parts, sides being the stringers and horizontal parts of treads.

rising: increasing in elevation; ascending; increasing in force; as, a *rising sea bottom; a rising gale.* Appearing above the horizon; *the rising land was still far off.* A stringer or stout batten secured to the frames, in the line of sheer of a boat, as a support for ends of the thwarts and, also, in larger craft, as an additional stiffener for upper sides of the boat. Any fore-and-aft timber serving as a support for beams of a deck; also, *rising piece.*

rising floors [ships]: floor frames which rise fore and aft above level of midship floors.

rising tide: portion of tide cycle between low water and following high water.

Rissoidae: shell small and spiral; aperture rounded with slightly expanded lip; eyes at base of tentacles. Found in marine or brackish water.

river: a natural stream, larger than a brook, creek, or rivulet, flowing into a lake, sea, or other stream. When flowing into another river, such stream is called an *affluent, branch,* or *tributary;* as, *the Missouri is a tributary of the Mississippi River.* Rivers of the world having greatest volume of flow in the order noted are: *Amazon* of Brazil, *Congo* of W. Africa, *La Plata* of Uruguay and Argentine,—fed by *Paraná* and *Uruguay Rivers,* and *Mississippi* of the U.S.; a few of greatest length in statute miles are: *Nile,* 3930; *Amazon,* 4050; *Yangtze Kiang,* 3500; *Congo,* 2700; *Amur,* 2700; *Hwang Ho (Yellow River),* 2700; *Mekong,* 2600; *Lena,* 2650; *Ob,* 2500; *Paraná,* 2450; *Volga,* 2300.

roach [ships]: curve cut into rear or bottom edge of sail.

roads: also roadstead; protected anchorage, usually offshore.

roadstead: place near shore where vessels may anchor; differing from harbor in not being sheltered.

robalo: a pike-like fish of West Indies and tropical America habitat. Upwards of three feet in length and having two large dorsal fins, is considered valuable as food; also called *snook.* A smaller species is known as *robalito.*

Robert's radio current meter: electromechanical current meter which measures current speed and direction. This meter can be suspended below an anchored buoy or ship which is equipped with radio transmitter that transmits current measurements to ship or shore-based monitor station.

rock borer: member of any one of several families, including *Mytilidae, Saxicavidae* and *Pholadidae,* of bivalves that live in cavities and bore in soft rock, concrete and other materials. Boring generally is accomplished by rotating the shell, which bears toothed or rasplike projections; chemical solution of rock may be a method used additionally by some.

rock crab, flat [*Percon planissimum*]: this little crab is very flat and measures a little more than 1 in. across carapace. It is green above and marked with a line down middle of back. Merus or thigh of walking legs is bordered in front by row of sharp spines. This common crab may be found in shallow water beneath rocks or hidden away in crevices.

rock crab, tuberculate [*Plagusia depressa tuberculata*]: carapace of this grapsoid crab is nearly circular in outline and covered with smooth, low rounded tubercles; it also bears spines along margin lateral to eyes. Pinchers are small, usually unequal in size and carried in front of body. Merus or thigh of each walking leg is flattened and bears a spine at forward outer edge. Carapace reaches a width of more than 2 in. This crab may usually be found inhabiting floating logs and timber.

rock crab, weak-shelled [*Grapus grapus tenuicrustatus*]: carapace is nearly circular in outline and contains no lobes on its margin between eyes. Each eye is protected at lateral edge by sharp spine which projects forward. Pinchers of first pair of legs are small, usually of different sizes and carried in front of body. Remaining legs are wide and flattened. Carapace reaches width 2¾ in. This crab lives on rock areas above waterline.

rock flour: finely ground rock particles, chiefly silt size, resulting from glacial abrasion; component of marine deposits off glacial stream mouths.

rock-forming minerals: minerals which occur as dominant constituents of igneous rocks; quartz, feldspars, micas, pyroxenes and olivine.

rock shell [*Francolin*]: this mollusc produces a shell which is firm and heavy in construction. Outside of shell is usually smooth, although it may exhibit fine striations in some specimens. It is variously colored with white, cream, yellow, brown and sometimes purple, and is further marked about center with irregular row of somewhat triangular area. It will reach a length of 2½ in. *Nassa francolinus*.

rockweed or popping wrack [*Fucus furcatus*]: this rockweed lies on the beach. It is a genus difficult to describe because of many variations. Rockweed is characterized by flattened, forked branches lying on one plane, more or less prominent midribs extending through entire length of alga, swelling at ends of branches, ability to remain for long time out of water without drying out and resistant to changes in temperature. Branches are rounded at ends, more or less sticky and have swollen bladders at ends. Swelling is caused by presence of mucilage.

rod: a slender batten or bar of wood or metal; a measuring strip or batten on which certain structural dimensions are indicated, as for use in ship construction. A connecting rod in an engine. A pole for a fishing line.

roll [ships]: sidewise motion of vessel caused by wind and wave.

roller: 1) indefinite term, sometimes considered to denote one of series of long crested, large waves which roll in upon a coast, as after a storm. 2) large breakers on exposed coasts formed by swell coming from great distance.

roncador: any of several fishes characterized by their croaking, drumming, or wheezing noises when taken from water, including the *croaker*, *drumfish*, *grunts*, and others of the American coasts.

room: extent or space; as, *sea room; swinging room*. Space enclosed by a bulkhead or partition; as, *radio room; state room*.

ropak: extreme formation of ridged ice; pinnacle or slab of heavy sea ice standing vertically on edge.

ropes [ships]: technically speaking there are but 3 ropes on a ship; footropes, manropes (handropes) and bucket-ropes. Remainder are halyards, stays, braces, lines, hawsers, lifts, etc.

rope yarn [ships]: yarn made usually from old ropes which sailors unlay.

rorqual: any baleen whale of family *Balaenopteridae*, group characterized by having triangular dorsal fin and series of parallel grooves running longitudinally in under surface of throat and chest region; e.g., blue whale, fin whale, sea whale, mink whale and humpback whale.

Rossel Current: seasoned current flowing westward and northward along both southern and northeastern coasts of New Guinea during May to September; southern part flows through Torres Strait and loses its identity in Arafura Sea and northern part curves northeastward to form Pacific Equatorial Countercurrent. Rossel Current is weak branch of South Equatorial Current. During Northern Hemisphere winter it is replaced by east flowing current from Indian Ocean.

rostral [reptile]: plate at tip of snout.

rostrate [*Mollusca*]: drawn out or produced into beaklike process.

rostrum: in *Crustacea*, forward prolongation of carapace beyond the head.

rotary current: tidal current that flows continually, changing direction during tidal cycle. Tendency to rotate is due to deflecting forces of earth's rotation. Unless modified by local conditions, current runs clockwise in Northern Hemisphere and counterclockwise in Southern Hemisphere. Speed of current usually varies throughout tidal cycle, with 2 maxima in opposite directions, and 2 minima with directions at approximately right angles from direction of maxima.

rotational and irrational motion: ideal nonviscous liquid must have irrational motion, as there is no internal friction between particles to make individual particles spin. Water has low viscosity, but nevertheless motion in it is probably irrational. One wave theory, however, demands rotational motion.

rotifer: member of *Rotifera*, group of very small aquatic animals which swim by cilia movements resembling a turning shell on front end of body.

rotten ice: ice that has become honeycombed during melting and is in advanced state of disintegration.

rough ice: expanse of ice having uneven surface caused by pressure ice formations or growlers frozen in place.

round of sights: observing series of angles between objects or observing series of bearings to objects relative to position of observer.

roving [ships]: twisted fibers of cloth used as filler.

rowlock [ships]: device on small boat's gunwale in or on which the oar rests and swings freely in rowing.

royal [ships]: square sail just above topgallant sail on square-rigged ship. Roach in foot is generally 2 ft. deep for main and fore royals and 2 ft. 6 in. on mizzen royal. Used only in light breeze.

rua: Siamese word for boat. Prefix on all Siamese boat names.

rua chalom: Gulf of Siam type name being applied to all sailing craft with high stern and sternpost, without distinction of rig. One large standing lugsail is carried on a mast which rakes extremely aft. Double quarter rudders are used.

rua pet: craft typical to Gulf of Siam. Deep hull has high overhanging "spoon" bow and pointed stern. Mainmast is set well forward of amidships and carried standing lugsail. Small lug foresail is set on light mast stepped in bow.

rua ta: Gulf of Siam type, somewhat resembling a "junk." Crude hull has overhanging stern gallery and eye painted on bow. It is lug-rigged with tall mainmast, shorter foremast set well forward and tiny mizzen at stern.

rubber ice: elastic young sea ice, not strong enough to bear the weight of a man standing still.

rubble: fragments of hard sea ice, roughly spherical and up to 5 ft. in diameter, resulting from disintegration of larger ice formations. When afloat, commonly called brash ice.

rub rail [ships]: strip of molding extending outward from boat's sides to protect topsides.

Ruchbah: star of magnitude 2.80 in the group *Cassiopeia*, having a right ascension of 1 hr. 22½ min. and declination of very nearly 60° N. When near the meridian above the pole, it may be recognized as second from the easternmost star, ϵ *Cassiopeiae*. It is within a minute of inferior transit when *Mizar*, second from end of the "handle" in the *Big Dipper* is on the meridian *above* the pole, and vice versa.

ruche or hidden rib [*Cryptopleura rupechtiana*]: seaweed attached to rocks between 0.5- and 1.5-ft. tide levels. Most conspicuous features are flat thallus divided like an open fan, network of veins and ribs that cover surface of blade and presence of densely crowded outgrowths on edges of blade. Outgrowths look like tiny ruching or ruffle 1/16-in. wide. This seaweed is a beautiful, bright, purplish-red with tissue-paper-thin texture.

rudder [ships]: device used in steering or maneuvering a vessel, usually a flat slab of steel or wood hung at stern of vessel and capable of being turned right or left as desired.

rudder bands [ships]: bands that extend on each side of rudder to help brace and tie it into pintles.

rudder bow [ships]: rudder placed at bottom of forward stem and maneuvered from forepeak.

rudder chains [ships]: chains whereby rudder is fastened to stern quarters. They are shackled to rudder by bolts just above waterline and hang slack enough to permit free motion of rudder. They are used as precaution against losing a rudder at sea.

rudderfish, banded: silvery brown or blue member of jack family found along Atlantic Coast from New England to Virginia; it rarely exceeds 18 in. in length and a weight of 4 lbs. Young rudderfish, abundant in northern part of range, are marked by 5 or 6 dark, vertical bars. They travel in schools following larger fishes and fishing boats.

rudder flange [ships]: flange which ties main part of rudder to rudder stem. It may be horizontal or vertical.

rudder frame [ships]: frame within inner shell, bolted through latter into main frame and shell, for purpose of stiffening the rudder.

rudder pilot [ships]: small rudder fastened to after part of regular rudder which, by mechanical attachment, pulls main rudder to either side.

rudder post [ships]: vertical part in stern of vessel on which rudder hangs.

rudder stock [ships]: vertical shaft having rudder attached to lower end and turned near upper end by quadrant or tiller.

rudder stop [ships]: fitting to limit swing of rudder.

rudder, streamlined [ships]: rudder with bullnosed, round forward edge which tapers regularly to thin after edge.

rudder trunk [ships]: well in stern which holds rudder stock.

rudimentary rays [fish]: unbranched, soft rays which may or may not reach margin of fin.

rudite: rocks or sediment deposits composed of grain larger than 2 mm.

Rugosa [*Tetracoralla*]: order ranges from Ordovician to Permian. Members may exist individually or colonially, but all are sessile benthos. Skeletons are calcareous. Calyx is bowl-shaped depression at oral end of corallite in which polyp rests. Columella is longitudinal rod in axis of corallite, formed by inner ends of septa. Mesenterial arrangement known from septal insertion which after insertion of first 6 septa, takes place in 4 quadrants, between cardinal and alar septa and between alar and counterlateral septa, with tendency to produce bilateral symmetry.

run [ships]: after part of vessel at waterline where lines converge toward sternpost.

runnel: trough or corrugation formed in foreshore

or in bottom immediately offshore, formed by waves or tidal currents.

runner: in a purchase, such as a fish tackle or one of the lower yard braces, a single rope rove in a fixed block and connected to the moving or hauling block of a tackle, its standing end and standing block of tackle terminating at a common point; such rig usually is termed a *runner and tackle*. Loosely, any whip or fall used as a working hoist. A vessel or person in charge of such that carries the catch of a fishing fleet to market. A smuggler or a vessel engaged in smuggling; as, a *rum-runner*. A person who solicits patronage of sailors at boarding house he represents; one employed by a tailor, shopkeeper, etc., for a similar purpose. One of a number of men engaged as a crew for the *run*, or passage from one place to another only. Man who attends to ships' mooring lines about a pier, wharf, set of dolphins, etc., as in landing a hawser by boat, making fast, or letting go as required. A carangoid fish, or one of the family including the *amberjack, cavalla, leather jack, moonfish*, etc., of warmer seas, so named from its swift swimming and leaping from the water; the *jurel* of U.S. Atlantic coast. Runner of a trawl is its main line to which the snells or snoods bearing the hooks are made fast.

running backstay [ships]: ropes or stays extending aft from mastheads to sides of boat. Unlike most stays, running backs are movable and part of running rigging.

running her longitude down [ships]: sailing ship terminology for vessel using west winds of "Roaring Forties" to run east making all longitude possible while going is good, and letting the making of latitude wait.

running rigging [ships]: all movable ropes and lines aboard sailing vessel that are pulled or hauled to control sails, booms, etc. Standing rigging includes all fixed supporting rigging (such as stays) that is not usually moved.

runoff: water derived from precipitation that ultimately reaches stream channels; has direct influence upon volume of river discharge.

runoff cycle: part of hydrologic cycle undergone by water between time it reaches land as precipitation and its subsequent evapotranspiration or discharge through stream channels.

run under [ships]: to sail under. Catastrophe, brought about by carrying too much sail, in which ship plunges into sea and disappears.

run-up: rush of water up a structure on breaking of wave. Amount of run-up is vertical height above still-water level that rush of water reaches.

S

S: in freeboard, or Plimsoll, marks on ship's side, denotes summer season line or limit to which a seagoing vessel may be immersed in seawater, or a lake or river vessel in fresh water. In ship's logbooks and weather records, abbreviation for *snow* or *snowing; south; smooth sea.* International Code flag, "Sugar," having a white ground with a central blue square about one-ninth of flag's area. Hoisted singly, flag S denotes "*My engines are going full speed astern*"; also, as a towing signal, displayed by *ship towed*, indicates "Go astern" and by *ship towing*, "My engines are going astern," or may be indicated by flashing the Morse Code S (. . .) as such towing signal.

Sabella: genus of polychaete worms characterized by having tubes fixed in position and made of fine sand particles.

saddle: low part on ridge or between seamounts.

sagged [ships]: said of ship which has been strained so that bottom drops lower in middle than it is at stem and stern.

Sagittarius: southern constellation, through which the sun passes at about the winter solstice, lying next to and east of *Scorpio*. The group contains two bright navigational stars; *Kaus Australis;* and *Nunki.*

Sahul Shelf: region of shallow water on northwest coast of Australia which reaches New Guinea; it was dry land during part of Pleistocene.

sail: 1) to make headway or be driven, as a boat, by wind pressure on a sail or sails; hence, by extension, to impel or be impelled, as a vessel, by means of steam or any other motive power. 2) to depart, as a vessel on a voyage. 3) to govern or direct a vessel; especially, by means of wind power; as, to *sail a schooner*. 4) a short passage or excursion; as, *we enjoyed the sail down the bay*. 5) any unidentified sailing craft sighted at sea; as, *a sail hove in sight;* or, collectively, as, *a fleet of ten sails*. 6) in plural, customary sailing ship short name for the *sailmaker*. 7) a sheet of canvas or any textile fabric that is spread to impel a boat or vessel by action of wind pressure on its surface. *Sails* are of two general classes; viz., *fore-and-aft*, or those having the *luff* or for-

ward edge attached to a stay or, either wholly or in part, to, or near, a mast; and *square*, or those spread from a *yard*, or spar lying at right angles to a mast. The former may be triangular in shape, as jibs, trysails, staysails, or jib-headed boom sails; or may be quadrilateral, usually with the after side *(leech)* of greater length than the other. Square sails take the name from their right-angled shape at the *head earings*, or points at which the *leeches* (vertical sides) meet the head at ends of the yard, rather than from their approximately rectilineal shape. Earliest sail used probably was of "square" pattern set only in fair winds, but the *three-sided lateen* with its long oblique hoisting yard apparently was foremost in utilizing the breezes for sailing *close-hauled*. The former is known to have been fitted to the roving Viking-ships, while the *lateen*, a favorite with the Venetians of the Middle Ages, was at least experimented with by the Phoenicians long before the Christian era. A combination of *square* and *lateen* sails appears to have been adopted in larger vessels of the 15th century, notably in the *caravel* of Columbus' time, but any kind of *top-sail*, or sail above a course, as all lower sails once were called, was a rarity as late as A.D. 1400. Square topsails may be said to date from 1500; probably a century later in the Spanish galleon a *top-gallant sail* appeared above the topsail. Meanwhile the *lateen* seems to have been favored as an *after sail* and ships of western Europe retained that canvas well into the 17th century. About 1700, the *royal* was first set above the *top-gallant* and continued as loftiest canvas until the days of the clippers. Outside of the historical all-lateen rigs peculiar to the Mediterranean, the credit for building and rigging, in about 1840, first vessels having an entire spread of pure *fore-and-aft sails* (jibs and gaff sails) on two or more masts goes to these United States. Such rig is the *schooner* type. Parts of a *triangular sail* are the *luff*, or forward edge; *leech*, or upper after edge; *foot*, or lower edge; angle of juncture of leech and foot, the *clew;* upper angle is the *head;* and foremost or lowest point, the *tack*. A *quadrilateral fore-and-aft sail* has a *luff*, the fore side; *leech*, or after side; *head*, or upper edge usually spread along a *gaff; foot*, often spread on a *boom;* its *tack* is lower forward corner; *throat*, upper forward corner; the *peak* is its highest or upper after point; and *clew*, its lower after corner. *A square sail* is bent to its yard by its *head;* its *leeches* are the two outer edges; and *foot*, its lower side. The *head-earings* are its upper corners, secured to the *yard-arms; clews*, lower corners to which the *sheets* are attached. *Roping*, or the bolt-rope secured to a sail along its edges, is named for its position; as, *luff-, head-, leech-*, and *foot-rope*. In a fore-and-aft sail, the roping is on *port side* of the canvas; in a square sail, on the *after side*. In square-rig, the *foresail* and all *lower topsails* are heavy-weather canvas, the strongest on board; in fore-and-aft rig, usually all lower canvas but that on after mast, where three or more masts are present. Names given to *sails* are legion, particularly in smaller vessels and the yachting field, and no doubt a good-sized volume might be used in their description. With the trading-vessel in mind, however, principal canvas is named for the mast on which it is set or to which its boom or yard is attached; thus, in square rig, we have the *foresail* set from the *fore yard*, which is slung from the *foremast* (or *forelowermast*); next above, the *lower* and *upper topsails* in way of the *topmast;* then the *topgallantsail* (sometimes also divided into *lower* and *upper*), fitted to its yard on the *topgallantmast;* and finally, the *royal* in way of the *royalmast*, if we omit, for the present, the lofty *skysails* hoisted on the *skysail pole. Staysails* take their name from the stays on which they are set; as, *fore staysails; main-topmast staysails;* and in this respect *jibs*, which are set on the *head stays*, also must be considered *staysails*. In the fore-and-aft rig, all *gaff sails* are named for their respective masts, excepting the *spanker*, or aftermost sail on a *mizzen* or *a jigger* mast, and their surmounting *gaff-topsails* for topmasts on which set; thus, *foresail; fore gaff-topsail; spanker; mizzen gaff-topsail.*

sailage: collectively, outfit of sails that a vessel may spread; sail area that is, or may be, spread.

sail battens [ships]: slender flexible strips generally placed on rear edge of a sail to help support it and hold its shape.

sailed: furnished with, or having all sails; especially, having all sail bent and ready for sea.

sailfin molly [*Mollienesia latipinna*]: pretty little fish with big dorsal fin. Anal fin with 8 rays; dorsal fin with 14—16 rays. Body oblong, compressed; head very small, depressed; mouth tiny, vertical, no lateral cleft; teeth small, pointed, in several bands. Ground color of male olive-greenish; females olivaceous. Each scale on back and sides with dark spots, thus forming indistinct rows of stripes. Breeding males beautifully tinged with bright greenish-blue or blue.

sailfish, Atlantic: readily recognizable by high sail-like dorsal fin. Like marlin, it carries a spear at top of nose. Dorsal fin and back are royal blue; rest of body is silvery with vertical rows of small dark spots. Dark, slender ventral fins are even more elongated than those of marlins. Sailfish make use of crescent-shaped and deeply forked tail fin to skip along surface as if sailing on water. Sailfish reach maximum length of 8 ft. and weight of 100 lbs.

sailing: 1) act or art of navigating or maneuvering a vessel that is driven by sail power; hence, by extension, art of directing; managing, and navigating a vessel propelled by any motive power; navigating; seagoing. In navigation, method followed in finding course to steer and distance from one point to another or resultant course and distance covered on several different courses, position arrived at, etc.; as, *great circle sailing; plane sailing; mercator sailing.* 2) act of departing, as a vessel from a port.

sailorman: a sailor in full sense of the name; as, *it takes a sailorman to rig a ship.*

sailor's purse: tough egg capsule of skates and certain rays, usually deposited on mud and sand-flats. Capsules are oblong with horn extending lengthwise from each of 4 corners; blackish when seen on beach.

Saint Elmo's Fire: also, *St. Elmo's Light.* See *corposant.*

Saint-Hilaire Method: Marcq St. Hilaire Method. See *intercept.*

Saint Ulmo's Fire: same as *St. Elmo's Fire.* See *corposant.*

saique: small vessel of Near East and Levant, popular prior to 19th century. Mainmast was square-rigged with 3 capped topmasts. Mizzenmast was lateen-rigged; spritsail carried on bowsprit. Hull had considerable sheer with flat stern.

salamander, Brimley's dusky [*Desmognathus fuscus brimleyorum*]: small, brownish salamander with light streak from eye to angle of jaw. Nasolabial grooves; light line from eye to angle of jaw; belly uniformly pale, not mottled.

salamander, Carr's dusky [*Desmognathus fuscus carri*]: small, blackish salamander with light streak from eye to angle of jaw. Nasolabial grooves; belly light to dark but throat region invariably pale; tail less than ½ of total length.

salamander, common dusky [*Desmognathus fuscus fuscus*]: small, brownish salamander with light streak from eye to angle of jaw. Nasolabial grooves present; belly pale, lightly mottled.

salamander, dwarf [*Manculus quadridigitatus*]: small, slender, long-tailed, yellow to brownish salamander. Nasolabial grooves present; 4 toes on hind foot. Head and body long and slender; head widest behind eyes; side of head converging abruptly before eyes to very short and bluntly rounded snout; eyes large for such a small salamander. Body slender, rounded slightly, flattened below; tail long and slender.

salamander, Eastern tiger [*Ambystoma tigrinum tigrinum*]: good-sized, bluish-gray salamander with yellow or gold blotches. No nasolabial grooves; costal grooves 12; pattern of large, irregular yellow or gold blotches.

salamander, frosted [*Ambystoma cingulatum cingulatum*]: dark, medium-sized salamander with lichenlike markings. Multiple rows of teeth in jaws; vomerine teeth generally in 3 rows. Belly with discrete white spots on black background.

salamander, Gulf Coast red [*Pseudotriton montanus flavissimus*]: orange or orange-red salamander with scattered small, round, dark spots. Nasolabial grooves; 16 to 18 costal grooves; orange or pale red in color with scattered, small, black dots both above and below.

salamander, marbled [*Ambystoma opacum*]: stout salamander about 4 in. long with white or silvery bars across back. No nasolabial grooves; 11 costal grooves; light bars across back. Head and body stout; head moderately broad, widest above angle of jaw. Tail rounded, not keeled, thicker above than below. Limbs stout; fingers 4, moderately slender, unwebbed; toes 4, moderately slender, unwebbed.

salamander, mole [*Ambystoma talpoideum*]: stout, gray or grayish-brown salamander, 3 to 4 in. long. No nasolabial grooves; 10 costal grooves; back brown or gray with small gray dots. Head and body stout; head broad, widest above angle of jaws; snout bluntly rounded. Very shallow middorsal groove; tail short, slightly keeled above, rounded below, compressed at tip. Fingers 4, toes 5, moderately slender, unwebbed.

salamander, reticulated [*Ambystoma cingulatum bishop*]: dark, medium-sized salamander with lichenlike markings. Multiple rows of teeth on jaws; vomerine teeth generally in 2 rows; belly with salt and pepper pattern.

salamander, rusty mud [*Pseudotriton montanus floridanus*]: dark, reddish-brown salamander with orange to red belly. Dorsum rusty or dark red; belly with scattered, round, dark spots on orange or reddish background. Nasolabial groove present. Costal grooves 17 to 18.

salamander, southern dusky [*Desmognathus fuscus auriculatus*]: small, brownish to blackish salamander with light streak from eye to angle of jaws. Nasolabial grooves present; light line from eye to angle of jaw; belly dark; throat region not much lighter than rest of belly; tail about ½ of total length.

salamander, southern slimy [*Plethodon glutinosus*

grobmani]: small, blue-black salamander with scattered whitish or golden flecks on back. Nasolabial grooves present; no fin on tail; tongue attached only at anterior margin; no light line from eye to angle of jaw.

salamander, southern two-lined [*Eurycea bislineata cirrigera*]: slender, yellowish salamander with 2 lines down back. Nasolabial grooves present; 5 toes on hind foot; no black middorsal stripe; vomerine teeth not continuous with parasphenoid teeth; tongue with central pedicle, its edge free all around.

salamander, three-lined [*Eurycea longicanda guttolincata*]: long, slender, yellowish salamander with 3 dark lines down back. Nasolabial grooves present; 5 toes on hind feet; black middorsal stripe; vomerine teeth not continuous with parasphenoid teeth; tongue with central pedicle and free edges all around.

salamander, Viosca's red [*Pseudotriton ruberi vioscai*]: stout-bodied, rusty brown, mottled salamander with speckled belly. Nasolabial grooves present; division rusty or dark red with numerous coalescing black spots, venter paler but heavily flecked. Costal grooves usually 16.

Salicornia: genus of shore plants also called glasswort or pickleweed. This herb has thick, fleshy branches with tiny, spiky leaves.

salient point: point formed by conspicuous projection extending outward from general trend of coast.

salina: salt marsh or salt pond separated from sea but flooded by high tides. Shallow salt ponds are used to evaporate water in commercial production of salt and are called salt gardens or salterns.

saline: having taste, characteristics and properties of sodium chloride, commonly known as salt.

salinity: measure of quantity of total dissolved solids in water. Salinity is visually expressed in total weight in grams of salts dissolved in 1 kilogram of ocean water; it is written $^\circ$/oo (parts per thousand). In open ocean salinity varies between 33 and 38°/oo. Sodium chloride (NaCl) would account for 77.8 percent of total salt contained in seawater of salinity 35°/oo.

salinometer: 1) in its most basic form, an ohmmeter-type of instrument for measuring electrical conductivity of seawater. More modern versions used inductance-type, media-coupling transformers. Device or instrument for determining salinity, especially one based on electrical conductivity methods. 2) instrument used to measure amount of salts in seawater.

salmon [family]: in addition to salmon and trout, salmon family includes whitefish and cisco, both important food fishes of Great Lakes region. Fishes in this family have graceful, elongated bodies covered with cycloid scales; single dorsal fin is located near middle of back above ventral fins; pectoral fins are set forward. Large mouth is provided with sharp jaw teeth indicating carnivorous habits of species. Family includes over 100 species of which 30 occur in U.S. Some species live entire life in freshwater, while others are marine species that migrate into streams to spawn. Common and scientific names of salmon came from Latin word *salio*, meaning "leap."

salmon, Atlantic: fresh from the sea, Atlantic salmon are glistening silver with blue back marked with x-shaped spots. Spawning salmon become reddish-brown; males develop elongated jaws with prominent hook to tip of lower jaw. Plump, searun salmon, 4 or 5 years old can be found in streams from mid-May to mid-July, growing to length of 30 in. and weighing at least 10 lbs. Smaller salmon, known as grills, that have spent only one year at sea weigh 5 lbs. or less. Many adults die after spawning. It has been estimated that only 15 percent of fishes return to spawn a second time.

salmon boat: open, double-ended model used in salmon gill-net industry near mouth of Columbia River, Oregon. It was carvel-built with nearly vertical stern and sternpost; washboards along sides; short deck at either end; 4 thwarts; cat-rigged.

salmon, chinook: also known as king salmon; largest species averaging 10 to 20 lbs. in weight, with some individuals attaining a record breaking 100 lbs. Typical chinook salmon has silvery sides and bluish-green back marked with small dark spots; it occurs over long range from California to Alaska.

salmon, coho: silvery salmon; small species, usually under 5 lbs. in weight. It has same range as chinook salmon. Coho salmon are abundant from Puget Sound to Alaska.

Salmonidae family: family *Salmonidae* includes salmon and trout and constitutes one of the most popular of game food fishes. These are long-bodied fishes with naked heads. Characterized by relatively small cycloid scales and well developed adipose fin. Anal fin has 9 to 16 rays; dorsal fin is single with 10 to 12 rays; no spines are present; ventral fins are located just below dorsal. A slit is present behind 4th gill; pseudobranchia are developed; gill membranes are not joined to isthmus; branchiostegal rays number from 10 to 20. Air bladder is large. Many pyloric caeca are present; are cold water fishes.

salmon, king [*Oncorhynchus tshawytscha*]: king salmon is large, weighing about 20 lbs., although weights up to 100 lbs. are known. This fish has dusky back and silvery sides; back and tail are covered with small black spots. Dorsal fin has 11 rays; anal fin usually has 16.

salmon, landlocked [*Salmo salar sebago*]: in certain lakes of Maine, Atlantic salmon has become landlocked forming a subspecies called sebago salmon. Sebago salmon has same general characteristics as Atlantic salmon but is smaller, averaging about 2 lbs.

salmon, Pacific: salmon of Pacific Coast belong to 5 different species; together they make up most valuable freshwater food fish in America. Salmon begin running in March and continue until spawning time from August to November. Some species are caught all seasons. Pacific salmon often reveal striking differences between sexes during spawning season. Snout of male becomes distorted, upper jaw becomes hooked and fleshy hump may develop in front of dorsal fin. In some species silvery color changes to brilliant red. Pacific salmon generally die after spawning; unlike Atlantic salmon they are rarely caught by hook in fresh water.

salmon, pink: also known as humpback salmon because of appearance of male during spawning; especially common in Alaska although it occurs as far south as Oregon. It usually weighs between 3 and 6 lbs. The flesh, somewhat inferior to that of sockeye or chinook, is canned as pink salmon.

salmon, sockeye or red: found from Oregon to Alaska; spawning males assume colorful attire with bright red body and green head. Average sockeye salmon is 2 ft. long and weighs up to 5 lbs.

saloon [ships]: main cabin on ship, occupied by officers and passengers.

salp: 1) any one of class (Thaliacea) of marine animals which are transparent pelagic representatives of tunicates. Body is more or less cylindrical and possesses conspicuous, ringlike muscle bands, contraction of which propels animal through water. Several kinds are bioluminescent. 2) member of genus of tunicates. Free swimming, cask-shaped animals, individual salps asexually produce clusters or chains of salps which in turn sexually produce more individual salps. Sexual forms (blastozooids) are in chains, while asexual oozooids are solitary and possess a stolon but no gonads. Branchial and atrial apertures are on anterior and posterior ends respectively, and test is thick. Distinctive feature of musculature is that it is incomplete ventrally. Alimentary canal may be straight or, more commonly, concentrated with gonads to form visceral mass.

salt: any substance which yields ions, other than hydrogen or hydroxyl ions. A salt is obtained by displacing hydrogen of an acid by a metal.

saltation: that method of sand movement in a fluid which individual particles leave the bed by bounding nearly vertically and, because motion of fluid is not strong or turbulent enough to retain them in suspension, return to bed at some distance downstream.

salt-flecked ice: ice-swept, clear snow except for wind ripples saturated with brine.

salt horse [ships]: sailor's slang for salt beef, also called bully beef.

salt marsh: flat, poorly drained, coastal swamp which is flooded by most high tides.

salt pans: shallow pools or brackish water used for natural evaporation of seawater to obtain salt.

salt pump: physiological mechanism that concentrates an ion against the osmotic gradient.

saltwater wedge: tidal, wedge-shaped estuary of seawater characterized by pronounced increase in salinity from surface to bottom.

salvage: act of voluntarily saving (or *salving*) a vessel, her cargo or part thereof, or a wreck (and in some cases lives of persons on a distressed vessel) from a peril of the sea or other extraordinary danger. That part of property that is salved. Compensation allowed *salvors* of ship and/or cargo. To *salve* or *save* that which is in peril; as, *the goods were salvaged in time.*

salvor: one who voluntarily renders services in salving property or lives of persons in distress or peril; especially, one who skillfully and enterprisingly salves or assists in salving a vessel, her cargo, or lives of her people. Such services usually meet with a generous award, particularly in cases involving exposure of salvor to personal danger or hardship and extreme difficulties in operation concerned, in order to encourage repetition of similar undertakings.

sambuk: small dhow of 18 to 20 tons used in Red Sea.

sampan: general term applied to all small, open or half-decked boats of Chinese build, used on coasts of China, Japan, Siam and other nearby Asiatic countries. These are two-masted, foremast with very forward rake and mainmast raked aft, and are rigged with battened lugsails.

sampan panjang: half-decked, keel sailing craft used at Jahore, Malay States. It has long, sharp, hollow bow with concave stern; long, sharp stern; practically no sheer; hollow, rising floor; rudder hung outside.

sampler, Heller: Heller sampler is a side intake sampler employed primarily in bogs or shallow lakes. It is a hollow tube, closed at both ends, about ½ meter long (1.6 ft.) and 4 cm. (about 1.5 in.) in diameter. It has a 90° slit cut lengthwise into tube. Larger, identically slit cylinder encloses this tube. To gather a sample, operator twists outer sleeve counterclockwise, covering inner slit. He then forces tubes into sediment with counterclockwise motion. When sampler has reached desired length, he twists cylinders clockwise, opening slits and filling inner cylinder. Before bringing them to the surface he reverses the cylinder again to sea and protects the sample.

sampler, Machreth: Machreth sampler is a piston sampler operated by air hoses. Compressed air rams sampler into bottom; then it floats to surface. This is an extremely manageable device, but its usefulness is limited to shallow-water depths of not more than 100 meters (328 ft.). A lone operator can obtain undisturbed cores up to 6 meters (19.7 ft.) long with Machreth sampler.

sampler, Swedish foil: Swedish foil sampler has many thin foils that join to a piston housed in the core head. Foils unroll as sampler penetrates sediment around piston. Foil prevents sliding of sleeve and alleviates friction between sampler and inside of sampler.

samson posts [ships]: short heavy masts used as boom supports and often used for ventilators.

sand: 1) separate grains of particles of detrital rock material, easily distinguished by unaided eye, but not large enough to be called pebbles; also a loose mass of such grains, forming incoherent arenaceous sediment. 2) loose materials consisting of grains ranging between 0.0625 and 2.0000 mm. in diameter.

sand apron: sand deposited along shore of reef lagoon.

sandbagger: sloop or cat-rigged racing boat, 18 to 28 ft. long, popular in New York and New England waters as early as 1855. Hull was quite flat and shallow with little freeboard; shifting ballast was used.

sandbar: in a river, ridge of sand built up to or near surface by river currents.

sand dollar: echinoid commonly known as sea urchin or sand dollar recognized longer than most other fossils. Prized as amulets by prehistoric peoples of Europe. Ordovician to Recent.

sand horn: pointed sand deposit extending from shore into shallow water.

sand lobe: rounded sand deposit extending from shore into shallow water.

sandstone: sedimentary rock consisting of sand grains cemented together by lime, etc. Used in building.

sapropel: aquatic ooze or sludge that is rich in organic matter.

saprophytic: mode of nutrition found in nongreen plants and many bacteria that require organic food absorbed through body surface. If substrate furnishing this food cannot be absorbed directly it is partly broken down or digested outside the organism by exoenzymes before absorption.

saprozoic: somewhat similar mode of nutrition in some animals such as tapeworms, differing in that subsequent metabolism of organic food is of different type than that found in plants.

saraggaso: loosely, a large floating mass of seaweeds.

sarcophagus: flesh-eating.

sardine, Pacific: pilchard, size of Atlantic herring, has distinctive dark spots along sides. Half billion pounds are harvested annually to be converted into fish oil and fish meal.

sardiner: early type of boat used in sardine fishery of Brittany, France. It was a two-masted, lug-rigged, open boat, very beamy with straight stem and vertical sternpost, long straight keel, outboard rudder, foremast stepped in bow and mainmast amidships. This type has been extinct for many years.

sardine, Spanish: similar in appearance to Atlantic herring. Smaller and more southern species, usually less than 6 in. long. Found from Cape Cod to Florida; of little economic importance except for use as bait.

Sargasso Sea: region of North Atlantic Ocean to east and south of Gulf Stream system. This is a region of convergence of surface waters and is characterized by clear, warm water, deep blue color and large quantities of floating *Sargassum* or gulfweed.

Sargassum: genus of seaweed; large brown alga with slender stalks, leaflike branches and gas bladders which aid in supporting the stalks by serving as float. It is normally attached to fixed objects on bottom, but often breaks loose and drifts, frequently washing ashore or floating in thick masses, as in well-known Sargasso Sea in Atlantic.

sargassum, frogfish: common frogfish found in warm waters. As its name indicates, it lives amid floating masses of brown seaweed known as *Sargassum*. Sargassum fish have developed art of camouflage to the point where the fish is practically indistinguishable from surrounding seaweeds. Its body and fins are mottled tan and brown, matching colors of *Sargassum*. Numerous flat tabs and outgrowths of various sizes, some resembling individual "leaves" of seaweed, clothe head, chin and body. Protected by this incredible mimicry, tiny fish crawls frog-fashion through seaweed pasture searching for meal of small invertebrates.

Sarsia eximia [phylum *Coelenterata*]: medusa of hydroid *Syncoryne eximia* and is mainly confined to coastal waters. It is fairly large and active even when first liberated from hydroid stage.

Sarsia gemmitera [phylum *Coelenterata*]: this has not been related to a hydroid. It is distinguished by ability to produce buds from wall of manubrium and by relatively short tentacles. It can reach a height of 5 mm. Ocelli are black.

Sarsia prolifera [phylum *Coelenterata*]: this medusa has not been related to hydroid but is presumably medusa of some species of *Syncoryne*. It differs from *S. eximia* most obviously when it has reached the stage at which secondary medusae are produced asexually by budding at base of tentacles. When fully grown it is only about 2 mm. tall.

Sarsia tubulosa [phylum *Coelenterata*]: probably medusa of *Syncoryne decipiens;* differs from 2 previous species in having long, tubular stomach and in growing much larger, sometimes attaining height of about 10 mm.

sastrugi: wavelike ridges of hard snow formed on level surface by action of wind.

satellite, transit type: space-borne instrumentation system used for navigation at sea. During its orbital journey apparatus may also collect and retransmit data from buoys and vessels at sea. It employs radar-type sensory or sensing devices for monitoring surface conditions and/or tracking worldwide migration of large marine animals equipped with transmitter devices.

saturated diving: diving technique in which human body is allowed to reach a condition of complete saturation with dissolved gases at pressure encountered in given working depth. Ascent from these depths requires considerable time so that saturated gases can escape gradually and not in large bubbles, causing the bends. To safely dive at these depths "saturated divers" use large quantities of helium gas which is relatively nontoxic when it saturates the body. Technique of maintaining divers in condition of maximum inert gas absorption for long periods of time.

saturation: condition in which partial pressure of any fluid constituent is equal to its maximum possible partial pressure under existing environmental conditions, such that any increases in amount of that constituent will initiate within it a change to a more condensed state.

saturation diving system [SAT system]: system consisting of one or more deck decompression chambers, personnel transfer capsule and either surface or sea-floor habitat. System is capable of supporting several teams of divers at elevated pressure for long periods of time.

saucer: 1) a socket for the pivot of a capstan. 2) a round flat caisson used in raising sunken vessels.

saucer lake: lake that occupies a shallow basin between natural level and valley wall.

sauger, eastern [*Stizostedion canadense canadense*]: eastern sauger is a smaller and more slender fish than walleye or pike perch, but otherwise its resemblance to walleye is very strong, so much so that when faded in color it is difficult to distinguish one from the other by casual examination. Usual color is grayish with brassy reflections and with dark mottlings on sides. Absence of black blotch in last dorsal spine and presence of black spot at base of each pectoral fin helps to distinguish it from walleye. Length of this species averages about 12 to 14 in.

saury: also called *skipper* and *billfish*, an edible slender long-beaked fish about 18 inches in length found in temperate waters on both sides of the North Atlantic. Swimming in large schools, the fish put up a good display of leaping from the water when pursued.

save all [ships]: "water sail."

Savonius rotor: special rotor used in some current meters. It spins in just one direction no matter at what angles a force strikes its curved surfaces. Current speed is proportional to rate of pulses triggered by turning rotor.

Savonius rotor current meter: low threshold, current speed sensor composed of 2 semicylindrical vanes disposed to form S-shaped rotor responsive to wide spectrum of horizontal flow components.

sawfish: intermediate in body form between rays and sharks. Flattened body is widest at head and bears broad but distinct pectoral fins; it is dark gray or brown with yellowish or whitish underside. Most distinctive feature is extension of upper jaw into long narrow blade whose edges are armed with stout peglike teeth. Three-foot-long "saw" grows to width of 9 in. and base, with as many as 32 pairs of teeth along edges of blade. Sawfishes usually occur near shore in shallow waters where they feed on small fishes; they are also found in brackish river mouths and any of the bayous.

sayke: old type of Turkish ketch.

scale: 1) incrustation on inside of a steam boiler, consisting of deposit of calcium, magnesium, and iron carbonates, calcium sulphate, among other impurities in fresh water. Black coating of oxide on surface of newly forged or rolled plates, etc.; usually called *mill scale;* sometimes, *forge scale, hammer scale.* 2) an accumulation of rust (ferro oxide) on iron and steel surfaces, as on ship's plating. 3) a graduated measure or rule. 4) ratio of linear measurements on a chart, drawing, or model to actual dimensions of body or object that is represented; as, *natural scale* of a chart or plan is 1:50,000; *scale* of ½ inch to a foot. 5) a system of numbers indicating, progressively, force, intensity, or amount; as, a *wind scale; state of sea scale; cloud scale.* 6) series of graded values; as, a *displacement scale; deadweight scale; tons per inch scale.* 7) to remove *scale*, as from an iron surface.

scaler: electronic device which registers current pulses received over given time interval.

scaler irradiance: quantitative measure of total radiant flux arriving at a point for all directions about a point. It is the measure of amount of radiant energy per unit volume of space at given point.

scallop: bivalve (having shell with 2 distinctive parts) mollusc. Scallops can swim by clapping shells together; flesh is popular seafood and familiar rigid shell is one of most common shells found.

scantling: in shipbuilding, sizes of structural parts, including frames, beams, girders, and plating, which must be adhered to according to specifications. Minimum scantling are prescribed for the various types and sizes of vessels by classification societies. Also, generally, softwood timber measuring less than 5″ x 5″.

Scaphopoda [class]: tooth shells are one of 5 large groups or classes of molluscs and receive common name from the fact that shells are somewhat like tusks or teeth of elephants. Like elephants' tusks, these shells are long, curved, tapering and hollow; but unlike teeth of other animals, these shells are open at both ends. Within this tubular shell is a tubular mantle which secretes the shell and encloses the body except at open ends of shell. Largest end of shell is anterior end and contains rudimentary head, muscular foot for burrowing in sand and some filaments which seem to serve as sense organs and help capture food. Heart and eyes are absent in molluscs and, although head is small and rudimentary, it bears characteristic radula. While alive, the head end of these animals lies buried in sand while smaller posterior end projects above surface. It is through this smaller posterior end of shell that water is drawn into and passes out of mantle cavity. Gills found in most molluscs are lacking in these forms so that duties of respiration are performed by mantle. Marine molluscs that make their home on bottom of ocean from shoreline down to considerable depths are sandy and free from organic material.

scapulet: in jellyfish of group rhizotomes, outgrowths of oral arms near bell, bearing supplementary mouth openings. Scapulets are not found in all rhizotomes, only in certain families and genera.

scarfing [ships]: method of cutting away 2 pieces so that they fit smoothly into each other to make one piece. They are fastened together by welding, bolting, riveting, etc.

scaridae: a family of brightly colored fishes, typical of which is the *parrot fish* or *parrot wrasse,* found in warmer seas. In many respects greatly resembles the *Labridae.*

scarp: sharp, steep slope along margin of undersea plateau, terrace, etc.

scattering: when sound wave travels outward from source into sea, energy produces primary directional wave and also secondary wavelets which travel in other directions. This phenomenon is called scattering.

Scheat: probably of Arabic origin, name given the star marking N.W. corner of the *Square of Pega-*

sus. Listed by astronomers as β *Pegasi*, it is located about 13° due north of *Markab (a Pegasi)*, S.W. member of the Square. A line joining these two, extended northward, passes close to *Polaris* at about 61° from *Scheat*; if extended southward, comes very near to *Fomalhaut* at 45° from *Markab.* The star has a magnitude of 2.61 and lies in declination 28° N., right ascension 23 hrs. Another name for it appears in older usage as *Menkib*, from Arabic *mankib*, meaning a *shoulder.*

Schedar: also written *Schedir*, one of *Cassiopeia's* brighter stars, having a magnitude varying from 2.1 to 2.6 and southernmost member of the group. When on the meridian below the pole, it is easily recognized as second star from western end of this constellation, otherwise known as the *Lady's Chair.* It is listed as a *Cassiopeiae.*

Schistomysis spiritus [mysid]: slender mysid whose carapace has rounded, blunt, anterior margin and slightly emarginated posterior, leaving whole of last and part of 7th thoracic segment exposed in dorsal view. Abdomen is long; long, narrow, antennal scale. General appearance of animal is long, slender and transparent, with long cylindrical eyes reaching beyond lateral margins of carapace. Very common in coastal waters.

schistosome dermatitis: irritating skin condition incurred by bathers in both fresh and salt waters and characterized by eruption of reddish welts and severe itching sensation. Cercarian larvae of certain parasitic trematode worms produce the dermatitis when they enter skin and die.

Schizopoda [*Crustacea*]: cleft-footed crustaceans, so-called because attached to thorax are 8 pairs of biramous legs.

schizopod stage: that stage in development of decapod crustaceans when they resemble adult.

Schnapper: an important food fish found in Australian and New Zealand waters. Of the *Spraidae* family, it has a long thorny dorsal fin, attains a length of 1½ to 2 feet, generally pinkish in color, and in profile, from back to mouth appears as a well-defined arc of a circle.

schnorkel: original tubular "breathing" apparatus developed by the Germans for use by submarines while the craft are cruising entirely submerged. The term appears to have been adopted from code word given the invention. Now called *snorkel* in U.S. navy and *snorter* by the British.

schokker: yacht of Netherlands, not unlike the "Botter," but having fuller stern which is straight and rakes at 60° with waterline.

school: large number of one kind of fish or other aquatic animals swimming or feeding together.

schoolmaster [*Lutjanus apodus*]: greenish-gray, faintly streaked, laterally compressed fish with long dorsal fin and tough mouth. Scales along lateral line 42—46; caninelike teeth on each side in front of upper jaw. Body comparatively elongate, compressed; back arched; mouth strong, conspicuous; jaws with bands of villiform teeth.

schooner: a two- or more masted vessel, fore-and-aft rigged. Essentials of schooner rig are 2 fore-and-aft sails and headsail (jib), any other sails being incidental.

schouw: small, shallow-draft, open pleasure craft of Holland and, to lesser extent, of Belgium. Hull is flat-bottomed and has pronounced sheer fore and aft. Both bow and stern have wide transom, former raking and latter vertical.

schuyt: contemporary, small, Dutch sailboat. Hull is sturdily built, rotund and shallow with outboard rudder and usual leeboards. It is sloop-rigged with 1 or 2 headsails and mainsail has short, curved gaff.

Scleractinia: madreporarian group of coral having calcareous exoskeleton, no siphonoglyph and small polyps. They are solitary or colonial and are reef formers.

scoopfish: device for collecting small samples of ocean floor surface while ship is underway.

scoopfish bottom sampler: small bottom sediment sampling device for underwater use, consisting essentially of streamlined weighted tube with stabilizing fins. Lead-end of tube is completely open so that scooping effect is achieved when sampler is towed. Bottom contact releases a spring activated cover over tube's open end so that any sediment sampled can be brought to surface.

scope [ships]: length of anchor chain out.

Scorpio: conspicuous southern constellation called by sailors the *Chain-hook* from its resemblance to that instrument. It extends from N.W. to S.E. between declinations 20 to 43 degrees and right ascension 16 to 17½ hours. The bright reddish *Antares* lies close to the *handle* and another bright member of the group, *Shaula (λ Scorpii)* marks the *point* of the *Hook* in 37° S. The sun passes through the northern part of this constellation during latter part of November.

scorpion fish: family includes numerous rockfish. Scorpion fish are sedentary, decorated with tentacles of various sizes on head and chin. Spiny portion of dorsal fin is large, as are winglike pectoral fins. Stonefish or rockfish is cousin of dragonfish, and like it, is member of family *Scorpaenidae.* It is venomous. Scorpion fish is repulsive in appearance; dragonfish is gorgeous. Called stonefish and rockfish because it lives on bottom among rocks, close to land in cold and in warm seas.

scorpion fish, spotted: West Indies species, which is a bewildering mixture of reds, greens, yellows, blues and browns in no regular pattern. Against coral reef background, such attire is practically invisible as fish rests motionless on bottom. Common scorpion fish grows to length of 12 in.

scour: downward and sideward erosion of sediment bed by wave or current action.

scour and fill: process of cutting and refilling channels in sediment deposited by aggrading stream. Associated with variations in flow velocity, as with rising and ebbing floods.

scour (erosion) of bottom sediments: process whereby sediments are transported from their resting place. Energy needed to carry out this process is supplied by water currents and wave oscillations.

scouring: said of eroding action of water flowing at high velocity. Sediments are transported during this action.

scow: 1) large, flat-bottomed, flat-decked vessel having broad square ends and straight side or sides. 2) flat-hulled sailing craft, usually sloop-rigged, used for racing or pleasure sailing. Typical scow has very flat floor and section that are generally parallel throughout and is of extremely shallow draft.

scow schooner: flat-bottomed, square-ended vessel of scow type with rig of two-masted coasting schooner, used in former days in vicinity of San Francisco, California.

scow sloop: New England scow, 50 to 60 ft. long, used for carrying ice, cordwood and stone in coastwide trade and on larger rivers. Hull was that of ordinary sand scow seen today. It was sloop-rigged and fast under favorable conditions.

scrag whale: any small whale of lean or shrivelled appearance; especially, a poor specimen of a finback or a right whale.

screw ice: small ice fragments in heaps or ridges produced by crushing together of ice cakes. Also applied to small formations of ridged ice, rafted ice and hummocked ice.

screwing pack: ice pack in which ice floes or ice cakes are in rotary motion due to influence of wind and current.

scrieve board [ships]: large section of flooring in mold loft in which lines of body are cut with knife. Used in making molds of frames, beams, floors, plates, etc.

scrimshaw: to engrave various fanciful designs on shells, whales' teeth, walrus tusks, etc. In general, to make useful or ornamental articles at sea, such as writing desks, toilet boxes and work boxes.

SCUBA: initials standing for Self Contained Underwater Breathing Apparatus, device perfected during World War II, which enables diver to remain underwater for considerable periods of time.

scud: 1) small shreds of clouds moving rapidly be-
low solid deck of higher clouds. 2) to be driven swiftly before a gale.

sculpin, Cabezone: grows to length of 30 in. and may weigh as much as 20 lbs. Its color varies with surroundings, being greenish amid eelgrass and green seaweeds but brownish in kelp beds. This species, also known as blue cod or butthead, is marketed on West Coast as food fish.

sculpin family [*Cottidae*]: grotesque fish. Body is elongate; head very large and much depressed; eyes are placed high in head, and space between them is narrow. Edge of preopercle has one or more spinous processes. Teeth are present on jaws and usually also on vomer and palatines; upper jaw is protractile; maxillary is without supplemental bone. Gill rakers are either short and tuberlike or absent. Body is naked or partially covered with scales, prickles or bony plates but never entirely scaled. Lateral line is present. Pectoral fins are very large; ventral fins are thoracic.

sculpin, slimy, or muddler: one of freshwater sculpins; as name implies, it has slimy coating. Unlike those of its saltwater relatives, spines are only feebly developed. This sculpin spends most of time hiding under stones; when venturing forth to feed on aquatic insects or algae, it is eaten by salmon and trout.

sculpture: elevated or depressed marks on a surface, as on a shell.

scupper: 1) any opening for carrying off water from a deck, either directly or through a *scupper pipe*. Scupper pipes and waste pipes leading from decks below a weather deck, or from enclosed superstructures usually are led to ship's bilges, but where leading overboard, their outboard ends are above load waterline and fitted with *storm*, or nonreturn, *valves.* 2) in plural, the waterways at side of a weather deck or in way of the scuppers.

scupper lip [ships]: projection on outside of vessel to allow water to drop free of ship's side.

scupper opening [ships]: hole longer than ordinary scupper with vertical bars, placed on side of ship at deck line to allow deck wash to flow over side of vessel. Also called freeing port.

scupper pipe [ships]: pipe connected to scupper of decks with outlet through side plating just above water. Water thus diverted from deck does not discolor ship's side plating or damage the paint.

scute: external horny plate found on some fish and many reptiles.

scuttle [ships]: small opening, usually circular in shape and generally fitted in decks to provide access as manhole or for stowing fuel, water and stores. Cover or lid is fitted so that scuttle may be closed when not in use.

scuttle butt [ships]: designation for container of

supply of drinking water for use of crew.

scutum: one of paired movable calcareous plates of barnacle.

scyphistoma: polyp stage of scyphozoan jellyfish with tetramerous symmetry and gastrovascular cavity of 4 divisions.

scyphomedusans: these members of class *Scyphozoa* are sometimes called "true jellyfish." Most familiar types are umbrella-shaped with tentacles at edge of body and 4 arms around central mouth. There is no real stomach, for it divides into 4 lobes that run out to edge of body and are joined by circular tube. Four U-shaped organs under "stomach" lobes produce reproductive cells. A band of muscles enables animals to swim by expanding and then contracting bodies. They range from early Cambrian to Recent in age.

Scyphozoa [phylum *Coelenterata*]: jellyfish in usual sense of the word. Large medusae lacking velum; usually free-swimming; tentacles from stomach; sense organs in form of tentaculocysts with no hydroid stage or perhaps with scyphistoma which buds off ephyrae.

sea: 1) subdivision of ocean. All seas except inland seas are physically interconnected parts of earth's total saltwater system. Two types are distinguished, Mediterranean and adjacent. Mediterranean are groups of seas, collectively separated from the major body as individual sea. Adjacent seas are those connected individually to larger body. 2) numerous Teutonic people of northern Europe had closely related words reserved to name continuous bodies of salt water. These Gothic, Old Norse, Old Frisian and Old Saxon terms are sufficiently alike to suggest common ancestry, though the word from which they were adapted is lost in mists of prehistory. As early as writing of epic poem *Beowulf*, inhabitants of Britain spoke of seemingly endless waters that surrounded their islands as *sae*. To them the earth was made up of just 2 components—land and sea. Even the most scrupulous early geographers did not attempt to specify the size of the sea. But very early a body of salt water smaller than an ocean customarily took a shorter title.

sea anchor [ships]: drag, such as piece of canvas in shape of a cone, thrown overboard to keep ship from drifting and help keep her pointing into wind.

sea anemones: sea anemones are *Cnidaria*, order *Actiniaria*, class *Anthozoa*. Although they are most common in warm shallow water, anemones are found in variety of environments all over the world. They are usually solitary, large and brightly colored. Slow-moving carnivores, they catch prey with stinging tentacles on flower-shaped oral discs. They are without skeletons and attach themselves with basal disc to rocks or, in some species, to shells. Although sedentary, they are able to move over very small area. They are found in cold and temperate seas as well as in the tropics. All sea anemones have same general form: muscular, cylindrical body surrounded by hollow tentacles, in center of which is anemone's body cavity; tentacles bear stinging cells which serve to capture food, tiny marine organisms, and even small fish and crabs and stuff it into cavity.

sea arch: wave erosion of cave or turned through headland leaving bridge of rock over water.

sea arrow: one of family *Ommastrephidea*, but more particularly one of genus *Ommastrephes* of cephalopods which are elongated and streamlined and possess terminal fins which unite in a point at terminus of body. These species are capable of rapid swimming and can overtake schools of fish on which they prey.

sea bass [*Serranidae*]: this family includes large number of marine fish. Several species are found in fresh water. Members of sea bass family are moderately deep-bodied and more or less compressed. Dorsal fins contain spines; ventral fins are thoracic and each usually has 1 spine and 5 soft rays; anal, if present, number 3. Lateral line does not extend on to caudal fin. Members of this family differ from those of centrarchid family in number of characteristics. They possess well-developed pseudobranchiae (gill-like structures on inside of opercle) which are very minute in centrarchids. Ribs are mostly attached to ends of transverse processes instead of on body of vertebrae.

sea belly [*Gastroclonium coulteri*]: neat looking seaweed adhering to rocks lying between 2- and 1.5-ft. tide levels. Has erect, cylindrical, sparsely arranged, forked branches, 5 to 8 in. high and 163 in. wide, which arise from broad, heavy disc-shaped holdfast. Lower part of branch is usually naked, while upper part has number of irregularly arranged, short, naked, lateral branchlets. Usually sea belly is dark olive-brown, sometimes dark green. Several species of *Gastrocolonium* found in warm seas are beautifully iridescent.

seaboard: general term for rather extensive coastal region bordering sea.

sea breeze: light wind blowing toward land caused by equal heating of land and water masses.

sea cabbage [*Hedophyllum sessile*]: common on rocky shores where tides beat hard. On exposed areas it forms dense beds near low-tide mark. Masses of wide blades are arranged in such dense clusters that general effect is that of head of cabbage. Almost circular blade is 15 to 18 in. long and about same width. Holdfast is composed of short, closely crowded fibers formed by thickened basal margins of blades. Sea cabbage is dark brown-green with texture of heavy leather. Fruiting bodies (sori) are present on both sides of blades near base.

sea cave: cave eroded in sea cliff by wave action. It usually is at sea level.

sea channel: long, narrow, U-shaped or V-shaped, shallow depression of sea floor, usually occurring on gently sloping plain or fan.

sea cliff: cliff situated at seaward edge of coast.

sea cock: valve for opening or closing a pipe connection through hull.

sea colander [*Agarum fimbriatum*]: attaches to rocks or wharf pilings from low-tide mark to depths of 50 ft. Prominent midrib about 1 inch wide extends like a smooth band through entire length of single blade. The blade, which may be 2 to 4 ft. long and 18 or more inches wide, widens quickly from short stipe until it becomes nearly circular or elliptical. It is thin and crinkly, perforated with holes near edges. Margins of blade are finely toothed, giving effect of minute ruffle or fringe. The seaweed is yellow-brown with texture of tissue paper. Holdfast is a cluster of many branched outgrowths.

sea comb [*Plocamium pacificum*]: attaches to rocks partially buried in sand in quiet waters between mean low tide and 1.5-ft. tide levels. Dainty sea comb reaches height of 3/8 in. with number of loose, narrow, subcylindrical or compressed branches spreading nearly as wide as high. Most noticeable features are almost transparent, elastic texture and 4 to 7 featherlike, curved branchlets. Holdfast is a tiny disc, or prostrate lower branches may attach to substratum to form the holdfast. Sea comb has rich rose hue, but sometimes color is obscured by sand or by being overgrown with diatoms.

sea cow: aquatic herbivorous mammal of order *Sirenia* which includes dugong, manatee and allegedly extinct Stellar's sea cow.

sea cucumber [*Holothuroidea*]: echinoderm, class *Holothuroidea*. It received popular name from Pliny, 1900 years ago, because this animal does in fact, resemble a cucumber. At top of its soft, tubular body is the mouth through which 10 tentacles draw mud, which passes through body and is expelled through cloaca at other end. Sea cucumber is able to resort to form of self evisceration by expelling internal organs through cloaca when frightened. These organs are regenerated in 4 to 6 weeks. Some species of sea cucumber secrete a strong poison called holothurin, which may prove valuable as a drug.

sea cucumber crab [*Lissocarcinus orbicularis*]: this little swimming crab has rather smooth, oval carapace which measures about ½ in. in diameter and which bears fine lobes upon anterolateral margin. It is symmetrically mottled above with light and dark areas which vary in color from almost black through purple to brown; lighter areas range from light yellow to white. Although

this crab belongs in family of swimming crabs (*Porfunidae*), it does not swim and does not have 5th leg flattened as do other members of this family. It lives among tentacles and in mouth cavity of sea cucumbers, particularly *Holothuria atra Jager*.

sea fans: same class (*Anthozoa*) of phylum *Cnidaria* as many jellyfish, are octocorallines. They are actually colonies of animals; large number of individual polyps spread over calcareous and flexible skeleton. They exist in brilliant reds, yellows, oranges and purples; attached to bottom or to rocks. Sea fans are found in all seas.

sea feathers: any of group of featherlike sessile crinoids.

sea fern [*Bryopsis corticulans*]: sea fern grows between 2- and 1.5-ft. tide levels on rocks exposed to strong surf. Most striking features are coarse, stiff branches which extend from conspicuous axis, 1/32 to 1/16 in. wide, glossy slippery texture and blackish-green color. Just as primary branches extend stiffly from axis, so secondary branches extend stiffly from primary branches. This gives the plant regular arrangement of a fern. This is an annual plant, fruiting during spring. Holdfast is a rhizoid from which several stiff, erect shoots arise.

sea fire: brilliant display of bioluminescence; more commonly described from tropical waters.

sea floor: bottom of ocean where there is generally smooth gentle gradient. In many uses depth is disregarded and term may be used to designate areas in basins or plains or on continental shelf.

sea floor habitat [diving]: undersea living quarters for aquanauts in saturated condition.

sea fog: type of advection fog formed when air, that has been lying over warm-water surface, is transported over colder water surface, resulting in cooling of lower layer of air below its dew point.

sea girdle or tangle [*Laminaria platymeris*]: sea girdle with single blade is one of largest and most conspicuous of big kelps; some Pacific beaches are dominated by it. Specimens differ greatly in length, thickness, degree of flattening of stipe, shape of blade and splitting of blade. Average specimen may be 3 ft. long and 1½ ft. wide, with blade divided 2 to 12 times. Holdfast is large, branched, rounded mass of fibers, strong enough to hold plant in place despite force of waves.

seagoing: designed or fitted for navigating the open sea or ocean, as distinguished from inland or sheltered water sailing; as, a *seagoing vessel;* a *seagoing tug.*

sea gooseberry: luminescent ctenophore (*Pleurobrachia*) found in coastal waters. Has appearance of transparent gooseberry.

sea grape: small ascidian, particularly of species

Molgula manhattensis, which grows in large clusters in piles, rocks and other underwater objects.

seagrass: 1) member of either of 2 families *(Hydrocharitaceae* and *Zosteraceae)* of usually grasslike marine spermatophytes. Sea grasses grow chiefly in sand or mud-sand bottoms and most abundantly in waters less than 30 ft., but some may grow on rock in intertidal zone, and others may range to depths of at least 200 ft. Eelgrass *(Zostera marina),* turtle grass *(Thalassia testudinum)* and manatee grass *(Syringodium filiforme)* are better known members of these families. 2) seed-bearing marine plants; some attain lengths of 8 ft. Found in shallow waters, both brackish and marine.

sea hare: large marine mollusks of class *Gastropoda.* Its arched, oval body has primitive internal shell nearly covered by mantle. Its 2 front tentacles resemble rabbit's ears and give animal its name.

sea horse, spotted: sea horse exhibits different color phases according to amount of light in environment. Sometimes it is gray, at other times greenish or brown, at still other times silvery black. It averages 5 or 6 in. long. Other species are smaller. But all sea horses are of similar appearance and habits. It is confined in straitjacket of armored rings with flattened sides, extending from head to tail. Arched head bears uncanny resemblance to head of a horse; eyes can move independently of each other, as those of a chameleon, aiding in its keen vision. Sea horses swim in vertical position, moved by whirling of tiny dorsal fin.

sea ice: specially, ice formed by freezing of seawater; opposed principally to land ice. In brief, it forms first as frazil crystals (lolly ice), thickens into sludge and coagulates into sheet ice, pancake ice or ice floes of various shapes and sizes. Thereafter, sea ice may develop into pack ice and/or become form of pressure ice.

sea ice shelf: sea ice floating in vicinity of its formation and separated from fast ice, of which it may have been a part, by tide crack or family of such cracks.

SEAL [Sea-Air-Land]: military assault force with underwater capability.

sea laurel [*Laurencia spectabilis*]: grows abundantly on rocks between mean low and 1.5-ft. tide levels. Striking feature is presence of smooth, blunt, flattened, cartilaginous branches which are without midribs, like on one plane, are free from one another and are naked on lower part. It is usually 5 to 7 in. high. Sea laurel is dull purplish-red. Like so many small, red seaweeds, sea laurel has tiny (1/16 in.) disclike holdfast.

sea lettuce [*Ulva lactuca*]: sea lettuce is found attached to rocks or other seaweed from 2-ft.-tide mark to mean low-tide mark. It is grass-green alga with texture of tissue paper. As it becomes old it may become brown or black. It has thin, broadly expanded blade, 8 to 12 in. long with width approximately 1/4 to 1/3 the length. Surface of 2-celled blade is perfectly smooth, although margins are often deeply cut and worn. Number of blades arise from holdfast so that they resemble head of loosely arranged leaf lettuce, branches falling gracefully over rock to which it is attached.

sea level: height of surface of sea at any time.

sea level datum: determination of mean sea level, having been adopted as standard for heights, although it may differ from later determination over longer period of time.

sea level pressure: atmospheric pressure at mean sea level, either directly measured or, most commonly, empirically determined from observed station pressure.

seam: 1) in reptiles, furrow separating laminae of shell of turtle. 2) in ships, space between planks in hull.

seamen's lien: that of a seaman against a vessel for wages due. Classed as a *preferred maritime lien,* it ranks first in priority claims.

seamen's records: U.S. Coast Guard maintains a record of all persons to whom documents have been issued authorizing them to serve as crew members of U.S. vessels of the *merchant marine;* also, all records of issues of licenses, suspensions and revocations of certificates of service and licenses, and current employment of merchant seamen. In Great Britain, the Registrar-General of Shipping and Seamen at London performs a similar national service.

seamount chain: several seamounts in a line with bases separated by relatively flat sea floor.

seamounts: 1) dotting the ocean floors are drowned, isolated, steep-sloped peaks called seamounts. They stand at least 3,000 ft. above surrounding ocean floor, their crests covered by depths of water measured in thousands of feet. Most seamounts have sharp peaks and, insofar as can be told, they are all of volcanic origin. 2) isolated, steep-sloped peak rising from deep ocean floor but submerged beneath ocean surface. Most have sharp peaks, but some have flat tops and are called guyots or tablemounts.

sea mud: rich saline deposit from salt marshes and seashores.

sea palm [*Postelsia palmaeformis*]: large conspicuous alga which thrives in upper tidal level where surf beats hard. Plant has olive-brown, glossy stipe, 2 ft. long and 1 to 2 in. in diameter, tapering slightly from base to top. Both branch and blade split longitudinally into 2 branches and blades of equal size. There may be as many as 100 pendent blades.

sea pansy: disc-shaped purple members of coelenterate subclass *Alcyonaria* or *Octocorallia*. Sea pansy is fleshy, colonial animal with many polyps.

sea pen: member of alcyonarian order *Pennatulacea* which exists as colony of specialized individuals. Sea pens are long, slender, feathery and bear polyps.

sea pork: compound tunicate that forms pale blue or pink masses on pilings or other solid objects.

sea puss: dangerous longshore current, a rip current, caused by return flow; loosely, the submerged channel or inlet through a bar caused by those currents.

sea raven [sculpin]: mottled reddish or purple-brown sculpin that grows to maximum length of 25 in. and weight of 7 lbs. Average individuals are 15 in. long. Sea ravens are found at depths of less than 300 ft. This unattractive fish is covered with tubercles and other outgrowths on head and chin and is armed with long, stiff spines on forward dorsal fin and on gill cover; ventral fins are small and stiff-rayed. They are voracious eaters preying on variety of aquatic invertebrates as well as fish, often tackling a fish larger than themselves.

sea reach: straight section of lower course of river between last bend and sea.

sea road: the course a ship takes on a voyage. Customary route taken by ships sailing between different places.

sea robin fish: have large grotesque heads and winglike pectoral fins, latter feature accounts for common name. Of 2 dorsal fins, forward one is very spiny; ventral fins are located far forward beneath head. Most distinctive feature consists of 3 fingerlike rays in front of each pectoral fin. These rays, hooked at tip, are used in grasping stones and other objects on sea bottom as fish crawls about in search of mollusks and crustaceans.

sea robin, northern: common sea robin is brown or gray with dark saddles across back and yellowish-white belly; it grows to length of 25 in.

sea robin, striped: same general appearance as northern sea robin, tan or brownish fish with spotted fins and striking brown-striped "fingers." It is slightly smaller, growing to length of 12 in.

sea rose [*Schizymenia pacifica*]: grows between mean low tide and 1.5-ft. tide level on rocks exposed to surf, or it is dredged from depth of 30 ft. Most noticeable features are rich brownish color and smooth, sticky, flat, relaxed blade which arises from extremely short (1/8 in.), cylindrical stipe and tiny holdfast. Almost at once stipe broadens into full membraneous blade which looks like torn petals of a rose.

sea sac [*Halosaccion gladiforme*]: grows abundantly in mid-tide range of 2.5- to 1-ft. tide levels in rather restricted areas. One of easiest seaweeds to identify, it is an erect, hollow alga standing upright on short, cylindrical stipe. It is approximately the length and circumference of human finger about 4 in. long, ½ to ¾ in. in diameter and rounded at top. Walls of sac are thin and smooth with texture of rubber gloves. Sea sac varies from yellowish-brown to olive-green to reddish-purple, color being determined by age of plant.

seashore lake: body of water isolated from sea by sediment bars or banks.

sea slick: area of sea surface, variable in size and markedly different in appearance, with color and/or oiliness; usually caused by plankton blooms.

sea slide: submarine sediment slump or mass movement which may evolve into turbidity flow. Analogous to landslide.

sea snail, neglected: this sea snail is oval and marked over outer surface of shell by spiral and longitudinal lines. Columella bears 7 or 8 teeth. Outer surface of shell is black and is spotted with white; shell is white within; it will reach length of about ½ in.

sea snail, pitchy: this species is oval and marked by fine spiral lines which may be either closely or widely spaced. Columella is broad, flat, slightly concave and bears few small teeth in middle. Shell is dark blue to black and often marked with fine, faint specks of white or gray; aperture is white. It will reach a length of about ¾ in.

sea snail, pleated: compact, solid species of somewhat hemispherical shape. It is covered over outer surface with 18 to 20 spiral ridges which are separated by grooves. Outer lip of aperture is crenated and bears within it a row of teeth which are bordered by larger tooth at each end. It is whitish to brownish in color and often spotted and streaked with black. Large specimens will reach a length of about 1½ in.

sea snake: reptile of family *Hydrophidae;* group comprising about 50 species of truly marine forms distantly related to cobras and possessing similar venom. All are inhabitants of warm coastal waters of Indian Ocean and western Pacific with one exception, yellow-bellied sea snake which is oceanic and ranges entirely across both Indian and Pacific Oceans in low latitudes.

sea snow: particles of organic detritus and living forms. Downward drift of these particles and living forms, especially in dense concentrations, appears similar to a snowfall when viewed by underwater investigators.

sea spatula [*Pleurophycus gardneri*]: lives in minus-tidal zone where currents run swiftly. Most conspicuous feature is broad band that extends length of blade. Blade is 18 to 30 in. long and 4 to 15 in. wide; midrib is 2 to 6 in. wide. Blade is broader at base, narrowing somewhat toward upper end. As far as is known, spatula is an annual plant. This seaweed is dark olive with texture of medium weight rubber gloves. Holdfast is composed of several whorls of strong branched fibers.

sea spider [*pycnogonid*]: one of class *Pycnogonida* of spiderlike benthic arthropods which range from shallow water to great depths. The species inhabiting shallow waters range in size from a fraction of an inch to a few inches; deepwater species may attain a spread of several feet.

sea stack: tall, columnar rock isolated from coast by differential wave erosion.

sea staghorn [*Codium fragile*]: grows rather commonly on tops and sides of rocks between 1½ ft. and mean low-tide levels. It is easy to recognize by erect, spongy, hairy, forked, cylindrical shoots; these are approximately 1/8 to 1/4 in. wide and 4 to 9 in. long. Both forking and texture reminds one of staghorns. Hairy exterior is covered with mucilage. Spongy shoots are usually greenish-black but they are sometimes covered with whitish fleece. Sea staghorn persists throughout winter, often living for several years.

sea star [starfish]: one of class *Asteroidea* of echinoderms having flat, usually fine-armed body. Body wall contains embedded calcareous plates bearing spines or tubercles. Some spines are modified into pincerlike organs called pedicellariae, which in some species are dangerously venomous to humans.

sea swallows [terns]: long-winged seabirds of rather small size with tapering pointed bills, straight or slightly curved at tip. Legs are very short; webbed feet are small. Most have long forked tails, outer tail feathers being exceptionally elongated in some of marine species. Mainly birds of coasts of warmer parts of the world, but a number of species migrate into north temperate regions during summer to breed.

sea turtle: any of various large marine turtles belonging to reptilian order, *Testidinata*, and having feet modified into paddlelike appendages, including leatherback, hawksbill, loggerhead, green and Ridley turtles; widely distributed in warm seas.

sea urchins: *one of a class (Echinoidea) of echino-* derms in which body is covered by hard shell (test) composed of fitted immovable plates; spines that are articulated at bases, of various sizes, often large and sharp are present on test; members of class may be spherical (regular sea urchins), depressed spherical (cake urchins), discoidal (sand dollars) or round elongate (heart urchins). Many species of urchins have venomous spines, over a foot long in some species, that

sea walnut: transparent, luminescent ctenophore. Often seen in large swarms on surface in coastal waters.

seaward: in the direction of or toward the sea; as, *the stream flows seaward.* Out from the coast or toward the offing; as, *the boat stood seaward on a long reach.*

seaward beach: seaward-facing beach of reef islands.

seaward reef margin: seaward edge of reef flat marked in place by algal ridge and cut by surge channels, which are landward extensions of reef-front grooves.

seaway: place where moderate seas are running.

seaweed: any macroscopic marine alga or sea grass.

seaweed bed: area of attachment and growth of many algae or eelgrass, most frequently in relatively shallow water.

sea whip: alcyonarian of order *Gorgonacea* with hard skeleton and long flexible body with few or no branching arms unlike its close relative, the sea fan.

seaworthiness: state of being seaworthy; that reasonably safe and proper condition in which a vessel's hull and equipment, her cargo and stowage thereof, machinery, and complement of crew are deemed adequate to undertake a specified sea voyage or to be employed in a particular trade.

secchi disc: white, black or varicolored disc, 30 cm. (about 11.7 in.) in diameter, used to measure water transparency (clarity). Disc is lowered in water and depth (in meters) at which it disappears from sight is averaged with depth at which it reappears. Average value is used to represent seawater transparency.

second: term used to describe distance or depth; one second refers to about 4,800 ft., or distance that sound will travel through seawater during one second. Two vessels may be said to be 10 seconds apart when their positions are separated by about 48,000 ft.

secondary current pattern: short period variation of prevailing current pattern.

secondary production: sum of organic matter pro- cover their bodies. Among the spines are tiny pedicles, which are small pincers, some possessing poison glands. Abundant in the tropics they are also found in colder waters as far north as Arctic Ocean. Body is generally knob-shaped; mouth with elaborate masticatory apparatus comprises 20 pieces and is located on lower surface. They sometimes live in holes which they dig to fit their bodies; diet normally consists of algae and minute organisms.

sea wall: man-made structure of rock or concrete built along portion of coast to prevent wave erosion of beach.

duced as result of predation on primary producers and their products. Net secondary production would be this figure less the loss due to catabolism. Organic matter produced by herbivores of zooplankton in given area or volume in given time. Second trophic level.

secondary tide station: place at which tide observations are made over short period.

sector: arc of the horizon through which a light is designed to show in a particular color, or is not visible therein. On charts, it usually is indicated by lines representing its limiting bearings.

secular changes: changes which are very slow and take many centuries to accomplish, they may apply to climate or level of land or sea. Increases or decreases of density and/or direction of earth's total magnetic field over period of many years; usually given as average gammas per year for intensity values and minutes per year for directional values.

sediment: 1) particulate organic and inorganic matter which accumulates in a loose, unconsolidated form. It may be chemically precipitated from solution, secreted by organisms or transported by air, ice, wind or water and deposited. 2) in the singular, term is usually applied to material in suspension in water or recently deposited from suspension. In the plural, term is applied to all kinds of deposits from waters of streams, lakes or seas, and in a more general sense, to deposits of wind and ice.

sedimentary cycle: every series of marine formations in given region is bounded by 2 regressions, constituting a sedimentary cycle. In reality this series necessarily begins with deposit of littoral, coastal facies, corresponding to coming of the sea. It will continue with deepwater formations, daily approximating maximum of transgressing and it will end finally with new littoral deposits, prelude to regression.

sedimentary facies: type of sediment within stratum of certain age that is distinct and different from other sediments of same age.

sedimentary rocks: rocks formed by accumulation of sediment in water (aqueous deposits) or from air (eolian deposits). Sediment may consist of rock fragments of particles of various sizes (conglomerate, sandstone, shale), of remains of products of animals or plants (certain limestone and coral), of product of chemical action or of evaporation (salt, gypsum, etc.) or of mixtures of these materials.

sedimentation: 1) process by which mineral and organic matter is deposited to make sediments. 2) process of breakup and separation of particles from parent rock, their transportation, deposition and consolidation into another rock.

sedimentation method: technique used in quanti-

tative estimation and identification of phytoplankton organisms. Plankton to be measured is concentrated by settling in glass cylinders and organisms are counted or identified by using inverted microscope.

sediment basin: depression, often marine, in which sediments are deposited. Deposits are usually thickest in center and thinner toward edges.

sediment transporters: denotes aquatic animals which stir up ocean bottom deposits and mix up organic and mineral constituents.

seersucker [*Costaria costata*]: seersucker kelp adorns wood, rocks and other large algae on exposed beaches at or just below tide mark. Outstanding characteristics are 5 prominent ribs which extend length of blade, each projecting on one side only and alternating, 3 on one side and 2 on the other. In mature specimens the portion between ribs is puckered or shirred, but edges of the blade are smooth. Plant is dark brown when alive but turns green when it dies.

seiche: stationary wave oscillation with a period varying from a few minutes to an hour or more (somewhat less than tidal periods), being dependent upon dimensions of basin in which it occurs. Seiches usually are attributed to strong winds, atmospheric pressure changes or seismic disturbances, and are found in enclosed bodies of water or superimposed upon tidal waves of open ocean.

seiche wave: oscillation wave on surface of lake caused by an earthquake.

seilsjegte: clinker-built, open skiff used by fishermen on southern coast of Norway; 18 to 20 ft. long and rigged with 1 or 2 spritsails.

seine: type of net used to catch fish by encirclement, usually by active closure of 2 ends but also including closure or pursing of the bottom (purse seine).

seismic profiler: continuous, deep-sea reflection system used to study structure beneath ocean floor to depths of 10,000 ft. or more. Reflections are recorded on a drum whose rotation is actuated by initial explosion.

seismic profiling: determining contours of ocean bottom, usually by continuous "reflection" obtained by measurement of sound waves reflected back from different bottom layers.

seismic reflection: measuring and recording, in wave form, of travel time of acoustic energy reflected back to detectors from rock or sediment layers which have different elastic wave velocities.

seismic sea wave: large amplitude, long period wave caused by submarine earthquake, "failure" or sliding of large masses of sediment on continental slope or submarine volcanic explosions. Describing seismic sea wave is considered incorrect because there is no known relation between tide and region of seismic sea wave. Tsunami is Japanese equivalent of seismic sea wave.

seize [ships]: to wrap, bind or secure with small staff.

seizure: arrest of a vessel and/or her cargo as by a writ of attachment with view of satisfying a lien or libel in admiralty; for violation of a public law, such as smuggling or carrying on an illicit trade; etc.

selenozone [*Gastropoda*]: band of closely-spaced crescentic growth lines on lateral surface of whorls. Typically, it marks positions of apertural notch or slit during earlier stages of growth.

Selsey galley: long, narrow, double-ended, clinker-built rowboat used by coast guard at Selsey, England, up to time of the Great War. It was about 40 ft. long and carried 22 men who pulled 11 pairs of oars.

semaphore: apparatus by which distant signals are shown, as by a system of lights, flags, disks, or movable arms, for controlling traffic in a canal or other waterway; indicating depth of water in a fairway, dock entrance, or on a bar; announcing local ice and weather conditions; etc. The *International Code* or military system of signaling in which letters of the alphabet are represented by various positions of one's outstretched arms, usually with the addition of short-staffed hand flags, with relation to the body; or, mechanically, by wooden or metal arms set at various angles with a post or pole. Messages always are made in plain language by this means. U.S. Hydrographic Office publication *H.O. 87, International Code of Signals, Vol. I,* contains instructions in *semaphore signaling.*

semidiurnal constituent: tidal constituent that has 2 maximums and 2 minimums each constituent day; its symbol is usually distinguished by subscript 2, as M_2, S_2, N_2, etc.

semidiurnal current: type of tidal current having 2 flood and 2 ebb periods of nearly the same duration during tidal day; usually associated with semidiurnal tide.

semidiurnal tides: having a period or cycle of approximately half a lunar day (12.42 solar hours). Tides and tidal currents are said to be semidiurnal when 2 flood and 2 ebb periods occur each lunar day. Type of tide having 2 high waters and 2 low waters each tidal day with small inequalities between successive high- and successive low-water heights and durations.

seminal vesicle: enlarged part of male reproductive system where sperm are stored; fluid may be secreted here also.

sensible heat: portion of energy exchanged between ocean and atmosphere which is utilized in changing temperature of medium into which it penetrates.

sensor: measuring device used to determine acoustic properties, height of waves, tides, temperatures, etc. A technical means, usually electronic, to extend man's natural senses by means of energy emitted or reflected.

septal groove [*Coelenterata*]: longitudinal groove on outer surface of corallite wall. Corresponds to position of septum on inner surface.

Septibranchia, subclass [phylum *Mollusca*]: gills absent; adductor muscles about equal; mantle partially open and divided horizontally by muscular partition (modified from gill); respiration through walls of suprabranchial chamber; muscular septum acting as pumping mechanism; marine. *Poromya, Cuspidaria.*

septum: 1) in *Coelenterata*, one of several longitudinal plates arranged radially between axis and wall of corallite. Presumably alternating in position with mesentaries and supported basal disk and lower wall of polyps. 2) in *Mollusca*, transverse plate of shelly material. 3) in cephalopods, partition which separates hollow chambers of shells.

sequence of current: order in which the 4 tidal current strengths occur daily, with special reference as to whether stronger flood immediately precedes or follows stronger ebb. Usually associated with mixed tidal currents having inequalities in speeds and durations.

sequence of tide: order in which the 4 tides of a day occur, with special reference as to whether higher high water immediately precedes or follows lower low water. Usually associated with mixed tide having inequalities in heights and duration.

sergeant fish: the *cobia* or *snook*, an edible pelagic fish found off the warmer coasts of America and in both East and West Indies waters. About four feet in length, has a stout body; somewhat of mackerel proportions, tapering to head and tail; a high mid-dorsal fin with added fringe to tail on upper and lower sides; and has a conspicuous full-length dark stripe along each side. The name sometimes is applied to the *robalo.*

sergestid: one of family *(Sergestidae)* of usually deep pelagic shrimps or prawns.

serial station: oceanographic station consisting of one or more Nansen casts.

Serpens: small constellation N.W. of, and adjoining, *Ophiuchus.* Its brightest member is *Unuk (a Serpentis)* of magnitude 2.75 located in 6° 35′ N. declination and 15 hrs. 42 min. right ascension, or 20° almost due south of *Alphacca* of the *Northern Crown.*

serpent shell, distorted [*Colubraria distorta*]: serpent shell is elongated, thick and solid; spire is bent; whorls are covered by granules and contain about 9 obliquely placed varices. Color of species is usually pinkish or yellowish-brown and marked with chestnut brown areas and spots. It ranges in length from 1½ to 2½ in.

serpent shell, pointed [*Colubraria muricata*]: this shell is elongated and has a somewhat turreted spire which is marked with about 11 varices. It appears to be longitudinally grooved and encircled by rows of tubercles. Anterior canal is short, columella is smooth and thickly enamelled and outer lip is toothed within. It is a light brownish color and marked with chestnut brown areas and with 1 or 2 encircling rows of brown spots. It ranges in length from 1½ to 2½ in.

serpulid: members of *Serpulidae*, family of polychaete worms that live in calcareous tubes.

serrate [*Mollusca*]: notched or like sawteeth; saw-edged in fish.

serve [ships]: to wrap ends of ropes with small staff so that they do not unlay.

serving ropes [ships]: small cordage wound around a rope in serving or wrapping it.

sessile: with respect to organisms, those which are fixed to substrate. With respect to structures that are sometimes stalked or raised, condition when they are not stalked or raised.

seston: living and nonliving bodies which swim or float in water.

set: 1) direction toward which current flows. Usually indicated in degrees true or points of the compass. 2) to attach to a surface, as by larvae of various marine invertebrates.

setae: bristlelike stiff cuticular structures, as in parapodia of polychaetes, on head of chaetographs or on appendages of various crustaceans, etc.

setee: long, sharp vessel formerly used in Mediterranean, rigged and navigated similarly to galley or xebec, but fitted with "setee" sails instead of lateens. Setee sail is quadrilateral with short luff, whereas lateen is triangular.

setee sail: quadrilateral sail, head of which was bent to lateen yard, which hung obliquely to mast at about 1/3rd length of yard, greater length being upper portion. Leech is generally 5/6ths the length of head, and luff 1/5th of depth of leech. Oriental setee sails have very short luff.

setose: having bristles, i.e., setae.

set piling [ships]: reinforcing piling in ground beneath the ways.

setting: act of placing, fitting, or securing something; as, *setting sail; setting of planking; setting of a sextant*. Designating that which sets; as, *settingmaul; settingpole; setting sun*.

settling volume: amount of plankton in container

concentrated by gravity and having variable quantities of interstitial water.

set up [ships]: to tighten.

Seven Seas: Seven Seas is a term generally applied to North and South Atlantic, North and South Pacific, Arctic and Antarctic and Indian Oceans.

sewing thread [*Gracilaria contervoies*]: lies half buried in sand or attaches itself to rocks at low-tide level or below. Cosmopolitan species growing throughout world. Easy to identify by its long, naked, whiplike shoots, from 2 to 6 ft. long and 1/32 in. wide. Shoots, which live from year to year, are cylindrical, irregular and sparingly branched, branching usually taking place near base. Texture is cartilaginous, becoming horny when dry; color varies from yellow to red-brown to purplish-black; branches taper to sharp points at apex.

sexern: 6-oared, open, double-ended, clinker-built boat from 20 to 23 ft. long, used in Shetland Islands off coast of Scotland. Stem and sternpost are raking and it is rigged with single, square lugsail. Single sail has been abandoned to great extent, however, in favor of standing lugsail and jib. It is used for inshore fishing and ferrying, but is rapidly becoming obsolete.

sextant: 1) navigational instrument used on ship to measure altitudes of sun, moon and stars. 2) literally, 6th part of a circle. An important instrument of navigation for measuring angular distance of 2 stars or other objects or altitude of sun or other celestial bodies above horizon.

sexual dimorphism: condition in which male and female of a species takes 2 distinct, different forms.

shackle [ships]: link with bolt fastened through its eyes, used for fastening chains and eye loops together.

shad: similar in appearance to alewives but grow to larger size, with average weight of 2 to 3 lbs. and occasional maximum weight of 10 lbs. Thus shad are largest members of herring family. Shad differ from alewives in having dark spots behind gills and notched upper jaw. Silvery area beneath eye deeper than it is long; in alewives this area is longer than it is deep.

shad, Alabama [*Alosa alabamae*]: large, silvery shad with small fins. Depth of body 1/3 the length; 55 scale rows along lateral line; about 40 gill rakers below angle of arch. Body deeply compressed, head deep; teeth in maxillary scarcely perceptible; upper jaw with small notch at top. Color bluish above, silvery white on side; small spot behind opercle.

shad, common [*Alosa sapidissima*]: large, silvery shad with small fins. Body deep, 1/3 the length; 60—65 scale rows along lateral line; about 60 gill rakers below angle of the arch. Body compressed;

head deep; positions of cheeks deeper than long. Peritoneum white. Color above bluish, silvery white on sides and ventrally; dark spot behind opercle, sometimes followed by several less conspicuous dots.

shade: one of the colored hinged glasses on a sextant for reducing the glare when taking a solar observation.

shad, Florida threadfin [*Dorosoma petenese vanhyningi*]: silvery fish with last ray of dorsal fin very long. Deep-bodied fish with 14—15 rays on dorsal fin, last ray of which is very elongate; 20—23 rays in anal fin; about 40 rows of scales along side of body. Stomach is very muscular like gizzard of a fowl. Color silvery with small round spot on shoulder region. Maximum length about 18 inches.

shad, gizzard [*Dorosoma cepedianum*]: gizzard shad is silvery with bluish back. Young fish have spot just posterior to pectoral fin. Belly is sharply serrated or keeled. This species is easily distinguished by last ray of dorsal fin, which is very long. Teeth are absent in adult, thorax present in young. Stomach is very muscular or gizzardlike and intestine is long and coiled. Gill rakers are long and extremely fine, reaching lengths of over 15 in. Gizzard shad frequent large rivers and muddy lakes.

shad, hickory [*Alosa mediocris*]: moderate-sized, silvery shad. Dorsal fin rays 15, anal fin rays 21, about 50 scale rows along side of body; lining of body cavity pale. Head long, profile straight and not very steep. Upper jaw emarginate, lower jaw strongly projecting. Color silvery, somewhat bluish above; sides with faint longitudinal stripes. Maximum length up to 2 ft.

shadow pin: the *style,* or vertical pin fitted in an azimuth instrument or in center of a compass card for indicating the bearing of the sun by shadow thrown on rim of the card. Bearing observed is then equal to number of degrees coinciding with shadow *minus* 180°.

shadow zone: sea area impervious to direct sound rays, due to refraction or reflecting conditions. Ideal place for submarine to hide.

shaft alley [ships]: passageway along shaft line between after bulkhead of engine room and sternpost, affording means of access to propeller shaft.

shaft coupling [ships]: flange on end of shaft section connecting 2 sections by bolts.

shaft pipe [ships]: pipe which passes through hole in sternpost and through frames with circular housing. In it are bearings on which propeller shaft rotates.

shaft strut [ships]: bracket supporting after end of propeller shaft and propeller in twin- or multi-

ple-screwed vessels having propeller shafts fitted off from center line.

shale: fine-grained rock formed by hardening of clay.

shallop: American "shallop" was nondescript type of small vessel, open or half-decked of various sizes. It was used in early colonial times for fishing.

shallow scattering layer: populations of organisms in water over continental shelf which scatter sound. Organisms usually occur as separate groups or patches and are discontinuous horizontally. Horizontal dimensions of such patches on echo-sounder record usually are less than vertical dimensions.

shallow sea: marginal or inland extension of ocean having prevailing depths of less than 600 ft.

shallow water constituent: short period, harmonic term introduced into formula of astronomical tide constituents to take account of change in form of tide wave resulting from shallow water conditions. Shallow water constituents include compound tides.

shallow water wave: progressive gravity wave which is, in water, less than 1/25 the wavelength in depth.

shank [ships]: main body of anchor.

shape: a ball, cone, or cylindrical drum, made of canvas or light metal, exhibited as a signal. A bar of structural metal having a curved or angular cross section, such as a *bulb angle, channel,* or a *T-bar.*

sharesman: member of a fishing vessel's crew who *shares* in profits of a voyage or season. He may be engaged on the "no catch-no pay" basis or may assume part of the capital risks involved.

shark: any of approximately 250 species of fish-like vertebrates belonging to elasmobranch order *Selachii.* Included are large, plankton-feeding basking whales and sharks, predacious white, mako, tiger, blue, hammerhead, sand and gray sharks, and variety of others, such as cow, frile, horn, thresher, nurse, cat, angel and dogfish sharks.

shark, basking: closely related to white shark, differing in having extremely long gill slits that almost meet under throat. It possesses very small teeth, peculiarity that makes it necessary for this shark to be a filter feeder. Basking sharks vary in color from brown and gray to black; in size they rate as second largest of all fishes, being outclassed only by whale sharks. A 30-ft. basking shark weighs over 4 tons.

shark, Bonito: similar in appearance and habits to porbeagle; grows to length of 20 ft.

shark, bull [*Carcharhinus leucas*]: grayish, rather stout shark with short, broad snout. Spiracles lacking, no pronounced labial grooves at corner of mouth; origin of anal fin slightly posterior to origin of second dorsal fin. Color grayish above, whitish below. Attains length of about 10 ft.

shark, Greenland: related to spiny dogfish but much larger; it is also an inhabitant of cold arctic waters. Entire body is one color, usually dark brown or grayish-black. Individuals reach length of 20 ft. and may weigh up to a ton. In spite of size, Greenland shark is harmless and sluggish, living most of the time on ocean bottom where it feeds on cod, halibut and haddock.

shark, leopard: relatively small shark, harmless, gray in color with saddlelike crossbars on back and spots along sides. It is usually less than 5 ft. long. Leopard shark is most common shark in California waters.

shark, mako: sharp-nosed mackerel shark, dark blue-gray species off Atlantic Coast. It is a medium-sized shark very similar to porbeagle except for minor anatomical features. Large individuals reach length of 12 ft. and weigh up to 1,000 lbs. Mako sharks are fast swimmers, usually found offshore where they prey on herring, mackerel and swordfish.

shark, nurse [*Cinglymostoma cirratum*]: harmless brown or gray shark with distinctive pair of barbels on either side of mouth; first dorsal fin is set far back above ventral fins. Nurse sharks reach length of 14 ft. but most individuals are half this size. This shark is sluggish, warm-water species. Nurse sharks feed on crustaceans, squid and refuse.

shark, porbeagle: common mackerel shark is gracefully proportional with blue-gray body and high dorsal fin situated far forward just behind pectoral fins. It has conspicuous keel on either side of tail. Porbeagle roams open seas preying on schools of mackerel and herring. They are medium-sized, harmless sharks ordinarily 4 to 5 ft. long.

shark, remora [*Echeneis naucrates*]: skinny, dark-striped fish with sucking grid on back. Anterior dorsal fin modified into sucker. Body slender and elongate, rounded in cross section; mouth moderate, terminal in position; lower jaw strongly protruding, tip flexible; teeth small, pointed and uniform in size in adults. Caudal fin lunate to truncate depending on age. Color grayish with dark stripe down each side, which is bordered above and below with lighter stripe.

shark, sand: harmless shark, brown or mottled in color, generally about 5 ft. long. Like other sharks with similar tail fins, dorsal fin is situated midway along back; upper lobe of tail fin is several times the size of lower lobe. Young sand sharks often have yellowish-brown spots along sides of body and on dorsal tail fins. Sand sharks

are sluggish fish, feeding on smaller aquatic animals in shallow waters off beaches.

shark, sandbar: also known as brown shark, it is medium-sized, attaining length of 8 ft. and weight of 200 lbs. Sandbar sharks are brownish with lighter underside; they are often found in shallow water over sandbars in bays and harbors.

shark, sharp-nosed [*Scoliodon terraenovae*]: small, slender, grayish shark, often with dark-bordered tail. Spiracles lacking; labial grooves at corners of mouth; origin of anal fin anterior to origin of 2nd dorsal fin. Color brownish to olive-gray above, whitish below.

shark, smooth dogfish: slaty gray species with yellowish underside usually 2 or 3 ft. long. It is omnivorous, thriving as well on refuse as on lobster and other crustaceans.

shark, smooth hammerhead: grayish or brownish shark with blunt head that extends laterally into fleshy projections. These grotesque appendages may serve as bow rudder aiding the shark to maneuver quickly as it pursues its prey. It is also thought that expanded head may be of use in detecting food, as nasal groove extends along entire forward edge. Hammerhead sharks have unusually keen sense of smell, being able to pick up a scent from great distance. Eyes are located on outer tip of appendages. Hammerheads are large sharks growing to length of 17 ft.; 13-ft. individual weighs 900 lbs. This species inhabits warm and temperate seas throughout the world.

shark, spiny dogfish: small, common shark that can be recognized by absence of anal fin and by sharp spine in front of each dorsal fin; cold-water species. Average individuals are 3 to 4 ft. long and weigh under 20 lbs. Slaty gray fish with lighter underparts, might be confused with smooth dogfish shark except for spines and lack of anal fin.

shark, thresher [*Alopias vulpinus*]: equipped with most massive and unsymmetrical tail of all sharks. Mammoth upper lobe is often as long as rest of shark's body. Thresher shark is brownish or bluish-gray with mottled or white underside. It is an inhabitant of temperate seas. Average individual is 15 ft. long and weighs over 500 lbs. Thresher sharks are usually encountered a few miles offshore roaming near surface after such schooling fishes as mackerel, menhaden and herring.

shark, tiger: largest member of the family, it is grayish or brown and found throughout the world in tropical and subtropical waters. Young individuals are conspicuously striped with vertical dark bars along sides. Tiger sharks have goatlike appetite feeding on variety of fishes and invertebrates as well as on all kinds of refuse thrown from ships.

shark, whale: harmless and inoffensive giant with authenticated length of over 30 ft. and weight well in excess of 12 tons. Whale sharks are relatively rare species of which little is known. They live in tropical waters. They are reddish or greenish-brown, decorated with bizarre checkerboard pattern made of crisscrossing white and yellowish lines. In some individuals center of each square has bright yellow spot. Huge size of this shark can be imagined when one realizes that one caught at Fire Island had tail-fin spread of 9 ft., head 5 ft. wide with a yard-wide mouth and dorsal fin 2 ft. tall.

shark, white: also known as man-eater shark, Except for greater size and strength, it is very similar to porbeagle. This ashy gray or leaden white shark is a heavyweight with added traits of great speed and voraciousness. A 21-ft. specimen weighs over 7,000 lbs. Worldwide in distribution. Its normal diet consists of large fishes such as tuna and sea turtles, seals and sea lions.

sharpie: small, flat-bottomed boat with outboard, usually cat schooner rigged with leg-of-mutton sail having horizontal sprits to extend to clews. Hull is open, carvel-built with long, sharp bow, slightly flowing sides, square stern and good sheer.

sharpshooter: small sailing boat of Bahamas. Hull has long run with short, hollow entrance. Greatest beam is well forward and there is drag to the keel. Stem and sternpost are straight and raking. Mast, which rakes aft, is set in bow and rigged with leg-of-mutton sail. No jib is carried.

Shaula: the star λ *Scorpii* marking the tip of the *Scorpion's tail*, or point of the *Chain-hook*. It is located in declination 37° S. and right ascension 17 hrs. 30 min.; magnitude 1.71.

shear crack: crack in sea ice caused by 2 different, simultaneous forces acting in parallel but opposite directions on adjacent portions of ice. Sheared parts undergo displacement parallel to plane of crack.

shear legs [ships]: usually 2 or more timbers or spars erected in shape of A-frame with lower ends spread out and upper ends fastened together from which lifting tackle is suspended. Used for raising and moving heavy weights where crane or derrick is not available.

shearwater, Christmas [*Puffinus nativitatis*]: chocolate-brown, bird somewhat lighter below, slightly grayish on throat; tail wedge-shaped; bill and feet black; length 14 in.

shearwater, Heinrots [*Puffinus heinrothi*]: brownish-black seabird with underparts somewhat paler than upper surface; throat and chin gray; underwing coverts whitish; bill grayish-black; feet flesh-colored with blackish margins; length 7.5 in.

shearwater, pale-footed [*Puffinus carneipes*]: seabird chocolate-black; bill fleshy white with line down center and tip brown; feet yellowish flesh color; length 19.5 in.

shearwater, short-tailed [*Puffinus tenuirostris*]: seabird sooty-brown, much paler on undersurface; underwing coverts grayish; bill blackish-brown, feet gray, outer toe blackish, web sometimes yellowish flesh color; length 13 in.

shearwater, sooty [*Puffinus griseus*]: seabird upperparts blackish-brown; underparts grayish-brown, paler on chin; underwing coverts grayish-white; bill blackish; feet slate-gray, outer toe blackish, webs sometimes yellowish; length 16 to 20 in.

shearwater, wedge-tailed [*Puffinus pacificus*]: seabird uppersurface dark chocolate brown, deepening into black on primaries and tail; tail strongly wedge-shaped; face and throat, dark brownish-gray; rest of under surface grayish-brown (dark phase) or white (light phase); bill reddish flesh color, darker on middle line and at tip; feet yellowish flesh color; length 15.5 in.

sheave [ships]: grooved wheel in block, mast or yard in which rope works, as wheel of a block.

shebek: Russian shebek of latter part of 18th century was probably an adaptation of Mediterranean "sebec" although it was more clumsily and heavily built. While retaining lateen rig on raking foremast, remainder was a mixture, square-rigged on mainmast, square topsail and fore-and-aft gaff driver or spanker on mizzenmast.

sheepshead [*Archosargus probatocephalus*]: laterally compressed fish with a pattern like a convict's uniform. Scales along lateral line 46—50; teeth incisorlike and protuberant. Body elongate, strongly compressed, strong arched above; mouth sturdy, but not large; both jaws with row of sharp incisorlike teeth; caudal fin shallow-forked. Color grayish with about 7 prominent dark vertical bars on each side, which are about as wide as interspaces.

sheepshead, California: also called fathead and California redfish. This is conspicuously marked fish with black or dusky body crossed vertically by broad saddle of bright red. Spiny dorsal fin and pectoral fins also are red. In profile this fish has very high "forehead." In breeding season head of male is elevated even more by development of fatty lump or lumps. This species weighs an average of 15 lbs.

sheer [ships]: upward curve of lines of vessel's hull. Amount by which longitudinal lines of hull of vessel depart from horizontal.

sheer plan [ships]: vertical, longitudinal midship section of vessel, showing plan elevation and end view on which are projected various lines as follows: waterline, diagonal line, buttock and bow lines, top-breadth lines, topside sheer lines.

sheer rail [ships]: rail surrounding ship on outside under gunwale; on small vessels, called guardrail.

sheer strakes [ships]: topmost plank of topsides.

sheet: 1) large broad piece of thin metal, distinguished from a plate by its thickness, usually taken as one-eighth inch or under. 2) an expanse of cloud; as, *a sheet of stratus*. 3) clear space amidst floating ice; as, *a sheet of open water*. 4) space in a boat forward of abaft the thwarts, usually in plural; as, *fore sheets, stern sheets*. 5) line or rope for extending and controlling angle of sail, as clew sheets.

sheet erosion: erosion caused by continuous sheet of surface water.

sheet ice: ice formed in smooth, thin layer on water surface by coagulation of frazil or sludge.

sheet-type luminescence: display of biological light appearing diffused or shimmering, often making sea surface appear milky or greenish in color. This type of display usually is caused by masses of microscopic or tiny organisms. Displays may cover large areas of sea surface, at time causing uniform glow from horizon to horizon, or they may appear as irregular patches or wide ribbons of light in an otherwise dark sea.

sheet winch [ships]: small winch for handling sheets, ropes used to adjust sails.

shelf: relatively broad area of shallow sea bottom adjacent to deeper water basin, as in western Texas during Permian time.

shelf edge: line along which there is marked increase of slope at outer margin of continental or island shelf.

shelf seas: shallow seas which occupy wide portions of continental shelf.

shell: 1) long, light, extremely narrow rowing craft employed only for racing or rowing exercises. Largest shell accommodates 8 oarsmen and the smallest but one. 2) hard outer covering of invertebrate; calcareous, siliceous, bony, horny or chitinous covering. 3) in *Gastropoda*, external calcareous skeleton. Consists of single plate, typically drawn into spirally coiled tube which encloses viscera and into which head and foot may be withdrawn. 4) in *Mollusca*, calcareous plate (or plates) deposited by cells in superficial layer of mantle and more or less covering body.

shellcracker: bright, silvery panfish with red margins on opercular spots. Tails emarginate; pectoral fin long and pointed; bright red posterior margin on opercular spot; no definite dark spot at base of posterior end of dorsal fin. Body compressed; ovate in profile; snout rather pronounced; palatine teeth absent. Color silvery olive or silvery bluish above, silvery below. Length up to 10 in.

shell expansion [ships]: plan showing shape and sizes of all plates of shell plating.

shellfish: any aquatic invertebrate with hard external covering, but more commonly any crustacean or mollusk, especially edible commercial species.

shell ice: ice on body of water that remains as an unbroken surface when water level drops so that a cavity is formed between water surface and ice.

shell landings [ships]: points on frames showing where edges of shell plates come.

shell structure: in its complete development, the pelecypod shell has 3 parts: ostracum, hypostracum and periostracum. Ostracum makes up most of calcareous shell; hypostracum is thin, filmlike calcareous layer secreted by cells of muscles at their insertions in shell; periostracum is thin layer of conchiolin covering outer surface of ostracum.

shelter deck [ships]: term applied to deck fitted from stem to stern on relatively light superstructure; main deck.

shelving coast: a coast in which the bottom gradually and constantly slopes from the shore into deep water, as opposed to a *bold, bluff,* or *steep* shore or coast.

Sheratan: star of magnitude 2.72 in *Aries*, lying about 4° S.W. of his brighter neighbor, *Hamal (a Arietis)*.

shift: 1) to change in direction or position; as, *the wind will shift to N.E.; shift the gaff-topsail tack!; shift the helm!; a heavy roll caused cargo to shift*. 2) act of *shifting*, as a vessel from one berth to another. A removal; change in direction or position; as, a shift of 10 feet; a shift of wind; a shift of the grain cargo.

shifting: 1) changeable; varying in position or direction; as, shifting sands; a shifting wind. Designating anything that is movable or may shift or move; as, shifting ballast; a shifting sand bar. 2) charge made by a tug for towing or assisting in moving a vessel from one berth to another.

shifting beam [ships]: portable beam fitted in hatchway to support hatch covers. Ends of beams are fitted in slotted carriers attached to inside of hatchway coamings.

shim [ships]: piece of metal or wood placed under bedplate or base of machine or fitting for purpose of truing it up. Also applied to pieces placed in slack places behind or under frames, plates or planks to preserve a fair surface.

shiner, blackchin [*Notropis heterodon*]: minnow moderately stout and has lateral band surrounding muzzle which is confined to chin and premaxillaries. Scales of first row above lateral line have dark bars which alternate with black marks on lateral line scales producing zigzag appearance. Scales are 5—36—3; 12 to 14 scales are in front of dorsal fin. Jaws are equal or nearly so, maxillary reaching posterior nostril; mouth is oblique, making angle of decidedly less than 60° with the vertical. The species reaches a length of 2½ in.

shiner, blacktail [*Notropis venustus*]: minnow with incomplete, dark lateral stripe and black spot at base of tail. About 15 scales from back of head to origin of dorsal fin; lateral line complete; rays in anal fin 8; head moderate, rather pointed. Brownish above; lighter below. A dark stripe along each side from tip of snout to base of caudal fin; this stripe becoming obsolete anteriorly in mature specimens. Very prominent, dark, oval spot on base of tail at end of lateral stripe. Tip of chin slightly darkened.

shiner, central big mouth [*Notropis dorsalis dorsalis*]: this minnow is greenish with dark lateral band on side. Head is long and flat; tail long and slender; about 35 scales in lateral line. Teeth are 1, 4—4, 1.

shiner, central weed [*Notropis roseus roseus*]: graceful minnow with dark stripe down side. Anal rays 7; 35—36 scales from back of head to origin of dorsal fin. Scales on side immediately below lateral stripe marginal with dark pigment. Head rather short, bluntly rounded. Olivaceous above, lighter below; prominent lateral dark stripe along each side from tip of snout to base of caudal fin.

shiner, eastern longnose [*Notropis longirostris*]: trim little minnow with hardly any color. Dark lateral stripe inconspicuous or absent; about 12 scales between back of head and origin of dorsal fin; lateral line complete; about 36 scales along lateral line; head small. Entire body straw-colored with faint, narrow, darker streak along each side from eye to base of tail; vertical fins slightly dusky. Small minnow is 2 in. long or less.

shiner, flagfin [*Notropis signipinnis*]: trim little minnow with dark stripe down side and 2 sulphur-yellow spots at base of tail. Membranes of dorsal and anal fins with little or no black pigment; scales in lateral line usually 34 or 35; anal fin with 11 rays. Rusty above, light band along side bordered below by dark lateral stripe which runs from tip of snout to base of caudal fin. Tip of chin dark; oval dark spot at base of tail bordered above and below by sulphur-yellow light spots. Vertical fins yellow at bases and red-orange at margins.

shiner, iron-colored [*Notropis chalybaeus*]: graceful minnow with dark stripe down side. Anal rays 7—8; 32—33 scales along lateral line; dark, lateral stripe not terminating in pronounced oval spot at base of tail; inside of mouth with dark pigment. Head flat above, rather narrow, tapering to some-

what parallel muzzle. Rusty-colored above, straw-colored below, prominent dark lateral stripe on each side from tip of snout to base of caudal fin; tip of chin black.

shiner, lowland [*Notropis cummingsae*]: trim little minnow with dark stripe down side. Scales in lateral line 38—40; fin rays 11; 18—20 scales from back of head to origin of dorsal fin. Head short, flattened above; muzzle rounded; mouth, large oblique. Dark olive above, light band of coppery-brown bordered below by lateral stripe of dull steel blue; tip of chin dark; fins very slightly pigmented.

shiner, northern blacknose [*Notropis heterolepis heterolepis*]: rather slender minnow with lateral band running over snout. Dark borders of lateral line pores are expanded to form prominent crescent-shaped black crossbars. Mouth is somewhat oblique but not as much so as in *N. heterodon*. Pharyngeal teeth are 4—4, those of outer row being absent. This minnow reaches length of over 2 in.

shiner, northern mimic [*Notropis volucellus volucellus*]: rather slender minnow with lateral band which is sometimes broken anteriorly. Lateral line scales number 35—38; exposed surface of lateral line scales is about 2 to 3 times as high as long. Mouth is small, length of upper jaw being about equal to diameter of eye; pharyngeal teeth are 4—4. This minnow reaches length of over 2 in.

shiner, northern weed [*Notropis xaenocephalus richardsoni*]: this minnow has slender dark olive body, dark lateral band and spot on tail. Anal rays number 7; these have about 37 scales on lateral line; pharyngeal teeth are 2, 4—4, 2; some are denticulate. Mouth is not oblique as in *N. heterdon* and snout is more blunt. This species reaches length of 2 in.

shiner, Peterson's [*Notropis petersoni*]: graceful, little minnow with dark stripe down side. Anal rays 7; 35—36 scales along lateral line; no pronounced, oval, black spot on base of tail; 13—15 scales from back of head to origin of dorsal fin; scale on side immediately below lateral stripe not margined with dark pigment. Olivaceous above, flesh-colored below with dark lateral stripe on each side from tip of snout to base of tail; lower lips pale.

shiner, pugnose [*Notropis anogenus*]: this minnow has a rather stout body with distinct lateral band and spot on tail. There are 34 to 37 scales in lateral line; pharyngeal teeth are 4—4. It reaches a length of 1½ in. Mouth is very small and oblique.

shiner, river [*Notropis blennius*]: this slender minnow is rather pale and has silvery lateral band. There are about 37 scales in lateral line. Teeth are 2, 4—4, 1.

shiner, rosefin [*Notropis roseipinnis*]: trim little minnow with dark lateral stripe down side and rose-colored fins. Eleven rays in anal fin; 41—44 scale rows along lateral line; 23—25 scales from back of head to origin of dorsal fin. Head short, muzzle pointed. Rusty above; dark lateral stripe from tip of snout to base of tail, this stripe somewhat obsolete in larger individuals; lateral stripe terminating in a small black spot at base of tail.

shiner, sailfin [*Notropis hypselopterus*]: trim, little minnow with dark stripe down side and 2 rose-colored spots at base of tail. Membranes of dorsal and anal fins with dark pigment; scales in lateral line 34—35; anal fin with 11 rays. Head short, flattened above, muzzle pointed. Rusty above, light band along side bordered below by dark lateral stripe which runs from tip of snout to base of tail; tip of chin dark; oval dark spot on base of tail bordered above and below by rosy-colored light spots; vertical fin membranes with dark pigment.

shiner, southeastern golden [*Notemigonus crysoleucas bosci*]: minnow deep-bodied, laterally compressed, golden and silvery fish with small delicate mouth. Rays of anal fins 14—17; no barbels at base of maxillary; dorsal fin with about 8 rays. Head rather flat between eyes; tapering to small terminal mouth. Colors of adults golden above, silvery below; young with dark lateral stripe. Length up to 12 in.

shiner, southwestern sand [*Notropis deliciosus deliciosus*]: this fish has stout body with dusky lateral band and 7 anal rays. There are 35 to 38 scales in lateral line; pharyngeal teeth are 4—4. This species reaches length of 2½ in.

shiner, spottail [*Notropis hudsonius hudsonius*]: this species has well defined spot at base of caudal fin. Color varies from yellow to dusky with silvery lateral band. Scales are 5—39—4; pharyngeal teeth are 1, 4—4, 0—2. This species reaches length of slightly over 4 in.

shiner, Topeka [*Notropis topeka*]: this shiner has stout body with lateral band ending in black caudal spot. Scales are 5—35—6. It reaches length of 3-3/5 in.

shingle: beach gravel composed of smooth, generally flattish pebbles and cobbles of roughly the same size; rounded, often flat, waterworn rock fragments larger than approximately 16 mm.

shingle barchanges: ridges of shingle, with intervening troughs of sand, formed in shallow water at right angles to beach.

shingle rampart: ridge of shingles, about 3 to 6 ft. (1 to 2 meters) high, built by waves on seaward edge of and parallel to reef flat.

ship: among seamen, a "ship" is a sailing vessel with bowsprit and 3 masts, i.e., foremast, mainmast and mizzenmast, and rarely with 4th mast, each composed of lower mast, topmast and topgallant mast, and sometimes higher masts (royal mast and skysail mast), in all of which square sails are set. As used in general, any large seagoing vessel is a "ship."

shipentine: four-masted sailing vessel with 3 square-rigged masts like a "ship"; fore-and-aft-rigged aftermast.

ship in stays [ships]: stopping the way of a ship by backing mainyards. In this maneuver yards are hauled around contrary to foresails.

ship of opportunity: ships used by government sponsored programs designed to reduce expenses of research ship time by providing space or having work done on vessels that coincidently are destined for an area of interest.

ship-of-the-line: large vessel falling into any one of 4 groups or rates of naval ships depending on size and number of guns. Ranging from 4th rate (50 to 60 guns) on 2 decks to first rate (100 guns) on 4 decks, a ship-of-the-line was of sufficient force to lie in line of battle; frigates (all vessels of war under 4th rate) were too small to appear on the line.

shipping: 1) vessels of all types, in a collective sense, as belonging to or frequenting a port, region, or country; vessels generally; commercial tonnage. 2) act or business of sending goods by ship (or other means of transportation) to a buyer or selling agent. 3) act or procedure of engaging seamen as members of a crew. 4) act of embarking or *taking ship*, as a passenger.

shipshape: in a seamanlike or orderly manner, as desirable on board ship; hence, well arranged; trim; neat; as expressed in the old English phrase, *"In shipshape and Bristol fashion."*

ship-sloop: ship-rigged naval vessel of 18 to 20 guns. *The Ranger*, which was commanded by John Paul Jones in the American Revolution, was a "ship-sloop."

shipway: sometimes called a *slipway*, space in a shipyard occupied by the blocks on which a vessel rests while being built and subsequently by the extended *ways* on which she slides in being launched.

shipworm [*teredo*]: one of a family *(Teredinidae)* of wormlike bivalves in which shells are limited to head end. Larvae penetrate wood, plastics and other material, and organisms excavate tunnels (in which they remain for life) as they grow by rasping away at surrounding material with ridged tooth shells. Incurrent and excurrent siphons project from original entrance hole, which is never enlarged. Shipworms are one of the two most destructive groups of marine borers.

shoal: submerged ridge, bank or bar consisting of or covered by unconsolidated sediments (mud, sand, gravel) which is at or near enough to water surface to constitute a danger to navigation. If composed of rock or coral, it is called a reef.

shoaling: bottom effect which describes height of waves but not direction. It can be divided into 2 parts which occur simultaneously. In one part waves become less dispersive close to shore; therefore, since same energy can be carried by high waves of lesser height, this effect causes gradual decrease in wave height. In the other part, waves slow down, crests move closer together, and since energy between crests remains relatively fixed, waves can become higher near shore.

shoaling coefficient: ratio of height of wave in water of any depth to its height in deep water with effect of refraction eliminated.

shoaling effect: alternation of wave proceeding from deep water into shallow water.

shoaling patches: individual and scattered elevations of bottom with depth of 10 fathoms or less, but composed of any material except rock or coral.

shole [ships]: piece of plank put under a shore where there is no groundway.

shoot: vernacular for "observe" using sextant, transit or alidade (azimuth instrument).

Shoran: precise short-range electronic navigation system which uses time divergence of pulse-type transmission from 2 or more fixed stations. Term is derived from words "short-range navigation."

shore: 1) narrow strip of land in immediate contact with sea, including zone between high and low waterlines. 2) in ships, one of many wooden props by which ribs or frames of a vessel are externally supported while building or by which vessel is held upright on ways. Timbers propping up a ship in dry dock.

shore current: movement of water parallel to shoreline.

shoreface: narrow zone seaward from low tide, over which beach sands and gravels actively oscillate with changing wave conditions.

shore ice: basic form of fast ice. It is a compact ice cover that is attached to shore and, in shallow water, also grounded.

shoreline: 1) juncture of land and sea during low tide, unless otherwise specified. 2) boundary line between body of water and land at high tide.

shoreline of emergence: shoreline resulting when water surface comes to rest against partially emerged sea floor.

shoreline of submergence: that shoreline produced when water surface comes to rest against partially submerged land area.

shore polynya: open water in sea ice along coast, formed either by current or wind.

shore profile: intersection of ground surface with vertical plane; may extend from top of dune line

to seaward of sand movement.

short-crested wave: system of short-crested waves having appearance of hills being separated by troughs.

shorten down: reducing extent of sail on sailing ship.

shorten sail [ships]: to reduce amount of canvas; to take in sail.

short-long flashing: abbreviation *S-L. Fl.*; a light having the characteristic phase of a *short flash* of about 0.4 second and a *long flash* of 4 times that duration, such group repeated about 8 times a minute.

shortwave radiation: in oceanography, term used loosely to distinguish radiation in visible and near visible portions of electromagnetic spectrum (roughly 0.5 to 1.0 micron in wavelength) from long-wave radiation.

short waves: waves under conditions where relative depth (water depth/wavelength) is greater than 0.5 and where phase velocity is independent of water depth, but dependent upon wavelength.

shotter: sailing craft used in British mackerel fisheries in middle 19th century. They ranged in tonnage from 6 to 25 tons. Rigs varied.

shrimp: any of several crustaceans, usually not more than a few inches in length and in appearance not unlike the *sea crayfish*. Related to the *lobster* and *prawn*, it is found in tropical and temperate regions in both fresh water and seawater, and, generally, is considered excellent food. The shrimp fishery of S.E. Atlantic coast of U.S. and Gulf of Mexico is an important one. Taken by a *dragnet* or *trawl*, they are pursued by *shrimp-draggers* or *shrimp-trawlers* in shallower coastal waters.

shrimp trawl: bottom trawl; i.e., bag net with triangular-shaped top and bottom, open end (base of triangle) fishes in oval-shaped spread laterally by other boards and vertically by floats on head or top rope by weights on lead or footrope. Fish entering open end are trapped in apex or "cod" end of net.

shrouds [ships]: rope or wire rope stays which brace a mast laterally, extending from masthead to chain plates on side of vessel. Lower ends are made fast to turnbuckles or deadeyes and lanyards, which in turn are secured to chain plates. Strong ropes extending from ship's masthead to each side of ship to support masts; part of standing rigging.

shuga: spongy white ice lumps a few centimeters in diameter (about 1 in.), formed by sludge and sometimes anchor ice, emerging on surface.

sial: a contraction of the term "silica-alumina" which is applied to the whole assemblage of relatively lightweight, high-standing, continental rocks including the granites granodiorites, and quartz diorites.

Siberian high: area of high pressure which forms over Siberia in winter, particularly apparent on mean charts of sea-level pressure. It is centered near Lake Baikal where average sea-level pressure is exceeding 1,030 millibars from late November to early March.

Siberian Shelf: rather poorly defined. Existence of very old platform has long been recognized, occupying almost all of northern Asia and extending as far south as district of Irkutsk.

sibling species: species that are very much alike but that occur in separated areas or ecological niches. Twin species.

side keelson [ships]: beam placed on side of hull about 2/3rds the distance from center line to bilgeway. This is used as a stiffener longitudinally for flat bottom of a vessel.

sidereal: relating to the stars; measured by apparent motion of a star or a fixed point in the heavens; as, a *sidereal year*.

side trawler: type of vessel engaged in ocean fishing that uses a trawl net, large, conical, open-mouthed net dragged along sea bottom. Unlike new trawlers which haul nets up a stern ramp, side trawlers work nets over the side, a less efficient and more dangerous procedure.

sieve: wire cloth container with mesh openings graded increasingly in fixed ratio. Coarse bottom sediments such as sand are usually analyzed for size by sieving.

sight: 1) sextant observation of a heavenly body; as, a *sight* of the sun. 2) device for setting an instrument in a desired direction of alignment by the eye, as a *pelorus* or a *gun*. 3) to observe or view, either with naked eye or as by a telescope; as, to sight the land, a whale, a boat, etc. 4) to direct or lay a gun at required elevation, etc., as by *sights*.

sight edges [ships]: edges of plating that are visible are called sight edges. Sight edge is on outside of shell, on tops of decks and inner bottom plating and on opposite side from stiffeners or bulkheads. Edge that is covered is called landing edge.

sighting: act of observing or first bringing into view; as, sighting a light; or of aiming, as a gun.

sign: 1) an indication, as of an approaching change in weather, a decreasing depth of water, etc. 2) a representation of a letter or number, or a symbol denoting a certain procedure, as in signaling by semaphore. 3) Morse code, etc.; as, the *J sign; call sign; repeat sign;* etc. 4) a mathematical symbol; as, *minus sign.* 5) a conspicuous lettered board, notice on a bulkhead, etc.; as, that marked *"Keep clear of Propellers"; "Fire Hydrant No. 10";* etc. 6) to write one's name as a token of obligation or assent.

signature: 1) characteristic frequency pattern of target displayed by detection and classification equipment. 2) graph of pressure versus time at a point as ship passes over it. Increased water velocity in constriction between ship and bottom of water basin causes pressure variation by Venturi effect.

significant wave: statistical term relating to 1/3rd highest waves of given group and defined by average of their heights and periods. Composition of higher waves depends upon extent to which lower waves are considered.

significant wave height: average height of the 1/3rd highest waves of given wave group.

significant wave period: arbitrary period generally taken as period of the 1/3rd highest waves within a given group.

sikussak: Eskimo name for very old sea ice, resembling glacier ice trapped in a fiord, and having snow accumulation on its surface which contributes to its formation and perpetuation.

silent zone: areas impervious to sound propagation due to refraction or reflecting conditions. Ideal zone for submarine to hide in.

silicate silicon: ionic form of silicon utilized by various plankters, principally diatoms and radiolarians. Measurement of silicates in seawater is useful for determining diatom productivity.

siliceous and horny sponges [*demosponges*]: largest and most complex group of sponges with longest history. It includes forms with needle-shaped or 4-branched siliceous spicules, which may or may not be supported by spongin. Spicules of demosponges have been found in Eozoic rocks, but first fossils that show entire bodies appear in middle Cambrian Burgess shale. Best and most varied fossil demosponges are found in Jurassic and Cretaceous rocks of France and Germany. Shapes range from stemmed goblets to flattened mushrooms, cones and crumpled cups.

siliceous ooze: fine-grained, pelagic sediment containing more than 30 percent siliceous skeletal remains of pelagic plants and animals.

silicoflagellate: any of a group of microscopic marine phytoplankton having siliceous shells with radiating spines; they are inhabitants principally of colder waters.

silk confetti [*Enteromorpha plumosa*]: looks like green scum or green silk floating on water. Silky appearance is due to matting together of exceedingly fine yellow-green branches which are usually 12 to 24 in. long. Cells are usually embedded in gelatinous substance and have but one nucleus; thalli multiply vegetatively by breaking away of outgrowths. Because of continuous ebb and flow of tides, the seashore affords 2 distinct habitats, the part of shore that is twice daily covered and uncovered by tides and the region below low tides where algae always remain submerged.

sill: low part of ridge or rise separating ocean basins from one another or from adjacent sea floor.

sill basin: submarine basin separated from main basin by narrow, submerged ridge. Deep water in silled basin may be stagnant and anaerobic.

silt: unconsolidated sediment whose particles range in size from 0.0039 to 0.625 mm. in diameter (between clay and sand sizes).

Silurian: period in Paleozoic era characterized by sea invasions, salt beds in eastern U.S. and first continental life.

silverside, Florida brook [*Labidesthes sicculus vanhynimgi*]: silvery-greenish, long-bodied fish. Scales along side 72—75; anal with about 23 soft rays; 2 dorsal fins; body very slender, fusiform; head flat above; mouth terminal, jaws produced into short depressed beak. Sides of head scaly. Color green with narrow pale stripe down each side.

silverside, northern brook [*Labidesthes sicculus sicculus*]: slender, beautiful little fish of transparent color. It has prominent and brilliant silver lateral band with dark lateral streak above it; back is dotted with black. Body is elongated and compressed; head is long and flattened above; snout is slender and considerably drawn out and longer than eye. Premaxillaries are very protractile; edge of upper jaw and scales are concave.

silverside, rough [*Membras martinica*]: silvery-greenish, streamlined little fish. Scales along side 45—47; anal with 16—17 soft rays; 2 dorsal fins; body slender, fusiform; mouth terminal, oblique; lower jaw short and weak; sides of head scaly. Color greenish with narrow silver stripe down each side.

sima: basic outer shell of earth under ocean basins and under sial layer of continents. Term is derived from abbreviations for silicon (Si) and magnesium (Mg). Major subdivision of earth's crust occurring mainly beneath ocean areas characterized by relatively high specific gravity (approximately 3.3), composed mainly of silicon (Si), magnesium (Mg) and aluminum (Al).

simultaneous altitudes: those of two or more celestial bodies observed at same instant, or reduced to their respective values at a common instant, for determining ship's position. Objects having a wide difference in azimuth are selected with the view of obtaining a definite intersection of at least two of the *lines of position* resulting from such observations.

Singora Lake boat: crude, shallow-draft, sailing craft of Singora Lake in Malay. Hull is a dugout with rough plank superstructure. Top strakes are extended aft over stern, forming sides of overhanging platform, while forward ends are turned up a little abaft the bow. One or 2 sails are high-peaked standing lugs of light matting.

sinistral: 1) direction of coiling. In orthostropic shells with axis of core held vertical, apex up and aperture facing observer, the aperture will be to left of axis. 2) *in Mollusca*, coiling in counter-clockwise direction.

sinkhole: topographic depression which results from collapse of the roof of a naturally-occurring subsurface limestone cavern.

sinking: downward movement of surface water generally caused by converging currents or when water mass becomes more dense than surrounding water.

sinus [*Gastropoda*]: groove or reentrant in lateral margin of aperture (outer lip) distinguished from slit by nonparallel margins.

sinusoidal: of or relating to sine curve.

sinus venosus: in primitive vertebrates, thin-walled chamber of head where blood from veins is collected before it enters auricle.

siphon: 1) specialized tube of mantle of certain pelecypods or test of tunicates for entrance of water. 2) in *Gastropoda*, tubular extensions of mantle border. Pierced by canal that opens into mantle cavity from exterior. May be indicated in shell by grooves or notch.

siphonal note [*Gastropoda*]: notch of anterior end of aperture occupied by siphon. When present it lies between and virtually separates the inner and outer.

Siphonariidae [family]: siphon shells are often called false limpets because of resemblance to members of limpet family. Like limpets they are conical in shape and usually circular in outline at base. Limpets possess a radial groove on inner side of shell which makes a projection along border of base of shell. These molluscs have gills together with a kind of lung which permits them to live between tides and to be out of water for great portion of time. For this reason they have at times been considered as intermediate between aquatic and terrestrial forms of molluscs. In their normal habitat they are attached to rocks along shoreline.

siphonoglyph: in most *Anthozoa* except corals, a ciliated canal at one or both ends of gullet serving as means of passing current of water on and out of gastrovascular cavity.

Siphonophora: *Cnidaria* of class *Hydrozoa;* one of an order of medusoid coelenterates. They are exclusively marine animals and are able to float. They are fragile, transparent, and often magnificently hued in iridescent colors. Syphonophores are hydrozoan colonies that are not fixed, but free-floating. Individuals of colony, therefore, develop in such a way as to be capable of performing special and distinct functions. Axis of colony is a stolon, at end of which is air-filled membrane (pneumatophore) that serves as a floater. Siphonophores feed on forms of marine life that they capture by means of venomous filaments. They reproduce by eggs and also by budding in form of medusae.

siphuncle: in early cephalopods, membranous tube connecting chambers made by coiled shells to posterior part of body.

sipunculid [peanut worm]: member of group of sausage-shaped, burrowing, marine worms; in mouth region they generally have either a crown of tentacles or proboscis that can be drawn inwards.

siren, great [*Siren lacertina*]: large, eel-shaped salamander with external gills, 2 small front legs and no hind legs. Four toes on each front leg; 38 costal grooves along sides between legs and anus. Color dark with series of yellowish dashes along side and often with indistinct, dark dots of mottling above. Venter slightly paler than back, with numerous light flecks. Attains length of 3 ft., but adults generally average smaller.

siren, Gulf hammock striped [*Pseudobranchus striatus lustricolus*]: eel-shaped salamander about the size of a pencil with external gills, 2 little front legs and no hind legs. Each of single pair of legs with 3 toes; about 34 costal grooves along sides of body between legs and anus; snout blunt-tipped; marked with bright yellow or orange stripes.

sirenian: of or pertaining to the *Sirenia*, an order of large, aquatic, herbivorous mammals, including the dugong, manatee, and sea cow. Any of the *Sirenia*.

siren, lesser [*Siren intermedia intermedia*]: large, eel-shaped salamander with external gills, 2 tiny front legs and no hind legs. Four toes on each front leg; 31—34 costal grooves along sides between legs and anus. Color dark above, slightly lighter below and usually with pattern of minute dark dots sprinkled on back, sides and tail. Adults usually between 8 and 12 in. long.

siren, narrow-headed striped: smaller than a pencil with external gills, 2 little front legs and no hind legs. Each of single pair of legs with 3 toes; about 34 costal grooves along sides between legs and anus; snout sharply pointed; marked with tannish-brown to yellowish-gray stripes.

siren, narrow-striped [*Pseudobranchus striatus axanthus*]: eel-shaped salamander about the size of a pencil with external gills, 2 little front legs and no hind legs. Each of single pair of legs with 3 toes; about 35 costal grooves along sides between legs and anus; snout blunt-tipped; no bright yellow or orange stripes. Marked with a lateral stripe of pearl gray; slightly darker dorsolateral stripe and sometimes with indistinct middorsal stripe.

Siriella armata [mysids]: long, slender mysid with long, pointed rostrum but small carapace which leaves last 3 thoracic segments uncovered. Long, slender antennary peduncle more than half the length of carapace; long, parallel-sided antennal scale whose outer margin is slightly concave and inner margin setose and slightly convex; outer margin ends in strong tooth. Eyes on long cylindrical stalks; telson long, slightly tapering with entire margin. Length about 21 mm. Widely distributed.

Sirus: brightest star in the heavens, of the group *Canis Major*, easily located just S.E. of *Orion*. With *Betelgeuse (a Orionis)*, reddish member a few degrees north of the *Belt* (three stars close in line), and bright *Procyon (a Canis Minoris)* to the N.E., *Sirius* stands at the southern corner of an equilateral triangle formed by lines joining all three. Classified as *a Canis Majoris*, its magnitude is given as -1.58; sidereal hour angle $259\frac{1}{4}°$; and declination as $16°\ 39'$ S.

sirocco: since it is often felt near Sahara Desert, one of the world's most unpleasant winds is popularly associated with land. Actually it often crosses the Mediterranean. Along north coast of Africa this intensely hot and dry wind seems to come directly from the blazing early-morning sun. So from Arabic *saraqua* "the sun rose," it took a name associated with dawn. Passing through Portuguese it entered 17th century French as sirocco. Later English mariners borrowed it unchanged. On land sirocco may cause great damage to crops. It has its own local name in many regions. Egyptians call it *khamsin;* in Tunis it is the *chili;* in Libya it is called *gibli.* Water-laden by the time it reaches southeastern Spain, it is known there as *leveche.* Called by whatever name, the wind that in some regions "blows from the rising sun" is always dreaded. Even after passing over miles of open water, the sirocco may make seamen and passengers acutely uncomfortable.

siscowet [*Cristivomer namaycush siscowet*]: also called fat trout, siscowet is a form of lake trout found only in deep waters of Lake Superior. In general it resembles lake trout, but differs in many details. Length is from 3 to 3½ times its depth. Margin of belly just anterior to vent is very much swollen, forcing vent to be directed posteriorly instead of ventrally as in typical lake trout. Body cavity is lined with very thick layer of fat. Color varies from light to dark but spots tend to be smaller than those of lake trout. Scales of siscowet are slightly longer, numbering about 175 in lateral line.

skaffie: type of Scotch lugger; double-ended; stem and sternpost raked; short, deep keel; lug-rig similar to that of the fife but with no jib. Some carried 3 masts. This type of boat has been supplanted by the "zulu" and none has been built for many years.

skag: heavy chain used when necessary in close waters as a drag for steadying a towed barge that has a tendency to sheer about.

skate: raylike fish of family *Rajidae* with highly developed pectoral on side fins and distinct slender tails. Skates generally lay a few eggs in well protected, rectangular, horny cases known as mermaid's purses. Skates, genus *Raja*, are related to sharks and have only a cartilaginous skeleton instead of bone.

skate, barn-door: has smoother skin than clearnose, but similar dark brown, spotted coloring. It attains length of 6 ft. and weight of 40 lbs. Barndoor skate is found in offshore waters where it feeds on crabs, lobsters, squids and smaller fishes.

skate, clearnose: brier skate is of same coloring and shape but differs in having row of spines along back and translucent areas on either side of snout. This is a larger skate reaching length of 31 in. and weighing up to 6 lbs. and found in shallow water.

skate, little: or common skate, it is eastern species. Upper surface of smooth-skinned body is spotted with dark brown, lower surface is white or gray. This is a normal skate, ordinarily under 2 ft. long and weighing less than 2 lbs. It haunts shallow waters for its diet of crustaceans, mollusks and small fishes.

skeg [ships]: afterpart of keel upon which sternpost rests.

skeid: large Viking longship with no figurehead.

skeleton: a vessel's principal framework fitted together without plating or planking, as in early stage of construction. Having the leading features only, or bare necessities; as, a *skeleton deck*, or platform deck having planks spaced an inch or two apart; a *skeleton rig*, or that of a *skeleton-rigged* vessel, in which all light yards, upper masts, etc., have been removed.

skerries: low, small island reefs and rocks which form broad belt (skjaerard) extending along coast for hundreds of miles. Skerries rise from shallow coastal strandflat.

skids [ships]: parallel timbers or other members upon which boats, casks and other objects are lashed.

skiff: light, open boat, usually for rowing, but sometimes equipped for sailing. Generally double-ended. Among eastern villages of Banffshire, Scotland, larger baldies of 25 ft. in the keel and upwards are known as skiffs.

skimmers [scissorbills]: very long-winged seabirds, resembling large terns with black or dark brown upper parts and white foreheads and underparts. Legs are short, feet small and webbed and tails moderately forked. Bills are quite unlike those of any other birds; lower mandible is much longer than upper one and both edges are compressed to knifelike thinness. Name skimmer has been bestowed upon them from their unique method of feeding. When seeking food they fly rapidly just over water with bill open and long, lower mandible cutting surface, so that they may be said literally to "plough the main."

skimmings: referred to damaged cargo, denotes the spoiled portion of a bagged commodity, such as coffee and cacao beans, lentils, peas, etc., separated from the unharmed and marketable goods.

skin [ships]: plating of ship.

skin diving: free diving with or without SCUBA gear.

skipjack: V-bottomed sloop, carrying leg-of-mutton mainsail and jib, generally clipper-bowed; centerboard was used. Popular on Chesapeake Bay.

skipjack, blue herring, golden shad [*Pomolobus chrysochloris*]: body is slender and elliptical with belly keeled like torpedo-boat chaser. Head is slender and pointed; lower jaw projects strongly; caudal fin is deeply forked and powerful. Back is a bright steel blue, sides have golden reflections and belly is silver. Even in perfectly clear water its movements are so extremely swift that the eye can seldom follow it.

skoffnar: lower Burmese coasting craft with combination of schooner and ketch rig of from 80 to 100 tons. Some carry topsails and sails are stowed up and down mast with brails. Very often masts are of same height. Single jib is generally carried, and sometimes a Chinese lug is used on raked foremast and fore-and-aft sail on aftermast.

skovshoved herring boat: Danish double-ended, spritsail-rigged, open boat used in herring fishery. Peak of spritsail is lower than the throat, and the foot shorter than the head. Two headsails and jib-headed topsail are carried.

skuas: members of this bird family are large, dark colored birds with some resemblance to immature gulls but characterized by stout, hooked beaks. Upper mandible is sharply curved downwards at tip and basal portion is covered by separate horny plate called the cere, front edge of mandible partly overhangs nostrils. The wings are long and legs have webbed feet that are rather stout. Skuas are mainly birds of high latitudes.

skuta: small, but very fast Viking ship.

skysail [ships]: square sail set above the royal on square-rigged ship.

skyscraper [ships]: same as moonraker.

slack [ships]: to ease off, as to slack a sheet or slack a dock line.

slack water [slack tide]: state of tidal current

when its velocity is near zero, especially moment a current reverses direction. Sometimes considered intermediate period between ebb and flood currents during which velocity of currents is less than 0.1 knot.

slant: transitory breeze or favorable wind, also period of its duration.

sleeper [*Gobiomorus dormitor*]: slender, high-finned, big-mouthed fish. Two dorsal fins; pelvic fins not united to form a disk; gill openings extending forward to below angles of jaws; 55—57 scale rows along sides. Head, large and elongate; mouth large; maxillary reaching to level of posterior margin of eye above gill openings; caudal fin rounded. Color brownish or olive, lighter below; spiny dorsal margined with black; head often with dark spots. Attains length of 2 ft.

sleeper, fat [*Dormitator maculatus*]: small, heavy-bodied, small-mouthed fish with high vertical fins. Two dorsal fins; pelvic fins not united at base to form disk; 30—35 scale rows along sides. Mouth small, maxillary not reaching level of posterior margin of eye; eye small. Color dark brown, often with lighter bluish spots. May attain length of 1 ft.

sleeper, slender [*Eleotris abacurus*]: slender, big-mouthed, big-finned fish. Two dorsal fins; pelvic fins not united at base to form disk; gill openings not extending below angles of jaws. Head long and depressed; mouth large, maxillary extending to level of posterior margin of eye. Eye small; body slender; dorsal fin high, divided into 2 portions. Body brownish with faint dots and darker on the scales.

sleepy sponge crab [*Domidiopsis dormia*]: large species which measures as much as 8 in. across carapace. Entire body is covered with brown fuzz which is usually longest on inner surface of pinchers or chelipeds. Legs are unequal in size and used for different purposes; front pair of legs bear a pair of beautiful ivory-white pinchers; 2nd and 3rd pairs of legs are about equal in size and used for walking; 4th and 5th pairs are smaller in size and do not touch the ground. Each of these last 2 pairs of legs terminates in fine, wirelike pinchers with which this crab carries a sponge aloft over its back. Eyes are very small and beady black in color; entire body is brown. Home of this crab is in outer edge of coral reef at depths which are usually in excess of 30 or 40 ft.

slewing: in ice navigation, act of forcing a ship through ice by pushing apart adjoining ice floes.

sliding gunter [ships]: triangular sail, upper part of luff of which is laced to topmast, which slides up and down lower mast by means of iron rings fastened to heel of topmast. Lower part of luff of sail is bent to hoops which encircle lower or standing mast. Sheet is fastened to clew and leads aft.

sliding ways [ships]: one of structures on each side of and parallel to the keel, supporting the cradle under bilgeways in which vessel rests in launching. Sliding ways form inclined plane down which vessel slides. It is made of planks laid on blocks of wood.

slime: soft, fine, oozy mud or other substance of similar consistency.

slip: 1) to let run overboard, as a cable, in sense of speeding ship's departure; as, to *slip and run*. 2) to release and let run out, as a mooring, a towing hawser, etc. 3) a device for releasing a hook. 4) in U.S., area of water between two wharves; a *ferry slip*. 5) inclined plane on which vessels are built; a *slipway;* place where vessels are hauled up for repairs; a *marine railway*. 6) difference between distance actually made through water and that as reckoned by revolutions of a paddle or a propeller; usually expressed as a *percentage of engine distance*, or that by revolutions. (This is *true slip*. In navigational practice slip is calculated regardless of presence of a current and thus may have a *minus value* where vessel has made good a distance *greater* than that indicated by shaft revolutions, in which case difference referred to is termed *negative slip*. In usual case of greater run according to engines, it is called *positive slip*.)

slipway: 1) the prepared and usually reenforced inclined surface on which *keel* and *bilge blocks* are laid for supporting a vessel under construction; a *building slip*. 2) also, a *patent slipway* or *marine* railway.

slit-band or selenizone: trace of a slit in outer lip of gastropod consisting of spiral band of crescentic growth lines ascending whorls of shell.

slob ice: accumulation of sludge so dense as to make passage of small craft impossible.

sloep: small, shallow-draft Dutch sailing craft originally rigged with sprit mainsail, but now sloop-rigged. It is equipped with leeboards and outboard rudder. Sloep was originated in Holland, probably in 17th century, for navigation of canals and coastal harbors.

sloop: craft with single mast and fore-and-aft rigged, in its simplest form a mainsail and jib. Sloop rig was introduced into America from England in latter 17th century.

sloop-of-war: war vessel armed on single deck and sometimes on quarter deck, rigged as ship, brig, brigantine, etc.

slop chest [ships]: supply of seamen's clothing and other supplies taken on board ship to sell to crew during voyage.

slope [*Mollusca*]: one face of bivalve shell, as anterior, central or posterior.

slope of foreshore: angle between tangent to the beach at high water line or some reference point and horizontal.

slough: 1) arm of a river flowing between islands and mainland, and separating islands from one another. 2) small, muddy marshland or tidal waterway usually connecting other tidal areas.

sludge: spongy, whitish ice lumps a few centimeters across. They consist of slush, snow slush and sometimes of spongy ice lumps formed on bottom of shallow sea and emerging at the surface.

sluice [ships]: opening in lower part of a bulkhead fitted with sliding watertight gate or door having an operating rod extending to upper deck or decks. These openings are useful in center line bulkheads, as in the case of damage to one side of the ship water may be quickly admitted to other side before ship is dangerously listed.

slump: slippage or sliding of a mass of unconsolidated sediment down submarine or subaqueous slope. Slumps occur frequently at heads or along sides of submarine canyons. Sediment usually moves as a unit mass initially but often becomes turbidity flow. It may be triggered by any small or large earth shock.

smack: general term for fore-and-aft rigged sailing vessel, used chiefly in fishing and coasting trades.

smackee: welled fishing boat of Key West, Florida. Typical size is about 24 ft. long by one third the beam. It is a carvel-built, keel boat with good sheer, long run and V-shaped raking stern. Sloop-rigged with leg-of-mutton mainsail and jib to a bowsprit; mast stepped well forward.

smak: Dutch fishing schooner or sloop.

small diurnal range: average difference in height between mean lower high water and mean higher low water, measured over 19-year period or its computed equivalent.

small tropic range: average difference in height between all tropic lower high waters and all tropic higher low waters which occur twice monthly when moon's north and south declinations are greatest.

smelling the bottom: also, *feeling the bottom, smelling the ground;* descreasing speed with more or less erratic steering observed as a vessel enters shallow water. This is attributed to restriction of displacement flow about ship's hull and so, in the steering, as the phrase more particularly refers to, unevenness of water's depth often bringing about unbalanced pressures on the hull which may result in vessel taking a broad and possibly dangerous sheer.

smelt: family of saltwater fishes that enters streams and ponds to spawn, in some cases becoming landlocked and never returning to sea. Ten species occur in U.S. on both Atlantic and Pacific coasts. Smelt is a small streamlined fish superficially like herring but possessing an adipose fin like salmon and trout. Body is covered with ctenoid scales; belly lacks saw-tooth ventral scales of alewife and shad.

smelt, American [*Osmerus mordax*]: slender, silvery fish with adipose fin. There are 2 to 4 large strong teeth on vomer; about 68 scales in lateral line; dorsal fin has 10 rays. These fishes are small, not exceeding 10 or 12 in. in length.

smoothing: averaging of data in space or time, designed to compensate for random errors or fluctuations of a scale smaller than that presumed significant to problem at hand, e.g., thermometer smooths the temperature on scale of its time constant.

SNAE: Systems for Nuclear Auxiliary Power. Fission-powered, electric generator used in Coast Guard's atomic-light buoy.

snaekka: Norwegian, clinker-built skiff. Often equipped for sailing either with sprit mainsail or jib.

snails: snails belong to phylum *Mollusca*, whose name comes from Latin word for "soft nut." Body is soft; lower part has become a muscular structure generally used for locomotion (foot). Upper part of body is spread out into a mantle that folds downward over rest of creature. Molluscan shell may be limy, chitinous or both.

snake: 1) to pass a *snaking* or line about two parallel ropes in zig-zag fashion; to finish off a flat seizing with zig-zag turns extending from each outside turn of such, called a *snaking-seizing,* and usually one of wire. 2) to flake down a rope or chain, as for clear running, in a continuous series of zig-zag turns.

snapper [*Lutianidae*]: many species of snapper are primarily tropical fish, although they are occasionally found in temperate waters, and all are highly thought of as food fish. Most specimens are 2 to 3 ft. long and weigh 5 to 6 lbs. They are basslike fishes with oblong body, large mouth provided with unequally sized teeth and slightly forked tail fin. Unlike groupers, snappers usually congregate in schools. Best known of the snappers is *Lutjanus campechanus* or common red snapper, immediately recognizable by brilliant scarlet color. Another common species is yellowtail snapper *(Ocyurus chrysurus)* with its deeply forked tail of yellow, yellow fins and yellow stripe along sides.

snapper, gray [*Lutjanus griseus*]: mangrove snapper is a grayish or coppery, laterally compressed fish with long dorsal fin and tough mouth. Scales along lateral lines 48—52; body comparatively elongate, compressed; back arched; head somewhat pointed; jaws with bands of villiform teeth and 2 or sometimes 4, enlarged canine teeth in front of upper jaw; caudal fin forked. Color grayish-green above, coppery below with indistinct and diffuse rows of spots corresponding to scale rows.

snapper, red: deep red or brick-colored fish with average length of 2 ft. and weight of less than 25 lbs. It is abundant in Gulf of Mexico, although individuals sometimes wind up on Atlantic Coast as far north as New York. Red snappers are an important food fish; center for commercial catch in Florida.

snapper samples: specially equipped devices that obtain samples of sea bottom.

snapper, vermilion: also called rockfish, it is a brilliantly colored species with red and yellow hues; usually 12 in. long and under 3 lbs. in weight. Bottom feeder found from Carolinas to Gulf of Mexico.

snapping shrimp: certain species of shrimp belonging to family *Alpheidae*, chiefly in genera *Alpheus* and *Synalpheus*, that are capable of producing sharp cracking sounds by rapid closure of enlarged claw. These shrimp form large populations in warm shallow waters on shell, rock or coral bottoms where their sounds constitute major component of underwater background noise. Shrimp noises range in frequency from about 500 to 50,000 cps with principal components between 2,000 and 20,000 cps.

sneak box: sailing punt used for duck hunting along New Jersey coast. Boats have draft of but a few inches with centerboard up to enable them to enter shallow marshes.

snekkja: early Norse ship of 12th and 13th centuries. Similar to Viking ship, but having raised platform or deck, fore-and-aft. Single mast was carried with standing yard to which square sail was bent. Above yard was a fighting top.

Snell's law: when wave (light or sound) travels obliquely from one medium into another, ratio of sine of angle of incidence to sine of angle of refraction is the same as ratio of respective wave velocities in this medium and is constant for two particular mediums.

snib: a fastening or catch; especially, one of the clamps or *dogs* for securing a bulkhead door.

snibs [ships]: handles that can be operated from both sides of watertight door.

snipe [ships]: to cut a sharp bevel on end of stiffener or beam.

snook [*Centropomus undecimalis*]: large fish with big mouth, 2 dorsal fins and narrow, dark stripe down side. Scales along lateral line 67—77; second spine not reaching to base of caudal fin; soft rays in anal fin 6. Body robust, little compressed; head depressed; mouth large, lower jaw projecting beyond upper. Dark olive to bluish above, whitish below, conspicuous narrow black strip along lateral line.

snorkel: 1) on submarines, device used to operate diesel engines and to recharge batteries while submerged. 2) for skin divers, breathing tube attached to face mask for shallow water observations.

snow: "snow" of early 19th century was similar to a brig except that an extra mast was carried close abaft the mainmast, and this carried the spanker or driver. Snows were usually larger vessels than brigs or brigantines.

snow blink: bright, white glare on underside of clouds, produced by reflection of light from snow-covered surface. This term is used in polar regions with reference to sky map.

snub [ships]: to check quickly around winch or cleat.

socket [*Brachiopoda*]: depression along hinge line of brachial valve which receives the hinge tooth of pedicle valve.

sofar: 1) acronym derived from expression "sound fixing and ranging." Position fixing system by which hyperbolic lines of position are determined by measuring at shore listening stations, difference in time of reception of sound signals produced in sound channel in sea. 2) sound rays will always be refracted toward region of decreased velocity—which means in region of minimum sound velocity, sound rays will remain in a narrow channel—remaining in it for tremendous distances with minimum attentuation.

soft coral: belonging to order *Alcyonacea* of subclass *Alcyonaria*; skeleton has isolated calcareous spicules scattered over coenenchyme; colonies may be mushroom-shaped or plantlike.

soft patch [ships]: plate put over break or hole and secured with tap bolts. It is made watertight with a gasket such as canvas saturated in red lead.

soft rays: fin rays which are segmented, flexible and often branched.

solar: pertaining to or measured by the sun.

solar constant: rate at which solar radiation is received outside earth's atmosphere on surface normal to incident radiation and at earth's mean distance from sun.

solar declination: angular distance of sun expressed north and/or south of celestial equator; it is indicated as (+) when north and (−) when south of equator. Maximum declination is about $23\frac{1}{2}°$ north and south of equator; maximum north declination occurs about June 21 and maximum south declination about December 21.

solar tide: tide caused solely by tide-producing forces of sun.

Solenacea [*Adapedonta*]: larvae of species belonging to this group are characterized by possession of external ligament which appears in 280μ larva and becomes larger with increasing size of larvae. In addition, right umbo is higher than left.

Solenacea [*Cultellus pellucidus*]: postero-dorsal edge of shell is concave, while umbo is shorter than the right. Length is approximately 330μ.

Solenacea [*Enis enis, Adapedonta*]: broad (posterior) end is sharply truncated and umbones are indistinct, left being lower. Larvae occur mainly in April and May, but also in June and July. Length of shell is approximately 250μ.

Solenacea [*Enis siliqua, Adapedonta*]: posterior end is not so truncated as in *E. ensis* and umbones are more pronounced. Larvae occur at same time as, but are rarer than, those of *E. ensis*. Length of shell is approximately 230μ.

solenopora: known to be red alga because its biscuits and heads are made of tiny calcareous tubes that formed around algal filaments.

sole, northern round [*Trinectes maculatus fasciatus*]: rounded, very compressed fish with both eyes and all its color on right side; pectoral fins absent; lateral line straight. Head small; mouth small, right lower lip fringed; body rounded, very compressed; depth contained nearly twice in standard length. Dorsal fin with 50—55 rays; caudal fin rounded; anal fin with 37—40 soft rays; pectoral fins absent. Color grayish with indefinite, narrow, darker, vertical bars.

sole plate [ships]: plate fitted to top of foundation to which base of machine is bolted. Also small plate fitted at end of stanchion.

solitary wave: wave consisting of single elevation (above water surface), its height not necessarily small compared to depth, and neither followed nor preceded by another elevation or depression of water surface.

solstice: 1) time of year when sun's vertical rays reach farthest north (June 21) or south (December 21) of Equator. 2) one of 2 points in sun's orbit (ecleptic) farthest from celestial equator; instant when sun's declination is maximum.

solstitial tide: tide occurring near times of solstices when sun reaches maximum north and south declinations; tropic range at these times is greatest.

solution basin: shallow depression on reef or beach rock surface produced by solution of current.

solution lake: body of water formed in basin dissolved from rock.

somatocyst: in many siphonophores, part of gastrovascular canal in front of proximal part of stem.

somite: any one of series of similar segments lining the body of a worm, crayfish, etc. at regular intervals along anteroposterior axis.

SONAR: Sound Navigation And Ranging device based on principle that underwater sound waves bounce back when they hit a target and can be measured in manner similar to radar on the surface. Active sonar emits a sound signal and detects its return from reflecting object. Variable depth sonar (VOS) is a sonar that may be towed by ship and its depth controlled by varying length of cable.

Sondfjord yawl: west coast Norwegian, open herring boat, double-ended with rounded stem and sternpost; deep hull and fine sea boat. Clinker-built with wide planking; single square sail used for sailing on short mast stepped a little forward of amidships.

Sondmoersk yawl: small, open fishing craft of west coast of Norway, not unlike old Viking long boat in line of hull, which is double-ended with heavy, rounded, ornamented stern and sternpost.

sonic bearing: bearing determined by measuring direction from which sound wave is coming.

sonic fishes: those fishes which are capable of producing sounds, usually by means of specialized organs such as air bladder or pharyngeal teeth. Spectra of fish sounds generally have limits between 50 and 5,000 cps with most of sound energy concentrated between 100 and 800 cps.

sonic layer depth: depth of surface layer into which sound rays are trapped by upward refraction effects. Sonic layer depth is indicated on sound velocity versus depth trace by point of near surface maximum sound velocity.

soniferous marine animals: species of fish, marine animals and crustaceans which may produce noise of sufficient intensity and frequency to interfere with sound ranging operations and acoustic mines.

sonne: radionavigational aid that provides a number of rotating characteristic signal zones. Bearing may be determined by observation of instant when transition occurs from one zone to following zone.

sonobuoy: free-floating or anchored device that includes a biway with radio telemetering equipment and hydrophone suspended beneath. Sound signal received at hydrophone is transmitted to nearby receiver for analysis.

sonoprobe: low frequency echo sounder which generates sound waves and records their reflections from one or more sediment layers beneath sediment/water interface.

soogee: 1) solution of washing soda, soap powder, soft soap, or the like, used for washing paint. 2) to wash or scrub paintwork, decks, etc., with *soogee*. 3) also spelled *sewgee, suegee, suji, sujee, sugee*.

sound: 1) periodic variation in pressure, particle displacement or particle velocity in elastic medium. 2) long arm of the sea which forms a channel between island and mainland or sea and ocean. There is a common impression that a sound, a waterway too long and broad to be called "strait," was named from practice of taking soundings in channels. This is not so, nor does the term have ties with any activity suggesting noise. Swimming called *sund* in both Old Norse and Old English has long been common practice on coastal waters of northern Europe. When nature provided a long inlet with calm waters, swimmers abounded. Before 14th century it was customary to name such a body of water from activity characteristic of it. Early metrical romance, "King Horn," has a character say, "Y fond a ship rower in ye sound." By the time Sir Francis Drake and his fellow adventurers dotted world's waterways with English names, "sound" was firmly established as proper term for stretch of water between the mainland and island or sandbar, regardless of whether or not it was a haven for swimmers.

sound boat: Danish, cutter-rigged fishing boat employed in fisheries of Strait of Kattegat and Oresmund Sound. These boats are known locally as "sound boats." They are double-ended, decked, sharp at bow and stern with raking curved stem and sternpost and have deep keel; clinker-built with oak frames and planking.

sound channel: region in water column where sound velocity first decreases to minimum value with depth and then increases in value as result of pressure. Above minimum value, sound rays are bent downward; below minimum value, sound rays are bent upward; rays are thus trapped in this channel.

sound channel axis: depth at which minimum sound velocity occurs.

sound energy density: sound energy density at point in sound field is sound energy contained in given infinitesimal part of medium divided by volume of that part of medium.

sounding: to measure depth of water usually in fathoms, by means of lead on line, on which is marked number of fathoms. Measuring water in ship's bilge with sounding rod.

sounding pipe [ships]: vertical pipe in oil or water tank, used to guide sounding device when measuring depth of liquid in tank.

sound intensity: at a point average rate of sound energy transmitted in specified direction through unit area normal to this direction at the point considered.

sound level: sound output of source as expressed in decibels relative to 1 dyne per square centimeter at distance of 1 yard from sound source.

sound pressure: instantaneous pressure at point in medium in presence of sound wave minus static pressure at that point.

sound pressure level: twenty times the logarithm to base 10 of ratio of pressure of sound to reference pressure in decibels at specific point. Reference pressure shall be explicitly stated.

sound velocimeter: instrument used to measure speed of sound in seawater directly (in situ), thus avoiding requirement for computing it from measured salinity, temperature and depth values.

sound velocity: rate of travel at which sound energy moves through medium, usually expressed in feet per second. Velocity of sound in seawater is function of temperature, salinity and changes in pressure associated with changes in depth. Increase in any of these factors tends to increase velocity.

source region: extensive area of ocean where water mass acquired its basic characteristics.

South Atlantic Current: eastward flowing current of South Atlantic Ocean that is continuous with northern edge of West Wind Drift.

South Equatorial Current: any of several ocean currents driven by southeast trade winds flowing over tropical oceans of Southern Hemisphere. In Atlantic Ocean it is known as Atlantic South Equatorial Current and flows westward with axis through 2° N, 25° W. Part flows northwest along northeast coast of South America (the Guianas) as Guiana Current. Other part turns below Natal and flows south along coast of Brazil as Brazil Current.

South Indian Current: eastward flowing current of southern Indian Ocean that is continuous with northern edge of West Wind Drift.

South Pacific Current: eastward flowing current of South Pacific Ocean that is continuous with northern edge of West Wind Drift.

sowbug [wood louse]: flat-bodied land crustacean of order *Isopoda*. Found under rocks or in trees, it eats plants and tree roots.

space: designated portion of a vessel's enclosed volume or a particularl area on board; as, *hold space; propelling power space; crew space; passenger deck space*.

spadefish, Atlantic: it is usually striped vertically with pearly gray body bearing several broad vertical bands of black. But like so many other tropical fishes, it can change color pattern at will, sometimes being entirely black, sometimes white. There are two distinct dorsal fins, posterior portion larger with conspicuous extension of first rays. Anal fin also has elongated anterior ray. Grows to length of 24 in.

spadefoot, common [*Scaphiopus holbrooki holbrooki*]: squat, brownish, big-eyed toad. Parotoid gland conspicuous, elevated and rounded rather than oblong; pupil of eye vertical; color dark brown or olive. Ground color brownish-tan to dirty brown with dorsal, light stripes running from behind eye to vent on each side; these stripes are tannish to lemon-yellow; belly pale.

spadefoot, Key West [*Scaphiopus holbrooki ablus*]: aquat, pale colored, big-eyed toad. Parotoid glands conspicuous, elevated and rounded rather than oblong; pupil of eye vertical; ground color pale dirty gray to nearly white. Stripes from eye to vent on each side of dorsum dirty yellow.

span: rope fastened at both ends so that purchase may be hooked to its bight; to confine with ropes.

spanker [ships]: 1) after-sail of ship or bark. Fore-and-aft sail extended by boom and gaff from after side of mizzenmast. 2) fore-and-aft sail set from aftermast of square-rigged ship. It was developed from lateen-mizzen, first by cutting sail vertically at mast and later cutting off lateen yard at mast.

spanner [ships]: form of open-head wrench.

spar [ships]: 1) general term for masts, booms, clubs, gaffs, poles and other slender pieces of wood including spar buoys. 2) seagoing platform for acoustic research. Steel tube, floating vertically is used as unmanned research station for open sea acoustic experiments. Also, type of navigation buoy.

spar deck [ships]: upper deck of flush-decked naval vessel.

sparker: geophysical-type echo-sounder or strong electrical discharge is used as sound source, otherwise very much similar to charting echo-sounding equipment. Variation of above is the boomer.

spark-type luminescence: display of biological light appearing as innumerable flickering pinpoints of light, particularly conspicuous in wake of ship, along hull line or in agitated waters. Crustaceans, such as copepods and euphausids, cause this type of display.

spat: spawn or young of bivalve mollusks.

spatangoids [heart urchins]: these echinoids, which are shaped like domes and biscuits as well as hearts, range from early Cretaceous to Recent. Ambulacra are petal-shaped and may number 4 instead of 5; mouth is forward from center; there is no lantern. Periproct lies in almost vertical area which is really part of dorsal surface. Spines are delicate and silky and either short or very long.

Spatangus: ovoid or heart-shaped sea urchin covered with short spines that lives on sandy bottom. It grows to approximate size of a man's fist. There are numerous species and they are sometimes called heart urchins or sand dollars.

specific gravity: 1) ratio of density of given substance to that of distilled water usually at 4° C and at pressure of one atmosphere. Since density of pure water depends on its isotopic composition, unless isotopic composition of water can be specified, term specific gravity should not be used when intention is to state a precise value. 2) substance's specific gravity is ratio between density (weight in air) and density of another substance (also weight in air) that is considered a standard of measurement.

specific volume: volume per unit mass of a substance or reciprocal of density. In oceanography practice, specific volume is taken as reciprocal of specific gravity.

specific volume anomaly: in oceanography, excess of actual specific volume of seawater at any point in ocean over specific volume of seawater of salinity 35 per mille and temperature 0° C at same pressure. Integral of specific volume anomaly with depth is dynamic height anomaly.

spectacle frame [ships]: single casting containing bearings for and supporting ends of propeller shafts in twin-screw vessel. It consists of arms of pear-shaped section extending outboard from each side of center line of ship to bosses, taking bearings of propeller shafts. Used in large merchant vessels in place of shaft struts or brackets.

spectrum: 1) spectrum of waves consists of the combination of large number of wave trains of different periods and amplitudes, moving in same or different direction. This gives complex pattern of waves normally to be found in ocean. 2) a visual display, photographic record or plat of the distribution of the intensity of energy dispersion of a given kind as a function of its wavelength, energy, frequency, momentum, mass or any related quantity.

Spelaeogriphacea [order]: body shrimplike with short carapace united to first thoracic segment; 2nd antennae with very long flagella; 3 pairs of oval gills attached to 5 to 7 thoracic appendages; 1st pair of thoracic limbs modified as maxillipeds; freshwater lake of South Africa. Spelaeogriphus.

speleology: scientific exploration and study of caves.

spencer [ships]: fore-and-aft sail carried on fore-and-aft mainmast of square-rigged ship, usually set to standing gaff.

spermaceti: in sperm whales, clear high-grade oil found in the melon or spermaceti organ in rostrum.

spermatophore: packet of sperm within complicated case secreted by male, as in copepods and cephalopods.

spermatophyte: one of division (Spermatophyta) of plants, most of which possess true stems, leaves and roots, and all of which produce seeds. Only small group of seed plants are marine.

sperm whale [Physeter macrocephalus]: sperm whale or cachalot, unlike most large whales, has teeth rather than horny strips of whalebone. These exist, however, only in lower jaw (20 to 30 on either side) and when mouth is closed they are sheathed in scabbardlike cavities in upper jaw. Male sperm whales grow up to 60 ft. long, while females are generally from 30 to 40 ft. long. It is one of the best divers of all whales, able to remain under water for about 90 minutes. Single species, Physeter catodon, is recognized as occurring in all warm seas.

spherical irradiance: limit of ratio of radiant flux onto spherical surface to area of surface, as radius of sphere tends toward zero with center fixed. Unit of measurement is watt per square meter (W/m2).

Spica: principal star in the group *Virgo* and listed in Nautical Almanac as a *Virginis*. Has a magnitude of 1.21; right ascension, 13h. 22m.; and declination, 11° S. It may be located by continuing the curve of the *Big Dipper's* handle through *Arcturus*, which star lies at half-way mark between tail of *Dipper* and *Spica*. The star lies in line with the gaff of the *Cutter's Mainsail*, or sail-shaped constellation *Corvus*, at about 11° northeastward of the latter.

spicula: minute, needlelike or multiradiate, calcareous or siliceous body in sponges, radiolarians, primitive chitons and echinoderms. They frequently are identified in marine sediment samples.

spider crab, simple [*Simocarcinus simplex*]: in this species males and females differ from each other in body shape. Males have carapace which is somewhat triangular in outline and larger rostrum or beak. In females rostrum is shorter, carapace more rectangular in outline and chelipeds are smaller than those of males. Body of this crab is about 1 in. long. Entire body is same brown color as seaweed in which it lives.

spider crab, spiny [*Hyastenus spinosus*]: body of this spider crab is pear-shaped and bears a few blunt spines. There are 4 blunt spines in midline of back which are distributed as follows: pair is placed in midline of back directly above mouth, single, very low, blunt spine lies in midline at widest point of carapace and single, low, blunt spine is located at posterior end of carapace. There is also a single, laterally directed spine on each side of carapace just behind widest point. Entire body is brown and usually covered to varying degree with marine growth including sponge, algae and hydroids.

Spilhaus Miller sea sampler: bathythermograph with attached container designed to collect seawater samples at predetermined depths. Sample bottles are triggered to close at both ends by pressure sensing element of bathythermograph.

spiling [ships]: curve of plate or strake as it narrows to a point.

spindrift: fine spray and foam swept by the wind from crests of the waves, or the resulting foamy streaks lying in the direction of the wind; also, *spoondrift. Scud,* or broken vapory clouds driven before the wind.

spine [fish]: median (unpaired) fin rays which are not suspended and are not branched at tip.

spinnaker [ships]: large, triangular sail made of light material having wide spread to its foot. It is set from masthead and tack is secured to outer end of boom called the "spinnaker boom", set horizontally from the mast to take it. Clew is controlled by a sheet belayed to cleat on deck. Boom is guyed by lines leading to fore and after part of boat. Spinnaker is used when going before wind and is set on weather side (side opposite mainsail) or, "wings and wing."

spinnaker pole [ships]: pole generally used to extend spinnakers.

spiny slipper limpet: this slipper limpet is low and domelike in shape and oval in outline at base. It possesses apex which is laterally placed at posterior end of shell. Outer surface of shell is marked by radiating ridges which are covered by spines of various lengths. On lower side of shell columella is expanded into shelf or septum which covers posterior half of aperture. Septum is usually slightly concave and margin is usually notched in middle and at both sides. Color of shell varies considerably. It ranges from white through yellow to brown above and is often marked with rays of brownish colors. Slipper limpet is a cosmopolitan species.

spiracel: blowhole or nostril on top of head in cetaceans (members of marine mammal order *Cetacea* that includes whales and porpoises); it is also an aperture carrying water to gills of rays.

spiral angle [*Gastropoda*]: angle formed between two lines tangent to periphery of two or more whorls and on opposite sides of shell. Angle may change from initial whorls to later ones.

spiralium [*Brachiopoda*]: one of a pair of spirally coiled calcareous ribbons that form the branchidium in some brachiopods.

spiral sea whip: type of sea whip, alcyonarian of class *Gorgonacea* with hard skeleton and long, flexible body with few or no branching arms, unlike its close relatives, sea fans.

spiral suture [*Foraminifera*]: line of contact between whorls in coiled test.

Spiratella [heteropods]: smallest of *Spiratella* species and perhaps most abundant of all pelagic gastropods. Shell, as in other thecosomatous pteropods, which is sinistrally spiralled, is made up of 5 whorls and is 2.8 mm. long. This species is characteristic of Atlantic.

Spiratella retroversa [*Aporrhaidae*]: most abundant species of thecosomatous pteropod is *Spiratella retroversa*. Eggs are found during most of year but are commonest in summer plankton. When shell is about 0.32 mm. long it is sinistrally coiled and two rudimentary lappets have formed at sides of foot. These rapidly develop into wings as velum regresses. At about same time a "balancer organ" is developed as projection from base of foot. Apart from brown digestive and anal glands larva is colorless.

spire [*Mollusca*]: visible part of all whorls in gastropod shell except the last which is body whorl.

Spiriferida: brachiopods, which range from mid Ordovician to Jurassic united by spiral structures (brachidia) supporting lophophore.

Spiriferoida: *Articulata* with calcareous spiralia or spirals; deltidial plates in some cases fused into single plate.

Spirula, pointed: shell of this mollusc is of usual cylindrical or conical tapering form with coils lying in one plane and with each chamber separated from last by partition or septum which is concave in shape toward open end and which is connected to preceeding septum and chamber by ventrally located, funnel-shaped, siphonal tube. Last chamber of shell is largest, while first or nuclear chamber is rounded or bulbous. Shell is white; will reach about ¾ in. in diameter. Species inhabits tropical Atlantic and Pacific Oceans; probably worldwide in warmer waters of globe.

Spirulidae: this family belongs in order *Decapoda* of two-gilled cephalopods. They are animals with elongated body and look much like small squid, covered over posterior end with small shell which is loosely coiled in one plane and chambered within, somewhat like *Nautilus*. Shell is held upright at end of body by mantle and is almost completely enclosed within it.

Spisula elliptica [*Mactracem cheterodonta*]: shell of this species has truncated broad end as in *Mactra corallina* but high umbones distinguish it from this species, as does presence of peglike process on provinculum. Larva reaches about 350μ in length and yellowish shell is crossed by groups of fine concentric lines.

spit: small point of land or long, narrow shoal, usually sand, extending from shore into body of water.

spitfire [ships]: small, storm jib.

Spitsberger Current: ocean current flowing northward and westward from point south of Spitzbergen and gradually merging with East Greenland Current in Greenland Sea. Spitsberger Current is continuation of northwestern branch of Norway Current.

splashnik: expendable, accelerometer, telemetry buoy which provides surface wave data.

splash zone: area high up shore, above tideline, which may be splashed with seawater from breaking waves.

splice [ships]: method of uniting ends of two ropes by first unlaying strands, then interweaving them so as to form continuous rope.

splitter: 1) tool used to partly split or open the edges of lapped plating preparatory to calking. 2) one of the crew in a fishing vessel who splits fish for cleaning.

split whip wrack [*Laminaria ander*]: split whip is fastened to substratum by many branched fibers, mass being 3 to 4 in. in diameter. Entire plant, stipe and blade may be 3 to 4 ft. long. Stipe is perennial, blade annual. When fruiting takes place late in autumn, spore cases produced in irregularly shaped patches nearly cover both surfaces of blade.

splosher: "coble" local to Staithes, Yorkshire, England, used in herring fishery. About 25 ft. long on keel, 30 ft. overall, beam about 10 ft.; square-sterned with rake of 3½ ft.

spoil banks: submerged accumulations of dumped material dredged from channels of harbors. Region where such material is dumped is called spoil ground.

spondylium [*Brachiopoda*]: curved plate in midline of beak of pedicle valve formed by union of dental plates from either side of midline and serving for muscle attachment.

sponges [*Porifera*, class *Demospongiae*]: sponges are simplest of multicellular animals, forming the phylum *Porifera*. Bodies are covered with holes through which water is drawn; food and oxygen are then extracted from this water. Sponges reproduce as primitively and as simply as they live. These animals are found in every sea, at every depth, in variety of shapes (fans, fingers, spheres, etc.) and colors (blue, yellow or red) and in sizes from ½ in. to 6 ft. long. There are about 5,000 distinct species. They are sedentary animals. Some have horny skeletons and others have harder skeletons made of silica.

spongin: fibrous, horny, flexible material making up skeleton of various *Demospongiae*. In order *Keratosa*, of which commercial sponges are representative, it comprises entire skeletal framework. Other groups also have spicules or may have only spicules.

spongy cushion [*Codium setchellii*]: grows on exposed faces of rocks between 1- and 1.5-ft. tide levels. Striking feature of this seaweed is unusual shape and texture, a felted, encrusted, dark green or black cushion shaped like a half moon. Flattened body is usually 1/3 in. high and 4 to 6 in. in circumference. Unusual shape is brought about by compact covering of noncalcareous, pith filaments which end in sacs perpendicular to surface and held together securely by a gelatinous substance. These filaments bind entire mass together.

spot: an edible fish, resembling and of same family as the *drumfish*, found on the U.S. Atlantic coast; averaging nine inches in length, the fish bears a remarkable black *spot* about two inches behind each eye and has 15 diagonal dark stripes across its back.

spot [*Leiostomus xanthurus*]: small croaker; laterally compressed fish with oblique yellow stripes on sides and back. Rays in soft dorsal 30—34; scales along lateral line 60—70; no barbels present on chin. Body moderately elongate, arched above; mouth moderate, terminal to subterminal in position; upper jaw with numerous minute teeth, lower jaw toothless in adults. Color bluish above, fading to off-white below; about 15 narrow, oblique yellowish bars on back and side and yellowish spot on each side in shoulder region.

spot [ship]: 1) to place in a desired position, as a sling of cargo being lowered, a vessel alongside a pier, ship's gangway, etc. 2) at hand and ready for use, shipment, etc., as, a *spot ship; spot cargo.*

spotted pebble crab [*Carpilius maculatus*]: most distinguishing feature is very hard and very heavy shell which covers body and legs. Carapace or back is convex, smooth, oval in outline and without spines. Species is easily recognized by 11 large, round, red spots which mark the back. Of these spots, 3 form crossward row in middle of back, 4 form a row across rear of carapace and 2 are located behind each of the eyes. Carapace may reach a width of 6 in. in large specimens.

spouting horn: marine caves eroded in coastal rocks which have openings to air through which water spouts or sprays as waves surge into cavern beneath.

spray ice: ice formed from blown spray which may occur along shore, on floating ice, on ships or seaplanes.

spray ridge: one of series of ice formations on ice foot, formed by freezing of spray blown from waves by wind.

spreaders: horizontal members of wood or metal attached to masts and used to give added tension to shrouds.

spreading: diminution of sound pressure level with distance according to various laws of behavior, such as spherical spreading, cylindrical spreading or dipolar spreading.

spring: current of round water issuing through natural opening where water table intersects surface.

spring line [ships]: line from the bow, aft or quarter, forward to prevent fore-and-aft motion at dock and to help hold vessel off dock.

spring maximum: abundance of marine phytoplankton (predominantly diatoms) after winter minimum. Production of phytoplankton is generally highest for the year during this period. This condition occurs most frequently in regions of higher latitudes which experience some form of vertical mixing.

spring rise: mean height of high water above chart datum during syzygy or periods of new and/or full moon.

spring tide: very high and low tides caused twice

monthly by combined "pull" of sun and full or new moon.

spritsail [ships]: 1) quadrilateral sail, head of which is extended and supported by small pole or "sprit," that extends upward diagonally from mast to peak. Fore-leech is attached to mast by lacing. Lower end of sprit rests in a collar of rope called a "snotter" which encircles mast near foot of sail. 2) sail extended by a sprit, hence sails on bowsprit (no longer in use) which were attached to a yard. It was often pierced by large hole at each lower corner to let out water with which it frequently filled when ship pitched. Columbus' ship, *Santa Maria,* was so equipped.

sprit topsail [ships]: small, square sail set on short vertical mast erected at outer end of bowsprit on larger ships of 16th and 17th centuries.

spud: 1) an armor-pointed vertical pile or post that may be dropped or lifted on end from a scow, dredge, etc., to serve as an anchor. 2) larger vessels of scow type having construction or dredging *plant* aboard usually are equipped with a *spud* at each corner of the hull.

spun yarn [ships]: line or cord formed of rope yarns twisted together, used for wrapping ropes to prevent chafing, binding, etc., with sails.

spur: 1) subordinate elevation, ridge or rise projecting outward from larger feature. 2) ridge, usually composed of sand or gravel, which extends into sea from shore or from larger submarine elevation.

squall: influenced by much older term, bawl; 17th century parents transformed the name of baby's squeal into a squall and used the new word to indicate an especially abrupt burst of noise. A household squall was no more welcome then than now. But association of the vivid term with sudden expulsion of air led it to be linked with short, sharp windstorms. Sailors were first to use the word in this sense; in 1725 it appeared in Defoe's famous "A New Voyage Round the World." From vernacular of the sea, landsmen borrowed back the nursery-born term and applied it to brief, violent gusts over land as well as over water.

squall line: line of thunderstorms at or ahead of fast-moving cold front.

square frame [ships]: frame having no bevel on its flange; midship frame.

square-rigged [ships]: describing a ship with square-rigging in which square sails are set across length of vessel and supported by yards carried athwart the masts. Fore-and-aft-rigged ship, far more common today, has differently rigged triangular or quadrilateral sails set more or less parallel to length of ship; having principal sails extended by yards joined to masses at the middle, and not by gaffs and booms. Bark or brig and a ship are square-rigged vessels, and are commonly called square-riggers.

square-rigger [ships]: sailing ships with square rigging in which sails hang across length of ship and are supported by yards carried athwart the masts.

square sail [ships]: 1) rectangular sail which hangs across length of ship and is supported by yards carried athwart a mast. Most sails today are fore-and-aft sails which are parallel to length of ship. 2) sails extended horizontally on yard secured to mast. Opposed to fore-and-aft sails extended by means of stays, gaffs, booms, etc.

squat [ships]: depression of after end of a vessel, or change of trim by the stern, due to motion through the water. Actually, in the case of ships having a *speed length ratio* of less than about 1.0, upon speed becoming great enough to produce wave making, the hull sinks bodily with little change of trim. With higher speed length ratios, however, *squat* appears under same conditions and in shallow water may increase to the undesirable extent of contact of the hull with the sea bottom. A good example of degree of *squat* is seen in the marked depression of a destroyer's after end when the vessel is proceeding at high speed.

squeeze [diving]: type of injury occurring in divers, usually during descent, which comes about because of inability to equalize pressure between closed air space, such as middle ear, and outside water pressure.

squid: one of an order *(Decapoda)* of cephalopods in which body is cigar-shaped or globose and bears 10 arms, 8 of which are of equal length with suckers along entire length and 2 are longer with suckers only on broad, terminal portion; shell, in most, is embedded in body or absent. Some species (sea arrows) are among faster nekton. One species, giant squid, is largest invertebrate and food of sperm whales.

squilla, banded [*Lysiosquilla maculata*]: stomatopods are unusual *Crustacea* for they have long, slender bodies which are usually larger toward posterior end. Carapace or shell is short and covers only front part of thorax; front end of body bears a pair of large, strong limbs which are adapted for seizing food; last 3 segments of thorax each bear a pair of leglike appendages. The banded squilla is easily recognized by alternating light and dark bands which cross body. Large individuals reach 8 in. in length. Lives on muddy bottoms along shoreline in fairly shallow water which is often somewhat brackish.

squilla, large white [*Squilla oratoria*]: this mantis shrimp is marked upon thorax and abdomen by longitudinal ridges. Carapace is narrower in front than behind and does not cover 4th to 8th thoracic segments; 3 pairs of leglike appendages arise on last thoracic segments. Eyes of this species are large and appear to be set somewhat crosswise on

eyestalks. Body is very light tan color above and lighter below; dark spot on uropod on each side of tail. Tail or telson bears 6 spines around margin. Most adult specimens range in length from 6 to 8 in. Lives on bottom in shallow water and is found in brackish esturaries where bottom is muddy and suitable for its burrows.

squirrelfish: especially named because of extremely large eyes, indicating that this species is nocturnal. When disturbed, these fishes chatter noisily, a trait reminding one of land animals from which squirrelfish get their name. A showy fish darting in and out of coral thickets, it is bright red on back and rosy-red on undersides; fins are bright red; dorsal fin has yellowish base. Forward portion of dorsal fin has large, tough spine that can spread the fin like a fan. Usually under 12 in. long.

squirrel hake: species of gadid fish, *Urophysischuss*, in North Atlantic waters. Valuable food fish.

Staballoy slide: trade name for gold-plated gas slide used in mechanical bathythermograph to record temperature versus depth trace.

stability: resistance to overturning or mixing in water column, resulting from presence of positive density gradient.

stable gravimeter: gravimeter having single weight or spring, such that sensitivity is proportional to square of its period.

stack: isolated, steep-sided rock mass standing as a small island in front of cliff line or off end of a promontory along coast.

stagger [ships]: to zigzag a line or row of rivet holes, etc.

staging [ships]: upright supports fastened together with horizontal and diagonal braces forming supports for planks which form working platform.

staircase shell [*Epitoniidae*]: staircase shells or wentletraps are beautiful, white, polished shells with high turreted spires composed of many rounded whorls which decrease gradually in size from body whorl to apex of spire. Outer surface of each whorl is covered by longitudinal varixes which are formed as reflected borders of outer lips and which become a new varix when animal moves forward to form a new lip. In addition to reflected border on each lip, shell has rounded aperture which is closed by horny operculum.

staircase shell, pleasing: this staircase shell is composed of loosely coiled whorls which are in contact with each other. Whorls are covered on outside by thin, longitudinal, slightly angled ribs. Umbilicus is partially covered by lip but is open between ribs on ventral surface. It is white and will reach more than ½ in. in length. *Epitonium* species.

staircase shell, pyramidal: this staircase shell is

composed of loosely coiled whorls which are decorated on outside by thin, longitudinal ribs. Umbilicus is completely covered by inner lip. It is whitish in color and will vary between 7/8 and 1 in. in length. *Epitonium* species.

stalked barnacle: barnacle whose body is differentiated into body proper, which usually is covered by 2-valved shell, and stalk at base, by which animal is attached to firm surface. Many are pelagic or deep living and some are attached to free-floating objects, e.g., floating seaweed, hulls of ships and whales.

stamuhka: Russian word for sea ice stranded on shoal or shallows.

stanch: also *staunch.* Seaworthy, tight, and sound; said of a vessel with respect to her fitness for carrying a prospective cargo.

stanchion [ships]: upright post or beam of different forms used to support deck, rails or awning on ship.

standard displacement: surface displacement of submarine, exclusive of water in nonwatertight structure, when fully manned, engined and equipped for sea duty, including all armament and ammunition, equipment, provisions for crews, miscellaneous, stores and implements of every description that are intended to be carried in war but excluding fuel, lubricating oil, fresh water or ballast water of any kind.

standard dress [diving]: diving system consisting of brass diving helmet, breastplate, heavy dry suit, weighted shoes, weight belt, hose, compressor and communications.

stand by [ships]: order to get ready, as "Stand by to drop anchor."

standing crop: refers to total quantity of any species living at any one time, which may be compared with quantity produced by reproduction.

standing port [ships]: right side of vessel, looking forward.

standing rigging [ships]: ropes or wire ropes which permanently support spars, such as shrouds and other stays, and are not moved when working sails.

standing wave: type of wave in which surface of water oscillates vertically between fixed points, called nodes, without progression. Points of maximum vertical rise and fall are called antinodes or loops. At nodes, underlying water particles exhibit no vertical motion but maximum horizontal motion. At antinodes, underlying water particles have no horizontal motion and maximum vertical motion.

stand of tide: interval at high or low water when there is no appreciable change in height of tide; duration will depend on range of tide, being longer when tide range is large. Where double

tide occurs, stand may last for several hours even with large range of tide.

stapling [ships]: collars, forged of angle bars, to fit around continuous members passing through bulkheads or decks for watertightness.

starboard [ships]: right-hand side of ship looking from aft toward forward; at night marked by green light.

starfish: member of a large class of echinoderms, the *Asteroidea,* whose bodies are in shape of a star with 5 branches or "arms." At extremity of each arm there is a short tentacle, and at base of that tentacle is bright red, light-sensitive, sensory organ. In addition, each arm carries on its underside, hundreds of tiny podia or tube feet equipped with suction discs. Starfish is much more mobile than its appearance. Mouth is located in central disc. Starfish is a dedicated carnivore which devours mollusks and crustaceans both living and dead. Method of digestion is unusual. Rather than swallowing its victim, the starfish regurgitates and applies results to its prey, whereupon victim is dissolved in starfish's digestive system.

starfish [*Acanthaster planci*]: numerous rays, as few as 5 and as many as 21, radiating from large disc that in life is raised, resembling a crown. Dorsal side of disc contains several madreporites. Both sides of animal are thickly covered with long, thorny spines which are poisonous and have been known to cause illness or death. Color varies from purplish, reddish-brown to sometimes yellow. Darker shading on central part of dorsal side; lighter on ventral side.

starfish [*Astropecten armatus*]: normally 5 rays radiating from small to medium-sized disc, flat dorsal surface, not arched. Large, marginal plates and long, lateral spines make row of bristling spines around long, tapering rays. Two rows of marginal plates always found along edge. Coloring on dorsal side runs from lavender to gray.

starfish [*Ctenodiscus crispatus*]: generally 5-rayed, but shape and length of rays are variable. Rays on dorsal side are edged with series of spines that give it a beaded appearance. Surface is closely covered with clusters of minute spines; length and closeness of spines vary. Having no intestine, intestinal caecum or anus, a large, single stomach serves this sea star. Sieve plate is prominent and very off-center.

starfish [*Diploteraster multipes*]: 5 short, blunt rays on thick, spiny disc. Dorsal side is purplish-red and ventral side is lighter. Rays turn up slightly. Ambulacral groove is very wide. This species bristles with stout central spines which push up membrane on dorsal surface and protrude through.

starfish [*Dipsacaster borealis*]: 5 rays evenly tapered. Purplish on dorsal side, lighter on ventral side. Dorsal side thickly covered with spinelets giving velvety appearance. Marginal plates are massive. Edges give appearance of being beaded. On ventral side, ambulacral groove is lined with spines.

starfish [*Henricia clarki*]: normally 5 long, slender, tapering rays whose undersides are flattened. These rays form 8 angles to each other. Disc is small and flat-topped. Surface feels velvety. Slightly raised granules in even and uneven formations on dorsal side. Ventral side has very small granules which are distributed evenly. Colors in life vary: blue on topside and bright orange-red on underside. Sieve plate or madreporite halfway between center of disc and ray angle, but not prominent.

starfish [*Henricia polyacantha*]: 5 moderately slender, almost round rays which taper gradually to bluntly pointed, upturned tips. Disc is small, slightly raised and almost flat. Rays form sharp, almost right angles to each other from the disc. Surface without spines but plates that form regular patterns. Madreporite is large, prominent and close to a right angle between 2 rays. Bright red-orange on ventral side.

starfish [*Leiaster callipeplus*]: 5 rays, not all equal in length. Rays are subcylindrical, nearly uniform in diameter, slightly constricted at base and tapered to blunt point. Disc is small with circular madreporite filter located nearer margin than midway between it and center of disc. Body is covered by thick, tough, smooth skin which, in living state, hides the plates, but when dried shrinks and allows plates to be clearly seen. Color in life is maroon-purple.

starfish [*Linckia guildingii*]: 5 long, slightly tapering rays which are rounded on dorsal side and flattened on ventral side. Surface covered with smooth skin which dries to smooth texture. Small plates are visible often curving with papulae shown only on dorsal surface. Only one madreporite filter visible. Color is muted green shading, lighter at tips of rays.

starfish [*Linckia multifora*]: 5 long, slender, gradually tapering rays which are cylindrical and unequal in length. They radiate from small, raised disc. Small, irregularly spaced plates on dorsal side. Color is orange-red with darker red spots. Two madreporite filters, circular in form, are located near edge of disc.

starfish [*Luidia foliolata*]: mottled greenish-colored ray on dorsal side and yellow on ventral side. Occasionally houses polynoid worm in ambulacral grooves. Normally, 5 long, evenly tapered rays with fringed edges. Intermediate plates are in single, longitudinal series on ray each bearing tuft of spinelets but no pedicellariae. Dorsal surface looks velvety.

starfish [*Nidorellia armata*]: 5 short, blunt rays

which radiate from elevated, pentagonal disc. Bordering rays are large marginal plates which on ventral side contain spines that are larger at mouth area; marginal plates on dorsal side do not bear spines. Young specimen has large conical-shaped spines arranged in 5 rows from center of disc down middle of each ray. These spines become smaller at end of rays. In mature specimen, spines are worn down on dorsal and extra spines are scattered between regular rows. Natural colors usually are grayish with black spines.

starfish [*Ophidiaster squameus*]: 4 or 5 rays that are unequal in length. Rays are cylindrical and scarcely tapered to blunt tip. At tip of ray is a large terminal plate which is conspicuous and smooth. Rays form right angles to each other from very small disc. Small prominent plates are arranged in regular longitudinal series. Color in life is vermilion with darker blotches.

starfish [*Ophidiaster triseriatus*]: usually 5 slightly tapering round rays which make fairly wide, acute angle from small disc. Surface is covered with tough, smooth skin that, when dry, shows even rows of skeletal plates and resembles snake's skin. Coloration is pinkish-tan with almost a lavender-blue. Irregular splotches are orange-red. Circular madreporite is situated between 2 radial plates.

starfish [*Pentacero hawaiiensis*]: dorsal surface maroon-colored and covered with prominent orange spines. Vertical surface is smooth, flat and colored an orange-red. Ambulacral grooves are very wide from which protrude large tube feet. This species has 1 madreporite filter located just off-center on dorsal side. This sea star has 5 rather short and tapering rays. Disc is convex, large and quite thick, especially in center.

starfish [*Pisaster giganteus capitatus*]: rays number 5 or 6 from medium-sized disc. Skeleton framework is rigid. Spines themselves and area around each one is light in color. These spines are numerous and prominent, but they do not form a network like pentagon shape on *Pisaster ochracens*. Color of this star is variable in shades of ochre or blue.

starfish [*Poraniopsis inflata*]: color from neutral beige to light tan; 5 rays tapering from broad disc with beautiful network of raised ridges which are pink in the live animal. Spines on raised areas. Rays are slightly inflated in middle and bluntly pointed.

starfish [*Pseudarchaster pareli alascensis*]: 5 rays tapering from broad disc. Flat-beaded edges on dorsal side on which are calcareous elevations that distinguish it from *Mediaster aequalis*. This star's surface is covered with calcareous elevations, but it does not have spines. Tips of rays taper into thin, tubular points.

starfish [*Pteraster tesselatus arcuatus*]: very thick

disc with short rays that turn slightly. Dorsal side is multicolored and ventral side is yellowish. On dorsal side, background color is beige with black and gray markings producing interesting designs. Sieve plate is not like other specimens but a small opening in center of disc that can be observed pulsating as animal takes in water.

starfish [*Stylasterias forreri*]: 5 long, slender rays extending from small disc. Spines on dorsal side are thin, tapered, smooth and spaced uniformly about their own length from each other. On ventral side spines are not present; pedicellarial and tube feet are, however. Color on dorsal side is deep brown between pedicellariae; overall appearance is of olive shades of brown with white spines on light raised area. Body is spiny and fragile.

starfish, basket star [*Gorgonocephalus caryi*]: this is probably most unusual of sea stars because of its shape and branching; 5 rays grow from disc; each ray branches up to 12 times and rolls toward mouth which allows the star to capture its food by snaring it. Surface is soft and granulated in colors of yellow. These rays, unlike most brittles, do not break off easily. Rays are often colored with orange markings. Extensive branching make it possible for animal to attach to rocks or seaweeds.

starfish, bat star [*Patiria miniata*]: normally, 5 triangular rays which radiate from broad, thick disc which becomes very thin at edges. Color variations are bright red or orange, purple, mottled-green and purple.

starfish, blood star [*Henricia leviuscula*]: color on dorsal side is blood-red, red-orange or on young specimen, light orange. Ventral side is usually yellow. Five rays are long and tapering from small disc. In its ambulacral groove it often hosts a scale worm called *Arctonoe vittata*. Rays are quite stiff with very short spine that give it a smooth appearance.

starfish, brittle star [*Opiopholis aculeata*]: well proportioned star with small disc and 5 thin, tapering rays. Between each ray is conspicuous lobe. In large specimens these lobes seem to be inflated on ventral surface. Rays are lined with spines perpendicular along sides. Color is variable with rusty-red being predominant and mottled-green being secondary. Red may be banded with red stripes.

starfish, leather star [*Dermasterias imbricata*]: 5 rays tapering from broad, thick disc. Dorsal side is sleek and smooth in colors of mottled delicate purple to deep red or neutral background; underside is yellow with tips of rays turning up slightly. Its only spines are on ventral side along ambulacral groove. Sea star has been known to scare stationary sea anemones into actually swimming.

starfish, long-rayed [*Orthasterias koehleri*]: spines on dorsal surface arranged in 5 or more indistinct longitudinal rows which extend from humped disc. Pliable skeleton from which rays break off easily, especially in northern species. Color in life is variable and runs from red to purple with white spines surrounded by light area.

starfish, morning sun [*Solaster dawsoni*]: rays number 8 to 15 but most commonly found with 11 or 13. Disc is broad with rays close together. Color varies from bright orange to dull yellow and blue-gray. Disc is slightly raised. On dorsal side this star has larger groups of flat-topped spinelets, those on edges are somewhat larger and longer along ambulacral groove.

starfish, mottled star [*Evasteria troschellii*]: small disc from which extend 5 long tapering rays. Dorsal surface spines are numerous and are arranged in a network or in clusters; 5 or 6 distinct lateral rows of spines start at margin of grooves on ventral side and extend up margin of rays. Color is variable and can be mottled shades of brown, blue, green or ochre. Although hybrids are not common among sea stars, this species often has hybrids. Skeletal framework is firm. Large, often reaches 2 ft. across.

starfish, pincushion [*Culcita noyae arenosa*]: large, thick and pentagonal-shaped; appears to be all disc and no rays. Thickness is fairly consistent; only one madreporite filter is visible. Dorsal surface is a blotchy, mottled maroon color covered with very short red spines. Ventral side is reddish-tan with short tan spines.

starfish, purple star or ochre star [*Pisaster ochracens*] rigid skeleton has, normally, 5 wide rays from substantial disc which is slightly humped. Short dorsal spines are arranged in close-set rows forming distinct network. Spines on disc form well-marked pentagon. Color ranges from deep purple to bright orange.

starfish, rose [*Crossaster papposus*]: one of the most beautiful stars which resembles a rose because of bright rose-pink, concentric bands of color on lighter pink shade. Ventral side is light beige. Rays number 8 to 14 radiating from large, flat disc. Dorsal surface has open network of calcareous stalks with clusters of spines at tips resembling tiny brushes.

starfish, six-rayed [*Leptasterias hexactis*]: sea star has normally 6 rays radiating from substantial disc. Color varies from dull pinks to dull greens. Its uneven spines give a rough appearance. Very small, 2 in. is considered large.

starfish, spiny red [*Hippasteria spinosa*]: 5 rays tapering from broad, thick disc. Firm skeleton. Color is bright red on dorsal side and yellow on ventral side. Dorsal side has numerous, raised spines.

starfish, sun [*Solaster stimpsoni*]: distinctive strip of blue-gray extending to tips of rays from a round center area on disc. On each side of stripe is a border of pink, red or orange. Rays are slim and uniformly tapered to a point; disc is large and slightly humped. Ventral side is light, almost white, except a gray stripe on each side of ambulacral grooves. Rays number 10 to 12.

starfish, sunflower [*Heliaster microbrachius*]: number of rays in adults varies from 30 to 44. Disc, very large with middle elevated like inverted saucer; proportionally short rays which taper to a point and are free less than 30%. Dorsal side dark gray to black, ventral side lighter shade of same color. Spines on both sides prominent because they are lighter shade. *Heliaster* is unable to extend its stomach outside its disc.

starfish, sunflower or twenty-rayed star [*Pycnopodia helianthoides*]: 20 to 24 rays from large disc in adult animal. Young specimen starts with 5 or 6 rays between existing ones. Rays break off easily when disturbed or when pulled from a rock. Coloring is variable from purple to mottled gray on disc and center of rays. Orange or salmon pink outline all rays. Dorsal surface is sparsely covered by spines with wreaths of pedicellariae and thick clusters of pedicellariae scattered over upper part of disc. Skeleton is not rigid.

starfish, vermilion star [*Mediaster aequatis*]: 5 rays tapering from broad disc. Color is bright red on dorsal side and shades of orange on lower side. Tube feet on ventral side are scarlet with flesh-colored tips. Dorsal side is covered with mail of raised calcareous elevations. Pedicellariae are present on both sides of surface.

stargazer: another name for a *moonsail*. Small spiny-rayed marine fish of the family *Uranoscopidae* so named because of upward-looking eyes. All in family are chunky fish with mouth located on top of head near eyes. Forward portion of dorsal fins bears a few short, stout spines; pectoral fins are smaller and more pointed than the toadfish. Stargazers seem harmless, but they carry a unique electric weapon on the head, undoubtedly useful in shocking an adversary or capturing prey.

stargazer, northern: dusky fish with irregular white spots on upper side and dark blotches on lower side. It grows to length of 12 in. and is found on ocean bottom. Stargazer often lies buried in sand waiting for a meal of small fishes or crustaceans, showing only its upturned eyes and protruding mouth.

star shells: tropical shells that can be ornamented with numerous spines or somewhat smooth. Star shells are vegetarians and like rocky beaches for their home. Operculum is limy and quite hard.

start [ships]: to start a sheet is to ease or loosen it.

station: 1) in oceanography, geographic location at which any set of oceanographic observations were taken. 2) when engineer makes a survey to locate a road, the term station applies to whole distance between 2 consecutive stakes, with the number written on last stake.

stationary front: boundary between two air masses that are not moving.

stationary wave theory: theory which assumes that basic tide motion in open ocean consists of a system of standing wave oscillations; progressive waves are of secondary importance except where tide advances into tributary waters.

station data: data collected by oceanographic ship while taking a station. Station data usually consist of identifying information, weather data, weather temperature, salinity and chemical composition at specified depths.

statocyst: lithocyst; small vesicle containing a statolith, serving as balancing organ.

statolith: in jellyfish, small calcareous concretion within a lithocyst.

statute mile: 4,280 ft. or 1.6093 km., or 0.869 nautical mile.

statutory deck line: datum line from which a vessel's *freeboard* is measured. It is painted black on a light ground or white on a dark ground on each side of the hull, at mid-distance between stem and stern, as a horizontal stripe 12 in. long by 1 in. in width, the upper edge of which indicates the exposed surface of freeboard deck plating or planking at vessel's side.

stay [ships]: heavy line, today usually of wire, used to support ship's mast. Stay attaches to head of mast and extends to another mast or deck. Those leading forward are called fore-and-aft stays, and those which lead down to vessel's side are backstays.

staysail [ships]: triangular fore-and-aft sail set from various stays and named for mast from which stays lead. On early frigates and men-of-war, quadrilateral staysails were often used.

staysail rig [ships]: modern rig used on schooner yachts in which mainsail is jibheaded with main staysail and upper staysails are set between fore-and mainmasts. Usual headsails are carried.

staysail schooner: type of schooner in which foresail is replaced by several smaller, triangular staysails.

Steady as you go: command to maintain course and speed.

stealer [ships]: foremost and aftermost plate in strake, which is dropped short of stem or sternpost of vessel.

steam fog: fog formed when water vapor is added to air which is much colder than vapor's source; most common when very cold air drifts across relatively warm water.

steerage [ships]: 1) portion of ship allotted to passengers who travel at cheapest rate; hence, steerage passengers. 2) act of steering.

steerageway [ships]: sufficient speed to keep vessel responding to rudder.

steering gear [ships]: term applied to steering wheels, leads, steering engine and fittings by which rudder is turned.

steering gear flat [ships]: deck above stern overhang on which rudder steering mechanism is installed.

steering sails [ships]: old term of "studding sails."

steeve [ships]: angle that bowsprit makes with horizontal.

stellar: of, pertaining to, or resembling a star or the stars. *Stellar* month equals sidereal month.

stem [ships]: 1) foremost upper timber in hull of vessel, all planks or plates being rabbeted or riveted to it. 2) foremost frame in vessel reaching from keel to meeting of port and starboard rails.

stem foot [ships]: forward end of keel into which stem is fitted.

stenobathic: having limited vertical range or range of depth tolerance.

stenohaline: capable of existence only within narrow range of salinity, as certain marine organisms.

stenothermal: having limited range of temperature tolerance.

step: 1) in ships, shaped and usually keyed receptacle affixed to keel to receive heel of mast. On some modern light sailboats, mast may be stepped to cabin top. 2) nearly horizontal section which more or less divides beach from shoreface.

stepping [ships]: manner of securing masts onto ship.

stereographic projection: perspective, conformal, azimuthal map projection in which points on surface of a sphere are conceived as projected by radial lines from any point on surface to a plane tangent to antipode of point of projection. Circles project as circles except for great circles through point of tangency which project as straight lines.

stereozone [*Coelenterata*]: zone of dense skeletal deposits, typically along or near wall of corallite.

steric level: mean dynamic depth (height) for the month minus annual, mean dynamic depth to same isobaric reference level.

stern [ships]: hind part of ship where rudder is placed. Part opposite stem or prow; after part of vessel.

stern frame [ships]: large casting attached to after end of keel to form ship's stern. Includes rudder post, propeller post and aperture for propeller.

stern pipe [ships]: pipe leading to opening at side of poop deck for passage of cables, chains, etc., for mooring purposes.

sternpost [ships]: afterpost to which rudder is hinged and placed on ship with sufficient clearance for propeller to revolve.

stern tube [ships]: bearing which supports propeller shaft where it emerges from ship.

sterodonts [sea urchins]: these echinoids which range from Triassic to Recent, are plump or almost spheroidal. Sterodonts seem to be Mesozoic descendants of early cidaroids with plates and spines much like those of their ancestors. Anus, however, is slightly off-center, and modern forms do most of breathing with specialized gills at edge of peristome.

steroid: one of numerous animal and plant compounds characterized by carbon ring system and including sterols (solid alcohol such as cholesterol) and many hormones.

stevedore: man whose duty or occupation is stowage of goods in ship's hold. One who loads or unloads vessels.

stick bag [*Coilodesme californica*]: stick bag is abundant at mean low to 1.5-ft. tide levels whenever host is present. It is a long or egg-shaped bag standing at right angles to branches of host plant. When young, epiphyte is smooth, inflated sack or bag, but when old, it becomes a thin, flat, eroded blade.

stickleback: small, spiny-rayed fish in which dorsal fin is reduced to separate, long spines varying in number from 3 to 9 according to species. Each ventral fin is also unusual in being reduced to single spine. About 12 species occur in both freshwater and marine habitats of north temperate regions; 5 species occur in U.S. Sticklebacks feed on aquatic plants, crustaceans and eggs and fry of fish.

stickleback, brook: lives in cool streams and small ponds of northern U.S. from Maine to Montana. It is mottled olive-green, yellowish on underside and armed with 5 or 6 dorsal spines. Full-grown individuals are only a few inches long yet males are ferocious fighters when disturbed, erecting their spines when meeting an adversary.

stiff [ships]: said of sailboat which does not heel readily in a breeze.

stiffener [ships]: angle bar or stringer fastened to surface to strengthen it and make it rigid.

stiff sea brush: stiff sea brush is found at all seasons of the year. Since usual habitat is below low-tide mark, specimens found on shore have been cast up by tides. Stiff sea brush, as name indicates, is coarse and brittle. It is dark brown or black. Species becomes 8 to 10 in. high; it has small, disk-shaped holdfast and stipe about 1 in. long. At upper end of stipe, 2 cylindrical branches with prominent midribs appear. Arising from midribs are widely and irregularly spaced alternate branches.

still-water level: level that sea surface would assume in absence of wind waves; not to be confused with mean sea level or half-tide level.

stingaree, southern stingray [*Dasyatis subina*]: circular, flat fish with long, whiplike tail and no dorsal fin. Body flattened, with no vertical fins or scales; mouth on ventral surface; tail more or less compressed with winglike expansion above, large one below. Anterior margin of body slightly indented anteriorly to produce a slightly elongated snout.

stingaree, whip stingray [*Dasyatis astata*]: flat fish with no scales or dorsal fins and with long, whiplike tail. Body flattened, without dorsal fins or scales; mouth, ventral surface; tail simple-keeled above but with a winglike expansion below. Anterior margins of body nearly straight, meeting in broad angle at tip of snout.

stingray: stingrays are skatelike fish with triangular outline when viewed from above, body sometimes being even greater in width than in length. Distinctive features are large spine and saw-toothed edge located on top of whiplike tail. Stingrays have strong, crushing teeth suited to diet of mollusks and crustaceans.

stingray, roughtail [northern stingray]: olive-brown ray, white on undersurface with long, slender tail. Stingray is found in shoal waters of inlets and bays. It is the largest stingray with reported length of 7 ft. and weight of 350 lbs.

stipe: 1) plant stalk, especially found between fronds and bases of some algae. 2) basal, stemlike part of thallus of alga beneath an erect blade. 3) in *Graptolithina*, branch of graptolite colony comprising series of tubes *(thecae)*.

stock: an anchor stock.

stock [ships]: crosspiece of anchor which fits through the shank. In yacht anchors, this piece unships for stowage, then, when positioned, is held in place with flat key.

stockless anchor: so-called *patent anchor;* or one without a *stock*.

stocks [ships]: timber on which vessel rests while it is being built.

Stokes law: expression of relation between size of spherical particles and their settling velocity in a fluid. The law is used in determining proportion and size distribution of silt and clay in sediment samplers.

stolon: 1) outgrowth from base of animal or colony of animals from which new individuals may grow by budding. Anthozoans, oscidians, hydrozoans and bryozoans all may develop stolons. 2) in *Graptolithina*, dense chitinous tubule extending through successive stolothecae and sending off branches to base of each autotheca and bitheca.

stolotheca [*Graptolithina*]: tube (theca) containing stolon and which gives rise to 3 new thecae (autotheca, litheca and stolotheca) by budding.

stomach [*Mollusca*]: pouch in anterior portion of digestive tube that serves primarily for digestion.

Stomatopoda: order of phylum *Arthropoda;* known as mantis shrimp, they are carnivorous marine crustaceans found in brackish water in tropical and subtropical regions. Stomatopods have 2 types of larvae: pseudozoea and antizoea.

stone: bottom sediment notation sometimes appearing on navigation charts. Stone is not differentiated from gravel in some charts.

stonecat [*Noturus flavus*]: this species is easily distinguished from bullheads of genus *Ameriurus* by the fact that long, low adipose fin is continuous with caudal except for shallow notch, whereas these fins are entirely separate in bullheads. Body is moderately elongate, broad and flat in front of dorsal, and subcylindrical behind it. It is yellowish-brown; sides of head shade to yellow; belly whitish. This species seldom exceeds length of 9 in.

stone reef: offshore bars converted into solid rock reefs by calcium carbonate cementation of sand grains in upper 10 to 15 ft. of reef.

stone sloop: sloop-rigged craft with various types of hull, used in stone trade of New England.

stopper [ships]: 1) short length of heavy rope or chain, or any contrivance, used temporarily to take the stress on a hawser, chain cable, halyard, etc. It is named for its location or for its particular use, as, bitt stopper, cable stopper, cathead stopper, clamp stopper, stern line stopper, deck stopper. 2) to stopper or stopper off a line, chain cable, etc., is to affix the appropriate stopper to such.

stops [ships]: bands of canvas wrapped around furled sail to keep it snug.

stop trim: condition of trim when net buoyancy is zero whereby stationary submarine can maintain its depth.

stopwater [ships]: wood plug driven through scarf joint to stop water from leaking into ship.

stores: 1) ship's stores are provisions and supplies for use on board ship at sea or in port. Such supplies are sealed, as nondutiable, by customs officer. 2) Scandinavian name for pack of heavy ice floes which drift from Arctic Ocean along east coast of Greenland, around Kap Farvel and northward along west coast of Greenland where it melts.

storm: archaeological evidence suggests that early Teutonic housewives had few utensils. Apparently they still managed to blend ingredients, for their verb "to stir" entered numerous European languages. Natives of Britain formed a noun from

it and used storm to name any violent disturbance of the atmosphere. Use of the term in this
sense began so early that in some passages that
include it, it is the only familiar word. A 9th
century version of Psalms includes the sonorous
line: "Ic bad hine se mechalne dyd from lythe-
lmodum and storm." Sailors of later epochs defined "storm" as "any movement of wind that
reduces a ship to her storm sails (bare poles)."
When meteorologists adopted the Beaufort Scale,
a disturbance intermediate between whole gale
and hurricane, with velocity between 55 and 75
miles per hour, took the name of the ancient
"stirring of the skies."

storm surge: phenomenon that causes flooding and
destruction along gentle coastline. Water piles up
near shoreline because of double action of wind
shearing and atmospheric pressure gradient.

Stornoway yawl: Scottish open skiff with lug rig,
sails being broad and low. Hull is clinker-built;
raked stem and sternpost; broad in beam and 25
to 30 ft. long.

stoss: side of glacially-shaped hill that faces direction from which glacier came.

stove-in [ships]: when shell of a boat is smashed in
by impact, craft is said to be stove-in.

stow [ships]: to pack or stow cargo in ship's hold.
Stowage is act of stowing.

stowage: 1) act or process of stowing goods, merchandise, or stores, gear, etc., on board a vessel.
State of being stowed, as, space economy demands compact stowage. 2) that which is stowed,
as, the stowage consists entirely of bagged grain.
3) Money paid for stowing goods. Supports,
chocks, lashings, special fittings, etc., collectively, for securing any or part of ship's equipment
or gear, such as those for stowing spare anchors,
boats, rafts, spars, and the like.

strain [ship construction]: amount of actual yield
of structural part to stress applied. Within elastic
limit, deformation or strain produced is proportional to stress.

strait: 1) narrow sea channel which separates 2
landmasses. 2) early Romans customarily used
leather thongs to bind bundles. From their verb
stringere (to tighten), they derived a noun to designate any constricted or closely bound object. It
was through this influence that Middle English
streit came to be regarded as just the right descriptive term for tight-fitting garment. But lin-
guistic bonds could not hold the vivid word. It
burst out of confinement and was applied to
such diverse things as a sailor's knot and a hearty
embrace. Small wonder, therefore, that it should
have entered the speech of navigators to name a
narrow or twisting passageway in which land
holds water so tightly that transit is difficult.
This literal usage is seldom employed today, but

the vivid imagery behind it is preserved in titles
such as the Strait of Gibraltar.

strake: one of the rows or strips of planking or
plating that constitute the outside surface, decks,
sides of deckhouses, or bulkheads in a vessel. In
shipbuilding, *strakes* are distinguished by letters,
each plate in a *strake* being numbered; thus, in
shell plating, second strake from the keel and
tenth from sternpost (or from stem) is designated
B-10; midship strake in a deck is composed of
plates *M-1*, *M-2*, etc; while port or starboard
strakes often are marked *P-A*, *P-B*, etc., starting
from midship, or *M strake*, with individual plates
indicated as *PA-1*, *PB-2*, *SA-1*, *SB-1*, etc. A
similar system is carried on in the preparation of
strakes for deck erections and bulkheads.

strake [ships]: continuous line of plates on vessel's
side, reaching from stem to stern. Plank or planks
running length of vessel.

strake, gore [ships]: strake which ends before
reaching stem or sternpost. Such strakes are laid
out at or near middle of ship's sides to lessen the
spiling of the plating.

strake, landing [ships]: second strake from gunwale.

strake, limber [ships]: strake on inner skin of
vessel which is nearest to keel.

strakes, sheer [ships]: top strake, just under gunwale.

strake, starboard [ships]: range of plating nearest
to keel on both port and starboard sides.

strand [ships]: 1) number of yarns twisted together. When strands are twisted together they
form rope. 2) vessel is said to be stranded when it
is aground. 3) portion of seashore between high
and low waterline.

strand flat: low, broad, constant flat, slightly submerged, supporting thousands of low small
islands, reefs and rocks. It may extend for hundreds of miles along coast.

stranding: in maritime law, action of a vessel in
running aground and being stuck fast in such pre-
dicament for a time. *Stranding* may be accidental
or purposely done to avoid a worse impending
peril, such as collision or foundering, in which
latter case the term *voluntary stranding* is applied.

strath: broad, elongated depression with relatively
steep walls located on continental shelf. Longitudinal profile of floor is gently modulating with
greatest depths often being found in inshore portion.

straticulate: having numerous thin layers, either of
sedimentary deposition from suspension as by
wave action or of deposition from solution.

stratification: state of fluid that consists of 2 or
more horizontal layers arranged according to
density, highest layer being on top and heaviest
at bottom.

stratified drift: deposits made by glacial meltwater

are known as stratified drift. Two requisites for stratified drift deposits are a supply of till which can be carried and sorted by meltwater and a check in velocity of transporting meltwater current. Like till, from which it is derived, stratified drift is largely composed of rock fragments of local origin.

stratosphere: in oceanography, nearly uniform masses of cold water in high latitudes and of cold bottom water in middle and low latitudes.

stratum: single, sedimentary bed or layer of generally homogeneous rock, independent of thickness.

streak: painted stripe, as that along a vessel's waterline or, in some small craft, a *sheer stripe* or *sheer streak* marking the line of sheer, just below the bulwarks. Same word as *strake*, but today not commonly used in that sense.

stream [trellis pattern]: trellis drainage pattern is one in which many of streams are subparallel and minor streams which join the parallel one do so at approximately right angles.

stream current: narrow, deep, fast-moving current as opposed to relatively wide and weak drift current; e.g., Gulf Stream, Kuroshio and Cromwell Undercurrent.

stream lines: paths followed by particles of water as they pass over immersed surface of a body moving through water.

stream the log [ships]: throwing the low (device to measure ship's speed) into ocean and trailing it behing a moving vessel.

strength of current: greatest speed of tidal current; usually referenced in knots and in hours before or after low and high water.

strength of ebb: ebb current at time of maximum speed.

strength of ebb interval: time interval between transit (upper or lower) of moon and next maximum ebb current at a place.

strength of flood interval: time interval between transit (upper or lower) of moon and next maximum flood current at a place. Usually shortened to flood interval.

Streptotheca [phytoplankton]: square, flat cell or cells with twist about middle. Probably widely distributed but mainly in inshore waters.

stress [ship construction]: amount of load to which particular member of the structure is subject. It is usually expressed in pounds per square inch of cross section.

striate: referring to fine sculpture that has appearance of minute scratches or grooves.

stridulatory sound: noise produced by hard skeletal parts of animal rubbing together or vibrating as rasping of pharyngeal teeth in certain fishes or rattle of spiny lobster's antennae against toothed

ridge in carapace.

stringer [ships]: large beam or angle fitted in various parts of vessel to give additional strength. Depending on location, stringers are known as bilge stringers, side stringers, hold stringers, etc. Fore and aft strengthening member, particularly sidepieces of ladder into which treads and risers are made fast.

stringer, plate [ships]: fore and aft member of deck plating which strengthens connection between beams and frames, and keeps beams square to the shell.

strip: long, narrow area of pack ice, more limited than a belt, bounded by open water or land.

stromatoporoids: colonial hydrozoans related to jellyfishes and corals (coelenterates). Found fossilized as large globular, concentrically thin-layered, onionlike rock masses. Ordovician to Devonian.

Strombidae [family]: conch shells are nearly all thick, solid, heavy shells with conical spires and greatly elongated body whorls. Aperture, which is long and notched at each end, is bordered on outside by thick, outer lip which in some species is greatly expanded. Operculum of animal is shaped like a claw and is much too small to close aperture. This operculum together with narrow foot is used for moving over bottom. They do not crawl as other snails do, but move by lifting up the shell and falling in such a manner that their gait is a series of leaps and jerks.

strombus, Hawaiian: Hawaiian conch shell is moderate in size with outer lip of shell extended laterally to form winglike expansion which ends posteriorly in a projection. Surface of shell is covered by encircling ribs which are more evident at anterior end. Each whorl also bears single, spiral row of large, blunt tubercles which on body whorl are placed just anterior to suture. Spire is well developed and turreted. Aperture of shell is marked with grooves which are more prominent at anterior and posterior ends than in the middle; aperture is white within while exterior surface is a cream color, speckled with brownish markings which develop into bands on upper side of wing lip. It will reach 3 in. in length.

strombus, Hell's conch: this little conch has inflated shell which is longitudinally ribbed. Aperture is narrow and ridged within; lip is thick. It is yellowish-brown without while columella and interior are purplish. It will reach length of about 1 in. *Strombus helli.*

strombus, spotted: spotted conch has shell which is heavy in form and which exhibits conical spire, long aperture and thickened, outer lip. It is spirally striated on exterior surface; these markings become more pronounced toward lip and base. Outer lip is finely grooved within. Color varies but is usually mottled white or clouded with brown, yellow or orange; it is white within aperture. It varies in length from ¾ to ½ in.

strombus, three-toothed conch [*Strombus tridentatus*]: this conch has elongated shell with smooth exterior which is marked by longitudinal ribs on upper part of body whorl. Anterior margin of outer lip bears 3 teeth. It is white and mottled with brown over outer surface; aperture is vivid purple color within. It varies in length from 1½ to 1 in.

Strophomenidae [family]: brachiopods most often referred to as "petrified butterflies." Shell has wide hinge line, costate surface and one concave valve, which may be either brachial or pedicle. Appearing in mid-Ordovician, Strophomenidae soon became both varied and abundant but declined after Devonian. A few species, however, survive in modern seas.

strut [ships]: supporting piece which holds propeller shaft in place between propeller and hull.

studding sail [ships]: commonly called "stun's'ls." Light sails, usually quadrilateral in shape, which were set from booms extended outwardly from yards of square-rigged ship. These sails were controlled by halyards, outhauls and sheets, and were named for square sails adjacent to them.

stud sail [ships]: extension on leech of fore-and-aft sail.

stuffing box [ships]: hull fitting through which propeller shaft passes, allowing shaft to turn freely without leaking water.

stump-knocker [*Lepomis punctatus punctatus*]: strongly compressed, brownish panfish with lots of black dots on sides. Tail emarginate; pectoral fin broad and rounded; scales on breast not much smaller than those on both sides; opercular spot without bright colored margin. Body ovate, strongly compressed; fins moderate; palatine teeth present. Color is dirty brown with numerous dark spots somewhat resembling flyspecks on sides of body and head.

stumpy: "Thames barge" with no topmasts.

sturgeon [family]: sturgeons are remnants of ancient and primitive group of fish in which primitive cartilaginous skeleton is retained and bony plates have appeared in skin. Distinguished by shovellike snout on underside with protractile, subterminal mouth with thick papillose lips extensible for sucking up food. Four barbels in transverse row are present under snout, anterior to mouth; no teeth are present except in very young. Internal skeleton is composed of cartilage and retains well-developed notochord. Head is covered by bony plates and rows of shieldlike plates occur on sides. Gills are 4 in number. There are no branchiostegal rays. Dorsal and anal fins are inserted far back.

sturgeon, Atlantic: bluish or olive-green fish that spends most of its life at sea but ascends coastal waters or rivers from New England to Carolinas to spawn. Today a large individual will not reach more than 7 ft. or weigh more than 200 lbs. A sturgeon this size is about 12 years old.

sturgeon, common [*Acipenser oxyrhynchus*]: big, roughly plated fish with ventral mouth. Tail heterocercal; snout elongated; mouth ventral. Dorsal plates 10—16, lateral plates 24—36; ventral plates 9—11; anal fin with 23—30 rays. Head pointed with elongated proboscis projecting anteriorly. Color dull tan. Sturgeons of this type attain length of 9 ft.

sturgeon, hackleback or shovelnose: hackleback or shovelnose sturgeon can be readily distinguished from lake sturgeon by longer snout and absence of spiracle. It rarely exceeds length of 3 ft. or weight of 5 or 6 lbs. Body of this species is more slender than that of lake sturgeon. Large caudal fin terminates in long filament nearly if not equaling rest of fin. It also differs from young rock sturgeons of corresponding size in that small bony shields completely cover tail, which is flattened from above. Snout is broad, flat and shovel-shaped. Unlike that of immature and adult rock sturgeon, its color is uniform pale yellowish-olive without spots or blotches.

sturgeon, rock [*Acipenser fulvescenes*]: rock sturgeon may be distinguished from shovelnose sturgeon by more pointed snout and presence of a pair of spiracles or openings in head, anterior to gills. Peduncle of tail is short and heavy. In appearance rock sturgeons change greatly with age and size. Young have sharp snouts and very rough shields with spine strongly hooked. Adults have blunt snouts and small, smooth shields, most of which disappear with age. Color also changes considerably; young are usually dark olive above and paler with dark blotches on sides; adults are greenish-olive or reddish and without spots.

sturgeon, white: white sturgeon of Pacific Coast is the giant of the family with maximum length of 12 ft. and weight of over 1,000 lbs. It is a greenish-gray fish whose body is covered by keeled or ridgelike plates, each terminating in spine. This species was formerly very common in Columbia and Fraser rivers, but building of dams has prevented this sturgeon from reaching its usual spawning grounds.

Stylaster: bright yellow hydrocoralline of phylum *Cnidaria* that branches into formations resembling thickets, which are sometimes of considerable size. *Stylaster* is a genus closely related to *Millepora*, and like them, is armed with stinging cells.

styliform: having form of dagger or stiletto.

subaqueous: 1) formed or occurring underwater; as, *subaqueous weeds.* 2) adapted for use beneath the water's surface; submarine; as, a *subaqueous helmet;* a *subaqueous suit.*

Subarctic Current: eastward-flowing ocean current which lies north of North Pacific Current. It originates from part of Aleutian Current and from outflow of water from Bering Sea. As it approaches coast of North America it divides to join northward-flowing Alaska Current and southward-flowing California Current.

subbottom reflection: return of sound energy from discontinuity in material below sea bottom surface.

subcaudals [reptile]: scales on underside of tail.

subcharter: an agreement made by a charterer whereby he hires all or part of vessel to another party. Usually authorized by shipowner to thus sublet, original charterer enters such contract independently of charter party signed by owner.

subchelate: chela in which dactyl simply presses back upon or opposes somewhat enlarged penultimate segment of appendage, rather than opposing a corresponding process of that segment.

subinternal mold: natural mold of outer calcite layer of shell often preserved in Paleozoic mollusks after there is no trace of inner or aragonite layer or hinge structure. Distinct growth lines and general ornamentation features may be preserved. Such a mold is striking but has misleading resemblance to external surface of shell; it is termed subinternal.

sublimation: process by which matter passes directly from solid state to vapor state.

sublittoral: coastal waters below littoral or intertidal zone. Sublittoral extends down to depth of about 21 meters (69 ft.) or to edge of continental shelf. That benthic region extending from mean low waters to depth of about 100 fathoms (200 meters) or edge of continental shelf.

submarginals [reptile]: few small scales between marginals and plastrals of alligator snapping turtle.

submarine canyon: long, narrow, steep-walled valley cut by turbid currents in sediments or sedimentary rocks of continental margin (continental shelf, continental slope, continental rise). Submarine canyons range from less than 1 mile to more than 10 miles wide, and can extend from water depths of 10 fathoms down to 1,000 fathoms.

submarine isthmus: submarine elevation joining 2 land regions and separating 2 basins by depth of less than that of basins.

submarine peninsula: elevated portion of submarine relief resembling peninsula.

submarine well: cavity in sea bottom; also called submarine pit.

submerged breakwater: breakwater with top below still water level. When this structure is struck by wave, part of wave energy is reflected seaward. Remaining energy is largely dissipated in a breaker, transmitted shoreward as multiple crest system or transmitted shoreward as simple wave system.

submergence: term which implies that part of land area has become inundated by sea but does not imply whether the sea rose over land or land sank beneath sea.

submersible decompression chamber or SDC [diving]: decompression chamber which diver enters underwater. After being sealed, chamber is hoisted to surface where diver undergoes decompression process.

suboculars [reptile]: scales between eye and labials.

subordinate station: one of places for which tide or tidal current predictions are determined by applying correction to predictions of reference station.

subpolar: pertaining to, or lying at, a point below the elevated pole of the heavens; as, *subpolar culmination of a star.* Located near the terrestrial pole; as, *northern subpolar latitudes.* A heavenly body is said to be *subpolar* when above the horizon at *lower transit (transit sub polo),* i.e., when observer's latitude is greater than 90°− body's declination, or its *polar distance.*

subpolar lows: stormy belts of low air pressure located at about 60° to 65° latitudes in both hemispheres.

subsequent: tributary to and subsequent in development to a primary consequent stream, but itself consequent upon structure brought out in degradation of region.

subsolar: having the sun in the zenith; beneath the sun; hence, *tropical.*

substrata: layer or base on which animal or plant lives.

subsurface current: current usually flowing below thermocline, generally at slower speeds and frequently in different direction from current near surface.

subtropical convergence: zone of converging currents generally located in midlatitudes. It is fairly well-defined in Southern Hemisphere where it appears as an earth-girding region wherein surface temperature increases equatorward.

subtropical high: one of semipermanent highs of subtropical high-pressure belt. They lie over ocean, and are best developed in summer season.

subumbrella: in jellyfish, lower or inner side of bell, usually concave side, bearing mouth or manubrium.

sucker [family *Catostomidae*]: body of fish of

sucker family is generally elongated and in some species is much compressed, but in others it is heavy and thick. Body is covered with smooth-edged scales; head is scaleless. Mouth varies in size but it always so constructed that it can be drawn out to considerable extent, thus enabling the fish to take food from bottom of stream or lake. No teeth are present on jaws; pharyngeal bones are set with numerous teeth that are some-what similar to those of a comb. Gill membranes are united to isthmus. Dorsal fin contains 10 or more soft rays but no spines; caudal fin is forked; ventral fins are inserted far back on abdomen.

sucker, blue [*Cycleptus elongatus*]: body of blue or Missouri sucker is elongated and only slightly compressed. Color ranges from dusky to bluish-black. Head is very small and slender, tapering to fleshy snout with bluntly pointed nozzle. Mouth is inferior; protractile lips are rather thick and directed downward; each lip has 5 or 6 rows of tuberclelike papillae; lower lip is encised behind. Long dorsal fin is elevated anteriorly and has from 30 to 32 rays; anal fin has 7 or 8 rays. This fish reaches length of over 2 ft.

sucker, chubsucker: widely distributed from New England to Great Lakes and southward to Texas. Its coloring often includes pattern of narrow, dusky bars. Chubsuckers are usually under 12 in. long with deeper body than that of suckers.

sucker, common white [*Catostomus commersoni commersoni*]: slender, cylindrical body with blunt snout. Upper lip is thin with 2 or 3 rows of papillae. Scales are larger than in northern stur-geon sucker, numbering about 70 (60—80) in lat-eral line. It is variable in coloration, particularly during spawning season, when it is so dark as to receive locally the name of black sucker. During spawning season males have well marked, black, lateral band, below which and parallel to it there is a salmon-colored or rosy one.

sucker, highfin [*Carpiodes velifer*]: this species differs from *Carpiodes carpio* in having the back elevated. It closely resembles *C. cyprinus* in form, color and character of dorsal fin, anterior rays of which are considerable elongated, some-times exceeding in length base of fin. Rays of dorsal fin range from 24 to 28. Snout is short and very blunt; nostrils are located over anterior tip of lower jaw. This species is small and of little value as food.

sucker, hog [*Hypentelium nigricans*]: well known by large head and dark cross blotches to almost every boy who has ever fished. Head is concave on top, eye posterior to middle of head. Scales are large and number 48—55 in lateral line. Hog sucker is found most frequently in clear, rapid streams where in midsummer it loves to bask in the sun, lying atop some large rocks or in shallow riffles.

sucker, longnose: averaging 2 lbs. in weight, it is caught as food fish in Great Lakes but its range extends eastward to St. Lawrence and westward to Columbia River. Longnose suckers resemble large, silvery minnows with blue-green backs.

sucker, northern redhorse: pinkish or yellowish fish with red fins; its stout body terminates in blunt snout that projects beyond mouth. Large individuals grow to length of 24 in. and weight of 10 lbs. This member of the family is found in central U.S.

sucker, northern sturgeon [*Catostomus catosto-mus catostomus*]: this species can usually be dis-tinguished from *C. commersoni* by its long, pointed snout which extends considerably be-yond mouth and by very small scales, much re-duced and crowded anteriorly and numbering more than 95 in lateral line. It is variable in coloration. Spring males are profusely tubercu-late on anal fin and have broad, rosy, lateral band which persists until late in summer. This species reaches length of over 2 ft.

sucker, river [*Carpiodes forbesi*]: adult river sucker is similar in body form and color to *C. carpio*. It differs in position of nostrils which are considerably posterior to tips of lips. Lips are plicate and not very thin; halves of lower lip meet in rather wide angle. Anterior rays of dorsal fin are slightly elevated and scarcely more than half the length of base of fin. Dorsal fin has from 25 to 30 rays. Lateral line has 38—40 scales.

sucker, Sacramento: olive-brown fish with silvery sides. This species, with habits similar to those of its eastern relative, is usually under 24 in. long and less than 2 lbs. in weight.

sucker, spotted [*Minytrema melanops*]: fish with suckerlike mouth and without spiny dorsal fin. Jaws toothless; 12 rays in dorsal fin; lateral line partially complete; 44—47 scale rows along side of body. Ground color of body pale; each scale with dark spot, hence dark spots are arranged in rows along side of body. Maximum length up to 18 in.

sued: said of a vessel that has grounded, having reference to a later depth of water, especially that occurring at a lower stage of tide; as, *ship is sued (or sued up) more than 3 ft.* i.e., water must rise at least that amount in order to refloat her.

Suez shoreboat: Arabian boat of Suez with long, sharp, overhanging bow with sharp sections, hull having great beam amidships to carry mast and sail weight. Ranking transom stern is used with outboard rudder. Lateen sail is of Arab cut with a few feet of luff below lower end of grade.

sugar sand: very fine sand common to delta areas.

sugar wrack [*Laminaria saccharina*]: attaches itself to rocks or other large algae at or just below minus-tide mark. It is found in temperate latitudes around the world, favoring quiet waters. Easily recognized by broadly oval or wedge-shaped blade, short stipe, rich yellow-brown color and thin texture. Blade may be 3 to 6 ft. long with width about ¼ the length. Sugar wrack is held to substratum by cone-shaped mass of fibers, 3 to 6 in. in diameter.

sulcus: 1) in *Brachiopoda*, major longitudinal depression, downarch along midline of valve; associated with up-arch, the fold. 2) in *Mollusca*, slit, fissure or deep furrow.

summer minimum: scarcity of phytoplankton (generally diatoms) noted after abundance in spring. Grazing by zooplankton and depletion of essential nutrients are main factors in reducing phytoplankton populations.

summer solstice: for either hemisphere, solstice at which sun is above that hemisphere. In northern latitudes, this occurs approximately on June 21.

sump tank: tank that collects and drains liquids.

sundial shell [*Architectonica*]: *Solariidae* or sundial shells are almost circular in appearance and usually have depressed spheres. They may be either conical-top shaped or flat, depending upon height of spire. Aperture is angular in outline and both columella and lip are simple. Umbilicus of these shells is wide, deep and marked along margin by knobby keel. They are found only in warm seas.

sundial shell, hybrid: this shell is somewhat conical in shape, is swollen about base and has small umbilicus. Whorls are convex, have smooth, shiny surface and bear 3 keels at margins. It is encircled by reddish-brown band below suture from which lines radiate to divide white portion of shell into irregular areas. It will reach a diameter of about 1 in.

sundial shell, Michel's: shell of this species is much more convex than others of family. Whorls are 4 or 5 in number and are longitudinally striated and grooved about periphery. Umbilicus is open and slightly crenulated along margin. Entire shell is ashen-gray in color. It will reach ½ in. in diameter.

sundial shell, perspective: this shell is low and conical in shape. Whorls have spiral groove below suture and 3 spiral ridges at outer edge which are separated by two grooves. Umbilicus is wide, deep and marked by spiral crenulated ridge along base of whorls. Shell is white to yellowish-brown and encircled by rows of brown spots which appear to form disconnected lines; it is lighter in color around edges and beneath. It will reach diameter of 2½ in.

sundial shell, variegated: this species exhibits depressed shell in which whorls are longitudinally striated and spirally grooved. Periphery of whorls bears about 10 grooves of which the one below

margin of whorl is largest. Umbilicus has margin and medial rib crenulated. It exhibits radiating pattern of white and brown; in some forms base is white. It will exceed ½ in. in diameter. This species extends from Hawaiian Islands across tropical Pacific and Indian Oceans to Red Sea.

sundial shell, wheellike: this shell is conically shaped and has whorls which are longitudinally striated, spirally grooved and contains 10 ribs. Ribs at periphery are elevated, beady and strong. Margins of umbilicus are crenulated and walls are marked with 2 spiral ribs. Shell is grayish in color and will reach ¾ of an inch in height or diameter.

sunfish [family *Centrarchidae*]: one of most important family of game fish, for it contains sunfish, crappies and largemouth and smallmouth bass. About 24 species are known in this family. Members of sunfish family are characterized by having more or less deep, flattened bodies with 2 dorsal fins in middle of back. These fins are confluent or jointed together. Front or anterior fin is supported by 5 to 13 sharp spines; hind or posterior fin is supported by soft rays. Ventral fins are thoracic and typically have 1 spine and 5 rays; anal fin has 2 to 8 spines. All are considered more or less warm-water fish and prefer fertile lakes of moderate temperatures.

sunfish, banded [*Enneacanthus obesus*]: small (3 in. or less), chubby sunfish with rounded tail margin. Median spines in dorsal fin not pronouncedly longer than other spines; usually 9 spines in dorsal fin; sides and vertical fins without bright blue spots. Body compressed. Color dark with 5—8 rather indistinct, vertical, dark bars along sides.

sunfish, banded pigmy [*Elassoma zonatum*]: tiny, perchlike fish with round tail margin. Dorsal spines 5; scale rows along sides. Body moderately elongate and compressed; mouth small, oblique; teeth stout and conical, in 2 or 3 rows; cheeks scaly; eye large. Ground color olive-greenish with about 10 vertical dark bars on each side; dark spot on each side below origin of dorsal fin.

sunfish, black-banded [*Enneacanthus chaetodon elizabethae*]: very small, strongly compressed sunfish with distinct, vertical, black bars on sides. Tail rounded, or truncate, not emarginate; median spines of spiny dorsal fin markedly longer than anterior and posterior spines; usually 9 spines in dorsal fin; 17—18 rows of scales around caudal peduncle; pattern without bright blue spots; body ovate. Color grayish or brownish with 4—6 strongly marked vertical black bars on sides of head and body. Length about 2 in.

sunfish, bluegill: largest sunfish, at times reaching length of 12 in. and weight slightly over 1 lb. It is brownish-green with reddish sides, marked by faint vertical bars and with orange-red breast; ear flaps are blue, tipped with black. Prefers ponds and quiet streams with dense bottom growth of plants where it can feed on insects, crustaceans and smaller fish.

sunfish, blue-spotted [*Enneacanthus gloriosus*]: small (3 in. or less), strongly compressed sunfish with scattered bright blue spots along sides. Tail rounded; median spines of dorsal fin not pronouncedly longer than other spines; usually 9 spines in dorsal fin; caudal fin rounded. Color dark; side of body and vertical fins with numerous, scattered, rounded, blue spots.

sunfish, dollar [*Lepomis marginatus*]: small, strongly ovate sunfish with green margin on opercular flap. Tail emarginate; pectoral fin broad and rounded; 12 rays in pectoral fin. Body short and rounded; mouth oblique; 4 rows of scales on cheeks. Color dark olive with darker vertical bars; head and body with numerous bluish-green stripes and spots. Size small, perhaps up to 7 in.

sunfish, Everglade pigmy [*Elassoma evergladei*]: tiny perchlike fish with rounded tail margin. Body moderately elongate and compressed; mouth small, oblique; teeth stout and conical, in 2 or 3 rows; cheeks scaly; eye large; fins moderately high; caudal fin rounded. Color gray to black often blotched with brilliant blue. Length up to 1½ in.

sunfish, Great Lakes longear [*Lepomis megalotis peltastes*]: Great Lakes longear is small with short, deep body colored with brilliant blue streaks and orange spots. Extremely long opercular flap is bordered with red. No black spots are present on either dorsal or anal fins. Fins are orange with blue rays. Pectoral fin is short and rounded and is contained 4 times in standard length. Gill rakers are short and knoblike.

sunfish, green [*Lepomis cyanellus*]: green sunfish is rather dull in color. When it is freshly removed from water, sides and back are colored olivegreen and each scale is flecked with yellow. Body is rather robust. This sunfish is not as deepbodied as pumpkinseed and black opercular lobe is shorter. Mouth is large; maxillary is 1/5 to 1/4 longer than distance from lower margin of orbit to lower posterior corner of preopercle. Gill rakers are long and slender.

sunfish, longear [*Lepomis megalotis megalotis*]: compressed, ovate sunfish with bright blue margin to opercular flap. Tail emarginate; pectoral fin broad and rounded; 13—15 rays in pectoral fin. Body compressed, short and deep; mouth small, oblique; fins moderately high. Color bluish above, orange below; cheeks orange with bright blue streaks.

sunfish, orange spot [*Lepomis humilis*]: small, rather slender sunfish may be recognized by bright orange spots scattered over body. Opercular lobe has pale margin and may be tinged with red or orange. Sometimes there are longitudinal orange bars on cheek. Pectoral fins are long and pointed and length is contained slightly more than 3 times in standard length. Gill rakers are long and slender. This species has little value as a panfish.

sun star: one of a group of starfish with many rays.

sun zenith distance: angle between sun and sun's disk.

supercargo: originally, an officer who superintended care of cargo, arranged for its sale at foreign ports, and managed all commercial business attending a merchant vessel's voyage. Now, one appointed by a charterer or shipper to supervise care of cargo with view of effecting sound and proper delivery of goods, livestock, etc. Also, in some cargo liners, a *freight clerk*, whose duties require arrangement and supervision of stowage and attention to all clerical matters connected with receipt and delivery of cargo at the several ports of call.

superstructure [ships]: any structure built above uppermost complete deck, such as pilothouse, bridge, etc.

suprabranchial: above gills.

supralittoral: shore zone immediately above high tide level. Commonly, zone kept more or less moist by waves and spray.

supraorbital semicircles: scales forming across top of head between eyes.

surf: collective term for breakers. Wave activity in area between shoreline and outermost limit of breakers.

surface current: general term meaning that part of directly observed movement of water which, in nearshore areas, does not extend more than 3 to 10 ft. (1 to 3 meters) below surface; in deep or open ocean areas, surface currents generally are considered to extend from surface to depths of about 33 ft. (10 meters).

surface density: density of surface material within range of elevation differences of gravitational survey. Both Bouguer correction and terrain corrections depend on density of surface materials.

surface duct: zone immediately below sea surface where sound rays are refracted toward surface and then reflected. They are refracted because sound velocity at some depth near surface is greater than at surface.

surface path: sound paths which go no deeper than 1,000 ft. from surface.

surface probe: thermistor that is towed along surface to record continuous sea-surface temperature.

surface reflection: return of sound rays to depth after striking sea surface.

surface scattering layer: population(s) of organisms on surface layers of ocean which scatter sound. Organisms may occur in uniform layer extending from surface to depth as great as 100 fathoms.

surface temperature: in oceanography, temperature of layer of seawater nearest atmosphere. It is generally determined either as bucket temperature or injection temperature.

surface wave: progressive gravity wave in which disturbance (i.e., particle movement in fluid mass as well as surface movement) is confined to upper limits of body of water.

surf beat: irregular oscillations of nearshore water levels, with periods on the order of several minutes.

surfperch: another small Pacific Coast family. As common name suggests, these fish live in surf zone along sandy shores. Surfperch have short, deep bodies with continuous, long dorsal fins. Family is one of the few marine bony fish that give birth to living young. Many species, though small, are considered good game fish.

surfperch, barbed: found from California to Washington, it is metallic blue with rosy belly and pattern of indistinct vertical bars on sides. It is usually under 8 in. long.

surf zone: area between outermost breaker and limit of wave uprush.

surge: long wave, which is longer than wind wave, but shorter than tidal wave. Also refers to movement at variable rate, as a vessel when making headway against heavy seas.

surge channel: transverse channel cutting outer edges of organic reef in which water level fluctuates with wave or tidal action.

suspension: particles of solid matter that are swept along in turbulent current of stream are said to be in suspension. This process of transportation is controlled by 2 factors: turbulence of water; characteristic known as terminal velocity of each individual grain. Terminal velocity is constant rate of fall that a particle eventually attains when acceleration caused by gravity is balanced by resistance of fluid through which grain is falling.

suture: 1) in mollusks, spiral line that marks junction of whorls in gastropod shell or junction between girdle and valve in chitons. 2) in reptiles, line where 2 bones meet. 3) in *Foraminifera*, line of contact between adjacent chambers of test.

swab[ships]: nautical term for mop.

swage [ships]: to bear or force down. Instrument having groove on underside for purpose of giving shape to any piece subjected to it when receiving blow from a hammer.

swallow float: 1) free-floating buoy which can be set for predetermined depth. Signals that it sends

out can be picked up by surface craft. Speed and direction of all submerged currents can thus be determined and traced. 2) tubular buoy, usually made of aluminum, that can be adjusted to remain at selected density level to drift with motion of that water mass. Float is tracked by shipboard listening devices and current velocities can be determined.

swamp: 1) lake basin that has become partly filled with decayed vegetation and sediment. 2) in ships, to sink by taking water over the rail.

swash: 1) movement of water up beach's slope from breaking wave. 2) narrow channel or sound within sandbank or between sandbank and shore.

swash channel: 1) in open shore, channel cut by flowing water in return to parent body (rip channel). 2) secondary channel passing through or shoreward of inlet or river bar.

swash mark: thin, wavy line of fine sand, mica scales, bits of seaweed, etc., left by uprush when it recedes from upward limit of movement on beach face.

swash plates [ships]: plates fixed in tanks to prevent excessive movement of contained liquid.

Swedish fishing boat: husky, flush-decked, clinker-built ketch or yawl-rigged vessel, used in mackerel fishery of Sweden. Hull has enormous beam, ¾ of length. It is double-ended with curved, very raking stem and sternpost; hollow floor and deep keel.

sweep: 1) track on which a quadrant or tiller travels. 2) long broad-bladed oar used either in steering or propelling a boat or small vessel. 3) range or motion of oars; as, to pull with a long *sweep*; *sweep* of the oars. 4) any lengthy arc of curvature in a vessel's structure; as, *sweep* of the counter; downward *sweep* of stem. 5) any curved line in a plan of a vessel. 6) curve or catenary in a hawser, cable, etc. 7) range or radius covered by a vessel in swinging at single anchor. 8) wire drag, such as is used to discover presence of sharp elevations in the sea bottom or to bring moored mines to surface.

sweepings: marketable remnants of a bulk cargo, such as grain, or spillage from broken bags or other faulty or damaged containers left in a vessel's hold; also called *spillage*.

swell: ocean waves which have traveled out of generating area. Swell characteristically exhibits more regular and longer period and has flatter crests than waves within their fetch.

swimmeret: in higher *Crustacea*, biramus appendage of abdominal segments; pleopods.

swimming crab, blood spotted [*Portunus sanguinoletus*]: this crab is large, edible, shoreline species. Carapace is smooth, convex and marked at lateral border by very large spine. There are 4 spines between eyes and 8 spines between eyes and large lateral spine. Rear of carapace is marked by 3 large, conspicuous, red spots. Last pair of legs is flattened for swimming. This species lives on sandy and muddy bottoms from shallow water to depths beyond 100 ft.

swimming crab, crenate [*Thalamita latreille*]: this crab is one of larger species of this genus and often measures more than 3½ in. across carapace. It can be identified by 6, nearly equal, rounded lobes along anterior margin of carapace between eyes and by fine sharp spines behind eye on each side. Chelipeds are quite large and strong. This crab inhabits shallow waters of shoreline where it frequents mouths of rivers and broad, muddy flats. It appears to prefer brackish water and is seldom found in clear seawater.

swimming crab, five-toothed [*Lupocyclus quinquedentaus*]: name of this crab is taken from 5 antero-lateral spines which border carapace on each side just posterior to eyes. There are also 6 pointed teeth along anterior margin of carapace between eyes. Carapace is crossed by curved lines, 2 of which are located near front, 2 near center and 5 are almost entirely red and marked with scattered, mottled, lighter areas. Walking legs and swimming legs are banded with alternating red and white. Each cheliped is marked with white stripe across pincher. Entire lower surface of body is white. Carapace is at least 1¾ in. wide.

swimming crab, hairy [*Portunus pubescens*]: this crab takes its name from the fact that body and legs are covered with hairs. Carapace is covered with small, short hairs. Edges of walking legs are quite thickly fringed with hair. Front edge of carapace is almost circular in outline. It bears 4 blunt teeth between eyes and 9 spines on each side of eyes, of which first 8 are almost equal in size and 9th, or last, is a little longer.

swimming crab, Hawaiian [*Charybdis hawaiiensis*]: 3-in.-wide carapace of this crab presents 6 blunt, rounded teeth in front plus one by each eye, totaling 8 teeth between eyes. There are 5 spines on edge of carapace plus another very small spine between 1st and 2nd. Line across top of carapace connects posterior spines of 2 sides. Inner side of cheliped is granular and pinching fingers are beautifully grooved and marked with black.

swimming crab, long-eyed [*Podophthalmus rigil*]: this crab is very easily identified by astonishing pair of eyes which are borne upon unusually long eyestalks. These eyes and their stalks may be held erect above body or horizontally in groove along front of carapace. Back or carapace of this species is smooth, wider in front than behind with strong spine at sides. Chelipeds are rather slender and armed with spines. Posterior pair of legs, as in the other members of this family, is adapted for swimming. This is large species which reaches width of over 5 in. across carapace. It is brown; a shoreline species which is often found in areas of brackish water.

swimming crab, red-legged [*Charybdis erythrodactyla*]: striking color pattern makes this crab easily identified. It can be recognized by blue spots upon yellowish-red carapace and by bright red legs. Carapace is marked with 6 blunt teeth along front margin between eyes. Anterolateral border bears 7 teeth of which 2nd and 4th are very small; larger teeth are sharp and point forward. This crab is reported to measure as much as 7 in. wide across carapace, although most individuals are usually 3 or 4 in. wide.

T

T: as an abbreviation, *t = time* or local hour angle, *thunder, ton* or *tons; T = tropical* in vessels' load-line marks; *true*, as in distinguishing a *true* from a compass or magnetic course or bearing; also = *time*, as in *G.C.T.* (Greenwich civil time). The letter is denoted by International Code flag "tare," showing red, white, and blue equal vertical divisions. Flown singly, it signifies "Do not pass ahead of me"; as a towing signal, by ship *towing*, means "I am increasing speed" and by ship *towed*, "Increase speed," or flashing Morse Code *T* which is a single *dash* (—).

tabellae [*Coelenterata*]: small horizontal plates near axis of corallite. In essence, incomplete tabulae.

tableknoll: knoll with comparatively smooth, flat top.

tablemount: a seamount having a comparatively smooth, flat top.

table reef: small, isolated reef, with or without islands, which has no lagoon.

Tables, Nautical: arrangement of mathematical values or other information in condensed tabular form for use of navigators in concisely determining ship's position by observation, as from *altitude table;* a heavenly body's true bearing, as from *azimuth table;* position arrived at in sailing given courses and distances, as from *traverse table;* information on tides and currents, as from *tide table* and *current table;* etc.

tabula: in corals, almost horizontal plate across center.

tabular iceberg: flat-topped iceberg showing horizontal firn snow layers, usually calved from ice shelf formation.

tabularium [*Coelenterata*]: axial portion of corallite in which tabulae occur.

tabulate [*Mollusca*]: shouldered; outline of upper part of gastropod whorls in which whorl meets previous whorl at approximately right angle and resulting flattened or horizontal ramp is bounded below by low carina.

tachometer: measuring device which indicates number of revolutions per minute.

tack: 1) change in direction of sailing vessel, when sailing into wind, so that wind strikes sails from other side. 2) to go about, to change from one tack to another, as from starboard to port tack. Heavy rope is used to confine foremast lower corner of course jibs or staysails. Course of ship in relation to position of sails; as "starboard tack" when ship is close-hauled with wind on starboard side, or "port tack" close-hauled with wind on starboard side, or "port tack" close-hauled with wind on port side. 3) length of halyard about 6 ft. long used to separate each group of flags which, if not separated, would convey different meaning to that intended.

tackle [ships]: combination of ropes and blocks for purpose of increasing pull. Also device or appliance for grasping or clutching an object. Purchase formed by rope running through one or more blocks.

tackle block [ships]: pulley over which rope runs.

tackline: a 6-ft. length of line used to separate groups or hoists of signal flags displayed on same halyard.

tadpole madtom: body of tadpole madtom is robust, short and deep; it is deepest in front of dorsal fin. Color is purplish-olive to dark brownish without noticeable speckling. There are 3 dark streaks on sides. Adipose fin is continuous with caudal. Premaxillary bands of teeth are truncate laterally and without backward, lateral extensions. Pectoral spines are smooth and unserrated. Species reaches length of 3 to 5 in.

taffrail [ships]: upper part of stern on wooden ship, usually ornamented with carvings; also railing on upper stern of vessel.

taffrail log: device consisting of counter, line and spinner, or "fish," which measures distance through water.

tail: short piece of rope attached to a block, larger rope, chain, etc. Rear end; inferior or diminishing end or limiting portion of anything; as, *tail* of a shaft, of a bank, of a gale, of a tidal stream, etc. To lie, as a vessel at anchor, with stern toward a certain direction or object; as, ship *tails* to the bank, up stream, down channel, etc. With *on,* to

316

lay hold of a line, as a number of men in hauling; as, to *tail* on to the main brace; also, to *tally on*. To attach a block or tackle to something by its tail.

tail shaft [ships]: aft section of shaft which receives propeller.

taken aback [ships]: said of vessel's sails when caught by wind in such a way as to press them aft against mast and often caused by sudden shift of wind.

talik: layer of unfrozen ground between seasonal frozen ground (active layer) and permafrost.

tally: an account or record of the number of packages, sometimes including identifying marks on such, loaded or discharged as cargo. To keep such account or record; as, to *tally* a shipment of goods. Old term meaning to haul in on the sheets of a course. With *on*, to lay hold of a rope, as a group of men, and haul; as *tally on the tops'l halyards!*

Tanaidacea, order: body with first 2 pairs of thoracic segments fused to head and covered by small carapace; respiratory chamber on each side enclosed by carapace; first pair of 8 thoracic appendages forming maxillipeds; second thoracic pair with chelae; exopodites absent in all thoracic appendages except second and third; last abdominal segment fused with telson; pleopods present or absent; mostly marine and cosmopolitan. *Tanais, Apseudes.*

tangential stress: components of stress tensor which are tangential to faces of fluid element.

tangue: very fine, calcareous silt and clay derived from banks of coquina limestone and which is deposited in estuaries along coast of Bay of Biscay.

tankage: capacity of a tank or tanks.

tanks [ships]: compartments for liquid or gases. They may be formed by ship's structure as double-bottom tanks, peak tanks, deep tanks, etc., or may be independent of ship's structure and installed on special supports.

tank top [ships]: plating laid on bottom floors of ship which forms top sides of tank sections or double bottom.

tannic acid: strong, complex substance found in plants with many commercial uses such as in tanning.

tape gage: tide gage which consists essentially of a flat attached to tape and counterpoise.

tarada: open, flat-bottomed boat used by Arab sheiks in marshes of southern Iraq. Gunwales curve up at ends to high peak and stem and stern rise gracefully from bottom to meet sheer line. Inside is decorated with hundreds of brass-headed nails. Tarada is usually punted and sheik sits amidships.

tarn [Icelandic]: small mountain lake or pool,

especially one that occupies ice-gouged basin on floor of a cirque.

taro: basic, starchy food in the tropics which is obtained from taro plant of Pacific islands. Edible portion of plant grows underground like the potato.

tarpon [*Tarpon atlanticus*]: large fish with big, silvery scales, deeply forked tail and last ray of dorsal fin very elongated. Scales large, 42—47 along lateral line; tail deeply forked; lower jaw projecting. Head moderate, 4 times in length; eye large with adipose lid. Color bluish-silver above, silvery on sides and below. Adults average about 60 lbs. but may attain weight of 300 lbs.

tarpon, Atlantic: iridescent, silvery fish with greenish-blue tints on back. Body is protected by extremely large cycloid scales often measuring 3 in. in diameter and used in making novelties and jewelry. Head terminates in broad mouth with outthrust lower jaw with small teeth. Distinctive feature is extension of last ray of dorsal fin into long, tapering filament. The filament is concave on lower side and can adhere to fish's body; this bends the dorsal fin in such a way as to determine direction of tarpon's fall. Average tarpon is 4 to 5 ft. long and weighs up to 30 lbs. Tarpon is carnivorous, feeding on smaller species such as mullet.

tar spot [*Ralfsia pacifica*]: looks like a splotch of very dark brown or black tar dropped on beach. Both size and shape are indefinite. At first the spot is circular, but later becomes irregularly lobed, 2 to 3 in. in diameter with rounded or scalloped edges. Tar spot is so thin it must be measured in millimeters. This seaweed is perennial; no specific holdfast, entire plant is encrusted on rock, probably held fast by rhizoids.

tartane: term generally applied to medium-sized vessels used on Mediterranean. They have tall mainmast with square sails and shorter mizzenmast, carrying either square sail or lateen.

tassel wing [*Pterochondria woodii*]: tassel wing is epiphytic on other algae. It is unmistakable as a species because it hangs in rather dense masses or tassels from stipes or branches of host plant. Although tassels are in dense masses, individuals thalli are delicate and lacy, usually 4 to 5 in. long. This seaweed is made up of freely branched thallus which is alternately and laxly divided into several orders of smaller branches. Lower part of alga is usually yellowish-brown, while upper is deep wine red. It is attached to host by minute rhizoids which penetrate deeply into host plant.

Taurus: a northern zodiacal constellation which the sun passes during June. Located north and west of *Orion*, it contains the bright reddish star *Aldebaran*, of magnitude 1.1, and a closely grouped cluster known as the *Pleiades* or *Seven Sisters*.

tautog [blackfish]: large, unprepossessing fish mottled brown in coloring. It grows to length of 36 in. and may weigh as much as 20 lbs. It differs from a cunner by having blunter snout. Jaws are armed with 2 rows of teeth, and additional pharyngeal teeth aid in crushing mollusks. Tautogs range from Cape Cod south to Delaware River, being found inshore during summer and in winter, offshore in deeper waters.

taut wire mooring: mooring arrangement in which submerged flat provides upward force necessary to maintain system in fixed position with reference to sea bottom. Taut wire moors may be single, double or multipoint, according to speed and variability of ambient currents.

taxodont [*Mollusca*]: hinge dentition composed of alternating teeth and sockets, mostly similar in form, in series of varying lengths.

taxon: category used in classification, e.g., a variety species, genus, family, etc. Living taxon is a reproducing natural population or system of populations of genetically related individuals.

taxonomic series: range of extant living organisms from simplest to most complex forms.

taxonomist: expert in taxonomy, scientific classification of animals and plants.

tchektirme: Turkish coasting vessel. Hull is low in waist; rounded bilges and high of stern. Low waist is sometimes protected by canvas strake or weather cloth.

tea clipper: large, fast, square-rigged "clipper ship" employed in China tea trade. Period of American tea clipper was from 1847 to 1860, and that of British tea clipper from 1850 to 1875.

Tealia crassicornis: intriguing marine animal that slides slowly along shallow floor of Alaskan seas looking more like a flower than the animal this sea anemone really is. During king crab moulting season, *Tealia* feed on king crab skeletons, food source available only at that time. *Tealia* belong to phylum *Coelenterata* which includes all sea anemones, jellyfish, hydroids and corals. One of characteristics of coelenterates is digestive cavity which has only one opening serving both as mouth and anus. Various muscles enable anemones to open their mouths widely, and large hollow intestines and extensive mesentary digestive system or surface enable them to consume objects almost as large as themselves, although most of their food is small. Mouth of *Tealia* is surrounded by ring of tentacles within which thousands of microscopic harpoons, called nematocysts, are embedded. Nematocysts contain venomous fluid and are spring-loaded, ready to fire upon contact to assist in food gathering. Tentacles contract when touched and bend toward mouth pushing food inside.

Tectibranchia, order: body with large head and with or without shell; when present, thin shell usually enclosed in mantle; operculum mostly lacking; one gill. *Aplysia* (sea hare), *Acteon*, *Bulla* (bubble shell).

tee bar [ships]: rolled shape generally of mild steel having cross section shaped like letter T. In ship work, it is used for bulkhead stiffeners, brackets, floor clips, etc. Size is denoted by dimensions of its cross section and weight per running foot.

teeth [*Mollusca*]: projections from dorsal margin of pelecypod valves, aperture in gastropods or around margins of chiton valves; stronger or larger than denticles.

tegmen: covering of oral disk of crinoids.

telegraph [ships]: means of signaling from bridge to engine room, etc.

telemetry: transmission of data (after conversion to radio waves) over distance and recording it at its destination. Oceanographic data may be telemetered to ship- or shore-based recording stations.

telemotor: hydraulic device for operating a steering engine from the navigating bridge or pilothouse. As steering wheel is turned, working fluid is compressed by a piston in one of two cylinders, which in turn transmits pressure to receiving piston and thence control valve system of steering engine is acted upon. Also, an electrically operated system for same use.

teleosts: fish with bony skeletons. They include common fish such as trout, bass, cod, tuna and mackerel. Teleosts occur in both salt and fresh water. Flexible-scaled fish with completely bony skeletons and powerful, well formed fins and tails. This is the group that dominates present-day seas and rivers.

Tellina crassa [*Tellinacea*]: this shell is crossed by a number of deep, concentric lines which become more widely spaced towards outer edge. These coarse striations are diagnostic of *T. crassa*. (*Heterodonta*.)

Tellina fabula [*Tellinacea*]: anterodorsal margin of shell is concave and shell is crossed by 5 concentric lines (*Heterodonta*).

telltale: an indicator, such as a pointer, for showing functional position or motion of a machinery part, etc.; any audible or visual device for warning, indicating, etc.

telluric currents: natural electric currents flowing on or near earth's surface in large "sheets." Geophysical methods have been developed for using these currents during earth-resistivity surveys.

telotroch: in trochophore larvae, circlet of cilia in front of anus.

telson: in higher *Crustacea*, caudal end of body behind last true somite. Telson contains anal opening, and together with uropods comprises tail fin.

temperature: measure of average energy of motion of molecules in an object. It is commonly measured in degrees on celsius, Fahrenheit or Kelvin scales.

temperature, absolute: temperature from absolute zero (-273.16° C.); thus absolute temperature is degrees celsius plus 273.16°.

temperature, celsius: thermometer scale in which water boils at 100° C. and freezes at 0° C. Absolute zero is 273° below celsius zero.

temperature, coefficient: coefficient expressing quantitative relation between change of temperature and constant variation of some other quality.

temperature, Fahrenheit: in this thermometer scale water boils at 212° F. and freezes at 32° F., above Fahrenheit zero. Absolute zero is -459.6° below Fahrenheit zero.

temperature inversion: in oceanography, layer in which temperature increases with depth.

temperature, Kelvin: temperature scale based on thermodynamic principles. Essentially it may be related to absolute temperature having same size of degrees as centigrade with freezing point at 273.16° K.

temperature, Rankine: temperature in which difference of boiling and freezing points of water is 212° and zero of which is absolute zero of temperature. Freezing point of water is 491.7° F., and one degree Rankine equals one degree Fahrenheit.

temperature salinity diagram: plot of temperature versus salinity data of water column. Result is diagram which identifies water masses within the column, the column's stability, indicates value and allows estimate of accuracy of temperature and salinity measurements.

temperature scale: graduated scale for measuring temperature of matter, usually based on freezing and boiling points of pure water at standard atmospheric pressure. Temperature scales most commonly used are Celsius (centigrade) scale, Kelvin (absolute) scale and Fahrenheit scale.

tempest: *tempus fugit,* "time flies," is one of the most widely known proverbs inherited from the Romans. Used in the general sense of "a season of the year," Latin term for time came to indicate a number of different seasons. Passing through old French and modified to tempest, the term was familiar in 12th century Britain. Though used a bit loosely, name usually had connotation of "falling weather," i.e., rain, hail or snow. A few early explorers, notably Sir Thomas Herbert, gave graphic but probably unreliable reports of tempests that lasted for many days. Our modern expression for great disturbance over a small matter, "a tempest in a teapot," did not originate in speech of men who sailed the seven seas. It first appeared in an 1854 Latin dictionary compiled by a scholar who had never been aboard ship.

tempolabile: tending to change with time.

temporals, posterior [reptiles]: one of two longitudinal, elongated scales, lying one above the other, behind postoculars and between parietals and upper labials.

tender [ships]: said of sailboat which heels quickly in a breeze. Also club or marine launch.

tenpounder [*Elops saurus*]: silvery, streamlined fish with deeply forked tail. Scales small, about 120 along lateral line; last ray of dorsal fin not elongate. Head moderately short, 4½ in. long; mouth moderate, oblique in position; head without scales. Color silverish.

tentacles: 1) in *Coelentarata,* armlike extension and mouth that serves primarily for food-getting. 2) in *Foraminifera,* slender armlike extension of cell periphery of variable length and shaped like a pseudopod but of fixed position. 3) in *Mollusca,* used in 2 senses, for short, slender, sensory head appendages and as grasping arms of cephalopods.

tentaculocyst: small, club-shaped, sense organ along margin of certain medusae in *Scyphozoa.*

tented ice: pressure ice formed when 2 ice floes have been pushed into the air leaving air space underneath.

tentilla: lateral branches of tentacle of gastrozooids in *Siphonophora.*

tenting: vertical displacement upward of ice under pressure to form an arch with cavity beneath.

tepukei: sailing, outrigger, dugout canoe of Matema Islands of Santa Cruz group which are located north of New Hebrides and east of Solomon Islands.

Terebratulina: these punctate shells apparently evolved from orthids in early or middle Silurian times and are characterized by short hinge lines and calcareous loops supporting lophophores. Early genera were almost circular to elongate-oval with smooth or finely costate shells. During Cretaceous and Tertiary periods, many shells became coarsely plicate. Terebratulids are important today, especially on Pacific Coast of North America. Some species inhabit rocky shores, though others are found in waters that are deep, quiet and cold.

terebridae [family]: auger shells are very slender, elongated seashells, many of which have beautiful colors and patterns. They are constructed of many flat-sided whorls which taper very gradually and evenly toward pointed apex. Aperture of these shells contains a small notch in front; columella is without plaits and operculum is of a horny texture. Found in warm waters of temperate and tropical seas where they burrow in sand. Family is a large one containing about 200 species.

Teredo: genus of molluscan borers. Also, common name of the animal.

tergum: in *Arthropoda*, skeletal plate covering dorsal part of each free segment.

terminal [*Mollusca*]: at extreme end, especially with reference to cylindrical or long, ovate, bivalve shell.

terminal moraine: rugged ridge or belt of unsorted till marking outermost margin of glacier.

terminus: end or outer margin of glacier.

ternary: consisting of 3 components, etc.

terns: sea swallows; long-winged seabirds of rather small size with tapering pointed bills, straight or slightly curved at tip. Legs are very short and webbed feet are small. Majority of species have long, forked tails, outer tail feathers being exceptionally elongated in some marine species. Terns are mainly birds of coasts of warmer parts of the world, but a number of species migrate into north temperate regions during the summer to breed.

tern schooner: three-masted schooner (tern means series of 3). Nova Scotia men use the term to denote any type of three-masted schooner, fisherman or coaster, but it is not commonly used in U.S.

terrace: benchlike structure bordering an undersea feature.

terrain correction: correction applied to observed terrain in geophysical surveys in order to remove effect of variations to observations due to topography in vicinity of site of observations.

terra-neuva: large, auxiliary, barkentine-rigged vessel of St. Malo, St. Sevan and other ports in Brittany, France, engaged in cod fishery off Newfoundland.

terrapin, Florida diamondback [*Malaclemys terrapin macrosipilota*]: medium-sized saltwater turtle with bulbous projections along central keel and spotted shell. This striking species may be recognized by combination of large yellow spot in center of each dorsal lamina, central keel in which individual sections terminate with strong bulb and by lack of dark borders along submarginal and plastral laminae. Yellow spots on upper shell make this the most easily recognized of all races of diamondbacks.

terrapin, mangrove [*Malaclemys terrapin rhizophorarum*]: strongly keeled saltwater turtle of medium size with no striking color pattern on upper shell. Although intermediate between adjacent subspecies of terrapins, this race may be recognized in a majority of specimens by terminally expanded, dorsal keels, lack of yellow centers in dorsal laminae and presence of black

borders along submarginal seams and also along some of plastral seams.

terrapin, Mississippi diamondback [*Malaclemys terrapin pileata*]: medium-sized saltwater turtle with no dorsal shell pattern. Relatively minor features by which this form is distinguished include central keel in which individual sections end in marked expansions, uniform dark color of carapace which is not marked with large, yellow, central spots in laminae and usually dark upper lip and upper surface of head.

terrapin, southern diamondback [*Malaclemys terrapin centrata*]: medium-sized, usually rough-shelled, saltwater turtle with no light head stripes. Recognized by broadly ovoid shell as seen from above, slightly convergent sides of posterior lobe of plastron, lack of terminal expansions in keels of centrals and lack of yellow spots on shell end of black borders on submarginal laminae.

terrestrial: pertaining to the earth; earthly; opposed to *celestial*; as, *terrestrial equator; terrestrial meridian*.

terrestrial magnetism: study of natural magnetic field within and surrounding earth and factors affecting it.

terrigenous: sediments of the continental shelf and continental slope, derived from adjoining continual masses, are referred to as terrigenous deposits. These usually reach the abyssal plain through turbid current transport.

terrigenous deposit: material derived from above sea level and deposited in deep ocean, e.g., volcanic ash.

terrigenous sediments: 1) those sediments that were deposited in shallow part of sea floor and composed of detritus derived from unsubmerged areas of land. 2) deposits consisting of debris derived from erosion of land areas and usually deposited in shallow parts of the sea.

Tertiary: period of Cenozoic era characterized by increase in mammals, appearance of primates.

test: 1) external shell or skeleton secreted by invertebrates which generally is divided into successive chambers. Hard covering or supporting structure of many invertebrates, it may be enclosed within outer layer of living tissue; shell. 2) in *Foraminifera*, skeleton of protozoan. Also refers to skeleton of some other kinds of animals.

test head [ships]: head of water corresponding to pressure prescribed as test bulkhead, tank, compartment, etc. Test heads are prescribed to insure satisfactory water- or oiltightness, and also as tests of strength.

Tethys Seaway: 1) greatest of all geosynclinal belts, extended halfway around the world, almost parallel with equator and occupied territory that is now within and adjacent to Mediterranean Sea and great east-west mountain systems of Europe and Asia. This belt was occupied by succession of shifting seas, coal-forming swamps, lakes and sandy lowlands which received a great variety of sediments. 2) long, relatively narrow tract of earth's crust that includes Mediterranean Sea and great ranges of Alpine-Himalayan chain as the world's most extensive geosynclinal belt. It lies between Baltic and Angara Shields on north and African and Indian shield areas on south. This was a position of instability and unrest, and with passage of time the belt subsided and accumulated a record of all geologic systems. During early Paleozoic it was not as active as Caledonian trough, but deposits of Cambrian, Ordovician and Silurian are known across its entire length from Spain to southeast Asia.

tetrasporic: pertaining to reproduction of plants which produce spores in groups of 4 that are found in "tetrasporangium" such as in red algae.

thalassic rocks: strata formed in deep, still water far from land, generally composed of very fine grains.

Thalassionema [phytoplankton]: rodlike cells united into zigzag or starlike colonies; numerous small chloroplasts. Subclass *Pennatae*.

Thalassiosira [phytoplankton]: cells are somewhat like those of *Coscinodiscus* but provided with numerous fine spines, often larger than the cell. Truly planktonic genus, although characteristic of inshore waters. *T. decipiens* has disc-shaped cells with curved spines; it unites to form chains with large spaces between cells which are from 12 to 40μ in diameter.

Thaliacea [*Urochordata*]: group of tunicates whose members may be either simple or compound but which never possess a notochord in adult stage. There is a test below which is a mantle containing muscle banks which are arranged transversely around body. Within mantle is a branchid sac or pharynx which communicates with peribranchial cavity via stigmata which may be few or numerous. Peribranchial cavity leads to exterior by posterior atrial aperture. *Thaliacea* are subdivided into three orders: *Pyrosomida*, *Doliolida* and *Salpida*.

thallatogenic: vertical movement of sea floor.

Thallophyta: one of artificial grouping of simple plants lacking true stems, leaves and roots and generally having one-celled sex organs. Algae, fungi and bacteria are included in this group.

thallus: plant body without true leaves, roots or stems.

thalweg: line connecting deepest points of channel of sea valley or submarine canyon.

thamakau: large, finely built, outrigger, dugout canoe of Fiji Islands used for interisland travel. Transversely the hull is ovate in section; washboard is added to each side. Outrigger or weather side of hull is straight from stem to stern, while lee side is bowed in regular manner.

Thames barge: sailing barge used on Thames River and nearby waters, rigged as ketch or yawl with large, loose-footed, boundless mainsail. It is fitted with rails and topsail with preparation of red ochre and oil to prevent weathering, for main and topsail are never covered up.

theca: 1) case, lorica or shell surrounding animal. 2) in *Coelenterata*, skeletal deposit enclosing corallite and presumably, side of polyp. 3) in *Graptholithina*, individual tube in graptolite colony.

thermal noise: very low level noise produced by molecular movements in sea.

thermal structure: refers to temperature variation with density of seawater.

thermal wake: temperature change produced on sea surface by passage of submerged submarine; although small, it can sometimes be detected with special sensors.

thermistor chain: temperature-sensing chain of thermistors (up to 1,200 ft. long) towed astern to get continuous data spectrum from upper water layers at sea. Scanner connects each sensor to readout facility in periodic intervals.

thermocline: usually horizontal layers of water in which there is rapid decrease of temperature with increasing depth. Commonly in existence at base of surface water masses. Sonar signals may be refracted or bent.

thermogenesis: ability to generate heat.

thermograph: self-recording thermometer. Thermometric element is most commonly either bimetal strip or Bourdon tube. In oceanography, 2 most commonly used thermographs are Geodyne (Bourdon) and Braincon (mercury thermometer, radioactive source and film).

thermohaline: processes which depend on variations of temperature and salinity, and thus on density which is dependent on these properties.

thermohaline circulation: vertical circulation induced by surface cooling which causes convective overturning and consequent mixing.

thermohaline convection: vertical movement of water observed when seawater, because of decreasing temperature or increasing salinity, becomes heavier than water underneath it and disturbed vertical equilibrium results.

thermometer: instrument for measuring temperature by utilizing variation of physical properties of substances according to their thermal states.

thermometer frame: frame designed to hold 2, 3 and in some cases, 4 reversing thermometers. It can quickly attach to or be removed from Nansen bottle. Frame consists of tubes arranged for reading thermometers and perforations to permit water circulation around mercury reservoir.

thermometric depth: depth in meters, at which paired and unprotected thermometers attached to Nansen bottle are reversed. Difference between corrected readings of the 2 thermometers represents effect of hydrostatic pressure at depth of reversal. Depth may then be determined by formula or form with depth anomaly graph. Depths obtained by this means are of greatest value when wire angle scale is used.

thermoprobe: transducer used to measure temperature in situ of ocean bottom sediments at depths beneath the bottom. Such measurements, when combined with heat conductivity information, provide measurement of heat flow through ocean bottom.

thermo-salinograph: graphic representation of relationship between temperature and salinity.

thermosonde: term from Russian language describing sensor that electronically measures temperature and depth.

thermosteric anomaly: specific volume anomaly (steric anomaly) that seawater at any point would attain if seawater were at atmosphere.

thief: 1) bung dipper or drinking can, usually made of tin and in elongate cylindrical form, so weighted that it tilts and fills upon reaching surface of liquid, as in a cask. 2) an auxiliary net for catching fish that drop out of main net while latter is hauled aboard, as in drift-net fishing.

thimbles [ships]: piece of shaped metal placed inside eye-splice in a line to protect rope or wire from chafing.

tholes [ships]: pins in gunwales of boat which are used for oarlocks.

thonnier [tunny fisherman]: modern, yawl-rigged fishing boat used on west coast of Brittany, about 50 to 60 ft. long with beam about 1/3 waterline length. Fore-and-aft, loose-footed main and boomless mizzen sheeted to long boomkin. Two headsails and topsails are carried and large balloon jib is used in favorable weather.

Thoracica [order]: mantle usually with calcareous plates; 6 pairs of biramous thoracic appendages; abdomen absent or represented by caudal furca; sessile or stalked with body in soft mantle (capitulum). Barnacles—*Lepas, Balanus.*

thoracic squeeze [diving]: development of differential pressure between environment and free air spaces of body. Lower pressure in lungs results in hemorrhage of pulmonary capillaries.

thorax: portion of body between head and abdomen; in vertebrates, enclosed by ribs.

thoroughfares: deep channels in lagoon marshes behind barriers and splits.

threefold block: tackle block having three sheaves; called also *treble block.* Two such blocks with fall working in all sheaves is a *threefold purchase.*

throat: upper corner of fore-and-aft sail adjacent to mast.

thurm: ragged, rocky headland by the sea.

thwarts [ships]: boards extending across rowboat, just below gunwale, to stiffen the boat and provide seats.

thwartship: extending, leading, or lying in, or nearly in, a horizontal plane at right angles to the fore-and-aft line; as, *thwartship bulkhead; thwartship bunker; thwartship alley.* Same as *athwartship.*

Thysanoessa [*Euphausida*]: rostrum has powerful, forwardly directed spine. Eye is not spherical, being narrowed dorsally. First 6 legs have full complement of joints; 2nd pair are often much longer than any of the others (this condition applies particularly to preadult stages); 7th leg has fully formed exopodite.

Thysanoessa inermis: may reach length of 32 mm. Rostrum is long and lanceolate, reaching as far forward as end of first antennular segment. Eyes are subspherical, slightly higher than broad. Last abdominal segment is much shorter than combined length of 2 preceding ones and bears large spine near distal end.

Thysanoessa longicaudata: small, slender species never more than 16 mm. long. Sharp, pointed rostrum reaches beyond middle of first antennular segment. There are no lateral denticles on carapace. Second legs are long and stout. Last abdominal segment is equal to, or slightly shorter than, combined lengths of 2 preceding ones.

Thysanoessa raschii: carapace bears small denticles in front of middle of lateral margins. Eyes are nearly spherical. Second pair of legs is never very long. Last abdominal segment is much shorter than combined length of 2 preceding ones, but bears no spine.

ticket: seamen's colloquialism for a personal license or a certificate; as, *an able seaman's ticket.* Especially among British merchant marine officers, a certificate of competency; as, *a master's ticket; chief's ticket* (that of a *1st. class engineer*); etc.

tidal: of or pertaining to a tide or tides; having a periodical flow and ebb or rise and fall, as a *tidal river;* caused by the tide, as a *tidal current; tidal action.*

tidal basin: basin affected by tides, particularly one in which water can be kept at desired level by means of a gate.

tidal bore: high waves that move up a river or estuary with incoming tide. They are caused when incoming tide is pushed back by water flowing out of river or estuary.

tidal constants: tidal relations that remain essentially the same for any particular locality. Tidal constants are classed as harmonic and nonharmonic. Harmonic constants consist of amplitudes and epochs, and nonharmonic constants include those values determined directly from observations, such as tidal ranges and intervals.

tidal correction: correction applied to gravitational observations to remove effect of earth tides or gravimetric observations. Value of gravity at any point varies in cyclical manner during course of a day, due to changing positions of sun and moon relative to area being investigated.

tidal current: alternating horizontal movement of water associated with rise and fall of tide caused by astronomical tide-producing forces.

tidal current chart: chart showing, by arrows and numbers, average direction and speed of tidal currents at particular part of current cycle. Number of such charts, one for each hour of current cycle, usually are published together.

tidal current cycle: complete oscillation of flood and ebb through all phases of tide from high water to next succeeding high waters. Duration of semidiurnal tide approximates 12.42 hours, while that of diurnal tide approximates 24.84 hours.

tidal delta: sandbars or shoals formed in entrance of inlets by reversing tidal currents.

tidal difference: difference in time or height of high or low water between subordinate station and reference station. Difference is applied to prediction at reference station to obtain time or height of tide at subordinate station. These differences are available in tide tables.

tidal flat: flat, soggy area, which emerges during low tide, characterized by simultaneous deposition of clay and sand by tidal waters. Marsh or sandy or muddy coastal flatland which is covered and uncovered by rise and fall of tide.

tidal glacier: glacier whose terminus is in tidewater.

tidal movement: movement which includes both vertical rise and fall of tides and horizontal flow of tidal currents. This movement is associated with astronomical tide-producing forces of moon and sun acting upon rotating earth.

tidal oscillations: very slow, rocking motions in parts of oceans, occurring in response to tidal bulges.

tidal pool: pool of water remaining on beach or reef after recession of tide.

tidal prediction: prediction of times and heights of high and low waters for various reference stations throughout the world. Tidal predictions generally are published by hydrographic departments of various countries, but in U.S. they are published by U.S. Department of Commerce, Coast and Geodetic Survey.

tidal pressure ridge: pressure ridge in sea ice caused by forces exerted on ice by tide.

tidal prism: 1) amount of water necessary to produce on flood tide, the rise of water level in fjord, bay, etc. 2) volume of water in prism-shaped cross section of moving stream or river.

tidal wave: in astronomical usage, restricted to periodic variations of sea level produced by gravitational attractions of sun and moon. Term is commonly and incorrectly used for large sea wave caused by submarine earthquake or volcanic eruption, which is properly called a seismic sea wave.

tide: changes in level of large volume of water masses due to effect of gravitational attraction of moon and to a lesser degree the sun. Periodic rising and falling of water level that results from gravitational attraction of moon and sun acting upon rotating earth.

tide amplitude: one-half of difference in height between consecutive high water and low water; hence, half of tide range.

tide curve: graphic presentation of rise and fall of tide; time (in hours or days) is represented by abscissa and height by ordinate.

tide cycle: period which includes complete set of tide conditions or characteristics, such as tidal day, lunar month or Metonic cycle.

tide gauge: instrument for determining variations of sea level with time.

tidehead: inland limit of water affected by tide.

tideland: land which is underwater at high tide and uncovered at low tide. Tidelands, beach, strand and seashore have nearly the same meanings. Tidelands refers to land sometimes covered by tidewater.

tidemark: 1) high-water mark left by tidal water. 2) highest point reached by high tide.

tide pool coral [*Corallina chilensis*]: common on rocks between 0.5- and 1.5-ft. tide levels. Graceful coral are calcified, hard and brittle through deposit of lime salts within segments of thallus. Portion between segments is not calcified, however, so that species have erect shoots with joined, flexible branches. It is 2 to 5 in. tall, freely branched several times with segments slightly broader than those of *Corallina gracilis*. Graceful corals are purple-red to deep purple. When exposed to strong light or at death, they bleach to white or pink.

tide race: very rapid tidal current in narrow channel or passage.

tide range: difference in height between consecutive high and low water. Where type of tide is diurnal, mean range is same as diurnal range.

tide rips: turbulent water body produced by opposition to tidal currents.

tide staff: tide gage consisting of vertical graduated staff from which height of tide at any time can be read directly.

tide tables: tables which give daily predictions usually a year in advance of time and heights of tide.

tidewater: water affected by tides or sometimes that part of it which covers tideland. Term is sometimes used broadly to designate the seaboard.

tidewater glacier: glacier which discharges into sea.

tide wave: long-period wave associated with tide-producing forces of moon and sun; identified with rising and falling of tide.

tideway: part of channel in which strong tidal currents run.

tie or **tye** [ships]: single part of halyard which hoists a yard.

tie plates [ships]: single fore-and-aft or diagonal course of plating attached to deck beams under wood deck to give extra strength.

tier: row or layer, as of similar pieces of cargo stowed in ship's hold; series of fakes of a hawser or chain cable as coiled down or ranged clear for running. Vessels are said to *lie in tier* when made fast or moored close alongside each other in ranks or rows, as a laid-up fleet.

tilefish: deep-bellied pelagic food fish of the North Atlantic. Attains a length of 3 ft.; has a protruding lower jaw; is covered with large round yellowish spots; and has a deep dorsal fringe extending almost full length of body.

till: unstratified, glacial drift of clay, sand and gravel, forming poor subsoil impervious to water.

tiller [ships]: bar of wood or iron connected with head of rudder post leading forward, by which rudder is moved to steer vessel.

tilt boat: sailing ferryboat formerly used for transporting passengers between London and ports on east coast of England, such as Margate and Gravesend. Name came from awning or "tilt," over portion of deck for protection of passengers.

time: measured or measurable duration; as, *steaming time; elapsed time.* A system by which days, hours, etc., are reckoned or computed; as, *apparent time; lunar time.* Instant of occurrence of an event; as, *time of observation; arrival time.* Hour of day as indicated by a clock, watch, or other means; as, *chronometer time; ship time.* Today it is usually customary to indicate *time* of day aboard ship by the 24-hour system, instead of the former use of a.m. and p.m.; thus *0030* takes the place of 12.30 a.m.; *1230* for 0.30 or 12.30 p.m.; *2210* for 10.10 p.m.; etc. In nautical astronomy, *time* in almost all calculations is a most essential element and involves use of one or more of the three systems, *apparent solar time, mean solar time,* and *sidereal time.*

time meridian: any standard meridian to which time is referred; Greenwich, standard or local.

tintinnid: any of suborder *(Tintinnoidea)* of microscopic, planktonic *Protozoa* which possess tubular or vase-shaped shell. Several species are luminescent.

Tintinnidae [phylum *Protozoa*]: mainly marine oligotropes which secrete vaselike shell or lorica into which body can be withdrawn and which is formed of hardened protein. Surface is often covered by diatoms, sponge spicules or other small particles. Body is often bell-shaped and attached to lorica by short, oblique stalk. Complicated, ciliated membranelles surround mouth and form feeding apparatus, together with series of contractile tentacles. *Tintinnidae* are widely distributed in open seas and coastal waters.

titration: chemical method for determining concentration of substance in solution. This concentration is established in terms of smallest amount of substance required to bring about given effect in reaction with another known solution or substance. Most common titration is that for chlorinity.

tjalk: small Dutch sailing vessel of about 60 tons used for sea and river navigation; usually with one mast. Hull is rotund in manner of Dutch boats; leeboards are used.

tjotter: beamy, round-bottomed, cat-rigged pleasure boat of Holland. Hull is on order of boeier and just as rotund, but has more pronounced bilge. Beam is apt to be ½ the length.

toadfish: bottom dwellers with flattened bodies, forward dorsal fin reduced to a few spines and long, low, posterior dorsal fin. Toadlike head, covered with warty outgrowths, terminates in large mouth with powerful jaws.

toadfish, oyster: squat, ugly fish growing to length of 15 in., protectively colored in mottled olive-green or brown. Pectoral fins are broad and fanlike; ventral fins are small, stiff and located beneath head. Toadfish live in shallow, weedy habitats where they hide beneath stones, darting out when hungry to catch crustaceans and mollusks.

toad, Fowler's [*Buto wood housei fowleri*]: short, fat toad with prominent parotid glands and head crests. Cranial crests not terminating in pronounced knobs in adults; parotid glands in contact with posterior margins of cranial crests. Back very warty; skin of belly, granular. Ground color grayish with 2 parallel series of darker spots along each side of back; belly gray-buff.

toad, oak [*Buto quercicus*]: tiny toad usually with thin, light line down middle of back. Parotid glands diverging posteriorly rather than parallel; cranial crests inconspicuous; upper jaw toothless; adult size less than 1½ in. Ground color grayish; reddish or blackish with light line generally along dorsum from tip of snout to anus; 3 to 5 pairs of unconnected, dark blotches on each side of light line along back.

toad, southern [*Buto terrestris terrestris*]: fair-sized, fat toad with prominent parotid glands and head crests. Cranial crests terminating in pronounced knobs in adults; parotid glands well separated from cranial crests or connected only by spurs extending from crests. Belly whitish with dark spots in pectoral region.

toe [ships]: edge of flange of angle.

toggle: piece of wood or metal fitted crosswise in end of a rope or a chain for purpose of quickly engaging or disengaging with a link, ring, or an eye; any small button, pin, knotted end of a rope, etc., serving such purpose, as that in a *becket* for holding a coil of rope clear of the deck, for connecting flags, etc. A movable barb in a harpoon for engaging the flesh and so preventing withdrawal of instrument from victim's body.

tombolo: sandbar connecting island with mainland or with another island. Result is called tied island.

tomcod: small gadoid edible fish found in northern latitudes of Pacific and Atlantic. Classified as of genus *Microgadus* (small cod) greatly resembles the common *cod*, except in size.

tomium [reptiles]: horny covering of jaws.

ton: unit of tonnage, which may be that of weight, as in deadweight tonnage, or burden, and displacement; or that of capacity, as in gross and net tonnage. In the former, it is equal to 2240 lbs.; in the latter, 100 cu. ft.

Tongan Archipelago: chain of islands in South Pacific, east of Figi Islands.

tongkang: large, open, Chinese ketch-rigged sailing lighter used mainly for carrying cargoes of logs from Dutch East Indies, Johore and other nearby places to Singapore. Hull has sharp, high bow with raking stem; vertical sternpost; straight keel; little dead rise; sharp buttocks; flaring sides.

tongue: 1) projection of ice edge up to several kilometers in length. Caused by winds or currents. 2) narrow peninsula formed by glacier and steep, narrow cliff of ice rising high above glacial neve is called an ice tongue. Extension of glacier into sea is called glacier tongue, and the end if afloat, an ice tongue afloat. 3) inlet.

tongue [ships]: tongue of a sternpost or propeller post is the raised middle section which is fastened to vertical keel. As a rule, tongue is raised twice as high as sides of dished keel.

tonguefish: lanceolate, very flattened fish with both eyes on left side. Anal fin rays 75-80, dorsal fins 85-95; dorsal and anal fins more or less confluent with caudal fin; pelvic fin of right side absent; eyes on left side of body. No pectoral

fins; mouth small, twisted toward blind side; body moderately elongate, very compressed. Caudal fin rather pointed; vertical fins more or less confluent. Color grayish with indistinct crossbars. Small fish less than 1 ft. long.

Tongue of the Ocean [TOTO]: steep-sided, deep-water embayment approximately 100 nautical miles long, 20 miles wide and 1 nautical mile deep, connected to Atlantic Ocean by Northwest Providence Channel and Northeast Providence Channel and trends southeast into Great Bahama Bank, terminating in circular cul-de-sac.

tongue on pedicel [amphibian]: mushroom-shaped tongue attached by central stalk.

tonnage, gross [ships]: entire internal cubic capacity of vessel expressed in "tons" taken at 100 cu. ft. each.

tonnage, net [ships]: internal cubic capacity of vessel which remains after capacities of certain specified spaces have been deducted from gross tonnage.

tonnage openings: openings in shelter deck bulkheads for purpose of economy in tonnage rating.

tony: curious open sailing canoe used for fishing at Bombay, India. It is long, narrow, double-ended and made of Malabar teak. Ends are strongly raking and sharp, rising abruptly to form high stem and sternpost, carvel on top. Rudder is attached to stern by rope beckets.

tooth [*Brachiopoda*]: projection along hinge line of pedicle valve that fits into socket on opposing valve.

toothed whale: member of cetacean suborder *Odontoceti*, which comprises dolphins, porpoises, killer whales, beaked whales and sperm whales.

tooth shell: one of class (*Scaphopoda*) of benthic marine mollusks having tubular, tapering, slightly curved shells, open at both ends; body has no distinct head but possesses a foot.

top [ships]: sort of platform surrounding head of lower mast on all sides. It serves to extend topmast shrouds. Tops are named after respective masts to which they are attached: foretop, maintop, mizzentop.

topa: small fishing boat of Venice. It has flat-bottomed, double-ended hull of light draft. Lugsail of varicolored pattern is carried in a mast stepped aft of center.

top breadth lines [ships]: width of vessel measured across shelter deck.

topgallant [ships]: square sail next above topsail or upper topsail on square-rigged ship. Roach or foot was 4 ft. on large ships and 3 ft. on smaller ones.

top hammer [ships]: sailing vessel's spars, upper rigging and any equipment not needed in upper part of ship.

topmast: mast extending above a lowermast; second mast above deck.

topminnow, banded [*Fundulus cingulatus*]: small fish with reddish fins and vertical bars on sides. Lateral lines absent; anal rays usually 9; no distinct dark spot under eye; anterior margin of dorsal fin above and slightly behind anterior margin of anal fin. Body short and robust, slightly arched above, compressed in region of caudal peduncle. Head short; mouth small and terminal. Color pale greenish or bronze with narrow vertical bars on sides but without gold flecks; fins reddish.

topminnow, eastern star-headed [*Fundulus notti lineolatus*]: little bait fish with dark patch under eye and light patch on head. No lateral line; pattern of about 6 longitudinal stripes along side (female) or of about 12 vertical dark bars (male); anterior margin of anal fin just about under anterior margin of dorsal fin. Scale rows 36-38. Color pale silvery; often orange-red around mouth and cheeks.

topminnow, golden [*Fundulus chrysatus*]: small fish with robust body and gold flecks on sides. Lateral line absent; rays usually 10; no distinct dark spot under eye; anterior margin of dorsal fin above or slightly behind anterior margin of anal fin. Body slightly arched above; compressed in region of caudal peduncle; head short; mouth small and terminal. Color pale to olive-brown with no or very few vertical dark bars on sides.

topminnow, southern star-headed [*Fundulus notti notti*]: little bait fish with dark patch under eye and light patch on head. No lateral line; pattern of longitudinal rows of disconnected spots; anterior margin of anal fin just about under anterior margin of dorsal fin. Scales along side 34—36. Color pale silvery with conspicuous dark spot under each eye and 6—8 longitudinal rows of spots along sides. Orange-red about mouth and cheeks.

topminnow, streaked [*Fundulus olivaceus*]: slender little fish with broad, dark band down each side from tip of snout to tail. No lateral line; scale rows along side about 34; anterior margin of dorsal fin just above anterior margin of anal fin. Body fusiform, compressed posteriorly; back not much arched; head rather elongate, flattened above. Color tannish-olive with broad, dark lateral stripe along each side from tip of snout to base of caudal fin.

top off [ships]: to fill up a tank.

topography: configuration of surface including its relief. In oceanography, term is applied to surface such as sea bottom or surface of given characteristic within water mass.

topping lift [ships]: rope or chain extending from head of boom or gaff to a mast or to vessel's structure for purpose of supporting weight of boom or gaff and its loads, and permitting them to be rotated at certain level.

topsail [ships]: sail next above "course" on square-rigged ship. About 1850, topsail was divided into upper and lower topsail for ease in handling. On fore-and-aft-rigged vessel, topsail is triangular and sets above mainsail gaff.

topsail schooner: fore-and-aft-rigged schooner with one or two square sails above foresail, on foremast and sometimes in mainmast.

top shells: somewhat dull in coloration. Genus *Calliostoma* contains some very colorful shells. Top shells are found on rocky beaches from high tide line to great depths. They are vegetarians. This is first of many groups to possess special "door" opening growing on their foot. This is called an operculum and snail uses it to close opening or aperture of shell when it is disturbed or when tide is out, thus protecting animal from drying effect of sun or from predators. Operculum of top shell is of horny material. Sometimes shells, especially in *Calliostoma* group, are ornamented with ribs, beads, etc.

topside [ships]: that portion of side of hull which is above designed waterline.

tornaria larva [*Hemichordata*]: pelagic larva characterized by sinuous ciliary bands and resembling bipinnaria larva of sea stars at a certain stage.

torpedo: high-speed, self-propelled, underwater explosive dirigible projected from war vessel against an enemy.

torpedo, Atlantic [*electric ray*]: ray with a short, thick tail and small tail fin; 2 small dorsal fins are located in front of tail. Unlike skates which have small, pointed snout, the torpedo has rounded outline to head. It is chocolate-brown or purplish-gray, well camouflaged when it lies partly buried in mud or sand. It reaches length of 5 ft. and may weigh as much as 75 lbs. Torpedo is common in waters from 60 to 300 ft. deep. This ray is unique in possessing electric organs on head.

torsion: in gastropods, twisting of visceral hump during larval life, bringing mantle cavity and gills to forward position.

tosca: applied in Argentina to white, calcareous marl. In Columbia it is synonymous with volcanic tufa.

total internal reflection: in wave refraction theory, term analogous to phenomenon of total internal reflection of light at 45-45-90 prism. It occurs at special type of caustic.

total magnetic intensity: vector resultant of intensity of horizontal and vertical components of earth's magnetic field at specified point.

total phosphorus: includes both soluble phosphorus (phosphate) and organic phosphorus contained in planktonic organisms and other organic material in water.

tow: to draw along through the water, as a vessel pulling a barge, raft, another vessel, etc. That which is *towed*, as, *we picked up a tow*. Act or condition of being towed, as, *barges taken in tow*. A *tow* or craft taken *in tow* has been extended to denote also a number of barges, scows, etc., being *pushed* by a powered vessel or *tug*, as is common practice on rivers and in sheltered waters, especially in U.S.A. Generally where liability for collision damage is in question, the *towing* vessel with her *tow* is considered a single vessel.

towage: act of *towing*, which includes assisting vessels in berthing, turning, shifting, etc., in harbor; also, the *towing* of a vessel in or out of port, through a narrow or dangerous passage, etc., in expediting her voyage, as opposed to *salvage*. Fee or charges made for such service.

towing: act of one who, or that which, *tows*; towage.

trabacola: Italian two-masted, lug-rigged vessel of Adriatic. Generally used as coastal trader. Hull is double-ended with curved stem and sternpost. Heavy outboard rudder is slung from the latter. Rig consists of balanced lugsail on each mast and 1 or 2 jibs to bowsprit.

Trabacoto: small southern European fishing boat which was popular in 17th century, but which has remained in use until quite recently. It was two-masted with gaily colored lateen or setee sails. Mainmast was vertical and foremast raked forward.

trabecula [*Coelenterata*]: rod of radiating calcite fibers forming an element of coral skeleton.

trace: line drawn on graph which shows variation of oceanographic element such as temperature and salinity usually with depth.

tracheae: air tube, respiratory system in insects and other arthropods.

Tracheophyta [phylum]: subdivision *Sphenopsida*: horsetail rushes and their kind constitute tribe characterized by regularly jointed stems. Existing horsetail or scouring rush (*Equisetum*) grows abundantly in moist places in many parts of U.S. In all horsetails stem has only thin cylinder of woody tissue around large center of pith. Reproduction is by means of spores which are borne in strobili (cones) at tops of stems. Modern horsetails are mostly small, and the race passed its climax in late Paleozoic, when giant scouring rushes (calamites) grew to height of trees and had stems as much as 12 in. in diameter.

Trachymedusae [phylum *Coelenterata*]: hydromedusae belonging to this suborder are characterized by practically hemispherical shape with thick nematocyst ring and by gonads usually confined to margins of radial canals. Marginal tentacles are solid in some species but hollow in others. There is no hydroid stage. *Trachymedusae* are separated from the *Narcomedusae* in that margins of umbrella are not lobed. There is a large muscular velum; marginal tentacles are easily detached.

trachyte: fine-grained, light-colored, igneous rock consisting largely of alkalic feldspars.

track: path or course of a vessel as indicated on a chart; wake of a vessel. A rail on which hanks of a sail travel, as on a gaff or a mast. To delineate, as on a chart, the path of a ship or of a hurricane, a stretch of submarine cable, or a line of soundings. *Bottle track* as indicated on a chart, path followed by a drifting bottle thrown overboard for purpose of estimating set and drift of surface current or currents.

traction load: bottom load or bed load of stream, carried by rolling, sliding or saltation.

trade winds: 1) wind system, occupying most of tropics which blows from subtropical highs toward equatorial trough; major component of general circulation of atmosphere. Winds are northeasterly in Northern Hemisphere and southeasterly in Southern Hemisphere. 2) tradition to the contrary, trade winds were not named because of their impact on commerce. Instead, title stems from early usage in which "trade" indicated any habitually followed path or track. Before end of 16th century it was known that over subtropical seas the wind often blew quite regularly during much of the year. It was a source of satisfaction to ship's master to find a wind belt where he could be sure the air would "blow trade" (follow a constant course). *Hakluyt's Voyages* (1591-1600) includes the phrase in this sense. From "blowing trade" it was a natural transition to "trade winds" as a title for steady currents on each side of equator in Atlantic and Pacific. First known use by a landsman was in a 1663 poem dedicated to Sir Francis Drake. With the early significance of "trade" forgotten it was inevitable that writers and some navigators should link steady winds with prosperous voyages and leap to the conclusion that their name originally had a commercial connotation.

traffic noise [ships]: general disturbance caused by ships, not associated with a specific ship, or more significant, which has no definite directional distribution relative to given observation point and which shows little change in intensity with change in position.

trail board [ships]: curved board extending from figurehead to bow, often carved or embellished.

trammel: fixed gill-net, loosely mounted for entangling fish; especially a set of three parallel nets, middle one of which is fine meshed and loosely hung, the others coarse meshed and stretched out. Fish entering from either side push fine-mesh middle net into one of the larger meshes of outer net and thus become entangled in the bight of fine-meshed netting.

transapical: width in diatom shell.

transgressions: when the sea invades a region formerly emerged, we say that there has been a transgression on this region and that deposits brought by this new sea are transgressive. Inversely, when region is abandoned by sea, we say there is a regression.

transgressive reef: one of a series of reefs or bioherms developed close to and parallel to shore by a net movement of sea over land.

transient thermocline: small decrease in vertical observed above thermocline. It is a short term phenomenon associated primarily with diurnal heating and wind mixing.

transition zone: 1) water area between 2 opposing currents manifested by eddies, upwelling rips and similar turbulent conditions occurring either vertically or horizontally. 2) zone between 2 water masses of differing physical characters, as temperature and/or salinity.

transmission anomaly: difference (in decibels) between total transmission loss in intensity and reduction in intensity due to assumed inverse square divergence.

transmission loss: as sound waves pass from one point to another some energy is lost, weakening the signal. This weakening is called transmission loss.

transom [ships]: one of several beams or timbers fixed across sternpost of a ship to strengthen after part and to give it the figure most suited to service for which vessel was intended.

transom beam [ships]: strong deck beam in after end of vessel directly over sternpost and connected at each end to transom frame. Cant beams supporting deck plating in overhang of stern radiate from it.

transom frame or plate [ships]: horizontal frame under ship's counter.

transom stern [ships]: flat type of stern.

transosondes: test balloon or balloons and their equipment for obtaining weather observation at high level winds. Navy balloons fly at preset, constant-pressure levels and are tracked by radio direction-finding equipment.

transparency: ability of water to transmit light of different wave lengths, usually measured in percent of radiation which penetrates a distance of 1 meter. Transparency is also measured by average of depths at which a Secchi disc (30 cm. in diameter) disappears and reappears.

transport: process by which substance or quantity is carried past a fixed point or across a fixed plane. In oceanography and meteorology, such quantities are heat, momentum, mass, dissolved impurities, suspended particles, etc.

transverse [ships]: placed at right angles to keel, such as transverse frame, transverse bulkhead, etc.

transverse bars: slightly submerged sand ridges which extend at right angles to shoreline.

transverse framing [ship construction]: made up of "ribs" of the body or parts whose chief function is to give transverse or athwartship strength.

transverse mercator projection: conformal, cylindrical, map projection in which points on surface of a sphere or spheroid, such as earth, are conceived as developed by Mercator principles on a cylinder tangent along a meridian. This projection is particularly useful for charts of polar regions and for those extending relatively short distance from tangent meridian. It is frequently used for star charts.

transverse section [TRANSEC]: line of survey used in underwater biological, military and geological surveys.

trash ice: also called *land trash*, broken-up ice on or along the shore in Arctic regions.

travel-time graph: in seismic refraction at sea, a plot of water wave travel-time (horizontal distance) against ground wave travel-time from which calculations of velocities and depths of oceanic structures are calculated.

trawl: bag or funnel-shaped net to catch bottom fish by dragging along bottom. Large research net designed on bottom trawl principles to catch large zooplankton and fish by towing in intermediate depths.

trawler: fishing vessel which tows large net called a "trawl," e.g., "Brixham trawler." Power-driven vessels have supplanted sailing trawlers almost entirely.

tread [ships]: length of vessel's keel.

treenails [ships]: wooden pins employed instead of nails or spikes to secure planking of wooden vessel to frame.

Trematoda: class of phylum *Platyhelminthes* that are mostly ectoparasites on gills, skin and external orifices of fish, a few amphibians and turtles. Distinctive characteristics are single host in life cycle, sexual reproduction and direct development.

trench: long, narrow and deep depression of sea floor with relatively steep sides.

trend: tendency toward, or inclination in, a given direction, as, *northerly trend of a coast*. Relative direction or angle with the fore-and-aft line in which ship's cable leads when swinging at single anchor. In an old-fashioned anchor, enlarged part of *shank* where it approaches and forms junction with the *arms*. To run, trend, or lead in direction, as, *the land trends to the eastward*.

trepang: certain species of large sea cucumbers that, boiled and dried, are used to make soup, especially in Orient.

trestletrees [ships]: short timbers running fore and aft on either side of mast that rests in the "hounds." They support top platform and cross-trees.

triangulation: measurement of series of angles between points on surface of earth. Used to establish relative positions of points in surveying.

Triassic: last period of Mesozoic Era during which small, primitive mammals began to appear.

triatic [ships]: supporting stay between main and mizzen or main and foremast of two-masted vessel.

trick [ships]: spell; turn; time alloted to a man to stand at the helm, generally 2 hours.

trickle: any narrow passage connecting 2 large bodies of water. In Gulf of Laurence it is restricted to an inlet between the sea and a lagoon.

Tridacna [giant clam]: lives on coral reefs where low tides expose most of shell, though high tides cover it. As water returns, valves open and mantle spreads out in thick, multicolored folds containing algae that grow on the flesh and use energy from sunlight to make food. Found in Tertiary rocks; fossil mollusks may or may not have grown algae in mantles.

trids: buds of *Thaliacea* in aggregate phase of life cycle.

trifid: three-pronged.

triggerfish: triggerfish of family *Balistidae* are notable for 2 characteristics. One is beauty of markings and monochromatic and polychromatic coloration, vivid blues, golds, browns and whites in variety of stripes, bars, speckles and spots. The other is defensive spine that can be raised at will and locked into place. Spine is part of dorsal fin. When triggerfish is pursued by an enemy, he flees into coral formation and uses his spines to lock himself into protected position among coral. Triggerfish has small mouth and leatherlike skin. It is found primarily in tropical and subtropical waters, where it rarely attains a length of more than 15 in.

triggerfish, queen: more brilliantly colored and grows to slightly larger size. This species is capable of rapid color changes but usual phase consists of yellow body, blue and yellow fins and blue bands across head. First rays of dorsal fin and 2 outer tips of tail are prolonged into tapering tips.

trigonal [*Mollusca*]: triangular in outline.

trilobite [three-lobed ones]: body consists of 3 parts: head, body and tail. Name actually refers to portions that run lengthwise and are separated by furrows, not joints. These grooves divide every trilobite into axial lobe in middle and 2 pleura, one at each side of body.

trim [ships]: to haul up to wind and brace yards sharp so as to receive wind to best advantage. Also to stow cargo properly so ship rides well. Difference in draft at bow of a vessel from that at stern. Attitude of submerged submarine with respect to neutral buoyancy and fore-and-aft balance.

Trimerellacea [*Brachiopoda*]: biconvex shells of circular-shaped outline with length up to 8 cm.; impunctate; composed of calcium carbonate. Muscle attached to platforms raised above floors of both valves and supported by median septum.

Triphora perversa [*Cerithidae*]: newly hatched veliger is 0 to 16 mm. long with sinistral one-whorled shell ornamented with fine raised dots, replaced by striae in later larvae. Shell is opaque brown and velum colorless; rest of animal is yellowish. Velum of newly hatched larva is 0.18 mm. across and formed of 2 round lobes. Later, shell becomes two-whorled, upper 1½ whorls being dotted and rest striated. At this stage it is 0.2 mm. high. When shell is 0.64 mm. high there are 6 or 7 whorls. When 7th and 8th whorls become tuberculate, velum is lost and larva settles.

triple rib [*Cyamathere triplicata*]: triple rib kelp has 3 conspicuous ridges and grooves alternating on upper and lower surfaces of smooth blade, giving well groomed, orderly appearance. Has exceedingly short, stout stipe, cylindrical below, flattened and slightly wider at point where blade begins. Blade is long and narrow, 4 to 6 ft. long and 6 to 8 in. wide. It is a rich yellow-brown with texture of heavy rubber gloves. Holdfast is a conical disc, 1 to 2 in. in diameter.

tripping bracket [ships]: flat bars placed at various points on deck girder or beams as reinforcement.

trirene: as applied to early Greek and Roman galleys, consensus is that the terms are used to denote number of men pulling on each oar. Trirenes were in use up to last of 15th century.

triton, anal [*Distorsio anus*]: shell of this species is covered with spiral rows of tubercles which are arranged to form a network over surface of shell. Columellar side of aperture is covered by large, calloused area; aperture is bordered with many teeth. Color is nearly white externally, but is often marked with reddish-brown bands. Ranges in length from 2 to 3 in.

triton, beaded or gem [*Cymatium gemmatum*]: beaded triton is marked by longitudinal varices and by revolving ribs and striae which are sometimes crossed by longitudinal ribs; it often bears 2 or 3 nodules between varices. Shell varies from whitish to orange-yellow in color. It will reach length of 1½ in.

triton, blood-spotted [*Bursa cruentata*]: this species is white, yellow or brown and is covered with tubercles, larger of which are often spotted with red; aperture is white or rosy within; red spots sometimes mark columella. It will reach length of 1½ in.

triton, clandestine or hidden [*Cymatium elandestinum*]: this triton has well-rounded whorls which usually bear single longitudinal varix and which are encircled by many regular, revolving, cordlike ribs. Outer lip bears teeth upon inner margin. Shell is light yellowish-brown color without and white within. Revolving ribs and teeth are dark brown. This species reaches about 2½ in. in length.

triton, family [*Cymatiidae*]: tritons are large family of thick, rugged, strong shells which exhibit spiral pattern of growth. These shells bear decorative pattern over exterior and have never more than 1 or 2 varices to a whorl. Shells of this family exhibit prominent anterior canal and usually have teeth upon inner surface of outer lip; operculum is present. They inhabit the bottom from shoreline to depth of 300 ft. or more and are found in both tropical and temperate waters.

triton, hairy [*Cymatium pileare*]: hairy triton is marked with spiral ribs and 7 to 9 varices which are separated by 3 to 5 longitudinal rows of tubercles. It is covered by thin, brown, bristly epidermis. This shell is white, yellow and brown in color, often in the form of revolving bands; aperture is orange-red with white plications. It measures between 2 to 5 in.

triton, lamp: lamp triton is large species with well-developed, turreted spire; it has more than 10 varices upon shell and, in addition, bears 2 prominent and several less prominent rows of tubercles upon each whorl together with smaller, revolving, granular ridges. Columella is wrinkled; outer lip is toothed. Shell is whitish to cream-colored and clouded with orange-brown; it is flesh-colored within and ranges in length from 3 to 9 in.

triton, little red [*Cymatium rubecula*]: surface of this shell is marked with 6 prominent varices and by spiral, granulose ridges about whorls. This species varies in color between lemon and orange-red. It is often marked with white or yellow band about middle of body whorl; other varices are banded with spots of white. Lips and columella resemble exterior of shell in color, but teeth and interior of shell are usually white. It will reach length of 2 in.

triton, Nicobar [*Cymatium nicobaricum*]: this triton is large, fairly heavy and marked with usual revolving ribs and longitudinal varices. Shell is whitish in color and marked with red or brown spots; lips, aperture and columella are bright orange. Ranges in length from ½ to 3 in.

triton, pear [*Cymatium pyrum*]: pear triton is

transversely ribbed and marked by 4 varices. Anterior canal is rather long and curved while spire is shorter than most other members of this group. Aperture bears teeth upon outer lip. In color this species is yellowish-orange or red, often with white spots upon varices. Aperture and teeth are light-colored or white.

triton, quilted or knobby [*Cymatium tuberosum*]: shell of this triton is spirally ribbed and covered by 6 or more rounded varices. Anterior canal is quite long and curved upwards. Outer lip and columella are heavily coated with enamel. It is brown without and orange or red within aperture. It will reach 2½ in. in length.

triton, related [*Bursa affinis*]: this triton is marked by varices on opposite sides of shell and by spiral rows of tubercles which cover shell; of several rows of tubercles, center row on each whorl is largest. Color ranges from fleshy-white to yellow; apex is rosy; surface is spotted and stained with brownish-red. It will reach 2 in. in length.

triton, toadlike [*Bursa bujonia*]: this species is marked by curved canal at each end of aperture. It is white in color, spotted with brown on outside and white or yellow within. It will reach length of 2½ in.

triton, trumpet [*Tritonalia tritonis*]: trumpet triton is one of largest and most beautiful shells in the sea. It is easily recognized by large size and by shell which is marked by encircling ribs, low rounded varices, long spire and large body whorl with still larger aperture. It is colored on outside of shell by white, yellow and brown; this color is often disposed in rows of moon-shaped blotches. Aperture is usually reddish-orange within, while columella is dark chocolate color crossed by light plications. Will reach length of at least 16 in.

Trivia monacha [*Cypraeidae*]: common inshore plankton but rather rare offshore. First larva has bilobed velum, accessory shell, small true shell and rudimentary tentacles. Body is full of orange-yellow yolk which later disappears. As tentacles become longer, animal becomes darker owing to development of brown liver and purple gut. Velum has brown border with lateral margin of each lobe slightly concave. Width of accessory shell of first larva is 0.36 mm. and true shell 0.16 mm. Anterior lobes become longer than hinder ones and scattered pigment appears on sole of foot which develops lateral lobes. Finally, before metamorphosis, accessory shell is covered by mantle and absorbed. Operculum and lateral lobes of foot disappear and larva settles.

Trochidae: mollusks of this family produce heavy conical shells of iridescent, nacreous material which are covered in life by periostracum. They are herbivorous and live among seaweed in warm waters of tropics.

Trochidae, top shell: this top shell is quite firm in construction and presents fairly symmetrical, conical outline because of large and straight spire. Entire outer surface of shell is covered by encircling ridges, each of which bears row of small beads upon it. Aperture is likewise spirally ridged. Shell is white or gray and marked near or over entire outer surface with variety of yellow, red and brown markings. It will measure over 1 in. in height or diameter.

trochoid: 1) in *Coelenterata*, corallite with angle of about 40° between sides expanding from apex. 2) in *Foraminifera*, coiled test in which whorls form a spiral on surface of cone.

trochoidal wave: progressive oscillatory wave whose form is that of prolate cycloid or trochoid. It is approximated by waves of small amplitudes.

trochophore: free-swimming larval stage in certain aquatic invertebrates, distinguished by ciliated, pear-shaped body. Free-swimming, pelagic larval stage of some annelids and mollusks.

troll: to fish with hook which has bait or bright lure attached. Line is drawn through water, generally to try to catch such surface-feeding species as bonito.

trophic: related to nutrition and foods of organisms. Trophic levels are steps along food chain from numerous small organisms to decreased numbers of large organisms.

trophic level: successive stage of nourishment as represented by links of food chain. Primary producers (phytoplankton) constitute first trophic level, herbivorous zooplankton the second trophic level and carnivorous organisms the third trophic level.

tropic: on both celestial and terrestrial spheres, either of two small circles parallel to and equidistant N. and S. of the equator about 23° 27'. The northern circle is called *Tropic of Cancer*; the southern one, *Tropic of Capricorn*. On the earth these mark the N. and S. limits of the *tropics*, or *torrid zone* or *belt*, extending between latitudes 23° 27' N. and S., within which, at any time of year at some place the sun passes through the zenith.

tropical cyclone: general term for cyclone that originates over tropical oceans. At maturity, tropical cyclone is one of the most intense and feared storms of the world; winds exceeding 175 knots (200 mph) have been measured and its rains are torrential.

tropic birds [bo'sun birds]: these white seabirds are almost exclusively confined to the tropics. They have straight, heavy beaks, long wings and short legs with all 4 toes webbed. Tails are web-shaped and in adult birds 2 central feathers are enormously elongated. They are commonly called "bo'sun birds" by sailors because they "carry a marlinspike on the tail." White plumage is more or less marked with black bars often crescentic in form and frequently more or less completely suffused with rosy or salmon color.

tropic currents: tidal currents occurring twice monthly when effect of moon's maximum declination is greatest. Greatest diurnal inequalities between speeds and duration of successive flood and successive ebb currents occur at this time.

tropic higher high water: the lunitidal interval pertaining to mean higher high waters at time of tropic tides.

tropic higher low water: the mean higher low water of tropic tides.

tropic inequalities: tropic high water inequality is average difference between 2 high waters at time of tropic tides. Tropic low water inequality is average difference between 2 low waters at time of tropic tides. Terms are applicable only when type of tide is semidiurnal or mixed.

tropic intervals: tropic higher high water interval is lunitidal interval of higher high waters at time of tropic tides. Tropic lower low water interval is lunitidal interval of lower low waters and time of tropic tides.

tropic lower low water: mean lower low water of tropic tides.

tropic lower low water interval: lunitidal interval pertaining to mean lower low waters and time of tropic tides.

tropic tides: tides occurring approximately every 2 weeks, when effect of moon's maximum declination north or south of equator is greater.

tropic velocity: speed of greater flood or greater ebb tidal currents at time of tropic tides.

troposphere: in oceanography, upper layer of oceanic waters in middle and low latitudes where there are strong currents and warm temperatures.

trough: long depression of sea floor normally wider and shallower than trench.

trout, brook: olive or yellowish-brown fish marked by lighter spots and occasional red dot. It is usually 7 to 16 in. long with average weight of 2 lbs., although large individuals weigh as much as 10 lbs. This species originally was found only in northern portion of U.S., east of Mississippi River; now it is widespread as result of artificial propagation, being found west to Pacific Coast.

trout, brown: European species that was introduced into U.S. over 60 years ago; it is now found from New England to California. It is able to survive in sluggish streams and small ponds; less sensitive to surroundings than other trout, it can thrive in habitats where our native trout are unable to live. Coloration is usually yellowish-brown with large dark spots, each surrounded by lighter halo. It also has silvery phase in which it easily can be mistaken for landlocked salmon. Usual weight ranges from 3 to 10 lbs.; large one may weigh as much as 30 lbs.

trout, coast rainbow [*Salmo gairdneri irideus*]: color of this rainbow trout is either blue or olive-green above and silver on sides with broad, pink lateral band. Back, sides, dorsal and caudal fins are profusely spotted. Scales are rather large and number 120 to 140 in lateral line. Tail fin is slightly forked; dorsal fin contains 11 rays; anal fin 10 to 12 rays.

trout, common brook or speckled [*Salvelinus fontinalis fontinalis*]: brook trout has dark olive back and sides with light, wormlike or marbled streaks across back. Numerous red spots margined with brown appear on sides. Scales are very small numbering about 230 in lateral line. Dorsal fin has 10 rays, anal fin 9. Caudal or tail fin is slightly forked.

trout, common lake [*Cristivomer namacycush namacycush*]: lake trout is frequently called "landlocked salmon" by anglers, but this name properly belongs to landlocked variety of Atlantic salmon. Lake trout is dark gray with round, pale spots sometimes tinged with pink. Although belly is usually pale, it may be dark and spotted. Length is about 4 times the depth. Dorsal and anal fins each have 11 rays; tail is deeply forked; scales are rather small, numbering 185-205 in lateral line.

trout, cutthroat: considered parent type of all American trout. It gets its name from bright red blotch beneath lower jaw; otherwise it is silvery with golden tints along sides and scattered spots which are often larger than those of a rainbow. Cutthroat is found in cold mountain streams from California to Alaska. Average size is under 12 in., but some individuals reach length of 36 in. and weigh up to 40 lbs.

trout, Dolly Varden: native of Pacific Coast. It resembles brook trout but is more slender, lacks dark markings and tail fin is slightly forked. Dolly Varden is common in streams but periodically migrates to sea. When it returns as searun trout, it is silvery, as are other members of trout and salmon group. Usual size is 8 to 20 in. and weight ranges from 2 lbs. for those found in streams to 20 lbs. for those in lakes.

trout, Lahontan cutthroat [*Salmo clarki henshawi*]: silvery trout has green back and coppery-silver sides. It is entirely covered by spots. Dorsal fin has 11 rays, anal fin 12; scales are moderate and number 160 to 170 in lateral line.

trout, lake: largest of trouts and, as name implies, inhabits ponds and lakes. It occurs from New England, where it is known as togue, across northern U.S. to Alaska. Lake trout prefer cool, deep water but come to surface for sunning and inshore for feeding. They have omnivorous appe-

tite, greedily eating anything from leaves and trash to smelts, eels and even small birds. Lake trout is variable in color, but commonly is brown or greenish-gray with silvery sides and numerous light spots scattered over darker gray background. Most trout have square-cut tail but that of lake trout is forked. Lake trout are usually 20 to 30 in. in length and weigh under 10 lbs.

trout, rainbow: named because of striking coloration. It has silvery and pink sides, greenish back and many colored spots scattered over body. This coloring is extremely variable, depending upon age and sex of trout and environment in which it has been living. Usual length is 8 to 20 in. with weight of from 2 to 8 lbs.

trout, speckled [*Cynoscion nebulosus*]: pale, handsome, yellow-washed, silver fish with conspicuous small black spots on sides and back. Scales along lateral line 90-102; rays in soft dorsal fin 25-27; no barbels present on chin. Body elongate, only slightly compressed laterally; back slightly arched; mouth slightly oblique, terminal in position. Color yellow above, paler below, with numerous distinct black spots on sides, back, dorsal and caudal fins. Maximum weight in excess of 15 lbs. but average much smaller.

trout, yellowstone cutthroat [*Salmo clarki lewisi*]: cutthroat trout has silvery color with black spots profusely scattered over back and sides. Lower jaw is streaked with red on creases along jawbone. Middle of side has rosy tinge. Scales are moderate in size and number 140-190 in lateral line.

trout-perch [*Percopsis omiscomaycus*]: although this fish bears general superficial resemblance to perch or small walleye, it may be distinguished from these species by presence of adipose fin, somewhat like that of trout or whitefish. When freshly caught, it has peculiar translucent appearance and is more or less mottled with light and dark colors with many small, black spots on and above lateral line. Head is conical and free from scales; head is contained 3.8 times in length and the depth 4.3 times. Dorsal fin is inserted about middle of body with 2 spines and 9 soft rays; anal fin has 1 spine and 7 soft rays; ventral fins each have 1 spine and 8 soft rays. This species reaches length of 8 in.

trout-perch, family [*Percopsidae*]: these fish have elongate bodies which are rather heavy anteriorly and compressed posteriorly. Head is rather pointed; mouth small; eye large; maxillary bones small. Premaxillaries border upper jaw which is protractile; jaws are set with weak teeth. Gill membranes are free from isthmus; pseudobranchia are developed; branchiostegal rays number 6; gill rakers are tuberlike. Bones of head are cavernous; scales are ctenoid; lateral spine is present. This family contains 2 genera, *Columbia* and

Percopsis.

trow: type of barge found in various British localities.

truck [ships]: circular piece of wood fixed on head of each of vessel's highest masts and having small sheave or holes in it through which flag halyards are rove.

true: correct; exact; in accord with fact or reality; not false, as, *true azimuth; true horizon; true time; true vertical.* Designating a corrected apparent or observed value; as, a *true altitude;* a *true course; true bearing; true place of a star; true wind.*

truncate [fish]: cut off square; not rounded or forked.

trunk: a casing or shaft entirely enclosing a hatchway between two or more decks; a *trunk-hatch* or *trunk hatchway.* A trunkway, passage, or conductor; a ventilating shaft or air duct. Upper part of a cabin extending above deck in a small vessel.

trunk bulkhead [ships]: casing or partition that forms enclosure running from deck to deck and surrounding hatch openings.

trunkfish: trunkfish have gone to an extreme in making use of armor, being encased entirely in rigid shell made of fused scales. They are aquatic armored tanks able to move only their eyes and small fins. When viewed from front, body has triangular outline with apex of triangle at top. With such rigid bodies, trunkfish swim sluggishly using only fins for locomotion. They exhibit wide range of colors: some are vivid green, others are white, still others are brown.

trunkfish, common: grows to length of 9 in. Frequent color phase is pearly gray background with dusky fins and dark, grayish band along upper sides.

try net: small shrimp trawl 12 to 24 ft. wide designed for exploration of shrimp grounds. Net is frequently used for biological sampling of benthic fish.

trysail [ships]: generally, triangular sail used in bad weather when regular working sails cannot be carried. Also used as "spanker" in connection with triangular ringtail.

tsukpin: outrigger sailing canoe of Yap Islands which lies at western end of Caroline Islands. It is employed by natives in catching flying fish.

tsunami: from Japanese term for "large waves in harbor"; geologist's word for "tidal wave." Tsunami are caused by seismic disturbance along ring of sea trenches. Submarine landslides, dropping of ocean floor, etc., may also cause tsunami. Waves are extremely long and reach enormous heights.

Tsushima Current: that part of Kuroshio flowing northeastward through Korea Strait and along Japanese coast in Sea of Japan; it sets strongly eastward through Tsugaru Strait at speeds up to 7 knots.

tuamotu Archipelago: group of islands of French Polynesia.

tube feet: little tentacle appendages with suckers on ends.

tube nose: describing birds whose nostrils are extended by horny tubes.

tubercle [reptiles]: wartlike projection.

tuberculate: characterized by small lumps or ridges.

tubeworm: any polychaete, chiefly serpulids or sabellids, that build calcareous or leathery tube on submerged surface. Tubeworms are notable fouling organisms.

Tubipora [*Tubipora musica*]: sometimes called organ-pipe coral, it is a colonial octocoralline allied to soft corals. Its skeleton is composed of complex of red, cylindrical tubes arranged side by side like a pipe organ. These tubes or pipes are not parallel but lean outward from base and are interconnected by means of occasional horizontal platforms. *Tubipora* grows vertically rather than horizontally and is a constituent element of coral massifs in which it is found.

Tubulariae: family of phylum *Coelenterata*, composed of mostly colonial hydromedusans.

tubulus: in some *Radiolaria*, wide radial cylindrical extension of skeleton.

Tucana: also, *Toucan;* a small southern constellation located nearly on opposite side of the pole to *Southern Cross* and having about same position in declination. Its brightest star is *a Tucanae,* of magnitude 2.91; right ascension 22 hrs. 15 min.; declination 60½° S.

tuck [ships]: after part of ship where shell plating meets in the run and is tucked together.

tuck boat: 19th century rowing boat of Cornwall, England. It was about 20 ft. long and carried a "stop net." It was carvel-built with sharp bow and square-transomed stern, 6-oared and used for pilchard fishing.

tufa: porous limestone formed by deposits from springs and streams.

tug: strongly built powered vessel of small tonnage specially designed for towing; a *tugboat* or *towboat.* There are two types, generally considered: the harbor or river tug and the sea-going tug.

Tuingutu: outrigger dugout canoe of Tongan Archipelago. Two or 3 outrigger booms, U-type or paired, are connected to float. Washboard is sewed to each side of hull. Decked at each end with boards.

tumble home [ships]: amount the topside of hull of vessel goes in toward center from the perpendicular above waterline. Said of sides of a vessel when they lean in at top.

tuna: tuna are members of *Scombridae* (mackerel) family. Although name tuna is used generally for albacore, bonito, yellowfin tuna, bluefin tuna, little tuna (false albacore) and skipjack, there is a great difference in size among various species. Pacific species of bonito *(Sarda sarda)*, e.g., grow to length of about 3½ ft. and weight of 25 lbs., while among bluefin tuna *(Thunnus thynnus)*, weight of from 200 to 500 lbs. is common. Bluefin is one of largest of bony fishes.

tuna, bluefin: largest member of mackerel family and also one of largest living fish. This "tiger of the sea" grows to length of 14 ft. and weighs as much as 1,500 lbs. Average bluefin, however, weighs under 200 lbs. Bluefin tuna is an iridescent fish with steely blue head and back, silvery sides and often a yellowish or purple stripe separating the blue and silver. Dusky fins may be tinged with yellow and small finlets are bright yellow. Soft-rayed dorsal and anal fins are long and taper to a point.

tuna, little: bluish fish with distinctive oblique wave lines on upper sides and spots behind pectoral fins. It is 24 in. or less in length and weighs 5 lbs. or under. False albacore roams entire Atlantic in large schools.

tuna, yellowfin: warm-water species found on Atlantic Coast, south of Maryland, and on southern Pacific Coast. It is dark blue with silvery sides and yellow fin and often with yellow stripe from eye to tail; these brilliant colors fade soon after fish is caught. Large individuals are 6 ft. long and weigh as much as 200 lbs.

Tundall flowers: small, water-filled cavities, often of basically hexagonal shape, which appear in interior of ice masses upon which light is falling. Their formation results from melting ice by radiative absorption at points of defect in ice lattice.

tunic: outer circular covering of tunicates.

Tunicata [subphylum]: phylum *Chordata*. Recent. Larva has notochord in tail region; notochord lost in adult but gill basket much enlarged; body enclosed in saclike cellulose tunic. Marine, predominantly sessile benthos; filter feeders.

tunicates: urochordates are primitive marine members of subphylum of *Chordata* (vertebrates). Like other vertebrates they possess, at some time in their lives even if it is before birth, dorsal (back or upper surface) nerve cords, gill slits and internal skeletons or notochords. Tunicates are characterized by hard outer coverings or tunics and large pharynxes. They include sea squirts.

tunny: large oceanic fish of the *mackerel* family, generally found in warmer latitudes. Usually called horse mackerel on the American Atlantic coast; tuna on the Pacific side; or, more widely known as the common, or great, tunny, representing the principal of several species. The little tunny of the North Atlantic and Mediterranean

and the long-finned tunny, or albacore, seldom attain a greater weight than 60 lbs., but the great tunny is known to have reached 14 ft. in length and a weight of 1500 lbs. Extensive tunny fishing is carried on in Pacific waters by hook and line; in the Mediterranean and near-by Atlantic also by heavy fixed nets extending 1 to 2 miles from shore. Largest tunny are captured in the latter region. The fish travel in schools, thrashing and jumping about as if continually in play. Its flesh is canned on a large scale on the U.S. Pacific coast.

tun shell [*Tonnidae*]: tun shells are small group of less than 30 species which inhabit Indo-Pacific area. They may be recognized by large, thin, globular shell, inflated body whorl, wide aperture and spiral ribs. *Doliidae.*

tun shell, apple [*Malea pomum*]: shell of apple tun is thicker than that of other species and bears teeth upon lips. It is white and amber in color and ranges from 2 to 3 in. long.

tun shell, black lipped [*Tonna melanostoma*]: black-lipped tun shell is thin, large and heavily ribbed species with large body whorl and large aperture. It is colored by black, brown, yellow and white markings which are arranged in longitudinal bands. Columella and outer lip are marked with black. It is a large species with shell ranging in size from 2 to at least 9 in. long.

tun shell, channeled [*Tonna canaliculata*]: shell of this species is large, thin and hard with large body whorl and large aperture. Suture is characteristically depressed and is the feature from which shell derives its name. It varies in length from 2 to 5 in.

tun shell, partridge [*Tonna perdix*]: partridge tun bears a shell that is large, thin and hard; body whorl is inflated; aperture is very wide. Shell is brownish and usually covered over outer surface by reticulated pattern of white lines. Shells are occasionally found, however, which have reticulated pattern lacking over part or all of shell.

tun shell, spotted [*Tonna dolium*]: this tun shell is a beautiful species with large, thin shell and inflated body whorl. It is white and bluish-white in color and is spotted with brown upon ridges. It ranges from 2 to 6 in. long.

turbidity: turbidity current deposits characterized by both vertical and horizontal graded bedding. Reduced water clarity resulting from presence of suspended matter. Water is considered turbulent when its load of suspended matter is visibly conspicuous, but all waters contain some suspended matter and therefore are turbid.

turbidity current: rapid, large-volume, downslope movement of sediment from continental slope. Usually turbidity current is triggered by an earthquake with epicenter at or near continental slope, by excessive sediment deposition on portion of slope which gives way (fails) under added weight or through slope disturbance of seismic sea waves.

turbinate [*Coelenterata*]: corallite with angle about 70° between sides expanding from apex.

turbine shell, ribbed: this turbine shell is quite heavy and solid and is marked over outside by many encircling grooves and ridges. Sometimes these ridges bear scalelike processes which in some individuals may be quite large and may project outward at an angle from ridges. Aperture of this species is circular; operculum is also circular and usually has external surface covered with granules. This shell is variously colored; background color is usually greenish or gray on which are irregular markings of black, green and brown. Outside of operculum is usually green in center and yellow about border; interior is silvery. Species will reach length of about 2 in.

Turbinidae: these mollusks produce solid, heavy, top-shaped shells which may be either smooth, rough or spiny on exterior surface. Exterior is covered by periostracum, beneath which shell is shiny and/or pearly. Aperture is usually oval and closed by heavy, calcareous operculum which is flat on inside and convex on outside. This operculum is commonly called a "cat's-eye" and is often worn as an ornament. Members of this family are herbivorous and live along shoreline; worldwide in warm waters.

turbot: large flounder of European coastal waters, greatly valued as a food fish. Attains a weight of 30 to 40 lbs. The name also designates several flounders or flatfishes similar in appearance to the true turbot; e.g., the American *plaice* or *summer flounder*, New Zealand *halibut*, California *halibut*, and European *brill*.

turbulence: mixed water, by physical action.

turema: Swedish armed craft of latter 18th century. Combination of galley and man-of-war. Armed with 26 guns with sweeps in pairs between guns; three-masted; square-rigged.

Turk's Head: kind of woven knot made by working one or more pieces of small line around a cylindrical object. In appearance like a turban, it is used as a finishing trim on ends of cross-pointing work, as on a stanchion or handrail, as a gripknot on a manrope, footrope, etc.; and is designated according to its number of strands, which are worked over and under each other; as 3-strand Turk's Head (its simplest form); 4-strand Turk's Head; etc.

turnbuckle [ships]: device at lower end of stays or other rigging ropes aboard ship. Turnbuckles are used to adjust length of these ropes and to pull objects together; limb threaded on both ends of short bar, one left-handed, the other right-handed.

turnover rate: usually net primary production per unit primary standing crop (phytoplankton) under natural light conditions, or more specifically, production divided by standing stock.

turreted [*Mollusca*]: tower-shaped with long spire (in gastropods) and somewhat shouldered whorls.

Turridae, family [*Pleurotomariidae*]: family of turret or slit shells is believed to be largest family of molluscs living in the ocean for they are reported to include several thousand species. In general these shells are spindle-shaped, bear turreted and pointed spire and usually have characteristic notch or slit in outer lip near suture. Columella is of varying length and usually ends in straight canal. Group exhibits wide variety of patterns and color markings and includes many species which are very beautiful. They vary in size from small, minute forms to species which are several inches long. Family lives in both temperate and tropical seas. Specimens are usually obtained by dredging in sand in coastal waters bordering tropical and semitropical islands.

Turritella: genus of gastropods commonly found as fossils, often as masses of high-spiraled, pointed shells or shell fragments. Probably used more than any other genus of gastropods for correlation of Cenozoic strata. Fossil Turritellas are often locally abundant enough to comprise veritable coquinas. Early Cretaceous to Recent.

tusks [*Scaphopoda*]: tusk shells are shaped, as name indicates, like elephant's tusks. They live buried in sand with just the small tip of shell extending above surface. In size shells range from tiny ½- to 6-in. Color is usually white, but a few species display browns, greens and reds. This small class contains only a few hundred species and are mostly found in beach drift or living below low-tide line.

twakow: Chinese craft of Singapore, used for general cargo carrying. Hull is flat-bottomed with flaring side; combination junk and sampan design with flat, rounded, V-shaped bow and wide transom stem, both raking.

Twister: 1) Spanish windlass. 2) waterspout or tornado.

tychoplankton: plankton consisting of animals and plants which have temporarily migrated or have been carried into plankton from normal benthic habitat.

tye yard: chain attached to middle of yard, leading through sheave in mast. Used in setting square hoisting sail.

Tyfon horn: patented sound-signal device used as a navigational aid during fog or poor visibility conditions at a lighthouse or coastal station. May be operated by steam or compressed air which produces the required blast by vibratory action of a special diaphragm.

Tyler standard grade scale: scale for sizing particles based on square root of 2 used as specifications for sieve mesh. Alternate class limits closely approximate class on Udden grade scale values; 0.50, 0.71, 1.00, 1.41, 2.00.

tympanum [amphibian]: eardrum of frogs, usually level with surface of head.

Tyne keel: coal-carrying "keel" used on Tyne river in England. This type is similar to "Mersey lighter."

typhoon: violent cyclonic storms in China seas awed first Europeans to sail there. From Cantonese for "big wind," natives called such a storm "ta feng." Seamen who tried to repeat the strange syllables, slurred them and telescoped the phrase into a single English word. It was spelled in many varied ways: tuffoon, tay-fum, tyfooning, tifoon and even tiffoon. Not until the last century was the name standardized as typhoon, big wind whose title still reveals kinship with tycoon, which stems from "ta kiun" (great prince).

typhoplankton: not regularly part of plankton; brought up from bottom by turbulence.

U

U: abbreviation in the form (U) denotes, on charts and in Light Lists, that light indicated is *unwatched* or *unattended,* thus warning the navigator of possible failure of such light; as *u* in logbooks and meteorological records, signifies *ugly, threatening appearance* of weather. In International Code of signals, *U* is a square flag showing two white and two red squares of equal size, alternately set. This flag, hoisted singly, denotes *"You are standing into danger,"* which signal also may be given by Morse Code flashing as . . —, or two dots and a dash, the symbol for *U.* Having resemblance in shape to letter *U; as U-bar; U-bolt; U-clip; U-section:* etc.

uba: dugout canoe used by Brazilian natives and Samaracas Indians of French Guiana on Oyapouk region of Amazon River delta.

uche: native name for "dugout canoe" in Hermit Islands. Last specimen of large, two-masted dugout canoes reposes in Berlin Museum. Above a high dugout are several rows of planks which form side of hull. Stern and sternpost are extended upwards and curve inboard. Whole hull is highly decorated.

Udden grade scale: grade scale for particle size with 1 millimeter as reference point and involving fixed ratio 2 to ½, depending on whether scale is increasing or decreasing, as ¼, ½ or 1, 2, 4.

udema: Swedish armed naval vessel of 18th century, mounted with 9 heavy caliber guns in center line of ship. It was three-masted, square-rigged on main and foremast, fore-and-aft sail on mizzenmast and 3 headsails.

ullage: inside measurement from surface of a liquid to the top or limit of space in a cask or tank: quantity of liquid by which containing vessel lacks of being full: deficiency, as of contents of a cask of liquor. In tank vessels, ullage is measured to inside of tank cover by an *ullage stick, ullage rod,* or *ullage gauge,* through the circular *ullage hole* which is about 10 in. in diameter and provided with an *ullage plug* capable of being closed airtight.

ultimate base level: ultimate base level is base level at sea level or below, to which lands may be reduced by processes acting upon them to lower and destroy them as land areas.

ultra plankton: plankton smaller than 5 microns; includes bacteria and small flagellate forms.

umbilical [diving]: normally a composite hose/cable for supplying breathing gas and communications to diver.

umbilical plug [*Foraminifera*]: deposit of skeletal material in axis of coiled test.

umbilicus: 1) in some conch shells, whorls diverge and axis of coiling lies free in open center (umbilicus) of spire. 2) in *Foraminifera,* depression in axis of coiled test. 3) in *Gastropoda,* opening along central axis of spiral where inner walls of whorls fail to meet. Typically a conical opening widest on body whorl.

umbo: 1) in *Brachiopoda,* relatively convex portion of valve next to beak. 2) in *Mollusca,* upper or early part of bivalve shell as seen from outside, opposite hinge; beak is terminal extension of umbo, best seen in an interior view of shell.

umbraculidae, family [*Umbrellidae*]: molluscs within this family are shaped somewhat like limpets, but unlike limpets are not completely covered by shell. They possess a large, cylindrical-shaped foot on top of which rests a very thin, flattened and calcareous shell. Family is small and contains about 6 species.

umbrella: gelatinous body of jellyfish, usually bearing prominent tentacles. It may be bell-, dome-, bowl-, or saucer-shaped.

umbrella [ships]: metal shield in form of frustrum of a cone, fitted to outer casing of smokestack over air casing to keep out weather.

umbrella shell, Chinese: Chinese umbrella shell is oval in outline and unusually thin for its size. It has very low conical shape with apex situated behind and to left of center of shell. Color of this species is variable. In general, shell is white and covered by yellowish cuticle. Interior of shell is usually darker than exterior and brown or orange-brown at center. This central area is in turn surrounded by yellowish band; it is encircled by band of white along outer margin. This shell will reach length of nearly 4 in.

umiak [oomiak]: open skin boat used by Eskimos of Greenland, Northern Canada and Alaska. It is made by stretching unhaired walrus- or sealskins over light wooden frame and lashed with thongs.

unaboat: English boat similar to American catboat.

unbroken ice: sea ice which has not been disturbed since its formation. It is usually fast ice, although a single, smooth ice floe could be said to be unbroken ice.

unconsolidated sediments: deposits consisting of uncemented or organic material.

uncovers: area of reef or other projection from bottom of body of water which periodically extends above and below surface.

unda: part of ocean floor which lies in zone of wave action, in which bottom sediments are repeatedly stirred and reworked; topographic expression is termed undaform and rock unit is termed undatherm.

undercurrent: water current flowing beneath surface current at different speed or in different direction.

undersea satellite: basketball-size device with gage (to measure tides), seismometer and transmitter.

undertow: 1) conjectural return of surf water beneath waves. 2) seaward flow near bottom of a sloping beach.

underwater navigation beacon: nuclear-powered device on sea bottom to enable submarines to operate about oceans without having to surface and seek any landmark for correct position.

underway: in progress; in motion; vessel that has weighed anchor or left moorings and is making progress through water is "underway."

unicuspid: single-cusped tooth, i.e., with one point.

unifoliate [*Bryozoa*]**:** colony form consisting of single layer of zooecia opening onto 1 surface.

uniform flow: any current in which neither convergence nor divergence is present.

union jack [ships]**:** blue field with 50 stars, carried on bow staff or jack staff.

uniserial [*Foraminifera*]**:** test in which chambers form single linear or curved series.

unlaw [ships]**:** to unreeve strands of rope.

unprotected thermometer: reversing thermometer for seawater temperature which is not protected against hydrostatic pressure. Mercury bulb is therefore squeezed and amount of mercury broken off on reversal is a function of both temperature and hydrostatic pressure.

unship [ships]**:** to remove from a place where it is fixed or fitted; as to unship oars, davits, etc.

unwatched light: lighthouse or beacon that is unmanned and automatically controlled.

up: in many instances used in nautical phraseology in an adverbial sense, as in *clew up; lie up; heave up; send up; set up; shore up;* as a preposition in *sail up the bay; climb up the rigging; leading up the foremast,* etc.; and in a verbal sense in such shortened commands as *Up anchor!* (for Heave up anchor!); *Up helm!* (for Put the helm up!); *Up behind!* (for Come up behind!).

up-and-down: lying or leading in a vertical line. An anchor cable is said to be *up-and-down* while hanging from the hawse pipe by its own weight, as when ship is lying in slack water; or when anchor lies directly beneath the fore foot, especially while being *broken out,* or just prior to being *aweigh.*

updrift: direction opposite that of predominant movement of littoral materials.

upper deck [ships]**:** partial deck above main deck amidships.

upper works [ships]**:** superstructures or deck erections located on or above weather deck.

uprush: rush of water onto foreshore following breaking of a wave.

uptake [ships]**:** sheet metal conduit connecting boiler furnace with base of smokestack. It conveys smoke and hot gases from boiler to stack.

upwelling: process by which water rises from lower to higher depth, usually as a result of divergence and offshore currents. Upwelling is most prominent where persistent wind blows parallel to coastline so that resultant wind-driven current sets away from coast.

urea: simple ammonia compound formed in liver which, as an end product of waste production of vertebrate protein metabolism, is excreted in body urine.

uropod: appendage of some crustaceans used for swimming and usually near the tail. Along with telson (end lobe of tail), it forms tail fan of the lobster.

urosome: part of body behind major joint. Includes abdominal somites, anal segment or telson; in some copepods, posterior thoracic segment.

Ursa Major: a conspicuous northern constellation also known as the *Great Bear, Dipper, Plough,* and *Charles' Wain* or *Charlie's Wagon,* easily recognized by the dipperlike formation of its seven principal stars. The two stars marking the outer limit of the "bowl" are called the *Pointers* for their use in locating *Polaris,* or *Pole Star.* Line of the Pointers extended from 28°, or about the length of *Great Bear* itself, comes close to *Polaris;* and when the tail star, or end of the *Dipper's* handle, is directly below or above *Polaris,* the latter bears very nearly *true north,* or has arrived at upper or lower culmination. Pointers are named *Dubhe* and *Merak,* or α (alpha) and β (beta) *Ursae Majoris,* respectively, the former marking the lip of the dipper-bowl. Tail-end star is *Alkaid* or *Benetnasch* (η *Ursae Majoris*).

Ursa Minor: called *Little Dipper.*

useful load: weight of cargo and necessary fuel, water, and stores that a vessel carries when floating at her load-line marks: also termed *net capacity.*

V

V: in the International Code of Signals, square flag having a white ground with an oblique or diagonal red cross; code-name *victor*. Hoisted singly or flashed in Morse by 3 dots and a dash (. . . —) denotes *"I require assistance"*; as a towing signal, by ship towing, means *"Set sails"* and by ship towed, *"I will set sails."* As a symbol in weather records, *v* equals variable, usually in describing winds.

vacuole: gas- or fluid-filled cavity outside of nucleus in living tissue.

vacuum filtration: method of extracting phytoplankton and bacteria from water sample.

vadose water: subsurface water in zone of aeration or leaching above zone of saturation.

vaka: 1) dugout canoe with single outrigger of Marquesas Islands. Modern "vakas" are simple in design, 12 to 18 ft. long and 12 to 18 in. wide and deep with narrow washboard nailed to each side of dugout. Two outrigger booms are secured to long, cylindrical pole floats near either end with crude slot connections. 2) outrigger sailing dugout canoe of Rennel Island. Sailing canoes are used only on inland lake on northeast portion of the island and not on the seashore. Hull is very narrow dugout, pointed and sharply raked.

vaka poti: Marquesan outrigger canoe, larger than vaka from these islands. Some have dugout underbody with wide washboard nailed from either side. Sides are clinker-built planking and short deck is often built at each end. In form this canoe resembles a narrow, double-ended rowboat.

valley: relatively shallow, wide depression with gentle slopes which grade continuously downward. Term is used for features that do not have canyonlike characteristics in any significant part of their extent.

valley glacier: streams of ice that flow down valleys of mountainous areas. Like streams of running water, they vary in width, depth and length.

valued policy: in marine insurance, one in which a *fixed value* is agreed upon as payable by insurer in event of partial or total loss of subject matter insured; opposed to an *unvalued* or *open policy*.

valve: 1) one of the pieces forming shell of diatom. Any of the pieces forming shell of certain invertebrates, such as mollusks and barnacles. 2) in *Brachiopoda*, one of the 2 curved, chitino-phosphatic or calcareous plates that form the brachiopod shell and surround and lie, respectively, along and below the ports.

vanagi: outrigger dugout canoe of Port Moresby. Hull is quite narrow, tapering towards the ends. These terminate in a point and curve up from bottom in sharp rake. Mangrove pole lies above each gunwale, rising at ends.

Van Dorn water bottle: water-sampling device consisting of tube open at both ends. Water is trapped inside by rubber stoppers that spring shut upon triggering.

vane: device fitted on the truck of a mast for indicating direction of wind, as an arrow of sheet metal, a long slender cone of light canvas or bunting, etc., free to swing about on a vertical spindle.

vangs [ships]: guy ropes extending from end of gaff to ship's rail or deck on each side to steady the peak of the gaff.

vanishing tide: when high and low water "melt" together into a period of several hours with nearly constant water level, tide is in diurnal category but is known as vanishing tide.

varagam oro: narrow dugout sailing canoe of Ceylon with outrigger. Transverse section is round and overhanging ends rake strongly. It is 25 to 30 ft. with about 1/10 the beam. Two curved bows are connected directly to a long float.

variability depth sonar: shipborne sonar system whereby transducer can be lowered below thermal layer.

variability of waves: variation of heights and periods between individual waves within wave train. Wave trains are not composed of waves of equal height and period, but rather of waves with heights and periods which vary in statistical manner. Variation in height along coast is usually called "variation along the wave."

variation: range within which values of a variable lie, as in diurnal or annual variation.

varix [*Mollusca*]: elevated axial sculpture in certain gastropods, more prominent than ribs and generally more widely spaced; evidence of periodic resting stages during growth in which thickened outer lip develops.

varve: sedimentary deposit bed or lamination deposited in one season. It is usually distinguished by color or composition and used as an index to changes in depositional environment.

veer [ships]: to change or alter course of ship by turning stern to windward; lay on different tack by turning vessel's head away from wind, as "to veer the ship."

veering [ships]: according to general international usage, change in wind direction in clockwise sense (e.g., south to southwest to west) in either hemisphere of earth; opposite of backing.

Vega: brightest star in the northern heavens, excepting, sometimes, the variable *Betelgeux* in *Orion.*

vein: narrow lead or lane in pack ice.

veined fan [*Hymenena flabelligera*]: veined fan is exposed on rocks between 1- and 1.5-ft. tide levels where surf beats hard. Some thalli are prostrate and some are erect, arising from broad disc. Erect branches are on one plane, fan-shaped and divided into long segments with rounded tips and smooth margins. Blades are tissue-paper thin; color ranges from deep salmon pink to dark red, verging on purple.

veliger: larval or immature mollusc characterized by velum or ring of hairlike cilia used for swimming; planktonic larval 2nd stage of many gastropods.

velocity discontinuity: abrupt change of rate of propagation of seismic waves within earth, as an interface.

velocity hydrophone: hydrophone in which electric output substantially corresponds to instantaneous particle velocity in impressed sound waves.

veloera: large three-masted coasting ship of Italy. Square-rigged on foremast, boomless fore-and-aft sail on main and lateen-rigged on mizzen. Bowsprit is carried as well as topmast on main.

velum: circular, muscular, locomotory membrane of hydromedusans.

veneer: thin layer of sediment covering rocky surface.

veneridae: family of phylum *Mollusca* characterized by heavy, regular shells, external ligament and hinge with 3 diverging teeth in each valve.

vent: posterior opening of digestive tract in fish.

ventilate [diving]: procedure in which diver increases gas flow to ventilate or flush life-support system.

ventral: pertaining to underside of body.

ventral fins [fish]: unpaired fins on median line of body; to wit, dorsal, caudal and anal fins.

ventral nerve cord [*Mollusca*]: one of pair of nerve bundles passing from head to foot.

ventrals [reptile]: laterally enlarged scales on lower surface of snake.

Venus ovata [*Heterodonta*]: larva is similar in structure to that of *V. striatula* but dorsolateral margin of narrow end is straight. Length is normally about 220μ and larvae occur in September and October, but mainly in October, i.e., autumn and winter. (Eulamellibranchs.)

Venus striatula: shell bears number of distinct concentric grooves. Dorsolateral margin of narrow end is convex, a feature which distinguishes it from *Venus ovata.* Length is about 220μ.

vermiculation [*Mollusca*]: surface sculpture of irregular wavy lines or grooves.

vermiform: shaped like a worm.

Verruca stroemia [crustacean larvae]: widely distributed but not as common as other species. Nauplii are triangular in outline; labrum has rounded tip. Caudal region is longer than that of *B. balanoides* and frontolateral horns are longer than in either of the other species. Final stage nauplius is approximately 0.6 mm. long.

vertebral centrum: body or main portion of vertebra; one of segments of spinal column.

Vertebrata phylum *Chordata* [subphylum]: Ordovician to Recent. Notochord primitive, large but not extending to tip of head; skeletal elements develop in mesenchyme; notochord supplemented or replaced by series of cartilaginous or bony vertebrae. Marine, freshwater and terrestrial; a wide variety of adaptation.

vertex: apex; highest point; zenith. Sun's or moon's *upper limb.* In a *great circle,* either of its diametrically opposite points lying nearest the pole; tangential point at which such circle meets with a latitude parallel—always 90°, or 5,400 nautical miles, from the circle's intersection with the equator.

vertex velocity: velocity at which sound wave becomes horizontal (grazing angle equals zero).

vertical: pertaining to the *vertex.* Plumb; upright; perpendicular to a horizontal base or plane of the horizon. A *vertical* line or plane.

vertical haul: lifting of open plankton net from certain depth to surface while ship or other platform is on station.

vertical keel [ships]: plate running in fore-and-aft direction connecting to flat keel and keel-rider plate. It is usually connected by 2 angles at top and bottom for riveted job or welded to keel and keel-rider.

vertically mixed estuary: estuary in which salinity is homogeneous with depth but increases along its length from head to mouth.

very shallow water: water of depths less than 1/25 the wavelength of surface waves.

vessel: as generally used among seamen, the term "vessel" means any craft that is protected from entrance of seawater by a continuous deck and is used for purposes of navigation; hence the difference between such craft and a "boat." In legal usage, however, the broader definition of *vessel*, especially where admiralty jurisdiction is concerned, may be stated as including "every description of water craft or other contrivance used, or capable of being used, as a means of transportation in water."

vibrating needle: as used in connection with compensating a vessel's magnetic compass, a small delicately pivoted magnetic needle by means of which the intensity of its directive power, as observed on shore free of any local attraction and at site of ship's compass, determines relative magnitude of horizontal component of vessel's magnetic field.

vibrating period: also, *oscillating period;* time, measured in seconds, occupied by a single oscillation or "swing" of the card of a magnetic compass upon being deflected through an arc of about 30° and instantly freed. Such observation being made as a test of card's comparative efficiency, period necessarily is a criterion of its directive power which depends upon the horizontal intensity of magnetic field, moment of inertia of card, and magnetic moment of card's needles.

vibrating wire pressure gauge: depth-measuring instrument consisting of thin wire stretched in magnetic field, with wire being fixed at one end and attached to pressure-sensing diaphragm at the other. The wire vibrates at frequency that is related to tension on it. Tension on wire, due to diaphragm action results in change of frequency. Electronic counter aboard ship provides data readout.

vigia: rock or shoal in sea whose existence or position is doubtful; also, warning note to the effect on a nautical chart.

vigilenga: "canoe" of Amazon delta having town of Vilgia as a base.

viking ship: early Norse "long ship" propelled mainly by oars, but also carrying single, demountable mast with square sail hung from horizontal yard. These vessels were clinker-built and sharp-ended with long easy sheer rising sharply at ends and rather flat bilge. Rounding stem and sternpost were elongated vertically and usually terminated in dragon's head, scroll or some such carving.

villiform band [teeth]: row of small teeth in some fish. They are closely set and resemble velvet pile.

vinco: three-masted vessel of Italy with high foremast, polacre-rigged and main and mizzen lateen-rigged.

vinella: vinella whose stolons resemble tubular threads is a ctenostome that appeared in middle Ordovician seas and lived in middle Silurian.

vinta: Philippine outrigger canoe.

violet snail shell [*Janthina fragilis*]: shell of this snail is globose in shape with low spire and with shoulder of body whorl somewhat angular in shape. Columella is nearly straight. It is pale violet above and dark violet below. It has maximum length of about 1½ in. Species is worldwide in warm waters.

violet snail shell [*Janthina globosa*]: this snail is named for its globose shape. It has low spire like *Janthina fragilis* but differs in having shoulder of body whorl rounded. It is white-violet but darker about spire and at base. It will reach length of about 1½ in. This is a pelagic species which is worldwide in warm waters.

violet snail shell [*Janthinidae*]: this family of molluscs is unusual in many ways. Its shells are among the very thinnest, most fragile and most delicate of all molluscs. These creatures produce shell of spiral design which is lavender or purple and somewhat transparent. They lack an operculum, and are also unusual in that they are pelagic or floating and drifting about freely over surface of sea. They are gregarious in their habits and are often found singly or in groups upon jellyfish commonly called Portuguese man-of-war and on which they are reported to feed. Eggs of these snails are attached to mucous bubbles and remain floating about in sea until they have hatched.

visceral hump [*Mollusca*]: portion of body behind head and above foot in which digestive and reproductive organs are concentrated. Not set off distinctly from foot though it may form a hump.

viscosity: ability of fluid to resist flow such as thickening of oil or molasses at decreased temperatures.

viscous stress: resistive force of water; it is proportional to speed of current but acts opposite to direction of flow.

visibility: ability to observe distant objects through water droplets in atmosphere. May vary from zero (dense fog) to 50 km. Curvature of horizon sets final limit for an (unaided) observation.

visor [ships]: small inclined awning running around pilothouse over windows or air ports to exclude glare of sun or to prevent rain or spray from coming in opening when glazed frames are dropped or opened.

vocal pouch [amphibian]: skin sac underneath or at side of throat in some frogs.

void ratio: ratio of intergranular voids to volume of solid material in sediment.

volcanic ash: uncemented pyroclastic material consisting of fragments most under 4 mm. in diameter. Carried coarse ash is ¼ to 4 mm. in grain size; fine ash is below ¼ mm. Constituent of some marine sediments.

volume transport: volume of moving water measured between 2 points of reference and expressed in cubic meters per second. It is determined by measuring cross-sectional areal limits of current and multiplying this figure by current speed.

volume velocity: rate of alternating flow of medium through specified surface due to sound wave.

voluntary loss: in connection with a *general average act*, such property as is sacrificed or expenditure incurred in the interests of common safety of ship, cargo, and freight.

volutions: series of turns or spirals of conch shell, typical of gastropods generally.

vomer: flat bone that separates nasal passages.

vomerine teeth [amphibian]: teeth on roof of mouth between or just behind internal naris, usually arranged in rounded patches or in transverse series.

Von Arx current meter: type of current measuring device using electromagnetic induction to determine speed and, in some models, direction of deep-sea currents. This meter provides continuous recordings of currents by transmitting through connecting cable, signals to deck unit that register speed, direction and instrument depth.

W

W: as an abbreviation, stands for compass point *West;* also *Winter,* in freeboard or load-line markings. In logbooks and weather records, *w* = heavy dew. In International Code of Signals, the square flag *"William,"* having a central red square set in a larger white square with an all-around blue border. Hoisted singly, flag *W* denotes *"I require medical assistance,"* which signal also may be used by flashing the Morse code *dot-dash-dash* (. — —). As a *towing* signal, *W* denotes by flag or flashing light *"I am paying out the towing hawser."* This may be used by either *vessel towing* or *vessel towed.*

wa: sailing, outrigger dugout canoe of Ninigo Islands which lie west of Admiralty Islands. This type is unique in that sides of narrow hull are straight and bottom flat. Ends sheer up somewhat. Hull is decorated with simple native designs.

wa'a: Hawaiian outrigger dugout canoe. Keelless bottom of hull is semicircular and sides are straight with thin plank washboard 6 or 8 in. high. Wa'a is very lightweight canoe, weighing not much over 50 lbs.

wa'a kaulua: double, Hawaiian dugout canoe. Hulls were similar to the wa'a although larger and were connected a short distance apart with 3 or 4 slightly arched booms. Platform made of a few poles or planks was usually laid on bows between hulls to carry passengers or cargo. Hawaiian canoes were paddled.

waga: outrigger dugout canoe is typical to Daui district of Papua. Ends of canoe are prolonged to blunt points which cut down obliquely. In elevation the ends raise the bottom in an easy raking "S."

wager policy: also called *honor policy;* in marine insurance, a policy under which assured party may recover without proof of his insurable interest, in event of loss; or, one in which actual possession of the document is sufficient proof of interest in property insured. Such policy contains the words, or their equivalent, "Interest or no interest," "This policy to be deemed sufficient proof of interest," etc.

wahoo: slender and elongated member of mackerel family, looking more like pike or barracuda than a tuna; another common name for this species is ocean barracuda. Wahoo is a sleek fish with long, low, spiny dorsal fin and smaller soft-rayed fin. Steel blue of dorsal fins and back blends into silvery blue sides that are sometimes marked indistinctly by vertical gray or yellow bars. Average individuals are 15 to 30 lbs. in weight. It occurs in warm Atlantic waters being especially abundant about Florida Keys.

Wain, The: Constellation *Ursa Major;* Charlie's Wain.

waist [ships]: middle portion of ship's upper deck.

waiver clause: conventional point of agreement in marine insurance policies, indicating that either insurer or insured may take such action or incur such necessary expense as will lessen loss to property insured, without disturbing the rights of either party under the insurance contract.

waka: dugout sailing canoe of Taku atoll group which lies north of Solomon Islands. Hull is fairly wide with heavy dugout, often with planks sewed on above to form washstrake. Outrigger float is supported by 3 transverse booms.

waka korari: woven punt-shaped boat raft formerly used by the Moriori of Chatham Islands. Having no trees for making canoes, natives used stalks of ferns, pieces of wood from shrubs and any other available vegetation to fashion their craft. This craft was never sailed. Kelp bladders were employed in larger boats to increase buoyancy.

waka taua: Maori war canoe of New Zealand. This was a very large type of dugout of average length of 60 to 70 ft. with freeboard increased by means of washstrake sewed to hull. Transverse section of hull was that of a wide "V" with curved sides. Floor grating of light rods lashed to crossbars was laid a little distance above bottom.

wake: region of turbulence immediately to rear of solid body in motion relative to a fluid. In the wake of; behind; water left astern of a vessel underway.

waku-amibune: open rowboat used in pound-net herring fishery off coast of Hokkaido, Japan. Bag net is suspended under boat to receive fish from pound net. Boat is flat-bottomed with raking stem projecting above bow; square, raking stern.

wa lap: outrigger sailing canoe of Marshall Islands in western Pacific. Outrigger is made up of 2 main straight booms flanked by 3 curved booms on each side. Latter are lashed directly to long float, while each straight boom is connected with short stanchion.

wale [ships]: strake of planking running fore and aft on outside of hull, heavier than regular planking.

walk: oceanographic walk is a platform situated near top of submerged cliff. Its width varies from a few inches to 6 ft. or more. Its origin is often due to chemical erosion, but its development is largely result of calcareous marine life such as madreporarians and lithothannion which is calcareous alga.

walleye [*Stizostedion vitreum vitreum*]: walleye varies considerably in color. It ranges from dark silver to dark olive-brown mottled with brassy specks. Large black spot is always present at base of last dorsal spine, though it may fade in dead walleyes. Lower lobe of tail or caudal fin has wide white margin. Jaws contain large canine or tearing teeth.

walrus: large mammal allied to the seals, found only in Arctic and contiguous waters. Often weighing more than a ton, the male has very heavy neck and shoulders, with two large tusks extending downward from his upper jaws. The female, much less weighty, has fine slender tusks, which, as also in the male, are a high-grade quality of ivory. Walrus hide produces a valuable leather and the blubber yields an oil of similar quality to that from seals. The walrus of Alaskan and Siberian northern coasts is a larger species than his cousin of Greenland, Spitzbergen, etc.

wardroom [ships]: room or space set aside for use of officers for social purposes and also used as their mess or dining room.

wa-ririk: outrigger canoe of Gilbert Islands.

warm [diving]: for definition, a diver is warm when his mean average weighted skin temperature is 94° or higher and his core temperature will not decrease with time below that of normal. Skin temperature in extremities is 85° or higher.

warmouth [*Chaenobryttus coronarius*]: warmouth resembles rock bass and may easily be mistaken for it. It has robust body of mottled olivaceous or gray color mixed with chocolate and purplish shades and sometimes flecked with gold or green. Belly is pale green or yellow speckled with dark dots or with gold. Cheek and opercle are streaked and have short black opercular flap. Dorsal fin 9 to 11 spines, usually 10 and 9 to 11 soft rays. This species reaches length of 8 to 10 in.

warm pool: body of warm water entirely surrounded by cold water.

warp [ships]: to move into some desired place or position by hauling on rope or warp which has been fastened to something fixed, as anchor or wharf. To warp ship into harbor or berth.

warp line: line with one end attached to boat and the other to towed object. It usually refers to line or lines used in towing in a net such as a trawl.

wash and strain ice foot: ice foot formed from ice casts and slush attached to shelving beach between high and low waterlines. High waves and spray may cause it to build up above high waterline.

washovers: small deltas built on lagoon sides of a bar separating lagoon from open sea. Storm waves breaking over bar deposit sediment on lagoon side in the form of deltas.

washstrake: thin plank above gunwale for keeping spray off or increasing freeboard; vertical in position.

watch [ships]: 4 hour stretch of duty for crew members. Watches are reckoned from midnight, each watch having 8 bells sounded successively each half hour. Dog watches are for 2 hours duration only, between 1600 and 1800 and 2000 hours (4 to 6 p.m. and 6 to 8 p.m.).

watch tackle [ships]: utility block and tackle. Same as handy billy.

water color: apparent color of surface layers of sea caused by reflection of certain components of visible light spectrum coupled with effects of dissolved material, concentration of plankton, detritus or other matter. Color of oceanic water varies from deep blue to yellow and is expressed by number values which are a variation of Frel scales. Plankton concentrations may cause temporary appearance of red, green, white or other colors.

water content: ratio; 100 multiplied by the weight of water in bottom sediment sample divided by weight of dried sample, expressed as percentage.

water dog, hog nosed [*Necturus beyeri*]: large, brownish salamander with external 4 toes on each foot. Known by large size, brownish color and by having most of belly mottled but with a few distinguishable small, dark spots; external gills present.

water exchange: volume and rate of water replacement in specific location, some of controlling factors being tides, winds, river discharges and currents.

water flea [*cladoceran*]: one of suborder (*Cladocera*) of small crustaceans that swim in jerky or jumpy manner. Although abundant in some shallow-water environments, they are not among more abundant marine plankton.

water gap: in stream that flows across tilled or folded strata, narrows or pass developed where valley crosses more resistant beds.

waterline: 1) one of horizontal lines supposed to be described by surface of water on ship's hull, and exhibited at certain depths upon sheer draft. Most important of these lines is light waterline, which marks depression of ship's body in water when ship is light or unladen; load waterline which marks ship's depression when loaded or laden. 2) a juncture of land and sea. This line fluctuates with tide or other changes in water level. Where waves are present on beach this line is also known as limit of backrush. Approximately intersection of land with still-water level.

water mass: body of water usually identified by T—S curve or chemical content, and normally consisting of mixture of 2 or more water types.

water pocket: water mass of limited size, frequently in form of a pocket and having properties different from those of surrounding water. Water pockets are often located at a meandering boundary where they usually are partly or completely cut off from original main body of water.

water sail: small sail, rectangular in shape, set under lower studding sail boom on square-rigged ship.

water sky: dark appearance of underside of cloud layer due to reflection of surface of open water surrounded or bounded by ice. Area of open water may be beyond range of visibility. This term is used largely in polar regions with reference to sky map; water sky is darker than land sky, and much darker than ice blink.

waterspout: funnel which contains an intense vortex, sometimes destructive, of small horizontal extent and which occurs over a body of water. In U.S. waterspouts are classified either as tornadoes (storms), spouts or fair-weather spouts, depending on formative processes. Usually a tornado occurring over water, rarely a lesser whirlwind over water comparable in intensity to dust devil over land. Waterspouts are most common over tropical and subtropical waters.

waterspout, fair weather: unlike tornadic spout this type is born solely over water, developing at sea level, and climbing skyward, much like old Indian rope trick. Spouts of this sort are usually small, of short duration and virtually harmless, being more curious than spectacular. Fair weather spouts usually favor equatorial regions, that broad variable band of doldrums with its fitful winds and sudden squalls straddling the equator, where humid, superheated air constantly circulates convectionally with cooler air overhead.

waterspout, tornadic: bona fide land tornadoes that literally go to sea or cross sizeable inland bodies of water. Frequently dangerous, they drop from thunderstorms, squall lines or leading edges of advancing cold fronts and closely resemble deadly "Texas Twisters" complete with sinister dark funnels and enormous "parent clouds." When fully developed, tornadic spouts are quite large and capable of considerable destruction. Tornadic spouts generally occur in middle latitudes, often developing off shores of large landmasses.

water tagging: process of introducing foreign substances (traces) into ocean to detect movement of waters by subsequent measurement of location and distribution of introduced substance.

water type: seawater of specified temperature and salinity and hence defined by single point.

waterway: gutterlike recess on shelter deck at midship section of ship which delivers excess water to scupper holes for discharge into sea.

waterway bar [ships]: angle or flat bar attached to deck stringer plate forming inboard boundary of waterway and serving as abutment for wood decking plate.

wattenschlick: tidal or intertidal mud.

wave: disturbance which moves through or over surface of medium (ocean) with speed dependent upon properties of medium; ridge deformation or undulation of surface of liquid.

wave age: state of development of wind-generated sea-surface wave, conveniently expressed by ratio of wave speed to wind speed. Wind speed is usually measured at about 25 ft. (8 meters) above still-water level.

wave base: depth at which wave action ceases to stir sediment.

wave-built terrace: embankment built along or near shore by aggradation work of waves.

wave celerity: magnitude of wave speed.

wave crest: highest part of wave. Also, that part of wave or waves above still-water level.

wave crest length: length of wave along its crest.

wave-cut terrace: leveled rock bench produced by retreat of sea cliff through wave erosion. Also called wave-platform and plain of marine abrasion.

wave decay: change which waves undergo after they leave generating area (fetch) and pass through calm or region of light or opposing winds. In process of decay, significant wavelength increases.

wave front: in seismology, surface of equal time elapse from point of detonation to position of resulting outgoing signal at any given time after charge has been determined and denotated. In more practical sense, surface whose phase is constant at given instant. Leading side of wave.

wave group: series of waves in which wave direction, length and height vary only slightly.

wave height: vertical distance between wave trough and wave crest, usually expressed in feet.

wave height coefficient: ratio of wave height at

selected point in shallow-water to deep-water wave height. Refraction coefficient multiplied by shoaling factor.

wave hindcasting: calculation from historic wind charts of wave characteristics that probably occurred at some past time.

wave interference: phenomenon which results when waves of same or nearly the same frequency are superimposed. It is characterized by spatial or temporal distribution of amplitude of some specified characteristic differing from that of intended superposed wave.

wavelength: the distance between corresponding points of 2 successive periodic waves in direction of propagation for which oscillation has same phase. Horizontal distance between points on 2 successive waves measured perpendicularly to wave crest.

wave level: position of sea surface above or below reference plane at any specific time in tide cycle.

wave meter: instrument to measure and record wave heights.

wave of translation: wave in which water particles are permanently displaced to significant degree in direction of wave travel. Wave in which there is pronounced forward movement of water.

wave period: time between 2 successive wave crests at given point. Time in seconds required for wave crest to traverse distance equal to one wavelength.

wave pole: device for measuring sea surface waves. It consists of weighted pole below which disk is suspended at depth sufficiently deep for wave motion associated with deep-water waves to be negligible. Pole will then remain nearly steady as if anchored to bottom, and wave height and period can be ascertained by observing or recording length of pole that extends above surface.

wave ray: line drawn everywhere perpendicular to wave crests on refraction diagram.

wave refraction: process by which direction of train of waves moving in shallow water at angle to contours is changed. Part of wave train advancing in shallow water moves more slowly than that part still advancing in deeper water, causing wave crest to bend toward alignment with true underwater contours.

wave signature: graph of pressure versus time and at a point as wave passes over it.

wave spectrum: in ocean wave studies, graph showing distribution of wave heights with respect to frequency in wave record.

wave steepness: ratio of wave height to wavelength.

wave-straightened coast: straight-cliffed coast which results from wave erosion of homogeneous coast rocks, along a contact between weak and resistant layers forming hogback coast or along a fault-line coast. It has wave-cut beach at base of sea cliffs and hanging valleys along coast.

wave train: series of waves moving in same direction.

wave trough: lowest part of wave form between successive wave crests. Also, that part of wave below still-water level.

wave velocity: speed at which individual wave form advances.

way: controlled motion through water. Legally, vessel may be under way although motionless in water, but vessel is said to "have way on" when moving; to have headway so as to answer helm.

ways [ships]: timber on which ship is built or supported before launching.

weakfish: also known as sea trout and squeteague. It occurs from New England to Florida, being caught only in summer in northern part of its range but year-round in south. In this member of drum family, spiny portion of dorsal fin is higher than soft-rayed portion and slightly separated from it. Weakfish is greenish-blue and silvery with upper sides marked by pattern of oblique wavy bars of brown-green. Lower jaw projects beyond upper which has 2 prominent front teeth. Average individual is 30 in. long and weighs 5 lbs.

wear or wear about [ships]: when ship shifts from one tack to the other by turning stern into wind.

weather [ships]: ship weathers when sailing past an object or another ship on windward side; mariners also use weather as adjective to describe everything lying to windward of particular situation.

weathered: descriptive of ice or rock that has been destroyed or partially destroyed by thermal, chemical or mechanical processes.

weathered ice: hummocked polar ice subjected to weathering which has given hummocks and pressure ridges a rounded form. If weathering continues, surface may become more or less level.

weathered iceberg: iceberg which is irregular in shape due to advanced stage of ablation. It may have overturned.

weatherly: ship is weatherly if able to work up to windward.

web [ships]: vertical portion of beam, athwartship portion of frame.

weeping [ships]: very slow issuance of water through seams of ship's structure or from containing vessel in insufficient quantity to produce stream.

weigh [ships]: to lift or raise, as a weighing anchor.

weigh anchor [ships]: to lift anchor off sea bottom.

weir: 1) a fence of stakes, brushwood, stones, etc.,

fixed in a tideway, river, or sheltered tidal water, for taking fish; a *fish weir*. Where set in a tideway, often is V-shaped, with apex toward, or facing, the flood stream; when set along a shore, with apex outward. Any net spread on stakes for taking fish at high water or ebb stage of tide; especially, in localities having a large tidal range. 2) weir is also that portion of canal bank, dam, or other embankment containing gates for release of waste water; sometimes termed a *waste weir*.

well [ships]: space between first bulkhead of long poop deck or deckhouse and forecastle bulkhead.

well deck [ships]: sunken deck on merchant vessel fitted between forecastle and long poop or continuous bridge house or raised quarterdeck.

Wentworth grade scale: logarithmic grade scale for size classification of sediment particles, starting at 1 millimeter and using ratio of ½ in one direction (2 in the other), providing diameter limits to size classes of 1, ½, ¼, etc., and 1, 2, 4, etc. This was adopted by Wentworth from Udden's scale with slight modification of grade terms and limits.

Wesphal balance: balance in which buoyance of a float is balanced by sliding weights. It is used for determining specific gravity of liquids, minerals, fragments, etc.

west: point of the compass lying on one's left hand when facing north; point on the horizon at which the sun *sets* at the equinoxes; opposite of *east*. Portion of a country lying toward the sunset; the *Occident, New World*, or the *West*, as indicating the Western Hemisphere from the European's homeland. Emanating from the west; as, a *west wind*. W. by N., point of the compass 11¼° *north* of *west*. W. by S., 11¼° or one point *south* of *west*. W.N.W., 22½° or two points *north* of *west*. W.S.W., 22½° or two points *south* of *west*. Magnetic West, the point West indicated by a correct *magnetic* compass. True West, geographical west; point in the celestial horizon diametrically opposite *true East*, or intersecting point of the equinoctial, horizon, and prime vertical at any place other than at either geographical pole.

West Australia Current: complex current flowing along coast of Australia. It flows northward and is stronger during November, December and January; it is weakest and tends to be variable in May, June and July. It curves toward west to join South Equatorial Current.

westerlies: winds in Northern Hemisphere between 30° and 60° latitude caused by flow of air from polar areas and deflected into west to east drift by earth's surface friction.

West Greenland Current: current flowing northward along west coast of Greenland into Davis Strait. It is formed by water of East Greenland and Irminger Currents. Part of West Greenland

Current turns to left when approaching Davis Strait and joins Labrador Current flowing southward; other part continues into Baffin Bay.

West Ice: drifting ice of Baffin Bay. To Norwegians, drifting ice off east coast of Greenland.

westing [ships]: distance in nautical miles made good by ship due west of point of departure, used in connection with sailing from Chilean ports toward Cape Horn as "running their westing down."

West Wind Drift: ocean current with largest volume transport (approximately 110 by 10⁶ cubic centimeters per second); it flows from west to east around Atlantic Continent and is formed partly by strong westerly wind in this region and partly by density differences.

wet density: ratio of weight of solid particles of bottom sediment and contained moisture to its total volume.

wet submersible [diving]: small, free-floating, underwater vehicle used for diver transport.

wet suit [diving]: closed-cell, neoprene, rubber diving suit that provides thermal barrier by insulating a thin layer of body-warmed water next to diver's skin.

wetted surface: measured outside area of that portion of vessel's hull below the waterline, including bilge keels, propeller bossing, and rudder. A close approximation to wetted surface of ordinary ship forms, expressed in *square feet*, may be found from the formula: $S = 15.8$ *times square root of product of Displacement (in tons) and Length of waterline (in feet)*. The value is taken into account chiefly in connection with determination of resistance and powering of vessels.

wet weight: quantitative measure of wet plankton; living weight. Although commonly used, this measurement may lead to erroneous results unless all extraneous water is removed by blotter or draining.

whaleboat: double-ended, single-banked rowing boat. It is very seaworthy and sometimes called a "whaler." Whaleboats were 28 to 30 ft. long with beam about 6 ft. 6 in.; sharp-ended; round, easy bilge; raking, curved stem and sternpost; good sheer; open with fine thwarts.

whalebone whale [*Mysticeti*]: any of suborder, e.g., gray whale, with toothless jaws, baleen in mouth and symmetrical skull.

whaler [ships]: any steel or wooden member for temporarily bracing bulkhead, deck, section, etc.

wharf: a waterside structure of wood, masonry, etc., at which vessels may be berthed for landing or taking in cargo, passengers, etc.; a large jetty; a pier.

wharfage: a charge per ton of cargo landed or loaded, per unit of registered tonnage, according to ship's length, etc., or a fee per day, for privilege of using a *wharfage; pierage; quayage*. Wharves of a port, collectively; accommodation or berthing at a wharf or wharves.

wheel [ships]: steering wheel connected to rudder by means of gears or tackle, located on poop deck. Also called helm.

whelk: large marine mollusks of class *Gastropoda*. They have spirally curved shells and are used for fish bait and human consumption.

wherry: wherry of Norfolk, England is light-draft, sailing cargo carrier about 50 ft. long and 13 ft. beam; greatest beam is well forward; bow short and hollow; low freeboard; stern sharp with fine run aft. Also, long, light, English rowboat.

whiff [*Citharichthys spilopterus*]: very flat fish with both eyes and all color on left side. Scales along lateral line 45—48; rays in dorsal fin 72—80; snout short, forming angle with the profile; jaws strongly curved, upper somewhat hooked over lower. Body moderately elongated, much compressed. Color on left side olive-brownish with scattered darker spots and blotches. Total length rarely exceeds 6 in.

whipping [ships]: light twine wrapped about end of rope to keep it from unlaying.

whip tube [*Scytosiphon lomentaria*]: this seaweed grows commonly on exposed rocks or in rock pools. It is partial to 2.5- to 1.5-ft. tide levels. Whip tube is easily recognized by long, olive-tan to dark brown whiplike shoots which arise from tiny disc. Flexible, unbranched shoots vary from 8 to 18 in. long and are 1/16 in. wide. They grow in extensive stands and look like long blades of dry grass. Found all over the world.

whirlpool: water moving rapidly in circular path; eddy or vortex of water.

whisker pole [ships]: light spar used on small sailboats to wing out jib when running.

white bass [*Lepibema chrysops*]: general color of white bass is silvery with yellowish underparts; sides are streaked with narrow, dusky, longitudinal lines, 5 of which are above lateral line. Body is compressed and deep; back is elevated; head is rather conical and scaly. Mouth is medium-sized and horizontal; jaws are about equal in length; maxillary extends to middle of eye with no supplemental bone. There is a deep notch in the subocular bone and preopercle is serrated. Gill rakes are bony and slender.

whitecaps: also called "skipper's daughters." Tall white-crested waves such as seen at sea in windy weather. On crest of a wave, white froth caused by wind.

whitefish [family]: fish of this family are more or less silvery in color with blue-green or pale green backs. Most have rather long, slender gill rakers.

They have a fin without rays behind dorsal fin. Mouth is small and either lacks teeth or has only a few small ones. All members of this family are coldwater fish.

whitefish, common menominnee [*Prosopium cylindraceum quadrilaterale*]: more or less ovate fish with silver sides and dark bronze back. Back is usually more deeply colored than those of common whitefish. Upper jaw contains large premaxillary which is greater in width than in length; mandible is contained more than 3.8 times the head; no vestigial teeth are present. Gill rakers number 15—20. During spawning season pearl organs are found on sides of bodies of both males and females, but not on heads. They reach a weight of 3 to 4 lbs.

whitefish, Great Lakes [*Coregonus clupeaformis clupeaformis*]: this common whitefish is a large, more or less ovate fish with silvery sides that shade to dark olive-brown back. It is characterized by presence of 2 flaps between opening of each nostril and by the snout which distinctly overhangs lower jaw. Upper jaw is characterized by wide premaxillary greater in width than in length; vestigial teeth may be present on premaxillaries, palatines, mandible and tongue. Gill rakers number more than 23 and less than 32. During spawning season pearl organs are developed by both sexes on sides of body and in head.

white ice: Russian term for sea ice of 30 to 70 cm. (12.0 to 27.5 in.) in thickness.

white noise: noise whose spectrum density (spectrum level) is substantially independent of frequency over specified range.

whiteout: atmospheric optical phenomenon of polar regions in which observer appears to be engulfed in uniform white flow. Neither shadows, horizon nor clouds are discernible; sense of depth and orientation is lost; only very dark nearby objects can be seen. Whiteouts occur over unbroken snow cover and beneath uniformly overcast sky, when, with the aid of snow blink effect, light from sky is about equal to that from snow surface. Blowing snow may be additional cause.

whorl: 1) in *Gastropoda*, single complete turn of spiral shell. 2) in *Mollusca*, same as volution, except that in spire whorls it is exposed portion between successive sutures.

wide branch color changer [*Desmarestia munda*]: attached usually to rocks lying just below low-tide mark, although it may be found 6 to 8 ft. below ebb-tide level. Most conspicuous feature of wide branch color changer is wide, flat, thin, central blade that extends length of plant. From this central blade (2 to 4 in. wide), primary, opposite branches of same width as central arise at intervals at 1 to 3 in. Texture of branches is thin and soft, when dry they become as crisp as tissue paper. Smaller, younger plants are yellow-brown;

larger specimens are dark brown. For size of plant holdfast is small, not more than 1/4 to 1/8 in. in diameter.

Williamson turn [ships]: maneuver developed by Commander John A. Williamson, USNR, during World War II, that enables ship to turn around and end up in approximately same position as when turn was started. It is particularly adaptable for rescuing a man overboard in rough weather, poor visibility or at night.

williwaw: 1) sudden, strong, cold wind from land, usually along mountainous coasts in northernmost and southernmost latitudes. 2) 18th century whalers learned to dread sudden, violent squalls in Strait of Magellan. Legend had it that the seas resented the effrontery that led men to sail around South American coast so it stirred up dangerous winds in retaliation. Often regarded half seriously as being of supernatural origin, a storm in this region came to be called a williwaw. There are no known words from which the name could have been formed. It is musical, but does not represent an attempt to imitate natural sounds heard during a storm. So its origin remains a mystery. Before 1850 the unusual word was part of sailor's talk. Seldom included in vocabulary of landsmen, it maintains its vitality by oral transmission from one generation of seamen to another. Probably through the influence of "williwaw," Australians call tropical cyclone of Timor Sea a willy-willy.

willy-willy: tropical cyclone in Pacific near Australia.

winch [ships]: device for hauling on a sheet, halyard or cable by means of turning a handle which revolves barrel of winch with mechanical advantage.

windage: surface of a vessel exposed to the wind. What is termed *wind drag* is force exerted by wind pressure against a vessel lying at anchor with head to wind, or stress borne by the anchor-cable due to such force, which depends upon vessel's windage.

wind gap: notch in ridge associated with abandoned water gap.

windjammers: name applied to old square-rigged sailing ships and to those who have deep regard for them.

windlass [ships]: apparatus in which horizontal or vertical drums or gypsies and wildcats are operated by means of steam engine or motor for purpose of handling heavy anchor chains, hawsers, etc. Device used for raising anchors or obtaining a purchase on other occasions; it consists of strong beam of wood placed horizontally and supported at ends by iron spindles which turn in collars or bushes inserted in what are called windlass-bitts. Windlasses on old sailing ships were operated by hand power applied in various ways to heave the axle around, while rope or chain for raising weight was wound around it.

windlop: state of water surface as disturbed by short, choppy, lopping waves; especially, those set up in a current or tideway running against the wind, as over shallows, in a river, etc.

windship: ship propelled by wind, same as sailing ship.

wind stress: force per unit area of wind acting on surface to produce waves and currents; its magnitude depends on wind speed, density and roughness of water surface.

windward [ships]: direction from which wind blows; opposite of leeward.

wind wave: wave resulting from action of wind on water surface. While wind is acting on it, it is a sea, thereafter a swell.

wing [ships]: overhanging part of deck on ferryboat or fore and aft of paddle boxes in sidewheeler. Also used to indicate outboard parts of ship, such as in wings of hold.

wing and wing [ships]: said of sailboat when running before the wind with main on one side and jib on the other.

wing brackets [ships]: large brackets which fasten margin plates to lower frame ends.

winged headland: seacliff with 2 bays or spits, one on either side.

wingsail [ships]: boomless fore-and-aft sail with gaff along head set from mainmast of square-rigged ketches of 18th century. Wingsail came into use after 1725.

wingtanks [ships]: tanks located outboard and usually just under weather deck.

Winkler method: chemical method for estimating dissolved oxygen in seawater. In this method manganese hydroxide is allowed to react with oxygen of the sample to produce a manganese compound which in presence of acid potassium iodide liberates an equivalent quantity of iodine that can be titrated with standard sodium thiosulphate.

winnow: in regard to a current acting to sort selectively and carry off fine sediment grains from heterogeneous sediment deposit, leaving coarse grains. Process by which wind separates fine particles from coarser or heavier ones.

winter drift ice: drift ice composed exclusively of winter ice.

winter fast ice: 1) fast ice in fiords, gulfs and straits mainly formed by growth from shore, but also by cementing of pack ice. Winter fast ice rises and falls according to tide. 2) fast ice made up of winter ice.

winter ice: generally unbroken level ice of less than one winter's growth. It is between 15 cm.

and 2 meters (6.0 in. to 6.6 ft.) thick. Sea ice more than 8 in. thick and less than one year old; stage which follows young ice.

winter solstice: for either hemisphere, solstice when sun is above opposite hemisphere. In northern latitudes time of this occurrence is approximately 22 December.

wire angle: angle measured between oceanographic wire and the vertical.

wire angle indicator: device used to measure angle of oceanographic wire from the vertical. It consists of protractor with weighted plumb iron. Indicator is suspended from wire at 2 points and plumb arm points to wire angle.

wishbone rig [ships]: recently invented rig used on various types of sailing yachts, in which triangular sail is used as a mainsail. Long side or luff is laced to mast and clew is extended by double-curved gaff which allows sail to take its natural curve. Triangular staysail fills in space underneath, if used on two-masted vessel. Mainsail or upper sail is placed in between 2 parts of gaff.

W/M: abbreviation *Weight or Measurement*, usually appearing in the phase: *W/M at ship's option.*

W N A: abbreviation *Winter North Atlantic.* Letters in freeboard or load-line marks indicating minimum freeboard allowed a vessel navigated in the North Atlantic during *winter.* For *sailing ships,* it is the only mark providing an increase of freeboard—in this case 3 inches—above the normal minimum, or that marked by the line passing through center of load-line disk. For *powered* vessels not exceeding 330 ft. in length (between perpendiculars) it is shown 2 in. below the mark *W* (= *Winter*); for those of greater length than 330 ft. it is the *W* mark.

wolf fish: a ferocious member of the *blenny* family inhabiting the North Atlantic and North Pacific. Has a blunt nose and strong ugly teeth; a dorsal fringe extending full length of body, which tapers to a small unforked tail; usually bluish or gray with dark cross-bars on back, or, as in the Pacific species, wholly brown. It attains a length of 4 to 6 ft.

woody chain bladder [*Cystoseira osmundacea*]: common between mean low tide and 1.5-ft. tide levels. This seaweed may reach length of 18 to 30 ft. Lower part is blackish-brown and upper part light tan. It has strong, conical holdfast, an inch or more in diameter from which arises a woody stipe. Short, angular stipe gives off several shoots from which arise primary branches, several feet long. Secondary branches arise from primary shoots. Both are flattened at lower end and upper portions of both are cylindrical.

wool clipper: large, square-rigged "ship" or "bark" of clipper type engaged in Australian-British trade from about 1866 until 1890's carrying passengers and supplies from England to Australia and returning with cargo of wool. Most wool clippers were built of iron and many had long, rounded poop.

working pressure [diving]: pressure to which high-pressure container can be repeatedly pressurized without causing structural fatigue.

work the ship [ships]: to direct course or movement of ship. To put forth effort for accomplishment of voyage.

worm tube: tube, usually of calcium carbonate or particles of mud or sand, built on submerged surface by polychaete worm.

wrack: species of algae or rockweed clinging to seashore rocks as film. Food for snails. General term usually applied to some rockweeds and kelp, but also, occasionally, to other kinds of seaweed.

wrasse: family of predominantly warm-water fish with over twenty species in U.S., all but three of which are found on Atlantic Coast. They have oblong bodies covered with cycloid scales; mouth is provided with strong jaw teeth as well as powerful pharyngeal teeth used in crushing mollusks. Many brilliant-colored species are inhabitants of coral reefs. Familiar northern members of family are cunner and tautog; hogfish and California sheepshead are southern and western species. Only a few species are considered game fish.

wreck: partial or total destruction of a vessel, as by stranding, collision, or force of the elements; shipwreck; a badly damaged vessel or remains of such vessel; property washed up on a shore, such as fragments of a ship or some of her cargo; shipwrecked property; flotsam, jetsam, or lagan; wreckage. To cause to suffer damage to, disable, or destroy a vessel, as by driving her, or causing her to drive, on the rocks, or by causing her to founder; to engage in *wrecking,* whether for plunder or for rescue or salvage purposes, as in boarding a wreck. According to U.S. law, a wreck or wreckage washed ashore becomes, in general, the property of person owning the shore, if not reclaimed by its original owner. In Great Britain, such material or goods, including *flotsam, jetsam,* and *lagan,* is forfeited to the crown, but may be recovered by the owner within a year, upon payment of certain charges, such as salvage or storage.

wreckage: goods or parts of a wrecked vessel washed ashore or afloat; remains of a *wreck;* that which has been *wrecked; wreck.*

W.T.: abbreviation *watertight;* also, W/T; as in *W.T. Door, W/T Flat, w.t. bulkhead,* etc.

X

X: square flag "X-ray" of the International Code, showing a white ground with a blue Greek cross extending full breadth and length of flag. Flown uppermost in a 4-flag hoist, it signifies a *true bearing* that is indicated by the other 3 flags; as, *X 0 0 5; X 3 5 0;* or, respectively, true bearings 5° and 350°. Hoisted singly, it means *"Stop carrying out your intentions and watch for my signals."* As a *towing signal,* hoisted or otherwise exhibited singly, by *ship towing* signifies *"Get spare towing hawser ready";* by *ship towed, "Spare towing hawser is ready."*

xanthophyll: yellow plant pigment.

xebec: A small Mediterranean and Oriental three-masted, narrow-hulled, trading vessel. The hull is generally terminated forward with a sharp beak and aft with an outer platform which comprises two wings. Foremast was square-rigged and raked forward and it had lateen sails on main and mizzen.

xiphias: 1) genus comprising the common swordfish, or that constituting the *Xiphiidae.* 2) another name for the small constellation *Dorado,* also called the *Swordfish.*

Y

Y: in the International Code of Signals, denoted by square flag *"yoke,"* which has a series of diagonal alternating yellow and red bars of equal width, having an upward slant at a 45° angle with the hoist. Displayed singly, it denotes *"I am carrying mails."* As a towing signal, the flag, or its Morse code equivalent by flashing light *dash-dot-dash-dash* (— . — —), signifies *"I can not carry out your order,"* as sent by either *vessel towing* or *vessel towed.* Having the shape of, or suggesting, the letter *Y*; as, a *Y-bend*; a *Y-branch* (in a pipe); a *wye*; *Y-gun*.

yardarm [ships]: either one of the ends of a yard.

yards [ships]: long cylindrical spars tapered toward ends and hung athwarthships on masts, upon which square sails are suspended.

Yarmouth yawl: long, narrow, double-ended, clinker-built boat used in England on Norfolk coast rigged with 3 lugsails and jib. In middle of 17th century these "yawls" were built up to 70 ft. in length and 500-footers with 10- or 11-ft. beam were common.

yaw: motion of vessel when thrown off course by heavy seas.

yawl: true "yawl" is the Yarmouth yawl and is descended from Scandinavian "yol." Modern yawl is fore-and-aft-rigged boat with mainmast stepped forward and small mizzenmast stepped in stern aft of helmsman. Mizzen sail sheets to a boomkin. There is a jib forward.

yawl boat: open boat used by coasting vessels, carried on the stern from davits. It also was used by fishing vessels previous to the 1870's before the dory was adopted. It is carvel-built keel boat with sharp flaring bow, curved stem and wide, heart-shaped stern. It has 4 or 5 thwarts and stern seat.

yol: Norwegian for yawl, meaning double-ended boat. Scandinavian yol is light, open, double, clinker-built boat; stem and stern alike. Used for rowing or sailing. Usual rig is single lugsail.

young ice: newly formed level ice generally in transition stage of development from ice rind or pancake ice to winter ice. It is 5 to 15 cm. (2 to 6 in.) thick.

young shore ice: primary stage of formation of shore ice. It is of local formation and usually consists of ice rind or thin young ice usually some 10 meters (32.8 ft.) wide, but sometimes as wide as 100 to 200 meters (328 to 656 ft.).

Yuloh [Formosan catamaran]: type of catamaran used at Takow, Formosa (Taiwan), Japan, for getting through heavy surf to vessels lying in open roadstead. Made up of 12 to 14 bamboo logs bound to several crosspieces on top with rattan lacings; bamboo gunwale runs along either side to which oarlocks are fastened. Single mast is stepped just forward of amidships on which single matting Chinese sail is carried. Steered with an oar.

Z

Z: International Code square flag *"zebra,"* consisting of four colored isosceles triangles of equal area having their apexes meeting at flag's center, *black* triangle being at the hoist; *blue,* at the fly; *yellow,* at top; and *red* one at bottom. Flown singly, the flag indicates *"I wish to address,* or *am addressing, a shore station"*; or its equivalent may be indicated by flashing the *Z* character in Morse code, *dash-dash-dot-dot* (— — . .). As a *towing signal,* hoisted or otherwise displayed singly by *ship towing,* Z-flag denotes *"I am commencing to tow"*; by *ship towed, "Commence towing."* Morse code *Z* by flashing also may be used for these signals. As an abbreviation, *Z = azimuth; z = zenith distance* and, in weather recording, *hazy.* Resembling the letter *Z* in form; as, *Z-crank; Z-iron; Z-beam.*

zabra: small sailing ship of 16th century.

Zanclea costata [phylum *Coelenterata*]: medusa of hydroid of same name. It has 4 exumbrellar patches of nematocysts. There are 4 marginal tentacles which are extensible and bear numerous stalked capsules of nematocysts. It is widely distributed but not very common medusa.

zarug: small, lateen-rigged craft of dhow family used mainly by Arabs for fishing in Red Sea. Zarugs are also often used clandestinely by Arabs in smuggling and in slave traffic carrying slaves from African to Arabian shore. It is a narrow, sometimes crudely built, double-ended, open boat with raking stem and sternpost, varying sheer and outboard rudder steered with a tiller.

zenith [ships]: when sun is in zenith and observed with a sextant, arc will be 90° from horizon.

Zephyr: Greeks of pre-Christian centuries often spoke of the wind as though it were a person or even a minor diety which they called *Zephyr.* Passing through Latin and somewhat modified, the word was current in Britain before the 10th century. Latin versing of the name retained their vitality as late as the time of Shakespeare. But in recent years scholars have successfully appealed for a return to the pure Greek form. Contemporary poets do not follow Chaucer in singing praises to "Zephirus with his swete breethe," but on land as well as on sea, gentle air movements once attributed to Zephyr's personal activity are received with gratitude even by persons who work and sleep in temperature-controlled buildings.

Z/L graph: graph used to determine in situ depths of oceanographic observations by thermometric-depth vs wire-depth ratio method.

Zoantharia: colonial coelenterates of class *Anthozoa.* They are closely related to coral, but have no skeleton and are sometimes encrusted with sand. Most common kinds are *Zoanthus* and *Polythoa,* and the latter is sometimes so thick it forms a "carpet" on a reef.

zoarium [*Bryozoa*]: skeleton of entire bryozoan colony; composed of calcite and/or chiton.

ZoBelle bottle: sterile bottle constructed to collect seawater samples at desired depth for bacteriological analysis. Multiple sampling can be accomplished in a manner similar to oceanographic cast.

Zodiac: imaginary belt in the heavens following and extending about 8° on each side of the *ecliptic,* while embracing also the orbits of our Moon and principal planets. What are called the *12 signs of the zodiac* take their names from the constellations through which the Sun successively passes in his apparent perennial path. These are, beginning with Sun's arrival at the *vernal equinox, Pisces,* or Latin word for *fishes; Aries*—ram; *Taurus*—bull; *Gemini*—twins; *Cancer*—crab; *Leo*—lion; *Virgo*—virgin; *Libra*—balance; *Scorpio*—scorpion; *Sagittarius*—archer; *Capricornus*—goat; *Aquarius*—waterbearer.

zoea: early larval form of certain decapod crustaceans.

zonal flow: currents or winds moving east or west along a latitude.

zone: an area or region of definite limits or generally distinct from an adjoining or surrounding region; as, *Canal Zone; danger zone; ice zone; zone of operations.* An encircling belt of a sphere; specifically, any of the great climatic-latitude divisions of the Earth, viz., the *Torrid Zone,* extending between the *Tropics of Cancer* (23° 27' N.) and *Capricorn* (23° 27' S.); *North Temperate Zone,* between 23° 27' N. and *Arctic Circle* (66° 33' N.); *North Frigid Zone,* or entire region poleward of last-named; *South Temperate*

Zone, between 23° 27' S. and *Antarctic Circle* (66° 33' S.); *South Frigid Zone*, or entire region south of last-named limit.

zone time: local mean time of reference or zone meridian whose time is kept throughout a designated zone. Zone meridian is usually nearest meridian whose longitude is exactly divisible by 15°.

zooecial wall [*Bryozoa*]: sides of skeleton (zooecium) of individual bryozoan.

zooecium: 1) secreted covering of individual making up colony of bryozoans. 2) in *Bryozoa*, chitinous or calcareous skeleton of individual bryozoan, consisting of tubular walls and various internal structures.

zoogeme: environment and deposits characterized by abundant lime-secreting organisms, such as reefs.

zoogeography: science dealing with geographical distribution of animals and relationship of animals and regions in which they live.

zooid: individual member of colony of animals.

zooplankton: 1) animal forms of plankton. They include various crustaceans, such as copepods and euphausiids, jellyfish, certain protozoans, worms, mollusks and larvae of benthic and nektonic animals. They are principal consumers of phytoplankton and in turn are principal food for large number of squids, fish and baleen whales. 2) in *Foraminifera*, rhizopods with branching and anastomosing pseudopodia which protrude through and form a network over shell or test. In vast majority the test is calcareous and perforated by minute pores. It may be a single shell, but most often is built of many chambers. Most many-chambered *Foraminifera* occur in 2 distinct forms: megalospheric with large initial chamber and microspheric with small initial chamber. Contents of microspheric forms undergo repeated divisions to form uninucleate young which are released and secrete initial chamber of megalospheric form, later chambers being added successively. Megalospheric forms undergo repeated division to form swarms of biflagellate gametes which fuse in pairs to form a zygote. Each zygote then secretes initial chamber of microspheric form. They are particularly abundant in warmer seas where tests of dead ones often accumulate on bottom to form deep layers of calcareous ooze.

zoosphere: flagellated plant spore capable of swimming.

zooxanthella: flagellate alga that lives in symbiotic relationships to various marine animals, such as scleractinians, certain alcyonarian corals and giant clams.

zulu: double-ended, lug-rigged, Scotch fishing boat, which is a compromise of fifie and skaffie dating from late 1870's. Straight stem and bow of fifie was retained with deep forefront, while stern was modeled after skaffie with more rake to sternpost.

zygote: 1) fertilized egg cell. 2) in *Bryozoa*, cell formed by union of egg and sperm cell.

TABLES

AREA, VOLUME AND MEAN DEPTH OF OCEANS AND SEAS
(IN METERS)

Body	Area (10^6 km^2)	Volume (10^6 km^3)	Mean depth (m)
Atlantic Ocean)	82.441	323.613	3926
Pacific Ocean) excluding adjacent	165.246	707.555	4282
Indian Ocean) seas	73.443	291.030	3963
All oceans) including adjacent			
seas	321.130	1322.198	4117
Arctic Mediterranean	14.090	16.980	1205
American Mediterranean	4.319	9.573	2216
Mediterranean Sea and Black Sea	2.966	4.238	1429
Asiatic Mediterranean	8.143	9.873	1212
Large Mediterranean seas	29.518	40.664	1378
Baltic Sea	0.422	0.023	55
Hudson Bay	1.232	0.158	128
Red Sea	0.438	0.215	491
Persian Gulf	0.239	0.006	25
Small Mediterranean seas	2.331	0.402	172
All Mediterranean seas	31.849	41.066	1289
North Sea	0.575	0.054	94
English Channel	0.075	0.004	54
Irish Sea	0.103	0.006	60
Gulf of St. Lawrence	0.238	0.030	127
Andaman Sea	0.798	0.694	870
Bering Sea	2.268	3.259	1437
Okhotsk Sea	1.528	1.279	838
Japan Sea	1.008	1.361	1350
East China Sea	1.249	0.235	188
Gulf of California	0.162	0.132	813
Bass Strait	0.075	0.005	70
Marginal Seas	8.079	7.059	874
All adjacent seas	39.928	48.125	1205
Atlantic Ocean)	106.463	354.679	3332
Pacific Ocean) including adjacent	179.679	723.699	4028
Indian Ocean) seas	74.917	291.945	3897
All oceans) including adjacent			
seas	361.059	1370.323	3795

AVERAGE SURFACE TEMPERATURE OF THE OCEANS
BETWEEN PARALLELS OF LATITUDE
(DEGREES CELCIUS)

North Latitude	Atlantic Ocean	Indian Ocean	Pacific Ocean	South Latitude	Atlantic Ocean	Indian Ocean	Pacific Ocean
70°–60°	5.66			70°–60°	-1.30	-1.50	-1.30
60 –50	8.66		5.74	60 –50	1.76	1.63	5.00
50 –40	13.16		9.99	50 –40	8.68	8.67	11.16
40 –30	20.40		18.62	40 –30	16.90	17.00	16.98
30 –20	24.16	26.14	23.38	30 –20	21.20	22.53	21.53
20 –10	25.81	27.23	26.42	20 –10	23.16	25.85	25.11
10 –0	26.66	27.88	27.20	10 –0	25.18	27.41	26.01

SALTS PRESENT IN THE OCEAN

		Percent
Sodium chloride	$NaCl$	77.758
Magnesium chloride	$MgCl_2$	10.878
Magnesium sulfate	$MgSO_4$	4.737
Calcium sulfate	$CaSO_4$	3.600
Potassium sulfate	K_2SO_4	2.465
Calcium carbonate	$CaCO_3$	0.345
Magnesium bromide	$MgBr_2$	0.217
		100.000

COMPARISON OF AVERAGE MINERAL MATTER
IN RIVER AND SEA WATER

	Percentage	
Constituent	River Water	Sea Water
Calcium	20.39	1.19
Silica, SiO_2	11.67	Trace
Sodium	5.79	30.59
Magnesium	3.41	3.72
Ferric and Aluminum oxides	2.75	0.00
Potassium	2.12	1.11
CO_3 radical	35.14	0.21
SO_4 radical	12.14	7.70
Cl radical	5.69	55.48
NO_3 radical	0.90	0.00
	100.00	100.00

COMPOSITION OF SEA WATER

Constituent	gm./kg. of water of salinity 35%
Chloride	19–353
Sodium	10–76
Sulphate	2–712
Magnesium	1–294
Calcium	0–413
Potassium	0–387
Bicarbonate	0–142
Bromide	0–067
Strontium	0–008
Boron	0–004
Fluoride	0–001

VELOCITY OF SOUND IN SEA WATER*

Pressure (db)	Temperature (°C)						
	0	5	10	15	20	25	30
0	1449–3	1471–0	1490–4	1507–4	1522–1	1534–8	1545–8
1000	1465–8	1487–4	1506–7	1523–7	1538–5	1551–3	1562–5
2000	1482–4	1504–0	1523–2	1540–2	1555–0	1567–9	1579–2
3000	1499–4	1520–7	1538–6	1555–6			
4000	1516–5	1537–7	1555–2	1572–2			
5000	1533–9	1554–8	1571–9	1588–9			
6000	1551–5	1572–1					
7000	1569–3						
8000	1587–3						
9000	1605–4						
10000	1623–5						

* Velocities in m./sec.
  Pressures in decibars above atmospheric.
  Salinity 35%.

DATE DUE
